ISDN AND BROADBAND ISDN, with FRAME RELAY AND ATM: THIRD EDITION An in-depth presentation of the technology and architecture of integrated services digital networks (ISDN). Covers the integrated digital network (IDN), ISDN services, architecture, signaling system no. 7 (SS7) and detailed coverage of the ITU-T standards. This new edition also provides detailed coverage of protocols and congestion control strategies for both frame relay and ATM.

BUSINESS DATA COMMUNICATIONS, THIRD EDITION A comprehensive presentation of data communications and telecommunications from a business perspective. Covers voice, data, image, and video communications and applications technology and includes a number of case studies.

PROTECT YOUR PRIVACY: A GUIDE FOR PGP USERS Provides detailed step-by-step instructions on the use of PGP on the most important computer platforms. It explains the fundamentals of encryption and digital signatures so that the reader will know what PGP can do for him or her. Also provides explicit instructions on solving the all-important problem of obtaining trusted public keys of other users.

Third Edition

BUSINESS DATA COMMUNICATIONS

William Stallings, Ph.D.

Richard Van Slyke, Ph.D.
Polytechnic University

Prentice Hall, Upper Saddle River, New Jersey 07458

Library of Congress Cataloging-in-Publication Data

Stallings, William.
    Business data communications / William Stallings, Richard Van
Slyke. — 3rd ed.
        p.   cm.
    Includes bibliographical references and index.
    ISBN 0-13-594581-X
    1. Business—Data processing. 2. Business—Communication systems—
Data processing. 3. Local area networks (Computer networks).
4. Data transmission systems. 5. Business enterprises—Computer
networks. 6. Electronic commerce. I. Van Slyke, Richard.
II. Title.
HF5548.2.S7728   1997
004.6–dc21   97-7154
                                                             CIP

Publisher: Alan Apt
Editor-in-Chief: Marcia Horton
Editor: Laura Steele
Assistant Vice President of Production and Manufac-
    turing: David W. Riccardi
Production Manager: Bayani Mendoza de Leon
Production Editor: Mona Pompili
Manufacturing Buyer: Donna Sullivan

Creative Director: Paula Maylahn
Art Director: Amy Rosen
Cover Designer: Tom Nery
Cover Illustrator: Wendy Grossman
Copy Editor: Barbara Zeiders
Editorial Assistant: Toni Chavez
Compositor: Preparé/Emilcomp

© 1998 by Prentice-Hall, Inc.
Simon & Schuster / A Viacom Company
Upper Saddle River, New Jersey 07458

Printed in the United States of America

10 9 8 7 6 5 4 3

ISBN 0-13-594581-X

PRENTICE-HALL INTERNATIONAL (UK) LIMITED, *London*
PRENTICE-HALL OF AUSTRALIA PTY. LIMITED, *Sydney*
PRENTICE-HALL CANADA, INC., *Toronto*
PRENTICE-HALL HISPANOAMERICANA, S.A., *Mexico*
PRENTICE-HALL OF INDIA PRIVATE LIMITED, *New Delhi*
PRENTICE-HALL OF JAPAN, INC., *Tokyo*
SIMON & SCHUSTER ASIA PTE. LTD., *Singapore*
EDITORA PRENTICE-HALL DO BRASIL, LTDA., *Rio de Janeiro*

To my loving wife, Tricia - W.S.
For Irene - R.V.S.

PREFACE

Background

Four trends have made a solid understanding of the fundamentals of **data communications** essential to business and information management students:

- *The increasing use of data processing equipment.* As the cost of computer hardware has dropped, data processing equipment has become an increasingly important and pervasive part of the office, factory, and engineering environments.

- *The increasing use of distributed systems.* The dropping hardware costs have resulted in the increasing use of small systems, including minicomputers, microcomputer workstations, and personal computers. These systems are distributed throughout a business and must be interconnected to exchange messages, share files, and share resources, such as printers.

- *The increasing diversity of networking options.* The emergence of a broad range of local area network (LAN) standards plus the evolution of LAN technology have led to a broad, overlapping range of products for local-area communications. Similarly, the planning for the next generation of telephone equipment and networks, and the evolution of new transmission and networking technologies have led to a broad, overlapping range of options for long-distance communications.

- *The sudden emergence of the Internet and the World Wide Web.* In a very short time, the Internet and especially the World Wide Web, have attracted millions of business and personal users. No business can ignore the potential of this enormous facility.

As a result of these factors, business data communications courses have become common in business and information management sequences, and this book intends to address the needs for such a course. However, a focus on data communications is no longer enough.

Over the past twenty years, as data processing capability has been introduced into the office, data communications products and services have gradually assumed increasing importance. Now, technological developments and the widespread acceptance of standards are transforming the ways in which information is used to support the business function. In addition to the traditional communications requirements for voice and data (meaning text and numerical data), there is now the need to deal with pictorial images and video information. These four types of information (voice, data, image, and video) are essential to the survival of any business in today's competitive international environment. What is needed is a treatment not just of data communications but of **information communications** for the business environment.

Information communications and computer networking have become essential to the functioning of today's businesses, large and small. Furthermore, they have become a major and growing cost to organizations. Management and staff need a thorough understanding of information communications in order to assess needs; plan for the introduction of products, services, and systems; and manage the systems and technical personnel that operate them. This understanding must comprise:

- *Technology:* the underlying technology of information communications facilities, networking systems, and communications software.
- *Architecture:* the way in which hardware, software, and services can be organized to provide computer and terminal interconnection.
- *Applications:* How information communications and networking systems can meet the requirements of today's businesses.

Approach

The purpose of this text is to present the concepts of information communications in a way that relates specifically to the business environment and to the concerns of business management and staff. To this end, the book takes an approach based on requirements, ingredients, and applications:

- *Requirements:* The need to provide services which enable businesses to utilize information is the driving force behind data and information communications technology. The text outlines the specific requirements that this technology is intended to address. This linkage between requirements and technology is essential to motivate a text of this nature.
- *Ingredients:* The technology of information communications includes the hardware, software, and communications services available to support distributed systems. An understanding of this technology is essential for a manager to make intelligent choices among the many alternatives.
- *Applications:* Management and staff must understand not only the technology but also the way in which that technology can be applied to satisfy business requirements.

These three concepts structure the presentation. They provide a way for the student to understand the context of what is being discussed at any point in the text, and they motivate the material. Thus, the student will gain a *practical* understanding of business information communications.

An important theme throughout the book is the essential role of standards. The proliferation of personal computers and other computer systems inevitably means that the manager will be faced with the need to integrate equipment from a variety of vendors. The only way to manage this requirement effectively is through standards. And, indeed, increasingly vendors are offering products and services that conform to international standards. This text addresses some of the key groupings of standards that are shaping the marketplace and that define the choices available to the decision-maker.

Intended Audience

This book is addressed to students and professionals who now have or expect to have some information communications responsibility. As a full-time job, some readers may have or plan to have responsibility for management of the company's telecommunications function. But virtually all managers and many staff personnel will need to have a basic understanding of business information communications to effectively perform their tasks.

For students, this text is intended as an introductory course in information communications for business and information management students. It does not assume any background in data communications, but does assume a basic knowledge of data processing.

The book is also intended for self-study, and is designed for use both as a tutorial and a reference book for those already involved in business information communications.

Plan of the Text

This text is a survey of the broad and fast-changing field of information communications. It is organized in such a way that new material is seen to fit into the context of the material already presented. By emphasizing requirements and applications as well as technology, the student is provided with motivation and a means of assessing the importance of a particular topic with respect to the whole. The book is divided into five parts:

1. *Requirements:* This part defines the needs for information communications in the business environment. It discusses the way in which various forms of information are used and the need for interconnection and networking facilities. An examination of the nature and role of distributed data processing is the highlight of this first part.

2. *Fundamentals:* This part deals with the basic technology of the communication of information. The emphasis is on digital communications techniques, since these are rapidly displacing analog techniques for all products and services related to information communications. Key topics include transmission media, data link control protocols, multiplexing, and compression.

3. *Networking:* This part examines the way in which communications facilities are organized into a network. There is a wide variety of options available to the manager and planner; this part intends to present the range of

options and compare their strengths and weaknesses, so that the reader can make informed choices based on specific requirements. Both wide-area networks (WANs) and local area networks (LANs) are covered.

4. *Applications:* This part deals with the specific business applications that require information communications facilities and networks. Following a look at the underlying TCP/IP protocol suite, this part presents key applications such as electronic mail, electronic document interchange, and the World Wide Web. The part closes with a discussion of client/server computing and intranets.

5. *Management Issues:* This part examines some of the most important issues that confront the manager with respect to the in-house implementation or the purchase of networking and communications services. It begins with the increasingly important issue of doing business on the Internet. This is followed by a discussion of network management and network security.

In addition, the book includes an extensive glossary, a list of frequently-used acronyms, and a bibliography. Each chapter includes problems and suggestions for further reading. Finally, a number of real-world cases studies are sprinkled throughout the book.

Note to the Instructor

The major goal of this text is to make it as effective a teaching tool for this exciting and fast-moving subject as possible. This goal is reflected both in the structure of the book and in the supporting material.

The text itself contains a number of features that provide strong pedagogical support for the instructor. Each chapter begins with a list of chapter objectives, which provides, in effect, an outline of the chapter and alerts the student to look for certain key concepts as the chapter is read. Key terms are introduced in bold face in the chapter, and all of the new key terms for that chapter are listed at the end of the chapter. In addition, all new acronyms are highlighted and listed at the end of the chapter; this is important because the field of information communications, unfortunately, is loaded with acronyms. A glossary and list of acronyms at the end of the book provide a handy summary of all key terms and acronyms. At the end of each chapter, there is a summary which highlights the key concepts and places them in the context of the entire book. In addition, there are questions and homework problems to reinforce and extend what has been learned. The book is also liberally supplied with figures, tables, and charts to enhance the points made in the text.

Throughout the book a number of case studies are presented. These are not "made-up" or "toy" cases, but actual cases reported in the literature. Each case is chosen to reinforce or extend the concepts introduced prior to the case study.

The text is also accompanied by supplementary material which will aid the instructor. A solutions manual provides answers to most of the problems at the end of each chapter. A test bank of additional problems is also available. A set of transparencies are available that reproduce all of the figures in the book.

Internet Services for Instructors and Students

An Internet mailing list has been set up so that instructors using this book can exchange information, suggestions, and questions with each other and with the author. There is a web page for this book that provides support for students and instructors. The page includes links to relevant sites, transparency masters of figures in the book in PDF (Adobe Acrobat) format, and sign-up information for the book's internet mailing list. The web page is at http://www.shore.net/~ws/BDC3e.html.

As soon as any typos or other errors are discovered, an errata list for this book will be available at http://www.shore.net/~ws.

Note to the Reader

In a book on this topic, for this sort of audience, it is tempting to launch immediately into a description of communications and networking technology, and to examine and compare the various approaches. Certainly, this is an essential element of a book that deals with business information communications. However, we believe that this approach is inappropriate. The business reader wants, and rightly so, to see the technical material in the context of the needs of the business and the ways in which communications and networking technology support desired business functions. Thus this book begins by defining the requirements for information communications in business. The types of information and their utility are examined first. This sets the stage for an examination of communications and networking alternatives. And, as these alternatives are presented and compared, the applications for which they are suited, as well as the underlying technology, are explored. It is hoped that this strategy will make the material more comprehensible and provides a structure that is more natural to a reader with a business orientation.

What's New in the Third Edition

This third edition is seeing the light of day less than eight years after the publication of the first edition. Much has happened during those years. Indeed, the pace of change, if anything, is increasing. The result is that this revision is more comprehensive and thorough than any of the previous ones. As an indication of this, about one-half of the figures and one-half of the tables in this edition are new. Every chapter has been revised and new chapters have been added.

To begin this process of revision, the second edition of this book was extensively reviewed by a number of professors who taught from that edition. The result is that, in many places, the narrative has been clarified and tightened and illustrations have been improved. Also, a number of new "field-tested" problems have been added.

Beyond these refinements to improve pedagogy and user-friendliness, there have been major substantive changes throughout the book. Highlights include:

- **The Internet, the Web, and Intranets:** The Internet was barely on the business radar screen when the second edition came out. What a difference it has made! Virtually all companies have or are planning some kind of Web presence and virtually all companies provide Internet access for their employees for electronic mail and information gathering. Most companies also have or are planning an internal Internet-style facility, known as an intranet. An entire new chapter of the book is devoted to doing business on the Internet. In addition, a section on the World Wide Web has been added to the chapter on distributed applications and a section on intranets has been added to the chapter on client/server computing. Finally, as mentioned above, this book itself takes advantage of the Internet and Web to provide services to the instructors and students.

- **Wireless Networks:** Wireless networking, both for local area networks (LANs), and wide-area networks (WANs), have become a significant component of many networking configurations. A new chapter explores this important technology.

- **High-speed LANs:** Coverage of this important area is introduced, and includes detailed treatment of leading-edge approaches, including Fast Ethernet (100BASE-T), Gigabit Ethernet, ATM LANs, and Fibre Channel.

- **TCP/IP:** TCP/IP has won the "protocol wars" with OSI, and is now the focus of the protocol coverage in this book.

- **Network Management:** SNMP and SNMPv2 have become essential tools in network management, and the book now contains an extensive discussion of these important protocols.

- **Network Security:** The chapter on network security has been completely rewritten and reorganized to provide a clearer presentation that emphasizes the important tools and strategies that management needs to implement. The chapter now also includes an extensive discussion of Web security.

In addition, throughout the book, virtually every topic has been updated to reflect the developments in standards and technology that have occurred since the publication of the second edition.

Acknowledgments

This new edition has benefited from review by a number of people, who gave generously of their time and expertise. We would like to thank the following who reveiwed part or all of the manuscript for the third edition: Gad Selig of St. Mary's College, Fairfield, CT; Arand Kunnathar of the University of Toledo; Glenn Shephard of San Jose State; Glenn Dietrich of the University of Texas - San Antonio; Cathy Bakes of Kent State University; Richard Kerns of East Carolina University; and Randy Smith of the University of Virginia.

BRIEF CONTENTS

xi

CONTENTS

CHAPTER 1

Introduction

1.1 INFORMATION AND COMMUNICATION

When Marshall McLuhan coined the term *global village* in the 1960s, he perhaps foresaw that General Motors would operate a network that linked more than 500,000 computing devices and telephones and connected 18,000 locations worldwide. Or that American Airlines' SABER reservations network, linking more than 60,000 video terminals all over the planet to six massive mainframe computers, sometimes would post larger annual revenues than did the airline itself.

By any name, a confluence of computers, communication technologies, and demographics is transforming the way any enterprise conducts itself and carries out its organizational mandate. And it's happening fast. A business that ignores it will fall hopelessly to the rear in the global race for the competitive edge.

At the heart of the transformation is information. No longer a by-product—no longer, in many cases, even a cost center—the generation and movement of information have been made profitable by those companies that have taken up the technological challenge posed by the myriad machines that automate so much of our lives.

We are unquestionably dependent on computers and the communications devices and services that connect them. The number of computers and terminals at work in the world today is over 100 million. It constitutes a critical mass: The overwhelming need of organizations and their workers now is for connectivity, for integration, for ease of access to information. So fundamental is information communications technology to business success that it is emerging as the foundation of a new strategy now taking shape in U.S. businesses—using management structures to gain a competitive advantage.

As businesses are challenged by such forces as global competition, mergers, and acquisitions, time-tested management structures are putting a strain on corporate bottom lines. In response, companies are breaking down divisional walls and flattening top-heavy management pyramids to create new corporate structures that help them to compete more effectively. The technology that is making much of this possible is *networking*.

Communications technology helps companies overcome three kinds of basic organizational difficulties: Good networks make geographically dispersed companies more manageable; they help top-heavy companies trim down middle management; and they also help companies break down barriers between divisions. As we examine the technology and applications throughout this book, we will see the ways in which information communications technology solves these and other vital business problems.

1.2 THE MANAGER'S DILEMMA

Effective management, use, and communication of information are essential for a business to remain competitive. In the 1960s and 1970s, this requirement placed a new burden on management: to understand and exploit the new technologies of data processing and telephone exchange systems. With respect to data processing, a business needed computing resources to store, process, and report information. Choices had to be made between the purchase of in-house computer systems and the use of time-sharing facilities from outside providers. Software was the central element that determined the effectiveness of the growing data processing budget in strengthening the company. Telephone systems began to offer more options and services, and again the choice was between an in-house private branch exchange (PBX) and a Centrex service from the local telephone company.

Several decades later, these challenges remain and indeed increase. As the cost of computing equipment drops, business relies more and more on in-house computing resources. But the choices proliferate: personal computers, Unix workstations, minicomputers, mainframes. The variety of software available has also increased dramatically. Because of lower costs today, it is tempting to buy a number of overlapping products and to decentralize the procurement authority to the divisional or even departmental level. But this approach makes the problems of managing and coordinating computing resources more difficult. In telephone exchange systems, also, the choices have become more complex. The introduction of computer technology into the private branch exchange and Centrex facility present the manager with more options.

1.3 NATURE OF BUSINESS INFORMATION REQUIREMENTS

A business survives and thrives on information: information within the organization and information exchanged with suppliers, customers, and regulators. Moreover, the information needs to be consistent, accessible, and at the right location. In Part 1, Chapters 2 and 3, we consider information in four forms—voice, data, image, and video—and the implications of distributed requirements.

In this book, the term **voice communications** refers primarily to telephone-related communications. By far the most common form of communication in any organization and for most personnel is direct telephone conversation. The telephone has been a basic tool of business for decades. Telephone communications has recently been enhanced by a variety of computer-based services, including voice mail and computerized telephone exchange systems. Voice mail provides the ability to send, forward, and reply to voice messages nonsimultaneously, and it has become a cost-efficient tool even for many midsize organizations. It provides savings on answering machines and services as well as a more responsive service to customers and suppliers. Advances have also been made in computerized telephone exchange systems, including in-house digital private branch exchanges (PBX) and Centrex systems provided by the local telephone company. These new systems provide a host of features, including call forwarding, camp-on call waiting, least-cost routing of long-distance calls, and a variety of accounting and auditing features.

The term **data communications** is sometimes used to refer to virtually any form of information transfer other than voice. It is sometimes convenient to limit this term to information in the form of text (such as reports, memos, and other documents) and numerical data (such as accounting files). The rapid changes in technology have created fresh challenges for management in making effective use of data communications. Later in this chapter we briefly outline the changes in technology in transmission, networks, and communications software that present the manager with new and powerful business tools but also the necessity of making choices among complex alternatives.

Image communications is just beginning to come into its own in the office environment. The best-known example of this technology is facsimile (fax). Like the tortoise who surprises the hare, facsimile machines have caught up with higher-tech alternatives and have achieved status over the past few years as the preferred method of sending documents over a long distance. With fax the document can have any content, including text, graphics, signatures, and even photographs. Newer machines can transmit these documents over telephone networks in seconds, and low-cost hardware, including personal computer attachments, is now available. In addition, image communication is coming to play an important role within the office. The arrival of the optical disk, based on the same technology as that of the familiar compact disk of the music industry, allows massive amounts of information to be stored inexpensively. Thus, all sorts of images, including engineering and design specifications, mixed documents (text, graphs, signatures, etc.), presentation material, and so on, can be moved quickly around the office and displayed on user workstations. This new technology for storing and transmitting images creates a demand for high-capacity networks and is one of the driving forces in the development of networking technology.

Video communications is also becoming important in the office environment. Traditionally, the technology has been used as a one-way delivery system of entertainment programs. Now, with the availability of high-capacity transmission links and networks, it has an increasing business application, most notably videoconferencing. Videoconferencing allows the linkup of two or more remotely located conference rooms to conduct such meetings as planning sessions, contract negotiations, and project reviews. The time and money saved on travel, food, and lodging make videoconferencing a powerful tool for increasing efficiency and productivity.

All these forms of information communications play a key role in today's businesses. The manager responsible for them must understand the technology sufficiently to be able to deal effectively with vendors of communications products and services and to make cost-effective choices among the growing array of options. In Chapter 2 we examine the business uses of these four classes of information and the communications requirements that they generate.

1.4 DISTRIBUTED DATA PROCESSING

The steady drop over many years in the cost of data processing equipment, coupled with an increase in the capability of such equipment, has led to the introduction of many small and medium-sized computers into the business environment. Traditionally, the data processing function was centrally organized around a mainframe computer. Today, however, it is much more common to find a distributed data processing configuration, one that consists of a number of computers and terminals linked together by networks. In Chapter 3 we examine the motivation for distributed data processing and discuss the various forms that it takes.

1.5 TRANSMISSION OF INFORMATION

The basic building block of any communications facility is the transmission line. Much of the technical detail of how information is encoded and transmitted across a line is of no real interest to the business manager. The manager is concerned with whether the particular facility provides the required capacity, with acceptable reliability, at minimum cost. However, there are certain aspects of transmission technology that a manager must understand to be able to ask the right questions and make informed decisions.

One of the basic choices facing a business user is the transmission medium. For use within the business premises, this choice is generally completely up to the business. For long-distance communications, the choice is generally but not always made by the long-distance carrier. In either case, changes in technology are rapidly changing the mix of media used. Of particular note are *fiber optic* transmission and *wireless* transmission (e.g., satellite and radio). These two media are now driving the evolution of data communications transmission.

The ever-increasing capacity of fiber optic channels is making channel capacity a virtually free resource. The growth of the market for optical fiber transmission systems since the beginning of the 1980s is without precedent. During the past 10 years, the cost of fiber optic transmission has dropped by more than an order of magnitude, and the capacity of such systems has grown at almost as rapid a rate. Long-distance telephone communications trunks within the United States will soon consist almost completely of fiber optic cable. Because of its high capacity and because of its security characteristics—fiber is almost impossible to tap—it is being used increasingly within office buildings to carry the growing load of business information. However, switching is now becoming the bottleneck. This problem is causing radical changes in communications architecture, including asynchronous transfer mode (ATM) switching, highly parallel processing in switches, and integrated network management schemes.

The second medium—wireless transmission—is a result of the trend toward universal personal telecommunications and universal access to communications.

The first concept refers to the ability of a person to identify himself or herself easily and to use conveniently any communication system in a large area (e.g., globally, over a continent, or in an entire country) in terms of a single account. The second refers to the capability of using one's terminal in a wide variety of environments to connect to information services (e.g., to have a portable terminal that will work in the office, on the street, and on airplanes equally well). This revolution in personal computing obviously involves wireless communication in a fundamental way.

Despite the growth in the capacity and the drop in cost of transmission facilities, transmission services remain the most costly component of a communications budget for most businesses. Thus, the manager needs to be aware of techniques that increase the efficiency of the use of these facilities. The two major approaches to greater efficiency are multiplexing and compression. *Multiplexing* refers to the ability of a number of devices to share a transmission facility. If each device needs the facility only a fraction of the time, a sharing arrangement allows the cost of the facility to be spread over many users.. As the name indicates, *compression* involves squeezing the data down so that a lower-capacity, cheaper transmission facility can be used to meet a given demand. These two techniques show up separately and in combination in a number of types of communications equipment. The manager needs to understand these technologies to be able to assess the appropriateness and cost-effectiveness of the various products on the market.

In Part 2, Chapters 4 through 6, we examine the key issues and technologies in the area of information transmission.

Transmission and Transmission Media

Information can be communicated by converting it into an electromagnetic signal and transmitting that signal over a medium such as a twisted-pair telephone line. The most commonly used transmission media are twisted-pair lines, coaxial cable, optical fiber cable, and terrestrial and satellite microwave. The data rates that can be achieved and the rate at which errors can occur depend on the nature of the signal and the type of medium. In Chapter 4 we examine the significant properties of electromagnetic signals. It also compares the various transmission media in terms of cost, performance, and applications.

Communication Techniques

The transmission of information across a transmission medium involves more than simply inserting a signal on the medium. The technique used to encode the information into an electromagnetic signal must be determined. There are various ways in which the encoding can be done, and the choice affects performance and reliability. Furthermore, the successful transmission of information involves a high degree of cooperation between the various components. The interface between a device and the transmission medium must be agreed on. Some means of controlling the flow of information and recovering from its loss or corruption must be used. The latter functions are performed by a data link control protocol. All these issues are examined in Chapter 5.

Transmission Efficiency

A major cost in any computer/communications facility is transmission cost. Because of this, it is important to maximize the amount of information that can be carried over a given resource or, alternatively, to minimize the transmission capacity needed to satisfy a given information communications requirement. Two ways of achieving this objective are multiplexing and compression. The two techniques can be used separately or in combination. In Chapter 6 we examine the three most common multiplexing techniques—frequency division, synchronous time division, and statistical time division—as well as the important compression techniques.

1.6 NETWORKS

The number of computers in use worldwide, according to the International Data Corporation, is in excess of 100 million. Moreover, because of the expanding memory and processing power of these computers, users can put the machines to work on new kinds of applications and functions. Accordingly, the pressure from the users of these systems for ways to communicate among all these machines is irresistible. It is changing the way vendors think and the way in which automation products and services are sold. This demand for connectivity is manifested in two specific requirements: the need for communications software, which is previewed in the next section, and the need for networks.

One type of network that has become increasingly common is the local-area network (LAN). Indeed, the LAN is to be found in virtually all medium-sized and large office buildings. As the number and power of computing devices have grown, so have the number and capacity of LANs to be found in an office. Although standards have been developed that reduce somewhat the number of types of LANs, there are still half a dozen general types of local-area networks to choose from. Furthermore, many offices need more than one such network, with the attendant problems of interconnecting and managing a diverse collection of networks, computers, and terminals.

Beyond the confines of a single office building, networks for voice, data, image, and video are equally important to business. Here, too, there are rapid changes. Advances in technology have led to greatly increased capacity and the concept of integration. *Integration* means that the customer equipment and networks can deal simultaneously with voice, data, image, and even video. Thus, a memo or report can be accompanied by voice commentary, presentation graphics, and perhaps even a short video introduction or summary. Image and video services impose large demands on wide-area network transmission. Moreover, as LANs become ubiquitous and as their transmission rates increase, the demands on the wide-area networks to support LAN interconnection have increased the demands on wide-area network capacity and switching. On the other hand, fortunately, the enormous and ever-increasing capacity of fiber optics transmission provides ample resources to meet these demands. However, developing switching systems with the capacity and rapid response to support these increased requirements is a challenge not yet conquered.

The opportunities for using networks as an aggressive competitive tool and as a means of enhancing productivity and slashing costs are great. The manager who understands the technology and can deal effectively with vendors of service and equipment is able to enhance a company's competitive position.

In Chapters 7 through 11, which make up Part 3, we examine the key alternatives for local networking (within a single building or cluster of buildings) and wide-area networking.

Wide-Area Networks

Wide-area networks provide the means for communication outside the office. The public telephone network is an effective and relatively inexpensive means of carrying voice traffic. For reasons of cost, security, or convenience, many companies supplement the public telephone network with private voice networks. In the latter case, the company usually leases communication lines from a provider of telephone or telecommunications service and uses the leased lines to connect switches at various customer sites.

For data transmission, the use of packet-switching networks has become common. Both public and private packet-switching networks are in operation. These networks often make use of an interface standard known as X.25. Integrated services digital network (ISDN) is a set of protocols and services now being implemented to support data, image, video, and voice communications efficiently and in a unified way. ISDN will be a worldwide public telecommunications network that will replace existing analog public telecommunications networks and deliver a wide variety of services.

In Chapters 7 and 8 we look at the various alternatives for wide-area networks, examine the technologies involved, and assess the applications for which each alternative is appropriate.

Local-Area Networks

Local networks are used to interconnect equipment within a single building or cluster of buildings. Some local networks rely on circuit-switching technology; these include digital private branch exchanges (PBXs) and digital data switches. This technology is suited primarily to telephone and terminal support. For higher-speed data support, networks that rely on a shared transmission medium and the use of packet transmission are needed. These are referred to as *local-area networks* (LANs). In Chapters 9 and 10 we look at various types of LANs, examine their strengths and weaknesses, and assess the role that each can play in business communications.

Wireless Networks

Wireless networks are assuming an increasingly important role in both wide-area and local area networking. Wireless networks provide advantages in the areas of mobility and ease of installation and configuration. In Chapter 11 we survey the field of wireless networks.

1.7 COMMUNICATIONS SOFTWARE

A business needs to be concerned with two dimensions of computer communications software: the application software that is provided for a community of terminals and computers, and the underlying interconnection software that allows these terminals and computers to work together cooperatively. The mere existence of a large population of computers and terminals creates a demand that these devices work together. For example, when most employees in an organization have access to a terminal or a personal computer (PC), one of the most effective means of communication within the organization is electronic mail (E-mail). If one employee needs to communicate with another, a message sent by E-mail can be far more effective than hit-or-miss attempts to reach the person by telephone. A detailed E-mail message can be left in the recipient's "electronic mailbox," to be read and answered when the recipient returns to the office. Other applications, such as the exchange of documents, the use of a database that is distributed among a number of computers, and the ability to access many different computers from a single terminal, can be provided with applications software that is geared for the new networked environment.

The key to the success of these applications is that all the terminals and computers in the community "speak" the same language. This is the role of the underlying interconnection software. This software must ensure that all the devices transmit messages in such a way that they can be understood by the other computers and terminals in the community. With the introduction of the systems network architecture (SNA) by IBM in the 1970s, this concept became a reality. However, SNA worked only with IBM equipment. Soon other vendors followed with their own proprietary communications architectures to tie their equipment together. Such an approach may be good business for the vendor, but it is bad business for the customer. Happily, that situation has changed radically with the adoption of standards for interconnection software. The manager needs to understand the scope and status of these standards to be able to exploit them in building a tailored multiple-vendor installation.

Modern data communications and microelectronics are radically changing the architecture of modern information systems. Most applications have evolved away from large, general-purpose mainframe computers to *distributed computing*. Instead of dumb terminals enslaved to mainframes, powerful workstations and PCs provide, local to the user, powerful graphical interfaces and much of the application computing. The local workstations and PCs are supported by specialized servers specifically designed for a single function, such as printing, storing files, or supporting database activities. The workstations and PCs are often connected to the servers by high-speed LANs. This approach, called *client–server architecture*, requires sophisticated, reliable, and secure data communications, but its inherent flexibility and responsiveness make it an essential tool in the businessperson's information systems repertoire.

In Part 4, Chapters 12 through 14, we examine the many issues that surround the topic of communications software and provide a framework within which the manager can define the needs of the business and assess various product options.

TCP/IP

One of the most difficult problems that has traditionally faced computer users is that different vendors have used different and incompatible architectures. In Chapter 12 we discuss the use of standardized communications protocols to integrate diverse equipment. The focus is on the TCP/IP (transmission control protocol/Internet protocol) protocol suite, which is now used universally for communications software functions across multiple-vendor equipment and is also the basis for operation of the Internet. We also review briefly two other approaches to organizing communications software: the opens system interconnection (OSI) architecture developed by the International Organization for Standardization (ISO), and IBM's proprietary systems network architecture (SNA).

Distributed Applications

Distributed information processing is essential in virtually all businesses. There is a growing use of applications that are designed to work among a distributed set of computers for both intracompany and intercompany information exchange. In Chapter 13 we examine three such applications that are likely to be the most important to a business:

- Electronic data interchange
- Electronic mail
- World Wide Web

Client–Server Architectures and Intranets

A remarkable transformation is taking place in the architecture of today's commercial computers. The large mainframe, although still important, is being replaced or supplemented in many applications by networked minicomputers and workstations, as illustrated by the increased manufacture of computers of different types. The number of PCs and workstations is growing at a much greater rate than that of mainframes and midrange computers, with the result that computing is being more widely distributed. Increasingly, computation is provided by the *client–server* model. Separate computers (servers) support database functions, store files, perform printing services, and provide other specialized functions on a shared basis for many users (clients). These servers, which can offer enhanced performance and cost savings through specialization, are accessed over LANs and other communications networks.

Even more recently, a new approach has gained widespread support within organizations: the intranet. An intranet provides the same sorts of applications and interfaces as found on the Internet, especially the World Wide Web. The difference is that an intranet is confined to use within the organization, with no access to outsiders. The intranet is a flexible, easy-to-use, and easy-to-implement approach to many business applications.

In Chapter 14 we look at both client–server computing and intranets.

1.8 MANAGEMENT ISSUES

In Part 5, Chapters 15 through 17, we conclude the book by examining key management issues related to business data communications.

Doing Business on the Internet

The Internet has become a central fact of life for corporations. For a number of years, the Internet has provided a vehicle by which employees can communicate with those outside the company using electronic mail and has provided a rich source of information that employees can tap to help in fulfilling their job functions. But it is the emergence of the World Wide Web that has created the most interest in corporate management. Virtually all companies have some sort of Web presence, even if it is a simple information-only Web page. But many companies now do business over the Internet, mainly through the use of the Web. Whether it is dealing with suppliers and corporate companies, or with individual consumers, the Web provides a great opportunity to expand business and simplify transactions. In Chapter 15 we examine the many issues associated with doing business on the Internet.

Network Management

In the early years of data communications, in the 1970s, the key focus was the functionality and performance of the technology. The key questions were: What could the technology do? How fast? For how many transactions? As electronic information systems became part of the basic fabric of many businesses, managers discovered that the operation of their businesses had become dependent on their information systems and that the economic performance of their firms depended on the cost-effective use of the technology. That is, like any resource, information technology had to be managed. For example, managers of data communications today are often most concerned about network reliability. Many of the management functions required are common to other aspects of business management, but the following requirements are special to information technology:

- Networks have evolved from an easily controlled master–slave (read: mainframe/dumb terminal) approach into peer-to-peer interconnections among highly distributed systems.
- Peer-to-peer networks have grown larger and larger—some have tens of thousands of attached devices—so that managing, monitoring, and maintaining them has become very complex.

- In many business sectors, such as banking, retailing, and other service industries, networks of computing devices constitute a critical strategic resource that cannot be allowed to fail.
- Communications costs, meanwhile, are climbing, and there is a shortage of skilled personnel to staff network command centers and to handle network management.

Network management must provide global visibility on corporate information flow. Techniques of centralized, remote monitoring and control provide rapid notification of failures and automatic invocation of recovery measures. On-the-fly analysis of network performance and dynamic adjustment of network parameters provide adaptation to varying cycles of business activity. Network management is a complex discipline, particularly in a multivendor environment. The manager must understand the requirements for network management and the tools and technologies available to be able to plan effectively for an automated network management strategy.

In Chapter 16 we focus on network management.

Network Security

As companies rely increasingly on networks and as access to outsiders via the Internet and other links grows, the vexing question of security becomes ever more important. Companies are at risk for the disclosure of confidential information and for the unauthorized altering of corporate data. In Chapter 17 we look at the basic tools for achieving network security and discuss how they can be adapted to meet a company's needs.

1.9 STANDARDS

Standards have come to play a dominant role in the information communications marketplace. Virtually all vendors of products and services are committed to supporting international standards. In Appendix A we explain the importance of standards and the current status of their use and provide an overview of the key organizations involved in developing these standards.

1.10 INTERNET RESOURCES

There are a number of resources available on the Internet for keeping up with developments in this field.

Web Sites for This Book

There is a Web page for this book that provides support for students and instructors. The page includes links to relevant sites, transparency masters of figures in the book in PDF (Adobe Acrobat) format, and sign-up information for the book's Internet mailing list. The mailing list has been set up so that instructors using this book can exchange information, suggestions, and questions with each other and with the author. The Web page is at http://www.shore.net/~ws/BDC3e.html.

As soon as any typos or other errors are discovered, an errata list for this book will be available at http://www.shore.net/~ws/. The file will be updated as needed. Please E-mail any errors that you spot to ws@shore.net. Errata sheets for other books by Bill Stallings are at the same Web site, as well as a discount ordering information for the books.

Other Web Sites

There are numerous Web sites that provide some sort of information related to the topics of this book. Here is a sample:

- http://web.syr.edu/~jmwobus/lans: links to most important sources of LAN information on the Internet, including all of the related FAQs (frequently-asked questions).
- http://www.spp.umich.edu/telecom/telecom-info.html: contains references to information sources relating to the technical, economic, public policy, and social aspects of telecommunications. All forms of telecommunication, including, voice, data, video, wired, wireless, cable TV, and satellite, are included.
- http://guide.sbanetweb.com: links to over 1000 hardware and software vendors who currently have WWW sites, as well as a list of thousands of computer and networking companies in a phone directory.

In subsequent chapters, pointers to more specific Web sites can be found in the "Recommended Reading" section.

USENET Newsgroups

A number of USENET newsgroups are devoted to some aspect of data communications and networking. As with virtually all USENET groups, there is a high noise-to-signal ratio, but it is worth experimenting to see if any meet your needs. Here is a sample:

- comp.dcom.lans, comp.dcom.lans.misc: general discussions of LANs.
- comp.std.wireless: general discussion of wireless networks including wireless LANs.
- comp.security.misc: computer security and encryption.
- comp.dcom.cell-relay: covers ATM and ATM LANs.
- comp.dcom.frame-relay: covers frame relay networks.
- comp.dcom.net-management: discussion of network management applications, protocols, and standards.
- comp.protocols.tcp-ip: TCP/IP protocol suite.

1.11 USEFUL PUBLICATIONS

This book serves as a tutorial for learning about the field of business data communications and a reference that can be turned to for help on a specific topic. However, with the rapid changes taking place in this field, no book can hope to

TABLE 1-1 Useful Periodicals

Name	*Web Site*
Business Communications Review	http://www.bcr.com Links to Web pages of vendors that advertise in the magazine.
Data Communications	http://www.data.com Well-organized archive of material from the magazine.
Telecommunications	http://www.telecoms-mag.com/tcs.html Articles and new product information from past issues, plus an extensive international listing of industry trade shows. Product listings include a brief description plus the ability to request product information from the vendor. A useful search capability can be used to search articles and product listing by keyword.
Network World	http://www.nwfusion.com The best Web site on this list. Contains a well-organized archive of the paper's contents. Also contains links to sites related to current news stories, sites related to various technical topics covered in the paper, and vendor information.
Network Computing	http://techweb.cmp.com/nwc Articles from magazine available plus pointers to advertisers. Site also includes a hypertext network design manual with useful practical tips for end-user network design.
LAN Magazine	http://www.lanmag.com Links to Web pages of vendors that advertise in the magazine.
Forbes/ASAP	http://www.forbes.com Copies of some articles from past issues are provided.
Business Week	http://www.businessweek.com Copies of some articles from past issues are provided.

stand alone for very long. If you are truly interested in this field, you will need to invest some of your time keeping up with new developments, and the best way to do that is by reading a few relevant periodicals. The list of publications that could be recommended is huge, and we have resisted the temptation to overwhelm you with quantity. Rather, we have listed in Table 1-1 a small, select list of publications that will repay the time that you devote to them.

Business-Oriented Publications

Because of the growing importance of information communications to business, virtually all business periodicals now provide some coverage of this field. Two of the best for providing such coverage are *Forbes* and *Business Week*. *Forbes* includes a regular "Computer/Communications" section that includes two or three articles plus a regular column in each issue. The articles are timely, to the point, and cover a broad range. Periodically, the supplement *ASAP* is included with *Forbes*. *ASAP* is a full-length magazine in its own right with broad coverage of business information systems and business data communications topics.

Business Week has a regular "Information Processing" section that includes two or three articles each week. The section is oriented more toward computers than communications but does provide coverage of the latter. In addition, from time to time the magazine has cover stories in this area that provide more in-depth discussion.

Trade/Technical Publications

The number of periodicals that cover some aspect of this field is vast and growing. A few of the most useful are discussed in this section.

Business Communications Review is a very useful monthly, oriented toward the business user, that integrates data and voice communications well. Besides clearly written features covering communications technology, management, and applications, it has a stable of well-qualified columnists writing on everything from the Washington regulatory scene and network management to the latest in broadband technologies.

Data Communications is a monthly magazine that provides excellent coverage of the industry, including a regular column on communication tariffs, articles on particular companies, statistics on communications-related stocks, and coverage of industry trends and regulatory issues. The magazine also regularly features buyers' guide articles on particular products and services. In addition, every month there are one or two case-study articles that relate the experience of a particular company that has installed some sort of distributed system or network. Usually, these articles are written by someone with the company. *Telecommunications* is a monthly magazine that contains both industry-related and technical articles. The magazine concentrates heavily on long-distance networking topics, such as telephone, telecommunications, and regulatory issues.

Network World is a weekly tabloid-size newspaper that is an excellent source of information about the industry and market for information communications products and services. The coverage is quite thorough and includes buyers' guides on products and services. Each week there are one or more in-depth articles that touch upon a single area, such as network management. The treatment is from a management rather than a technical orientation. The newspaper also provides product comparisons.

LAN Magazine and *Network Computing* both focus on networking products. Both magazines have some technical articles but deal more with vendor offerings. Together, they provide an excellent means for tracking new product releases and for obtaining comparative analyses of product offerings.

QUESTIONS

1. What three kinds of basic organizational difficulties can communications technology help companies overcome?
2. Name four types of information that are found on networks.

3. How has the technology of the compact disk used in the music industry been used in image communications?

4. Why are the burdens on the manager today greater than in previous years when it comes to using new technology efficiently?

5. Why has optical fiber transmission become more popular in the past few years?

6. Name three approaches to organizing communications software.

7. Name two approaches that can be used for increasing the efficiency of transmission services.

8. Contrast the function of application software with that of interconnection software.

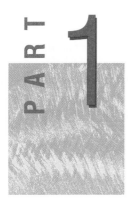

PART 1

REQUIREMENTS

CHAPTER 2

Business Information

CHAPTER OBJECTIVES

After reading this chapter, you should be able to:

- Distinguish between digital and analog information sources.

- Characterize business information types into one of four categories: voice, data, image, and video.

- Estimate quantitatively the communication resources required by the four types of information sources.

- Explain why system response time is a critical factor in user productivity.

*I*t is important to understand how information communication relates to business requirements. A first step in this understanding is to examine the various forms of business information. There is a wide variety of applications, each with its own information characteristics. For the analysis and design of information networks, however, the kinds of information usually can be categorized as requiring one of a small number of services: **voice**, **data**, **image**, and **video**. Our examination covers the following topics:

- How the impact of information sources on communications systems is measured.

- The nature of the four major forms of business information: voice, data, image, and video.

- The types of business services that relate to each of these forms of information.

- An introductory look at the implications of these services from the point of view of the communications requirements that they generate.

Information sources can produce information in **digital** or **analog** form. *Digital information* is represented as a sequence of discrete symbols from a finite "alphabet." Examples are text, numerical data, and binary data. For digital communication, the information rate and the capacity of a digital channel are measured in bits per second (bps).

Analog information is a continuous signal, for example, a voltage, that can take on a continuum of values. An example is the electrical signal coming out of a microphone when someone speaks into it. In this case, the analog electrical signal represents the continuous acoustic changes in air pressure that make up sound. For analog communication, information rate and channel capacity are measured in hertz (Hz) of bandwidth (1 Hz = 1 cycle per second). Virtually any communication signal can be expressed as a combination of pure oscillations of various frequencies. The bandwidth measures the limits of these frequencies. The higher the frequencies allowed, the more accurately a complex signal can be represented.

The *bit* is the fundamental unit of discrete information. It represents the outcome of one choice: 1 or 0, yes or no, or on or off. A bit is usually represented as a choice of a one or a zero. Thus, in this representation, the two potential outcomes are 0 and 1. The outcome of choices represents information. One bit represents two potential outcomes. So, for example, one bit can represent the on–off state of a switch. Two bits can represent four outcomes: 00, 01, 10, 11, for example. Three bits represent eight outcomes: 000, 001, 010, 011, 100, 101, 110, 111, for example. Each time another bit is added, the numbers of outcomes double. A *byte* (or octet) is the name given to 8 bits. The number of potential outcomes a byte represents is $2 \times 2 \times 2 \times 2 \times 2 \times 2 \times 2 \times 2 = 2^8 = 256$. Bytes are usually used in representing quantities of storage in computers. Bits are traditionally used in communications. It is also common in discussions involving computers to use the term *kilo* to refer to $2^{10} = 1024$, whereas in communications, *kilo* virtually always means 1000. Thus, in referring to computer storage, 64 kilobytes of memory usually means $2^{16} = 65,536$, whereas a communication channel of 64 kilobits per second means 64,000 bits per second. In a communications context, we take *kilo* to mean 1000, *mega* to mean 1,000,000, and *giga* to mean 1,000,000,000. In discussing computer storage, the terms *kilo*, *mega*, and *giga* refer to $2^{10} = 1024$, $2^{20} = 1,048,576$, and $2^{30} = 1,073,741,824$, respectively. It is useful to memorize some of the common and fundamental relations between the number of bits and the corresponding number of outcomes, some of which are given in Table 2-1.

2.1 VOICE

The voice service supports applications based on sound, usually of the human voice. The primary application using voice service is telephone communication. Other applications include telemarketing, voice mail, audio teleconferencing, and entertainment radio. The quality of sound is characterized mainly by the bandwidth used. Voice on a telephone is limited to about 3000 Hz of bandwidth, which is of moderate quality. Voice of teleconference quality requires about 7000 Hz of bandwidth. For reasonably high-fidelity sound, about 15,000 Hz (approximately the range of the human ear) is needed. For compact disks, 20,000 Hz is supported for each of two channels for stereo.

TABLE 2-1 Bits and Outcomes

Number of Bits	Number of Outcomes	Typical Use
1	2	Basic unit of information
2	4	
4	16	Hexadecimal digit
7	128	ASCII character without parity bit
8	256	Byte; character with parity bit
10	1,024	Kilobit of storage
13	8,192	Kilobyte of storage
16	65,536	Address size in older computers
20	1,048,576	Megabit of storage
23	8,388,608	Megabyte of storage
32	4.3×10^9	Modern address size

Voice (audio) information can also be represented digitally. The details are given in Chapter 5. We give an abbreviated discussion here. To get a good representation of sound in digital format, we need to sample its amplitude at a rate (samples per second, or smp/sec) equal to at least twice the maximum frequency (in hertz) of the analog signal. For voice of telephone quality, one usually samples at a rate of 8000 smp/sec. For high-quality sound on compact disks, 44,100 smp/sec is the rate used on each channel. After sampling, the signal amplitudes must be put in digital form. Eight bits per sample are usually used for telephone voice and 16 bits per sample for each channel for stereophonic compact disk. In the first case, 256 levels of amplitude can be distinguished, and in the second, more than 65,536. Thus, without compression, digital voice requires 8 bits/smp $\times$ 8000 smp/sec = 64,000 bps. In the case of CDs, a straightforward multiplication of the foregoing parameters leads to a data rate of 1.41 Mbps for both channels. A CD is usually rated at a capacity of about 600 megabytes (MB). This leads to an audio capacity of about 1 hr of stereo sound.

Typical telephone conversations have an average length in the range 1 to 5 min. For ordinary voice telephone communication, information in either direction is transmitted less than half the time; otherwise, the two parties would be talking at once. Speech typically takes place in bursts that average about 350 milliseconds (msec), separated by silent periods of about 650 msec [SPIR88].

Networking Implications

The requirements just discussed suggest the need for an intralocation facility that is both powerful and flexible, plus access to a variety of outside telephone services. Outside services are provided by public telephone networks, including the local telephone company and long-distance carriers such as AT&T or a national PTT (postal, telegraph, and telephone) authority. In addition, various private networking facilities and leased-line arrangements are possible. All of these are discussed in Chapter 7.

Intralocation services, plus access to outside services, is provided by means of either in-house equipment, often called customer premises equipment, such as

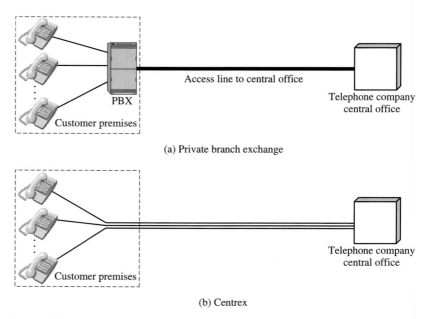

FIGURE 2.1 Business Telephone Configurations.

Private Branch Exchange (PBX)
A telephone exchange on the user's premises.

Centrex
A service offered by operating telephone companies that provides functions and features comparable to those provided by a PBX.

a private branch exchange, or by Centrex. The most effective way of satisfying the requirements just listed is to tie all of the phones at a given site into a single system. There are two main alternatives for this: the private branch exchange and Centrex. A **private branch exchange** (**PBX**) is an on-premises switching facility, owned or leased by an organization, that interconnects the telephones within the facility and provides access to the public telephone system (Figure 2.1a). Typically, a telephone user on the premises dials a three- or four-digit number to call another subscriber on the premises and dials one digit (usually 8 or 9) to get a dial tone for an outside line, which allows the caller to dial a number in the same fashion as a residential user.

Centrex is a telephone company offering that provides the same sort of service as a PBX but performs the switching function in equipment located in the telephone company's central office as opposed to the customer's premises (Figure 2.1b). All telephone lines are routed from the customer site to the central switch. The user can still make local calls with a short extension number, giving the appearance of an on-premises switch. Either a PBX or a Centrex facility can support a wide variety of voice-related services. Both voice mail and audio teleconferencing can be supported by either approach.

2.2 DATA

Data consist of information that can be represented by a finite alphabet of symbols, such as the digits 0 through 9 or the symbols represented on a terminal keyboard. Common examples of data include text and numerical information.

Symbols are quite often represented in computers or for transmission by groups of 8 bits (octets or bytes).

To get some practice in using the concepts introduced so far, let us estimate approximately how many bits are required to transmit a page of text. Commonly, a letter of the alphabet or a typographical symbol is represented by a byte, or 8 bits. Let us consider an 8- by-11-in. sheet, with a 1-in. margin on all sides. This leaves a 6- by-9 in. message space. A double-spaced page ordinarily has three lines to the inch, or 27 lines for the page. In a common typeface, there are 10 characters per inch, or 60 characters per line. This gives us a total $8 \times 27 \times 60 =$ 12,460 bits. This overstates the situation because contiguous spaces at the ends of lines are not ordinarily included, and some pages are not full. As a round number, 10,000 bits per page is probably a fair estimate. For a PC or a terminal communicating with a computer over a telephone line using a modem, a typical channel capacity is 28,800 bps. Thus it would take about 0.35 sec to transmit a page. For a medium-speed line of 56,000 bps, it would take about 0.17 sec.

To test our theory, we analyzed an 84-page report that was formatted with 1-in. margins and used a 10-pitch font except for headings. The formatted report consisted of 115,325 characters, which comes out to 1373 characters per page, or 10,984 bits, which is quite close to our rough estimate.

This is by no means the whole story. For example, English text is very redundant. That is, the same information can be sent by using many fewer bits. In the experiment just described, we used a standard compression routine to reduce the file to less than 40% of its size, or 4098 bits per page. We explore data compression techniques in Chapter 6. Another feature that characterizes many data-oriented information sources is the response time required, discussed later in this chapter.

2.3 IMAGE

The image service supports the communication of individual pictures, charts, or drawings. Image-based applications include facsimile, computer-aided design (CAD), publishing, and medical imaging. As an example of the types of demands that can be placed by imaging systems, consider medical image transmission requirements. Table 2-2 summarizes the communication impact of various medical image types. As well as giving the bits per image and the number of images per exam, the table gives the transmission time per exam for three standard digital transmission rates: DS-0 = 56 kbps, DS-1 = 1.544 Mbps, and DS-3 = 44.736 Mbps.

Again, compression can be used. If we allow some barely perceivable loss of information, we can use "lossy" compression, which might reduce the data by factors of roughly 10:1 to 20:1. On the other hand, for medical imaging lossy compression usually is not acceptable, so compression ratios for these applications run below 5:1.

Networking Implications

The various configurations by which image information is used and communicated do not differ fundamentally from the configurations used for text and numerical data. The key difference is in the volume of data. A page of text may

TABLE 2-2 Transfer Time for Digital Radiology Images[a]

Image Type	*Mbytes per Image*	*Images per Exam*	*DS-0 Time per Exam (sec)*	*DS-1 Time per Exam (sec)*	*DS-3 Time per Exam (sec)*
Computerized tomography (CT)	0.52	30	2229	81	3
Magnetic resonance imagery (MRI)	0.13	50	928	34	1
Digital angiography	1	20	2857	104	4
Digital fluorography	1	15	2142	78	3
Ultrasound	0.26	36	1337	48	2
Nuclear medicine	0.016	26	59	2	0.1
Computerized radiography	8	4	4571	166	6
Digitized film	8	4	4571	166	6

Source: [DWYE92].
[a] *DS-0 = 56 kbps; DS-1 = 1.544 Mbps; DS-2 = 44.736 Mbps.*

contain 300 words, which can be represented with about 13,000 bits (assuming 8 bits per character and an average of 5.5 characters per word). The bit image of a good-quality personal computer screen, such as that of the Macintosh, requires over 300,000 bits. A facsimile page with a resolution of 200 points per inch (which is an adequate but not unnecessarily high resolution) generates 3,740,000 bits. Thus, for image information, a tremendous number of bits are needed for representation in the computer.

The number of bits needed to represent an image can be reduced by the use of image compression techniques. In a typical document, whether it contains text or pictorial information, the black and white areas of the image tend to cluster. This property can be exploited to describe the patterns of black and white in a manner that is more concise than simply providing a listing of black and white values, one for each point in the image. Compression ratios (the ratio of the number of points in the image to the number of bits in the representation) of from 8 to 16 are readily achievable.

Even with compression, the number of bits to be transmitted for image information is large. As usual, there are two concerns: response time and throughput. In some cases, such as a CAD/CAM application, the user is interactively manipulating an image. If the user's terminal is separated from the application by a communications facility, the communications capacity must be substantial to give adequate response time. In other cases, such as facsimile, a delay of a few seconds or even a few minutes is usually of no consequence. However, the communications facility must still have a capacity great enough to keep up with the average rate of facsimile transmission. Otherwise, delays on the facility will grow over time as a backlog develops.

2.4 VIDEO

The video service carries sequences of pictures in time. Applications based on video include instructional and entertainment television, teleconferencing,

TABLE 2-3 Digital Television Formats

Format	*Spatiotemporal Resolution*	*Sampling Rate (MHz)*
CIF	$360 \times 288 \times 30$	3
CCIR	$720 \times 576 \times 30$	12
HDTV	$1280 \times 720 \times 60$	60

closed-circuit TV, and multimedia. For example, a black-and-white TV signal for video conferencing might have a frame resolution of 360 by 280 pixels[1] sent every 1/30 sec with an intensity ranging from black through gray to white represented by 8 bits. This would correspond to a raw data rate, without compression, of about 25 Mbps. To add color, the bit rate might go up by 50%. Table 2-3 gives the sampling rate in pixels per second for three common types of video. The table gives only the rates for luminance because color is treated differently in the three formats. At the extreme, uncompressed high-definition color television would require more than a gigabit per second to transmit. As with images, lossy compression can be used. Moreover, use can be made of the fact that video scenes in adjacent frames are very similar. Compression ratios from about 20:1 to 100:1 can be used, with reasonable quality being achieved.

2.5 RESPONSE TIME

Response Time
The elapsed time between the end of transmission of an enquiry and the beginning of the receipt of a response, measured at the enquiry terminal.

Response time is the time it takes a system to react to a given input. In an interactive transaction, it may be defined as the time between the last keystroke by the user and the beginning of the display of a result by the computer. For different types of applications, a slightly different definition is needed. In general, it is the time it takes for the system to respond to a request to perform a particular task.

Ideally, one would like the response time for any application to be short. However, it is almost invariably the case that shorter response time imposes greater cost. This cost comes from two sources:

- *Computer processing power.* The faster the computer, the shorter the response time. Of course, increased processing power means increased cost.

- *Competing requirements.* Providing rapid response time to some processes may penalize other processes.

Thus the value of a given level of response time must be assessed versus the cost of achieving that response time.

Table 2-4 lists six general ranges of response times. Design difficulties are faced when a response time of less than 1 second is required. That rapid response time is the key to productivity in interactive applications has been confirmed in a number of studies [SHNE84; THAD81; GUYN88]. These studies show that when a computer and a user interact at a pace that ensures that neither has to

---

[1] A **pixel**, or picture element, is the smallest element of a digital image that can be assigned a gray level. Equivalently, a pixel is an individual dot in a dot-matrix representation of a picture.

TABLE 2-4 Response-Time Ranges

Greater than 15 seconds

This rules out conversational interaction. For certain types of applications, certain types of users may be content to sit at a terminal for more than 15 sec waiting for the answer to a single simple inquiry. However, for a busy person, captivity for more than 15 sec seems intolerable. If such delays will occur, the system should be designed so that the user can turn to other activities and request the response at a later time.

Greater than 4 seconds

This is generally too long for a conversation requiring the operator to retain information in short-term memory (the operator's memory, not the computer's). Such delays would be very inhibiting in problem-solving activity and frustrating in data-entry activity. However, after a major closure, delays of from 4 to 15 sec can be tolerated.

2 to 4 seconds

A delay longer than 2 sec can be inhibiting to terminal operations that demand a high level of concentration. A wait of 2 to 4 sec at a terminal can seem surprisingly long when the user is absorbed and emotionally committed to complete what he or she is doing. Again, a delay in this range may be acceptable after a minor closure has occurred.

Less than 2 seconds

When the terminal user has to remember information throughout several responses, the response time must be short. The more detailed the information remembered, the greater the need for responses of less than 2 sec. For elaborate terminal activities, 2 sec represents an important response-time limit.

Subsecond response time

Certain types of thought-intensive work, especially with graphics applications, require very short response times to maintain the user's interest and attention for long periods of time.

Decisecond response time

A response to pressing a key and seeing the character displayed on the screen or clicking a screen object with a mouse needs to be almost instantaneous, less than 0.1 sec after the action. Interaction with a mouse requires extremely fast interaction if the designer is to avoid the use of alien syntax (one with commands, mnemonics punctuation, etc.)

Source: Based on [MART88].

wait on the other, productivity increases significantly, the cost of the work done on the computer therefore drops, and quality tends to improve. It used to be widely accepted that a relatively slow response, up to 2 sec, was acceptable for most interactive applications because the person was thinking about the next task. However, it now appears that productivity increases as rapid response times are achieved.

The results reported on response time are based on an analysis of on-line transactions. A transaction consists of a user command from a terminal and the system's reply. It is the fundamental unit of work for on-line system users. It can be divided into two time sequences:

- *User response time*: the time span between the moment a user receives a complete reply to one command and enters the next command. People often refer to this as *think time*.

- *System response time:* the time span between the moment the user enters a command and the moment a complete response is displayed on the terminal.

As an example of the effect of reduced system response time, Figure 2.2 shows the results of a study carried out on engineers using a computer-aided design graphics program for the design of integrated-circuit chips and boards [SMIT88]. Each transaction consists of a command by the engineer that alters in some way the graphic image being displayed on the screen. The results show that the rate of transactions increases as system response time falls and rises dramatically once system response time falls below 1 sec. What is happening is that as the system response time falls, so does the user response time. This has to do with the effects of short-term memory and human attention span.

In terms of the types of computer-based information systems that we have been discussing, rapid response time is most critical for transaction processing systems. The output of management information systems and decision support systems is generally a report or the results of some modeling exercise. In these cases, rapid turnaround is not essential. For office automation applications, the need for rapid response time occurs when documents are being prepared or modified, but there is less urgency for things such as electronic mail and computer teleconferencing. The implication in terms of communications is this: If there is a communications facility between an interactive user and the application and a rapid response time is required, the communications system must be designed so that its contribution to delay is compatible with that requirement. Thus, if a transaction processing application requires a response time of 1 sec and the average time it takes the computer application to generate a response is 0.75 sec, the delay due to the communications facility must be no more than 0.25 sec.

Another area where response time has become critical is the use of the World Wide Web, either over the Internet or over a corporate intranet.[2] The

FIGURE 2.2 Response Time Results for High-Function Graphics.

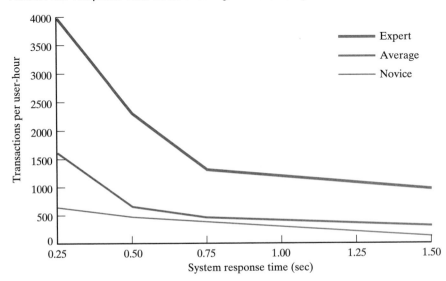

---

[2] **Intranet** is a term used to refer to the implementation of Internet technologies within a corporate organization rather than for external connection to the global Internet; this topic is explored in Chapter 14.

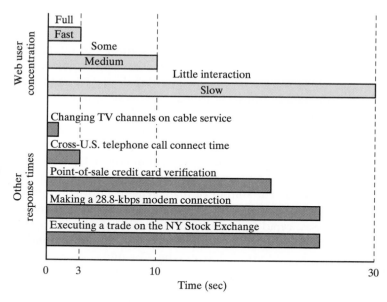

FIGURE 2.3 Response Time Requirements [SEVC96].

time it takes for a typical Web page to come up on the user's screen varies greatly. Response times can be gauged based on the level of user involvement in the session; in particular, systems with very fast response times tend to command more user attention.

As Figure 2.3 indicates, Web systems with a 3-sec or better response time maintain a high level of user attention. With a response time of between 3 and 10 sec, some user concentration is lost, and response times above 10 sec discourage the user, who may simply abort the session. For an organization that maintains an Internet Web site, much of the response time is determined by forces beyond the organization's control, such as the Internet throughput and the end user's access speed. In such circumstances the organization may consider keeping the image content of each page low and relying heavily on text, to promote rapid response time. For intranets, the organization has more control over delivery data rates and can afford more elaborate Web pages.

SUMMARY

The trend toward higher and higher transmission speed makes possible increased support for different services [e.g., integrated services digital network (ISDN) and broadband-based multimedia services] that once seemed too demanding for digital communication. To make effective use of these new capabilities, it is essential to have a sense of the demands each service puts on the storage and communications of integrated information systems. Services can be grouped into data, voice, image, and video, whose demands on information systems vary widely. Figure 2.4 gives an indication of the data rates required for various information types. Table 2-5 estimates the types of data rates that can be achieved with the use of compression. Data compression is discussed in Chapter 6. The compression values given in Table 2-5 are rough values of what is achievable with little or no noticeable degradation in quality.

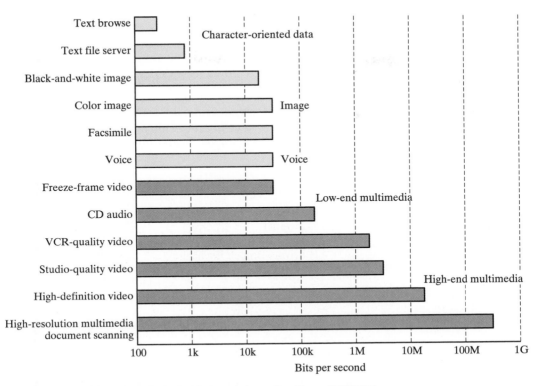

FIGURE 2.4 Required Data Rates for Various Information Types [TEGE95].

TABLE 2-5 Data Rate Requirements for Various Information Types

Information Type	*Uncompressed Date Rate*	*Compressed Data Rate*
Voice	64 kbps	8 kbps
Stereo audio	88.2 kbps	12 kbps
Full-motion video	45 Mbps	1 Mbps
Broadcast-quality NTSC video	120 Mbps	3–6 Mbps
Studio-quality NTSC video	216 Mbps	10–30 Mbps
High-definition video, broadcast quality	1500 Mbps	20–30 Mbps
Visualization imagery, full motion at 60 ft/sec, 1000 × 1000 pixels	1500–2500 Mbps	50–200 Mbps
Monochrome binary still images, 600 × 600 pixels/in., 135 pages/min	120 Mbps	5–50 Mbps
Full-color still images, 400 × 400 pixels/in., 60 pages/min	500 Mbps	45 Mbps

Source: Based on [COX95] and [LYLE92].

RECOMMENDED READING

[FREE91] provides a detailed survey of the communications requirements of all the information types discussed in this chapter. A good discussion of the many networking issues raised by multimedia applications is provided by [COX95].

COX95   COX, N., MANLEY, C., and CHEA, F. *LAN Times Guide to Multimedia Networking.* New York: Osborne/McGraw-Hill, 1995.
FREE91   FREEMAN, R. *Telecommunication Transmission Handbook.* New York: Wiley, 1991.

KEY TERMS

Analog	Image	Response Time
Centrex	Intranet	Video
Data	Pixel	Voice
Digital	Private Branch Exchange (PBX)	

PROBLEMS

1. How many bits will it take to represent the following sets of outcomes?
   a. The uppercase alphabet A, B, . . . , Z.
   b. The digits 0, 1, . . . , 9.
   c. The seconds in a 24-hr day.
   d. The people in the United States (about 248,000,000 of them).
   e. The world population (about 6 billion).

2. When examining x-rays, radiologists often deal with four to six images at a time. For a faithful digital representation of an x-ray photograph, a pixel array of 2048 × 2048 is typically used with a gray scale of intensity for each pixel of 12 bits. As you would hope, radiologists do not look kindly on compression that degrades quality.
   a. How many levels of gray scale are represented by 12 bits?
   b. How many bits does it take to represent an x-ray based on these parameters?
   c. Suppose that five x-rays have to be sent to another site over a T-1 line (1.544 Mbps). How long would it take at best, ignoring overhead?
   d. Suppose now that we wish to build a communications system that will provide the five x-rays of part c upon demand; that is, from the time the x-rays are requested, we want them available within 2 sec. What is a lowest channel rate that can support this demand?
   e. The next generation of displays for x-rays is planned for 4096 by 4096 pixels with a 12-bit gray scale. What does the answer to part d become when using this resolution?

3. A multimedia version of a multivolume reference book is being prepared for storage on compact disk (CD). Each disk can store about 600 MB. The input to each volume consists of 1000 pages of text typed 10 characters to the inch, six lines to the inch, on 8-by-11-in. paper with 1-in. margins. Each volume also has about 100 pictures, which will be displayed in color at Super VGA resolution (1024 × 768 pixels, 8 bits/pixel). Moreover, each volume is enhanced for the CD version with 30 min of audio of teleconferencing quality (16,000 smp/sec, 6 bits/smp).

    a. How many bits are there on a 600-MB CD (a megabyte = 2^{20} bytes).

    b. Without compression and ignoring overhead, how many volumes can be put on one CD?

    c. Suppose that the material is to be transmitted over a T-1 facility (1.544 Mbps). How long will it take, exclusive of overhead, to transmit a volume?

    d. Suppose that the text can be compressed at a 3:1 rate, the pictures at 10:1, and the audio at 2:1. How many volumes, exclusive of overhead, will fit on a CD? How long will it take to transmit a compressed volume on a T-1 channel?

4. The text of the *Encyclopaedia Britannica* is about 44 million words. For a sample of about 2000 words, the average word length was 5.1 characters per word.

    a. Approximately how many characters are there in the encyclopedia? (Be sure to allow for spaces and punctuation between words.)

    b. How long would it take to transmit the text over a T-1 line at 1.544 Mbps? On a fiber optic link at 2.488 Gbps?

    c. Could the text fit on a 600-MB CD?

5. Commonly, medical digital radiology ultrasound studies consist of about 25 images extracted from a full-motion ultrasound examination. Each image contains a 512×512 pixels, each with 8 bits of intensity information.

    a. How many bits are there in the 25 images?

    b. Ideally, however, the doctors would like to use $512 \times 512 \times 8$-bit frames at 30 ft/sec. Ignoring possible compression and overhead factors, what is the minimum channel capacity required to sustain this full-motion ultrasound?

    c. Suppose that each full-motion study consists of 25 sec of frames. How many such studies could fit on a 600-MB CD ROM?

CHAPTER **3**

Distributed Data Processing

CHAPTER OBJECTIVES

After reading this chapter, you should be able to:

- Describe the difference between centralized and distributed data processing and discuss the pros and cons of each approach.

- Explain why a distributed data processing system needs to be interconnected with some sort of data communications or networking facility.

- Describe the various forms of distributed data processing for applications.

- Describe the various forms of distributed databases.

- Discuss the implications of distributed data processing in terms of the requirements for data communications and networking facilities.

- Understand the motivation behind the trend to client–server architectures.

*I*n Chapter 2 we looked at the overall requirement for information in an organization and found that four types of information are vital to the competitive health of any business: data, voice, image, and video. In terms of data communications and networking facilities, it is the first of these types of information, data, that has shaped corporate strategy. Until recently, voice was treated as an entirely separate requirement, and indeed it still is treated that way in many organizations. As we shall see as the book progresses, the advent of digital transmission and networking facilities, plus the use of flexible transmission protocols such as ATM (asynchronous transfer mode), make it feasible for businesses to integrate voice, data, image, and in some cases video to provide cost-effective networking solutions.

Voice, image, and video have each produced separate communications technologies and what must be considered relatively straightforward solutions from the user's point of view. The situation with respect to data is much more complex, both because the variety of data processing facilities is wide and because the range of approaches to support the business data communications function is large. Therefore, so that the various approaches to business data communications and networking can be seen in context, we devote this chapter to looking at the types of data processing systems that are typical in organizations. We begin with a look at the two extremes in organization of the computing function: centralized and distributed data processing. The computing function in most organizations is implemented somewhere along a spectrum between these two extremes. By examining this spectrum, we can see the nature of the communications and networking requirements for business begin to emerge. We then focus on distributed data processing, examine various approaches, and look at the communications implications of these approaches. In particular, we examine the recent trend toward client–server architectures as one approach to achieving the best of centralized and decentralized architectures.

3.1 CENTRALIZED VERSUS DISTRIBUTED PROCESSING

Centralized and Distributed Organization

Traditionally, the data processing function was organized in a centralized fashion. In a **centralized data processing** architecture, data processing support is provided by one or a cluster of computers, generally large computers, located in a central data processing facility. Many of the tasks performed by such a facility are initiated at the center with the results produced at the center. An example is a payroll application. Other tasks may require interactive access by personnel who are not physically located in the data processing center. For example, a data-entry function such as inventory update may be performed by personnel at sites throughout the organization. In a centralized architecture, each person is provided with a local terminal that is connected by a communications facility to the central data processing facility.

A fully centralized data processing facility is centralized in many senses of the word:

- *Centralized computers.* One or more computers are located in a central facility. In many cases, there are one or more large mainframe computers, which require special facilities such as air conditioning and a raised floor. In a smaller organization, the central computer or computers are large minicomputers, or midrange systems. The AS/400 series from IBM is an example of a midrange system.
- *Centralized processing.* All applications are run on the central data processing facility. This includes applications that are clearly central or organization-wide in nature, such as payroll, as well as applications that support the needs of users in a particular organizational unit. As an example of the latter, a product design department may make use of a computer-aided design (CAD) graphics package that runs on the central facility.
- *Centralized data.* All data are stored in files and databases at the central facility and are controlled by and accessible by the central computer or computers. This includes data that are of use to many units in the organization, such as inventory figures, as well as data that support the needs

of, and should be used by, only one organizational unit. As an example of the latter, the marketing organization may maintain a database with information derived from customer surveys.

- *Centralized control.* A data processing or information systems manager has responsibility for the centralized data processing facility. Depending on the size and importance of the facility, control may be exercised at the middle-management level or may be very high in the organization. It is quite common to have control exercised at the vice-presidential level, and a number of organizations have the equivalent of a corporate information officer who has authority at the board level. In the case of very senior management, a subordinate generally has control of the centralized data processing facility, whereas the top data processing (DP) or information officer has broader authority in matters related to corporate acquisition, use, and protection of information.
- *Centralized support staff.* A centralized data processing facility must include a technical support staff to operate and maintain the data processing equipment. In addition, some (and in many cases all) programming is done by a central staff.

Such a centralized organization has a number of attractive aspects. There may be economies of scale in the purchase and operation of equipment and software. A large central DP shop can afford to have professional programmers on staff to meet the needs of the various departments. Management can maintain control over data processing procurement, enforce standards for programming and data file structure, and design and implement a security policy.

An example of a centralized data processing facility is that of Holiday Inn, shown in general terms in Figure 3.1. Holiday Inn's corporate offices in Atlanta are supported by a number of workstations and personal computers connected by internal local-area networks (LANs) to a variety of server machines. The servers maintain many of the files used in day-to-day operation and in running the headquarters organization. The company's data center is located about 15 miles away; a leased 44-Mbps digital line connects the networked equipment in the two locations. The heart of the data center is a pair of IBM mainframe computers: one for running a transaction processing application that handles bookings by travel agents, hotels, and individuals; and the other for running core business applications such as financial and human resources. The data center is also linked via satellite to each of the approximately 1600 U.S. hotels, as well as having satellite links to Europe.

This centralized configuration meets a number of business objectives for Holiday Inn. The mainframe reservation system is the largest of its kind in the world, handling around 25 million calls per year. The single central reservation system means that there is one place with up-to-date information about availability in all the hotels; this timely information contributes to Holiday Inn's high occupancy rate. In addition, the central system collects and maintains detailed information on customer behavior and other details of individual hotel operation. This information can be analyzed in many different ways to provide top manage-

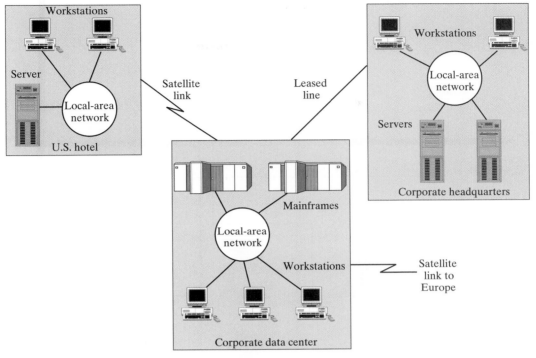

FIGURE 3.1 Holiday Inn Information Systems Architecture [LIEB95].

ment with valuable guidance in meeting customer satisfaction objectives. Without a centralized system, it would be difficult to gather and use the many different types of data that go into the customer analysis applications.

A data processing facility may depart in varying degrees from the centralized data processing organization by implementing a **distributed data processing (DDP)** strategy. A distributed data processing facility is one in which computers, usually smaller computers, are dispersed throughout an organization. The objective of such dispersion is to process information in a way that is most effective based on operational, economic, and/or geographic considerations, or all three. A DDP facility may include a central facility plus satellite facilities, or it may more nearly resemble a community of peer computing facilities. In either case, some form of interconnection is usually needed; that is, the various computers in the system must be connected to one another. As may be expected, given the characterization of centralized data processing provided here, a DDP facility involves the distribution of computers, processing, and data.

An example of a distributed data processing facility is that of J. P. Morgan Securities' fixed-income market department, shown in general terms in Figure 3.2. The main business of the department is trading mortgage-backed securities. These financial instruments provide their purchasers with interest payments for as long as the mortgages behind them are earning interest. Determining the value of such securities is a complex process that involves making estimates of how long

Distributed Data Processing
Data processing in which some or all of the processing, storage, and control functions are dispersed.

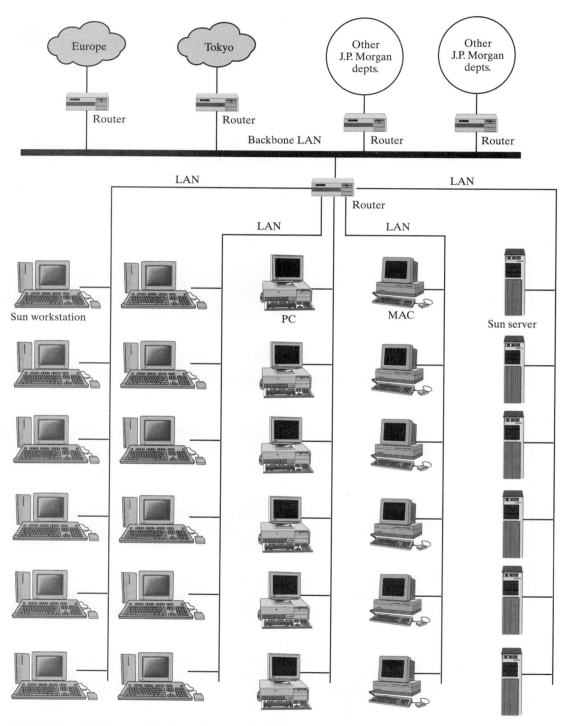

FIGURE 3.2 J. P. Morgan's Distributed Systems Architecture [HAIG92].

the underlying mortgages will generate interest (interest stops if the property is sold, refinanced or repossessed), and of future changes in interest rates. Traders compete by using a variety of algorithms to make these projections. Input to the algorithms include a number of current factors as well as historical data from J. P. Morgan's huge database of previous transactions. For individual traders to have access to the required data to be able to tailor the algorithms to their use and to get immediate answers, each trader is equipped with his or her own fast computer to run the algorithms, with access to updated databases when needed.

As the figure shows, individual traders have some leeway in choosing a computer. Depending on the trader's volume of work, personal preference, and chosen algorithms, a PC, Macintosh, or high-power Sun workstation is most appropriate. Dozens of these machines are hooked together by means of LANs. Machines are grouped on a single LAN based on the need of the trader's to exchange data with each other. All of the trader machines are in turn connected to a LAN[1] that supports a set of high-performance, large-storage servers. The servers maintain a centralized database as well as supporting some specialized applications, such as accounting and report preparation, that need not run on the individual trader's machines. Finally, links are maintained to other Morgan departments and to offices in Tokyo and Europe.

Technical Trends Leading to Distributed Data Processing

Until the early 1970s, the centralized data processing approach enjoyed nearly universal use in businesses. Since that time, there has been a steady evolution to distributed processing. We can address this trend from two points of view: means and motive. First, let us look at the changes in the data processing industry that have given companies the means to choose distributed processing. We then turn to the question of why distributed data processing is coming to be preferred to centralized data processing.

The key factor that has made DDP possible is the dramatic and continuing decrease in cost of computer hardware, accompanied by an increase in its capabilities. Today's personal computers have speeds, instruction sets, and memory capacities comparable to those of minicomputers and even mainframes of just a few years ago. Equally important, today's personal computers boast graphical user interfaces (GUIs) that provide unprecedented ease of use and responsiveness.

Management and Organizational Considerations

The increasing availability of inexpensive yet powerful systems with a growing repertoire of applications software has made it possible for organizations to disperse computing capability throughout the organization rather than to continue to rely on a centralized facility with, at most, distributed terminals for access. However, the centralized option is still very much available to the organization.

---

[1] Multiple LANs are used to limit the amount of traffic on any given LAN. The LANs are connected by routers, which are devices that can route traffic between stations on different networks. Routers are described in Chapter 12.

TABLE 3-1 Requirements for the Corporate Computing Function

1. Provide computing capability to all organizational units that legitimately require it.
2. Contain the capital and operations cost in provision of computing services within the organization.
3. Satisfy special computing needs of user departments.
4. Maintain organizational integrity in operations that are dependent on computing (i.e., avoid mismatches in operation among departments).
5. Meet information requirements of management.
6. Provide computing services in a reliable, professional, and technically competent manner.
7. Allow organizational units sufficient autonomy in the conduct of their tasks to optimize creativity and performance at the unit level.
8. Preserve autonomy among organizational units and, if possible, increase their importance and influence within the larger organization.
9. Make the work of employees enjoyable as well as productive.

As with other types of computers, the powerful mainframes that are the heart of a centralized facility have also dropped in price and increased in power.

To begin, let us consider the requirements for the corporate computing function, that is, those needs that the computing facility must fulfill. Table 3-1 suggests nine specific requirements for the computing facility. A case can clearly be made that requirements 1, 3, 7, 8, and 9 can be satisfied with a distributed arrangement of low-cost servers, workstations, and personal computers. Widespread use of small computers can provide highly individualistic service to all the departments needing computing, allow users to establish and maintain autonomy in their operations using their own equipment, and provide users with hands-on opportunity to enjoy computing use while improving departmental productivity.

Two aspects of the needs of users demonstrate the truth of the preceding statement: the need for new applications and the need for short response time. First, consider the need for new applications. For any organization to remain competitive, each department within the organization must strive continually to improve productivity and effectiveness. A major source of such improvement is increasing reliance on data processing and computers. The result is that in most well-managed organizations, the demand for new applications is rising faster than the central data processing service can develop them. There are a variety of reasons for this, including the inadequacy of techniques for communicating requirements from users to professional programmers and the fact that much of the time of programmers in any mature data processing facility is taken up with software maintenance. For these reasons, the backlog of needed applications is growing. Indeed, a waiting time of from two to seven years for new user applications on central computer systems is not uncommon. A way around this dilemma is to make use of distributed servers, workstations, and personal computers. If end users have access to such machines, the application logjam can be broken in two ways:

- *Off-the-shelf applications.* There is a long list of applications software for common machines, such as Unix-based servers and workstations, and for Windows-based and Macintosh personal computers.
- *End-user programming.* Many tools are available on small systems that allow users to construct modest applications without needing to use a traditional programming language. Examples are spreadsheet programs and project management tools.

The second need mentioned earlier is for short response time. As described in Chapter 2, in many applications it is critical to productivity that response time be short. On a mainframe computer with a complex operating system that is being time-shared by many users, it is often difficult to achieve reasonable response times, but a user on a dedicated personal computer or workstation or a user who is one of only a few sharing a powerful minicomputer can often experience extremely fast response times.

We can see, then, that with distributed small systems that are both physically closer to the user and more dedicated to the user's particular applications, user productivity and computing effectiveness may be improved. However, the manager must exercise caution in adopting a distributed strategy. The lack of centralized computing may result in the loss of centralized control. Individual departments may adopt incompatible systems, making interdepartmental cooperation difficult. Procurement decisions may be made without systematic forecasts of requirements and cost and with no enforcement of standards for hardware, software, or departmental programming practices. These effects jeopardize objectives 4 and 6 of Table 3-1. Equally important, the devolvement of data processing activities to the departmental level can increase the difficulty of obtaining data for use by top management (objective 5). The adoption of differing departmental standards and means of summarizing data makes uniform collection of data for upward reporting more difficult.

Tables 3-2 and 3-3 summarize some of the key potential benefits and potential drawbacks of distributed data processing.

Client–Server Architecture

An organizational approach that is becoming increasingly popular is client–server architecture, an attempt to provide the best aspects of both distributed and centralized computing. Users work on powerful workstations or PCs, which support the end-user programming, provide the ability to use off-the-shelf software, and give the immediate response inherent in distributed architecture. These workstations, or "clients," are supported by specialized "servers." Examples of servers are specialized computers for providing database services, printing and fax services, file storage, and communications front ends, gateways, and bridges. This architecture has been made possible by the advent of high-speed LANs and LAN interconnections, along with more sophisticated systems software to provide intermachine processing.

Client–server architecture is attractive for several reasons. First, it is cost-effective and achieves economies of scale by centralizing support for specialized

TABLE 3-2 Potential Benefits of Distributed Data Processing

Responsiveness
Local computing facilities can be managed in such a way that they can more directly satisfy the needs of local organizational management than can a central facility intended to satisfy the needs of the entire organization.

Availability
With multiple interconnected systems, the loss of any one system should have minimal impact. Key systems and components (e.g., computers with critical applications, printers, mass storage devices) can be replicated so that a backup system can quickly take up the load after a failure.

Correspondence to organizational patterns
Many organizations employ a decentralized structure with corresponding policies and operational procedures. Requirements for data files and other automated resources tend to reflect these organizational patterns.

Resource sharing
Expensive hardware, such as a laser printer, can be shared among users. Data files can be centrally managed and maintained, but with organization-wide access. Staff services, programs, and databases can be developed on an organization-wide basis and distributed to the dispersed facilities.

Incremental growth
In a centralized facility, an increased workload or the need for a new set of applications usually involves a major equipment purchase or software upgrade. This involves significant expenditure. In addition, a major change may require conversion or reprogramming of existing applications, with the risk of error and degraded performance. With a distributed system, it is possible to replace applications or systems gradually, avoiding the "all-or-nothing" approach. In addition, old equipment can be left in the facility to run a single application if the cost of moving the application to a new machine is not justified.

Increased user involvement and control
With smaller, more manageable equipment physically located close to the user, the user has greater opportunity to affect system design and operation, either by direction interaction with technical personnel or through the user's immediate superior.

Decentralized operation and centralized control
Decentralized applications and facilities can be tailored to the individual organizational unit's requirements and be enhanced by centralized services and databases with varying degrees of centralized control.

End-user productivity
Distributed systems tend to give more rapid response time to the user, since each piece of equipment is attempting a smaller job. Also, the applications and interfaces of the facility can be optimized to the needs of the organizational unit. Unit managers are in a position to assess the effectiveness of the local portion of the facility and to make the appropriate changes.

Distance and location independence
Distributed systems introduce interfaces and access methods for utilizing computing services. These interfaces and access methods become independent of location or distance. Hence the user has access to organization-wide facilities with little or no additional training.

Privacy and security
With a distributed system, it is easier to assign responsibility for security of data files and other resources to the owners and users of those resources. Physical and software means can be employed to prevent unauthorized access to data and resources.

Vendor independence
Properly implemented, a distributed system will accommodate equipment and software from a variety of suppliers. This provides greater competition and enhanced bargaining power on the part of the buyer. The organization is less likely to become dependent on a single vendor with the risks that such a position entails.

Flexibility
Users may be in a position to adapt their application software to changing circumstances if they have control over program maintenance and day-to-day running. Because the equipment is not used by other users, they are able to change the configuration if they need to, with little trouble.

TABLE 3-3 Potential Drawbacks of Distributed Data Processing

More difficult test and failure diagnosis
Particularly when there is a high degree of interaction between elements of a distributed system, it is difficult to determine the cause of failure or performance degradation.

More dependence on communications technology
To be effective, a distributed system must be interconnected by communication and networking facilities. These facilities become critical to the day-to-day operation of the organization.

Incompatibility among equipment
Equipment from different vendors may not connect and communicate easily. To guarantee avoidance of this problem, the user must restrict applications and resources to those for which standards exist.

Incompatibility among data
Similarly, data generated by one application may not be usable in the form generated by another application. Again, the user may need to restrict applications to those that are standardized.

Network management and control
Because equipment is physically dispersed, may involve multiple vendors, and may be controlled by various organizational units, it is difficult to provide overall management, to enforce standards for software and data, and to control the information available through the network. Thus, data processing facilities and services may evolve in an uncontrolled fashion.

Difficulty in control of corporate information resources
Data may be dispersed, or if not, at least access to data is dispersed. If distributed users can perform the update function (essential in many applications), it becomes difficult for a central authority to control the integrity and security of the data needed at the corporate level. In some cases, it may even be difficult to gather required management information from the dispersed and dissimilar detailed databases.

Suboptimization
With the dispersal of computer equipment and the ease of adding equipment and applications incrementally, it becomes easier for managers of suborganizations to justify procurement for their unit. Although each procurement may be justifiable individually, the totality of procurements throughout an organization may well exceed the total requirement.

Duplication of effort
Technical personnel in various units may individually develop similar applications or data files, resulting in unnecessary and costly duplication of effort.

---

functions. File servers and database servers also make it easier to provide universal access to information by authorized users and to maintain consistency and security of files and data. The physical architecture of the computers used can be designed especially to support their service function. Finally, this architecture is very flexible. One reason is that functional services are not necessarily in a one-to-one relation with physical computers. That is, file service and database services can be on the same computer, or for an example at the other extreme, database services can be provided by several geographically dispersed machines. Services can share processors for smaller information systems, and they can be split among processors in larger systems to provide redundancy, increased capacity, and increased responsiveness. This increasingly popular approach is examined in more detail in Chapter 14.

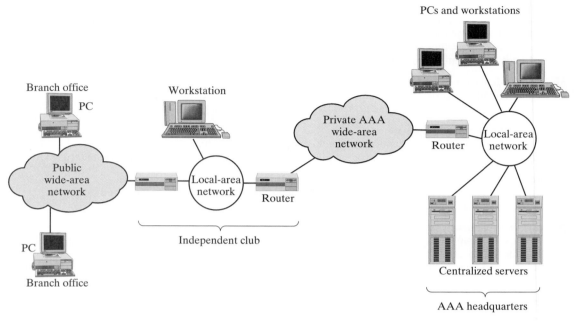

FIGURE 3.3 AAA Client–Server Architecture [GARE95].

An example of a client–server architecture is that used by the American Automobile Association (AAA), shown in general terms in Figure 3.3. This system ties together over 1000 branch offices and independent AAA clubs with the headquarters data processing facility. Corporate headquarters is home to five vertical service groups: automotive, travel, insurance, publishing, and financial. Another 15 horizontal departments, including purchasing, facilities, and benefits, are also located there. Using the resources of this central facility are over 100 independent clubs with nearly 40 million members; each club in turn operates a number of branch offices for in-person service.

In 1991, this vast organization was ill-served by a number of separate data processing facilities run by different divisions or even departments, with little or no connectivity or cooperation among them. For example, the travel and insurance groups maintained their own databases of customer profiles, even though it would have been more efficient for the insurance group to use travelers' lists as the basis for mailings and solicitations.

In four years, this unpromising situation was transformed into a flexible and efficient integrated system based on client–server principles. All databases are maintained on servers at the headquarters site, with high-speed local- and wide-area networks allowing individual users access. In addition to maintaining member information, the central servers include data and applications that are needed by all clubs and branch offices. For example, the application TravelMatch allows clubs to access a centralized database containing information about hotels, cities, and routes.

Intranets

The latest development in the ongoing evolution of distributed data processing is the intranet. In essence, an intranet provides users the features and applications of the Internet but isolated within the organization. Key features of an intranet:

- Uses Internet-based standards, such as the hypertext markup language (HTML) and the simple mail transfer protocol (SMTP).[2]
- Uses the TCP/IP protocol suite for local- and wide-area networking.[3]
- Comprises wholly owned content not accessible to the general Internet even though the corporation has Internet connections and runs a Web server on the Internet.
- Can be managed, unlike the Internet.

In general terms, an intranet can be considered as a form of client–server architecture. The advantages of the intranet approach include ease of implementation and ease of use. Intranets are examined in detail in Chapter 14.

3.2 FORMS OF DISTRIBUTED DATA PROCESSING

We have defined a DDP system as a computing facility in which computers are dispersed within an organization with some means of interconnection among them. This general definition conceals the wide variety of forms that DDP can take. One way to gain an appreciation of this variety is to consider in more detail the following functions or objects that are supported by distributed processors:

- Applications
- Data
- Device controllers
- Control

It is often the case that more than one of these functions or objects is distributed in a DDP system. For our purposes it is sufficient to examine them one at a time to gain insight into the configurations that are implemented in DDP.

Distributed Applications

Two dimensions characterize the distribution of applications. First, there is the allocation of application functions:

- One application split up into components that are dispersed among a number of machines
- One application replicated on a number of machines
- A number of different applications distributed among a number of machines

---

[2] HTML and SMTP are described in Chapter 13.
[3] TCP/IP is discussed in Chapter 12.

Distributed application processing can also be characterized by whether the distribution is vertical or horizontal. In general, vertical partitioning involves one application split up into components that are dispersed among a number of machines, whereas horizontal partitioning involves either one application replicated on a number of machines or a number of different applications distributed among a number of machines.

With **vertical partitioning**, data processing is distributed in a hierarchical fashion. This distribution may reflect organizational structure or may simply be most appropriate for the application. Several examples:

1. *Insurance.* Data processing distribution is often a two-level hierarchy. Each branch has a computer system that it uses for preparing new contracts and for processing claims. In most cases these transactions can be handled directly by the local office. Summary information is sent to a head office. The head office uses contract and claim information to perform risk analysis and actuarial calculations. On the basis of the company's financial position and current exposure, the head office can adjust rates and communicate the changes to the branches.

2. *Retail chain.* Each retail store includes point-of-sale terminals and terminals for use by sales and office personnel. A convenient arrangement is a single powerful workstation or server that houses all the information used at the store. An interconnected set of personal computers is also possible, but the nature of the application lends itself more readily to a single site for storing all branch information. Point-of-sale terminals make use of pricing information from the computer system. Sales transactions record sales and changes in inventory and accounts receivable. Sales and office personnel can use terminals to display summary sales information, inventory, accounts receivable, and customer statements. Store management can display information on sales performance, goods aging, and other analyses. Periodically, perhaps once a day, sales and inventory information is transmitted to the head office system.

3. *Process control.* The process-control function in a factory adapts readily to a vertical DDP system. Each major operational area is controlled by a workstation, which is fed information from individual process-control microprocessors. The microprocessors are responsible for the automated control of sensors and effector devices on the shop floor. The operations workstation scans sensor readings looking for exceptions or analyzing trends. It may also control part of the operation to vary the rate or mix of production. These distributed workstations ensure rapid response to conditions at the process level. All the workstations are linked to a higher-level computer concerned with operations planning, optimization, providing management information, and general corporate data processing.

As these examples illustrate, a vertically partitioned DDP system generally consists of a central computer system with one or more levels of satellite systems. The nature of the partition reflects organizational structure or the structure of the task to be performed, or both. The objective is to assign processing load to the level of the hierarchy at which it is most cost-effective. Such an arrangement combines some of the best features of both centralized and distributed data processing.

With **horizontal partitioning**, data processing is distributed among a number of computers that have a peer relationship. That is, there is no concept of master–slave. Computers in a horizontal configuration normally operate autonomously, although in some cases this configuration is used for load leveling. In many cases, horizontal partitioning reflects organizational decentralization. Two examples follow:

1. *Office automation support system.* Typically, secretarial staff and other personnel are equipped with personal computers linked together by a network. Each user's personal computer contains software packages useful to that user (e.g., word processing, spreadsheet). The systems are linked together so that users may exchange messages, files, and other information.

2. *Air traffic control system.* Each regional center for air traffic control operates autonomously of the other centers, performing the same set of applications. Within the center, several computers are used to process radar and radio data and to provide a visual status to the air traffic controllers.

It is more often the case that an organization's computing function will include both horizontal and vertical partitioning. Corporate headquarters may maintain a mainframe computer facility with a corporate management information system and decision support system. Central staff functions such as public relations, strategic planning, and corporate finance and accounting may be supported here. A vertical partition is created by providing subordinate computing facilities at branch offices. Within each branch office, a horizontal partition will provide office automation support.

Distributed Data

Before beginning our discussion of distributed data, it is necessary to say something about the nature of the organization of data in a computer system. In some cases, an organization can function with a relatively simple collection of files of data. Each file may contain text (e.g., copies of memos and reports) or numerical data (e.g., spreadsheets). A more complex file consists of a set of records. However, for an organization of any appreciable size, a more complex organization known as a database is required. A **database** is a structured collection of data stored for use in one or more applications. In addition to data, a database contains the relationships between data items and groups of data items. As an example of the distinction between data files and a database, consider the following. A simple personnel file might consist of a set of records, one for each employee. Each record gives the employee's name, address, date of birth, position, salary, and other details needed by the personnel department. A personnel database includes a personnel file, as just described. It may also include a time and attendance file, showing for each week the hours worked by each employee. With a database organization, these two files are tied together so that a payroll program can extract the information about time worked and salary for each employee to generate paychecks.

A **distributed database** is one in which portions of the data are dispersed among a number of computer systems. A distributed database must include a directory that identifies the physical location of each data element in the database.

In general terms, we can distinguish three ways of organizing data for use by an organization: centralized, replicated, and partitioned. A **centralized database** is housed in a central computer facility. If the computing function is distributed, users and application programs at remote locations may have access to the centralized database. A centralized database is often used with a vertical DDP organization. It is desirable when the security and integrity of the data are paramount, because the central facility is more easily controlled than is a dispersed collection of data. On the other hand, there are a number of reasons why a distributed data organization might be attractive, including the following:

1. A distributed design can reflect an organization's structure or function. This makes the design of the data organization and the use of the data more understandable and easier to implement and maintain.

2. Data can be stored locally, under local control. Local storage decreases response times and communications costs and increases data availability.

3. Distributing data across multiple autonomous sites confines the effects of a computer breakdown to its point of occurrence; the data on the surviving computers can still be processed.

4. The size of the total collection of data and the number of users of those data need not be limited by a computer's size and processing power.

When data are distributed, one of two overall strategies may be adopted. In a **replicated database**, all or part of the database is copied at two or more computers. A retail chain is a good example of where replication is appropriate. Each store maintains a database of its own inventory and sales and of customer accounts. During the day, activity is posted to the local database. At the end of the day, the results are transmitted to the head office, which updates the central database. Charges by customers at branches other than their own are consolidated into the records. At the beginning of each day, the updated records reflecting customer activity at other branches are transmitted to each branch.

In a **partitioned database**, the database exists as distinct and nonoverlapping segments that are dispersed among multiple computer systems. In general, there is no duplication of data among the segments of a partitioned database. This strategy can be used with either a horizontal or vertical DDP organization.

Table 3-4 provides a simplified comparison of these three approaches to database organization. In practice, a mixture of strategies will be used. A more detailed look at strategies for database organization is provided in Table 3-5. For

TABLE 3-4 Advantages and Disadvantages of Database Distribution Methods

Type of Distribution	Advantages	Disadvantages
Common database accessed by all processors (centralized)	No duplication of data; little reorganization required	Contention among multiple processors attempting to access data simultaneously; database is large, so response time is slow; during disk failures, all processors lose access to data
Copy of the common central database stored at each processor (replicated)	Each processor has access to database without contention; fast response time; during failure, new copy can be obtained	High storage cost due to extensive duplication of data; updates of one copy must subsequently be made on all other copies; high database reorganization costs
Individual database for each processor (partitioned)	No duplication of data minimizes storage cost; size of database determined by application of node, not total corporate requirement; fast response time	Ad hoc or management reports must be obtained from different databases

replicated databases, two strategies are possible. First, a central database is maintained, and copies of portions of the database may be extracted for local use. Typically, such systems lock the affected portion of the central database if the satellite computer has the authority to update. If this is the case, the remote computer transmits the updates back to the central database upon completion of the task. Alternatively, a more elaborate synchronization technique can be employed so that updates to one copy of a replicated database are propagated automatically throughout the DDP system to update all copies. This strategy requires considerably more software and communications load but provides the user with a more flexible system.

The simplest partitioned strategy is one in which there are a number of independently operated databases with remote access allowed. In effect, we have a collection of centralized databases, with more than one center. A more complex system is one in which the databases are integrated so that a single query by the user may require access to any of the databases. In a sophisticated system, this access is invisible to the user, who need not specify where the data are located and who need not use a different command style for different portions of the distributed database.

Thus we can see that a variety of strategies is possible. In designing a distributed database, two sets of objectives are paramount: database objectives and communications objectives. *Database objectives* include accessibility of the data, security and privacy, and completeness and integrity of the data. *Communications objectives* are to minimize the communications load and the delays imposed by the use of communications facilities.

TABLE 3-5 Strategies for Database Organization

Strategy	Reliability	Expandability	Communications Overhead	Manageability	Data Consistency or Integrity
Centralized					
Centralized database Database resides in one location on host; data values may be distributed to geographically dispersed users for local processing	Poor	Poor	Very high	Very good	Excellent
Replicated					
Distributed snapshot databases Copy of portion of the central database created by extraction and replication for use at remote sites	Good	Very good	Low to medium	Very good	Medium
Replicated, distributed database Data are replicated and synchronized at multiple sites	Excellent	Very good	Medium because of synchronization requirements	Medium	Medium to very good, depending on synchronization technique
Partitioned					
Distributed, nonintegrated databases Independent databases that can be accessed by applications on remote computers	Good	Good	Low	Very good	Low
Distributed, integrated database Data span multiple computers and software	Very good	Very good	Low to medium if most requests are local	Difficult to very difficult	Very good

Other Forms of DDP

In addition to, or instead of, the distribution of applications or data, a DDP system may involve the distribution of device controllers, or network management. Let us briefly examine each of these possibilities.

Distributed Devices One natural use of DDP is to support a distributed set of devices that can be controlled by processors, such as automatic teller machines or laboratory interface equipment. One common application of this approach is in factory automation. A factory may contain a number of sensors, programmable controllers, microprocessors, and even robots that are involved in the automation of the manufacturing process. Such a system involves the distribution of processing technology to the various locations of the manufacturing process.

Network Management Any distributed system requires some form of management and control, including control of access to some of the facilities in the distributed system, monitoring of the status of various components of the distributed system, and management of the communications facility to ensure availability and responsiveness. In most cases, some sort of central network management system is required. However, such a system needs to obtain status information from the various computers in the distributed system and to issue commands to those computers. Thus, each computer in the distributed system must include some management and control logic to be able to interact with the central network management system. We provide more detail on these issues in Chapter 16.

3.3 NETWORKING IMPLICATIONS OF DDP

We can characterize the requirements for communications and networking generated by the use of distributed data processing as falling into three key areas: connectivity, availability, and performance. The **connectivity** of a distributed system refers to the ability of components in the system to exchange data. In a vertically partitioned DDP system, components of the system generally need links only to components above and below them in the hierarchical structure. Such a requirement can often be met with simple direct links between systems. In a horizontally partitioned system, it may be necessary to allow data exchange between any two systems. For example, in an office automation system, any user should be able to exchange electronic mail and files with any other user, subject to any security policy. In a system requiring high connectivity, some sort of network may be preferable to a large number of direct links. To see this, consider Figure 3.4. If we have a distributed system requiring full connectivity and use a direct link between each pair of systems, the number of links and the communication interfaces needed grow rapidly with the number of systems. With four computers, six links are required; with five computers, 10 links are required. Instead, suppose that we create a network by providing a central switch and connecting each computer

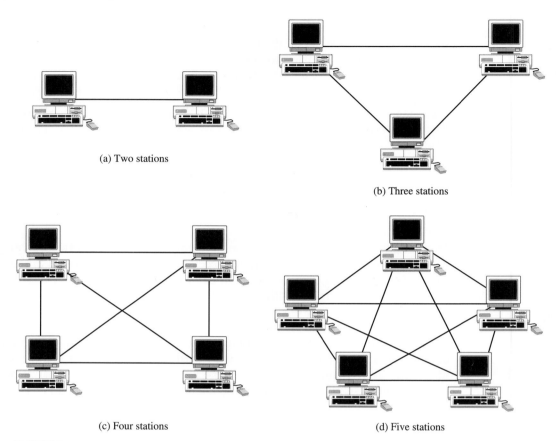

(a) Two stations

(b) Three stations

(c) Four stations

(d) Five stations

FIGURE 3.4 Full Connectivity Using Direct Links.

system to that switch. The results are shown in Figure 3.5. In this case, with four computers, four links are required, and with five computers, five links are required. If the components of a distributed system are dispersed geographically, the requirement for connectivity dictates the need for a method of transmitting data over long distances. This involves the use of public telecommunications facilities or a private installation.

Availability refers to the percentage of time that a particular function or application is available for users. Depending on the application, availability may be merely desirable or it may be essential. For example, in an air traffic control system, the availability of the computer system that supports the air traffic controllers is critical. High availability requirements mean that the distributed system must be designed in such a way that the failure of a single computer or other device will not deny access to the application. For example, backup processors can be employed. High availability requirements also mean that the communications facility must be highly available. Thus, some form of redundancy and backup in the communications facility is needed.

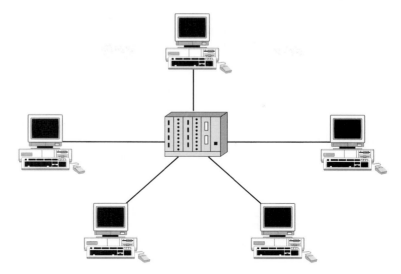

FIGURE 3.5 The Use of a Central Switch for Full Connectivity.

Finally, the **performance** of the communications facility can be assessed, given the nature of the DDP system and the applications that it supports. In a highly interactive system such as a data-entry system or a graphics design application, we have seen that response time is critically important. Thus, not only must the processors that execute the applications respond rapidly but also, if the interaction involves transmission across a network, the network must have sufficient capacity and flexibility to provide the required response time. If the system is used instead to move a lot of data around but without the time being critical, the concern may be more one of throughput. That is, the communications facility must be designed to handle large volumes of data.

Once we have examined the details of the available data communications techniques and facilities, we will return to this topic and examine strategies for communications and network planning.

SUMMARY

With the increasing availability of inexpensive yet powerful personal computers and workstations, there has been an increasing trend toward distributed data processing (DDP). With DDP, processors, data, and other aspects of a data processing system may be dispersed within an organization. This provides a system that is more responsive to user needs, is able to provide better response times, and may minimize communications costs compared to a centralized approach. A DDP system involves either the horizontal or vertical partitioning of the computing function and may also involve a distributed organization of databases, device control, and interaction (network) control. This trend has been facilitated by the advent of client–server architectures.

At this stage we are not yet ready to translate our description of DDP characteristics into an analysis of the needed data communications and networking facilities. In general terms, we can say that a DDP system involves requirements in the areas of connectivity, availability, and performance. These requirements, in turn, dictate the type of data communications or networking approach that is appropriate for a given DDP system.

RECOMMENDED READING

One of the best treatments of distributed data processing is [COUL94]. This book is a broad survey of the issues involved, including networking, file and database design, protocols, transaction issues, and security. [MULL93] is a much more technical book, getting into details of operating system and protocol design, but it also has some worthwhile, readable chapters on overall distributed system design. [CASA94] is a collection of reprints on the subject; many of the articles provide useful elaboration on the material in this chapter.

CASA94   CASAVANT, T., and SINGHAL, M., eds. *Distributed Computing Systems.* Los Alamitos, CA: IEEE Computer Society Press, 1994.
COUL94   COULOURIS, G., DOLLIMORE, J., and KINDBERG, T. *Distributed Systems: Concepts and Design.* Reading, MA: Addison-Wesley, 1994.
MULL93   MULLENDER, S., ed. *Distributed Systems.* New York: ACM Press, 1993.

KEY TERMS

Availability	Database	Partitioned Database
Centralized Database	Distributed Database	Performance
Centralized Data Processing	Distributed Data Processing (DDP)	Replicated Database
Connectivity	Horizontal Partitioning	Vertical Partitioning

QUESTIONS

1. What are some functions that are centralized in a fully centralized data processing facility?

2. What are some advantages of a centralized data processing facility?

3. What is a distributed data processing (DDP) strategy?

4. What major problems for the data processing manager result from distributed small systems?

5. What are some reasons for wanting to interconnect distributed data processing systems?

6. Distinguish between horizontal and vertical partitioning of applications.

7. Why would a company want a distributed database?

8. In designing a distributed database, database objectives and communications objectives are not always the same. Distinguish between these two sets of objectives.

9. How does a factory often reflect the use of distributed devices?

10. Name three types of communications networking requirements generated by the use of distributed data processing.
11. What are the key features of an intranet?

PROBLEM

1. How many direct connections does it take to connect *n* computers together? *Hint:* Count the number of "ends" of connections and divide by 2. Suppose that you have a computer in each of the 50 states: How many direct connections would you need?

PART 2

FUNDAMENTALS

CHAPTER 4

Data Transmission
and Transmission Media

CHAPTER OBJECTIVES

After reading this chapter, you should be able to:

■ Explain the various ways in which voice, data, image, and video can be represented by electromagnetic signals.

■ Discuss the various transmission impairments that affect the quality and transfer rate of information.

■ Describe the various transmission media: twisted pair, coaxial cable, optical fiber, terrestrial microwave, satellite, and broadcast radio; and discuss their applications and transmission characteristics.

*I*n this book we are concerned with one particular means for communicating information: the transmission of electromagnetic waves. All of the forms of information that we have discussed (voice, data, image, video) can be represented by electromagnetic signals and transmitted over a suitable transmission medium. Figure 4.1 illustrates this. Information is generated by a source (such as a telephone handset, computer terminal, facsimile scanner, video camera) and is then transformed into an electromagnetic signal. The signal is then applied to a transmission medium and propagates from a transmitter to a receiver. The receiver is able to recover the information from the electromagnetic signal to reproduce, either approximately or exactly, the original information.

The purpose of this chapter is to focus on this process and discuss the various transmission media that are in common use. First we look at the types of electromagnetic signals that are used to convey information. In doing so we describe

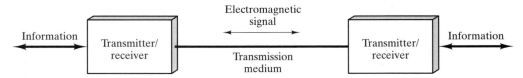

FIGURE 4.1 Information Transmission.

the most straightforward way in which each of the four types of information can be represented. Then we discuss the sad fact that such transmission is subject to impairments that can introduce errors and inefficiencies. Finally, we look at the various transmission media that can be used to convey information.

One note of caution: The material in this chapter and the next deals with fundamental aspects of communications technology. In a business context it is important to have at least a modest level of understanding of these technologies to be able to assess various products and services. However, in most cases, the choices facing the decision maker do not boil down to a simple selection of a technology but rather, to a product or service that exploits a variety of technologies. Thus, it is only in later chapters (Chapter 7 onward) that we will be able to relate effectively the concepts being discussed to the needs of the business.

4.1 SIGNALS FOR CONVEYING INFORMATION

Electromagnetic Signals

As illustrated in Figure 4.1, information is transmitted by means of an electromagnetic signal. An electromagnetic signal is a function of time, but it can also be expressed as a function of frequency; that is, the signal consists of components of different frequencies. It turns out that the *frequency-domain* view of a signal is far more important to an understanding of data transmission than a *time-domain* view. Both views are introduced here.

Analog Signal
A continuously varying electromagnetic wave that may be propagated over a variety of media.

Digital Signal
A discrete or discontinuous signal, such as a sequence of voltage pulses.

Time-Domain Concepts Viewed as a function of time, an electromagnetic signal can be either analog or digital. An **analog signal** is one in which the signal intensity varies in a smooth fashion over time. In other words, there are no breaks or discontinuities in the signal. A **digital signal** is one in which the signal intensity maintains a constant level for some period of time and then changes to another constant level. Figure 4.2 shows examples of both kinds of signals. The analog signal might represent speech, and the digital signal might represent binary 1's and 0's.

The simplest sort of signal is a **periodic signal**, in which the same signal pattern repeats over time. Figure 4.3 shows an example of a periodic analog signal (sine wave) and a periodic digital signal (square wave). The sine wave is the fundamental analog signal. A general sine wave can be represented by three parameters: amplitude (A), frequency (f), and phase (ϕ). The **amplitude** is the peak value or strength of the signal over time; typically, this value is measured in volts. The **frequency** is the rate [in cycles per second, or hertz (Hz)] at which the signal repeats. An equivalent parameter is the **period** (T) of a signal, which is the amount of time it takes for one repetition; therefore, $T = 1/f$. **Phase** is a measure of the relative position in time within a single period of a signal, as illustrated below.

The general sine wave can be written $s(t) = A \sin(2\pi ft + \phi)$. Figure 4.4 shows the effect of varying each of the three parameters. In part (a) of the figure, the frequency is 1 Hz; thus the period is $T = 1$ sec. Part (b) has the same frequency and phase but an amplitude of $\frac{1}{2}$. In part (c) we have $f = 2$, which is

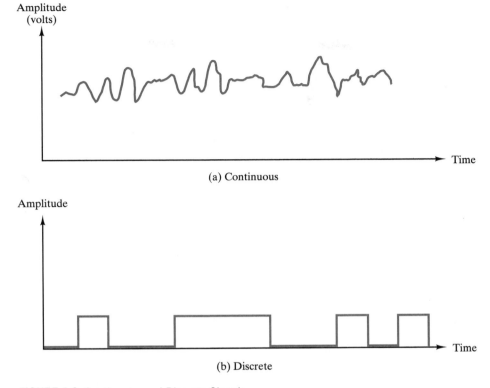

(a) Continuous

(b) Discrete

FIGURE 4.2 Continuous and Discrete Signals.

equivalent to $T = \frac{1}{2}$. Finally, part (d) shows the effect of a phase shift of $\pi/4$ radians, which is 45°.

In Figure 4.4 the horizontal axis is time; the graphs display the value of a signal at a given point in space as a function of time. These same graphs, with a change of scale, can apply with horizontal axes in space. In this case the graphs display the value of a signal at a given point in time as a function of distance. For example, for a sinusoidal transmission (say, an electromagnetic radio wave some distance from a radio antenna or sound some distance from loudspeaker) at a particular instant of time, the intensity of the signal varies in a sinusoidal way as a function of distance from the source.

A little thought should convince you that there is a simple relationship between the two sine waves, one in time and one in space. Define the **wavelength** (λ) of a signal as the distance occupied by a single cycle, or put another way, the distance between two points of corresponding phase of two consecutive cycles. Assume that the signal is traveling with a velocity v. Then the wavelength is related to the period as follows: $\lambda = vT$. Equivalently, $\lambda f = v$. Of particular relevance to this discussion is the case where $v = c$, the speed of light in free space, which is 3×10^8 m/sec.

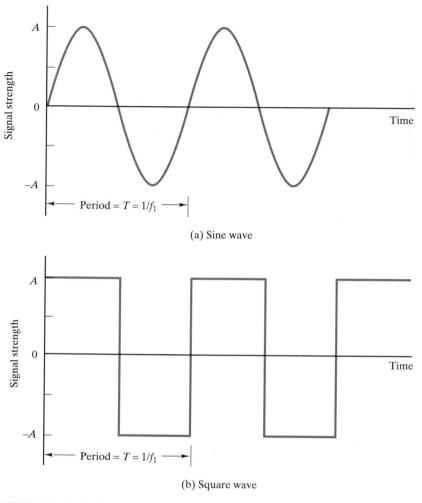

FIGURE 4.3 Examples of Periodic Signals.

Frequency-Domain Concepts   In practice, an electromagnetic signal will be made up of many frequencies. For example, the signal

$$s(t) = \sin(2\pi f_1 t) + \tfrac{1}{3}\sin[2\pi(3f_1)t]$$

is shown in Figure 4.5. The components of this signal are just sine waves of frequencies f_1 and $3f_1$; parts (a) and (b) of the figure show these individual components. There are several interesting points that can be made about this figure:

- The second frequency is an integer multiple of the first frequency. When all of the frequency components of a signal are integer multiples of one frequency, the latter frequency is referred to as the *fundamental frequency*.

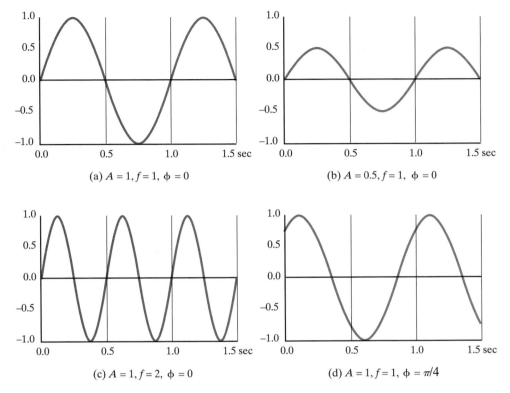

FIGURE 4.4 $A \sin(2\pi ft + \phi)$.

- The period of the total signal is equal to the period of the fundamental frequency. The period of the component $\sin(2\pi f_1 t)$ is $T = 1/f_1$, and the period of $s(t)$ is also T, as can be seen from Figure 4.5c.

By adding together enough sinusoidal signals, each with the appropriate amplitude, frequency, and phase, any electromagnetic signal can be constructed. Put another way, any electromagnetic signal can be shown to consist of a collection of periodic analog signals (sine waves) at different amplitudes, frequencies, and phases. The importance of being able to look at a signal from the frequency perspective (frequency domain) rather than a time perspective (time domain) should become clear as the discussion proceeds.

Several more terms need to be introduced. The **spectrum** of a signal is the range of frequencies that it contains. For the signal of Figure 4.5, the spectrum extends from f_1 to $3f_1$. The **bandwidth** of a signal is the width of the spectrum. In our example, the bandwidth of the signal is $2f_1$.

There is a direct relationship between the information-carrying capacity of a signal and its bandwidth: The greater the bandwidth, the higher the information-carrying capacity. As a very simple example, consider the square wave of Figure 4.3b. Suppose that we let a positive pulse represent binary 1 and a negative pulse represent binary 0. Then the waveform represents the binary stream

Spectrum
Refers to an absolute, contiguous range of frequencies.

Bandwidth
The difference between the limiting frequencies of a continuous frequency band.

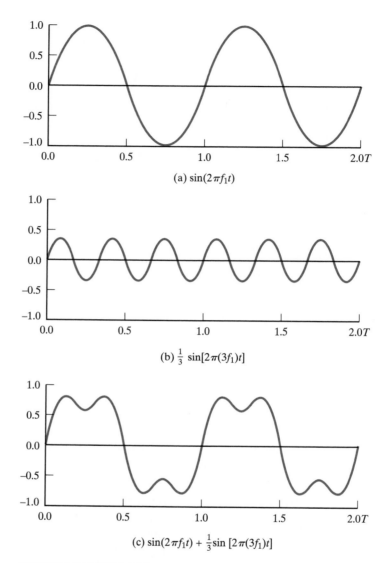

FIGURE 4.5 Addition of Frequency Components ($T = 1/f_1$).

1010.... The duration of each pulse is $1/2f_1$; thus the data rate is $2f_1$ bps. What are the frequency components of this signal? To answer this question, reconsider Figure 4.5. By adding together sine waves at frequencies f_1 and $3f_1$, we get a waveform that resembles the square wave. Let us continue this process by adding a sine wave of frequency $5f_1$, as shown in Figure 4.6a, and then adding a sine wave of frequency $7f_1$, as shown in Figure 4.6b. As we add additional odd multiples of f_1, suitably scaled, the resulting waveform approaches that of a square wave more and more closely.

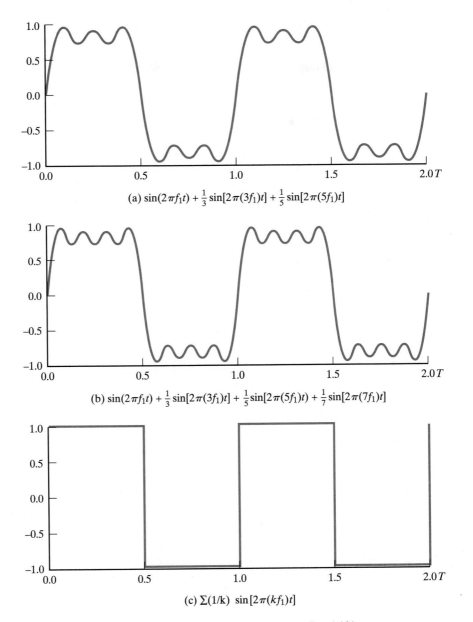

(a) $\sin(2\pi f_1 t) + \frac{1}{3}\sin[2\pi(3f_1)t] + \frac{1}{5}\sin[2\pi(5f_1)t]$

(b) $\sin(2\pi f_1 t) + \frac{1}{3}\sin[2\pi(3f_1)t] + \frac{1}{5}\sin[2\pi(5f_1)t] + \frac{1}{7}\sin[2\pi(7f_1)t]$

(c) $\Sigma(1/k) \ \sin[2\pi(kf_1)t]$

FIGURE 4.6 Frequency Components of a Square Wave ($T = 1/f_1$).

Indeed, it can be shown that the frequency components of the square wave, $s(t)$, can be expressed as follows:

$$s(t) = A \times \sum_{k=1,3,\ldots}^{\infty} \frac{1}{k} \sin(2\pi k f_1 t)$$

Thus, this waveform has an infinite number of frequency components and hence an infinite bandwidth. However, the amplitude of the kth frequency component, kf_1, is only $1/k$, so most of the energy in this waveform is in the first few frequency components. What happens if we limit the bandwidth to the first three frequency components? We have already seen the answer, in Figure 4.6a. As we can see, the shape of the resulting waveform is reasonably close to that of the original square wave.

We can use Figures 4.5 and 4.6 to illustrate the relationship between data rate and bandwidth. Suppose that we are using a digital transmission system that is capable of transmitting signals with a bandwidth of 4 MHz. Let us attempt to transmit a sequence of alternating 1's and 0's as the square wave of Figure 4.6c. What data rate can be achieved? Well, let us approximate our square wave with the waveform of Figure 4.6a. Although this waveform is a "distorted" square wave, it is sufficiently close to the square wave that a receiver should be able to discriminate between a binary 0 and a binary 1. Now, if we let $f_1 = 10^6$ cycles/second = 1 MHz, the bandwidth of the signal

$$s(t) = \sin[(2\pi \times 10^6)t] + \tfrac{1}{3}\sin[(2\pi \times 3 \times 10^6)t] + \tfrac{1}{5}\sin[(2\pi \times 5 \times 10^6)t]$$

is $(5 \times 10^6) - 10^6 = 4$ MHz. Note that for $f_1 = 1$ MHz, the period of the fundamental frequency is $T = 1/10^6 = 10^{-6} = 1$ μsec. Thus, if we treat this waveform as a bit string of 1's and 0's, one bit occurs every 0.5 μsec, for a data rate of 2×10^6 = 2 Mbps. Thus, for a bandwidth of 4 MHz, a data rate of 2 Mbps is achieved.

Now suppose that we have a bandwidth of 8 MHz. Let us look again at Figure 4.6a, but now with $f_1 = 2$ MHz. Using the same line of reasoning as before, the bandwidth of the signal is $(5 \times 2 \times 10^6) - (2 \times 10^6) = 8$ MHz. But in this case $T = 1/f_1 = 0.5$ μsec. As a result, one bit occurs every 0.25 μsec for a data rate of 4 Mbps. Thus, other things being equal, by doubling the bandwidth, we double the potential data rate.

But now suppose that the waveform of Figure 4.5c is considered adequate for approximating a square wave. That is, the difference between a positive and a negative pulse in Figure 4.5c is sufficiently distinct that the waveform can be used successfully to represent a sequence of 1's and 0's. Now, let $f_1 = 2$ MHz. Using the same line of reasoning as before, the bandwidth of the signal of Figure 4.5c is $(3 \times 2 \times 10^6) - (2 \times 10^6) = 4$ MHz. But in this case $T = 1/f_1 = 0.5$ μsec. As a result, one bit occurs every 0.25 μsec, for a data rate of 4 Mbps. Thus, a given bandwidth can support various data rates, depending on the requirements of the receiver.

We can draw the following general conclusions from the foregoing observations. In general, any digital waveform will have infinite bandwidth. If we attempt to transmit this waveform as a signal over any medium, the nature of the medium will limit the bandwidth that can be transmitted. Furthermore, for any given medium, the greater the bandwidth transmitted, the greater the cost. Thus, on the one hand, economic and practical reasons dictate that digital information be approximated by a signal of limited bandwidth. On the other hand, limiting the bandwidth creates distortions, which makes the task of interpreting the received signal more difficult. The more limited the bandwidth, the greater the distortion, and the greater the potential for error by the receiver.

Analog Signals

Voice Signals   Just as an analog signal is one whose value varies in a continuous fashion, we can say that analog information is information that takes on continuous values. The most familiar example of analog information is audio, or acoustic, information, which, in the form of sound waves, can be perceived directly by human beings. One form of acoustic information, of course, is human speech, which has frequency components in the range 20 Hz to 20 kHz. This form of information is easily converted to an electromagnetic signal for transmission (Figure 4.7). In essence, all of the sound frequencies, whose amplitude is measured in terms of loudness, are converted into electromagnetic frequencies, whose amplitude is measured in volts. The telephone handset contains a simple mechanism for making such a conversion.

Thus, the voice sound wave can be represented directly by an electromagnetic signal occupying the same spectrum. However, there is a need to compromise between the fidelity of the sound as transmitted electromagnetically and the cost of transmission, which increases with increasing bandwidth. Although, as mentioned, human speech has a spectrum of 20 Hz to 20 kHz, tests have shown that a much narrower bandwidth, the range 300 to 3400 Hz, will produce acceptable voice reproduction. That is, if the frequency components outside that range are subtracted, the remainder sounds quite natural. For this reason, telephone networks are able to use communication facilities that limit the transmission of sound to that narrower bandwidth (Figure 4.8). This reduction in the capacity requirement for the transmission of speech results in a corresponding reduction in the cost of the facility.

FIGURE 4.7 Conversion of Voice Input to Analog Signal.

In this graph of a typical analog signal, the many variations in amplitude and frequency convey the gradations of loudness and pitch in speech or music. Similar signals are used to transmit television pictures, but at much higher frequencies.

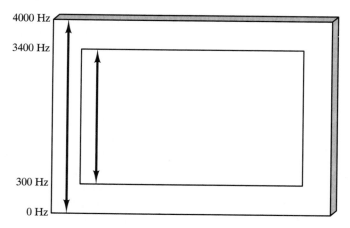

The human voice creates waves of many frequencies, but natural-sounding speech can be limited to a frequency range, or band, of 300 to 3400 Hz. Telephone equipment allows the voice a bandwidth of 4000 Hz, which includes a guardband at top and bottom to prevent interference. TV signals need a bandwidth of 4 million hertz (4 MHz).

FIGURE 4.8 The Voice Band.

Note from Figure 4.8 that the actual bandwidth used by the telephone transmission facility is 4 kHz, not 3.1 kHz. The extra bandwidth serves the purpose of isolating the sound signal from interference from signals in adjacent bandwidths. [1] For transmission, then, the telephone handset converts the incoming voice-produced sound wave into an analog electromagnetic signal over the range 300 to 3400 Hz. This signal is then transmitted over the telephone system to a telephone receiver, which reproduces a sound wave from the incoming electromagnetic signal.

Video Signals To describe the video signal, it is best to begin with the viewpoint of the receiver. To produce a picture on the screen, an electron beam scans across the surface of the screen from left to right and top to bottom. For black-and-white television, the amount of illumination produced (on a scale from black to white) at any point is proportional to the intensity of the beam as it passes that point. Thus, at any instant in time the beam takes on an analog value of intensity to produce the desired brightness at that point on the screen. Further, as the beam scans, the analog value changes. Thus, the video image can be viewed as a time-varying analog signal.

Figure 4.9 depicts the scanning process. At the end of each scan line, the beam is swept rapidly back to the left (horizontal retrace). The beam is turned off (blanked out) during the retrace intervals. At all times, the intensity of the beam is determined by the incoming video signal.

---

[1] We will see in Chapter 6 that it is common to have a number of signals at different areas of the spectrum occupy the same transmission medium, a process known as *multiplexing*. The extra bandwidth, or guardbands, prevent adjacent signals from interfering with each other.

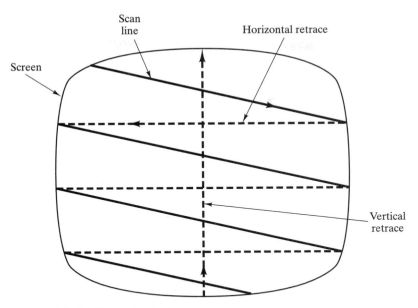

FIGURE 4.9 TV Picture Production.

To produce a video signal, a TV camera, which performs a function similar to that of a TV receiver, is used. One component of the camera is a photosensitive plate, upon which a scene is optically focused. An electron beam sweeps across the plate from left to right and top to bottom, as depicted in Figure 4.9 for the receiver. As the beam sweeps, an analog electric signal is produced proportional to the brightness of the scene at a particular spot.

To transmit analog video information at the necessary rate, a bandwidth of about 4 MHz is needed. As with voice transmission over the telephone network, video signaling over cable TV or via broadcast involves the use of extra bandwidth or guardbands to isolate video signals. With these guardbands, the standard bandwidth for color video signaling is 6 MHz.

Digital Signals

Digital Data Signaling   The term *digital signaling* usually refers to the transmission of electromagnetic pulses that represent the two binary digits, 1 and 0. For example, a constant-positive-voltage pulse could represent binary 0 and a constant negative voltage pulse could represent binary 1. Another alternative is to have one binary digit represented by a constant-voltage pulse and the other represented by the absence of any voltage. In either case, what is being represented is binary information. Binary information is generated by terminals, computers, and other data processing equipment and then converted into digital voltage pulses for transmission, as illustrated in Figure 4.10. In the context of this book, the data in which we are interested are in the form of numbers or text. In either case, we must convert this information into binary form; in binary form, it can then be converted into a digital signal.

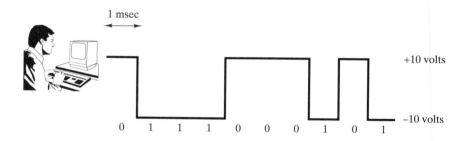

User input at a terminal is converted into a stream of binary digits (1's and 0's). In this graph of a typical digital signal, binary one is represented by –10 volts and binary zero is represented as +10 volts. The signal for each bit has a duration of 1 ms, giving a data rate of 1000 bits per second (bps).

FIGURE 4.10 Conversion of Terminal Input to Digital Signal.

For humans, *numbers* are represented in decimal form. In the decimal system, 10 different digits are used to represent numbers. The position of each digit in a number determines its value. Thus, the decimal number 83 means eight tens plus three:

$$83 = 8 \times 10 + 3$$

and the number 4728 means

$$4728 = 4 \times 1000 + 7 \times 100 + 2 \times 10 + 8$$

The decimal system is said to have a *base* of 10. This means that each digit in the number is multiplied by 10 raised to a power corresponding to that digit's position. Thus,

$$83 = 8 \times 10^1 + 3$$

$$4728 = 4 \times 10^3 + 7 \times 10^2 + 2 \times 10^1 + 8$$

In the binary system, we have only two digits, 1 and 0. Thus, numbers in the binary system are represented to the base 2. As with decimal notation, each digit in a binary number has a value depending on its position:

$$10 = 1 \times 2 + 0 = \text{decimal } 2$$

$$11 = 1 \times 2 + 1 = \text{decimal } 3$$

$$100 = 1 \times 2^2 + 0 \times 2 + 0 = \text{decimal } 4$$

where the first number on each line is a binary number. The binary notation can be extended to represent fractional values and negative numbers. The details are not of concern here.

The other form of what in this book is referred to as data is *text*. Text is nothing more than a string of characters. While textual data are most convenient for human beings, they cannot, in character form, be easily stored or transmitted by data processing and communications system. Such systems are designed for binary data. Thus, a number of codes have been devised by which characters are represented by a sequence of bits. Perhaps the earliest common example of this is the Morse code. The most commonly used code is ASCII (American Standard Code for Information Interchange) in the United States and ITU-T Alphabet Number 5 internationally. Each character in this code is represented by a unique 7-bit binary code; thus 128 different characters can be represented.[2] Table 4-1 lists all the code values. In the table, the bits of each character are labeled from b_1, which is the least significant bit, to b_7, which is the most significant bit. ASCII characters are of two types: printable and control (Table 4-2). *Printable characters* are the alphabetic, numeric, and special characters that can be printed on paper or displayed on a screen. For example, the bit representation of the character "K" is 1001011 (the bits, reading from left to right, are listed in order from b_7 to b_1). Some of the *control characters* have to do with controlling the printing or displaying of characters; an example is carriage return. Other control characters are concerned with communications procedures and are discussed later.

TABLE 4-1 American Standard Code for Information Interchange (ASCII) [a]

Bit Position							b_7=0 b_6=0 b_5=0	0 0 1	0 1 0	0 1 1	1 0 0	1 0 1	1 1 0	1 1 1
b_7	b_6	b_5	b_4	b_3	b_2	b_1								
			0	0	0	0	NUL	DLE	SP	0	@	P	`	p
			0	0	0	1	SOH	DC1	!	1	A	Q	a	q
			0	0	1	0	STX	DC2	"	2	B	R	b	r
			0	0	1	1	ETX	DC3	#	3	C	S	c	s
			0	1	0	0	EOT	DC4	$	4	D	T	d	t
			0	1	0	1	ENQ	NAK	%	5	E	U	e	u
			0	1	1	0	ACK	SYN	&	6	F	V	f	v
			0	1	1	1	BEL	ETB	'	7	G	W	g	w
			1	0	0	0	BS	CAN	(	8	H	X	h	x
			1	0	0	1	HT	EM	)	9	I	Y	i	y
			1	0	1	0	LF	SUB	*	:	J	Z	j	z
			1	0	1	1	VT	ESC	+	;	K	[	k	{
			1	1	0	0	FF	FS	,	<	L	\	l		
			1	1	0	1	CR	GS	-	=	M	]	m	}
			1	1	1	0	SO	RS	.	>	N	^	n	~
			1	1	1	1	SI	US	/	?	O	_	o	DEL

[a] *This is the U.S. national version of ITU-T International Alphabet Number 5 (T.50). The control characters are explained in Table 4-2.*

[2] ASCII-encoded characters are almost always stored and transmitted using 8 bits per character (a block of 8 bits is referred to as an *octet*, or *byte*). The eighth bit is a parity bit used for error detection. This bit is set such that the total number of binary 1's in each octet is always odd (odd parity) or always even (even parity), depending on the convention being used. It is easy to see that an error which alters a single bit can be detected using the parity bit. The parity bit is in the most-significant-bit position, and therefore would be labeled b_8. This topic is pursued in Chapter 5.

TABLE 4-2 ASCII Control Characters

Format Control

BS (backspace): indicates movement of the printing mechanism or display cursor backward one position.

HT (horizontal tab): indicates movement of the printing mechanism or display cursor forward to the next preassigned "tab" or stopping position.

LF (line feed): indicates movement of the printing mechanism or display cursor to the start of the next line.

VT (vertical tab): indicates movement of the printing mechanism or display cursor to the next of a series of preassigned printing lines.

FF (form feed): indicates movement of the printing mechanism or display cursor to the starting position of the next page, form, or screen.

CR (carriage return): indicates movement of the printing mechanism or display cursor to the starting position of the same line.

Transmission Control

SOH (start of heading): used to indicate the start of a heading, which may contain address or routing information.

STX (start of text): used to indicate the start of the text and so also indicates the end of the heading.

ETX (end of text): used to terminate the text that was started with STX.

EOT (end of transmission): indicates the end of a transmission, which may have included one or more "texts" with their headings.

ENQ (enquiry): a request for a response from a remote station. It may be used as a "WHO ARE YOU" request for a station to identify itself.

ACK (acknowledge): a character transmitted by a receiving device as an affirmation response to a sender. It is used as a positive response to polling messages.

NAK (negative acknowledgment): a character transmitted by a receiving device as an negative response to a sender. It is used as a negative response to polling messages.

SYN (synchronous/idle): used by a synchronous transmission system to achieve synchronization. When no data are being sent, a synchronous transmission system may send SYN characters continuously.

ETB (end of transmission block): indicates the end of a block of data for communication purposes. It is used for blocking data where the block structure is not necessarily related to the processing format.

Information Separator

FS (file separator)
GS (group separator)
RS (record separator)
US (united separator)

Information separators to be used in an optional manner except that their hierarchy shall be FS (the most inclusive) to US (the least inclusive)

Miscellaneous

NUL (null): no character. Used for filling in time or filling space on tape when there are no data.

BEL (bell): used when there is need to call human attention. It may control alarm or attention devices.

SO (shift out): indicates that the code combinations that follow shall be interpreted as outside the standard character set until a SI character is reached.

SI (shift in): indicates that the code combinations that follow shall be interpreted according to the standard character set.

DEL (delete): used to obliterate unwanted characters: for example, by overwriting.

SP (space): a nonprinting character used to separate words or to move the printing mechanism or display cursor forward by one position.

DLE (data link escape): a character that shall change the meaning of one or more contiguously following characters. It can provide supplementary controls, or permits the sending of data characters having any bit combination.

DC1, DC2, DC3, DC4 (device controls): characters for the control of ancillary devices or special terminal features.

CAN (cancel): indicates that the data that precede it in a message or block should be disregarded (usually because an error has been detected).

EM (end of medium): indicates the physical end of a tape or other medium, or the end of the required or used portion of the medium.

SUB (substitute): substituted for a character that is found to be erroneous or invalid.

ESC (escape): a character intended to provide code extension in that it gives a specified number of continuously following characters an alternate meaning.

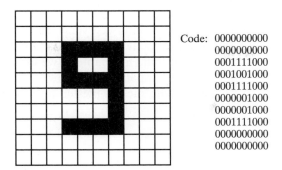

Code: 0000000000
0000000000
0001111000
0001001000
0001111000
0000001000
0000001000
0001111000
0000000000
0000000000

FIGURE 4.11 A 100-Pixel Image and Its Binary Code.

Image Signaling There are a variety of techniques used to represent image information. Among the approaches:

- *Analog facsimile.* This technique is very similar to the video scanning technique just outlined. The image is represented as a set of horizontal lines, and each horizontal line is represented by a continuously varying intensity pattern.
- *Digital facsimile.* This technique is gradually replacing analog facsimile because of its superior quality and performance. With digital facsimile, the image is represented as a two-dimensional array of spots, called pixels, each pixel being either black or white.
- *Raster-scan computer graphics.* A graphic image on a computer screen is represented in the same fashion as facsimile representation, as a two-dimensional array of pixels.
- *Object-oriented computer graphics.* A graphic image on a computer screen is represented by means of descriptions of predefined objects (e.g., squares, rectangles, lines, arcs, characters). The description of each object gives its position, orientation, and size.

With analog facsimile, an image can be converted into an analog signal in the same fashion as we saw for video. For the remainder of the techniques, the image is converted into binary digits. For example, Figure 4.11 shows a simple 10 × 10 representation of an image. This could be a facsimile or raster-scan computer graphics image. The 10 × 10 representation is easily converted to a 100-bit code for the image. Object-oriented computer graphics involves the use of binary codes to represent object type, size, and orientation. In all these cases, the image is represented and stored as a set of binary digits and can be transmitted using digital signals.

4.2 TRANSMISSION IMPAIRMENTS AND CHANNEL CAPACITY

With any communications system, the signal that is received will differ from the signal that is transmitted, due to various transmission impairments. For analog signals, these impairments introduce various random modifications that degrade the signal quality. For digital signals, bit errors are introduced: A binary 1 is transformed into a binary 0, and vice versa. In this section we examine the various impairments and comment on their effect on the information-carrying capacity of a communications link; in Chapter 5 we look at measures that can be taken to compensate for these impairments.

For guided media such as twisted pair, coaxial cable, and optical fiber, the most significant impairments are:

- Attenuation and attenuation distortion
- Delay distortion
- Noise

With wireless transmission, the concerns are:

- Free-space loss
- Atmospheric absorption
- Multipath
- Refraction
- Thermal noise

Guided Media

Attenuation   When an electromagnetic signal is transmitted along any medium, it gradually becomes weaker at greater distances; this is referred to as **attenuation**. Attenuation introduces three considerations for the transmission engineer:

1. A received signal must have sufficient strength so that the electronic circuitry in the receiver can detect and interpret the signal.
2. The signal must maintain a level sufficiently higher than noise to be received without error.
3. Attenuation is greater at higher frequencies, and this causes distortion.

The first and second considerations are dealt with by attention to signal strength and the use of amplifiers or repeaters. The simplest sort of link between transmitter and receiver is shown in Figure 4.1. Data transmission occurs between a *transmitter* and a *receiver* over a *transmission medium*. For a very short link, no measures may need to be taken. For distances at which the attenuation becomes significant, one or more intermediate devices may be used to compensate. In the case of analog signals, an *amplifier* is used; the amplifier boosts the amplitude, or strength, of the signal. In the ideal case, the amplifier will not alter the information content of the signal. In practice, however, the amplifier will introduce some distortion to the signal. This distortion will be cumulative if multiple amplifiers are used along the path between the transmitter and receiver. In the case of digital signals, the intermediate devices are one or more repeaters. The *repeater* receives the incoming signal on one side, recovers the binary data, and transmits a new digital signal on the other side (Figure 4.12). Thus, there is not an accumulation of distortion. However, any error made in recovering the binary data from the incoming signal persists for the remainder of the transmission path.

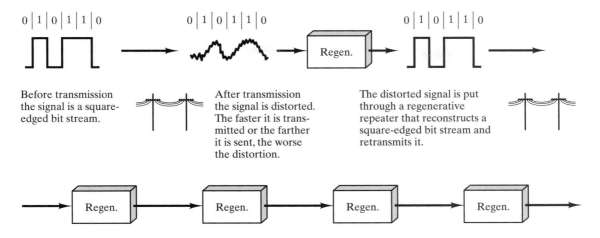

A digital transmission line has many regenerative repeaters. If they are at sufficiently frequent intervals, a much higher bit rate can be transmitted than with analog transmission.

FIGURE 4.12 Regenerative Repeaters.

The third consideration, known as *attenuation distortion,* is particularly noticeable for analog signals. Because attenuation is different for different frequencies, and the signal is made up of a number of frequencies, the received signal is not only reduced in strength but is also distorted. To overcome this problem, techniques are available for equalizing attenuation across a band of frequencies. This is commonly done for telephone lines by using loading coils that change the electrical properties of the line to smooth out attenuation effects.

Digital signals are also made up of a number of frequencies. However, most of the energy in a digital signal is concentrated in a reasonably narrow band. Hence, attenuation distortion is less of a problem than it is for analog signals.

Delay Distortion Delay distortion is a phenomenon that occurs in transmission cables (such as twisted pair, coaxial cable, and optical fiber, discussed in the next section); it does not occur when signals are transmitted through the air by means of antennas. Delay distortion is caused by the fact that the velocity of propagation of a signal through a cable is different for different frequencies. For a signal with a given bandwidth, the velocity tends to be highest near the center frequency of the signal and to fall off toward the two edges of the band. Thus, various components of a signal will arrive at the receiver at different times.

This effect is referred to as *delay distortion* because the received signal is distorted due to a variable delay in its frequency components. Delay distortion is particularly critical for digital data. Because of delay distortion, some of the signal energy in one bit position will spill over into other bit positions, which may cause errors on reception; this is a major limitation to the data rate for digital data.

Noise When information is transmitted in the form of an electromagnetic signal, the received signal will consist of the transmitted signal, modified by attenuation and the various distortions imposed by the transmission system, plus the addition of unwanted electromagnetic energy that is inserted somewhere between transmission and reception. The latter, undesired signals are referred to as **noise**. It is noise that is the major limiting factor in communications system performance.

Noise may be divided into four categories:

Noise
Unwanted signals that combine with and hence distort the signal intended for transmission and reception.

- Thermal noise
- Intermodulation noise
- Crosstalk
- Impulse noise

Thermal noise is due to thermal agitation of electrons in a conductor. It is present in all electronic devices and transmission media and is a function of temperature. Thermal noise is uniformly distributed across the frequency spectrum and hence is often referred to as **white noise**. Thermal noise cannot be eliminated and therefore places an upper bound on communications system performance.

White Noise
Noise that has a flat, or uniform, frequency spectrum in the frequency range of interest.

When signals of different frequencies share the same transmission medium, the result may be *intermodulation noise*. The effect of intermodulation noise is to produce signals at a frequency that is the sum or difference of the two original frequencies or multiples of those frequencies. For example, if two signals, one at 4000 Hz and one at 8000 Hz, share the same transmission facility, they might produce energy at 12,000 Hz. This noise could interfere with an intended signal at 12,000 Hz.

Intermodulation noise is produced when there is some nonlinearity in the transmitter, receiver, or intervening transmission system. Normally, these components behave as linear systems; that is, the output is equal to the input times a constant. In a nonlinear system, the output is a more complex function of the input. Such nonlinearity can be caused by component malfunction or the use of excessive signal strength. It is under these circumstances that the sum and difference terms occur.

Crosstalk has been experienced by anyone who, while having a telephone conversation, has been able to hear another telephone conversation; it is an unwanted coupling between signal paths. It can occur by electrical coupling between nearby cables or by the overlap of signals transmitted by antennas. Typically, crosstalk is of the same order of magnitude as, or less than, thermal noise.

All of the types of noise discussed so far have reasonably predictable and reasonably constant magnitudes. Thus, it is possible to engineer a transmission system to cope with them. *Impulse noise*, however, is noncontinuous, consisting of irregular pulses or noise spikes of short duration and of relatively high amplitude. It is generated from a variety of causes, including external electromagnetic disturbances, such as lightning, and faults and flaws in the communications system. Impulse noise is generally only a minor annoyance for analog data. For example, voice transmission may be corrupted by short clicks and crackles with no loss of intelligibility. However, impulse noise is the primary source of error in digital data communication. For example, a sharp spike of energy of 0.01 sec duration

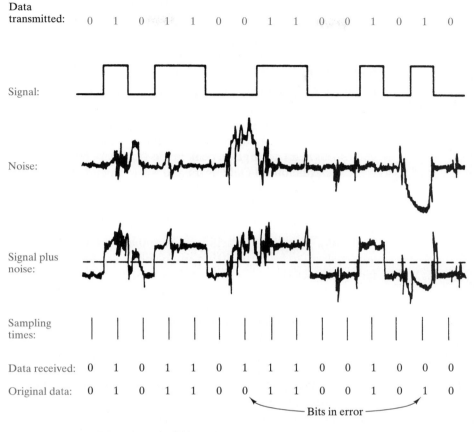

FIGURE 4.13 Effect of Noise on a Digital Signal.

would not destroy any voice information but would wash out about 50 bits of data being transmitted at 4800 bps. Figure 4.13 is an example of the effect on a digital signal. Here the noise consists of a relatively modest level of thermal noise plus occasional spikes of impulse noise. The digital data are recovered from the signal by sampling the received waveform once per bit time. As can be seen, the noise is occasionally sufficient to change a 1 to a 0 or a 0 to a 1.

Unguided Media

Free-Space Loss For any type of wireless communication the signal disperses with distance. Therefore, an antenna with a fixed area will receive less signal power the farther it is from the transmitting antenna. For satellite communication this is the primary mode of signal loss. Under idealized conditions, the ratio of the power P_r received by the antenna to the radiated power P_t is given by

$$\frac{P_r}{P_t} = \frac{A_r A_t f^2}{(cd)^2}$$

where A_r is the area of the receiving antenna, A_t the area of the transmitting antenna, d the distance between the antennas, f the carrier frequency, $\lambda = f/c$ the wavelength, and $c = 300,000$ km/sec the speed of the electromagnetic wave. Thus, for the same antenna dimensions and separation, the higher the carrier frequency f, the lower is the free-space path loss.

Atmospheric Absorption   An additional loss between the transmitting and receiving antennas is atmospheric absorption. Water vapor and oxygen contribute most to attenuation. A peak attenuation occurs in the vicinity of 22 GHz due to water vapor. At frequencies below 15 GHz, the attenuation is less. The presence of oxygen results in an absorption peak in the vicinity of 60 GHz, but contributes less at frequencies below 30 GHz. Rain and fog (suspended water droplets) cause scattering of radio waves that results in attenuation. This can be a major cause of signal loss. Thus, in areas of significant precipitation, either path lengths have to be kept short or lower-frequency bands should be used.

Multipath   For wireless facilities where there is a relatively free choice of where antennas are to be located, they can be placed so that if there are no nearby interfering obstacles, there is a direct line-of-sight path from transmitter to receiver. This is generally the case for many satellite facilities and for point-to-point microwave. In other cases, such as mobile telephony, there are obstacles in abundance. The signal can be reflected by such obstacles so that multiple copies of the signal with varying delays can be received. In fact, in extreme cases, there may be *no* direct signal. Depending on the differences in the path lengths of the direct and reflected waves, the composite signal can be either larger or smaller than the direct signal. Reinforcement and cancellation of the signal resulting from the signal following multiple paths can be controlled for communication between fixed, well-sited antennas, and between satellites and fixed ground stations, but for mobile telephony and communication to antennas that are not well sited, multipath considerations can be paramount.

Refraction   Additionally, radio waves are refracted (or bent) when they propagate through the atmosphere. The refraction is caused by changes in the speed of the signal with altitude or by other spatial changes in the atmospheric conditions. Normally, the speed of the signal increases with altitude, causing radio waves to diffract downward. However, on occasion, weather conditions may lead to variations in speed with height that differ significantly from the typical variations. This may result in a situation in which only a fraction or no part of the line-of-sight wave reaches the receiving antenna.

Thermal Noise   Thermal or white noise is inescapable. It arises from the thermal activity of the devices and media of the communication system. Because of the weakness of the signal received by satellite earth stations, thermal noise is particularly important for satellite communication.

Channel Capacity

We have seen that there are a variety of impairments that distort or corrupt a signal. For digital data, the question that then arises is to what extent these impairments limit the data rate that can be achieved. The rate at which data can be transmitted over a given communication path, or channel, under given conditions, is referred to as the **channel capacity**.

There are four concepts here that we are trying to relate to one another:

- *Data rate:* the rate, in bits per second (bps), at which data can be communicated.
- *Bandwidth:* the bandwidth of the transmitted signal as constrained by the transmitter and the nature of the transmission medium, expressed in cycles per second, or hertz.
- *Noise*: the average level of noise over the communications path.
- *Error rate:* the rate at which errors occur, where an error is the reception of a 1 when a 0 was transmitted or the reception of a 0 when a 1 was transmitted.

The problem we are addressing is this: Communications facilities are expensive, and in general, the greater the bandwidth of a facility, the greater the cost. Furthermore, all transmission channels of any practical interest are of limited bandwidth. The limitations arise from the physical properties of the transmission medium or from deliberate limitations at the transmitter on the bandwidth to prevent interference from other sources. Accordingly, we would like to make as efficient use as possible of a given bandwidth. For digital data, this means that we would like to get as high a data rate as possible at a particular limit of error rate for a given bandwidth. The main constraint on achieving this efficiency is noise.

We have already shown the relationship between bandwidth and data rate in Figure 4.5. All other things being equal, doubling the bandwidth doubles the data rate. Now consider the relationship between data rate, noise, and error rate. This can be explained intuitively by again considering Figure 4.13. The presence of noise can corrupt one or more bits. If the data rate is increased, the bits become "shorter," so that more bits are affected by a given pattern of noise. Thus, at a given noise level, the higher the data rate, the higher the error rate.

All of these concepts can be tied together neatly in a formula developed by the mathematician Claude Shannon. As we have just illustrated, the higher the data rate, the more damage that unwanted noise can do. For a given level of noise, we would expect that a greater signal strength would improve the ability to receive data correctly in the presence of noise. The key parameter involved in this reasoning is the *signal-to-noise ratio* (*S/N*), which is the ratio of the power in a signal to the power contained in the noise that is present at a particular point in the transmission. Typically, this ratio is measured at a receiver, because it is at this point that an attempt is made to process the signal and eliminate the unwanted noise. The signal-to-noise ratio is important in the transmission of digital data because it sets the upper bound on the achievable data rate. Shannon's result is that the maximum channel capacity, in bits per second, obeys the equation

$$C = W \log_2 \left(1 + \frac{S}{N} \right)$$

where *C* is the capacity of the channel in bits per second and *W* is the bandwidth of the channel in hertz. This represents the theoretical maximum that can be achieved. In practice, however, only much lower rates are achieved. One reason for this is that the formula assumes white noise (thermal noise). Impulse noise is not accounted for, nor are attenuation or delay distortion.

Several observations concerning the Shannon equation can be made. The measure of efficiency of a digital transmission is the ratio *C/W*, which is the bps per hertz value that is achieved. For a given level of noise, it would appear that the data rate could be increased by increasing the signal strength or bandwidth. However, as the signal strength increases, so do nonlinearities in the system, leading to an increase in intermodulation noise. Note also that because noise is assumed to be white, the wider the bandwidth, the more noise is admitted to the system. Thus, as *W* increases, *S/N* increases.

4.3 TRANSMISSION MEDIA

Transmission Medium
The physical medium that conveys data between data stations.

The **transmission medium** is the physical path between transmitter and receiver in a data transmission system. Transmission media can be classified as guided or unguided. In both cases, communication is in the form of electromagnetic waves. With **guided media**, the waves are guided along a solid medium, such as copper twisted pair, copper coaxial cable, and optical fiber. The atmosphere and outer space are examples of **unguided media**, which provide a means of transmitting electromagnetic signals but do not guide them; this form of transmission is usually referred to as **wireless transmission**.

The characteristics and quality of a data transmission are determined by both the characteristics of the medium and the characteristics of the signal. In the case of guided media, the medium itself is more important in determining the limitations of transmission. For unguided media, the bandwidth of the signal produced by the transmitting antenna is more important than the medium in determining transmission characteristics. One key property of signals transmitted by antenna is directionality. In general, signals at lower frequencies are omnidirectional; that is, the signal propagates in all directions from the antenna. At higher frequencies, it is possible to focus the signal into a directional beam.

In considering the design of data transmission systems, a key concern is generally data rate and distance: The greater the data rate and distance, the better. A number of design factors relating to the transmission medium and the signal determine the data rate and distance:

- *Bandwidth.* All other factors remaining constant, the greater the bandwidth of a signal, the higher the data rate that can be achieved.
- *Transmission impairments.* Impairments, such as attenuation, limit the distance. For guided media, twisted pair generally suffers more impairment than coaxial cable, which in turn suffers more than optical fiber.
- *Interference.* Interference from competing signals in overlapping frequency bands can distort or wipe out a signal. Interference is of particular concern for unguided media but is also a problem with guided media. For guided media, interference can be caused by emanations from

nearby cables. For example, twisted pairs are often bundled together and conduits often carry multiple cables. Interference can also be experienced from unguided transmissions. Proper shielding of a guided medium can minimize this problem.

■ *Number of receivers.* A guided medium can be used to construct a point-to-point link or a shared link with multiple attachments. In the latter case, each attachment introduces some attenuation and distortion on the line, limiting distance and/or data rate.

Figure 4.14 depicts the electromagnetic spectrum and indicates the frequencies at which various guided media and unguided transmission techniques operate. In this section we examine guided transmission media. In all cases we describe the systems physically, discuss applications briefly, and summarize key transmission characteristics. Section 4.4 is devoted to wireless transmission.

For guided transmission media, the transmission capacity, in terms of either data rate or bandwidth, depends critically on the distance and on whether the medium is point-to-point or multipoint, such as in a local-area network (LAN). Table 4-3 indicates the type of performance typical for the common guided

TABLE 4-3 Point-to-Point Transmission Characteristics of Guided Media

Transmission Medium	Total Data Rate	Bandwidth	Repeater Spacing (km)
Twisted Pair	4 Mbps	3 MHz	2–10
Coaxial Cable	500 Mbps	350 MHz	1–10
Optical Fiber	2 Gbps	2 GHz	10–100

FIGURE 4.14 Electromagnetic Spectrum for Telecommunications.

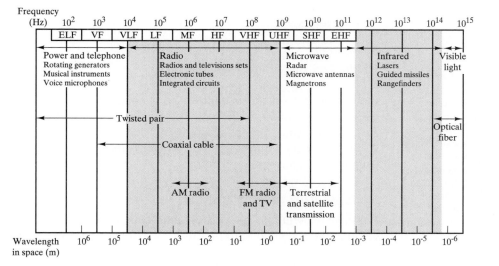

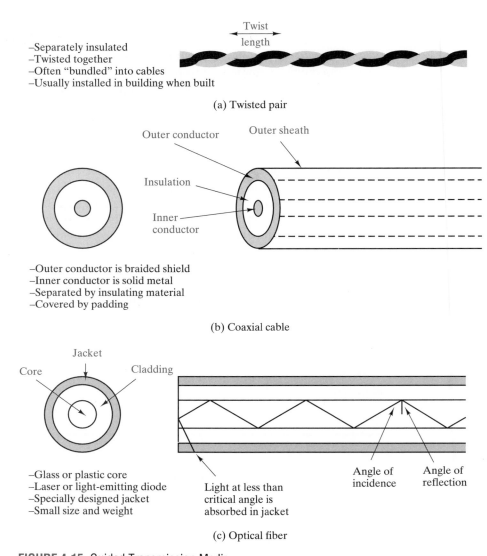

–Separately insulated
–Twisted together
–Often "bundled" into cables
–Usually installed in building when built

(a) Twisted pair

–Outer conductor is braided shield
–Inner conductor is solid metal
–Separated by insulating material
–Covered by padding

(b) Coaxial cable

–Glass or plastic core
–Laser or light-emitting diode
–Specially designed jacket
–Small size and weight

(c) Optical fiber

FIGURE 4.15 Guided Transmission Media.

medium for long-distance point-to-point applications; we defer a discussion of the use of these media for LANs to Part 3. The three guided media commonly used for data transmission are twisted pair, coaxial cable, and optical fiber (Figure 4.15). We begin with twisted pair, which is the least expensive and most widely used guided transmission medium.

Twisted Pair
A transmission medium that consists of two insulated conductors twisted together to reduce noise.

Twisted Pair

Physical Description   A **twisted pair** consists of two insulated copper wires arranged in a regular spiral pattern. A wire pair acts as a single communication link. Typically, a number of these pairs are bundled together into a cable by wrapping them in a tough protective sheath. Over longer distances, cables may contain hundreds of pairs. The twisting tends to decrease the crosstalk interference between adjacent pairs in a cable. Neighboring pairs in a bundle typically have somewhat different twist lengths to enhance the crosstalk interference. On long-distance links, the twist length typically varies from 2 to 6 in.

Applications By far the most common transmission medium for both analog and digital signals is twisted pair. It is the most commonly used medium in the telephone network as well as the workhorse for communications within buildings. In the telephone system, individual residential telephone sets are connected to the local telephone exchange, or *end office*, by twisted-pair wire. These are referred to as *subscriber loops*. Within an office building, each telephone is also connected to a twisted pair, which goes to the in-house private branch exchange (PBX) system or to a Centrex facility at the end office. These twisted-pair installations were designed to support voice traffic using analog signaling. However, by means of a modem, these facilities can handle digital data traffic at modest data rates.

Twisted pair is also the most common medium used for digital signaling. For connections to a digital data switch or digital PBX within a building, a data rate of 64 kbps is common. Twisted pair is also commonly used within a building for local-area networks supporting personal computers. Data rates for such products are typically in the neighborhood of 10 Mbps. However, recently, twisted-pair networks with data rates of 100 Mbps have been developed, although these are quite limited in terms of the number of devices and geographic scope of the network. For long-distance applications, twisted pair can be used at data rates of 4 Mbps or more. An increasingly common long-distance application of twisted pair is to provide a digital link from a residential subscriber to an ISDN (integrated services digital network). Twisted pair is much less expensive than the other commonly used guided transmission media (coaxial cable, optical fiber) and is easier to work with. It is more limited in terms of data rate and distance.

Transmission Characteristics Twisted pair may be used to transmit either analog or digital signals. For analog signals, amplifiers are required about every 5 to 6 km. For digital signals, repeaters are required every 2 or 3 km. Compared to other commonly used guided transmission media (coaxial cable, optical fiber), twisted pair is limited in distance, bandwidth, and data rate. The medium is quite susceptible to interference and noise because of its easy coupling with electromagnetic fields. For example, a wire run parallel to an ac power line will pick up 60-Hz energy. Impulse noise also easily intrudes into twisted pair. Several measures are taken to reduce impairments. Shielding the wire with metallic braid or sheathing reduces interference. The twisting of the wire reduces low-frequency interference, and the use of different twist lengths in adjacent pairs reduces crosstalk.

For analog signaling, a bandwidth of up to about 250 kHz is possible. This accommodates a number of voice channels. For long-distance digital point-to-point signaling, data rates of up to a few Mbps are possible; for very short distances, data rates of up to 100 Mbps have been achieved in commercially available products.

Unshielded and Shielded Twisted Pair   Twisted pair comes in two varieties: unshielded and shielded. Unshielded twisted pair (UTP) is ordinary telephone wire. Office buildings, by universal practice, are prewired with a lot of excess unshielded twisted pair, more than is needed for simple telephone support. This is the least expensive of all the transmission media commonly used for local-area networks and is easy to work with and to install.

Unshielded twisted pair is subject to external electromagnetic interference, including interference from nearby twisted pair and from noise generated in the environment. A way to improve the characteristics of this medium is to shield the twisted pair with a metallic braid or sheathing that reduces interference. This shielded twisted pair (STP) provides better performance at lower data rates. However, it is more expensive than unshielded twisted pair and more difficult to work with.

Category 3 and Category 5 UTP   Most office buildings are prewired with a type of 100-ohm (Ω) twisted-pair cable commonly referred to as voice grade. Because voice-grade twisted pair is already installed, it is an attractive alternative for use as a LAN medium. Unfortunately, the data rates and distances achievable with voice-grade twisted pair are limited.

In 1991, the Electronic Industries Association published standard EIA-568, "Commercial Building Telecommunications Cabling Standard," which specified the use of voice-grade unshielded twisted pair as well as shielded twisted pair for in-building data applications. At that time the specification was felt to be adequate for the range of frequencies and data rates found in office environments. Up to that time, the principal interest for LAN designs was in the range of data rates from 1 to 16 Mbps. Subsequently, as users migrated to higher-performance workstations and applications, there was increasing interest in providing LANs that could operate up to 100 Mbps over inexpensive cable. In response to this need, EIA-568-A was issued in 1995. The new standard reflects advances in cable and connector design and test methods. It covers 150-Ω shielded twisted pair and 100-Ω unshielded twisted pair.

EIA-568-A recognizes three categories of UTP cabling:

- *Category 3:* UTP cables and associated connecting hardware whose transmission characteristics are specified up to 16 MHz
- *Category 4:* UTP cables and associated connecting hardware whose transmission characteristics are specified up to 20 MHz
- *Category 5:* UTP cables and associated connecting hardware whose transmission characteristics are specified up to 100 MHz

Of these, it is category 3 and category 5 cable that have received the most attention for LAN applications. Category 3 corresponds to the voice-grade cable found in abundance in most office buildings. Over limited distances and with proper design, data rates of up to 16 Mbps should be achievable with category 4. Category 5 is a data-grade cable that is becoming increasingly common for prein-stallation in new office buildings. Over limited distances and with proper design, data rates of up to 100 Mbps should be achievable with category 5.

A key difference between category 3 and category 5 cable is the number of twists in the cable per unit distance. Category 5 is much more tightly twisted, typically three to four twists per inch compared to three to four twists per foot for category 4. The tighter twisting is more expensive but provides much better performance than category 4.

Table 4-4 summarizes the performance of category 3 and category 5 UTP, as well as the STP specified in EIA-568-A. The first parameter used for comparison, attenuation, is fairly straightforward. The strength of a signal falls off with distance over any transmission medium. For guided media attenuation is generally logarithmic and therefore is typically expressed as a constant number of decibels[3] per unit distance. Attenuation introduces three considerations for the designer: (1) a received signal must have sufficient magnitude so that the electronic circuitry in the receiver can detect and interpret the signal; (2) the signal must maintain a level sufficiently higher than noise to be received without error; and (3) attenuation is an increasing function of frequency.

Near-end crosstalk as it applies to twisted-pair wiring systems is the coupling of the signal from one pair of conductors to another pair. These conductors may be the metal pins in a connector or wire pairs in a cable. *Near end* refers to coupling that takes place when the transmit signal entering the link couples back to the receive conductor pair at that same end of the link (i.e., the near-transmitted signal is picked up by the near-receive pair).

TABLE 4-4 Comparison of Shielded and Unshielded Twisted Pair

Frequency (MHz)	Attenuation (dB per 100 m)			Near-End Crosstalk (dB)		
	Category 3 UTP	*Category 5 UTP*	*150-Ω STP*	*Category 3 UTP*	*Category 5 UTP*	*150-Ω STP*
1	2.6	2.0	1.1	41	62	58
4	5.6	4.1	2.2	32	53	58
16	13.1	8.2	4.4	23	44	50.4
25	—	10.4	6.2	—	32	47.5
100	—	22.0	12.3	—	—	38.5
300	—	—	21.4	—	—	31.3

[3] The decibel (dB) measures the relative strength of two signals. The number of dB is 10 times the log of the ratio of the power of two signals, or 20 times the log of the ratio of the voltage of two signals. A loss of 3 dB halves the voltage level; a gain of 3 dB doubles the voltage level.

Coaxial Cable

Coaxial Cable
A cable consisting of one copper conductor within and insulated from another copper conductor.

Physical Description   Like twisted pair, **Coaxial cable** consists of two conductors but is constructed differently to permit it to operate over a wider range of frequencies. It consists of a hollow outer cylindrical conductor that surrounds a single inner wire conductor (Figure 4.15b). The inner conductor is held in place by either regularly spaced insulating rings or a solid dielectric material. The outer conductor is covered with a jacket or shield. Because of its shielded, concentric construction, coaxial cable in much less susceptible to interference and crosstalk than is twisted pair. Coaxial cable can be used over longer distances than twisted pair and can support more stations on a shared line.

Applications   Coaxial cable is perhaps the most versatile transmission medium and enjoys widespread use in a wide variety of applications. The most important of these are:

- Television distribution
- Long-distance telephone transmission
- Short-run computer system links
- Local-area networks

Coaxial cable is commonly used as a means of distributing TV signals to individual homes—cable TV. From its modest beginnings as community antenna television (CATV), designed to provide service to remote areas, cable TV will eventually reach almost as many homes and offices as the telephone. A cable TV system can carry dozens or even hundreds of TV channels at ranges up to a few tens of miles.

Coaxial cable has traditionally been an important part of the long-distance telephone network. Today, it faces increasing competition from optical fiber, terrestrial microwave, and satellite. Using frequency-division multiplexing (FDM; see Chapter 6), a coaxial cable can carry over 10,000 voice channels simultaneously.

Coaxial cable is also commonly used for short-range connections between devices. Using digital signaling, coaxial cable can be used to provide high-speed I/O channels on computer systems. Another application area for coaxial cable is local-area networks. Coaxial cable can support a large number of devices with a variety of data and traffic types, over distances that encompass a single building or a complex of buildings.

Transmission Characteristics   Coaxial cable is used to transmit both analog and digital signals. As can be seen from Figure 4.14, coaxial cable has frequency characteristics that are superior to those of twisted pair and thus can be used effectively at higher frequencies and data rates. Because of its shielded, concentric construction, coaxial cable is much less susceptible than twisted pair to interference and crosstalk.

For long-distance transmission of analog signals, amplifiers are needed every few kilometers, with closer spacing required if higher frequencies are used. The usable spectrum for analog signaling extends to about 400 MHz. For digital signaling, repeaters are needed every kilometer or so, with closer spacing needed for higher data rates.

Optical Fiber

Optical Fiber
A thin filament of glass or other transparent material through which a signal-encoded light beam may be transmitted.

Physical Description An **optical fiber** is a thin, flexible medium capable of conducting an optical ray. Various glasses and plastics can be used to make optical fibers. The lowest losses have been obtained using fibers of ultrapure fused silica. Ultrapure fiber is difficult to manufacture; higher-loss multicomponent glass fibers are more economical and still provide good performance. Plastic fiber is even less costly and can be used for short-haul links, for which moderately high losses are acceptable.

An optical fiber has a cylindrical shape and consists of three concentric sections (Figure 4.15c). The two innermost are two types of glass with different indexes of refraction. The center one is called the *core*, and the next layer the *cladding*. These two sections of glass are covered by a protective and light absorbing *jacket*. Optical fibers are grouped together into optical cables.

Applications One of the most significant technological breakthroughs in data transmission has been the development of practical fiber optic communications systems. Optical fiber already enjoys considerable use in long-distance telecommunications, and its use in military applications is growing. The continuing improvements in performance and decline in prices, together with the inherent advantages of optical fiber, have made it increasingly attractive for local-area networking. The following characteristics distinguish optical fiber from twisted pair or coaxial cable:

- *Greater capacity.* The potential bandwidth, and hence data rate, of optical fiber is immense; data rates of 2 Gbps over tens of kilometers have been demonstrated. Compare this to the practical maximum of hundreds of Mbps over about 1 km for coaxial cable and just a few Mbps over 1 km or up to 100 Mbps over a few tens of meters for twisted pair.

- *Smaller size and lighter weight.* Optical fibers are considerably thinner than coaxial cable or bundled twisted-pair cable—at least an order of magnitude thinner for comparable information transmission capacity. For cramped conduits in buildings and underground along public rights-of-way, the advantage of small size is considerable. The corresponding reduction in weight reduces structural support requirements.

- *Lower attenuation.* Attenuation is significantly lower for optical fiber than for coaxial cable or twisted pair and is constant over a wide range of frequencies.

- *Electromagnetic isolation.* Optical fiber systems are not affected by external electromagnetic fields. Thus, the system is not vulnerable to interference, impulse noise, or crosstalk. By the same token, fibers do not radiate energy, causing little interference with other equipment and providing a high degree of security from eavesdropping. In addition, fiber is inherently difficult to tap.

- *Greater repeater spacing.* Fewer repeaters means lower cost and fewer sources of error. From this point of view the performance of optical fiber systems has been steadily improving.

Five basic categories of application have become important for optical fiber:

- Long-haul trunks
- Metropolitan trunks
- Rural exchange trunks
- Subscriber loops
- Local-area networks

Long-haul fiber transmission is becoming increasingly common in the telephone network. Long-haul routes average about 900 miles in length and offer high capacity (typically, 20,000 to 60,000 voice channels). These systems compete economically with microwave and have so underpriced coaxial cable in many developed countries that coaxial cable is rapidly being phased out of the telephone network in such countries.

Metropolitan trunking circuits have an average length of 7.8 miles and may have as many as 100,000 voice channels in a trunk group. Most facilities are installed in underground conduits and are repeaterless, joining telephone exchanges in a metropolitan or city area. Included in this category are routes that link long-haul microwave facilities that terminate at a city perimeter to the main telephone exchange building downtown.

Rural exchange trunks have circuit lengths ranging from 25 to 100 miles and link towns and villages. In the United States, they often connect the exchanges of different telephone companies. Most of these systems have fewer than 5000 voice channels. The technology used in these applications competes with microwave facilities.

Subscriber loop circuits are fibers that run directly from the central exchange to a subscriber. These facilities are beginning to displace twisted pair and coaxial cable links as the telephone networks evolve into full-service networks capable of handling not only voice and data but also image and video. The initial penetration of optical fiber in this application is for the business subscriber, but fiber transmission into the home will soon begin to appear.

A final important application of optical fiber is for local-area networks. Recently, standards have been developed and products introduced for optical fiber networks that have a total capacity of 100 Mbps and can support hundreds or even thousands of stations in a large office building or a complex of buildings. The advantages of optical fiber over twisted pair and coaxial cable become more compelling as the demand for all types of information (voice, data, image, video) increases.

Transmission Characteristics Optical fiber systems operate in the range of about 10^{14} to 10^{15} Hz; this covers portions of the infrared and visible spectrums. The principle of optical fiber transmission is as follows. Light from a source enters the cylindrical glass or plastic core. Rays at shallow angles are reflected and propagated along the fiber; other rays are absorbed by the surrounding material. This form of propagation is called *multimode*, referring to the variety of angles that will reflect. When the fiber core radius is reduced, fewer angles will reflect. By reducing the radius of the core to the order of a wavelength, only a single angle or mode can pass: the axial ray. This single-mode propagation provides superior performance, for the following reason. With multimode transmission, multiple propagation paths exist, each with a different path length and hence time to traverse the fiber. This causes signal elements to spread out in time, which limits the rate at which data can be accurately received. Because there is a single transmission path with single-mode transmission, such distortion cannot occur. Finally, by varying the index of refraction of the core, a third type of transmission, known as *multimode graded index,* is possible. This type is intermediate between the other two in characteristics. The variable refraction has the effect of focusing the rays more efficiently than ordinary multimode, also known as *multimode step index.* Table 4-5 compares the three fiber transmission modes.

Two different types of light source are used in fiber optic systems: the light-emitting diode (LED) and the injection laser diode (ILD). Both are semiconductor devices that emit a beam of light when a voltage is applied. The LED is less costly, operates over a greater temperature range, and has a longer operational life. The ILD, which operates on the laser principle, is more efficient and can sustain greater data rates.

There is a relationship among the wavelength employed, the type of transmission, and the achievable data rate. Both single mode and multimode can support several different wavelengths of light and can employ laser or LED light source. In optical fiber, light propagates best in three distinct wavelength "windows," centered on 850, 1300, and 1550 nanometers (nm). These are all in the infrared portion of the frequency spectrum, below the visible-light portion, which

TABLE 4-5 Typical Optical Fiber Characteristics

Fiber Type	*Core Diameter (μm)*	*Cladding Diameter (μm)*	*Maximum Attenuation (dB/km)*			*Maximum Bandwidth (MHz/km)*
			850 nm	*1300 nm*	*1500 nm*	
Single mode	5.0	85 or 125	2.3			5000 at 850 nm
	8.1	125		0.5	0.25	
Graded index	50	125	2.4	0.6	0.5	600 at 850 nm
						1500 at 1300 nm
	62.5	125	3.0	0.7	0.3	200 at 850 nm
						1000 at 1300 nm
	100	140	3.5	1.5	0.9	300 at 850 nm
						500 at 1300 nm
Step index	200 or 300	380 or 440	6.0			6

is 400 to 700 nm. The loss is lower at higher wavelengths, allowing greater data rates over longer distances (Table 4-5). Most local applications today use 850-nm LED light sources. Although this combination is relatively inexpensive, it is generally limited to data rates under 100 Mbps and distances of a few kilometers. To achieve higher data rates and longer distances, a 1300-nm LED or laser source is needed. The highest data rates and longest distances require 1500-nm laser sources.

4.4 WIRELESS TRANSMISSION

For unguided media, transmission and reception are achieved by means of an antenna. For transmission, the antenna radiates electromagnetic energy into the medium (usually air), and for reception, the antenna picks up electromagnetic waves from the surrounding medium. There are basically two types of configurations for wireless transmission: directional and omnidirectional. For the directional configuration, the transmitting antenna puts out a focused electromagnetic beam; the transmitting and receiving antennas must therefore be carefully aligned. In the omnidirectional case, the transmitted signal spreads out in all directions and can be received by many antennas. In general, the higher the frequency of a signal, the more it is possible to focus it into a directional beam.

Three general ranges of frequencies are of interest in our discussion of wireless transmission. Frequencies in the range of about 2 GHz (gigahertz = 10^9 Hz) to 40 GHz are referred to as **microwave frequencies**. At these frequencies, highly directional beams are possible, and microwave is quite suitable for point-to-point transmission. Microwave is also used for satellite communications. Frequencies in the range 30 MHz to 1 GHz are suitable for omnidirectional applications. We refer to this range as the broadcast radio range.

Another important frequency range, for local applications, is the infrared portion of the spectrum. This covers, roughly, from 3×10^{11} to 2×10^{14} Hz. Infrared is useful to local point-to-point and multipoint applications within confined areas such as a single room.

Terrestrial Microwave

Physical Description   The most common type of microwave antenna is the parabolic *dish.* The antenna is fixed rigidly and focuses a narrow beam to achieve line-of-sight transmission to the receiving antenna. Microwave antennas are usually located at substantial heights above ground level in order to extend the range between antennas and to be able to transmit over intervening obstacles. To achieve long-distance transmission, a series of microwave relay towers is used, and point-to-point microwave links are strung together over the desired distance.

Applications   The primary use for terrestrial microwave systems is in long-haul telecommunications service, as an alternative to coaxial cable or optical fiber. The microwave facility requires far fewer amplifiers or repeaters than coaxial cable requires over the same distance, but necessitates line-of-sight transmission. Microwave is commonly used for both voice and television transmission.

TABLE 4-6 Typical Digital Microwave Performance

Band (GHz)	Bandwidth (MHz)	Data Rate (Mbps)
2	7	12
6	30	90
11	40	90
18	220	274

Another increasingly common use of microwave is for short point-to-point links between buildings. This can be used for closed-circuit TV or as a data link between local-area networks. Short-haul microwave can also be used for "bypass" applications. A business can establish a microwave link to a long-distance telecommunications facility in the same city, bypassing the local telephone company.

Transmission Characteristics Microwave transmission covers a substantial portion of the electromagnetic spectrum. Common frequencies used for transmission are in the range 2 to 40 GHz. The higher the frequency used, the higher the potential bandwidth and therefore the higher the potential data rate. Table 4-6 indicates bandwidth and data rate for some typical systems.

As with any transmission system, a main source of loss is attenuation. This loss is proportionally less than with twisted pair or coaxial cable, allowing repeaters or amplifiers to be placed farther apart for microwave systems—10 to 100 km is typical. Attenuation is increased with rainfall. The effects of rainfall become especially noticeable above 10 GHz. Another source of impairment is interference. With the growing popularity of microwave, transmission areas overlap and interference is always a danger. Thus, the assignment of frequency bands is strictly regulated.

Satellite Microwave

Physical Description A communication satellite is, in effect, a microwave relay station. It is used to link two or more ground-based microwave transmitter/receivers, known as *earth stations* or *ground stations*. The satellite receives transmissions on one frequency band (uplink), amplifies or repeats the signal, and transmits it on another frequency (downlink). A single orbiting satellite will operate on a number of frequency bands, called *transponder channels* or simply *transponders*.

Figure 4.16 depicts in a general way two common configurations for satellite communication. In the first, the satellite is being used to provide a point-to-point link between two distant ground-based antennas. In the second, the satellite provides communications between one ground-based transmitter and a number of ground-based receivers.

For a communication satellite to function effectively, it is generally required that it remain stationary with respect to its position over the earth. Otherwise, it would not be within the line of sight of its earth stations at all times. To remain

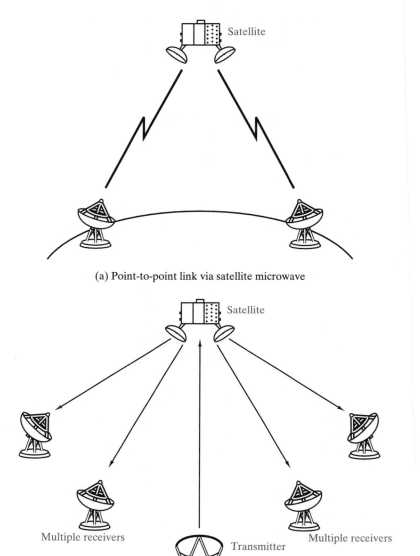

(a) Point-to-point link via satellite microwave

(b) Broadcast link via satellite microwave

FIGURE 4.16 Satellite Communications Configurations.

stationary, the satellite must have a period of rotation equal to the earth's period of rotation. This match occurs at a height of 35,784 km.

If close enough together, two satellites using the same frequency band will interfere with each other. To avoid this, current standards require a 4° spacing (angular displacement as measured from the earth) in the 4/6-GHz band and a 3° spacing at 12/14 GHz. Thus, the number of possible satellites is quite limited.

Applications   The communication satellite is a technological revolution as important as fiber optics. Among the most important applications for satellites:

- Television distribution
- Long-distance telephone transmission
- Private business networks

Because of their broadcast nature, satellites are well suited to television distribution and are being used extensively for this purpose in the United States and throughout the world. In its traditional use, a network provides programming from a central location. Programs are transmitted to the satellite and then broadcast down to a number of stations, which then distribute the programs to individual viewers. A more recent application of satellite technology to television distribution is direct broadcast satellite (DBS), in which satellite video signals are transmitted directly to the home user.

Satellite transmission is also used for point-to-point trunks between telephone exchange offices in public telephone networks. It is the useful medium for high-usage international trunks and is competitive with terrestrial systems for many long-distance intranational links, particularly in remote and undeveloped areas.

Finally, there are a number of business data applications for satellite. The satellite provider can divide the total capacity into a number of channels and lease these channels to individual business users. A user equipped with the antennas at a number of sites can use a satellite channel for a private network. Traditionally, such applications have been quite expensive and limited to larger organizations with high-volume requirements. Today, the very small aperture terminal (VSAT) system, which provides a low-cost alternative. Figure 4.17 depicts a typical VSAT configuration. A number of subscriber stations are equipped with low-cost VSAT antennas. Using some discipline, these stations share a satellite transmission capacity for transmission to a hub station. The hub station can exchange messages with each of the subscribers and can relay messages between subscribers.

Transmission Characteristics   The optimum frequency range for satellite transmission is in the range 1 to 10 GHz. Below 1 GHz, there is significant noise from natural sources, including galactic, solar, and atmospheric noise, and human-made interference from various electronic devices. Above 10 GHz, the signal is severely attenuated by atmospheric absorption and precipitation.

Most satellites providing point-to-point service today use a frequency bandwidth in the range 5.925 to 6.425 GHz for transmission from earth to satellite (uplink) and a bandwidth in the range 4.7 to 4.2 GHz for transmission from satellite to earth (downlink). This combination is referred to as the 4/6-GHz band, or C band. Note that the uplink and downlink frequencies differ. For continuous operation without interference, a satellite cannot transmit and receive on the same frequency. Thus, signals received from a ground station on one frequency must be transmitted back on another.

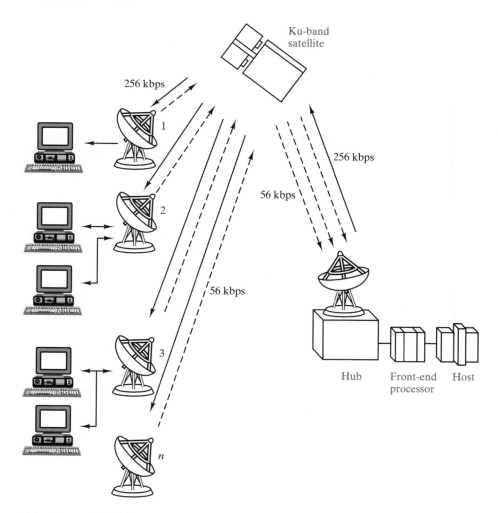

FIGURE 4.17 VSAT Configuration.

The 4/6-GHz band is within the optimum zone of 1 to 10 GHz but has become saturated. Other frequencies in that range are unavailable because of sources of interference operating at those frequencies, usually terrestrial microwave. Therefore, the 12/14-GHz band (K band) has been developed (uplink: 14 to 14.5 GHz; downlink: 11.7 to 12.2 GHz). At this frequency band, attenuation problems must be overcome. However, smaller and cheaper earth-station receivers can be used. It is anticipated that this band will also saturate, and use is projected for the 19/29-GHz band (uplink: 27.5 to 31.0 GHz; downlink: 17.7 to 21.2 GHz). This band experiences even greater attenuation problems but will allow greater bandwidth (2500 MHz versus 500 MHz) and even smaller and cheaper receivers.

Several properties of satellite communication should be noted. First, because of the long distances involved, there is a propagation delay of about 0.25 sec from transmission from one earth station to reception by another earth station. This delay is noticeable in ordinary telephone conversations. It also introduces problems in the areas of error control and flow control, which we discuss in later chapters. Second, satellite microwave is inherently a broadcast facility. Many stations can transmit to the satellite, and a transmission from a satellite can be received by many stations.

Optical Fiber versus Satellite Communications

Up until around 1990, the dominant transmission media for information communications of various sorts have been twisted pair, coaxial cable, and terrestrial microwave. With the exception of twisted pair, these older technologies will be almost completely crowded off the scene by the rapid price/performance advances of optical fiber and satellite and the inherent advantages of these newer technologies over the older ones. Twisted pair will continue to have a role to play inside buildings and for residential local loops for some time to come because it is low cost and a large amount is already installed. For metropolitan and long-distance applications, the combination of satellite and optical fiber is in the process of completely displacing terrestrial microwave, coaxial cable, and twisted pair.

A tremendous expansion of the optical fiber cable network is under way in the telecommunications industry. This expansion has produced an enormous capacity, particularly in the United States, Japan, and Western Europe. There have been three important effects:

- The prices for data, voice, and video transmission are dropping.
- A host of services, including electronic mail and teleconferencing, is more widely available.
- The role of the satellite is becoming increasingly limited in the face of the fiber competition.

So, while optical fiber and satellite have become the two dominant means of intersite communication, the manager with a choice to make needs to ask whether an investment in satellite is worthwhile if it too will be displaced by fiber. The answer is that in some application areas, satellite retains an advantage over optical fiber or any other transmission system. In those areas, satellite remains a sensible choice.

The shift from satellite to fiber is especially pronounced in high-usage, point-to-point applications. In sparsely populated regions with relatively low traffic volumes, satellites will remain strong; the cost of installing optical fiber cable is not justified. For now, the satellite also retains an advantage for broadcast applications such as television. Even this advantage may dwindle as the fiber-based telecommunications networks mature in the late 1990s. Finally, there is an issue of the speed of installation and flexibility of configuration. To hook into an available satellite channel, the subscriber simply needs to install an earth station or to obtain a terrestrial link to an existing earth station. A network based on fiber requires that all the points to be connected be linked by installing fiber cable.

TABLE 4-7 Comparison of Optical Fiber and Satellite Transmission

Characteristic	Optical Fiber	Satellite
Bandwidth	Theoretical limit of 1 terahertz; currently 1–10 GHz	Typical transponder has a bandwidth of 36–72 MHz
Immunity to interference	Immune to electromagnetic interference	Subject to interference from various sources, including microwave
Security	Difficult to tap without detection	Signals must be encrypted for security
Multipoint capability	Primarily a point-to-point medium	Point-to-multipoint communications easily implemented
Flexibility	Difficult to reconfigure to meet changing demand	Easy to reconfigure
Connectivity to customer site	Local loop required	With antenna installed on customer premises, local loop not required

This is a costly and time-consuming process. Thus, despite the strengths of optical fiber and the remarkable speed with which fiber capacity is being deployed, a role for the satellite will remain for many years to come.

Table 4-7 offers a comparison of key characteristics of optical fiber and satellite transmission services.

Broadcast Radio

Physical Description The principal difference between broadcast radio and microwave is that the former is omnidirectional and the latter is directional. Thus, broadcast radio does not require dish-shaped antennas, and the antennas need not be rigidly mounted to a precise alignment.

Applications *Radio* is a general term used to encompass frequencies in the range 3 kHz to 300 GHz. We are using the informal term *broadcast radio* to cover the VHF and part of the UHF band: 30 MHz to 1 GHz. This range covers FM radio and UHF and VHF television. This range is also used for a number of data networking applications.

Transmission Characteristics The range 30 MHz to 1 GHz is effective for broadcast communications. Unlike the case for lower-frequency electromagnetic waves, the ionosphere is transparent to radio waves above 30 MHz. Thus, transmission is limited to the line of sight, and distant transmitters will not interfere with each other due to reflection from the atmosphere. Unlike the higher frequencies of the microwave region, broadcast radio waves are less sensitive to attenuation from rainfall.

A prime source of impairment for broadcast radio waves is multipath interference. Reflection from land, water, and natural or human-made objects can create multiple paths between antennas. This effect is frequently evident when TV reception displays multiple images as an airplane passes by.

Infrared

Infrared communications is achieved using transmitters/receivers (transceivers) that modulate noncoherent infrared light. Transceivers must be with line of sight of each other either directly or via reflection from a light-colored surface such as the ceiling of a room. One important difference between infrared and microwave transmission is that the former does not penetrate walls. Thus, the security and interference problems encountered in microwave systems are not present. Furthermore, there is no frequency allocation issue with infrared because licensing is not required.

SUMMARY

All of the forms of information that are discussed in this book (voice, data, image, video) can be represented by electromagnetic signals and transmitted over a suitable transmission medium. Depending on the transmission medium and the communications environment, either analog or digital signals can be used to convey information. Any electromagnetic signal, analog or digital, is made up of a number of constituent frequencies. A key parameter that characterizes the signal is bandwidth, which is the width of the range of frequencies that comprise the signal. In general, the greater the bandwidth of the signal, the greater its information-carrying capacity.

A major problem in designing a communications facility is transmission impairment. The most significant impairments are attenuation, attenuation distortion, delay distortion, and the various types of noise. The various forms of noise include thermal noise, intermodulation noise, crosstalk, and impulse noise. For analog signals, transmission impairments introduce random modifications that degrade the quality of the received information and may affect intelligibility. For digital signals, transmission impairments may cause bit errors.

The designer of a communications facility must deal with four factors: the bandwidth of the signal, the data rate that is used for digital information, the amount of noise and other impairments, and the level of error rate that is acceptable. The bandwidth is limited by the transmission medium and the desire to avoid interference with other nearby signals. Because bandwidth is a scarce resource, we would like to maximize the data rate that is achieved in a given bandwidth. The data rate is limited by the bandwidth, the presence of impairments, and the error rate that is acceptable. The efficiency of a transmission system is measured by the ratio of data rate (in bps) to bandwidth (in Hz). Efficiencies of between 1 and 5 bps/Hz are considered good.

The transmission media that are used to convey information can be classified as guided or unguided. Guided media provide a physical path along which the signals are propagated; these include twisted pair, coaxial cable, and optical fiber. Unguided media employ an antenna for transmitting through air, vacuum, or water. The techniques commonly used for information communications include broadcast radio, terrestrial microwave, and satellite. Traditionally, twisted pair has been the workhorse for communications of all sorts, and terrestrial microwave and coaxial cable have been heavily used for long-distance telecommunications trunks. More recently, optical fiber and satellite have come to play a dominant role and have displaced other media in many applications. Of these two, optical fiber has the most promising future for the widest range of applications.

RECOMMENDED READING

All of the material in this chapter is covered in greater detail in [STAL97a]. A thorough treatment of both analog and digital communications can be found in [COUC97]. Detailed descriptions of the transmission characteristics of the transmission media discussed in this chapter can be found in [FREE91]. [REEV95] provides an excellent treatment of twisted pair and optical fiber. A thorough explanation of structured cabling systems is provided in [MCEL93].

COUC97   COUCH, L. *Digital and Analog Communication Systems.* Upper Saddle River, NJ: Prentice Hall, 1997.

FREE91   FREEMAN, R. *Telecommunication Transmission Handbook.* New York: Wiley, 1991.

MCEL93   McELROY, M. *The Corporate Cabling Guide.* Boston: Artech House, 1993.

REEV95   REEVE, W. *Subscriber Loop Signaling and Transmission Handbook.* Piscataway, NJ: IEEE Press, 1995.

STAL97a   STALLINGS, W. *Data and Computer Communications, 5th ed.* Upper Saddle River, NJ: Prentice Hall, 1997.

Recommended Web Site

- http://snapple.cs.washington.edu/mobile/mobile.html: source for information about wireless technology, products, conferences, and publications.

KEY TERMS

Amplitude	Guided Media	Transmission Medium
Analog Signal	Microwave Frequencies	Twisted Pair
Attenuation	Noise	Unguided Media
Bandwidth	Optical Fiber	Wavelength
Channel Capacity	Period	White Noise
Coaxial Cable	Periodic Signal	Wireless Transmission
Digital Signal	Phase	
Frequency	Spectrum	

QUESTIONS

1. Differentiate between a continuous and a discrete electromagnetic signal.
2. What are three important characteristics of a periodic signal?
3. What is the relationship between a signal's spectrum and its bandwidth?
4. How can telephone networks use communication facilities that limit the transmission of sound to a narrow bandwidth?
5. What is attenuation?
6. How does delay distortion place a limitation on the data rate for digital data?
7. What is white noise?
8. Differentiate between guided media and unguided media.
9. Why are the wires twisted in twisted-pair copper wire?
10. What are some major limitations of twisted-pair wire?
11. Describe the components of optical fiber cable.
12. What are some major advantages and disadvantages of microwave transmission?

13. What is direct broadcast satellite (DBS)?

14. Why must a satellite have uplink and downlink frequencies?

15. Indicate some significant differences between broadcast radio and microwave.

16. Using Table 4-7 as a guide, speculate on whether fiber optics or satellite will dominate in the future.

PROBLEMS

1. Indicate the decimal equivalent of the following numbers
   a. 101
   b. 111
   c. 110

2. *a.* Using the ASCII code in Table 4-1, indicate the 7-bit ASCII code for the following:
   (1) D
   (2) d
   (3) H
   (4) h
   b. Repeat part a, but this time show the 8-bit code that includes an odd parity bit.

3. Express the following in the simplest form you can:
   a. $\sin(2\pi ft - \pi) + \sin(2\pi ft + \pi)$
   b. $\sin 2\pi ft + \sin(2\pi ft - \pi)$

4. Explain the logical flaw in the following argument. According to Table 4-3, a twisted pair can carry a digital data rate of 4 Mbps. Home computers can use a modem with the telephone network to communicate with other computers. The telephone outlet is connected to the central exchange by a local loop, which is a twisted pair. It is very difficult to establish communication by this method at a data rate higher than 28,800 bps. This is much lower than 4 Mbps. Therefore, a mistake must have been made in Table 4-3.

5. It turns out that the depth in the ocean to which airborne electromagnetic signals can be detected grows with the wavelength. Therefore, the military got the idea of using very long wave lengths, corresponding to about 30 Hz, to communicate with submarines throughout the world. It is desirable to have an antenna that is about $\frac{1}{2}$ wavelength long. How long would that be?

6. The audio power of the human voice is concentrated at about 300 Hz. Antennas of the appropriate size for this frequency are impracticably large, so that to send voice by radio the voice signal must be used to modulate a higher (carrier) frequency for which the natural antenna size is smaller.
   a. What is the length of an antenna one half wavelength long for sending radio at 300 Hz?
   b. Suppose we would like a half-wave antenna to have a length of 1 meter. What carrier frequency would we use?

7. If the dotted curve in Figure 4.18 represents $\sin 2\pi t$ what does the solid curve represent? That is, the solid curve can be written in the form $A \sin(2\pi ft + \xi)$; what are $A, f,$ and ξ?

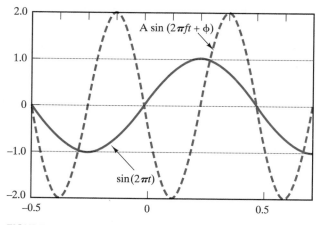

FIGURE 4.18

8. The highest generally available data rate for modems operating on general voice grade circuits is 28.8 Kbps. Some claim that this is very close to the Shannon limit. Suppose that 28.8 Kbps. is the Shannon limit and assume a voice channel bandwidth of 3,300 Hz. What signal to noise ratio does this imply?

9. Stories abound of people who receive radio signals in fillings in their teeth. Suppose you have one filling that is 2.5 mm (0.0025 m) long that acts as a radio antenna. That is, that it is equal in length to one-half the wavelength. What frequency do you receive?

10. You are communicating between two satellites. The transmission obeys the free space law. The signal is too weak. Your vendor offers you two options. They can use a higher frequency that is twice the current frequency or they can double the effective area of **both** of the antennas. Which will offer you more received power or will both offer the same improvement, all other factors remaining equal? How much improvement in the received power do you obtain from the best option?

CHAPTER 5

Data Communication Fundamentals

CHAPTER OBJECTIVES

After reading this chapter, you should be able to:

- Describe how digital data can be encoded by means of a modem so that they can be transmitted over analog telephone lines.

- Describe how analog data, such as voice, can be encoded by means of a codec so that it can be transmitted over digital facilities.

- Explain the differences between asynchronous and synchronous transmission and when each technique is used.

- Describe the purpose of EIA-232 and other interfacing standards.

- Discuss the various control mechanisms required for two devices to exchange data: flow control, error detection, and error control.

- Explain the need for a data link control protocol.

- Describe the basic operation of a data link control protocol such as the widely used HDLC.

*I*n Chapter 4 we described the basic elements of data transmission. But the transmission of data across a transmission medium involves more than simply inserting a signal on the medium. A considerable degree of cooperation between the two sides is needed. In this chapter we explore the essential mechanisms involved in the successful transmission of data between two devices across a transmission medium. First, we discuss the ways in which signals can be encoded for effective and efficient communication. Next, we look at the issue of synchronization: To interpret an incoming signal correctly the receiver must know when each arriving bit begins and ends so that it can keep pace with the transmitter. Several common techniques for synchronizing the receiver with the transmitter are described. We then turn to the issue of interfacing: How does a device actually attach to a medium? We shall see that the interface defines not only the physical attachment, but also the techniques for sending data onto the medium.

Next we look at a set of techniques that, collectively, is embodied in a control mechanism known as a data link control protocol. These mechanisms include techniques for coordinating the presence of more than two devices on a line, as well as techniques for regulating the flow of data and for compensating for transmission errors. After all these techniques have been introduced, we turn to a discussion of a specific data link control protocol, HDLC. This protocol, one of the most commonly used, illustrates the techniques used in such protocols.

5.1 ANALOG AND DIGITAL DATA COMMUNICATION

Electromagnetic signals, which are capable of propagation on a variety of transmission media, can be used to convey data. The exact way in which these signals are encoded to convey data will determine the efficiency and reliability of the transmission. We begin with some basic definitions that are essential to the discussion and then look at the alternative encoding techniques in current use.

Analog and Digital Transmission

The terms *analog* and *digital* correspond, roughly, to *continuous* and *discrete*, respectively. These two terms are frequently used in data communications in at least three contexts:

- Data
- Signaling
- Transmission

Analog Data
Data represented by a continuous physical quantity whose magnitude is proportional to a suitable function of the data.

Digital Data
Data represented by discrete values or conditions.

Analog Signal
A continuously varying electromagnetic wave that may be propagated over a variety of media.

Digital Signal
A discrete or discontinuous signal, such as a sequence of voltage pulses.

The use of these terms in different contexts is often the source of confusion in articles and books. In this section we clarify the various uses of these two terms. We have already had occasion to use these terms in the first two contexts. **Analog data** take on continuous values on some interval. For example, voice and video are continuously varying patterns of intensity. Most data collected by sensors, such as temperature and pressure, are continuous-valued. **Digital data** take on discrete values; examples are text and integers.

In a communications system, data are propagated from one point to another by means of electromagnetic *signals*. An **analog signal** is a continuously varying electromagnetic wave that may be transmitted over a variety of media, depending on frequency. A **digital signal** is a sequence of voltage pulses that may be transmitted over a wire medium; for example, a constant positive voltage may represent binary 1, and a constant negative value may represent binary 0. The principal advantages of digital signaling are that it is generally cheaper than analog signaling and is less susceptible to noise interference. The principal disadvantage is that digital signals suffer more from attenuation than do analog signals. However, note that digital signaling is possible only on copper media (Table 5-1).

Both analog and digital data can be represented, and hence propagated, by either analog or digital signals; this is illustrated in Figure 5.1. Generally, analog data are a function of time and occupy a limited frequency spectrum. Such data can be represented directly by an electromagnetic signal occupying the same spectrum (e.g., voice data in the telephone voice band). In addition, we shall see

TABLE 5-1 Signals and Transmission Media

Transmission Medium	Analog Signaling	Digital Signaling
Copper media (twisted pair, coaxial cable)	Yes; see Figure 4.14 for possible range of frequencies.	Yes
Optical fiber	Yes; see Figure 4.14 for possible range of frequencies.	No
Unguided media (terrestrial radio and microwave; satellite microwave; infrared)	Yes; see Figure 4.14 for possible range of frequencies.	No

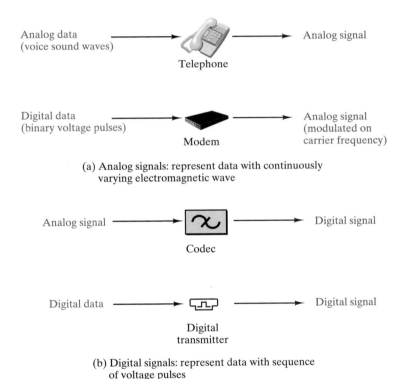

(a) Analog signals: represent data with continuously varying electromagnetic wave

(b) Digital signals: represent data with sequence of voltage pulses

FIGURE 5.1 Analog and Digital Signaling of Analog and Digital Data.

Modem
A device that converts digital data to an analog signal that can be transmitted and converts the received analog signal to data.

that various forms of encoding can be used to provide an analog signal at a different portion of the spectrum. This is done to improve signal quality or transmission efficiency.

Digital data can also be represented by analog signals, by use of a **modem** (modulator/demodulator). The modem converts a series of binary voltage pulses into an analog signal by modulating a *carrier frequency*. The resulting signal occupies a certain spectrum of frequency centered about the carrier and may be propagated across a medium suitable for that carrier. The most common modems represent digital data in the voice spectrum and hence enable digital data to be propagated over ordinary voice-grade telephone lines. At the other end of the line, a modem demodulates the signal to recover the original data. Various modulation techniques are discussed here.

In an operation very similar to that performed by a modem, analog data can be represented by a digital signal. The device that performs this function for voice is a **codec** (coder/decoder). In essence, the codec takes an analog signal that directly represents the voice data and approximates that signal by a bit stream. At the other end of a line, the bit stream is used to reconstruct the analog data.

Finally, digital data can be represented directly, in binary form, by two voltage levels. To improve propagation characteristics, however, the binary data are often encoded, as explained subsequently.

Each of the four combinations just described is in widespread use. The reasons for choosing a particular combination for any given communications task vary. We list here some representative reasons:

- *Digital data, digital signal.* In general, the equipment for encoding digital data into a digital signal is less complex and less expensive than digital-to-analog equipment.

- *Analog data, digital signal.* Conversion of analog data to digital form permits the use of modern digital transmission and switching equipment.

- *Digital data, analog signal.* Some transmission media, such as optical fiber and satellite, will only propagate analog signals.

- *Analog data, analog signal.* Analog data are easily converted to an analog signal.

A final distinction remains to be made. Both analog and digital signals may be transmitted on suitable transmission media. The way these signals are treated is a function of the transmission system. Table 5-2 summarizes the methods of transmission. *Analog transmission* is a means of transmitting analog signals without regard to their content; the signals may represent analog data (such as voice) or digital data (such as data that pass through a modem). In either case, the analog signal will suffer attenuation, which limits the length of the transmission link. To achieve longer distances, the analog transmission system includes amplifiers that boost the energy in the signal. Unfortunately, the amplifier also boosts the noise components. With amplifiers cascaded to achieve long distance, the signal becomes more and more distorted. For analog data such as voice, quite a bit of distortion can be tolerated and the data remain intelligible. However, for digital data transmitted as analog signals, cascaded amplifiers will increase the number of errors.

Digital transmission, in contrast, is concerned with the content of the signal. We have mentioned that a digital signal can be propagated only a limited distance before attenuation endangers the integrity of the data. To achieve greater distances, repeaters are used. A repeater receives the digital signal, recovers the pattern of 1's and 0's, and retransmits a new signal. Thus the attenuation is overcome.

Codec

Transforms analog data into a digital bit stream (coder) and digital signals into analog data (decoder).

TABLE 5-2 Analog and Digital Transmission

(a) DATA AND SIGNALS		
	Analog Signal	*Digital Signal*
Analog Data	Two alternatives: (1) signal occupies the same spectrum as the analog data; (2) analog data are encoded to occupy a different portion of spectrum.	Analog data are encoded using a codec to produce a digital bit stream.
Digital Data	Digital data are encoded using a modem to produce analog signal.	Two alternatives: (1) signal consists of two voltage levels to represent the two binary values; (2) digital data are encoded to produce a digital signal with desired properties.
(b) TREATMENT OF SIGNALS		
	Analog Transmission	*Digital Transmission*
Analog Signal	Is propagated through amplifiers; same treatment whether signal is used to represent analog data or digital data.	Assumes that the analog signal represents digital data. Signal is propagated through repeaters; at each repeater, digital data are recovered from inbound signal and used to generate a new analog outbound signal.
Digital Signal	Not used.	Digital signal represents a stream of 1's and 0's, which may represent digital data or may be an encoding of analog data. Signal is propagated through repeaters; at each repeater, a stream of 1's and 0's is recovered from an inbound signal and used to generate a new digital outbound signal.

The same technique may be used with an analog signal if it is assumed that the signal carries digital data. At appropriately spaced points, the transmission system has retransmission devices rather than amplifiers. The retransmission device recovers the digital data from the analog signal and generates a new, clean analog signal. Thus noise is not cumulative.

The question naturally arises as to which is the preferred method of transmission. The answer being supplied by the telecommunications industry and its customers is digital, this despite an enormous investment in analog communications facilities. Both long-haul telecommunication facilities and intrabuilding services are gradually being converted to digital transmission and, where possible, digital signaling techniques. The most important reasons for this are summarized in Table 5-3.

We now turn to an examination of each of the four signal encoding options.

TABLE 5-3 Advantages of Digital Transmission

Cost

The advent of large-scale integration (LSI) and very-large-scale integration (VLSI) has caused a continuing drop in the cost and size of digital circuitry. Analog equipment has not shown a similar drop. Further, maintenance costs for digital circuitry are a fraction of those for analog circuitry.

Data integrity

With the use of digital repeaters rather than analog amplifiers, the effects of noise and other signal impairments are not cumulative. Thus it is possible to transmit data longer distances and over lesser-quality lines by digital means while maintaining the integrity of the data.

Capacity utilization

It has become economical to build transmission links of very high bandwidth, including satellite channels and optical fiber. A high degree of multiplexing is needed to utilize such capacity effectively, and this is more easily and cheaply achieved with digital (time-division) rather than analog (frequency-division) techniques (see Chapter 6).

Security and privacy

Encryption techniques can readily be applied to digital data and to analog data that have been digitized.

Integration

By treating both analog and digital information digitally, all signals have the same form and can be treated similarly. Thus economies of scale and convenience can be achieved by integrating voice, video, image, and digital data.

5.2 DATA ENCODING TECHNIQUES

As we have pointed out, data, either analog or digital, must be converted into a signal for purposes of transmission. In the case of digital data, different signal elements are used to represent binary 1 and binary 0. The mapping from binary digits to signal elements is the *encoding scheme* for transmission. Encoding schemes are designed to minimize errors in determining the start and end of each bit and errors in determining whether each bit is a 1 or a 0. For analog data, the encoding scheme is designed to enhance the quality, or fidelity, of transmission. That is, we would like the received analog data to be as close as possible to the transmitted data.

Analog Encoding of Digital Information

The basis for analog encoding is a continuous constant-frequency signal known as the *carrier signal*. Digital information is encoded by means of a *modem* that modulates one of the three characteristics of the carrier: amplitude, frequency, or phase, or a combination of these. Figure 5.2 illustrates the three basic forms of modulation of analog signals for digital data:

- Amplitude-shift keying
- Frequency-shift keying
- Phase-shift keying

In all these cases, the resulting signal contains a range of frequencies on both sides of the carrier frequency, which is the bandwidth of the signal.

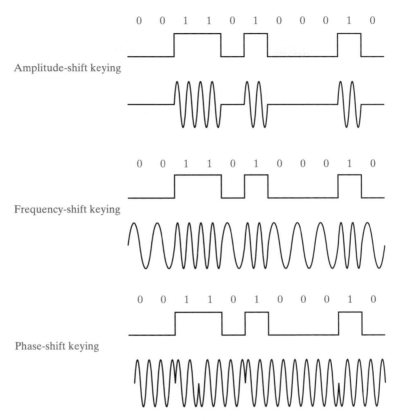

FIGURE 5.2 Modulation of Analog Signals for Digital Data.

In *amplitude-shift keying (ASK),* the two binary values are represented by two different amplitudes of the carrier frequency. In some cases, one of the amplitudes is zero; that is, one binary digit is represented by the presence, at constant amplitude, of the carrier, the other by the absence of the carrier. Amplitude-shift keying is susceptible to sudden gain changes and is a rather inefficient modulation technique. On voice-grade lines, it is typically used only up to 1200 bps.

The amplitude-shift keying technique is commonly used to transmit digital data over optical fiber. For LED transmitters, binary 1 is represented by a short pulse of light and binary 0 by the absence of light. Laser transmitters normally have a fixed "bias" current that causes the device to emit a low light level. This low level represents binary 0, while a higher-amplitude lightwave represents binary 1.

In *frequency-shift keying (FSK),* the two binary values are represented by two different frequencies near the carrier frequency. This scheme is less susceptible to error than is amplitude-shift keying. On voice-grade lines, it is typically used up to 1200 bps. It is also commonly used for high-frequency (4 to 30 MHz) radio transmission.

In *phase-shift keying (PSK),* the phase of the carrier signal is shifted to encode data. Figure 5.2c is an example of a two-phase system. In this system, a 0 is represented by sending a signal burst of the same phase as the preceding signal burst sent. A 1 is represented by sending a signal burst of opposite phase to the preceding one. Phase-shift keying can use more than two phase shifts. A four-phase system would encode two bits with each signal burst. The phase-shift keying technique is more noise-resistant and efficient than frequency-shift keying; on a voice-grade line, rates up to 9600 bps are achieved.

Finally, the techniques just discussed may be combined. A common combination is phase-shift keying and amplitude-shift keying, where some or all of the phase shifts may occur at one or two amplitudes. Using these more complex techniques, data rates as high as 56 kbps on a voice-grade line have been achieved. These techniques are referred to as *multilevel* signaling because each signal element represents multiple bits. Note that four-phase phase-shift keying also falls into this category. With multilevel signaling, we must distinguish between *data rate,* which is the rate, in bits per second, that bits are transmitted, and *modulation rate,* or *signaling rate,* which is the rate at which signal elements are transmitted. The latter rate is expressed in *bauds*, signal elements per second.

Modems   Although both public and private telecommunications facilities are becoming increasingly digital, the use of analog facilities for data transmission will be substantial for many years to come. Thus, the modem is one of the most widely used pieces of communications gear. Modems are offered in several different forms for use in different applications. Stand-alone modems, for instance, are self-contained, with internal power supplies, and are used with separate information products. Where a number of circuits come together—as at the interface to a large computer system—rack-mounted modems are often used, sharing power supplies and packaging. Modems can also be packaged inside an information product (such as personal computer or a terminal). Such integrated modems usually lower overall cost but increase the complexity of the information product and the cost of designing it. Integrated modems are usually offered as an option, because to standardize on a particular modem type with a product might restrict the usefulness of the product.

Because modems are used in pairs for communications, and because this use often occurs over the public telephone network, allowing many different modems to be paired, standards are essential. Table 5-4 lists the most popular modem types, as designated by the ITU-T Recommendation that defines them.[1] The table also lists the applications of each standard.

Digital Encoding of Analog Information

The evolution of public telecommunications networks and private branch exchanges to digital transmission and switching requires that voice data be represented in digital form. It is important to note that this does not necessarily imply

---

[1] See Appendix A for a discussion of ITU-T and other standards bodies.

TABLE 5-4 Modem Specifications

ITU-T Recommendation	*Data Rate (bps)*	*Dial-Up*	*Half-Duplex*	*Full-Duplex*
V.29	9,600		×	×
V.32	9,600	×		×
V.32bis	14,400	×		×
V.33	14,400			×
V.34	28,800	×	×	×

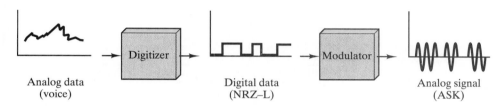

Analog data (voice) → Digitizer → Digital data (NRZ–L) → Modulator → Analog signal (ASK)

FIGURE 5.3 Digitizing Analog Data.

that the voice data be transmitted using digital signals. Figure 5.3 illustrates a common situation. Analog voice signals are digitized to produce a pattern of 1's and 0's. As a digital signal, this pattern of 1's and 0's may be fed into a modem so that an analog signal may be transmitted, for example by satellite or optical fiber. However, this new analog signal differs significantly from the original voice signal, in that it represents an encoding of a binary stream. Hence, the digital transmission techniques just discussed can be applied. In particular, retransmission devices rather than amplifiers are used to extend the length of a transmission link. Ultimately, of course, the new analog signal must be converted back to analog data that approximate the original voice input. For the remainder of this discussion, we can safely ignore the step of converting the digital data back into analog form and concentrate on the voice digitization process.

Pulse-Code Modulation (PCM) A process in which a signal is sampled, and the magnitude of each sample is quantized and converted by coding to a digital signal.

The best-known technique for voice digitization is **pulse-code modulation (PCM)**. PCM is based on the sampling theorem, which states that if a signal is sampled at regular intervals of time and at a rate higher than twice the highest significant signal frequency, the samples contain all the information of the original signal. A proof of this theorem can be found in [STAL97a].

If voice data are limited to frequencies below 4000 Hz, as is done in the analog telephone network, 8000 samples per second would be sufficient to completely characterize the voice signal. Note, however, that these are analog samples. To convert to digital, each of these analog samples must be assigned a binary code. Figure 5.4 shows an example in which each sample is approximated by being "quantized" into one of 16 different levels. Each sample can then be represented by 4 bits. Because the 4-bit value only approximates the analog value, it is now impossible to recover the original signal exactly. By using an 8-bit sample,

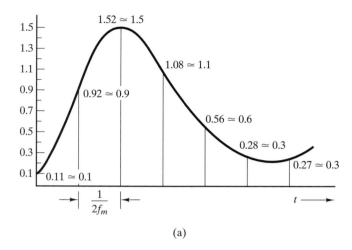

(a)

Digit	Binary equivalent	Pulse-code waveform
0	0000	
1	0001	
2	0010	
3	0011	
4	0100	
5	0101	
6	0110	
7	0111	
8	1000	
9	1001	
10	1010	
11	1011	
12	1100	
13	1101	
14	1110	
15	1111	

(b)

FIGURE 5.4 Pulse-Code Modulation.

which allows 256 quantizing levels, the quality of the recovered voice signal is comparable to that achieved via analog transmission. Note that this implies that a data rate of 8000 samples per second × 8 bits per sample = 64 kbps is needed for a single voice signal.

PCM can, of course, be used for other than voice signals. For example, a color TV signal has a useful bandwidth of 4.6 MHz, and reasonable quality can be achieved with 10-bit samples, for a data rate of 92 Mbps. In recent times, variations on the PCM technique, as well as other encoding techniques, have been used to reduce the digital data rate required to carry voice. Good-quality voice transmission can be achieved with a data rate of 8 kbps. With video, advantage can be taken of the fact that from frame to frame most picture elements will not change. Interframe coding techniques should allow the video requirement to be reduced to about 15 Mpbs, and for slowly changing scenes, such as those in a video teleconference, down to 1.5 Mbps or less. Indeed, recent advances have resulted in commercial videoconference products with data rates as low as 64 kbps.

Digital Encoding of Digital Data

The most common, and easiest, way to transmit digital signals is to use two different voltage levels for the two binary digits. Typically, a negative voltage is used to represent binary 1 and a positive voltage is used to represent binary 0 (Figure 5.5a). This code is known as *nonreturn-to-zero-level (NRZ-L)* (meaning that the signal never returns to zero voltage, and the value during a bit time is a level voltage). NRZ-L is often used for very short connections, such as between a personal computer and an external modem or a terminal and a nearby computer.

A variation of NRZ is *NRZI (NRZ, invert on ones).* As with NRZ-L, NRZI maintains a constant-voltage pulse for the duration of a bit time. The data themselves are encoded as the presence or absence of a signal transition at the beginning of the bit time. A transition (low-to-high or high-to-low) at the beginning of

FIGURE 5.5 Examples of Digital Signal Encoding Schemes.

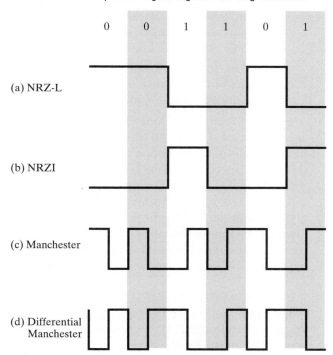

a bit time denotes a binary 1 for that bit time; no transition indicates a binary 0 (Figure 5.5b). NRZI is used on low-speed (64 kbps) ISDN connections.

NRZI is an example of *differential encoding*. In differential encoding, the signal is decoded by comparing the polarity of adjacent signal elements rather than determining the absolute value of a signal element. One benefit of this scheme is that it may be more reliable to detect a transition in the presence of noise than to compare a value to a threshold. Another benefit is that with a complex cabling layout, it is easy to lose the sense of the polarity of the signal. For example, if the leads from an attached device to a twisted-pair cable are accidentally inverted, all 1's and 0's will be inverted for NRZ-L. This does not happen with differential encoding.

A significant disadvantage of NRZ transmission is that it is difficult to determine where one bit ends and another begins. To picture the problem, consider that with a long string of 1's or 0's for NRZ-L, the output is a constant voltage over a long period of time. Under these circumstances, any drift between the timing of transmitter and receiver will result in the loss of synchronization between the two.

There is a set of alternative coding techniques, grouped under the term *biphase*, that overcomes this problem. Two of these techniques, Manchester and differential Manchester, are in common use. All of the biphase techniques require at least one transition per bit time and may have as many as two transitions. Thus, the maximum modulation rate is twice that for NRZ; this means that the bandwidth required is correspondingly greater. To compensate for this, the biphase schemes have several advantages:

- *Synchronization.* Because there is a predictable transition during each bit time, the receiver can synchronize on that transition. For this reason, the biphase codes are known as self-clocking codes.

- *Error detection.* The absence of an expected transition can be used to detect errors. Noise on the line would have to invert both the signal before and after the expected transition to cause an undetected error.

In the *Manchester* code (Figure 5.5c), there is a transition at the middle of each bit period. The midbit transition serves as a clocking mechanism and also as data: A high-to-low transition represents a 1, and a low-to-high transition represents a 0. Manchester coding is used in Ethernet and a number of other local-area networks (LANs). In *differential Manchester* (Figure 5.5d), the midbit transition is used only to provide clocking. The encoding of a 0 is represented by the presence of a transition at the beginning of a bit period, and a 1 is represented by the absence of a transition at the beginning of a bit period. Differential Manchester is used in token-ring LANs. Differential Manchester has the added advantage of employing differential encoding.

Analog Encoding of Analog Information

Analog information can be converted directly into an analog signal that occupies the same bandwidth. The best example of this is voice. Voice-generated sound wave in the range 300 to 3400 Hz can be represented by an electromagnetic signal with the same frequency components. This signal can then be directly transmitted on a voice-grade telephone line. It is also possible to use an analog signal to modulate a carrier to produce a new analog signal that conveys the same information but occupies a different frequency band. There are two principal reasons for doing this:

- A higher frequency may be needed for effective transmission. For unguided media, it is virtually impossible to transmit low-frequency signals; the required antennas would be many kilometers in diameter. Guided media also have constraints on frequency range. Optical fiber, for example, requires that the frequency be on the order of 10^{14} Hz.
- Analog-to-analog modulation permits frequency-division multiplexing, an important technique explored in Chapter 6.

As with digital-to-analog modulation, analog-to-analog modulation involves an information source that is used to modulate one of the three principal characteristics of a carrier signal: amplitude, frequency, or phase. Figure 5.6 illustrate the three possibilities. With amplitude modulation (AM), the amplitude of the carrier varies with the pattern of the modulating signal. Similarly, frequency modulation (FM) and phase modulation (PM) modulate the frequency and phase of a carrier, respectively.

5.3 ASYNCHRONOUS AND SYNCHRONOUS TRANSMISSION

Recall from Figure 4.13 that the reception of digital data involves sampling the incoming signal once per bit time to determine the binary value. One of the difficulties encountered in such a process is that various transmission impairments will corrupt the signal so that occasional errors will occur. This problem is compounded by a timing difficulty: For the receiver to sample the incoming bits properly, it must know the arrival time and duration of each bit that it receives.

Suppose that the sender simply transmits a stream of data bits. The sender has a clock that governs the timing of the transmitted bits. For example, if data are to be transmitted at 10,000 bps, one bit will be transmitted every $1/10,000 = 0.1$ msec, as measured by the sender's clock. Typically, the receiver will attempt to sample the medium at the center of each bit time. The receiver will time its samples at intervals of one bit time. In our example, the sampling would occur once every 0.1 msec. If the receiver times its samples based on its own clock, there will be a problem if the transmitter's and receiver's clocks are not aligned precisely. If there is a drift of 1% (the receiver's clock is 1% faster or slower than the transmitter's clock), the first sampling will be 0.01 of a bit time (0.001 msec) away from the center of the bit (center of bit is 0.05 msec from beginning and end of bit). After 50 or more samples, the receiver may be in error because it is sampling in the wrong bit time ($50 \times 0.001 = 0.05$ msec). For smaller timing differences, the error would occur later, but eventually the receiver will be out of step with the transmitter if the transmitter sends a sufficiently long stream of bits and if no steps are taken to synchronize the transmitter and receiver.

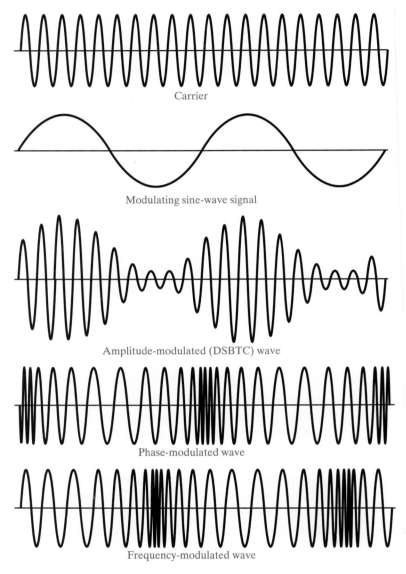

Carrier

Modulating sine-wave signal

Amplitude-modulated (DSBTC) wave

Phase-modulated wave

Frequency-modulated wave

FIGURE 5.6 Amplitude, Phase, and Frequency Modulation of a Sine-Wave Carrier by a Sine-Wave Signal.

Asynchronous Transmission
Transmission in which each information character is individually synchronized.

Asynchronous Transmission

Two approaches are common for achieving the desired synchronization. The first is called, oddly enough, **asynchronous transmission**. The strategy with this scheme is to avoid the timing problem by not sending long, uninterrupted streams of bits. Instead, data are transmitted one character at a time, where each character is 5 to

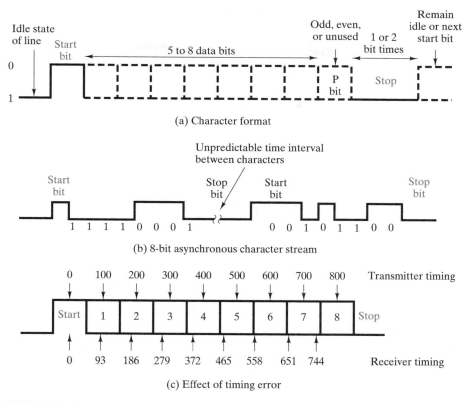

(a) Character format

(b) 8-bit asynchronous character stream

(c) Effect of timing error

FIGURE 5.7 Asynchronous Transmission.

8 bits in length.[2] Timing or synchronization must only be maintained within each character; the receiver has the opportunity to resynchronize at the beginning of each new character.

The technique is easily explained with reference to Figure 5.7. When no character is being transmitted, the line between transmitter and receiver is in an "idle" state. The definition of idle is equivalent to the signaling element for binary 1. Thus, for NRZ-L signaling (see Figure 5.5), which is common for asynchronous transmission, idle would be the presence of a negative voltage on the line. The beginning of a character is signaled by a *start bit* with a value of binary 0. This is followed by the 5 to 8 bits that actually make up the character. Usually, this is followed by a **parity bit**. The parity bit is set by the transmitter such that the

Parity bit
A check bit appended to an array of binary digits to make the sum of all the binary digits always odd or always even.

---

[2] The number of bits that comprise a character depends on the code used. We have already seen one common example, the ASCII code, which uses 7 bits per character (Table 4-1). Another common code is the Extended Binary Coded Decimal Interchange Code (EBCDIC), which is an 8-bit character code used on all IBM machines except for IBM PCs.

total number of 1's in the character, including the parity bit, is even (even parity) or odd (odd parity), depending on the convention being used. This bit is used by the receiver for error detection, as discussed in Section 5.6. The final element is a *stop*, which is a binary 1. A minimum length for the stop is specified, and this is usually 1, 1.5, or 2 times the duration of an ordinary bit. No maximum value is specified. Because the stop is the same as the idle state, the transmitter will continue to transmit the stop signal until it is ready to send the next character.

If a steady stream of characters is sent, the interval between two characters is uniform and equal to the stop element. For example, if the stop is one bit time and the ASCII characters ABC are sent (without parity bit), the pattern[3] is 0<u>1000001</u>1<u>0010000</u>1<u>1011000</u>01111...111. The start bit (0) starts the timing sequence for the next eight elements, which are the 7-bit ASCII code and the stop bit. In the idle state, the receiver looks for a transition from 1 to 0 to signal the beginning of the next character and then samples the input signal at 1-bit intervals for seven intervals. It then looks for the next 1-to-0 transition, which will occur no sooner than one more bit time.

The timing requirements for this scheme are modest. For example, ASCII characters are typically sent as 8-bit units, including the parity bit. If the receiver is 5% slower or faster than the transmitter, the sampling of the eighth information bit will be displaced by 45% and still be sampled correctly. Figure 5.7c shows the effects of a timing error of sufficient magnitude to cause an error in reception. In this example we assume a data rate of 10,000 bits per second (10 kbps); therefore, each bit is of 0.1 msec, or 100 nanoseconds (nsec), duration. Assume that the receiver is off by 7%, or 7 nsec per bit time. Thus, the receiver samples the incoming character every 93 nsec (based on the transmitter's clock). As can be seen, the last sample is erroneous.

Asynchronous transmission is simple and cheap but requires an overhead of 2 to 3 bits per character. For example, for a 7-bit code, using a 1-bit-long stop bit and no parity bit, 2 of every 9 bits convey no information but are there merely for synchronization; thus the overhead is $2/9 \times 100\% = 22\%$. To achieve greater efficiency, a different form of synchronization, synchronous transmission, is used.

Synchronous Transmission

Synchronous Transmission
Data transmission in which the time of occurrence of each bit is related to a fixed time frame.

With **synchronous transmission**, a block of bits is transmitted in a steady stream without start and stop codes. The block may be many characters in length. To prevent timing drift between transmitter and receiver, their clocks must somehow be synchronized. One possibility is to provide a separate clock line between transmitter and receiver. One side (transmitter or receiver) pulses the line regularly with one short pulse per bit time. The other side uses these regular pulses as a clock. This technique works well over short distance, but over longer distances the clock pulses are subject to the same impairments as the data signal, and tim-

---

[3] Each character is transmitted starting with the least significant bit (b1 in Table 4-1). In the text above, the transmission is shown from left (first bit transmitted) to right (last bit transmitted).

ing errors can occur. The other alternative is to embed the clocking information in the data signal. For digital signals, this can be accomplished with Manchester or differential Manchester encoding, as explained in Section 5.2. For analog signals, a number of techniques can be used; for example, the carrier frequency itself can be used to synchronize the receiver based on the phase of the carrier.

With synchronous transmission, there is another level of synchronization required, to allow the receiver to determine the beginning and end of a block of data. To achieve this, each block begins with a *preamble* bit pattern and generally ends with a *postamble* bit pattern. In addition, other bits are added to the block that convey control information used in the data link control procedures discussed later in this chapter. The data plus preamble, postamble, and control information are called a **frame**. The exact format of the frame depends on which data link control procedure is being used.

For sizable blocks of data, synchronous transmission is far more efficient than asynchronous. Asynchronous transmission requires 20% or more overhead. The control information, preamble, and postamble in synchronous transmission are typically less than 100 bits. For example, one of the more common schemes, HDLC, contains 48 bits of control, preamble, and postamble. Thus, for a 1000-character block of data, each frame consists of 48 bits of overhead and $1000 \times 8 = 8000$ bits of data, for a percentage overhead of only $48/8048 \times 100\% = 0.6\%$.

For applications involving low-speed terminals or personal computers, asynchronous transmission is the most common technique. The technique is inexpensive, and its inefficiency is not a problem in most interactive applications, where more time is spent in looking at the screen and thinking than in transmission. However, the overhead of asynchronous transmission would be a heavy price to pay in more communications-intensive applications. For large systems and computer networks, the efficiency of synchronous transmission is needed, even though it introduces the technical problem of synchronizing the clocks of transmitter and receiver.

In addition to the requirement for efficiency, large transfers introduce a requirement for error checking. The interactive user checks his or her own input and output for errors by looking at the screen and rekeying or asking for retransmission of portions that contain errors. Such a procedure is clearly impractical for long file transfers that occur at fast rates and often without an operator present. As we will see, synchronous transmission involves the use of a data link control procedure, which will automatically detect transmission errors and cause a frame in error to be retransmitted.

5.4 INTERFACING

Most digital data processing devices are possessed of limited data transmission capability. Typically, they generate a simple digital signal, such as NRZ-L, and the distance across which they can transmit data is limited. Consequently, it is rare for such a device (terminal, computer) to attach directly to a transmission or networking facility. The more common situation is depicted in Figure 5.8. The

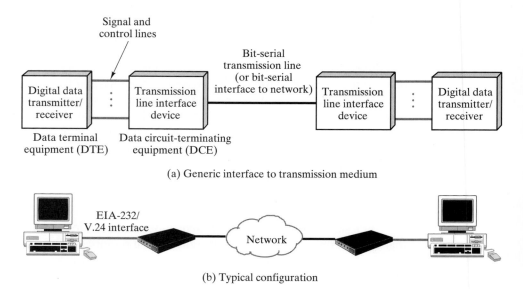

(a) Generic interface to transmission medium

(b) Typical configuration

FIGURE 5.8 Data Communications Interfacing.

Data Terminal Equipment (DTE)
Converts user information into data signals for transmission or reconvert the received data signals into user information.

Data Circuit-terminating Equipment
Provides the signal conversion and coding between the data terminal equipment (DTE) and the line.

devices we are discussing, which include terminals and computers, are referred to generically as **data terminal equipment (DTE)**. A DTE makes use of the transmission system through the mediation of **data circuit-terminating equipment (DCE)**. An example of the latter is a modem.

On one side, the DCE is responsible for transmitting and receiving bits, one at a time, over a transmission medium or network. On the other side, the DCE must interact with the DTE. In general, this requires both data and control information to be exchanged. This is done over a set of wires referred to as **interchange circuits**. For this scheme to work, a high degree of cooperation is required. The two DCEs that exchange signals over the transmission line or network must understand each other. That is, the receiver of each must use the same encoding scheme (e.g., Manchester, PSK) and data rate as the transmitter of the other. In addition, each DTE–DCE pair must be designed to interact cooperatively. To ease the burden on data processing equipment manufacturers and users, standards have been developed that specify the exact nature of the interface between the DTE and the DCE. Such an interface has four important characteristics:

- *Mechanical:* pertains to the actual physical connection of the DTE to the DCE. Typically, the signal and control interchange circuits are bundled into a cable with a terminator plug, male or female, at each end. The DTE and DCE must present plugs of opposite genders at one end of the cable, effecting the physical connection. This is analogous to the situation for residential electrical power. Power is provided via a socket or wall outlet, and the device to be attached must have the appropriate male plug (two-pronged, two-pronged polarized, or three-pronged) to match the socket.

- *Electrical:* concerned with the voltage levels and timing of voltage changes. Both DTE and DCE must use the same code (e.g., NRZ-L), must use the same voltage levels to mean the same things, and must use the same duration of signal elements. These characteristics determine the data rates and distances that can be achieved.
- *Functional:* specifies the functions that are performed, by assigning meanings to each of the interchange circuits. Functions can be classified into the broad categories of data, control, timing, and electrical ground.
- *Procedural:* specifies the sequence of events for transmitting data, based on the functional characteristics of the interface. The examples that follow should clarify this point.

A variety of standards for interfacing exist, of which we present here one of the most important: V.24/EIA-232-E.

V.24/EIA-232-E

The most widely used interface is one that is specified in the ITU-T standard, V.24. In fact, this standard specifies only the functional and procedural aspects of the interface; V.24 references other standards for the electrical and mechanical aspects. In the United States, there is a corresponding specification, virtually identical, that covers all four aspects: **EIA-232**. The correspondence is as follows:

- *Mechanical:* ISO 2110
- *Electrical:* V.28
- *Functional:* V.24
- *Procedural:* V.24

EIA-232 was first issued by the Electronic Industries Association in 1962, as RS-232. It is currently in its fifth revision EIA-232-E, issued in 1991. The current V.24 and V.28 specifications were issued in 1993. This interface is used to connect DTE devices to voice-grade modems for use on public analog telecommunications systems. It is also widely used for many other interconnection applications.

The *mechanical specification* for EIA-232-E is illustrated in Figure 5.9. It calls for a 25-pin connector with a specific arrangement of leads. This connector is the terminating plug or socket on a cable running from a DTE (e.g., personal computer) or DCE (e.g., modem). Thus, in theory, a 25-wire cable could be used to connect the DTE to the DCE. In practice, far fewer interchange circuits are used in most applications.

The *electrical characteristics* specify the signaling between DTE and DCE. Digital signaling is used on all interchange circuits. The convention specifies that with respect to a common ground, a voltage more negative than −3 V is interpreted as binary 1 and a voltage more positive than +3 V is interpreted as binary 0. The interface is rated at a signal rate of <20 kbps and a distance of <15 m. Greater distances and data rates are possible with good design, but it is prudent to assume that these limits apply in practice as well as in theory.

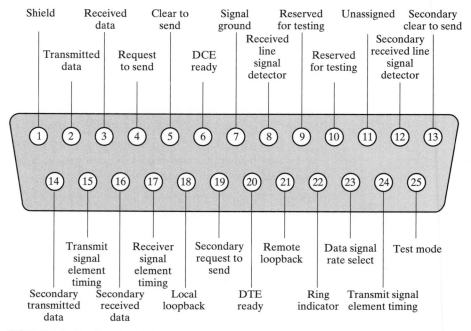

FIGURE 5.9 Pin Assignments for V.24/EIA-232.

Table 5-5 summarizes the *functional specification* of the most important interchange circuits, and Figure 5.9 illustrates the placement of these circuits on the plug. There is one data circuit in each direction, so full-duplex operation is possible. The timing signals provide clock pulses for synchronous transmission. When the DCE is sending synchronous data over the received data circuit (BB), it also sends 1–0 and 0–1 transitions on the receiver signal element timing circuit (DD), with transitions timed to the middle of each BB signal element. When the DTE is sending synchronous data, either the DTE or DCE can provide timing pulses, depending on the circumstances. The control signals are explained by *procedural specifications*, and a few examples are given here.

The first example is a very common one for connecting two devices over a short distance within a building. It is known as an asynchronous private-line, or limited-distance, modem. As the name suggests, the limited-distance modem accepts digital signals from a DTE, such as a terminal or computer, converts these to analog signals, and transmits the signals over a short length of medium, such as twisted pair. On the other end of the line is another limited-distance modem, which accepts the incoming analog signals, converts them to digital, and passes them on to another terminal or computer. Of course, the exchange of data is two-way. The EIA-232 interface between the terminal or computer and the modem serves three functions:

- It provides a means of attachment.
- Asynchronous digital data are exchanged between terminal or computer and modem over the interface.

TABLE 5-5 V.24/EIA-232-E Interchange Circuits

V.24	EIA-232	Name	Direction to:	Function
Data Signals				
103	BA	Transmitted data	DCE	Transmitted by DTE
104	BB	Received data	DTE	Received by DTE
118	SBA	Secondary transmitted data	DCE	Transmitted by DTE
104	SBB	Secondary received data	DTE	Received by DTE
Control Signals				
105	CA	Request to send	DCE	DTE wishes to transmit
106	CB	Clear to send	DTE	DCE is ready to receive; response to request to send
107	CC	DCE ready	DTE	DCE is ready to operate
108.2	CD	DTE ready	DCE	DTE is ready to operate
125	CE	Ring indicator	DTE	DCE is receiving a ringing signal on the channel line
109	CF	Received line signal detector	DTE	DCE is receiving a signal within appropriate limits on the channel line
110	CG	Signal quality detector	DTE	Indicates whether there is a high probability of error in the data received
111	CH	Data signal rate selector	DCE	Selects one of two data rates
112	CI	Data signal rate selector	DTE	Selects one of two data rates
133	CJ	Ready for receiving	DCE	On/off flow control
120	SCA	Secondary request to send	DCE	DTE wishes to transmit on reverse channel
121	SCB	Secondary clear to send	DTE	DCE is ready to receive on reverse channel
122	SCF	Secondary received line signal detector	DTE	Same as 109, for reverse channel
140	RL	Remote loopback	DCE	Instructs remote DCE to loop back signals
141	LL	Local loopback	DCE	Instructs DCE to loop back signals
142	TM	Test mode	DTE	Local DCE is in a test condition
Timing Signals				
113	DA	Transmitter signal element timing	DCE	Clocking signal; transitions to ON and OFF occur at center of each signal element
114	DB	Transmitter signal element timing	DTE	Clocking signal; both 113 and 114 relate to signals on circuit 103
115	DD	Receiver signal element timing	DTE	Clocking signal for circuit 104
Ground				
102	AB	Signal ground/common return		Common ground reference for all circuits

- The modem and terminal or computer cooperate by the exchange of control signals over the interface.

For this simple application, only the following interchange circuits are actually required:

- Signal ground (102)
- Transmitted data (103)
- Received data (104)
- Request to send (105)
- Clear to send (106)
- DCE ready (107)
- Received line signal detector (109)

Let us consider the case of an asynchronous terminal connected to a computer by a pair of private-line modems and a short length of cable between the two modems. When the modem is turned on and is ready to operate, it asserts (applies a constant negative voltage to) the DCE ready line. When the DTE is ready to send data (the terminal user has entered a character), it asserts a request to send. The modem responds by asserting a clear to send, indicating that data may be transmitted over the transmitted data line. The DTE may now transmit data over the transmitted data line. When data arrive from the remote modem (attached to the remote computer), the local modem asserts the received line signal detector to indicate that the remote modem is transmitting and delivers the data on the received data line. Note that it is not necessary to use timing circuits, because this is asynchronous transmission.

The circuits just listed are sufficient for private-line point-to-point modems, but additional circuits are required to use a modem to transmit data over the telephone network. In this case the initiator of a connection must call the destination device over the network. Two additional leads are required:

- DTE ready (108.2)
- Ring indicator (125)

With the addition of these two lines, the DTE can effectively use the telephone network in a way analogous to voice telephone use. Figure 5.10 depicts the steps involved in dial-up operation. When a call is made, either manually or automatically, the telephone system sends a ringing signal. A telephone set would respond by ringing its bell; a modem responds by asserting the ring indicator. A person answers a call by lifting the handset; a DTE answers by asserting DTE ready. A person who answers a call will listen for another's voice, and if nothing is heard, hang up. A DTE will listen for the received line signal detector, which will be asserted by the modem when a signal is present; if this circuit is not asserted, the DTE will drop DTE ready. You might wonder how this last contingency might arise. One common way is if a person accidentally dials the number of a modem. This activates the modem's DTE, but when no carrier tone comes through, the problem is resolved.

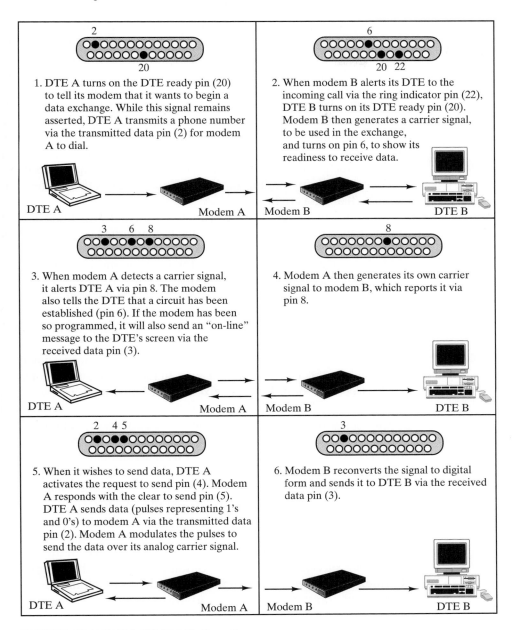

2

1. DTE A turns on the DTE ready pin (20) to tell its modem that it wants to begin a data exchange. While this signal remains asserted, DTE A transmits a phone number via the transmitted data pin (2) for modem A to dial.

DTE A · Modem A

6

2. When modem B alerts its DTE to the incoming call via the ring indicator pin (22), DTE B turns on its DTE ready pin (20). Modem B then generates a carrier signal, to be used in the exchange, and turns on pin 6, to show its readiness to receive data.

Modem B · DTE B

3 6 8

3. When modem A detects a carrier signal, it alerts DTE A via pin 8. The modem also tells the DTE that a circuit has been established (pin 6). If the modem has been so programmed, it will also send an "on-line" message to the DTE's screen via the received data pin (3).

DTE A · Modem A

8

4. Modem A then generates its own carrier signal to modem B, which reports it via pin 8.

Modem B · DTE B

2 4 5

5. When it wishes to send data, DTE A activates the request to send pin (4). Modem A responds with the clear to send pin (5). DTE A sends data (pulses representing 1's and 0's) to modem A via the transmitted data pin (2). Modem A modulates the pulses to send the data over its analog carrier signal.

DTE A · Modem A

3

6. Modem B reconverts the signal to digital form and sends it to DTE B via the received data pin (3).

Modem B · DTE B

FIGURE 5.10 V.24/EIA-232 Dial-Up Operation.

5.5 FLOW CONTROL

Suppose that we wish to write a program, called a printer driver, to pass data from a computer to a printer. We connect the two with the appropriate cable to an EIA-232 port on the host machine. The host port is programmable to match the peripheral device. In this case, let us say that the printer is set up for ASCII 7-bit characters, odd parity, a stop of 1-bit length, and a data rate of 9600 bps. We use these parameters on the host port, write the program, and try to send a page of text to the printer. The result is that after the first few lines of text, there are a number of missing characters: in fact, more missing characters than are printed.

What is the problem? First, let's calculate the character transfer rate. We have 7 bits for the character, 1 for the start bit, 1 for parity, and 1 for stop, for a total of 10 bits per character. Because the computer is transmitting at 9600 bps, the character rate is 960 characters per second. Checking the printer manual, we find that the printer can print at a maximum rate of 80 characters per second. This means that we are sending 12 times as much data as the printer can accept. No wonder that data are lost.

It may seem odd that the printer is equipped with a higher data-rate capability than printing capability, but this is common. The printer includes a small buffer (perhaps 200 characters) so that it can accept characters in a burst of speed, print those characters, and then accept another burst. This allows the printer to be used on a shared multidrop line that is running at a sufficiently high speed to service a number of printers and terminals. For example, a 9600-bps multidrop line could easily accommodate 5 or 10 such printers. However, because the data rate is higher than the printing rate, it is possible for the overrun condition described previously to occur.

Flow Control
A function performed by a receiving entity to limit the amount or rate of data sent by a transmitting entity.

Flow control is a technique for assuring that a transmitting entity does not overwhelm a receiving entity with data. In the case of an electromagnetic device, such as a printer or disk drive, a fixed buffer is provided, as described previously. In the case of data being transmitted to a computer, they are typically destined for an application or system program. The receiving computer allocates a data buffer of some maximum length for that application or system program. When data are received, the computer must do a certain amount of processing before passing the data to the higher-level software. In the absence of flow control, the receiver's buffer may fill up and overflow while it is processing old data.

In this section we examine mechanisms for flow control in the absence of errors. As we discussed previously for synchronous transmission, the data are sent in a sequence of frames, with each frame containing a portion of the data and some control information. For now, we assume that all frames that are transmitted are successfully received; no frames are lost and none arrive with errors. Furthermore, frames arrive in the same order in which they are sent. However, each frame transmitted suffers an arbitrary and variable amount of delay before reception.

Stop-and-Wait Flow Control

The simplest form of flow control, known as *stop-and-wait flow control,* works as follows. A source entity transmits a frame. After reception, the destination entity indicates its willingness to accept another frame by sending back an acknowledgment to the frame just received. The source must wait until it receives the acknowledgment before sending the next frame. The destination can thus stop the flow of data simply by withholding acknowledgment. This procedure works fine and, indeed, can hardly be improved upon when a message is sent in a few large frames. However, it is often the case that a source will break up a large block of data into smaller blocks and transmit the data in many frames. This is done for the following reasons:

- The buffer size of the receiver may be limited.
- The longer the transmission, the more likely that there will be an error, necessitating retransmission of the entire frame. With smaller frames, errors are detected sooner, and a smaller number of data need to be retransmitted.

With the use of many frames for a single message, the stop-and-wait procedure may be inadequate. The essence of the problem is that only one frame at a time can be in transit. In situations where the link is relatively long, serious inefficiencies result. This is illustrated in Figure 5.11. In this figure we assume that transmission is to be made over a long-distance link of 40 km at a data rate of 10 Mbps and that we will be transmitting frames of 1000 bits each. To perform the necessary calculations, you also need to know that the speed of propagation of a signal in a copper transmission medium is about 2×10^8 m/sec. The figure shows a workstation connected to a server by a direct link. The workstation begins to transmit a 1000-bit frame. At a data rate of 10 Mbps, this takes $1000/10^7 = 0.1$ msec. The propagation delay from one end of the link to the other is $(40,000 \text{ m})/(2 \times 10^8 \text{ m/sec}) = 0.2$ msec, so the leading edge of the frame arrives at the other side 0.2 msec after the beginning of transmission. It is not until 0.1 msec later (0.3 msec after the beginning of transmission) that the trailing edge of the frame reaches the destination. It then takes an additional 0.2 msec for a short acknowledgment frame to be returned to the workstation, allowing it to send the next frame. So, while the transmission took only 0.1 msec, the line was tied up for a total of 0.5 msec; efficiency is only 20%.

Sliding-Window Flow Control

Efficiency can be greatly improved by allowing multiple frames to be in transit at the same time. Let us examine how this might work for two stations, A and B, connected via a full-duplex link. Station B allocates buffer space for seven frames instead of the just one discussed . Thus, station B can accept seven frames, and station A is allowed to send seven frames without waiting for an acknowledgment. To keep track of which frames have been acknowledged, each is labeled with a sequence number. Station B acknowledges a frame by sending an acknowledgment that includes the sequence number of the next frame expected. This acknowledgment also implicitly announces that station B is prepared to receive the next seven frames, beginning with the number specified. This scheme can also be used to acknowledge multiple frames. For example, station B could receive frames 2, 3, and 4, but withhold acknowledgment until frame 4 has arrived. By then returning an acknowledgment with sequence number 5, station B acknowledges frames 2, 3, and 4 at one time. Station A maintains a list of sequence numbers that it is allowed to send, and station B maintains a list of sequence numbers

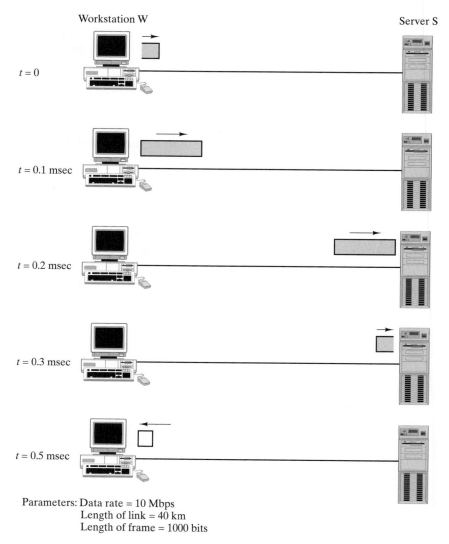

Workstation W

Server S

$t = 0$

$t = 0.1$ msec

$t = 0.2$ msec

$t = 0.3$ msec

$t = 0.5$ msec

Parameters: Data rate = 10 Mbps
Length of link = 40 km
Length of frame = 1000 bits

FIGURE 5.11 Use of Stop-and-Wait Link.

that it is prepared to receive. Each of these lists can be thought of as a *window* of frames. The operation is referred to as sliding-window flow control.

Note that because the sequence number to be used occupies a field in the frame, it is clearly of bounded size. For example, for a 3-bit field, the sequence number can range from 0 to 7. Accordingly, frames are numbered modulo 8; that is, after sequence number 7, the next number is 0. With this in mind, Figure 5.12 is a useful way of depicting the sliding-window process. It assumes the use of a 3-bit sequence number, so that frames are numbered sequentially from 0 through 7, and then the same numbers are reused for subsequent frames. The shaded rectangle represents the window of frames that may be transmitted. The figure indi-

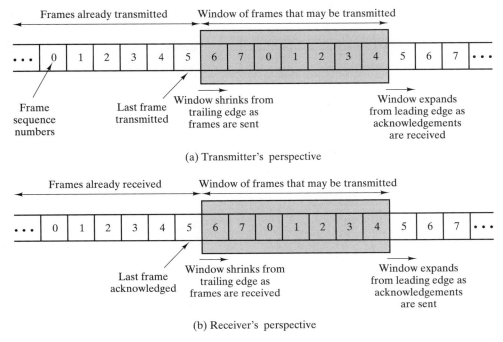

FIGURE 5.12 Sliding-Window Depiction.

cates that the sender may transmit seven frames, beginning with frame 6. Each time a frame is sent, the shaded portion will shrink; each time a new acknowledgment is received, the shaded portion will grow.

An example is shown in Figure 5.13. The example assumes a 3-bit sequence number field and a maximum window size of seven. Initially, stations A and B have windows indicating that station A may transmit seven frames, beginning with frame 0 (F0). After transmitting three frames (F0, F1, F2) without acknowledgment, station A has shrunk its window to four frames. The window indicates that station A may transmit four frames, beginning with frame 3. Station B then transmits an ACK3, which means: "I have received all frames up through frame 2 and am ready to receive frame 3; in fact, I am prepared to receive seven frames, beginning with frame 3." With this acknowledgment, station A is back up to permission to transmit seven frames, still beginning with frame 3. Station A proceeds to transmit frames 3, 4, 5, and 6, and station B returns an ACK7, which acknowledges all of these frames and permits station A to send 7 frames, beginning with frame 7.

The mechanism so far described does indeed provide a form of flow control: The receiver must only be able to accommodate seven frames beyond the one it has last acknowledged. To supplement this, most protocols also allow a station to cut off completely the flow of frames from the other side by sending a receive not ready (RNR) message, which acknowledges former frames but forbids transfer

Source System A   Destination System B

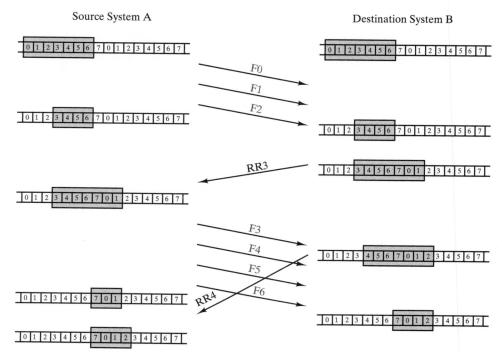

FIGURE 5.13 Example of a Sliding-Window Protocol.

of future frames. Thus, RNR 5 means: "I have received all frames up through 4 but am unable to accept any more." At some subsequent point, the station must send a normal acknowledgment to reopen the window.

In the example that was just given, a 3-bit sequence number was used, allowing a maximum of seven frames to be outstanding. In some circumstances, a bigger maximum window size is desirable. For example, on a satellite link, the delay between transmitter and receiver is so great that many more than seven frames could be in the pipeline at a time. To provide for more efficient transmission on such long-delay links, longer sequence numbers are used. A common alternative is the 7-bit sequence number, which allows up to 127 frames to be outstanding at any time.

So far, we have discussed transmission in one direction only. If two stations exchange data, each needs to maintain two windows, one for transmit and one for receive, and each side needs to send the data and acknowledgments to the other. To provide efficient support for this requirement, a feature known as *piggybacking* is typically provided. Each *data frame* includes a field that holds the sequence number of that frame plus a field that holds the sequence number used for acknowledgment. Thus, if a station has both data and an acknowledgment to send, it sends them together in one frame, saving communication capacity. Of course, if a station has an acknowledgment but no data to send, it sends a separate *acknowledgment frame*. If a station has data to send but no new acknowledgment, it must repeat the last acknowledgment that it sent. This is because the data frame includes a field for the acknowledgment number and some value must be put into that field. When a station receives a duplicate ACK, it simply ignores it.

5.6 ERROR DETECTION

Need for Error Control

As discussed in Chapter 4, any transmission facility has the potential of introducing errors. The ability to control those errors is an increasingly important task of a data communications system. This is partly because the issue of data integrity is becoming increasingly important. There is downward pressure on the allowable error rates for communication and mass storage systems as bandwidths and volumes of data increase. Certain data cannot be wrong; for example, no one can be complacent about the effect of an undetected data error on an electronic funds transfer. More generally, in any system that handles large amounts of data, uncorrected and undetected errors can degrade performance, response time, and possibly increase the need for intervention by human operators.

Error control   The process of **error control** involves two elements:

- *Error detection.* Redundancy is introduced into the data stream so that the occurrence of an error will be detected.
- *Error correction.* Once an error is detected by the receiver, the receiver and the transmitter cooperate to cause the frames in error to be retransmitted.

We look at the error detection process in this section and examine error correction in the next section.

Parity Checks

The simplest approach to error detection is to append a parity bit to the end of a block of data. A typical example is ASCII transmission, in which a parity bit is attached to each 7-bit ASCII character. The value of this bit is selected so that the character has an even number of 1's (even parity) or an odd number of 1's (odd parity). So, for example, if the transmitter is transmitting an ASCII G (1110001) and using odd parity, it will append a 1 and transmit 11100011. The receiver examines the received character, and if the total number of 1's is odd, assumes that no error has occurred. If one bit (or any odd number of bits) is erroneously inverted during transmission (e.g., 11000011), the receiver will detect an error.

Frame Check Sequence
An error-detecting code inserted as a field in a block of data to be transmitted. The code is used to check for transmission errors.

Error-Detecting Code
A code attached to transmitted data and recalculated on received data, to detect transmission errors.

Note, however, that if two (or any even number) of bits are inverted due to error, an undetected error occurs. Typically, even parity is used for synchronous transmission and odd parity for asynchronous transmission.

The use of the parity bit is not foolproof, because noise impulses are often long enough to destroy more than one bit, particularly at high data rates.

Cyclic Redundancy Check

When synchronous transmission is used, it is possible to employ an error detection technique that is both more efficient (lower percentage of overhead bits) and more powerful (more errors detected) than the simple parity bit. This technique requires the addition of a **frame check sequence (FCS)**, or **error-detecting code**, to each synchronous frame. The use of an FCS is illustrated in Figure 5.14, using the CRC code described below. Upon transmission, a calculation is performed on the bits of the frame to be transmitted; the result is inserted as an additional field in the frame. On reception, the same calculation is performed on the bits received and the result calculated is compared to the value stored in the incoming frame. If there is a discrepancy, the receiver assumes that an error has occurred.

FIGURE 5.14 Error Detection Using CRC.

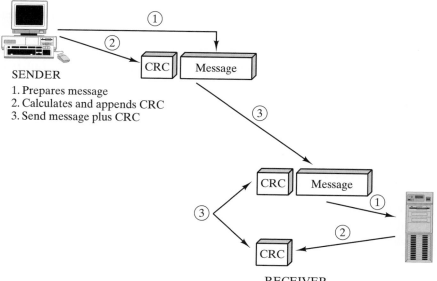

SENDER
1. Prepares message
2. Calculates and appends CRC
3. Send message plus CRC

RECEIVER
1. Receives message plus CRC
2. Calculates CRC from message
3. Compares received CRC wih calculated CRC; signals error if not identical

One of the most common, and one of the most powerful, of the error-detecting codes is the **cyclic redundancy check (CRC)**. For this technique, the message to be transmitted is treated as one long binary number. This number is divided by a unique prime binary number (a number divisible only by itself and 1), and the remainder is attached to the frame to be transmitted. When the frame is received, the receiver performs the same division, using the same divisor, and compares the remainder calculated with the remainder received in the frame. The most commonly used divisors are a 17-bit divisor, which produces a 16-bit remainder, and a 33-bit divisor, which produces a 32-bit remainder.

The measure of effectiveness of any error-detecting code is what percentage of errors it detects. For a CRC of length N, the rate of undetected errors is on the order of 2^{-N} (see [STAL97a] for details). In summary, the CRC is a very powerful means of error detection and requires very little overhead. As an example, if a 16-bit FCS is used with frames of 1000 bits, the overhead is only 1.6%. With a 32-bit FCS, the overhead is 3.2%.

5.7 ERROR CORRECTION

So far, we have discussed techniques that enable a receiver to detect errors that occur in the transmission and reception process. To correct these errors, data link control provides mechanisms by which the two sides cooperate in the retransmission of frames that suffer from errors on the first try. These mechanisms extend the flow control techniques discussed in Section 5.5. Again, data are sent as a sequence of frames; frames arrive in the order in which they are sent; and each frame transmitted suffers an arbitrary and variable amount of delay before reception. In addition, we admit the possibility of two types of errors:

- *Lost frame.* A frame fails to arrive at the other side. In the case of a network, the network may simply fail to deliver a frame. In the case of a direct point-to-point data link, a noise burst may damage a frame to the extent that the receiver is not aware that a frame has been transmitted.
- *Damaged frame.* A recognizable frame does arrive, but some of the bits are in error (have been altered during transmission).

The most common techniques for error control are based on some or all of the following ingredients:

- *Error detection.* The destination detects frames that are in error, using the techniques described in the preceding section, and discards those frames.
- *Positive acknowledgment.* The destination returns a positive acknowledgment to error-free frames received successfully.
- *Retransmission after time-out.* The source retransmits a frame that has not been acknowledged after a predetermined amount of time.
- *Negative acknowledgment and retransmission.* The destination returns a negative acknowledgment to frames in which an error is detected. The source retransmits such frames.

Collectively, these mechanisms are all referred to as **automatic repeat request (ARQ)**. The effect of ARQ is to turn a potentially unreliable data link into a reliable one. The two most common forms of ARQ are stop-and-wait ARQ and go-back-N ARQ. We examine each of these in turn.

Stop-and-Wait ARQ

Figure 5.15[4] illustrates stop-and-wait ARQ. The source station transmits a single frame and then must await an acknowledgment. No other data frames can be sent until the destination station's reply arrives at the source station. Two sorts of errors can occur. First, the frame that arrives at the destination could be damaged. The receiver detects this using the error detection technique described ear-

FIGURE 5.15 Stop-and-Wait ARQ.

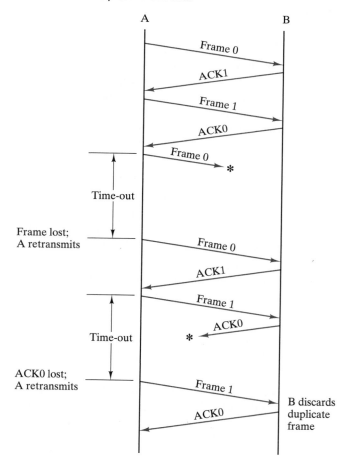

---

[4] The figure is a vertical time-sequence diagram. Each arrow represents a single frame transiting a data link between two stations. This type of figure shows time dependencies and illustrates the correct send–receive relationship.

lier and simply discards the frame. To account for this possibility, the source station is equipped with a timer. After a frame is transmitted, the source station waits for an acknowledgment. If no acknowledgment is received by the time the timer expires, the frame is sent again. Note that this method requires that the transmitter maintain a copy of a transmitted frame until an acknowledgment is received for that frame.

The second sort of error is a damaged acknowledgment. Consider the following situation. Station A sends a frame. The frame is received correctly by station B, which responds with an acknowledgment (ACK). The ACK is damaged in transit and is not recognizable by station A, which will therefore time out and resend the frame. This duplicate frame arrives and is accepted by station B; B has therefore accepted two copies of the same frame as if they were separate. To avoid this problem, frames are alternately labeled with 0 or 1, and positive acknowledgments are of the form ACK0 and ACK1. In keeping with the sliding-window convention, an ACK0 acknowledges receipt of a frame numbered 1 and indicates that the receiver is ready for a frame numbered 0.

Go-Back-N ARQ

The principal advantage of stop-and-wait ARQ is its simplicity. Its principal disadvantage is that of the underlying stop-and-wait flow control technique: It is inefficient. However, just as the stop-and-wait flow control technique can be used as the basis for error control, so can the sliding-window flow control technique be adapted. The form of error control based on sliding-window flow control that is most commonly used is called go-back-N ARQ.

In go-back-N ARQ, a station may send a series of frames sequentially numbered up to some maximum value, after which the sequence numbers start over again at zero. The number of unacknowledged frames outstanding is determined by window size, using the sliding-window flow control technique. While no errors occur, the destination will acknowledge (RR = receiver ready) incoming frames as usual. If the destination station detects an error in a frame, it sends a negative acknowledgment (REJ = reject) for that frame. The destination station will discard that frame and all future incoming frames until the frame in error is correctly received. Thus, the source station, when it receives a REJ, must retransmit the frame in error plus all succeeding frames that had been transmitted in the interim.

Figure 5.16 is an example of the frame flow for go-back-N ARQ. Because of the propagation delay on the line, by the time that an acknowledgment (positive or negative) arrives back at the sending station, it has already sent two additional frames beyond the one being acknowledged. Thus, when a negative acknowledgment is received for frame 5, not only frame 5 but also frames 6 and 7 must be retransmitted. Thus, the transmitter must keep a copy of all unacknowledged frames.

5.8 DATA LINK CONTROL

Physical interface standards such as EIA-232 provide a means by which a stream of data can be transmitted, either synchronously or asynchronously, onto a

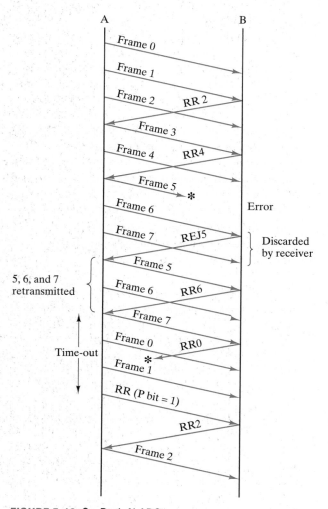

FIGURE 5.16 Go-Back-N ARQ.

transmission medium. However, these interfaces do not include all of the functions required for data communication. Among the most important items lacking are flow control and error control.

To provide these needed functions, a data link control protocol is used. Such protocols are generally used only for synchronous transmission. The basic scheme is as follows. The data to be transmitted by an application are sent to the data link module, which organizes the data into a set of frames. Each frame is supplemented with control bits that allow the two sides to cooperate to deliver the data reliably. The control bits are added by the sender of the frame. When the frame arrives, the receiver examines the control bits and, if the data arrive successfully, strips off the control bits and delivers the pure data to the intended destination point within the system. Figure 5.17 illustrates the process.

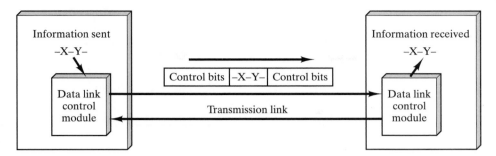

FIGURE 5.17 Operation of a Data Link Control Module.

With the use of control bits, a number of functions can be performed, including error control and flow control. In this section we examine these functions and look specifically at one data link control protocol, known as **HDLC (high-level data link control)**. HDLC, and some very similar variants, are the most widely used data link control standards.

HDLC Frame Structure

Perhaps the best way to begin an explanation of HDLC is to look at the frame structure. The operation of HDLC involves the exchange of two sorts of information between the two connected stations. First, HDLC accepts user data from some higher layer of software and delivers those user data across the link to the other side. On the other side, HDLC accepts the user data and delivers them to a higher layer of software on that side. Second, the two HDLC modules must exchange control information, to provide for flow control, error control, and other control functions. The method by which this is done is to format the information that is exchanged into a *frame*. A frame is a predefined structure that provides a specific location for various kinds of control information and for user data.

Figure 5.18 depicts the format of the HDLC frame. The frame has the following fields:

- *Flag:* used for synchronization. It appears at the beginning and end of the frame and always contains the pattern 01111110.
- *Address:* indicates the *secondary station* for this transmission. It is needed in the case of a multidrop line, where a primary may send data to one of a number of secondaries, and one of a number of secondaries may send data to the primary. This field is usually 8 bits long but can be extended (Figure 5.18b).
- *Control:* identifies the purpose and functions of the frame. It is described below.
- *Information:* contains the user data to be transmitted.
- *Frame check sequence:* contains a 16- or 32-bit cyclic redundancy check, used for error detection.

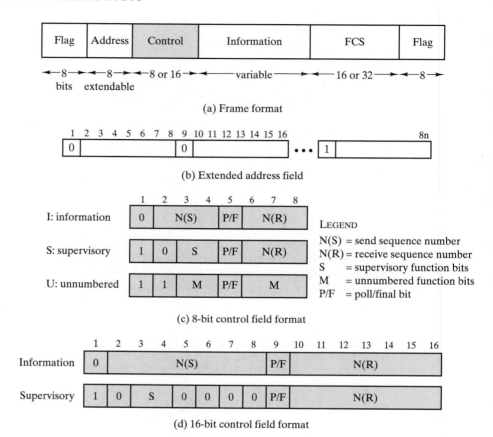

(a) Frame format

(b) Extended address field

LEGEND

N(S) = send sequence number
N(R) = receive sequence number
S   = supervisory function bits
M   = unnumbered function bits
P/F = poll/final bit

(c) 8-bit control field format

(d) 16-bit control field format

FIGURE 5.18 HDLC Frame Structure.

HDLC defines three types of frames, each with a different control field format. Information frames (I-frames) carry the user data to be transmitted for the station. Additionally, the information frames contain control information for flow control and error control. The supervisory frames (S-frames) provide another means of exercising flow control and error control. Unnumbered frames (U-frames) provide supplemental link control functions.

The first 1 or 2 bits of the control field serve to identify the frame type. The remaining bit positions are organized into subfields as indicated in Figure 5.18c and d. Their use is explained in the discussion of HDLC operation that follows. Note that the basic control field for S- and I-frames uses 3-bit sequence numbers. With the appropriate set-mode commands, an extended control field can be used that employs 7-bit sequence numbers.

HDLC Operation

HDLC operation consists of the exchange of I-frames, S-frames, and U-frames between two stations. The various commands and responses defined for these

TABLE 5-6 HDLC Commands and Responses

Name	Command/Response	Description
Information (I)	C/R	Exchange user data
Supervisory (S)		
Receive ready (RR)	C/R	Positive acknowledgment; ready to receive I-frame
Receive not ready (RNR)	C/R	Positive acknowledgment; not ready to receive
Reject (REJ)	C/R	Negative acknowledgment; go back N
Selective reject (SREJ)	C/R	Negative acknowledgment; selective reject
Unnumbered (U)		
Set normal response/extended mode (SNRM/SNRME)	C	Set mode; extended = 7-bit sequence numbers
Set asynchronous response/extended mode (SARM/SARME)	C	Set mode; extended = 7-bit sequence numbers
Set asynchronous balanced/extended mode (SABM, SABME)	C	Set mode; extended = 7-bit sequence numbers
Set initialization mode (SIM)	C	Initialize link control functions in addressed station
Disconnect (DISC)	C	Terminate logical link connection
Unnumbered acknowledgment (UA)	R	Acknowledge acceptance of one of the set-mode commands
Disconnected mode (DM)	C	Terminate logical link connection
Request disconnect (RD)	R	Request for DISC command
Request initialization mode (RIM)	R	Initialization needed; request for SIM command
Unnumbered information (UI)	C/R	Used to exchange control information
Unnumbered poll (UP)	C	Used to solicit control information
Reset (RSET)	C	Used for recovery; resets N(R), N(S)
Exchange identification (XID)	C/R	Used to request/report status
Test (TEST)	C/R	Exchange identical information fields for testing
Frame reject (FRMR)	R	Reports receipt of unacceptable frame

frame types are listed in Table 5-6. In describing HDLC operation, we discuss these three types of frames.

The operation of HDLC involves three phases. First, one side or another initializes the data link so that frames may be exchanged in an orderly fashion. During this phase, the options that are to be used are agreed upon. After initialization, the two sides exchange user data and the control information to exercise flow and error control. Finally, one of the two sides signals termination of the operation.

Initialization   Initialization may be requested by either side by issuing one of the six set-mode commands. This command serves three purposes:

1. It signals the other side that initialization is requested.

2. It specifies which of the three modes is requested; these modes have to do with whether one side acts as a primary and controls the exchange or whether the two sides are peers and cooperate in the exchange.

3. It specifies whether 3- or 7-bit sequence numbers are to be used.

If the other side accepts this request, the HDLC module on that end transmits an unnumbered acknowledged (UA) frame back to the initiating side. If the request is rejected, a disconnected mode (DM) frame is sent.

Data Transfer   When initialization has been requested and accepted, a logical connection is established. Both sides may begin to send user data in I-frames, starting with sequence number 0. The N(S) and N(R) fields of the I-frame are sequence numbers that support flow control and error control. An HDLC module sending a sequence of I-frames will number them sequentially, modulo 8 or 128, depending on whether 3- or 7-bit sequence numbers are used, and place the sequence number in N(S). N(R) is the acknowledgment for I-frames received; it enables the HDLC module to indicate which number I-frame it expects to receive next.

S-frames are also used for flow control and error control. The receive ready (RR) frame is used to acknowledge the last I-frame received by indicating the next I-frame expected. The RR is used when there is no reverse user data traffic (I-frames) to carry an acknowledgment. Receive not ready (RNR) acknowledges an I-frame, as with RR, but also asks the peer entity to suspend transmission of I-frames. When the entity that issued RNR is again ready, it sends an RR. REJ initiates the go-back-N ARQ. It indicates that the last I-frame received has been rejected and that retransmission of all I-frames beginning with number N(R) is required. Selective reject (SREJ) is used to request retransmission of just a single frame.

Disconnect   Either HDLC module can initiate a disconnect, either on its own initiative if there is some sort of fault, or at the request of its higher-layer user. HDLC issues a disconnect by sending a disconnect (DISC) frame. The other side must accept the disconnect by replying with a UA.

Examples of Operation   To better understand HDLC operation, several examples are presented in Figure 5.19. In the example diagrams, each arrow includes a legend that specifies the frame name, the setting of the P/F bit, and, where appropriate, the values of N(R) and N(S). The setting of the P or F bit is 1 if the designation is present and 0 if absent.

Figure 5.19a shows the frames involved in link setup and disconnect. The HDLC entity for one side issues an SABM command to the other side and starts a timer. The other side, upon receiving the SABM, returns a UA response and sets local variables and counters to their initial values. The initiating entity receives the UA response, sets its variables and counters, and stops the timer. The logical connection is now active, and both sides may begin transmitting frames. Should the timer expire without a response, the originator will repeat the

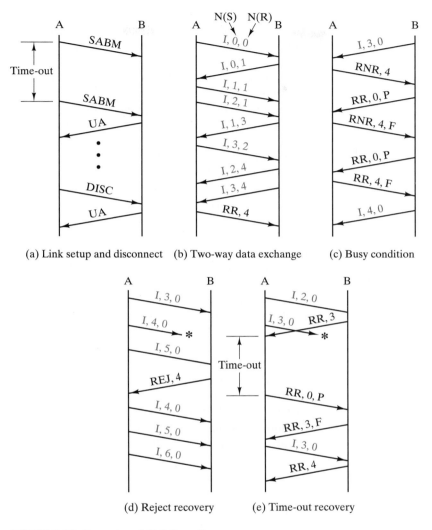

(a) Link setup and disconnect (b) Two-way data exchange (c) Busy condition

(d) Reject recovery (e) Time-out recovery

FIGURE 5.19 Examples of BLC Operation.

SABM, as illustrated. This would be repeated until a UA or DM is received or until, after a given number of tries, the entity attempting initiation gives up and reports failure to a management entity. In such a case, higher-layer intervention is necessary. The same figure (Figure 5.19a) shows the disconnect procedure. One side issues a DISC command, and the other responds with a UA response.

Figure 5.19b illustrates the full-duplex exchange of I-frames. When an entity sends a number of I-frames in a row with no incoming data, the receive sequence number, N(R), is simply repeated (e.g., I,1,1; I,2,1 in the A-to-B direction). When an entity receives a number of I-frames in a row with no outgoing frames, the receive sequence number in the next outgoing frame must reflect the cumulative activity (e.g., I,1,3 in the B-to-A direction). Note that in addition to I-frames, data exchange may involve supervisory frames.

Figure 5.19c shows an operation involving a busy condition. Such a condition may arise because an HDLC entity is not able to process I-frames as fast as they are arriving, or the intended user is not able to accept data as fast as they arrive in I-frames. In either case, the entity's receive buffer fills up and it must halt the incoming flow of I-frames, using an RNR command. In this example, station A issues an RNR, which requires the other side to halt transmission of I-frames. The station receiving the RNR will usually poll the busy station at periodic intervals by sending an RR with the P bit set. This requires the other side to respond with either an RR or an RNR. When the busy condition has cleared, A returns an RR, and I-frame transmission from B can resume.

An example of error recovery using the REJ command is shown in Figure 5.19d. In this example, A transmits I-frames 3, 4, and 5. Frame 4 suffers an error. B detects the error and discards the frame. When B receives I-frame 5, it discards this frame because it is out of order and sends an REJ with an N(R) of 4. This causes A to initiate retransmission of all I-frames sent, beginning with frame 4. It may continue to send additional frames after the retransmitted frames.

An example of error recovery using a timeout is shown in Figure 5.19e. In this example, A transmits I-frame 3 as the last in a sequence of I-frames. The frame suffers an error. B detects the error and discards it. However, B cannot send an REJ. This is because there is no way to know if this was an I-frame. If an error is detected in a frame, all of the bits of that frame are suspect, and the receiver has no way to act upon it. A, however, started a timer as the frame was transmitted. The duration of this timer is long enough to span the expected response time. When the timer expires, A initiates recovery action. This is usually done by polling the other side with an RR command with the P bit set, to determine the status of the other side. Because the poll demands a response, the entity will receive a frame containing an N(R) field and be able to proceed. In this case, the response indicates that frame 3 was lost, which A retransmits.

These examples are not exhaustive. However, they should give the reader a good feeling for the behavior of HDLC.

Other Data Link Control Protocols

HDLC is only one of a number of data link control protocols. All of them follow a similar strategy of defining a frame structure that is used to carry both user data and control information. Table 5-7 lists the most widely used data link control protocols.

SUMMARY

Both analog and digital information can be encoded as either analog or digital signals. The particular encoding that is chosen depends on the specific requirements to be met and the media and communications facilities available. For example, to transmit digital information over an analog telephone line, a modem is used to convert the digital data into analog form. Similarly, there is an increasing use of digital facilities, and voice information must be encoded in digital form to be transmitted on these digital facilities.

TABLE 5-7 Common Data Link Control Protocols

HDLC (high-level data link control)
One of the most widely used link control protocols. Generally used on direct point-to-point links and on multidrop links between a primary and multiple secondaries.

LAPB (link access protocol, balanced)
Used as part of the X.25 standard to connect a device to a packet-switching network. LAPB is a subset of HDLC and uses the same frame format.

LAPD (link access protocol, D channel)
Used on ISDN. It is based on HDLC, with the principal difference related to addressing (discussed in Chapter 7).

LLC (logical link control)
Part of the IEEE 802 family of standards for operation over a local-area network (LAN). LLC lacks some features found in HDLC and adds some new ones (discussed in Chapter 9).

LAPF (link access protocol, frame relay)
Provides the data link control function for frame relay networks. Similar to HDLC but provides more flexibility to streamline operation (discussed in Chapter 8).

The transmission of a stream of bits from one device to another across a transmission link involves a great deal of cooperation and agreement between the two sides. One of the most fundamental requirements is *synchronization*. The receiver must know the rate at which bits are being received so that it can sample the line at regular intervals to determine the value of each bit received. Two techniques are in common use for this purpose. In asynchronous transmission, each character of data is treated independently. Each byte begins with a start bit that alerts the receiver that a character is arriving. The receiver samples each bit in the character and then looks for the beginning of the next character. This technique would not work well for long blocks of data because the receiver's clock might eventually drift out of synchronization with the transmitter's clock. However, sending data in large blocks is more efficient than sending data one character at a time. For large blocks, synchronous transmission is used. Each block of data is formatted as a frame which includes a starting and ending flag. Some form of synchronization, such as the use of Manchester encoding, is employed to maintain synchronization.

For a device to transmit across a medium, it must be attached through some sort of *interface*. The interface defines not only the electrical characteristics of the signal but also the physical means of attachment and the procedures for sending and receiving bits of data. There are a number of interfaces in use; the most common standard is EIA-232.

Because of the possibility of transmission errors and because the receiver of data may need to regulate the rate at which data arrive, synchronization and interfacing techniques are insufficient by themselves. It is necessary to impose a layer of control in each communicating device that provides functions such as flow control, error detection, and error control. This layer of control is known as a *data link control protocol*. The most common of these is HDLC. Similar data link control protocols are also in use.

RECOMMENDED READING

[BLAC96a] provides detailed, broad coverage of many physical layer interface standards. [BLAC95] focuses on modem interfaces and the ITU-T V series recommendations. [SEYE91] is an easy-to-read and thorough introduction to EIA-232. Error detection and correction is dealt with in most textbooks on data communications. One of the more readable treatments can be found in [MART88]. [BLAC93] provides a useful overview of various data link control protocols.

BLAC93   BLACK, U. *Data Link Protocols.* Upper Saddle River, NJ: Prentice Hall, 1993.

BLAC95   BLACK, U. *The V Series Recommendations: Standards for Data Communications over the Telephone Network.* New York: McGraw-Hill, 1995.

BLAC96a   BLACK, U. *Physical Level Interfaces and Protocols.* Los Alamitos, CA: IEEE Computer Society Press, 1995.

MART88   MARTIN, J., and LEBAN, J. *Principles of Data Communication.* Upper Saddle River, NJ: Prentice Hall, 1988.

SEYE91   SEYER, M. *RS-232 Made Easy: Connecting Computers, Printers, Terminals, and Modems.* Upper Saddle River, NJ: Prentice Hall, 1991.

KEY TERMS

Analog Data	Data Link Control Protocol	Frame Check Sequence
Analog Signal	Data Terminal Equipment	(FCS)
Asynchronous Transmission	(DTE)	High-Level Data Link
Automatic Repeat Request	Digital Data	Control (HDLC)
(ARQ)	Digital Signal	Interchange Circuits
Codec	EIA-232	Modem
Cyclic Redundancy Check	Error Control	Parity bit
(CRC)	Error-Detecting Code	Pulse-Code Modulation
Data Circuit-Terminating	Flow Control	(PCM)
Equipment (DCE)	Frame	Synchronous Transmission

QUESTIONS

1. What function does a modem perform?
2. Indicate three major advantages of digital transmission over analog transmission.
3. How are binary values represented in amplitude shift keying, and what is the limitation of this approach?
4. What are the three basic forms of modulation of analog signals for digital data?
5. What is NRZ-L? What is a major disadvantage of this data encoding approach?
6. How is the transmission of a single character differentiated from the transmission of the next character in asynchronous transmission?
7. What is a major disadvantage of asynchronous transmission?
8. What is a DCE, and what is its function?
9. Explain how stop-and-wait flow control works when a printer receives information from a computer.
10. How is sliding-window flow control superior to stop-and-wait flow control?
11. What two key elements comprise error control?
12. Explain how go-back-N ARQ works.

PROBLEMS

1. Suppose that a file of 10,000 characters is to be sent over a line at 2400 bps.
   a. Calculate the overhead in bits and time in using asynchronous communication. Assume 1 start bit and 1 stop bit, and 8 bits to send the character itself for each character.

b. Calculate the overhead in bits and the time using synchronous communication. Assume that the data are sent in frames. Each frame consists of 1000 characters = 8000 bits, an overhead of 48 bits per frame of control, and error detection.

c. What would the answers to parts a and b be for a file of 100,000 characters?

d. What would the answers to parts a and b be for the original file of 10,000 characters except at a data rate of 9600 bps?

2. A data source produces 7-bit ASCII characters. Derive an expression of the maximum effective data rate (rate of ASCII data bits) over a B-bps line for the following:

a. Asynchronous transmission, with a 1.5-unit stop bit and a parity bit.

b. Synchronous transmission, with a frame consisting of 48 control bits and 128 information bits. The information field contains 8-bit (parity included) ASCII characters.

c. Same as part b, except that the information field is 1024 bits.

3. In Figure 5.20, frames generated by node A are sent to node C through node B. Determine the minimum transmission rate required between nodes B and C so that the buffers of node B are not flooded, based on the following:

- The data rate between A and B is 100 kbps.
- The propagation delay is 10 μsec/mile for both lines.
- There are full-duplex lines between the nodes.
- All data frames are 1000 bits long; ACK frames are separate frames of negligible length.
- Between A and B, a sliding-window protocol with a window size of 3 is used.
- Between B and C, a stop-and-wait protocol is used.
- There are no errors.

Hint: In order not to flood the buffers of B, the average number of frames entering and leaving B must be the same over a long interval.

4. When President Franklin Delano Roosevelt gave his first inaugural speech—"the only thing we have to fear is fear itself…."—it lasted about 23 minutes. In printed form it takes about 4 pages. The part that is printed on a page is about $4\frac{1}{2}$" wide and $7\frac{3}{8}$" vertically. There are about 77 characters per line, and there are about $5\frac{2}{3}$ lines per vertical inch. Suppose you wished to represent the speech in a CD ROM encyclopedia.

a. How many 8-bit bytes would it take to store a recording of FDR giving the speech using PCM without compression assuming a bandwidth of 22,000 Hz, monaural. Ignore any overhead. You wish to pick a sample discretization which can encode about 64,000 amplitude levels. Use the minimum sampling rate implied by the sampling theorem.

b. Suppose the speech was stored as text, one text character per byte without compression. How much space, in bytes, on the CD ROM now?

c. Suppose the speech was stored as an image of the text as specified above. That is, you only scan the area with text. Suppose the image is scanned at 1200 pixels per inch in both the horizontal and vertical directions, and that the image is stored as

FIGURE 5.20 Configuration for Problem 3.

black and white (no color or gray scale). Again ignore overhead and assume no compression. How much CD ROM storage in bytes for this representation?

Note: The relative size of the results of a), b), and c) make qualitative sense. The reading carries the most information, including inflection, pacing, etc. in addition to the text itself. This representation takes the most space. The image carries more information than the text, such as fonts, page layout, etc., but less information than the reading. The text as an ASCII string carries no additional information beyond the text itself, but is the most compact.

5. On December 7, 1995, after more than 6 years and $2\frac{1}{3}$ billion miles traveled, the atmospheric probe of the Galileo orbiter entered the planet Jupiter's atmosphere. NASA and the Jet Propulsion Laboratory reported that at noon (EDT) the next day, the orbiter was 581,751,114.1196 miles or 936,237,665.3592 km. from Earth. Let us consider communication between Galileo and Earth.

   a. At the planned on data rate of 134,400 bps, what was the propagation delay for transmission from the Earth to Galileo?

   b. Suppose we wish to use HDLC type communication with window flow control, and that we wish not to delay transmission waiting for acknowledgments when there are no errors. Suppose the frame size is 2,000 bytes and the channel data rate is 134,400 bps. What window size W is implied by this data?

   c. You should have found that W is very much larger than standard HDLC can support. That is, the window count fields must be very much larger. What size count fields will be required to support the W you calculated in part b)?

   d. The main high gain Galileo antenna which was designed to operate at 134,400 bps. malfunctioned and another low gain antenna is being used instead which has a data rate of approximately 8 bps! Redo parts b) and c) for this latter data rate.

Transmission Efficiency

CHAPTER OBJECTIVES

After reading this chapter, you should be able to:

- Explain the need for transmission efficiency and list the two major approaches used to achieve efficiency.

- Discuss the use of frequency-division multiplexing in video distribution and in voice networks.

- Explain the difference between synchronous TDM and statistical TDM, list the benefits of each, and discuss the applications for each.

- Describe the use of multiplexing in digital carrier systems.

- Discuss the T-1 service and describe its importance and the applications that use it.

- Discuss the SONET standard and its significance for wide-area networking.

- Understand the performance benefits and limitations of statistical multiplexing.

- Describe the compression techniques used in V.24 modems and in the popular ZIP compression algorithm.

- Explain the importance of data compression for image transmission and describe some of the techniques that can be used.

A major source of expense in any distributed or networked environment is transmission cost. Because of the critical nature of transmission in such environments and their potentially high cost, it is important to maximize the amount of information that can be carried over a given resource, or alternatively, to minimize the transmission capacity needed to satisfy a given business information communications requirement. In this chapter we look at the two most important approaches to achieving transmission efficiency: multiplexing and data compression.

■ Illustration: Problem Statement

A semiconductor chip manufacturer is faced with a moving problem. The company is housed in a set of buildings providing space for 8000 employees. All the space at that site is filled up with buildings (and parking lots). When it came time to expand, the company purchased several acres across the river, about a mile away from the main site, and erected three buildings. Management has found it less expensive to equip the new buildings for "dry" (technical and administrative) workers than for "wet" (manufacturing) operations. Manufacturing is to remain at its current location. So too, are the manufacturing personnel and process engineers. The company's design engineers, who work with such "dry" things as data, are to move, as is the data center that supports them.

Left at the original site after the move is completed will be fifty 9600-bps terminals that require access to the data center on a fairly regular basis. After examining a number of alternatives, including dial-up support, the company concluded that leased analog lines that can support the use of 28,800-bps modems would be the most cost-effective way of linking the terminals to the new data center. In the worst case, the company would have to lease 50 such lines. What can be done to reduce transmission costs? (The problem solution appears at the end of the chapter.) ■

6.1 NEED FOR TRANSMISSION EFFICIENCY

As we have already pointed out, the creation, use, and communication of information within an organization have become vital business requirements. A major challenge in meeting these requirements is the high cost of voice and data communication facilities and services, as well as the use and management of those facilities and services. The costs include the personnel needed to operate and manage the communications function, leased and owned equipment, the maintenance of equipment, and the training of operators and users. But by far the most significant cost is the actual transmission service, which is provided by a carrier or networking service that sells transmission capacity to organizations. Included in this category are the public telephone systems (e.g., AT&T, the Bell operating companies), transmission lines that are leased from various providers, and packet-switched network services.

Because of the large dollar volume spent on transmission services, and because it represents the major portion of a typical organization's communications budget, an opportunity exists to achieve meaningful savings. In general terms, two approaches are taken to achieve greater efficiency in the use of transmission services: multiplexing and compression. With **multiplexing**, several information sources, each of which requires a given transmission capacity, share a larger transmission capacity. The larger facility is of sufficient capacity that it can keep up with the needs of the various sources sharing that facility. With compression, techniques are used to reduce the number of bits required to represent a given amount of information and hence reduce the capacity needed for a given information source. Thus, several sources can be compressed and multiplexed to

Multiplexing
A function that permits two or more data sources to share a common transmission medium such that each data source has its own channel.

share a transmission capacity that is less than the sum of the capacity requirements of the individual sources. If there is but a single source, compression can be used to reduce the transmission capacity required.

These two techniques, multiplexing and compression, are independent of one another and may be employed separately. However, it is not uncommon to use both techniques together to obtain a powerful approach to transmission efficiency. Before looking at each of these two techniques in detail, it is worth describing the specific benefits that each of these techniques offers.

Motivation for Multiplexing

Figure 6.1 depicts the multiplexing function in its simplest form. There are *n* inputs to a multiplexer. The multiplexer is connected by a single data link to a demultiplexer. The link is able to carry *n* separate channels of data. The multiplexer combines (multiplexes) data from the *n* input lines and transmits over a higher-capacity data link. The demultiplexer accepts the multiplexed data stream, separates (demultiplexes) the data according to channel, and delivers them to the appropriate output lines.

Two facts, which are nearly universally applicable to the field of data communications, explain the pervasiveness of multiplexing:

1. The higher the data rate, the more cost-effective the transmission facility. That is, for a given application and over a given distance, the cost per kbps almost invariably declines with an increase in the data rate of the transmission facility. Similarly, the cost of transmission and receiving equipment, relative to data rate, declines with increasing data rate. Thus, even if a user owns the transmission lines and need not pay lease charges, the relative cost of the use of that line declines with increasing capacity.

2. Most individual data communicating devices require relatively modest data-rate support. For example, for most terminal applications, a data rate of between 4800 bps and 64 kbps is generally more than adequate. Table 6-1 gives some examples.

The preceding two statements were phrased in terms of data communications devices. Similar statements apply to voice communications. That is, the greater the capacity of a transmission facility in terms of voice channels, the less the cost per individual voice channel, and the capacity required for a single voice channel is modest.

FIGURE 6.1 Multiplexing.

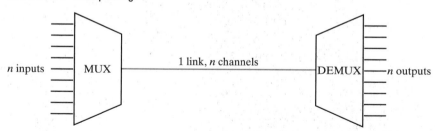

TABLE 6-1 Data Rates of Some Typical User and Peripheral Devices

Device	Data Rate (kbps)
Security and environmental sensors	0.1
Text-oriented terminal (e.g., point of sale)	1.2–9.6
Teletex terminal	2.4
Facsimile	4.8–9.6
Line printer	19.2
Internet-connected PC or web browser	28.8–64

Let us illustrate this principle with several applications. First consider the support of a number of 4800-bps point-of-sale terminal devices by a host computer. Four alternative approaches are shown in Figure 6.2. In part (a), we see the simplest approach, which is to provide a direct, point-to-point link between each terminal and the host system. This requires a single I/O port for each terminal and a single transmission line for each terminal. If all the terminals are in the

FIGURE 6.2 Alternative Approaches to Terminal Support.

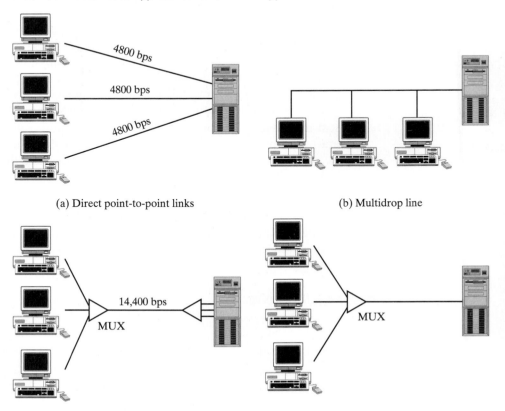

(a) Direct point-to-point links

(b) Multidrop line

(c) Multiplexer

(d) Integrated MUX function in host

same room as the computer, the transmission line cost is negligible. However, even under those circumstances, there is a substantial cost associated with the number of I/O ports on the host system.

An alternative, shown in (b), is the multidrop line. The multidrop line takes advantage of the fact that a typical terminal is transmitting only a fraction of the time. All of these terminals can share a single line into the host system. The host controls the transmission process by polling each terminal in turn for data. With this alternative, not only is there is savings in I/O port costs, but there is also a savings in communication line costs. Consider a situation in which the host computer is in one building and all the terminals are in another building some distance away. A digital leased line is obtained from the local phone company to link the two. Because a multidrop discipline is being used, only a single leased line is needed.

Alternative (b) is appropriate if all the terminals are operating at the same data rate and if the total communications load is no greater than that data rate. If either assumption is invalid, some form of multiplexing is needed. For example, you have a set of 10 terminals, all of which operate at 9600 bps, and the total traffic generated by all 10 together is no greater than 9600 bps; thus, on average, each terminal is active less than 10% of the time.

Alternative (c) depicts a basic multiplexer. In this example, all the terminals are connected to one multiplexer, which is connected by a single data link to another multiplexer, which is in turn connected to the host computer. The number of lines between the host and its multiplexer is the same as the number of terminals on the other end (three, in this case). The link between the two multiplexers is able to carry multiple separate *channels* of data. The multiplexer on the terminal end combines (multiplexes) data from all the terminal lines and transmits them over a higher-capacity data link. The multiplexer on the other end accepts the multiplexed data stream, separates (demultiplexes) the data according to channel, and delivers them to the appropriate host computer line. The multiplexers are actually symmetric and full-duplex. That is, terminal data destined for the host are multiplexed and transmitted in some form of channel structure over the common link, and all host data travel over the same link in the reverse direction and are demultiplexed for delivery to the appropriate terminal.

One requirement for multiplexing and demultiplexing that should be evident is that there must be some way for the demultiplexing function to determine which destination port is to receive the data. Some control structure or convention is needed for that purpose. Thus, data presented to a multiplexer must be tagged or ordered in some fashion so that the destination may be determined. This leads to a consideration of alternative (d). In this configuration, the logic for multiplexing and demultiplexing on the computer end has been incorporated in the host software and firmware. Thus, there is a savings not only in communications line costs, but also in I/O port costs.

As a second example, consider the requirement for long-distance communication of voice and data. Public facilities are provided for this, in the form of the digital and voice services available from telephone companies, such as the Bell operating companies, AT&T, MCI, and Sprint in the United States, and the postal, telegraph, and telephone (PTT) authorities in most other countries. In addition, private networks are commonly set up by large, geographically dispersed organizations to handle their in-house voice and/or data needs. In either case, the network consists of a collection of interconnected switches. Connections between switches are referred to as *trunks;* a connection between a switch and an end user is referred to as a *subscriber line.* All the traffic from all the subscribers at a particular switch destined for subscribers attached to other switches must be multiplexed for transmission over the trunks to other switches. Internal to the network, traffic from subscribers is routed and switched from source to destination, with each trunk carrying multiplexed traffic from a variety of sources. This scheme clearly requires that the traffic on the trunks be multiplexed.

Further examples of multiplexing are given in the remainder of this chapter and throughout the remainder of this book.

Motivation for Data Compression

The most obvious motivation for the use of data compression is the same one that we saw for multiplexing: the increase in the efficiency of transmission. Data compression will permit an increase in the amount of information transferred over a data link per unit time interval. Thus, for a link of a given data rate, a greater information load can be supported. Conversely, by compressing data, a given source or set of sources can be supported on a lower-speed data link, resulting in a reduction in cost compared with the expense of a data link operated at a higher data rate.

Other benefits can also be gained from the use of data compression. It can be used as a technique to reduce the duration of a transmission session. For example, there are products available that can reduce the transmitted data for a facsimile image by a factor of 15. Thus, a 3-min transmission session can be reduced to approximately 12 sec. If the transmission occurs over the public telephone network, substantial savings in facsimile transmission costs can be achieved for heavy facsimile users. When a number of terminals share the same facility, such as a multidrop line, the use of compression can improve response time, because it takes less time to transmit the data and there is less competition for the use of the line. Finally, because compression involves some encoding of the original data, it may offer some security against illicit monitoring, improving security.

The benefits of data compression extend to the ability to affect the structure of a communications network needed to satisfy user needs. Consider the multidrop-line configuration of Figure 6.2b. The major bottleneck in this configuration is the data rate on the line. If the total load on the line increases, system response time will increase. Thus, the number of terminals on the line must be limited to achieve adequate response time. A typical limit on such a configuration is about 20 terminals per line. An application requiring the support of 30 terminals would probably necessitate two multidrop lines, with the attendant increase in line costs and I/O hardware on the host. However, with data compression, it should be possible to increase the number of terminals on a single line from 20 to 30 with no degradation of response time.

As another example of network structure, consider the use of multiplexers in Figure 6.2c. One of the types of multiplexers that we will look at is a conventional time-division multiplexer. With such a multiplexer, the aggregate input data rate from the connected terminals cannot exceed the data rate of the line between the multiplexer and the computer. For instance, a 64-kbps leased line used to connect a terminal multiplexer to a host multiplexer could service six 9600-kbps terminals. Suppose that an installation were required to support 12 simultaneous users at the remote location. Planners would be faced with the need to install a second multiplexer pair and lease a second line. However, with data compression, it may be possible to support all 12 terminals on a single line. This is an example of the joint use of multiplexing and compression.

We now turn to a more detailed discussion of these two techniques, beginning with a look at various forms of multiplexing.

6.2 FREQUENCY-DIVISION MULTIPLEXING

Frequency-Division Multiplexing (FDM)
Division of a transmission facility into two or more channels by splitting the frequency band.

Frequency-division multiplexing (FDM) is a familiar and widely used form of multiplexing. A simple example is its use in cable TV systems, which carry multiple video channels on a single cable. FDM is possible when the useful bandwidth of the transmission medium exceeds the required bandwidth of signals to be transmitted. A number of signals can be carried simultaneously if each signal is modulated onto a different carrier frequency and the carrier frequencies are sufficiently separated that the bandwidths of the signals do not overlap. A general case of FDM is shown in Figure 6.3a. Six signal sources are fed into a multiplexer, which modulates each signal onto a different frequency (f1,...,f6). Each modulated signal requires a certain bandwidth centered around its carrier frequency, referred to as a **channel**. To prevent interference, the channels are separated by guardbands, which are unused portions of the spectrum.

The composite signal transmitted across the medium is analog. Note, however, that the input signals may be either digital or analog. In the case of digital input, the input signals must be passed through modems to be converted to analog. In either case, each input analog signal must then be modulated to move it to the appropriate frequency band.

A simple example of FDM is illustrated in Figure 6.4, which shows the transmission of three voice signals simultaneously over a transmission medium. The bandwidth of a voice signal is generally taken to be 4 kHz, with an effective spectrum of 300 to 3400 Hz. Using amplitude modulation on a 64-kHz carrier, this voice signal can be raised to a bandwidth extending from 60 to 64 kHz. Similarly, the two other voice signals can be modulated to fit into the ranges 64 to 68 kHz and 68 to 72 kHz, respectively. These signals are then combined in the multiplexer to produce a single signal with a range of 60 to 72 kHz. At the receiving end, the demultiplexing process involves splitting the received signal into three frequency bands and then demodulating each signal back to the original voice band (0 to 4 kHz). Note that there is only a minor amount of overlap between the multiplexed signals. Because the effective bandwidth of each signal is actually less than 4 kHz, no interference results.

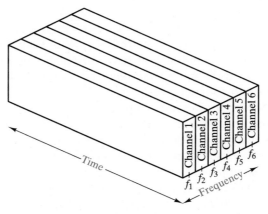

(a) Frequency-division multiplexing

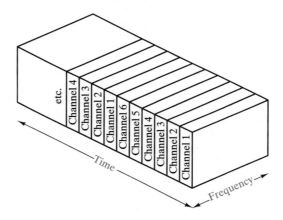

(b) Time-division multiplexing

FIGURE 6.3 FDM and TDM.

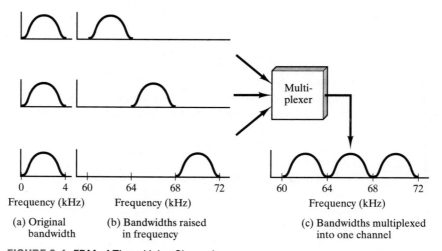

(a) Original
bandwidth

(b) Bandwidths raised
in frequency

(c) Bandwidths multiplexed
into one channel

FIGURE 6.4 FDM of Three Voice Channels.

FDM has been the mainstay of telephone transmission for many years; it is actually more efficient than digital systems in terms of bandwidth. The problem is that noise is amplified along with the voice signal. This fact, and the great decrease in the cost of digital electronics, has led to the widespread replacement of FDM systems with TDM systems in telephone networks.

Although the use of FDM for voice transmission is declining rapidly, it is still used almost exclusively for television distribution systems, including broadcast television and cable TV. The analog television signal discussed in Chapter 4 fits comfortably into a 6-MHz bandwidth. Figure 6.5 depicts the transmitted video signal and its bandwidth. The black-and-white video signal is amplitude-modulated on a carrier signal. The resulting signal has a bandwidth of about 5 MHz, most of which is above the carrier signal. A separate color subcarrier is used to

FIGURE 6.5 Transmitted TV Signal.

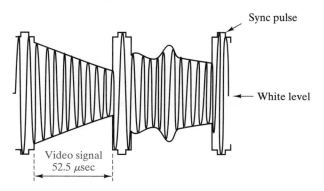

(a) Amplitude modulation with video signal

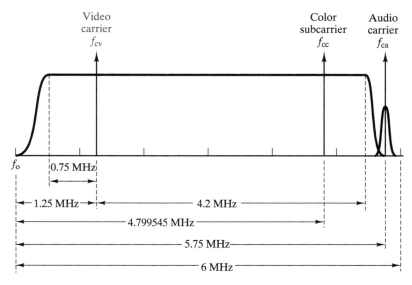

(b) Magnitude spectrum of RF video signal

TABLE 6-2 Cable Television Channel Frequencies

Channel Number	Band (MHz)	Channel Number	Band (MHz)	Channel Number	Band (MHz)
2	54–60	22	168–174	42	330–336
3	60–66	23	216–222	43	336–342
4	66–72	24	222–228	44	342–348
5	76–82	25	228–234	45	348–354
6	82–88	26	234–240	46	354–360
7	174–180	27	240–246	47	360–366
8	180–186	28	246–252	48	366–372
9	186–192	29	252–258	49	372–378
10	192–198	30	258–264	50	378–384
11	198–204	31	264–270	51	384–390
12	204–210	32	270–276	52	390–396
13	210–216	33	276–282	53	396–402
FM	88–108	34	282–288	54	72–78
14	120–126	35	288–294	55	78–84
15	126–132	36	294–300	56	84–90
16	132–138	37	300–306	57	90–96
17	138–144	38	306–312	58	96–102
18	144–150	39	312–318	59	102–108
19	150–156	40	318–324	60	108–114
20	156–162	41	324–330	61	114–120
21	162–168				

Time-division Multiplexing
The sharing of a transmission facility by allotting a common channel to several different information channels, one at a time.

transmit color information. This is spaced far enough from the main carrier that there is essentially no interference. Finally, the audio portion of the signal is modulated on a third carrier, outside the effective bandwidth of the other two signals. The composite signal fits into a 6-MHz bandwidth with the video, color, and audio signal carriers at 1.25 MHz, 4.799545 MHz, and 5.75 MHz above the lower edge of the band, respectively. Thus, multiple TV signals can be frequency-division multiplexed on a cable, each with a bandwidth of 6 MHz. Given the enormous bandwidth of coaxial cable (as much as 500 MHz), dozens of video signals can be carried simultaneously using FDM. Table 6-2 shows the frequency allocation for cable television in the United States.

6.3 SYNCHRONOUS TIME-DIVISION MULTIPLEXING

TDM Mechanism

Synchronous Time-division Multiplexing
A method of TDM in which time slots on a shared transmission line are assigned to devices on a fixed, predetermined basis.

The other major form of multiplexing is **time-division multiplexing (TDM)**. There are two variants of TDM in common use: synchronous TDM and statistical TDM. In this section we examine **synchronous TDM**.

Time-division multiplexing is possible when the data rate of the transmission medium exceeds the required data rate of signals to be transmitted. A number of digital signals, or analog signals carrying digital data, can be carried simultaneously by interleaving portions of each signal in time. A general case of TDM is shown in Figure 6.3b. Six signal sources are fed into a multiplexer, which interleaves the bits from each signal by taking turns transmitting bits from each of

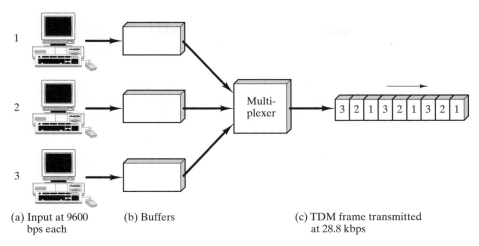

(a) Input at 9600   (b) Buffers   (c) TDM frame transmitted
bps each   at 28.8 kbps

FIGURE 6.6 Synchronous TDM of Three Data Channels.

the signals in a round-robin fashion. For example, the multiplexer in Figure 6.3b has six inputs which might be, say, 9.6 kbps each. A single line with a capacity of at least 57.6 kbps accommodates all six sources.

A simple example of TDM is illustrated in Figure 6.6, which shows the transmission of three data signals simultaneously over a transmission medium. In this example, each source operates at 9600 bps. The output from each source is briefly buffered. Each buffer is typically one bit or one character in length. The buffers are scanned in round-robin fashion to form a composite digital data stream. The scan operation are sufficiently rapid that each buffer is emptied before more data can arrive. The scanned data are combined by the multiplexer into a composite data stream. Thus, the data rate transmitted by the multiplexer must at least equal the sum of the data rates of the three inputs (3×9.6 = 28.8 kbps). The digital signal produced by the multiplexer may be transmitted digitally or passed through a modem so that an analog signal is transmitted. In either case, transmission is typically synchronous (as opposed to asynchronous). At the receiving end , the demultiplexing process involves distributing the incoming data among three destination buffers.

The data transmitted by a synchronous TDM system have a format something like that of Figure 6.7. The data are organized into **frames**, each of which contains a cycle of time slots. In each frame one or more slots is dedicated to each

FIGURE 6.7 TDM Frame Structure.

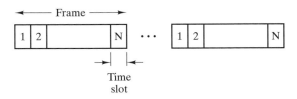

data source. Transmission consists of the transmission of a sequence of frames. The set of time slots dedicated to one source, from frame to frame, is called a **channel**. Note that this is the same term used for FDM. The two uses of the term *channel* are logically equivalent. In both cases, a portion of the transmission capacity is dedicated to signals from a single source; that source sees a constant-data-rate or constant-bandwidth channel for transmission.

The slot length equals the transmitter buffer length, typically a bit or a character. The *character-interleaving* technique is used with asynchronous sources. Each time slot contains one character of data. Typically, the start and stop bits of each character are eliminated before transmission and reinserted by the receiver, thus improving efficiency. The *bit-interleaving* technique is used with synchronous sources.

Synchronous TDM is called synchronous not because synchronous transmission is used but because the time slots are preassigned to sources and are fixed. The time slots for a given source are transmitted whether or not the source has data to send. This is, of course, also the case with FDM: A frequency band is dedicated to a particular source whether or not the source is transmitting at any given time. In both cases, capacity is wasted to achieve simplicity of implementation. Even when fixed assignment is used, however, it is possible for a synchronous TDM device to handle sources of different data rates. For example, the slowest input devices could be assigned one slot per frame, while faster devices are assigned multiple slots per frame.

Digital Carrier Systems

The long-distance carrier system provided in the United States and throughout the world was designed to transmit voice signals over high-capacity transmission links, such as optical fiber, coaxial cable, and microwave. Part of the evolution of these telecommunications networks to digital technology has been the adoption of synchronous TDM transmission structures. In the United States, AT&T developed a hierarchy of TDM structures of various capacities; this structure is used in Canada and Japan as well as the United States. A similar, but unfortunately not identical, hierarchy has been adopted internationally under the auspices of ITU-T (Table 6-3).

TABLE 6-3 North American and International TDM Carrier Standards

NORTH AMERICAN			INTERNATIONAL (ITU-T)		
Designation	*Number of Voice Channels*	*Data Rate (Mbps)*	*Level*	*Number of Voice Channels*	*Data Rate (Mbps)*
DS-1	24	1.544	1	30	2.048
DS-1C	48	3.152	2	120	8.448
DS-2	96	6.312	3	480	34.368
DS-3	672	44.736	4	1920	139.264
DS-4	4032	274.176	5	7680	565.148

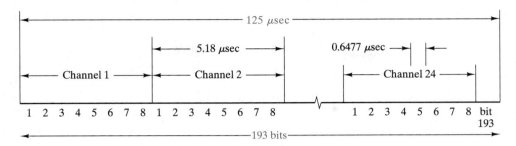

Notes:
1. Bit 193 is a framing bit, used for synchronization.
2. Voice channels:
    • 8-bit PCM used on five of six frames.
    • 7-bit PCM used on every sixth frame; bit 8 of each channel is a signaling bit.
3. Data channels:
    • Channel 24 used for signaling only in some schemes.
    • Bit 8 is a control bit.
    • Bits 1–7 used for 56-kbps service.
    • Bits 2–7 used for 9.6-kbps, 4.8 kbps, and 2.4-kbps service.

FIGURE 6.8 DS - 1 Transmission Format.

The basis of the TDM hierarchy (in North America and Japan) is the DS-1 transmission format (Figure 6.8), which multiplexes 24 channels. Each frame contains 8 bits per channel plus a framing bit for $24 \times 8 + 1 = 193$ bits. For voice transmission, the following rules apply. Each channel contains one word of digitized voice data. The original analog voice signal is digitized using pulse-code modulation (PCM) at a rate of 8000 samples per second. Therefore, each channel slot and hence each frame must repeat 8000 times per second. With a frame length of 193 bits, we have a data rate of $8000 \times 193 = 1.544$ Mbps. For five of every six frames, 8-bit PCM samples are used. For every sixth frame, each channel contains a 7-bit PCM word plus a *signaling bit*. The signaling bits form a stream for each voice channel that contains network control and routing information. For example, control signals are used to establish a connection or terminate a call.

The same DS-1 format is used to provide digital data service. For compatibility with voice, the same 1.544-Mbps data rate is used. In this case, 23 channels of data are provided. The twenty-fourth channel position is reserved for a special sync byte, which allows faster and more reliable reframing following a framing error. Within each channel, 7 bits per frame are used for data, with the eighth bit used to indicate whether the channel for that frame contains user data or system control data. With 7 bits per channel, and because each frame is repeated 8000 times per second, a data rate of 56 kbps can be provided per channel. Lower data rates are provided using a technique known as *subrate multiplexing*. For this technique, an additional bit is robbed from each channel to indicate which subrate multiplexing rate is being provided. This leaves a total capacity per channel of $6 \times 8000 = 48$ kbps. This capacity is used to multiplex five 9.6-kbps channels, ten

4.8-kbps channels, or twenty 2.4-kbps channels. For example, if channel 2 is used to provide 9.6-kbps service, up to five data subchannels share this channel. The data for each subchannel appear as 6 bits in channel 2 every fifth frame.

Finally, the DS-1 format can be used to carry a mixture of voice and data channels. In this case, all 24 channels are utilized; no sync byte is provided.

Above this basic data rate of 1.544 Mbps, higher-level multiplexing is achieved by interleaving bits from DS-1 inputs. For example, the DS-2 transmission system combines four DS-1 inputs into a 6.312-Mbps stream. Data from the four sources are interleaved 12 bits at a time. Note that $1.544 \times 4 = 6.176$ Mbps. The remaining capacity is used for framing and control bits.

The designations DS-1, DS-1C, and so on, refer to the multiplexing scheme used for carrying information. AT&T and other carriers supply transmission facilities that support these various multiplexed signals, referred to as carrier systems. These are designated with a "T" label. Thus, the T-1 carrier provides a data rate of 1.544 Mbps and is thus capable of supporting the DS-1 multiplex format, and so on for higher data rates.

T-1 Facilities

The **T-1** facility is widely used by companies as a way of expanding networking capability and controlling costs. The most common external use (not part of the telephone network) of T-1 facilities is for leased dedicated transmission between customer premises. These facilities allow the customer to set up private networks to carry traffic throughout an organization. Examples of applications for such private networks:

- *Private voice networks.* When there is a substantial amount of intersite voice traffic, a leased private network can provide significant savings over using dial-up facilities.
- *Private data network.* Similarly, high data volumes between two or more sites can be supported by T-1 lines.
- *Video teleconferencing.* Allow high-quality video to be transmitted. As the bandwidth requirement for video declines, private video conferencing links can share T-1 facilities with other applications.
- *High-speed digital facsimile.* This permits rapid transmission of facsimile images and, depending on the facsimile load, may be able to share the T-1 link with other applications.
- *Internet access.* If a high volume of traffic between the site and the Internet is anticipated, a high-capacity access line to the local Internet service provider is needed.

For users with substantial data transmission needs, the use of private T-1 networking is attractive for two reasons: (1) T-1 permits simpler configurations than is available from a mix of lower-speed offerings, and (2) T-1 transmission services are less expensive. Another popular use of T-1 is to provide high-speed access from the customer's premises to the telephone network. In this application, a local-area network or telephone exchange on the customer's premises supports a number of devices that generate sufficient off-site traffic to require the use of a T-1 access line to the public network. This particular application is similar to the *primary service* of ISDN, which is in Chapter 7.

SONET/SDH

SONET (synchronous optical network) is an optical transmission interface originally proposed by BellCore and standardized by ANSI. A compatible version, referred to as **synchronous digital hierarchy (SDH)**, has been published by ITU-T in Recommendations G.707, G.708, and G.709.[1] SONET is intended to provide a specification for taking advantage of the high-speed digital transmission capability of optical fiber.

Signal Hierarchy   The SONET specification defines a hierarchy of standardized digital data rates (Table 6-4). The lowest level, referred to as STS-1 (synchronous transport signal level 1) or OC-1 (optical carrier level 1),[2] is 51.84 Mbps. This rate can be used to carry a single DS-3 signal or a group of lower-rate signals, such as DS-1, DS-1C, DS-2, plus ITU-T rates (e.g., 2.048 Mbps).

Multiple STS-1 signals can be combined to form an STS-N signal. The signal is created by interleaving bytes from N STS-1 signals that are mutually synchronized. For the ITU-T synchronous digital hierarchy, the lowest rate is 155.52 Mbps, which is designated STM-1. This corresponds to SONET STS-3. The reason for the discrepancy is that STM-1 is the lowest-rate signal that can accommodate an ITU-T level 4 signal (139.264 Mbps).

Frame Format   The basic SONET building block is the STS-1 frame, which consists of 810 octets and is transmitted once every 125 μsec, for an overall data rate of 51.84 Mbps (Figure 6.9a). The frame can logically be viewed as a matrix of 9 rows of 90 octets each, with transmission being one row at a time, from left to right and top to bottom.

TABLE 6-4 SONET/SDH Signal Hierarchy

SONET Designation	ITU-T Designation	Data Rate (Mbps)	Payload Rate (Mbps)
STS-1/OC-1		51.84	50.112
STS-3/OC-3	STM-1	155.52	150.336
STS-9/OC-9	STM-3	466.56	451.008
STS-12/OC-12	STM-4	622.08	601.344
STS-18/OC-18	STM-6	933.12	902.016
STS-24/OC-24	STM-8	1244.16	1202.688
STS-36/OC-36	STM-12	1866.24	1804.032
STS-48/OC-48	STM-16	2488.32	2405.376

[1] In what follows, we use the term SONET to refer to both specifications. Where differences exist, these are addressed.

[2] An OC-N rate is the optical equivalent of an STS-N electrical signal. End-user devices transmit and receive electrical signals; these must be converted to and from optical signals for transmission over optical fiber.

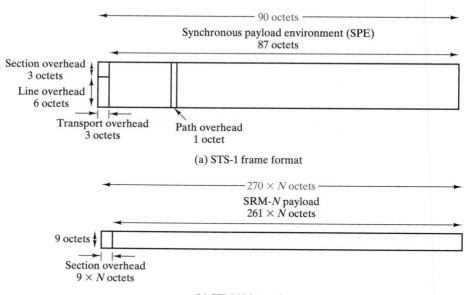

FIGURE 6.9 SONET/SDH Frame Formats.

The first three columns (3 octets × 9 rows = 27 octets) of the frame are devoted to overhead octets, called *section overhead* and *line overhead,* which relate to different levels of detail in describing a SONET transmission. These octets convey not only synchronization information but also network management information. The remainder of the frame is payload, which is provided by the logical layer of SONET called the *path layer.* The payload includes a column of path overhead, which is not necessarily in the first available column position; the line overhead contains a pointer that indicates where the path overhead starts. Figure 6.9b shows the general format for higher-rate frames using the ITU-T designation.

6.4 STATISTICAL TIME-DIVISION MULTIPLEXING

In a synchronous time-division multiplexer, it is generally the case that many of the time slots in a frame are wasted. A typical application of a synchronous TDM involves linking a number of terminals to a shared computer port. Even if all terminals are actively in use, most of the time there is no data transfer at any particular terminal. Table 6-5 shows the results of a study conducted by a group developing standards for local-area networks (discussed in Chapter 9). The table shows some representative data rates for various types of terminal equipment. In addition, the table shows the percentage of time that a terminal device, on average, is using its communications link. For example, a data-entry terminal is used for entering information from paper forms into a computer database. A typical data rate for such a terminal is 9600 bps. However, because typing is a relatively slow process and because the handling of forms is also slow, the actual load

TABLE 6-5 Workload Generated by Various Terminal Types

Terminal Type	Peak Data Rate (kbps)	Duty Factor[a] (%)
Line printer	19.2	50–90
Data-entry terminal	9.6	0.1–1.0
Data-enquiry terminal	9.6	10–30
Laser printer	64	20–50
Fax machine	256	5–20
Graphics terminal (noncompressed)	9.6	1–10
Graphics terminal (compressed)	64	10–30
Optical character reader	2.4	50–90

[a] *Duty factor is the percentage of time that the device is transmitting or receiving.*

imposed by such a terminal may average somewhere between 10 and 100 bps. It is therefore clear that the use of a synchronous time-division multiplexer for a group of such devices would be extremely inefficient.

Statistical time-Division Multiplexing
A method of TDM in which time slots on a shared transmission line are assigned to devices on demand.

A much more efficient scheme than synchronous TDM is **statistical TDM**, also knows as *asynchronous TDM* or *intelligent TDM*. The statistical multiplexer dynamically allocates time slots on demand. As with a synchronous TDM, the statistical multiplexer has a number of I/O lines on one side and a higher-speed multiplexed line on the other. Each I/O line has associated with it a buffer. In the case of the statistical multiplexer, there are more attached devices than there are time slots available within a frame for transmission. For input, the function of the multiplexer is to scan the input buffers, collecting data until a frame is filled, and then to send the frame. On output, the multiplexer receives a frame and distributes the slots of data to the appropriate output buffers.

Because statistical TDM takes advantage of the fact that the attached devices are not all transmitting all of the time, the data rate on the multiplexed line is less than the sum of the data rates of the attached devices. Thus, a statistical multiplexer can use a lower data rate to support as many devices as a synchronous multiplexer. Alternatively, if a statistical multiplexer and a synchronous multiplexer operate at the same data rate, the statistical multiplexer can support more devices.

Figure 6.10 contrasts statistical and synchronous TDM. The figure depicts four data sources and shows the data produced in four time intervals (t_0, t_1, t_2, t_3). In the case of the synchronous multiplexer, the effective output rate is four times the data rate of any of the input devices. During each interval, data are collected from all four sources and sent out. For example, in the first interval, sources C and D produce no data. Thus, two of the four time slots transmitted by the multiplexer are empty.

In contrast, the statistical multiplexer does not send empty slots when there are no data to send. Thus, during the first time interval, only slots for sources A and B are sent. However, the positional significance of the slots is lost in this scheme. It is not known ahead of time which source's data will be in any particular slot. Because data arrive from and are distributed to I/O lines unpredictably, address information is required to assure proper delivery. Thus, there is more

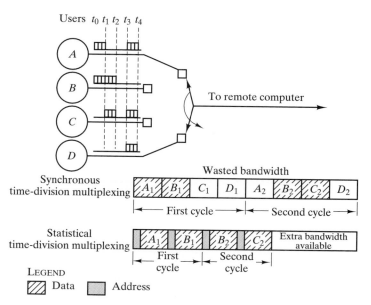

FIGURE 6.10 Synchronous TDM Contrasted with Statistical TDM.

overhead per slot for statistical TDM because each slot carries an address as well as data.

We have said that the data rate on the multiplexed side of a statistical multiplexer is less than the sum of the data rates of the individual lines. This is allowable because it is anticipated that the average amount of input is less than the capacity of the multiplexed line. The difficulty with this approach is that while the average aggregate input may be less than the multiplexed line capacity, there may be peak periods when the input exceeds capacity.

The solution to this problem is to include a buffer in the multiplexer to hold temporary excess input. Table 6-6 gives an example of the behavior of such sys-

TABLE 6-6 Example of Statistical Multiplexer Performance

Input	Capacity = 5000 bps		Capacity = 7000 bps	
	Output	Backlog	Output	Backlog
6	5	1	6	0
9	5	5	7	2
3	5	3	5	0
7	5	5	7	0
2	5	2	2	0
2	4	0	2	0
2	2	0	2	0
3	3	0	3	0
4	4	0	4	0
6	5	1	6	0
1	2	0	1	0
10	5	5	7	3

tems. We assume 10 sources, each capable of 1000 bps, and we assume that the average input per source is 50% of its maximum. That is, each source generates an average of 500 bps, for a total average load of 5000 bps. Two cases are shown: multiplexers of output capacity 5000 bps and 7000 bps. The entries of the table show the total number of bits input from the 10 devices each millisecond and the output from the multiplexer. When the input exceeds the output, backlog develops that must be buffered. As might be expected, the backlog tends to be higher for the lower-speed multiplexer.

There is a trade-off between the size of the buffer used and the data rate of the line. To minimize cost we would like to use the smallest possible buffer and the smallest possible data rate, but a reduction in one requires an increase in the other. Note that we are not so much concerned with the cost of the buffer—memory is cheap—as we are with the fact that the more buffering there is, the longer the delay. Thus, the trade-off is really one between system response time and the speed of the multiplexed line. Figure 6.11 gives some insight into the nature of the trade-off. It assumes that data are being transmitted in 1000-bit frames. Part (a) of the figure shows the average number of frames that must be buffered as a function of the average utilization of the multiplexed line. The utilization is expressed as a percentage of the total line capacity. Thus, if the average input load is 5000 bps, the utilization is 100% for a line capacity of 5000 bps and about 71% for a line capacity of 7000 bps. Part (b) of the figure shows the average delay experienced by a frame as a function of utilization and data rate. Note that as the utilization rises, so do the buffer requirements and the delay. A utilization above 80% is clearly undesirable.

The reader may wonder at the rather dramatic shapes of the curves in Figure 6.11. Actually, this phenomenon is by no means unique to statistical multiplexers. The same sort of behavior is found in any situation in which a number of devices share a communications facility. The result, in fact, appears in any situation in which a server (e.g., transmission line, bank teller) is providing service to a number of users (e.g., terminals, customers). Using a mathematical discipline known as *queuing theory,* it can be shown that the shape of the curves in Figure 6.11 is accurate. That is, as the utilization of a server approaches 100%, the delay experienced by users becomes infinite.

Despite the buffering requirements and overflow risk associated with statistical multiplexers, they have by and large supplanted synchronous multiplexers for many data communications applications, especially the support of terminal-to-host traffic. This is because the statistical multiplexer allows a significant savings in transmission costs. Synchronous multiplexers still have an important role to play in long-distance private and public networks, especially where a mix of traffic, including voice, is to be handled.

Data Compression
The process of eliminating redundancies in data to shorten the length of records or blocks.

6.5 DATA COMPRESSION

The principle of **data compression** is quite straightforward. Virtually all forms of data (text, numerical, image, video) contain redundant elements. The data can be compressed by eliminating these redundant elements. However, when

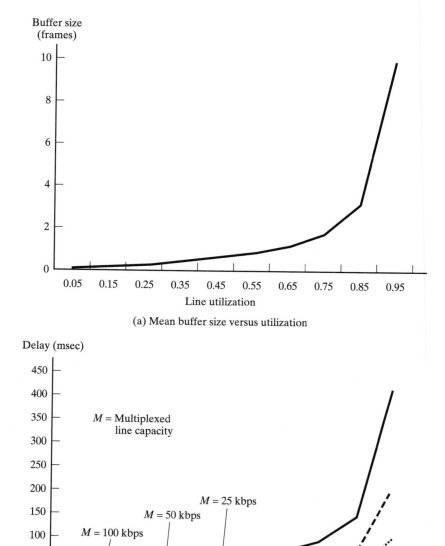

(a) Mean buffer size versus utilization

(b) Mean delay versus utilization

FIGURE 6.11 Buffer Size and Delay for a Statistical Multiplexer.

compressed data are received over a communications link, it must be possible to expand the data back to the original form. For this purpose, when the data are compressed, some sort of code must be substituted for the elements eliminated so that the receiver can, based on the code, reconstruct the original data. As long as the coding scheme is such that the code is shorter than the eliminated data, compression will occur.

A variety of forms of data compression are in use and available in such products as statistical multiplexers, modems, and image transmission and storage systems. An important distinction is between lossless (or reversible) compression and lossy compression. For many kinds of digital information it is imperative that the information reconstituted from the compressed data be exactly the same as the original information. Data such as payroll files form one such example. Compression techniques that enable recovery of the exact original are called *lossless compression techniques.* On the other hand, digital audio, image, and video information, which often require large volumes of data to be transmitted in real time or stored, make more compression essential. In these cases, one may only insist that the reconstituted information be "perceptually equivalent' to the original. By this we mean that as far as human beings can tell, the reconstituted information sounds or appears like the original. This less demanding standard makes much higher degrees of compression possible. This type of compression is referred to as *lossy compression.* We begin with a description of two lossless techniques and then introduce some of the newer lossy techniques used for modern multimedia systems.

Run-Length Encoding

Run-length encoding is used to compress any type of repeating character sequence. Figure 6.12 summarizes the technique when applied to character data and gives some examples. The transmitter looks for sequences of repeating characters to replace. Any sequence of repeating characters can be eliminated and replaced by a three-character code. The code consists of a special character that

FIGURE 6.12 Run-Length Encoding.

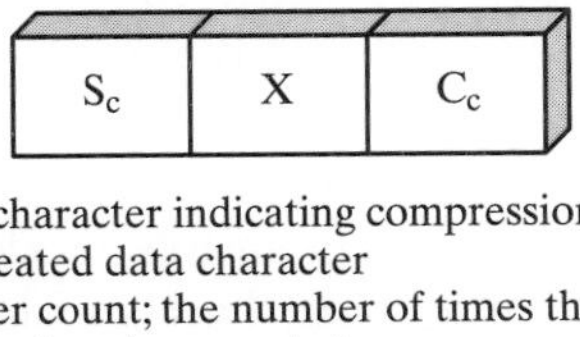

S_c = special character indicating compression follows
X = any repeated data character
C_c = character count; the number of times the compressed
       character is to be repeated

(a) Compression format

Original Data String	Encoded Data String
\$******55.72	\$$S_c$*655.72
---------	S_c-9
Gunsbbbbbbbbbbbbbb Butter	GunsS_cb9Butter

(b) Compression format

indicates suppression, followed by the character to be suppressed, followed by a count of the number of characters suppressed. Thus, any sequence of four or more identical characters can be suppressed, with a net reduction in the total number of characters transmitted.

Run-length encoding efficiency depends on the number of repeated character occurrences in the data to be compressed and the average repeated character length. The standard measure of compression efficiency is the compression ratio, which is the ratio of the length of the uncompressed data to the compressed data (including any necessary codes). [HELD96] reports compression ratios of up to 1.5, depending on the characteristics of the input text.

V.42bis Compression and ZIP

To make efficient use of voice-grade lines, the incorporation of compression technology in modems has become increasingly popular. The technique that has achieved the most widespread use is specified in ITU-T standard **V.42bis**. The algorithm used in V.42bis, known as the *Lempel–Ziv* (LZ) *algorithm*, is also the basis of a widely used compression package known as ZIP. ZIP is a freeware package written in C that runs as a utility on Unix and some other systems. ZIP is functionally equivalent to PKZIP, a widely available shareware package for MSDOS systems developed by PKWARE, Inc. The ZIP algorithm is perhaps the most commonly used cross-platform compression technique on the Internet; freeware and shareware versions are available for Macintosh and other systems as well as Windows and Unix systems.

The LZ algorithm uses a fixed-length code to represent variable-length input. Furthermore, the LZ code is adaptable, with the code assignments changing in response to the changing characteristics of the input. The LZ algorithm is well suited for use in transmitting text via modem.

The LZ algorithm is used to encode character strings. For this purpose, a dictionary of strings, with their codes, is maintained by both transmitter and receiver. When any of the strings in the dictionary appears in the input to the transmitter, the code for that string is substituted; the receiver, when it receives such a code, replaces it with the corresponding string from the dictionary. As transmission occurs, new strings are added to the dictionaries of the transmitter and receiver, and older strings are deleted.

Before describing the algorithm, we define the following quantities, using the notation in the standard:

C_1 = next available unused codeword

C_2 = codeword size; the default is 9 bits

N_2 = maximum size of the dictionary = number of codewords = 2^{C_2}

N_3 = character size; the default is 8 bits

N_5 = first codeword used to represent a string of more than one character

N_7 = maximum string length that can be encoded

At any time, the dictionary contains all one-character strings plus some multiple-character strings. Due to the mechanism by which strings are added to the dictionary, for any multiple-character string in the dictionary, all of its leading substrings are also in the dictionary. Thus, if the string MEOW is in the dictionary, with a unique codeword, the strings MEO and ME are also in the dictionary, each with its own unique codeword.

The dictionary can logically be represented as a set of trees, with each tree having a root corresponding to a character in the alphabet. So in the default case ($N_3 = 8$ bits) there are 256 trees. An example is shown in Figure 6.13. Each tree represents the set of strings in the dictionary that begin with a specific character, and each node represents a particular string, consisting of the characters defined by the path from the root. The trees in Figure 6.13 indicate that the following strings are in the dictionary: A, B, BA, BAG, BAR, BAT, BI, BIN, C, D, DE, DO, and DOG.

The number in parentheses is the codeword for the corresponding string. Note that the codes for the one-character strings are just the ASCII codes for the characters (Table 4.1). The first code available for assignment to a multiple-character string is N_5, which in this example is 256. Thus, with a 9-bit code, a total of 256 multiple-character strings can be represented in addition to the 256 single-character strings.

The LZ algorithm consists of three main ingredients:

- String matching and encoding
- Addition of new strings to the dictionary
- Deletion of old strings from the dictionary.

The LZ algorithm will always match the input to the longest matching string in the dictionary. The transmitter partitions the input into strings that are in the dictionary and converts each string into its corresponding codeword. Since all one-character strings are always in the dictionary, all of the input can be

FIGURE 6.13 Tree-Based Representation of V.42bis Dictionary.

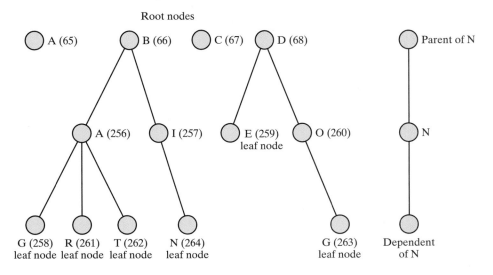

partitioned into strings in the dictionary. The receiver accepts a stream of code-words and converts each codeword to its corresponding character string.

The algorithm is always seeking to add new strings to the dictionary, replacing older strings, which may not be as likely to appear in the future. The procedure is as follows:

1. Process incoming characters to produce the longest matching string.
2. If the matched string is of maximum length (N_7 characters), go to step 1.
3. Otherwise, append the next character to the matched string, add this string to the dictionary, and assign a code to it. However, since this new string does not yet exist in the receiver's dictionary, transmit the code for the original matched string and use the remaining character to begin again at step 1.

The procedure for adding a new string to the dictionary depends on whether or not the dictionary is full. In either case, the transmitter maintains a variable C_1, which is the value of the next available codeword. When the system is initialized, C_1 is initialized to have the value N_5, which is the first value after all one-character strings are assigned values. Thus, in the default, C_1 begins with a value of 256. As long as the dictionary remains empty, as each new string is defined it is assigned the code value of C_1, and C_1 is incremented by 1.

When the dictionary is full, the following procedure is adopted. As each new string is defined, it is assigned the code value of C_1. Then:

1. C_1 is incremented by 1.
2. If C_1 equals N_2, C_1 is set equal to N_5. That is, once C_1 reaches its maximum value, it cycles back to its minimum value.
3. If the node identified by the value of C_1 is not a leaf node, go to step 1.
4. If the node is a leaf node, delete it from the dictionary.

At the end of this procedure, there is room for one new entry in the dictionary, and C_1 is the unused code to be assigned to that entry. The system is now ready to define the next new string for the dictionary. As an example, assume that the dictionary is in the state shown in Figure 6.13 and the next three input characters are BAY. The first character B is read and the dictionary searched. Since this character is present, the next character A is read and appended, forming the string BA. The dictionary is searched and the string is found. Then Y is appended, forming BAY. The dictionary search fails for this string. Y is removed and the string-matching procedure exits with BA as the matched string and Y as the unmatched character.

BA is encoded with the 9-bit binary value of 256 and passed to the control function for transmission. The string BAY is added to the dictionary by appending Y to BA under the B tree. The next available code (265) is assigned to this new string. C_1 is incremented to the value 266. The character Y is then used to start a new string search.

Video Compression Standards

Full-motion video is becoming increasingly common for desktop computers and is making some inroads on the Internet. An uncompressed, digitized video signal involves enormous amounts of data, exceeding the capacities of both transmission and computer storage systems. Fortunately, because the high level of redundancy in video, it is readily amenable to compression. There is ongoing research and development to design compression algorithms that are computationally fast and result in high degrees of compression. Here we briefly summarize approaches that have been standardized.

The three most important video-compression standards are:

- *M-JPEG.* Motion-JPEG was developed by ISO's Joint Photographic Experts Group (JPEG). This approach involves the independent compression of each individual frame in a video signal and is therefore known as an *intraframe* technique.

- *ITU-T H.261.* This technique was designed for use over ISDN lines and attempts to produce a high-quality image at a data rate of $p \times 64$ kbps, where p ranges between 1 and 30 (i.e., a data rate of from 64 kbps to 1.92 Mbps). H.261 does intraframe compression is a manner similar to M-JPEG. In addition, the algorithm allows for interframe encoding: Some frames are coded on the basis of changes from the preceding frame. The use of interframe encoding results in a considerable improvement in compression, particularly for video sequences in which there are only gradual changes between frames.

- *MPEG.* The MPEG algorithms were developed by ISO's Motion Picture Experts Group. Like H.261, MPEG relies on both intraframe and interframe techniques. MPEG-1 is designed to produce a good-quality image at a data rate of 1.5 Mbps. MPEG-2 is aimed at data rates above 2 Mbps and supports a wide variety of formats for multimedia applications that require better quality than MPEG-1 can achieve.

All of these techniques use what are known as *lossy algorithms*. These algorithms produce a final image that is only an approximation of the original analog video image. To give some feeling for the operation of these algorithms, let us look in general terms at the MPEG algorithms. MPEG involves seven steps of processing:

1. *Preliminary scaling and color conversion.* Each frame is converted into a standardized representation known as Source Input Format (SIF), and color information is translated into a scheme known as YUV.

2. *Color subsampling.* Brightness is the dominant component of color seen by the human eye, while hue is less important. Accordingly, the algorithm is able to reduce the hue information by about 75% with little effect on subjective fidelity.

3. *Discrete cosine transformation* (DCT). This process maps each 8×8 block of points (pixels) into a set of numbers similar to a Fourier transform of the block. In essence, the DCT provides a frequency-domain

representation of the image. This transformation does not result in compression but provides suitable input for later stages.

4. *Quantization.* The DCT values are quantized into a finite number of possible values (similar to pulse-code modulation quantization). The more quantization levels that are used, the greater the picture fidelity, but the less the amount of compression.

5. *Run-length encoding.* The quantized DCT values are represented using a run-length encoding technique.

6. *Huffman coding.* The data stream from the preceding step is compressed using Huffman coding, a lossless compression technique that assigns the most common bit sequences from the preceding step to symbols that are as short as possible.

7. *Interframe compression.* Identical blocks of pixels common to two or more successive frames are replaced by a pointer that references a single copy of the block.

Steps 2 and 4 make use of an understanding of human perception to increase compression in such a way that the reconstituted images, while differing slightly from the original images, appear virtually identical. The JPEG compression technique involves essentially only the first six steps.

Fractal Compression

There is a limit to practical use of the standardized video compression algorithms discussed in the preceding section, all of which are based on the use of DCT transformations. The DCT approach is effective at compression ratios up to about 25:1. Greater degrees of compression generally result in a seriously degraded picture quality.

To achieve greater compression efficiency, there has been much interest in a very different lossy approach known as **fractal compression**. Fractal compression is based on the concept of self-similarity. A common way of explaining this concept is to consider the question: How long is a coastline? The answer depends on how closely you examine the coastline. Measuring the coastline at any particular resolution, a given length is arrived at. But as you look closer at the boundary between land and water, the coastline gets longer as more and more kinks are seen in it. In fact, the small-scale view looks remarkably like a miniature version of the large-scale view. This tendency for an object or data series to exhibit similar properties at different scales is referred to as *self-similar*.

The mathematical properties of fractal images can be used to perform compression. The process is complex to explain mathematically. In very general terms, recurring patterns in an image are identified regardless of size, and a single copy of each pattern is stored. Information about the actual size and position of copies of the pattern is also stored. The result is an extremely efficient method of image compression.

Fractal compression appears to achieve superior compression ratios than current techniques for images up to 100 and for video. The major drawback to fractal compression has been the immense processing resources required. However, fractal compression algorithms continue to evolve in the direction of greater efficiency, suggesting that this technique will eventually become a widely used approach to image and video compression.

Illustration: Problem Solution

The use of synchronous multiplexers would allow three terminals to be supported on each line, reducing the line requirement to 17 lines. With the use of a statistical multiplexer, greater savings can be achieved. How many terminals can be accommodated by each 28,800-bps statistical multiplexer will depend on the nature of the application, but it might be reasonable to expect that from six to eight terminals could be accommodated on each multiplexer. The other approach would be to use data compression equipment, which may allow as much as a 30% reduction. A combined statistical multiplexer and data compresser would be the most effective, possibly allowing as many as 10 to 12 terminals to be clustered. Thus, the company may be able to get by with as few as five circuits. ■

SUMMARY

Transmission costs are the most substantial portion of most data communications and voice communications budgets. Organizations that are faced with increasing needs for business information communications must exploit techniques for increasing transmission efficiency. Two complementary approaches are in common use. Multiplexing allows several transmission sources to share a larger transmission capacity. This allows the user to realize the economies of scale of using fewer higher-capacity lines rather than many lower-capacity lines. Compression is used to reduce the capacity required for a given transmission source. This allows more sources to share a given transmission capacity or allows less capacity to be used to support a single source. Multiplexing and compression can be combined to provide even greater improvements in efficiency.

Frequency-division multiplexing can be used with analog signals. A number of signals can be carried simultaneously on the same medium by allocating each signal a different frequency band. Modulation equipment is needed to move each signal to the required frequency band, and multiplexing equipment is needed to combine the modulated signals. This technique is used in both broadcast and cable TV video distribution systems. It has also been widely used in telephone networks to multiplex voice signals. However, the latter use is being displaced by synchronous time-division multiplexing techniques as telephone networks convert to digital operation.

Synchronous time-division multiplexing can be used with digital signals or analog signals carrying digital data. In this form of multiplexing, data from various sources are carried in repetitive frames. Each frame consists of a set of time slots, and each source is assigned one or more time slots per frame. The effect is to interleave bits of data from the various sources. This technique is widely used in digital telephone networks and in data communications facilities within organizations. One of the most popular forms of synchronous TDM is known as T-1. This refers to a leased transmission facility of 1.544 Mbps available from various sources and the specific multiplex format used on this facility. T-1 is popular for constructing private networks within geographically dispersed organizations and is used increasingly to provide business-user access to public telephone networks.

Statistical time-division multiplexing provides a generally more efficient service than synchronous TDM for the support of terminals. With statistical TDM, time slots are not preassigned to particular data sources. Rather, user data are buffered and transmitted as rapidly as possible using available time slots. Statistical TDM has largely supplanted synchronous TDM for terminal networking applications.

A variety of data compression techniques are in common use. All of them take advantage of redundancy in the data to be transmitted. In lossless methods, redundant information is compressed and replaced by short codes that can be used by the receiver to reconstruct the original data exactly. For audio, image, and video, greater compression can be achieved by using lossy compression, which allow reconstitution of sound or image that is very similar to the original.

RECOMMENDED READING

A discussion of FDM and TDM carrier systems can be found in [BELL90] and [FREE94]. Two useful books on data compression are [NELS96] and [HELD96]. Both books contain a number of programs to compress and decompress data and to analyze the susceptibility of data to compression. These programs are also available on disk. A more technical treatment can be found in [STAL98]. A detailed discussion of V.42bis is contained in [BLAC95].

BELL90 BELLCORE (Bell Communications Research). *Telecommunications Transmission Engineering.* Three volumes. 1990.

BLAC95 BLACK, U. *The V Series Recommendations: Standards for Data Communications over the Telephone Network.* New York: McGraw-Hill, 1995.

FREE94 FREEMAN, R. *Reference Manual for Telecommunications Engineering.* New York: Wiley, 1994.

HELD96 HELD, G. *Data and Image Compression: Tools and Techniques.* New York: Wiley, 1996.

NELS96 NELSON, M., and GAILLY, J. *The Data Compression Book.* New York: M&T Books, 1996.

STAL98 STALLINGS, W. *High-Speed and Gigabit Networks: TCP/IP and ATM Design Principles.* Upper Saddle River, NJ: Prentice Hall, 1998.

Recommended Web Site

- http://www.atis.org/atis/sif/sifhom.htm: SONET Interoperability Forum site. Discusses current projects and technology.

KEY TERMS

Channel	Multiplexing	Synchronous Time-Division Multiplexing
Cursor	Run-Length Encoding	
Data Compression	SDH	T-1
Fractal Compression	SONET	Time-Division Multiplexing (TDM)
Frame	Statistical Time-Division Multiplexing	
Frequency-Division Multiplexing (FDM)		V.42bis

QUESTIONS

1. Why is multiplexing so cost-effective?
2. How is interference avoided by using frequency-division multiplexing?
3. Explain how synchronous time-division multiplexing (TDM) works.
4. What are some of the major uses of T-1 lines?
5. Why is the use of private T-1 lines attractive to companies?
6. Why is a statistical time-division multiplexer more efficient than a synchronous time-division multiplexer?
7. What is run-length encoding?
8. Using Table 6.3 as a guide, indicate the major difference between North American and international TDM carrier standards.
9. Using Figure 6.11 as a guide, indicate the relationship between buffer size and line utilization.
10. What is the difference between lossless and lossy compression, and in what applications are each used?

PROBLEMS

1. How do we achieve a data rate of 56 kbps in 23 channels using a DS-1 format?
2. To get some indication of the relative demands of voice and data traffic, consider the following:
   a. Calculate the number of bits used to send a 3-min telephone call using standard PCM.
   b. How many pages of ASCII text with an average of 65 characters a line and 55 lines a page correspond to one telephone call?
   c. How many pages of facsimile at standard resolution [i.e., 200 dpi (dots per inch) horizontally and 100 dpi vertically] corresponds to one 3-minute phone call? Assume that the effective page is 8 in. wide and 10.5 in. long. Moreover, assume an effective compression ratio of 10:1.
3. Recently, a new scanner was announced that provided 1200 dpi resolution and over 1 billion colors.
   a. How much memory in bytes would it take to store a bit map of an 8- by 10-in. monochrome picture at 1200 dpi with a 10-bit gray scale?
   b. Suppose that the colors are represented as a combination of three colors—red, blue, green—each with n bits to represent its intensity. What is the least value of n that will provide over 1 billion colors?
   c. How long would it take to send a color representation of an 8- by 10-in. picture at 1200 dpi over a T-1 line (1.544 Mbps)?
4. Phototypesetters often print black-and-white material at a resolution of 2400 dots per linear inch. Suppose that you want to send a 7- by 11-in. page of material generated by your PC to be printed by such a typesetter.
   a. If you store it, uncompressed, as pixels in your PC, how much memory do you need in bytes?
   b. Suppose you have a modem that transmits at 19,200 bps. How long would it take you to send the file to the typesetter?
5. Assume that you are to design a TDM carrier, say T-489, to support 30 voice channels using 6-bit samples and a structure similar to T-1. Determine the bit rate required.

PART 3

NETWORKING

7

Traditional Wide-Area Networks

CHAPTER OBJECTIVES

After reading this chapter, you should be able to:

- Explain the need for a communications network for wide-area voice and data communications.

- Define circuit switching and describe the key elements of circuit-switching technology.

- Discuss the important applications of circuit switching, including public networks, private networks, and software-defined networks.

- Define packet switching and describe the key elements of packet-switching technology.

- Discuss the important applications of packet switching, including public and private networks.

- Discuss the relative merits of circuit switching and packet switching and analyze the circumstances for which each is most appropriate.

- Explain why ISDN is important to the plans of telecommunications managers.

- Discuss the transmission options available under ISDN.

- Describe some of the anticipated benefits of ISDN.

- Explain the role of standards in the definition of ISDN and in its practical application.

- Understand the importance of planning for ISDN.

*I*n Part 2 we described how information can be encoded and transmitted over a communications link. We turn now to the broader discussion of networks, which can be used to interconnect many devices. The chapter begins with a general discussion of types of networks. The remainder of the chapter focuses on wide-area networks and, in particular, on traditional approaches to wide-area network design.

■ Illustration: Problem Statement

An automobile insurance company maintains a headquarters in Hartford, Connecticut, with eight offices in major metropolitan areas throughout the United States. Each of the city offices services a number of suburban agents' offices. Every day, claims information is transmitted from the suburban offices to the regional offices. The regional centers collect, record, and sort the claims information and transfer the processed information to corporate headquarters.

Initially, the transfers from the suburban offices were handled at the end of each business day, averaging 65 claims of 5000 8-bit characters apiece from each of 10 offices per city. The total daily traffic from each agent site was 2.6 Mbits. At these levels, each suburban site transmitted for 1 to 2 hours a day, and each downtown area transmitted for about 4 hours daily.

Over time, the volume of claims to be processed grew. Although no additional agent or central sites were added, the volume grew to five times the previous amount. With the growth in business, the company recognized the competitive value of interactive claims processing, allowing agents to access and update records immediately in the regional and corporate centers. The new service was installed and averaged 500 to 1000 daily 1000-character queries from each agent site. All queries were directed primarily to data bases at the downtown offices. Unresolved queries were redirected to Hartford headquarters. This type of traffic load required an average of two terminals at each agent's site to be able to access either the downtown or the corporate center on demand. Transmissions were sporadic, with total daily traffic under 1 million characters.

The company then embarked on a major expansion. Suburban offices increased to an average of 25 to 30 per downtown site. Downtown locations increased to 50, and regional centers were established in New York, Chicago, and San Francisco. Traffic volumes for both end-of-day processing and interactive queries experienced a 10- to 20-fold growth.

At each stage of the company's growth, what is the appropriate communications approach for supporting data transmission requirements? (The problem solution appears at the end of the chapter.) ■

7.1 LANs, MANs, AND WANs

Local-area networks (LANs), metropolitan-area networks (MANs), and wide-area networks (WANs) are all examples of communications networks. A communications network is a facility that interconnects a number of devices and provides a means for transmitting data from one attached device to another.

There are a number of ways of classifying communications networks. One way is in terms of the technology used: specifically, in terms of topology and transmission medium. This part of the book indeed addresses these technology features. It will be useful first to look at another commonly used means of classification, which is on the basis of geographical scope. Traditionally, networks have been classified as either LANs or WANs. A category that recently begun to receive much attention is the MAN. Figure 7.1 illustrates these categories. By

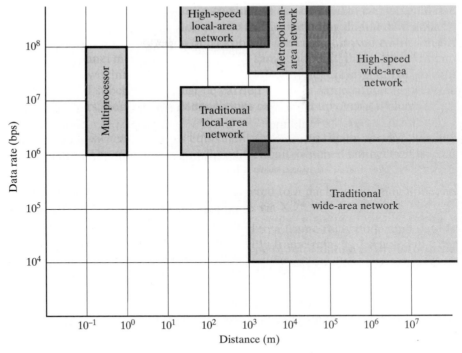

FIGURE 7.1 Comparison of Multiprocessor Systems, LANs, MANs, and WANs.

way of contrast, the typical range of parameters for a multiple-processor computer is also depicted.

Wide-Area Network

Wide-area networks cover a large geographical area, often require the crossing of public rights-of-way, and often rely at least in part on circuits provided by a common carrier. Typically, a WAN consists of a number of interconnected switching nodes. A transmission from any one device is routed through these internal nodes to the destination device specified.

Traditionally, WANs have provided only relatively modest capacity to subscribers. For data attachment, either to a data network or to a telephone network by means of a modem, data rates of 9600 bps or even less have been common. Business subscribers have been able to obtain higher rates: for example, T-1, which operates at 1.544 Mbps, being common. The most important recent development in WANs in this range of performance has been the development of the integrated services digital network (ISDN), which provides network services at rates up to 1.544 Mbps (2.048 Mbps in Europe).

The continuing development of practical optical fiber facilities has led to the standardization of much higher data rates for WANs, and these services are becoming more widely available. These high-speed WANs provide user connections in the tens and hundreds of Mbps, using transmission techniques known as *frame relay* and *asynchronous transfer mode* (ATM).

Local-Area Network

As with wide-area networks, a local-area network is a communications network that interconnects a variety of devices and provides a means for information exchange among those devices. There are several key distinctions between LANs and WANs:

1. The scope of the LAN is small, typically a single building or a cluster of buildings. This difference in geographic scope leads to different technical solutions, as we shall see. In particular, most LAN designs involve the shared use of a transmission medium rather than an interconnected set of network switching nodes.

2. It is usually the case that the LAN is owned by the same organization that owns the attached devices. For WANs, this is less often the case, or at least a significant fraction of the network assets are not owned. This has two implications. First, care must be taken in the choice of LAN, since there may be a substantial capital investment (compared to dial-up or leased charges for wide-area networks) for both purchase and maintenance. Second, the network management responsibility for a local network falls solely on the user.

3. The internal data rates of LANs are typically much greater than those of wide-area networks.

Traditional LANs have provided data rates in a range from about 1 to 20 Mbps. These data rates, though substantial, have become increasingly inadequate with the proliferation of devices, the growth in multimedia applications, and the increased use of the client–server architecture. As a result, much of the effort in LAN development has been in the development of high-speed LANs, with data rates of 100 Mbps or more.

Metropolitan-Area Networks

As the name suggests, a MAN occupies a middle ground between LANs and WANs. Interest in MANs has come about as a result of a recognition that the traditional point-to-point and switched network techniques used in WANs may be inadequate for the growing needs of organizations. While frame relay and ATM promise to meet a wide range of high-speed needs, there is a requirement now for both private and public networks that provide high capacity at low costs over a large area. The high-speed shared-medium approach of the LAN standards provides a number of benefits that can be realized on a metropolitan scale.

The primary market for MANs is the customer that has high-capacity needs in a metropolitan area. A MAN is intended to provide the required capacity at lower cost and greater efficiency than would be possible with an equivalent service from the local telephone company. There is nothing unique about the design of MANs. Some designs use LAN technology, extended over a larger area, whereas other designs use WAN technology, restricted to a metropolitan area. Thus, we do not specifically address MAN design in these chapters.

7.2 CIRCUIT-SWITCHING TECHNOLOGY

For transmission of data[1] beyond a local area, communication is typically achieved by transmitting data from source to destination through a network of intermediate switching nodes; this switched network design is sometimes used to implement LANs and MANs as well. The switching nodes are not concerned with the content of the data; rather, their purpose is to provide a switching facility that will move the data from node to node until they reach their destination. The end devices that wish to communicate may be referred to as *stations*. The stations may be computers, terminals, telephones, or other communicating devices. We will refer to the switching devices whose purpose is to provide communication as *nodes*. The nodes are connected to each other in some topology by transmission links. Each station attaches to a node, and the collection of nodes is referred to as a *communications network*.

Figure 7.2 illustrates a simple network. Signals entering the network from a station are routed to the destination by being switched from node to node. For example, information from station A intended for station F is sent to node 4. It may then be routed via nodes 5 and 6 or nodes 7 and 6 to the destination. Several observations are in order:

FIGURE 7.2 Simple Switching Network.

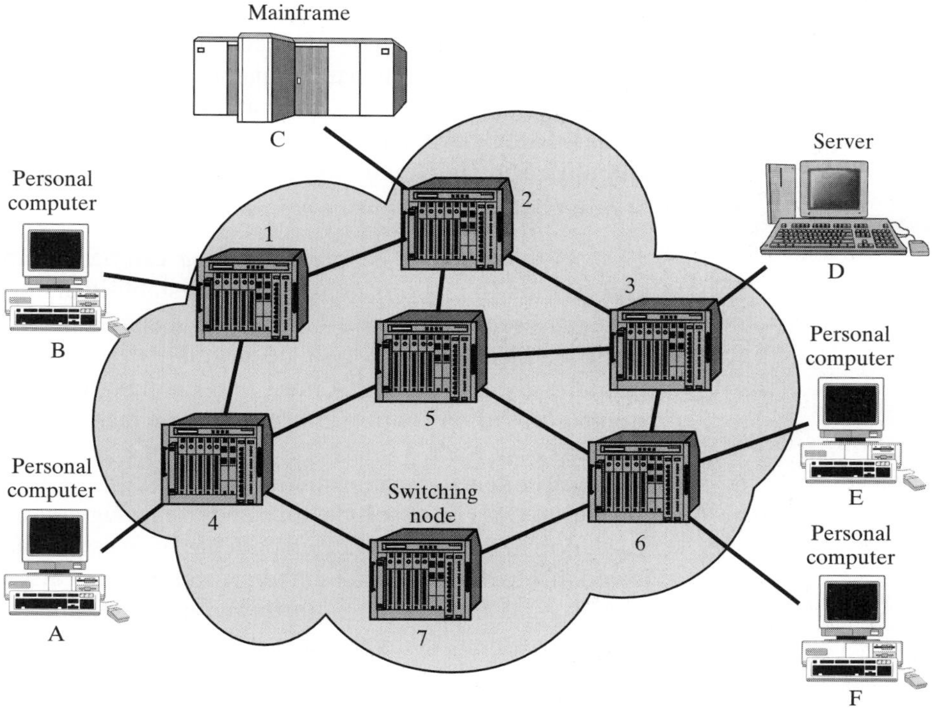

---

[1] We use this term here in a very general sense, to include voice, image, and video, as well as ordinary data (e.g., numerical, text).

1. Some nodes connect only to other nodes (e.g., 5 and 7). Their sole task is the internal (to the network) switching of information. Other nodes have one or more stations attached as well; in addition to their switching functions, such nodes accept information from and deliver information to the attached stations.

2. Node–station links are generally dedicated point-to-point links. Node–node links are usually multiplexed links, using either frequency-division multiplexing (FDM) or some form of time-division multiplexing (TDM).

3. Usually, the network is not fully connected; that is, there is not a direct link between every possible pair of nodes. However, it is always desirable to have more than one possible path through the network for each pair of stations. This enhances the reliability of the network.

Two quite different technologies are used in wide-area switched networks: circuit switching and packet switching. These two technologies differ in the way the nodes switch information from one link to another on the way from source to destination. In this chapter we look at the details of both of these technologies, beginning with circuit switching.

External Operation

Circuit Switching
Communication in which a dedicated communications path is established between two devices through one or more intermediate switching nodes.

Circuit switching is the dominant technology for both voice and data communications today and will remain so for the foreseeable future. Communication via circuit switching implies that there is a dedicated communication path between two stations. That path is a connected sequence of links between network nodes. On each physical link, a channel is dedicated to the connection. The most common example of circuit switching is the telephone network.

Communication via circuit switching involves three phases, which can be explained with reference to Figure 7.2.

1. *Circuit establishment.* Before any signals can be transmitted, an end-to-end (station-to-station) circuit must be established. For example, station A sends a request to node 4 requesting a connection to station E. Typically, the link from A to 4 is a dedicated line, so that part of the connection already exists. Node 4 must find the next leg in a route leading to node 6. Based on routing information and measures of availability and perhaps cost, node 4 selects the link to node 5, allocates a free channel (using frequency-division multiplexing, FDM, or time-division multiplexing, TDM) on that link, and sends a message requesting connection to station E. So far, a dedicated path has been established from station A through 4 to 5. Because a number of stations may attach to 4, it must be able to establish internal paths from multiple stations to multiple nodes. How this is done is discussed later in the section. The remainder of the process proceeds similarly. Node 5 dedicates a channel to node 6 and ties that channel internally to the channel from node 4. Node 6 completes the connection to station E. In completing the connection, a test is made to determine if E is busy or is prepared to accept the connection.

2. *Information transfer.* Information can now be transmitted from station A through the network to E. The transmission may be analog voice, digitized voice, or binary data, depending on the nature of the network. As the carriers evolve to fully integrated digital networks, the use of digital (binary) transmission for both voice and data is becoming the dominant method. The path is: A–4 link, internal switching through 4, 4–5 channel, internal switching through 5, 5–6 channel, internal switching through 6, 6–E link. Generally, the connection is full duplex, and signals may be transmitted in both directions simultaneously.

3. *Circuit disconnect.* After some period of information transfer, the connection is terminated, usually by the action of one of the two stations. Signals must be propagated to nodes 4, 5, and 6 to deallocate the dedicated resources.

Note that the connection path is established before data transmission begins. Thus, channel capacity must be reserved between each pair of nodes in the path and each node must have available internal switching capacity to handle the connection requested. The switches must have the intelligence to make these allocations and to devise a route through the network.

Circuit switching can be rather inefficient. Channel capacity is dedicated for the duration of a connection even if no data are being transferred. For a voice connection, utilization may be rather high, but it still does not approach 100%. For a terminal-to-computer connection, the capacity may be idle during most of the time of the connection. In terms of performance, there is a delay prior to signal transfer for call establishment. However, once the circuit is established, the network is effectively transparent to the users. Information is transmitted at a fixed data rate with no delay other than the propagation delay through the transmission links. The delay at each node is negligible.

Circuit switching was developed to handle voice traffic but is now also used for data traffic. Some of the key applications of circuit switching are summarized in Table 7-1. The best-known example of a circuit-switching network is the public telephone network (Figure 7.3). This is actually a collection of national networks interconnected to form the international service. Although originally designed and implemented to service analog telephone subscribers, it handles substantial data traffic via modem and is well on its way to being converted to a digital network. Another well-known application of circuit switching is the private branch exchange (PBX), used to interconnect telephones within a building or office. Circuit switching is also used in private networks. Typically, such a network is set up by a corporation or other large organization to interconnect its various sites. Such a network usually consists of PBX systems at each site interconnected by dedicated, leased lines obtained from one of the carriers, such as AT&T. A final common example of the application of circuit switching is the data switch. The data switch is similar to the PBX but is designed to interconnect digital data processing devices, such as terminals and computers.

A public telecommunications network can be described using four generic architectural components:

TABLE 7-1 Applications of Circuit Switching and Packet Switching

Circuit Switching	*Packet Switching*
Public telephone network Provides interconnection for two-way voice exchange between attached telephones. Calls can be placed between any two subscribers on a national and international basis. This type of network handles an increasing volume of data traffic.	**Public data network (PDN)/value-added network (VAN)** Provides a wide-area data communications facility for computers and terminals. The network is a shared resource, owned by a provider who sells the capacity to others. Thus, it functions as a utility service for a number of subscriber communities.
Private branch exchange Provides telephone and data exchange capability within a single building or cluster of buildings. Calls can be placed between any two subscribers within the local site; interconnection is also provided to public or private wide-area circuit-switched networks.	**Private packet-switching network** Provides a shared resource for one organization's computers and terminals. A private packet-switching network is justified if there are a substantial number of devices with a substantial amount of traffic in one organization.
Private wide-area network Provides interconnection among a number of sites. Generally used to interconnect PBXs that are part of the same organization.	
Data switch Provides for the interconnection of terminals and computers within a local site.	

FIGURE 7.3 Public Circuit-Switching Network.

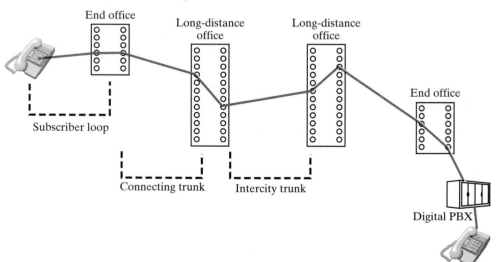

- *Subscribers*: the devices that attach to the network. It is still the case that most subscriber devices to public telecommunications networks are telephones, but the percentage of data traffic increases year by year.
- *Local loop*: the link between the subscriber and the network, also referred to as the *subscriber loop*. Almost all local loop connections use twisted-pair wire. The length of a local loop is typically in a range from a few kilometers to a few tens of kilometers.
- *Exchanges*: the switching centers in the network. A switching center that supports subscribers directly is known as an *end office*. Typically, an end office will support many thousands of subscribers in a localized area. There are over 19,000 end offices in the United States, so it is clearly impractical for each end office to have a direct link to each of the other end offices; this would require on the order of 2×10^8 links. Rather, intermediate switching nodes are used.
- *Trunks*: the branches between exchanges. Trunks carry multiple voice-frequency circuits using either FDM or synchronous TDM. Earlier, these were referred to as *carrier systems*.

Subscribers connect directly to an end office, which switches traffic between subscribers and between a subscriber and other exchanges. The other exchanges are responsible for routing and switching traffic between end offices This distinction is shown in Figure 7.4. To connect two subscribers attached to the same end office, a circuit is set up between them in the same fashion as described before. If two subscribers connect to different end offices, a circuit between them consists of a chain of circuits through one or more intermediate offices. In the figure, a connection is established between lines a and b simply by setting up the connection through the end office. The connection between lines c and d is more

FIGURE 7.4 Circuit Establishment.

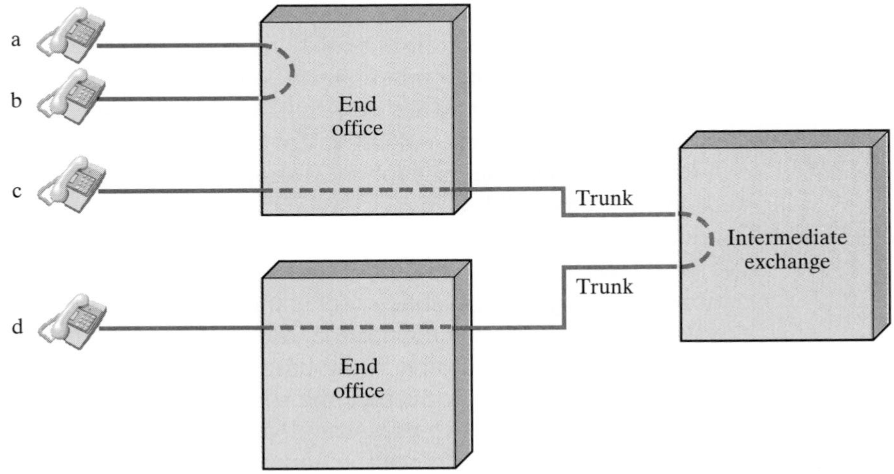

complex. In c's end office, a connection is established between line c and one channel on a TDM trunk to the intermediate switch. In the intermediate switch, that channel is connected to a channel on a TDM trunk to line d's end office. In that end office, the channel is connected to line d.

Circuit-switching technology has been driven by those applications that handle voice traffic. One of the key requirements for voice traffic is that there must be virtually no transmission delay and certainly no variation in delay. A constant signal transmission rate must be maintained, because transmission and reception occur at the same signal rate. These requirements are necessary to allow normal human conversation. Further, the quality of the received signal must be sufficiently high to provide, at a minimum, intelligibility.

Circuit switching achieved its widespread, dominant position because it is well suited to the analog transmission of voice signals. In today's digital world, its inefficiencies are more apparent. However, despite the inefficiency, circuit switching is and will remain an attractive choice for both local-area and wide-area networking. One of its key strengths is that it is transparent. Once a circuit is established, it appears like a direct connection to the two attached stations; no special networking logic is needed at the station.

Internal Operation

The technology of circuit switching is best approached by examining the operation of a single circuit-switched node. A network built around a single circuit-switching node consists of a collection of stations attached to a central switching unit. The central switch establishes a dedicated path between any two devices that wish to communicate. Figure 7.5 depicts the major elements of such a one-node network. The dashed lines inside the switch symbolize the connections that are currently active.

The heart of a modern system is a *digital switch*. The function of the digital switch is to provide a transparent signal path between any pair of attached devices. The path is transparent in the sense that it appears to the attached pair of devices that there is a direct connection between them. Typically, the connection must allow full-duplex transmission.

The *network interface* element represents the functions and hardware needed to connect digital devices, such as data processing devices and digital telephones, to the network. Analog telephones can also be attached if the network interface contains the logic for converting to digital signals. Trunks to other digital switches carry TDM signals and provide the links for constructing multiple-node networks.

The *control unit* performs three general tasks. First, it establishes connections. This is generally done on demand, that is, at the request of an attached device. To establish the connection, the control unit must handle and acknowledge the request, determine if the intended destination is free, and construct a path through the switch. Second, the control unit must maintain the connection. Because the digital switch uses time-division principles, this may require ongoing manipulation of the switching elements. However, the bits of the communication are transferred transparently (from the point of view of the attached devices).

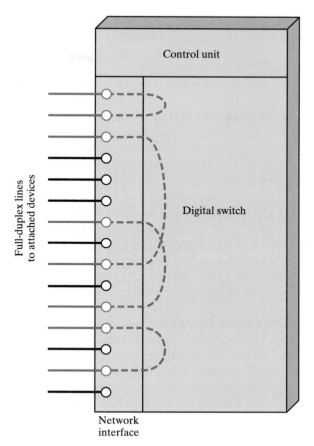

FIGURE 7.5 Elements of a Circuit-Switching Node.

Third, the control unit must tear down the connection, either in response to a request from one of the parties or for its own reasons.

An important characteristic of a circuit-switching device is whether it is blocking or nonblocking. Blocking occurs when the network is unable to connect two stations because all possible paths between them are already in use. A **blocking network** is one in which such blocking is possible. Hence a **nonblocking network** permits all stations to be connected (in pairs) at once and grants all possible connection requests as long as the called party is free. When a network is supporting only voice traffic, a blocking configuration is generally acceptable, because it is expected that most phone calls are of short duration and that therefore only a fraction of the telephones will be engaged at any time. However, when data processing devices are involved, these assumptions may be invalid. For example, for a data-entry application, a terminal may be continuously connected to a computer for hours at a time. [BHUS85] reports that typical voice connections on a private branch exchange (PBX) have a duration of 120 to 180 sec, whereas data calls have a range of from 8 seconds to 15 hr. Hence, for data applications there is a requirement for a nonblocking or "nearly nonblocking" (very low probability of blocking) configuration.

We turn now to an examination of the switching techniques internal to a single circuit-switching node. In general terms, digital switches operate in one of two ways: space-division switching or time-division switching.

Space-division Switching
A circuit-switching technique in which each connection through the switch takes a physically separate and dedicated path.

Space-Division Switching   **Space-division switching** was originally developed for the analog environment and has been carried over into the digital realm. The fundamental principles are the same, whether the switch is used to carry analog or digital signals. As its name implies, a space-division switch is one in which the signal paths are physically separate from one another (divided in space). Each connection requires the establishment of a physical path through the switch that is dedicated solely to the transfer of signals between the two endpoints. The basic building block of the switch is a metallic crosspoint or semiconductor gate that can be enabled and disabled by a control unit. Figure 7.6 shows the simplest type of crosspoint matrix. Each station attaches to the matrix via one input and one output line. Interconnection is possible between any two lines by enabling the appropriate crosspoint switch.

Time-division Switching
A circuit-switching technique in which time slots are manipulated to pass data from an input to an output.

Time-Division Switching   Time-division switches can be used in digital transmission systems. With **time-division switching**, the signals on each input line are treated as streams of digital bits. In effect, the switch multiplexes all of these input streams onto a common internal transmission path and then demultiplexes this common internal stream of bits, to route the appropriate bits to each output line.

To give the reader some feeling for time-division switching, we examine one of the simplest but most popular techniques, referred to as TDM bus switching,

FIGURE 7.6 Space-Division Switch.

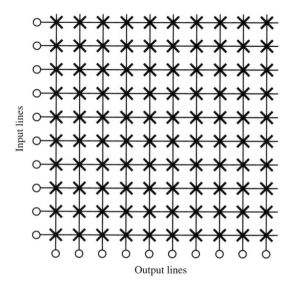

Output lines

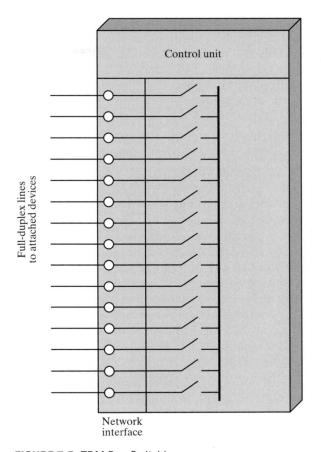

FIGURE 7.7 TDM Bus Switching.

which is illustrated in Figure 7.7. Each device attaches to the switch through a full-duplex line. Each line is connected through a buffer and a controlled gate to a high-speed digital bus. Each line is assigned a time slot for providing input. For the duration of the slot, that line's gate is enabled, allowing a small burst of data onto the bus. For that same time slot, one of the other line gates is enabled for output. Thus, during that time slot, data are switched from the enabled input line to the enabled output line. During successive time slots, different I/O pairings are enabled, allowing a number of connections to be carried over the shared bus. An attached device achieves full-duplex operation by transmitting during one assigned time slot and receiving during another. The other end of the connection is an I/O pair for which these time slots have the opposite meanings. For this scheme to work, the internal bus must have a data rate significantly higher than the data rate on each I/O line.

7.3 CIRCUIT-SWITCHING NETWORKS

As illustrated in Figure 7.4, the operation of a circuit-switching network involves the establishment of a circuit between two end systems that may be attached to different switching nodes. Two essential functions are involved in establishing such circuits: routing and control signaling.

Routing

In a large circuit-switching network such as the AT&T long-distance telephone network, many of the circuit connections will require a path through more than one switch. When a call is placed, the network must devise a route through the network from calling subscriber to called subscriber that passes through some number of switches and trunks. There are two main requirements for the network's architecture that bear on the routing strategy: efficiency and resilience. First, it is desirable to minimize the amount of equipment (switches and trunks) in the network subject to the ability to handle the expected load. The load requirement is usually expressed in terms of a *busy-hour traffic load*. This is simply the average load expected over the course of the busiest hour of use during the course of a day. From a functional point of view, it is necessary to handle that amount of load. From a cost point of view, we would like to handle that load with minimum equipment. However, there is another requirement, resilience. Although the network may be sized for the busy-hour load, it is possible for the traffic to surge above that level temporarily (e.g., during a major storm). It will also be the case that from time to time, switches and trunks will fail and be temporarily unavailable (unfortunately, perhaps during the same storm). We would like the network to provide a reasonable level of service under such conditions.

The key design issue that determines the nature of the trade-off between efficiency and resilience is the routing strategy. Traditionally, the routing function in public telecommunications networks has been quite simple. In essence, the switches of a network were organized into a tree structure, or hierarchy. A path was constructed by starting at the calling subscriber, tracing up the tree to the first common node, and then tracing down the tree to the called subscriber. To add some resilience to the network, additional high-usage trunks were added that cut across the tree structure to connect exchanges with high volumes of traffic between them. In general, this is a static approach. The addition of high-usage trunks provides redundancy and extra capacity, but limitations remain in terms of both efficiency and resilience. Because this routing scheme is not able to adapt to changing conditions, the network must be designed to meet some typical heavy demand. As an example of the problems raised by this approach, the busy hours for east–west and north–south traffic do not coincide and place different demands on the system. It is difficult to analyze the effects of these variables, which leads to oversizing and therefore inefficiency. In terms of resilience, the fixed hierarchical structure with supplemental trunks may respond poorly to failures. Typically in such designs the result of a failure is a major local congestion near the site of the failure.

To cope with the growing demands on public telecommunications networks, virtually all providers have moved away from the static hierarchical approach to a dynamic approach. A dynamic routing approach is one in which routing decisions are influenced by current traffic conditions. Typically, the circuit-switching nodes have a peer relationship with each other rather than a hierarchical one. All nodes are capable of performing the same functions. In such an architecture, routing is both more complex and more flexible. It is more complex because the architecture does not provide a "natural" path or set of paths based on hierarchical structure. But it is also more flexible, because more alternative routes are available.

As an example, we look at a form of routing in circuit-switching networks known as *alternate routing.*

Alternate Routing   The essence of alternate routing schemes is that the possible routes to be used between two end offices are predefined. It is the responsibility of the originating switch to select the appropriate route for each call. Each switch is given a set of preplanned routes for each destination, in order of preference. If a direct trunk connection exists between two switches, this is usually the preferred choice. If this trunk is unavailable, the second choice is to be tried, and so on. The routing sequences (sequence in which the routes in the set are tried) reflect an analysis based on historical traffic patterns and are designed to optimize the use of network resources.

If there is only one routing sequence defined for each source–destination pair, the scheme is known as a fixed alternate routing scheme. More commonly, a dynamic alternate routing scheme is used. In the latter case, a different set of preplanned routes is used for different time periods, to take advantage of the differing traffic patterns in different time zones and at different times of day. Thus, the routing decision is based both on current traffic status (a route is rejected if busy) and on historical traffic patterns (which determines the sequence of routes to be considered).

A simple example is shown in Figure 7.8. The originating switch, X, has four possible routes to the destination switch, Y. The direct route (a) will always be tried first. If this trunk is unavailable (busy, out of service), the other routes will be tried in a particular order, depending on the time period. For example, during weekday mornings, route b is tried next.

A form of the dynamic alternate routing technique is employed by the Bell operating companies for providing local and regional telephone service [BELL90]; it is referred to as *multialternate routing* (MAR). This approach is also used by AT&T in its long-distance network [ASH90], and is referred to as *dynamic nonhierarchical routing* (DNHR).

Control Signaling

Control signals are the means by which the network is managed and by which calls are established, maintained, and terminated. Both call management and overall network management require that information be exchanged between

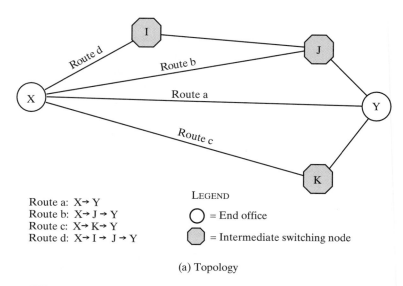

Route a: X→Y
Route b: X→J→Y
Route c: X→K→Y
Route d: X→I→J→Y

LEGEND

○ = End office

⬡ = Intermediate switching node

(a) Topology

Time Period	First Route	Second Route	Third Route	Fourth and Final Route
Morning	a	b	c	d
Afternoon	a	d	b	c
Evening	a	d	c	b
Weekend	a	c	b	d

(b) Routing table

FIGURE 7.8 Alternate Routes From End Office X to End Office Y.

subscriber and switch, among switches, and between switch and network management center. For a large public telecommunications network, a relatively complex control signaling scheme is required.

Signaling Functions   Control signals affect many aspects of network behavior, including both network services visible to the subscriber and internal mechanisms. As networks become more complex, the number of functions performed by control signaling necessarily grows. The following functions, listed in [MART90], are among the most important:

1. Audible communication with the subscriber, including dial tone, ringing tone, busy signal, and so on.
2. Transmission of the number dialed to switching offices that will attempt to complete a connection.
3. Transmission of information between switches indicating that a call cannot be completed.
4. Transmission of information between switches indicating that a call has ended and that the path can be disconnected.

5. A signal to make a telephone ring.
6. Transmission of information used for billing purposes.
7. Transmission of information giving the status of equipment or trunks in the network. This information may be used for routing and maintenance purposes.
8. Transmission of information used in diagnosing and isolating system failures.
9. Control of special equipment such as satellite channel equipment.

As an example of the use of control signaling, consider a typical telephone connection sequence from one line to another in the same central office:

1. Prior to the call, both telephones are not in use (on-hook). The call begins when one subscriber lifts the receiver (off-hook), which is automatically signaled to the end office switch.
2. The switch responds with an audible dial tone, signaling the subscriber that the number may be dialed.
3. The caller dials the number, which is communicated to the switch as a called address.
4. If the called subscriber is not busy, the switch alerts that subscriber to an incoming call by sending a ringing signal, which causes the telephone to ring.
5. Feedback is provided to the calling subscriber by the switch:
   a. If the called subscriber is not busy, the switch returns an audible ringing tone to the caller while the ringing signal is being sent to the called subscriber.
   b. If the called subscriber is busy, the switch sends an audible busy signal to the caller.
   c. If the call cannot be completed through the switch, the switch sends an audible "reorder" message to the caller.
6. The called party accepts the call by lifting the receiver (off-hook), which is signaled to the switch automatically.
7. The switch terminates the ringing signal and the audible ringing tone, and establishes a connection between the two subscribers.
8. The connection is released when either subscriber hangs up.

When the called subscriber is attached to a different switch than the calling subscriber, the following switch-to-switch trunk signaling functions are required:

9. The originating switch seizes an idle interswitch trunk, sends an off-hook indication on the trunk, and requests a digit register at the far end, so that the address may be communicated.
10. The terminating switch sends an off-hook followed by an on-hook signal, known as a *wink*. This indicates a register-ready status.
11. The originating switch sends the address digits to the terminating switch.

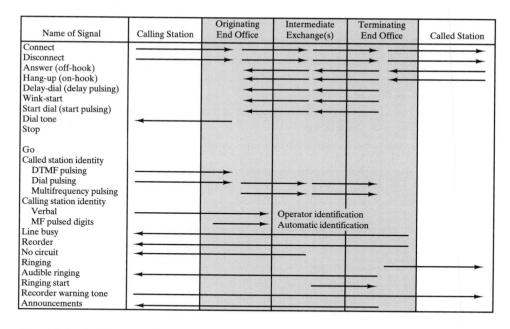

Name of Signal	Calling Station	Originating End Office	Intermediate Exchange(s)	Terminating End Office	Called Station
Connect					
Disconnect					
Answer (off-hook)					
Hang-up (on-hook)					
Delay-dial (delay pulsing)					
Wink-start					
Start dial (start pulsing)					
Dial tone					
Stop					
Go					
Called station identity					
DTMF pulsing					
Dial pulsing					
Multifrequency pulsing					
Calling station identity					
Verbal			Operator identification		
MF pulsed digits			Automatic identification		
Line busy					
Reorder					
No circuit					
Ringing					
Audible ringing					
Ringing start					
Recorder warning tone					
Announcements					

Note: A broken line indicates repetition of a signal at each office, whereas a solid line indicates direct transmittal through intermediate offices.

FIGURE 7.9 Control Signaling Through a Circuit-Switched Telephone Network.

This example illustrates some of the functions performed using control signals.

Figure 7.9, based on one in [FREE94], indicates the origin and destination of various control signals. Signaling can also be classified functionally as supervisory, address, call information, and network management.

The term *supervisory* is generally used to refer to control functions that have a binary character (true/false; on/off), such as request for service, answer, alerting, and return to idle. They deal with the availability of the called subscriber and of the needed network resources. Supervisory control signals are used to determine if a needed resource is available and, if so, to seize it. They are also used to communicate the status of requested resources.

Address signals identify a subscriber. Initially, an address signal is generated by a calling subscriber when dialing a telephone number. The resulting address may be propagated through the network to support the routing function and to locate and ring the called subscriber's phone.

The term *call information* refers to those signals that provide information to the subscriber about the status of a call. This is in contrast to internal control signals between switches used in call establishment and termination. Such internal signals are analog or digital electrical messages. In contrast, call information signals are audible tones that can be heard by the caller or an operator with the proper phone set.

Supervisory, address, and call information control signals are directly involved in the establishment and termination of a call. In contrast, *network management* signals are used for the maintenance, troubleshooting, and overall operation of the network. Such signals may be in the form of messages, such as a list of preplanned routes being sent to a station to update its routing tables. These signals cover a broad scope, and it is this category that will expand most with the increasing complexity of switched networks.

Location of Signaling   Control signaling needs to be considered in two contexts: signaling between a subscriber and the network, and signaling within the network. Typically, signaling operates differently within these two contexts. Signaling between a telephone or other subscriber device and the switching office to which it attaches is, to a large extent, determined by the characteristics of the subscriber device and the needs of the human user. Signals within the network are entirely computer to computer. Internal signaling is concerned not only with the management of subscriber calls but with the management of the network itself. Thus, for internal signaling a more complex repertoire of commands, responses, and set of parameters is needed.

Because two different signaling techniques are used, the local switching office to which the subscriber is attached must provide a mapping between the relatively less complex signaling technique used by the subscriber and the more complex technique used within the network. For intranetwork signaling, Signaling System Number 7 (SS7) is used on most digital networks.

Common-Channel Signaling   Traditional control signaling in circuit-switching networks has been on a per-trunk or inchannel basis. With *in-channel signaling,* the same channel is used to carry control signals as is used to carry the call to which the control signals relate. Such signaling begins at the originating subscriber and follows the same path as the call itself. This has the merit that no additional transmission facilities are needed for signaling; the facilities for voice transmission are shared with control signaling.

As public telecommunications networks become more complex and provide a richer set of services, the drawbacks of in-channel signaling become more apparent. The information transfer rate is quite limited with in-channel signaling because the same capacity is shared with the information being transmitted. With such limits, it is difficult to accommodate, in a timely fashion, any but the simplest form of control messages. However, to take advantage of the potential services and to cope with the increasing complexity of evolving network technology, a richer and more powerful control signal repertoire is needed.

A second drawback of inchannel signaling is the amount of delay from the time a subscriber enters an address (dials a number) and the connection is established. The requirement to reduce this delay is becoming more important as the network is used in new ways. For example, computer-controlled calls, such as with transaction processing, use relatively short messages; therefore, the call setup time represents an appreciable part of the total transaction time.

Both of these problems can be addressed with *common-channel signaling,* in which control signals are carried over paths completely independent of the voice channels. One independent control signal path can carry the signals for a number of subscriber channels and hence is a common control channel for these subscriber channels.

Internal to the network, common-channel signals are transmitted on paths that are logically distinct from those that carry the subscriber information. In some cases these may be physically distinct transmission facilities; in other cases, separate logical channels on shared trunks are used. The common channel can be configured with the bandwidth required to carry control signals for a rich variety of functions. Thus, both the signaling protocol and the network architecture to support that protocol are more complex than inchannel signaling. However, the continuing drop in computer hardware costs makes common-channel signaling increasingly attractive. The control signals are messages that are passed between switches and between a switch and the network management center. Thus, the control signaling portion of the network is in effect a distributed computer network carrying short messages.

With in-channel signaling, control signals from one switch are originated by a control processor and switched onto the outgoing channel. On the receiving end, the control signals must be switched from the voice channel into the control processor. With common-channel signaling, the control signals are transferred directly from one control processor to another without being tied to a voice signal. This is a simpler procedure, and one that is less susceptible to accidental or intentional interference between subscriber and control signals. This is one of the main motivations for common-channel signaling. Another key motivation for common-channel signaling is that call setup time is reduced. Consider the sequence of events for call setup with inchannel signaling when more than one switch is involved. A control signal will be sent from one switch to the next in the intended path. At each switch, the control signal cannot be transferred through the switch to the next leg of the route until the associated circuit is established through that switch. With common-channel signaling, forwarding of control information can overlap the circuit-setup process.

Packet Switching
Method of transmitting messages through a communications network, in which long messages are subdivided into short packets.

Common-channel techniques can also be used external to the network, at the interface between the subscriber and the network. This is the case with ISDN and many other digital networks. For external signaling, a logically distinct channel on the subscribe-network link is devoted to control signaling, used for setting up and tearing down connections on other logical channels on that link. Thus, a multiplexed link is controlled by a single channel over that link.

7.4 PACKET-SWITCHING NETWORKS

Around 1970, research began on a new form of architecture for long-distance digital data communications: **packet switching**. Although the technology of packet switching has evolved substantially since that time, it is remarkable that (1) the basic technology of packet switching is fundamentally the same today as it was in the early-1970s networks, and (2) packet switching remains one of the few effective technologies for long-distance data communications. The two newest WAN technologies, frame relay and ATM, are essentially variations on the basic packet-switching approach. In this chapter we provide an overview of the original packet-switching design, which is still in very widespread use; frame relay and ATM are discussed in Chapter 8.

We will see that many of the advantages of packet switching (flexibility, resource sharing, robustness, responsiveness) come with a cost. The packet-switching network is a distributed collection of packet-switching nodes. In the ideal, all packet-switched nodes would always know the state of the entire network. Unfortunately, because the nodes are distributed, there is always a time delay between a change in status in one portion of the network and the knowledge of that change elsewhere. Furthermore, there is overhead involved in communicating status information. As a result, a packet-switching network can never perform "perfectly," and elaborate algorithms are used to cope with the time delay and overhead penalties of network operation.

Basic Operation

The long-haul circuit-switched telecommunications network was originally designed to handle voice traffic, and the majority of traffic on these networks continues to be voice. A key characteristic of circuit-switching networks is that resources within the network are dedicated to a particular call. For voice connections, the resulting circuit will enjoy a high percentage of utilization because, most of the time, one party or the other is talking. However, as the circuit-switching network began to be used increasingly for data connections, two shortcomings became apparent:

- In a typical terminal-to-host data connection, much of the time the line is idle. Thus, with data connections, a circuit-switched approach is inefficient.

- In a circuit-switching network, the connection provides for transmission at a constant data rate. Thus, each of the two devices that are connected must transmit and receive at the same data rate as that of the other device. This limits the utility of the network in interconnecting a variety of host computers and terminals.

With packet switching, data are transmitted in short blocks called *packets*. A typical upper bound on packet length is 1000 octets (bytes). If a source has a longer message to send, the message is broken up into a series of packets (Figure 7.10). Each packet contains a portion (or all for a short message) of the user's data plus some control information. The control information, at a minimum, includes the information that the network requires to be able to route the packet through the network and deliver it to the intended destination. At each node en route, the packet is received, stored briefly, and passed on to the next node.

Figure 7.11 illustrates the basic operation. A transmitting computer or other device sends a message as a sequence of packets (a). Each packet includes control information indicating the destination station (computer, terminal, etc.). The packets are initially sent to the node to which the sending station attaches. As

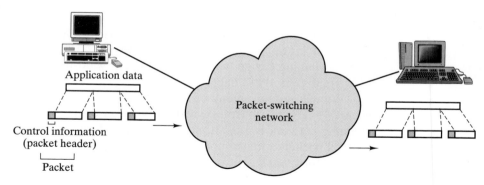

Application data

Control information
(packet header)

Packet

Packet-switching
network

FIGURE 7.10 The Use of Packets.

each packet arrives at this node, it stores the packet briefly, determines the next leg of the route, and queues the packet to go out on that link. When the link is available, each packet is transmitted to the next node (b). All of the packets eventually work their way through the network and are delivered to the intended destination.

The packet-switching approach has a number of advantages over circuit switching:

- Line efficiency is greater, because a single node-to-node link can be dynamically shared by many packets over time. The packets are queued up and transmitted over the link as rapidly as possible. By contrast, with circuit switching, time on a node-to-node link is preallocated using synchronous time-division multiplexing. Much of the time, such a link may be idle because a portion of its time is dedicated to a connection that is idle.

- A packet-switching network can carry out data-rate conversion. Two stations of different data rates can exchange packets, because each connects to its node at its proper data rate.

- When traffic becomes heavy on a circuit-switching network, some calls are blocked; that is, the network refuses to accept additional connection requests until the load on the network decreases. On a packet-switching network, packets are still accepted but delivery delay increases.

- Priorities can be used. Thus, if a node has a number of packets queued for transmission, it can transmit the higher-priority packets first. These packets will therefore experience less delay than will lower-priority packets.

Packet switching also has disadvantages relative to circuit switching:

- Each time a packet passes through a packet-switching node it incurs a delay not present in circuit switching. At a minimum, it incurs a transmission delay equal to the length of the packet in bits divided by the incoming channel rate in bits per second; this is the time it takes to

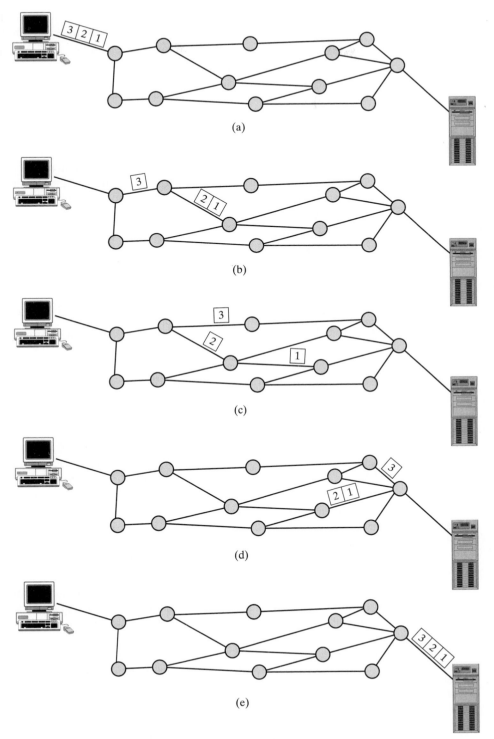

FIGURE 7.11 Packet Switching: Datagram Approach.

absorb the packet into an internal buffer. In addition, there may be a variable delay due to processing and queuing in the node.

- Because the packets between a given source and destination may vary in length, may take different routes, and may be subject to varying delay in the switches they encounter, the overall packet delay can vary substantially. This phenomenom, called *jitter*, may not be desirable for some applications: for example, in real-time applications, including telephone voice and real-time video.

- To route packets through the network, overhead information, including the address of the destination and often sequencing information, must be added to each packet, which reduces the communication capacity available for carrying user data. This is not needed in circuit switching once the circuit is set up.

- More processing is involved in the transfer of information using packet switching than in circuit switching at each node. In the case of circuit switching, there is virtually no processing at each switch once the circuit is set up.

Switching Technique

A station has a message to send through a packet-switching network that is of greater length than the maximum packet size. It therefore breaks the message up into packets and sends these packets, one at a time, to the network. A question arises as to how the network will handle this stream of packets as it attempts to route them through the network and deliver them to the intended destination. Two approaches are used in contemporary networks: datagram and virtual circuit.

Datagram
A self-contained packet, independent of other packets, that carries information sufficient for routing.

In the **datagram** approach, each packet is treated independently, with no reference to packets that have gone before. This approach is illustrated in Figure 7.11. Each node chooses the next node on a packet's path, taking into account information received from neighboring nodes on traffic, line failures, and so on. So the packets, each with the same destination address, do not all follow the same route (c), and they may arrive out of sequence at the exit point. In this example, the exit node restores the packets to their original order before delivering them to the destination. In some datagram networks, it is up to the destination rather than the exit node to do the reordering. Also, it is possible for a packet to be destroyed in the network. For example, if a packet-switching node crashes momentarily, all of its queued packets may be lost. Again, it is up to either the exit node or the destination to detect the loss of a packet and decide how to recover it. In this technique, each packet, treated independently, is referred to as a datagram.

Virtual-Circuit
A packet-switching mechanism in which a logical connection (virtual circuit) is established between two stations.

In the **virtual-circuit** approach, a preplanned route is established before any data packets are sent. Once the route is established, all the packets between a pair of communicating parties follow this same route through the network. This is illustrated in Figure 7.12. Because the route is fixed for the duration of the logical connection, it is somewhat similar to a circuit in a circuit-switching network and is

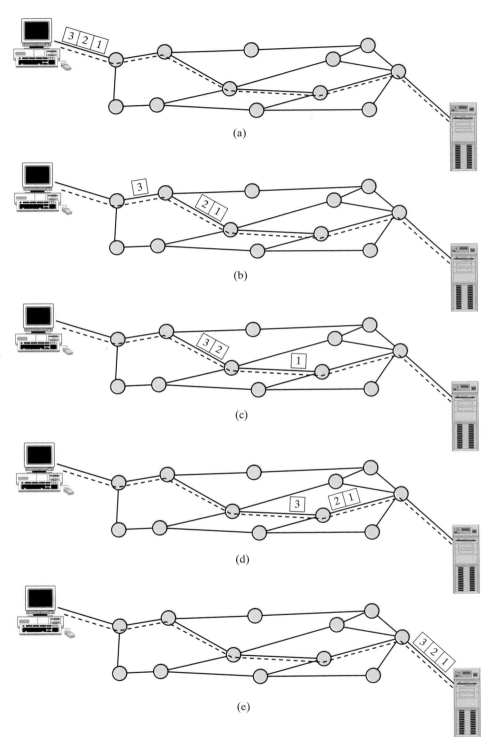

FIGURE 7.12 Packet Switching: Virtual-Circuit Approach.

referred to as a virtual circuit. Each packet now contains a virtual circuit identifier as well as data. Each node on the preestablished route knows where to direct such packets; no routing decisions are required. At any time, each station can have more than one virtual circuit to any other station and can have virtual circuits to more than one station.

So the main characteristic of the virtual-circuit technique is that a route between stations is set up prior to data transfer. Note that this does not mean that this is a dedicated path, as in circuit switching. A packet is still buffered at each node and queued for output over a line. The difference from the datagram approach is that, with virtual circuits, the node need not make a routing decision for each packet. It is made only once for all packets using that virtual circuit.

If two stations wish to exchange data over an extended period of time, there are certain advantages to virtual circuits. First, the network may provide services related to the virtual circuit, including sequencing and error control. *Sequencing* refers to the fact that because all packets follow the same route, they arrive in the original order. *Error control* is a service that assures not only that packets arrive in proper sequence, but that all packets arrive correctly. For example, if a packet in a sequence from node 4 to node 6 fails to arrive at node 6, or arrives with an error, node 6 can request a retransmission of that packet from node 4. Another advantage is that packets should transit the network more rapidly with a virtual circuit; it is not necessary to make a routing decision for each packet at each node.

One advantage of the datagram approach is that the call setup phase is avoided. Thus, if a station wishes to send only one or a few packets, datagram delivery will be quicker. Another advantage of the datagram service is that because it is more primitive, it is more flexible. For example, if congestion develops in one part of the network, incoming datagrams can be routed away from the congestion. With the use of virtual circuits, packets follow a predefined route, and thus it is more difficult for the network to adapt to congestion. A third advantage is that datagram delivery is inherently more reliable. With the use of virtual circuits, if a node fails, all virtual circuits that pass through that node are lost. With datagram delivery, if a node fails, subsequent packets may find an alternate route that bypasses that node.

Most currently available packet-switching networks make use of virtual circuits for their internal operation. To some degree, this reflects a historical motivation to provide a network that presents a service as reliable (in terms of sequencing) as a circuit-switching network. There are, however, several providers of private packet-switching networks that make use of datagram operation. From the user's point of view, there should be very little difference in the external behavior based on the use of datagrams or virtual circuits. If a manager is faced with a choice, other factors, such as cost and performance, should probably take precedence over whether the internal network operation is datagram or virtual circuit.

Routing

Two related functions, congestion control and routing, are essential to the operation of a packet-switching network. In virtually all packet-switching networks, some sort of adaptive routing technique is used. That is, the routing decisions that are made change as conditions in the network change. The principal conditions that influence routing decisions are the following:

- *Failure.* When a node or trunk fails, it can no longer be used as part of a route.
- *Congestion.* When a particular portion of the network is heavily congested, it is desirable to route packets around rather than through the area of congestion.

For adaptive routing to be possible, information about the state of the network must be exchanged among the nodes. There is a trade-off here between the quality of the information and the amount of overhead. The more information that is exchanged and the more frequently it is exchanged, the better will be the routing decisions that each node makes. On the other hand, this information is itself a load on the network, causing performance degradation.

Congestion Control

The objective of congestion control is to maintain the number of packets within the network or a region of the network below the level at which queuing delays become excessive. In essence, a packet-switching network is a network of queues. At each node there is a queue of packets for each outgoing link. If the rate at which packets arrive and queue up exceeds the rate at which packets are transmitted, the queue size grows without bound and the delay experienced by a packet goes to infinity. Even if the packet arrival rate is less than the packet transmission rate, queue length will grow dramatically as the arrival rate approaches the transmission rate. As a rule of thumb, when the line for which packets are queuing becomes more than 80% utilized, the queue length grows at an alarming rate.

The object of all congestion-control techniques is to limit queue lengths at the nodes so as to avoid throughput collapse. This control involves some unavoidable overhead. Thus, a congestion-control technique cannot perform as well as the theoretical ideal. However, a good congestion-control strategy will avoid throughput collapse and maintain a throughput that differs from the ideal by an amount roughly equal to the overhead of the control. This control overhead is generally in the form of status information exchanged among the nodes, so that each node can determine the relative congestion in various regions of the network.

As with routing, congestion control is based on the exchange of status information among the various nodes of the network. In addition, congestion control requires that the network provide control signals to the attached stations regulating the flow of data. The latter function is performed using an interface protocol, usually X.25, which is discussed next.

7.5 X.25

One technical aspect of packet-switching networks remains to be examined: the interface between attached devices and the network. We have seen that a circuit-switching network provides a transparent communications path for attached devices that makes it appear that the two communicating stations have a direct link. However, in the case of packet-switching networks, the attached stations must organize their data into packets for transmission. This requires a certain level of cooperation between the network and the attached stations. This cooperation is embodied in an interface standard. The almost universally used standard for this purpose is X.25.

X.25 is an ITU-T[2] standard that specifies an interface between a host system and a packet-switching network. The functionality of X.25 is specified on three levels:

- Physical level
- Link level
- Packet level

The physical level deals with the physical interface between an attached station (computer, terminal) and the link that attaches that station to the packet-switching node. It makes use of the physical-level specification in a standard known as X.21, but in many cases, other standards, such as EIA-232, are substituted. The link level provides for the reliable transfer of data across the physical link, by transmitting the data as a sequence of frames. The link-level standard is referred to as LAPB (link access protocol—balanced). LAPB is a subset of HDLC, described in Chapter 5.

The packet level provides a virtual-circuit service. This service enables any subscriber to the network to set up virtual circuits to other subscribers. An example is shown in Figure 7.13 (compare Figure 7.2). In this example, station A has a virtual-circuit connection to C; station B has two virtual circuits established, one to C and one to D; and stations E and F each have a virtual-circuit connection to D. In this context the term *virtual circuit* refers to the logical connection between two stations through the network; this is perhaps best termed an *external virtual circuit*. Earlier, we used the term *virtual circuit* to refer to a specific preplanned route through the network between two stations; this could be called an *internal virtual circuit*. Typically, there is a one-to-one relationship between external and internal virtual circuits. However, it is also possible to employ X.25 with a datagram-style network. What is important for an external virtual circuit is that there be a logical relationship, or logical channel, established between two stations, and all of the data associated with that logical channel be considered as part of a single stream of data between the two stations. For example, in Figure 7.13, station D keeps track of data packets arriving from three different workstations (B, E, and F) on the basis of the virtual-circuit number associated with each incoming packet.

Figure 7.14 illustrates the relationship between the levels of X.25. User data are passed down to X.25 level 3, which appends control information as a header, creating a packet. This control information serves several purposes, including:

---

[2] The International Telecommunication Union Telecommunication Standardization Sector. See Appendix A for a discussion of ITU-T and other standards-making organizations.

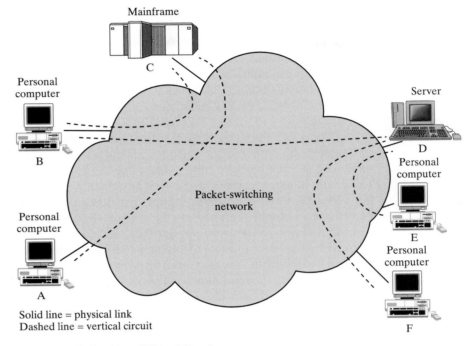

FIGURE 7.13 The Use of Virtual Circuits.

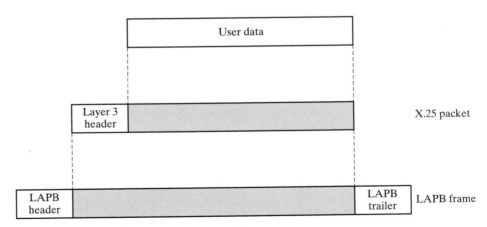

FIGURE 7.14 User Data and X.25 Protocol Control Information.

1. Identifying by number a particular virtual circuit with which these data are to be associated.
2. Providing sequence numbers that can be used for flow and error control on a virtual-circuit basis.

The entire X.25 packet is then passed down to the LAPB entity, which appends control information at the front and back of the packet, forming a LAPB frame (see Figure 5.18). Again, the control information in the frame is needed for operation of the LAPB protocol.

The operation of the X.25 packet level is actually quite similar to that of HDLC as described in Chapter 5. Each X.25 data packet includes send and receive sequence numbers. The send sequence number, P(S), is used to sequentially number all outgoing data packets on a particular virtual circuit. The receive sequence number, P(R), is an acknowledgment of packets received on that virtual circuit.

Figure 7.15 shows the packet formats used in X.25. For user data, the data are broken up into blocks of some maximum size, and a 24-bit header is appended to each block to form a *data packet*. The header includes a 12-bit virtual circuit number (expressed as a 4-bit group number and an 8-bit channel number). The P(S) and P(R) fields support the functions of flow control and error control on a virtual-circuit basis as they do on a link basis in HDLC.

In addition to transmitting user data, X.25 must transmit control information related to the establishment, maintenance, and termination of virtual circuits. Control information is transmitted in a *control packet*. Each control packet includes the virtual circuit number; the packet type, which identifies the particular control function; and additional control information related to that function. For example, a call request packet includes the following additional fields:

- *Calling DTE address length* (4 bits): length of the corresponding address field in 4-bit units.

- *Called DTE address length* (4 bits): length of the corresponding address field in 4-bit units.

- *DTE addresses* (variable): the calling and called DTE addresses.

- *Facility length:* length of the facility field in octets.

- *Facilities:* a sequence of facility specifications. Each specification consists of an 8-bit facility code and zero or more parameter codes. An example of a facility is reverse charging.

FIGURE 7.15 X.25 Packet Formats.

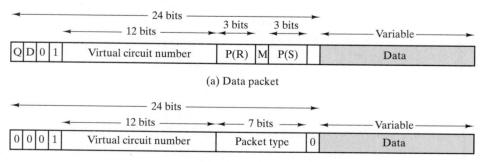

(a) Data packet

(b) Control packet

7.6 NARROWBAND ISDN

Rapid advances in computer and communication technologies have resulted in the increasing merger of these two fields. The lines have blurred among computing, switching, and digital transmission equipment, and the same digital techniques are being used for data, voice, and image transmission. Merging and evolving technologies, coupled with increasing demands for efficient and timely collection, processing, and dissemination of information, are leading to the development of integrated systems that transmit and process all types of data. The ultimate goal of this evolution is the **integrated services digital network (ISDN)**.

Integrated Services Digital Network
Telecommunication service that uses digital transmission and switching technology to support voice and digital data communications.

The ISDN is intended to be a worldwide public telecommunications network to replace existing public telecommunications networks and deliver a wide variety of services. The ISDN is defined by the standardization of user interfaces and is implemented as a set of digital switches and paths supporting a broad range of traffic types and providing value-added processing services. In practice, there are currently multiple networks, implemented within national boundaries, but from the user's point of view, there will ultimately be a single, uniformly accessible, worldwide network.

The impact of ISDN on both users and vendors will be profound. To control ISDN evolution and impact, a massive effort at standardization is under way. Although ISDN standards are still evolving, both the technology and the emerging implementation strategy are well understood.

Despite the fact that ISDN has yet to achieve the universal deployment hoped for, it is already in its second generation. The first generation, sometimes referred to as *narrowband ISDN,* is based on the use of a 64-kbps channel as the basic unit of switching and has a circuit-switching orientation. The major technical contribution of the narrowband ISDN effort has been frame relay. The second generation, referred to as *broadband ISDN (B-ISDN),* supports very high data rates (hundreds of Mbps) and has a packet-switching orientation. The major technical contribution of the broadband ISDN effort has been asynchronous transfer mode (ATM), also known as *cell relay.*

Next, we provide an overview of narrowband ISDN. Frame relay, cell relay, and broadband ISDN are addressed in Chapter 8.

Principles of ISDN

ITU-T has developed a long and growing collection of standards that define ISDN. ITU-T Recommendation I.120 lists the following principles that govern the ISDN design effort:

1. *Support of voice and nonvoice applications using a limited set of standardized facilities.* This principle defines both the purpose of ISDN and the means of achieving it. The ISDN supports a variety of services related to voice communications (telephone calls) and nonvoice communications (digital data exchange). These services are to be provided in conformance with standards (ITU-T recommendations) that specify a small number of interfaces and data transmission facilities.

2. *Support for switched and nonswitched applications.* ISDN supports both circuit switching and packet switching. In addition, ISDN supports non-switched services in the form of dedicated lines.

3. *Reliance on 64-kbps connections.* ISDN provides circuit-switched and packet-switched connections at 64 kbps. This is the fundamental building block of ISDN. This rate was chosen because, at the time, it was the standard rate for digitized voice, and hence was being introduced into the evolving digital networks. Although this data rate is useful, it is unfortunately restrictive to rely solely on it. Future developments in ISDN will permit greater flexibility.

4. *Intelligence in the network.* An ISDN is expected to be able to provide sophisticated services beyond the simple setup of a circuit-switched call.

5. *Layered protocol architecture.* The protocols being developed for user access to ISDN exhibit a layered architecture and can be mapped into the OSI model, which is examined in Part 4. This has a number of advantages:

    a. Standards already developed for OSI-related applications may be used on ISDN. An example is X.25 level 3 for access to packet-switching services in ISDN.

    b. New ISDN-related standards can be based on existing standards, reducing the cost of new implementations. An example is LAPD, which is based on LAPB.

    c. Standards can be developed and implemented independently for various layers and for various functions within a layer. This allows for the gradual implementation of ISDN services at a pace appropriate for a given provider or a given customer base.

6. *Variety of configurations.* More than one physical configuration is possible for implementing ISDN. This allows for differences in national policy (single-source versus competition), in the state of technology, and in the needs and existing equipment of the customer base.

User Interface

Figure 7.16 is a conceptual view of the ISDN from a user or customer point of view. The user has access to the ISDN by means of a local interface to a digital "pipe" of a certain bit rate. Pipes of various sizes will be available to satisfy differing needs. For example, a residential customer may require only sufficient capacity to handle a telephone and a personal computer. An office will typically wish to connect to the ISDN via an on-premises digital PBX or LAN and will require a much-higher-capacity pipe.

At any given point in time, the pipe to the user's premises has a fixed capacity, but the traffic on the pipe may be a variable mix up to the capacity limit. Thus, a user may access circuit-switched and packet-switched services, as well as other services, in a dynamic mix of signal types and bit rates. The ISDN will require rather complex control signals to instruct it how to sort out the time-multiplexed

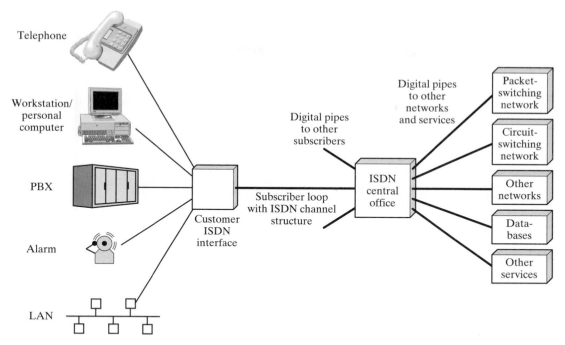

FIGURE 7.16 Conceptual View of ISDN Connection Features.

data and provide the services required. These control signals will also be multiplexed onto the same digital pipe.

An important aspect of the interface is that the user may, at any time, employ less than the maximum capacity of the pipe and will be charged according to the capacity used rather than *connect time.* This characteristic significantly diminishes the value of current user design efforts that are geared to optimize circuit utilization by use of concentrators, multiplexers, packet switches, and other line-sharing arrangements.

Network Architecture

Figure 7.17 is an architectural depiction of ISDN. The ISDN specifies a physical connector for subscribers, a digital link from the subscriber to the network, and ISDN-specific features for the network switching offices. The common physical interface provides a standardized means of attaching to the network. The same connector is usable for telephone, computer, and other devices. Protocols are required to define the exchange of control information between user device and the network. Provision must be made for high-speed interfaces to, for example, a digital PBX or a LAN. This interface is defined between the customer's equipment, referred to generically as *terminal equipment* (TE) and a device on the customer's premises known as a *network termination* (NT). The NT forms the boundary between the customer and the network.

The physical signal path from subscriber to ISDN central office is generally referred to as the *subscriber loop,* or **local loop**. This link must support full-duplex

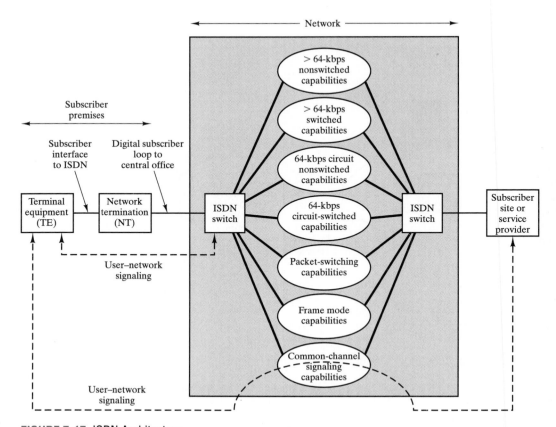

FIGURE 7.17 ISDN Architecture.

digital transmission at ISDN data rates. Initially, much of the subscriber loop plant will be twisted pair. As the network evolves and grows, optical fiber will increasingly be used.

The ISDN central office connects the numerous subscriber loops to the digital network. This provides access to a variety of transmission functions, including circuit-switched, packet-switched, and dedicated facilities. In addition, common channel signaling, used to control the network and provide call management, is accessible to the user. This signaling will allow user-network control dialogue.

Transmission Structure

The digital pipe between the central office and the ISDN subscriber carries a number of communication channels. The capacity of the pipe, and therefore the number of channels carried, may vary from user to user. The transmission structure of any access link is constructed from the following types of channels:

- *B channel:* 64 kbps
- *D channel:* 16 or 64 kbps
- *H channel:* 384, 1536, or 1920 kbps

The **B channel** is the basic user channel. It can be used to carry digital data, digitized voice, or a mixture of lower-rate traffic, including digital data and digitized voice encoded at a fraction of 64 kbps. In the case of mixed traffic, all traffic of the B channel must be destined for the same endpoint; that is, the elemental unit of circuit switching is the B channel. If a B channel consists of two or more subchannels, all subchannels must be carried over the same circuit between the same subscribers. Four kinds of connections can be set up over a B channel:

- *Circuit-switched.* This is equivalent to switched digital service, available today. The user places a call and a circuit-switched connection is established with another network user.

- *Packet-switched.* The user is connected to a packet-switching node, and data are exchanged with other users via X.25.

- *Frame mode.* The user is connected to a frame relay node, and data are exchanged with other users via LAPF; frame relay is discussed in Chapter 8.

- *Semipermanent.* This is a connection to another user set up by prior arrangement and not requiring a call establishment protocol. This is equivalent to a leased line.

The **D channel** serves two main purposes. First, it carries signaling information to control circuit-switched calls on associated B channels at the user interface. That is, if a user wishes to place a call on a B channel, a control message is sent to the ISDN central office on the D channel requesting the connection. The D channel is used to set up calls on all of the B channels at the customer's interface. This technique is known as *common-channel signaling*, as the D channel is a common channel for providing control signals for all the other channels. Common-channel signaling allows the other (B) channels to be used more efficiently. In addition to its use for control signaling, the D channel may be used for packet switching or low-speed telemetry at times when no signaling information is waiting. Table 7-2 summarizes the types of data traffic to be supported on B and D channels.

TABLE 7-2 ISDN Channel Functions

B Channel (64 kbps)	*D Channel (16 kbps)*
Digital voice	Signaling
64-kbps PCM	Basic
Low bit rate (32 kbps)	Enhanced
High-speed data	Low-speed data
Circuit-switched	Videotex
Packet-switched	Teletex
Other	Terminal
Facsimile	Telemetry
Slow-scan video	Emergency services
	Energy management

H channels are provided for user information at higher bit rates. The user may use such a channel as a high-speed trunk or subdivide the channel according to the user's own TDM scheme. Examples of applications include fast facsimile, video, high-speed data, high-quality audio, and multiplexed information streams at lower data rates.

These channel types are grouped into transmission structures that are offered to the user as a package. The best-defined structures at this time (Figure 7.18) are the basic channel structure (basic access) and the primary channel structure (primary access).

Basic access consists of two full-duplex 64-kbps B channels and a full-duplex 16-kbps D channel. The total bit rate, by simple arithmetic, is 144 kbps. However, framing, synchronization, and other overhead bits bring the total bit rate on a basic access link to 192 kbps. The basic service is intended to meet the needs of most individual users, including residential subscribers and very small offices. It allows simultaneous use of voice and several data applications, such as packet-switched access, a link to a central alarm service, facsimile, Teletex, and so on. These services could be accessed through a single multifunction terminal or several separate terminals. In either case, a single physical interface is provided. Most existing twisted-pair local loops can support this interface.

In some cases, one or both of the B channels remain unused. This results in a B + D or D interface rather than the 2B + D interface. However, to simplify the network implementation, the data rate at the interface remains at 192 kbps. Nevertheless, for those subscribers with more modest transmission requirements, there may be a cost savings in using a reduced basic interface.

Primary access is intended for users with greater capacity requirements, such as offices with a digital PBX or a LAN. Because of differences in the digital

FIGURE 7.18 ISDN Channel Structure.

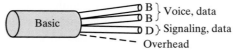

1. Basic service
   Rate: 192 kbps
   Composition: B + B + D channels,
          + synchronization and framing

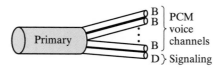

2. Primary service
   Rate: 1.544/2.048 Mbps
   Composition: 2.048 Mbps: 30 B channels at 64 kbps each
                       1 D channel at 64 kbps
              1.544 Mbps: 23 B channels at 64 kbps each
                       1 D channel at 64 kbps

transmission hierarchies used in different countries, it was not possible to get agreement on a single data rate. The United States, Canada, and Japan make use of a transmission structure based on 1.544 Mbps; this corresponds to the T-1 transmission facility of AT&T. In Europe, 2.048 Mbps is the standard rate. Both of these data rates are provided as a primary interface service. Typically, the channel structure for the 1.544-Mbps rate will be 23 B channels plus one 64-kbps D channel, and for the 2.048-Mbps rate, 30 B channels plus one 64-kbps D channel. Again, it is possible for a customer with lesser requirements to employ fewer B channels, in which case the channel structure is $nB + D$, where n ranges from 1 to 23 or from 1 to 30 for the two primary services. Also, a customer with high-data-rate demands may be provided with more than one primary physical interface. In this case, a single D channel on one of the interfaces may suffice for all signaling needs, and the other interfaces may consist solely of B channels (24B or 31B).

The primary interface may also be used to support H channels. Some of these structures include a 64-kbps D channel for control signaling. When no D channel is present, it is assumed that a D channel on another primary interface at the same subscriber location will provide any signaling required.

Benefits

The principal benefits of ISDN to the *customer* can be expressed in terms of cost savings and flexibility. The integration of voice and a variety of data on a single transport system means that the user does not have to buy multiple services to meet multiple needs. The efficiencies and economies of scale of an integrated network allow these services to be offered at lower cost than if they were provided separately. Further, the user needs to bear the expense of just a single access line to these multiple services. The requirements of various users can differ greatly in a number of ways: for example, in information volume, traffic pattern, response time, and interface types. The ISDN allows the user to tailor the service purchased to actual needs to a degree not possible in older network technologies. In addition, customers enjoy the advantages of competition among equipment vendors. These advantages include product diversity, low price, and wide availability of services. Interface standards permit selection of terminal equipment and transport and other services from a range of competitors without changes in equipment or use of special adapters. Finally, because the offerings to the customer are based on the ISDN recommendations, which of necessity are slow to change, the risk of obsolescence is reduced.

Network providers, on a larger scale but in a similar way, profit from the advantages of competition, including the areas of digital switches and digital transmission equipment. Also, standards support universality and a larger potential market for services. Interface standards permit flexibility in selection of suppliers, consistent control signaling procedures, and technical innovation and evolution within the network without customer involvement.

Manufacturers can focus research and development on technical applications and be assured that a broad potential demand exists. In particular, the cost of developing chip implementations is justified by the potential market.

Specialized niches in the market create opportunities for competitive, smaller manufacturers. Significant economies of scale can be realized by manufacturers of all sizes. Interface standards assure that the manufacturer's equipment will be compatible with the equipment across the interface.

Finally, *enhanced service providers,* such as for information retrieval or transaction-based services, will benefit from simplified user access. End users will not be required to buy special-access arrangements or terminal devices to gain access to particular services.

Of course, any technical innovation comes with penalties as well as benefits. The main penalty here is the cost of migration. This cost must, however, be seen in the context of evolving customer needs. There will be changes in the telecommunications offerings available to customers, with or without ISDN. It is hoped that the ISDN framework will at least control the cost and reduce the confusion of migration. Another potential penalty of ISDN is that it will retard technical innovation. The process of adopting standards is long and complex. The result is that by the time a standard is adopted and products are available, more advanced technical solutions have appeared. This is always a problem with standards. By and large, the benefits of standards outweigh the fact that they are always at least a little way behind the state of the art.

Role of ISDN

It is important to balance our presentation of the many potential benefits of ISDN with the recognition that a number of alternatives to ISDN exist and that the reality may be that ISDN will play much less of a role than originally intended by its designers. An article in the *Economist* [CARR90] made a startling comparison between telex and ISDN. Ten years ago, telex dominated the text-transmission market; however, it was provided primarily as a monopoly service belonging to carriers. The telecommunications industry did little to respond to improvements in technology or to the growing sophistication of customer demands. As a result, telex failed and has been virtually replaced by the fax machine.

Similarly, ISDN was dreamed up when telephone companies still thought like utilities that provide a blanket public service. Market forces have driven telecommunication technology, products, and services beyond the slow pace of ISDN standardization, with the result that ISDN is fated to be a special service, one among a variety of alternatives for the business user. As [CARR90] put it: "ISDN is not a universal service, the next step to the future and all that jazz. If it is sold as such, it will be nothing but a disappointment to those that subscribe to it." This sober publication is not normally given to exaggeration. Indeed, it is not alone in rethinking the potential role of ISDN in the telecommunications market. ISDN was intended to be the master plan for an advanced, all-digital network and was to completely replace today's telecommunications networks. A much more modest role appears certain.

One short-term trend that should improve the penetration of ISDN into the residential market is the demand for access to the Internet and the World Wide Web. Web access, in particular, suffers at speeds below 64 kbps. However, over the longer run, other competing techniques for accessing the web at higher speeds may reduce residential ISDN demand. One example is the cable modem, which enables a cable TV subscriber to use the cable link for access at speeds greater than 1 Mbps.

Fundamentally, ISDN provides a circuit-switching service coupled with an anemic (64-kbps access) packet-switching service. On the one hand, this set of services must compete with a variety of alternatives, as discussed in the next section. On the other hand, ISDN is inadequate to meet a number of high-capacity requirements generated by the fast-moving pace of performance improvement in data-processing and telecommunications equipment; we return to this issue in Chapter 8.

7.7 TRADITIONAL WIDE-AREA NETWORK ALTERNATIVES

Value-added Network (VAN)
A privately owned packet-switched network whose services are sold to the public.

Public Data Network (PDN)
A packet-switched network that is publicly available to subscribers.

As Table 7-1 indicates, packet switching adds several new alternatives for wide-area networking in addition to those that can be provided using circuit-switching technology. Just as there are public and private circuit-switching networks, there are public and private packet-switching networks. A public packet-switching network works much like a public telephone network. In this case the network provides a packet transmission service to a variety of subscribers. Typically, the network provider owns a set of packet-switching nodes and links these together with leased lines provided by a carrier such as AT&T. Such a network is called a **value-added network (VAN)**, reflecting the fact that the network adds value to the underlying transmission facilities. In a number of countries, there is a single public network owned or controlled by the government and referred to as a **public data network (PDN)**. The other packet-switching alternative is a network dedicated to the needs of a single organization. The organization may own the packet-switching nodes or lease an entire dedicated packet-switching network from a network provider. In either case, the links between nodes are again leased telecommunications lines.

Thus, a business is faced with an array of choices for meeting wide-area networking needs. This choice includes a number of high-speed options, such as frame relay and ATM. In this section we explore the various traditional WAN options, to get some feeling for the types of trade-offs involved. The issues are revisited in Chapter 8. Before beginning our evaluation of these alternatives, it is useful to consider the overview of circuit switching and packet switching provided in Table 7-3. While both circuit switching and packet switching can be used for data transmission, each has particular strengths and weaknesses for a given application.

Wide-Area Networks for Voice

Although there has been a certain amount of research on the use of packet-switching networks to handle voice, this approach is not in current commercial use. With packetized voice, the voice signal is digitized and broken up into packets to be transmitted across the network. There are two important requirements for voice communication that are difficult to satisfy with packet switching. First,

TABLE 7-3 Relative Merits of Circuit Switching and Packet Switching of Data

Advantages	*Disadvantages*
Circuit Switching	
Compatible with voice. Economies of scale can be realized by using the same network for voice and data. Commonality of calling procedures for voice and data. No special user training or communication protocols are needed to handle data traffic. Predictable, constant rate for data traffic.	Subject to blocking. This makes it difficult to size the network properly. The problem is less severe with the use of dynamic nonhierarchical routing techniques. Requires subscriber compatibility. The devices at each end of a circuit must be compatible in terms of protocol and data rate since the circuit is a transparent connection. Large processing and signal burden. For transaction-type applications, data calls are of short duration and need to be set up rapidly. This increases proportionally the overhead burden on the network.
Packet Switching	
Provides speed conversion. Two attached devices with different data rates may exchange data; the network buffers the data and delivers them at the appropriate data rate. Appears nonblocking. As the network load increases, the delay increases, but new exchanges are usually permitted. Efficient utilization. Switches and trunks are used on demand rather than dedicating capacity to a particular call. Logical multiplexing. A host system can have simultaneous conversations with a number of terminals over a single line.	Complex routing and control. To achieve efficiency and resilience, a packet-switched network must employ a complex set of routing and control algorithms. Delay. Delay is a function of load. It can be long and it is variable.

the overall delay should be small, to permit natural two-way conversation. This is difficult to guarantee with a packet-switching network. Second, and even more difficult to achieve with packet switching, the delay should not be variable. The speech signal must emerge at a smooth rate, matching the rate at which it is generated. Typically, delays on a packet-switching network vary with load, which would sound most unnatural.

Accordingly, the preferred business alternatives for wide-area voice communications all employ circuit switching. With the increasing competition and advancing technology of recent years, this still leaves the manager with many choices, including private networks, software-defined networks, ordinary telephone service, and a variety of special services such as 800 numbers and WATS. Further complicating the choice is the gradual introduction of services related to ISDN.

With all of these choices, and with the constantly changing prices attached to the various choices, it is difficult to generalize. What can be said is that business relies heavily on the public telephone networks and related services, such as 800 and WATS. Private networks are appropriate for an organization with a number of sites and with a substantial amount of voice traffic between them.

Wide-Area Networks for Data

For data traffic, the number of wide-area networking choices is even broader. Roughly, we can list the following categories as alternatives:

- *Public packet-switching networks.* There are a number of such networks in the United States and at least one in most industrialized countries. Invariably, the interface to such a network is X.25. Typically, the user must lease a line from the user's computing equipment to the nearest packet-switching node.
- *Private packet-switching networks.* In this case the user owns or leases the packet-switching nodes, which are generally collocated with the user's data processing equipment. Leased lines, typically 56- or 64-kbps digital lines, interconnect the nodes.
- *Private leased lines.* Dedicated lines can be used between sites. No switching is involved, so a leased line is needed between any pair of sites that wish to exchange data.
- *Public circuit-switching networks.* With the use of modems or switched digital service, the user can employ dial-up telephone lines for data communications.
- *Private circuit-switching networks.* If the user has an interconnected set of digital PBXs, either by leased 56-kbps lines or T-1 lines, this network can carry data as well as voice.
- *ISDN.* ISDN offers both X.25 packet switching and traditional circuit switching in an integrated service.

The last two alternatives are likely to be justified on the basis of the voice traffic, with data traffic being a sort of bonus that comes with the network. Because this approach is therefore not directly comparable to the others, we do not consider it further in this chapter.

As with voice, the choice of approach for data networking is complex and depends on current prices. In comparing the alternatives for wide-area data networks, we look first at the cost and performance considerations, which are more easily quantified and analyzed. Then we consider some other issues that are also important in selecting a network.

Cost/Performance Considerations   Data communications traffic can be roughly classified into two categories: stream and bursty. Stream traffic is characterized by lengthy and fairly continuous transmission. Examples are file transfer, telemetry, other sorts of batch data processing applications, and digitized voice communication. Bursty traffic is characterized by short, sporadic transmissions. Interactive client–server traffic, such as transaction processing, data entry, and time sharing, fits this description. Facsimile transmission is also bursty.

The public circuit-switching network approach makes use of dial-up lines. The cost is based on data rate, connection time, and distance. As we have said, this is quite inefficient for bursty traffic. However, for occasional stream-oriented requirements, this may be the most appropriate choice. For example, a corporation may have distributed offices. At the close of the day, each office transfers a file to headquarters summarizing the activities for that day. A dial-up line used for the single transfer from each office appears to be the most cost-effective solution. When there is a high volume of stream traffic between a few sites, the most economical solution is to obtain dedicated circuits between sites. These circuits, also known as *leased lines* or *semipermanent circuits,* may be leased from a telecommunications provider, such as a telephone company, or from a satellite provider. The dedicated circuit carries a constant fixed cost based on data rate and, in some cases, distance. If the traffic volume is high enough, the utilization will be high enough to make this approach the most attractive.

On the other hand, if the traffic is primarily bursty, packet switching has the advantage. Furthermore, packet switching permits terminals and computer ports of various data rates to be interconnected. If the traffic is primarily bursty but is of relatively modest volume for an organization, a public packet-switching network provides the best solution. In this case the network provides a packet transmission service to a variety of subscribers, each of which has moderate traffic requirements. If there is a number of different subscribers, the total traffic should be great enough to result in high utilization. Hence, the public network is cost-effective from the provider's point of view. The subscriber gets the advantages of packet switching without the fixed cost of implementing and maintaining the network. The cost to the subscriber is based on both connection time and traffic volume but not distance.

If the volume of an organization's bursty traffic is high and is concentrated among a small number of sites, a private packet-switched network is the best solution. With a lot of bursty traffic between sites, the private packet-switching network provides much better utilization and hence lower cost than using circuit switching or simple dedicated lines. The cost of a private network (other than the initial fixed cost of the packet-switching nodes) is based solely on distance. Thus, it combines the efficiencies of public packet switching with the time and volume independence of dedicated circuits.

Other Considerations In addition to the issues of cost and performance, the choice of network should also take into account control, reliability, and security. An organization large enough to need a wide-area data network will come to rely heavily on that network. Accordingly, it is vital that management be able to maintain proper control of the network to provide an efficient and effective service to users. We will explore this topic at some length in Chapter 16. For our purposes here, we can say that three aspects of control are significant in comparing various network approaches: strategic control, growth control, and day-to-day operation of the network.

Strategic control involves the process of designing and implementing the network to meet the organization's unique requirements. With public packet switching, the subscriber has virtually no strategic control over service levels, reliability, or maintenance. The network is intended as a public utility to serve the average customer. With either dedicated lines or a private packet-switching network, the user organization can decide on the capacity and level of redundancy that it is willing to pay for. *Growth control* allows users to plan for network expansion and modifications arising as their needs change. A private packet-switching network provides the most flexibility in accommodating needs for growth. Additional packet-switching nodes, more trunks, and higher-capacity trunks can be added as needed. These raise the overall capacity and reliability of the network. Although the user has control over the number and capacity of lines in a dedicated-line design, there is less flexibility for expanding the network incrementally. Again, with a public packet-switching network, the user has no control over growth. The user's needs are satisfied only if they happen to be within the capabilities of the public network. With respect to *day-to-day operation,* the user is concerned with accommodating peaks of traffic and in quickly diagnosing and repairing faults. Packet-switching networks can be designed with effective centralized network control that allows the network to be adjusted to changing conditions. Of course, in the case of the public network, the user is dependent on the network provider. As in any public utility, such as a transportation system, there tend to be "rush hours" in public networks when service levels decline. Day-to-day control is more difficult to automate in the case of dedicated lines; available tools are comparatively few and crude, because we are not dealing with a unified network.

The inherent *reliability* of a packet-switching network is higher than that of a collection of dedicated lines. The network consists of a set of shared facilities and is equipped with centralized, automated network control facilities. Faults can easily be located and isolated and the traffic shifted to the healthy part of the network. A public network may be able to afford a greater investment in redundancy and control tools because the cost is spread over many users. Further, the user is relieved of the burden of developing the expertise required to keep a large data communications network operational.

Finally, data *security* is vital to most corporations. We explore this topic in detail in Chapter 14. For purposes of the present discussion, we can say that use of a private network or dedicated lines will clearly afford greater security than will use of a public packet-switching network. Public networks can use various access control mechanisms to limit the ways in which users can obtain data across the network. Those same control mechanisms are useful in private networks, because an organization may wish to segregate various communities of users.

Table 7-4 summarizes the difference among the various communications approaches.

TABLE 7-4 Features of Wide-Area Networks

Feature	Dedicated (leased lines)	Public Packet	Private Packet
Strategic control	Network design, service, and maintenance can be given priority and controlled by user.	Service limited to that which suits the average customer.	Network design, service, and maintenance can be given priority and controlled by user.
Growth control and operation control	Not integrated; decentralized fault detection may be expensive.	Provided by service supplier to satisfy average requirements.	Integrated into all equipment; centralized fault isolation and detection.
Reliability	Manual and user-visible recovery from failure.	Transparent and automatic recovery from failure.	Transparent and automatic recovery from failure.
Security	Private users only.	Public users, network access control.	Private users only, network access control.

Illustration: Problem Solution

The initial volumes of traffic are relatively modest, so the insurance company would not be advised to invest in special equipment or services. Simple dial-up service using modems should suffice. As the traffic volume grows, a dedicated-circuit service would be more cost-effective. The company can lease lines between each suburban site and its downtown office and between each downtown office and headquarters.

With the introduction of interactive traffic, the application is well suited to a public packet-switching network. The combination of both interactive low-volume queries from many agent offices and multiple destinations (downtown and Hartford centers) warrants a volume-sensitive pricing approach.

With the expansion of the number of offices, a private packet-switching network appears to be the most cost-effective approach. It eliminates the time-duration and volume-sensitive tariffs. Also, although traffic volumes are high, the large interactive component favors this solution over the dedicated-circuit alternative. ■

SUMMARY

The use of a direct point-to-point link for information communications is impractical for all but the most limited requirements. For cost-effective, practical information communications, some sort of communications network is needed. For communications outside the range of a single building or a cluster of building, a *wide-area network* (WAN) is employed. Two basic technologies are employed: circuit switching and packet switching.

Circuit switching is used in public telephone networks and is the basis for private networks built on leased lines and using on-site circuit switches. Circuit switching was developed to handle voice traffic but can also handle digital data, although the latter use is often inefficient. With circuit switching, a dedicated path is established between two stations for communication. Switching and transmission resources within the network are reserved for the exclusive use of the circuit for the duration of the connection. The connection is transparent: Once it is established, it appears to attached devices as if there were a direct connection.

Packet switching is employed to provide an efficient means of using the shared facilities in a data communications network. With packet switching, a station transmits data in small blocks called packets. Each packet contains some portion of the user data plus control information needed for proper functioning of the network. Public packet-switching networks are available, to be shared by a number of separate subscriber communities. The technology may also be employed to build a private packet-switching network.

The choice between circuit and packet switching depends on a host of considerations, including cost, performance, reliability, and flexibility. Both technologies will continue to be important in wide-area networking.

Beyond the traditional alternatives for packet-switching and circuit-switching services, a new wide-area networking alternative is rapidly becoming widely available: ISDN. The ongoing introduction of the integrated services digital network (ISDN) provides both opportunities and challenges for the manager. The ISDN service is based on the concept of providing a set of channels at a single interface. The B channel, at 64 kbps, is the principal channel used for circuit switching, packet switching, and dedicated (leased) circuits. The D channel is used for control signaling (call setup) and may also carry some data. For residential users and small businesses, a basic access service of two B channels and one D channel is adequate. For customers with digital PBX or LAN installations, a primary access service of either 23 B channels or 30 B channels and one D channel can be used.

RECOMMENDED READING

As befits its age, circuit switching has inspired a voluminous literature. Two good books on the subject are [BELL91] and [FREE96]. The literature on packet switching is also enormous. Books with good treatments of this subject include [SPOH93], [BERT92], and [SPRA91]. A detailed technical treatment of ISDN and broadband ISDN can be found in [STAL95a]. Other book-length treatments include [KESS93] and [HELG91].

BELL91   BELLAMY, J. *Digital Telephony.* New York: Wiley, 1991.

BERT92   BERTSEKAS, D., and GALLAGER, R. *Data Networks.* Upper Saddle River, NJ: Prentice Hall, 1992.

FREE96   FREEMAN, R. *Telecommunication System Engineering.* New York: Wiley, 1996.

HELG91   HELGERT, H. *Integrated Services Digital Networks: Architectures, Protocols, and Standards.* Reading, MA: Addison-Wesley, 1991.

KESS93   KESSLER, G. *ISDN: Concepts, Facilities, and Services.* New York: McGraw-Hill, 1993.

SPOH93   SPOHN, D. *Data Network Design.* New York: McGraw-Hill, 1994.

SPRA91   SPRAGINS, J., HAMMOND, J., and PAWLIKOWSKI, K. *Telecommunications Protocols and Design.* Reading, MA: Addison-Wesley, 1991.

STAL95a   STALLINGS, W. *ISDN and Broadband ISDN, with Frame Relay and ATM*, 3rd ed. Upper Saddle River, NJ: Prentice Hall, 1995.

Recommended Web Sites

- http://alumni.caltech.edu/~dank/isdn: information on ISDN tariffs, standards status, and links to vendors.

- http://www.isdn.ocn.com: provided by Open Communication Networks, Inc., gives basic (and not so basic) information about setting up an ISDN connection. Dear Mr. ISDN answers E-mail questions about ISDN and includes a "propeller heads" section for more technical questions. The site also provides ISDN ordering links to major national ISDN providers, information about hardware, and other ISDN links.

KEY TERMS

B Channel	Integrated Services Digital	Space-Division Switching
Basic Access	Network (ISDN)	Time-Division Switching
Blocking Network	Local Loop	Value-Added Network (VAN)
Circuit Switching	Nonblocking Network	Virtual Circuit
D Channel	Packet Switching	X.25
Datagram	Primary Access	
H Channel	Public Data Network (PDN)	

QUESTIONS

1. Differentiate between WANs and LANs.

2. Why is it useful to have more than one possible path through a network for each pair of stations?

3. Describe three functions of a control unit on a circuit-switching device.

4. Distinguish between a blocking network and a nonblocking network.

5. What is a busy hour?

6. What are some advantages of private networks?

7. What are some of the limitations of using a circuit-switched network for data transmission?

8. What is a value-added network (VAN)?

9. Why is packet switching impractical for digital voice transmission?

PROBLEMS

1. Define the following parameters for a switching network:

   - N: number of hops between two given stations
   - L: message length, in bits
   - B: data rate, in bps, on all links
   - P: packet size, in bits
   - H: overhead (header), in bits per packet
   - S: call setup time (circuit-switched or virtual circuit), in seconds
   - D: propagation delay per hop, in seconds

   a. For $N = 4$, $L = 3200$, $B = 9600$, $P = 1024$, $H = 16$, $S = 0.2$, $D = 0.001$, compute the end-to-end delay for circuit switching, virtual circuit packet switching, and datagram packet switching. Assume that there is no node delay.
   b. Derive general expressions for the three techniques, taken two at a time (three expressions in all), showing the conditions under which delays are equal.

2. Consider a packet-switched network of *N* nodes, connected by the following topologies:

   a. *Star:* one central node with no attached station; all other nodes attach to the central node.

   b. *Loop:* each node connects to two other nodes to form a closed loop.

   c. *Fully connected:* each node is directly connected to all other nodes.

   For each case, give the average number of hops between stations.

3. Flow control mechanisms are used at both levels 2 and 3 of X.25. Are both necessary, or is this redundant? Explain.

4. In X.25, the virtual-circuit number used by one station of two communicating stations is different from the virtual-circuit number used by the other station. Why would this be so? After all, it is the same full-duplex virtual circuit.

CHAPTER **8**

High-Speed Wide-Area Networks

CHAPTER OBJECTIVES

After reading this chapter, you should be able to:

■ Discuss the reasons for the growing interest in and availability of high-speed alternatives for wide-area networking.

■ Describe the features and characteristics of frame relay networks.

■ Describe the features and characteristics of ATM networks.

■ Describe the features and characteristics of SMDS networks.

■ Describe the features and characteristics of B-ISDN networks.

■ Assess the pros and cons of these alternative services.

*A*s the speed and number of local-area networks (LANs) continue their relentless growth, increasing demand is placed on wide-area packet-switching networks to support the tremendous throughput generated by the LANs. In the early days of wide-area networking, X.25 was designed to support direct connection of terminals and computers over long distances. At speeds up to 64 kbps or so, X.25 copes well with these demands. As LANs have come to play an increasing role in the local environment, X.25, with its substantial overhead, is being recognized as an inadequate tool for wide-area networking. Fortunately, several new generations of high-speed switched services for wide-area networking are moving rapidly from the research lab and the draft standard stage to the commercially available, standardized-product stage. There are, in fact, three such high-speed WAN services available:

■ Frame relay
■ Switched multimegabit data service (SMDS)
■ Asynchronous transfer mode (ATM), also known as cell relay

In addition, there is a follow-on specification for a second-generation ISDN, known as broadband ISDN (B-ISDN), that is based on the use of ATM. Indeed, the network manager may now be faced with too many choices for solving capacity problems. In this chapter we examine these four new services and try to show where the strengths and weaknesses lie. But we begin with an overall look at the business requirements for wide-area networking and the general strategies that have evolved.

8.1 WIDE-AREA NETWORKING ALTERNATIVES

In considering wide-area networking strategies for business and other organizations, two distinct but related trends need to be analyzed. The first is the distributed processing architecture used to support applications and to meet an organization's needs, and the second is the wide-area networking technologies and services available to meet those needs.

New Corporate Strategy

As recently as the early 1990s, there was an emphasis in many organizations on a centralized data processing model. In a typical environment, there might be significant computing facilities at a few regional offices, consisting of mainframes or well-equipped midrange systems. These centralized facilities could handle most corporate applications, including basic finance, accounting, and personnel programs, as well as many of the business-specific applications. Smaller, outlying offices (e.g., a bank branch) could be equipped with terminals or basic personal computers linked to one of the regional centers in a transaction-oriented environment.

This model began to change in the early 1990s and the change accelerated through the mid-1990s. Many organizations have dispersed their employees into many smaller offices and there is a growing use of telecommuting. Most significantly, the nature of the application structure has changed. First, client–server computing, and more recently, intranet computing have fundamentally restructured the organizational data processing environment. There is now much more reliance on personal computers, workstations, and servers and much less use of centralized mainframe and midrange systems. Furthermore, the virtually universal deployment of graphical user interfaces to the desktop enables the end user to exploit graphic applications, multimedia, and other data-intensive applications. In addition, most organizations require access to the Internet. When a few clicks of the mouse can trigger huge volumes of data, traffic patterns have become more unpredictable while the average load has risen.

WAN Alternatives

To meet the demands of the new corporate computing paradigm, service and equipment providers have developed a variety of high-speed services. These include faster multiplexed line schemes, such as T-3 and SONET/SDH, as well as switched network schemes, including frame relay, SMDS, and ATM.

Figure 8.1 lays out the primary alternatives available from public U.S. carriers; a similar mix is available in other countries. A nonswitched, or dedicated line

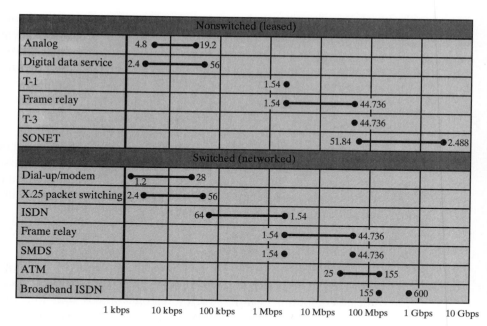

FIGURE 8.1 U.S. Carriers' Communications Services.

is a transmission link leased for a fixed price. Such lines can be leased from a carrier and used to link offices of an organization. Common offerings include:

- *Analog.* The least expensive option is to lease a twisted-pair analog link. With dedicated private-line modems, data rates of 4.8 to 19.2 kbps are common.

- *Digital data service.* High-quality digital lines that require digital signaling units rather than modems are more expensive but can be leased at higher data rates.

- *T-1, T-3.* For many years, the most common leased line for high-traffic voice and data needs was the T-1 line, which is still quite popular. For greater needs, the T-3 is widely available.

- *Frame relay.* Although a switched network technology, the frame relay protocol can be used over a dedicated line to provide a convenient and flexible multiplexing technique. For this use frame relay devices are required at the customer's premises.

- *SONET.* The highest-speed leased lines that are available use SONET/SDH, discussed in Chapter 6.

Public switched services include:

- *Dial-up/modem.* Modems connected to the public telephone network provide a relatively inexpensive way to obtain low-speed data services. The modems themselves are inexpensive and the telephone rates are reasonable for modest connect times. This is the nearly universal access technique for residential users. In organizations, many LANs and PBXs are equipped with modem banks to provide low-cost, supplemental data transmission service.

- *X.25 packet switching.* This elderly standby is still widely used to provide a switched data transfer service. With the increasing use of graphic and multimedia applications, X.25 at its traditional data rates is becoming increasingly inadequate. Typically, network charges are based on the volume of data transferred.

- *ISDN.* This service provides both circuit switching and X.25 packet switching over 64-kbps B channels. With a primary rate interface, higher data rates are achievable. Typically, network charges are based on the duration of call regardless of the amount of data transferred.

- *Frame relay.* This service provides switched capability at speeds equivalent to the leased T-1 rate and, in some offerings, higher rates up to T-3. Its low overhead makes it suitable for interconnecting LANs and high-speed stand-alone systems.

- *SMDS.* This is a high-speed switched offering that overlaps the capacities of frame relay and ATM.

- *ATM.* Asynchronous transfer mode has achieved the unusual position of being viewed almost unanimously as the universal networking technology for networking, destined to replace many of the current offerings.

Choosing among the various leased and switched alternatives is no easy task, and the proliferation of alternatives in the 1990s has increased the difficulty. Table 8-1 indicates common pricing practices in the United States; comparable

TABLE 8-1 WAN Alternatives (U.S. Pricing)

Service	*Usage Rate*	*Distance Rate*
Leased line	Fixed price per month for a specific capacity (e.g., T-1 or T-3) and no additional fee for usage.	More for greater distance.
ISDN	Fixed price per month for service plus a usage charge based on amount of connect time.	Long-distance charges apply.
Frame relay	Fixed price per month for a port connection and a flat rate for a permanent virtual circuit (PVC) based on the capacity of the link.	Not distance sensitive.
SMDS	Monthly port connection charge based on the capacity of the connection, plus a monthly usage charge based on volume of traffic over the link.	Not distance sensitive.
ATM	Pricing policies vary.	Not distance sensitive.

practices are used in other countries. As can be seen, the pricing structures of the various services are not directly comparable. This is one complication. Other issues that complicate the selection process include the difficulty of forecasting future traffic volumes by organizations with wide-area networking requirements, and difficulty in forecasting traffic distributions given the flexibility of applications and the mobility of users.

Evolution of WAN Architectures

Figure 8.2a shows the type of architecture that was dominant in business networks until just a few years ago and continues to be a popular model. In a typical configuration, all the devices at a customer's premises are fed through a synchronous time-division multiplexer onto a high-speed subscriber line to a carrier. This includes a PBX that controls phone and fax machines for voice and fax traffic as well as an interface to a LAN. Typically, the LAN is interfaced through a device called a router, discussed in Part Four. There may also be a number of dumb terminals connected to a controller that interfaces to the multiplexer. The line itself can be either T-1 or T-3; as demand rises, SONET links will become more common.

At the carrier end, the multiplexed traffic can be split up into a number of leased circuits. These enable the creation of a private network linking to PBXs, LANs, and mainframe hosts at other locations for this customer. In addition, for data traffic, the carrier can provide an interface to a public high-speed switched network. Most commonly today, that network is frame relay, but SMDS and ATM networks are also offered. Finally, a link to the Internet may be provided.

The configuration of Figure 8.2a is an attractive one. It integrates all of the customer's voice and data traffic onto a single external line, which simplifies network management and configuration. One drawback is its relative lack of flexibility. The capacity on the synchronous TDM line is divided into fixed partitions allocated to the various elements at the customer site, such as PBX, LAN, and terminal controller. This makes it difficult, if not impossible, to dynamically allocate capacity as needed.

With the advent of faster and faster public switched networks, a more flexible solution is now possible, an example of which is shown in Figure 8.2b. In this arrangement, the high-speed external line connects directly to a public switched network, such as frame relay, SMDS, or ATM. Although frame relay was offered initially as a data network, some recent offerings have sufficient capacity to handle voice as well, and both SMDS and ATM are well capable of handling voice traffic. Thus, it is possible to link all of the site equipment onto this single line into the switched network. Virtual connections (the equivalent of X.25 virtual circuits) can be used to set up temporary "pipes" to various destinations. In addition, most frame relay and ATM suppliers offer what are called *permanent virtual connections*; these provide the equivalent of dedicated synchronous TDM channels and can be used to set up private networks. However, the permanent virtual connections can be changed from time to time to alter capacity. For maximum

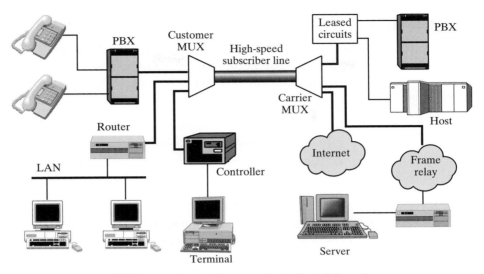

(a) Integrated network access using dedicated channels

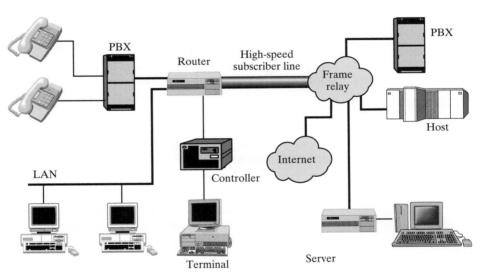

(b) Integrated network access using public switched WAN

FIGURE 8.2 Integrated Network Strategies.

flexibility, the customer can rely on *switched virtual connections* that are set up and torn down dynamically. Each time a connection is set up, the customer can configure that connection to carry a particular capacity of traffic. Thus, as the mix of traffic into and out of the site changes, the customer can dynamically change the capacity mix to provide optimum performance.

8.2 FRAME RELAY

The traditional approach to packet switching makes use of X.25, which not only determines the user–network interface but also influences the internal design of the network. There are several key features of the X.25 approach:

- Call control packets, used for setting up and clearing virtual circuits, are carried on the same channel and the same virtual circuit as data packets. In effect, inband signaling is used.
- Multiplexing of virtual circuits takes place at layer 3.
- Both layer 2 and layer 3 include flow control and error control mechanisms.

This approach results in considerable overhead. Figure 8.3a indicates the flow of data across a packet-switching network through just three nodes between source and destination.[1] Data are taken from the source device and stored to make retransmission possible. The data are organized as a sequence of blocks. For each block, an X.25 header is added to form a packet. Then, routing calculations are made. Finally, the packet is enclosed in a LAPB frame by adding a LAPB header and trailer. The frame is then transmitted over a data link to the next packet-switching node. The node performs flow- and error-control functions at the data link layer, which involves sending an acknowledgment back across the link and may require retransmission. Then the node removes the data link layer fields to examine the packet header for routing purposes. This entire process is repeated at each hop across the network.

All of this overhead may be justified when there is a significant probability of error on any of the links in the network. But this approach is not appropriate for modern digital communication facilities. Today's networks employ reliable digital transmission technology over high-quality, reliable transmission links, many of which are optical fiber. In addition, with the use of optical fiber and digital transmission, high data rates can be achieved. In this environment, the overhead of X.25 is not only unnecessary but degrades the effective utilization of the available high data rates.

Frame relay is designed to eliminate much of the overhead that X.25 imposes on end-user systems and on the packet-switching network. The key differences between frame relay and a conventional X.25 packet-switching service are:

Frame Relay
A streamlined form of packet switching. Many of the basic functions have been eliminated to provide for greater throughput.

- Call control signaling is carried on a separate logical connection from user data. Thus, intermediate nodes need not maintain state tables or process messages relating to call control on an individual per-connection basis.
- Multiplexing and switching of logical connections takes place at layer 2 instead of layer 3, eliminating one entire layer of processing.

[1] To simplify the picture, the processing between each end system and the packet-switching node to which it is attached is ignored.

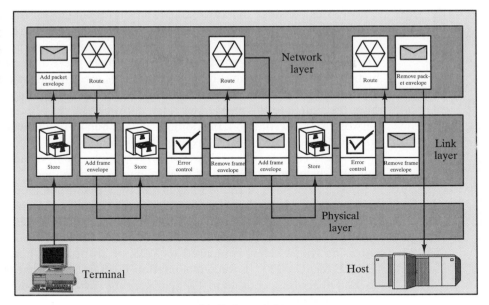

(a) Packet switching

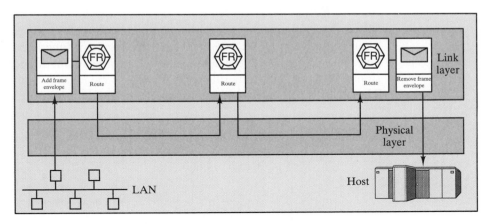

(b) Frame relay

FIGURE 8.3 Packet Switching and Frame Relay Operation.

- There is no hop-by-hop flow control and error control. End-to-end flow control and error control are the responsibility of a higher layer, if employed at all.

Figure 8.3b indicates the operation of frame relay, in which a single user data frame is sent from source to destination through three frame relay nodes. This frame contains the addressing information necessary to route the data through the frame relay network. No flow or error control is performed between frame relay nodes.

Let us consider the advantages and disadvantages of this approach. The principal potential disadvantage of frame relay, compared to X.25, is that we have lost the ability to do link-by-link flow and error control. (Although frame relay does not provide end-to-end flow and error control, these are easily provided at a higher layer.) In X.25, multiple virtual circuits are carried on a single physical link, and LAPB is available at the link level for providing reliable transmission from the source to the packet-switching network and from the packet-switching network to the destination. In addition, at each hop through the network, the link control protocol can be used for reliability. With the use of frame relay, this hop-by-hop link control is lost. However, with the increasing reliability of transmission and switching facilities, this is not a major disadvantage.

The advantage of frame relay is that we have streamlined the communications process. The protocol functionality required at the user–network interface is reduced, as is the internal network processing. As a result, lower delay and higher throughput can be expected. Studies indicate an improvement in throughput using frame relay, compared to X.25, of an order of magnitude or more [HARB92]. The ITU-T Recommendation I.233 indicates that frame relay is to be used at access speeds up to 2 Mbps. Recently, however, frame relay service at even higher data rates has become available.

Frame Relay Architecture

Figure 8.4 compares the protocol makeup of frame relay with that of X.25. As we discussed in Chapter 7, X.25 involves three layers of functionality. The physical layer is concerned with the details of the transmission medium and the transmission of bits at a given data rate using a particular signal encoding (e.g., EIA-232). The LAPB protocol provides a reliable data link control protocol across a link.

FIGURE 8.4 Comparison of X.25 and Frame Relay Protocol Stacks.

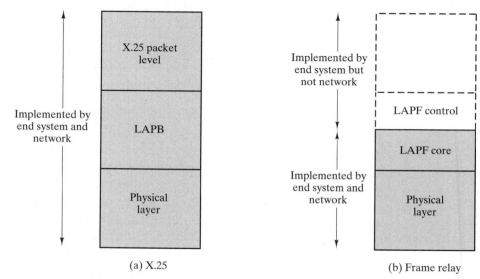

(a) X.25

(b) Frame relay

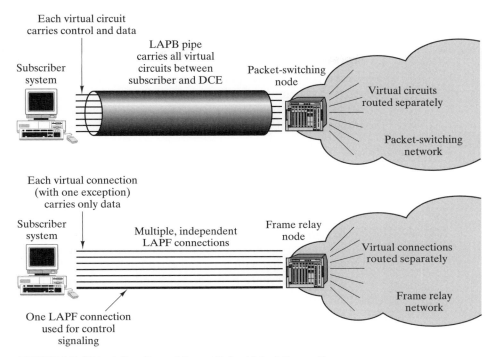

FIGURE 8.5 Virtual Circuits and Frame Relay Virtual Connections.

The packet level is used to define virtual circuits. The relationship between LAPB and the packet level is illustrated in Figure 8.5a. Between the subscriber device (DTE) and the packet-switching node to which it is attached (DCE), a LAPB protocol is used to assure reliable transfer of frames. Each frame contains a packet that includes a virtual-circuit number in its header (see Figure 7.15). Thus, a number of different virtual circuits can be supported through the LAPB "pipe." As Figure 8.5a shows, these virtual circuits can have different routes through the network going to different destinations. Thus, a subscriber can maintain a number of virtual circuits to other subscribers on the network.

In contrast, frame relay involves the physical layer and a data link control protocol known as LAPF. In fact, two versions of LAPF are defined. All frame relay networks involve implementation of the *LAPF core* protocol on all subscriber systems and on all frame relay nodes. LAPF core provides a minimal set of data link control functions, consisting of the following:

- Frame delimiting, alignment, and transparency
- Frame multiplexing/demultiplexing using the address field
- Inspection of the frame to ensure that it consists of an integer number of octets prior to zero-bit insertion or following zero-bit extraction
- Inspection of the frame to ensure that it is neither too long or too short
- Detection of transmission errors

- Congestion control functions

Above this, the user may choose to select additional data link or network-layer end-to-end functions. One possibility is known as the *LAPF control* protocol. LAPF control is not part of the frame relay service but may be implemented only in end systems to provide flow and error control.

The frame relay service using LAPF core has the following properties for the transmission of data:

- Preservation of the order of frame transfer from one edge of the network to the other
- A small probability of frame loss

As with X.25, frame relay involves the use of logical connections, in this case called *virtual connections* rather than virtual circuits. Figure 8.5b emphasizes that the frames transmitted over these virtual connections are not protected by a data link control pipe with flow and error control.

Another difference between X.25 and frame relay is that the latter devotes a separate virtual connection to call control. The setting up and tearing down of virtual connections is done over this permanent control-oriented virtual connection. This is the same principle as the common-channel signaling technique described for ISDN.

The frame relay architecture significantly reduces the amount of work required of the network. User data are transmitted in frames with virtually no processing by the intermediate network nodes other than to check for errors and to route based on connection number. A frame in error is simply discarded, leaving error recovery to higher layers.

User Data Transfer

The operation of frame relay for user data transfer is best explained by beginning with the frame format, illustrated in Figure 8.6. The format is similar to that of other data link control protocols, such as HDLC and LAPB, with one omission: There is no control field. In traditional data link control protocols, the control field is used for the following functions:

- Part of the control field identifies the frame type. In addition to a frame for carrying user data, there are various control frames. These carry no user data but are used for various protocol control functions, such as setting up and tearing down logical connections.
- The control field for user data frames includes send and receive sequence numbers. The send sequence number is used to number each transmitted frame sequentially. The receive sequence number is used to provide a positive or negative acknowledgment to incoming frames. The use of sequence numbers allows the receiver to control the rate of incoming frames (flow control) and to report missing or damaged frames, which can then be retransmitted (error control).

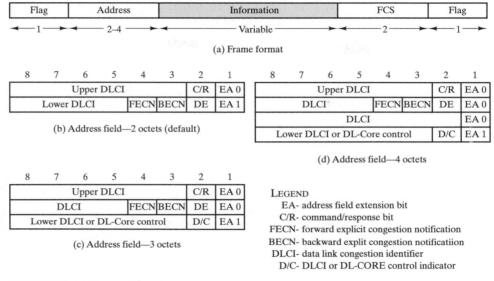

FIGURE 8.6 LAPF-core Formats.

The lack of a control field in the frame relay format means that the process of setting up and tearing down connections must be carried out on a separate channel at a higher layer of software. It also means that it is not possible to perform flow control and error control.

The flag and frame check sequence (FCS) fields function as in HDLC. The flag field is a unique pattern that delimits the start and end of the frame. The FCS field is used for error detection. On transmission, the FCS checksum is calculated and stored in the FCS field. On reception, the checksum is again calculated and compared to the value stored in the incoming FCS field. If there is a mismatch, the frame is assumed to be in error and is discarded.

The information field carries higher-layer data. The higher-layer data may be either user data or call control messages, as explained below.

The address field has a default length of 2 octets and may be extended to 3 or 4 octets. It carries a data link connection identifier (DLCI) of 10, 17, or 24 bits. The DLCI serves the same function as the virtual circuit number in X.25: It allows multiple logical frame relay connections to be multiplexed over a single channel.

The length of the address field, and hence of the DLCI, is determined by the address field extension (EA) bits. The C/R bit is application-specific and not used by the standard frame relay protocol. The remaining bits in the address field have to do with congestion control and are explained below.

Frame Relay Call Control

The actual details of the call control procedure for frame relay depend on the context of its use. The standards that have been developed assume the use of frame relay over ISDN. When frame relay is used over a point-to-point link between a pair of bridges or routers, a simpler protocol may suffice. Here we summarize the essential elements of frame relay call control.

As with X.25, frame relay supports multiple connections over a single link. In the case of frame relay, these are called data link connections, and each has a unique data link connection identifier (DLCI). Data transfer involves the following stages:

1. Establish a logical connection between two endpoints, and assign a unique DLCI to the connection.
2. Exchange information in data frames. Each frame includes a DLCI field to identify the connection.
3. Release the logical connection.

The establishment and release of a logical connection is accomplished by the exchange of messages over a connection dedicated to call control, with DLCI = 0. A frame with DLCI = 0 contains a call control message in the information field. At a minimum, four message types are needed: SETUP, CONNECT, RELEASE, and RELEASE COMPLETE.

Either side may request the establishment of a logical connection by sending a SETUP message. The other side, upon receiving the SETUP message, must reply with a CONNECT message if it accepts the connection; otherwise, it responds with a RELEASE COMPLETE message. The side sending the SETUP message may assign the DLCI by choosing an unused value and including this value in the SETUP message. Otherwise, the DLCI value is assigned by the accepting side in the CONNECT message.

Either side may request to clear a logical connection by sending a RELEASE message. The other side, upon receipt of this message, must respond with a RELEASE COMPLETE message.

Congestion Control

Congestion control for a frame relay network is challenging because of the limited tools available to the frame handlers. The frame relay protocol has been streamlined to maximize throughput and efficiency. A consequence of this is that a frame handler cannot control the flow of frames coming from a subscriber or an adjacent node using the typical flow control mechanism of other data link control protocols.

Congestion control is the joint responsibility of the network and the end users. The network (i.e., the collection of frame-handling nodes) is in the best position to monitor the degree of congestion, while the end users are in the best position to control congestion by limiting the flow of traffic. With the above in mind, two general congestion control strategies are supported in frame relay: congestion avoidance and congestion recovery.

Congestion avoidance procedures are used at the onset of congestion to minimize the effect on the network. At a point at which the network detects a buildup of queue lengths and the danger of congestion, there would be little evidence available to end users that congestion is increasing. Thus, there must be some *explicit signaling* mechanism from the network that will trigger the congestion avoidance.

Congestion recovery procedures are used to prevent network collapse in the face of severe congestion. These procedures are typically initiated when the network has begun to drop frames due to congestion. Such dropped frames will be reported by some higher layer of software and serve as an *implicit signaling* mechanism.

For explicit signaling, two bits in the address field of each frame are provided. Either bit may be set by the frame handler that detects congestion. If a frame handler forwards a frame in which one or both of these bits are set, it must not clear the bits. Thus, the bits constitute signals from the network to the end user. The two bits are:

- *Backward explicit congestion notification (BECN):* notifies the user that congestion avoidance procedures should be initiated where applicable for traffic in the direction opposite to the received frame. It indicates that the frames that the user transmits on this logical connection may encounter congested resources.

- *Forward explicit congestion notification (FECN):* notifies the user that congestion avoidance procedures should be initiated where applicable for traffic in the same direction as the received frame. It indicates that this frame, on this logical connection, has encountered congested resources.

Implicit signaling occurs when the network discards a frame, and this fact is detected by the end user at a higher layer. The network role, of course, is to discard frames as necessary. One bit in the address field of each frame can be used to provide guidance:

- *Discard eligibility (DE):* Indicates a request that a frame should be discarded in preference to other frames in which this bit is not set, when it is necessary to discard frames.

The DE capability makes it possible for the user temporarily to send more frames than it is allowed to on average. In this case, the user sets the DE bit on the excess frames. The network will forward these frames if it has the capacity to do so. The DE bit also can be set by a frame handler. The network can monitor the influx of frames from the user and use the DE bit to protect the network with flexible "firewalls." That is, if the frame handler to which the user is directly connected decides that the input is potentially excessive, it sets the DE bit on each frame and then forwards it farther into the network.

The DE bit can be used in such a way as to provide guidance for the discard decision and at the same time as a tool for providing a guaranteed level of service. This tool can be used on a per logical connection basis to ensure that heavy users can get the throughput they need without penalizing lighter users. The mechanism works as follows: each user can negotiate a **committed information rate (CIR)** (in bits per second) at connection setup time. The requested CIR

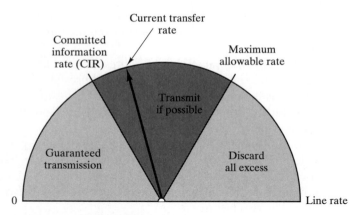

FIGURE 8.7 Operation of the CIR.

represents the user's estimate of its "normal" traffic during a busy period; the granted CIR, which is less than or equal to the requested CIR, is the network's commitment to deliver data at that rate in the absence of errors. The frame handler to which the user's station attaches then performs a metering function (Figure 8.7). If the user is sending data at less than the CIR, the incoming frame handler does not alter the DE bit. If the rate exceeds the CIR, the incoming frame handler will set the DE bit on the excess frames and then forward them; such frames may get through or may be discarded if congestion is encountered. Finally, a maximum rate is defined, such that any frames above the maximum are discarded at the entry frame handler.

8.3 ASYNCHRONOUS TRANSFER MODE

As the speed and number of local-area networks (LANs) continue their relentless growth, increasing demand is placed on wide-area packet-switching networks to support the tremendous throughput generated by these LANs. In the early days of wide-area networking, X.25 was designed to support direct connection of terminals and computers over long distances. At speeds up to 64 kbps or so, X.25 copes well with these demands. As LANs have come to play an increasing role in the local environment, X.25, with its substantial overhead, is being recognized as an inadequate tool for wide-area networking. This has led to increasing interest in frame relay, which is designed to support access speeds up to 2 Mbps. But now, even the streamlined design of frame relay is faltering in the face of a requirement for wide-area access speeds in the tens and hundreds of megabits per second. To accommodate these gargantuan requirements, a new technology has emerged: **asynchronous transfer mode (ATM)**, also known as **cell relay**.

Cell relay is perhaps the most important technical innovation to come out of the standardization work on broadband ISDN (B-ISDN). Cell relay is similar in concept to frame relay. Both frame relay and cell relay take advantage of the reliability and fidelity of modern digital facilities to provide faster packet switching than X.25. Cell relay is even more streamlined than frame relay in its functional-

Asynchronous Transfer Mode (ATM)
A form of packet switching in which fixed-size cells of 53 octets are used.

Cell Relay
Another term for asynchronous transfer mode.

ity and can support data rates several orders of magnitude greater than frame relay.

In addition to their technical similarities, cell relay and frame relay have similar histories. Frame relay was developed as part of the work of ISDN but is now finding wide application in private networks and other non-ISDN applications, particularly in bridges and routers. Cell relay was developed as part of the work on broadband ISDN but is beginning to find application in non-B-ISDN environments, in which very high data rates are required.

Virtual Channels and Virtual Paths

ATM is a packet-oriented transfer mode. Like frame relay and X.25, it allows multiple logical connections to be multiplexed over a single physical interface. The information flow on each logical connection is organized into fixed-size packets, called **cells**. As with frame relay, there is no link-by-link error control or flow control.

Logical connections in ATM are referred to as **virtual channels**. A virtual channel is analogous to a virtual circuit in X.25 or a frame relay virtual connection. It is the basic unit of switching in an ATM network. A virtual channel is set up between two end users through the network and a variable-rate, full-duplex flow of fixed-size cells is exchanged over the connection. Virtual channels are also used for user–network exchange (control signaling) and network–network exchange (network management and routing).

For ATM, a second sublayer of processing has been introduced that deals with the concept of **virtual path** (Figure 8.8). A virtual path is a bundle of virtual channels that have the same endpoints. Thus, all of the cells flowing over all of the virtual channels in a single virtual path are switched together.

Several advantages can be listed for the use of virtual paths:

- *Simplified network architecture.* Network transport functions can be separated into those related to an individual logical connection (virtual channel) and those related to a group of logical connections (virtual path).
- *Increased network performance and reliability.* The network deals with fewer, aggregated entities.
- *Reduced processing and short connection setup time.* Much of the work is done when the virtual path is set up. The addition of new virtual channels to an existing virtual path involves minimal processing.

FIGURE 8.8 ATM Connection Relationships.

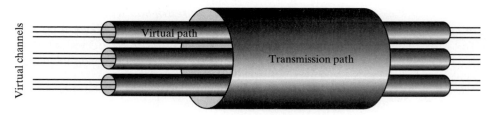

- *Enhanced network services.* The virtual path is used internal to the network but is also visible to the end user. Thus, the user may define closed user groups or closed networks of virtual-channel bundles.

Virtual-Path and Virtual-Channel Characteristics   ITU-T Recommendation I.150 lists the following as characteristics of virtual-channel connections:

- *Quality of service.* A user of a virtual channel is provided with a quality of service specified by parameters such as cell loss ratio (ratio of cells lost to cells transmitted) and cell delay variation.
- *Switched and semipermanent virtual-channel connections.* Both switched connections, which require call-control signaling, and dedicated channels can be provided.
- *Cell sequence integrity.* The sequence of transmitted cells within a virtual channel is preserved.
- *Traffic parameter negotiation and usage monitoring.* Traffic parameters can be negotiated between a user and the network for each virtual channel. The input of cells to the virtual channel is monitored by the network to ensure that the negotiated parameters are not violated.

The types of traffic parameters that can be negotiated include average rate, peak rate, burstiness, and peak duration. The network may need a number of strategies to deal with congestion and to manage existing and requested virtual channels. At the crudest level, the network may simply deny new requests for virtual channels to prevent congestion. Additionally, cells may be discarded if negotiated parameters are violated or if congestion becomes severe. In an extreme situation, existing connections might be terminated.

I.150 also lists characteristics of virtual paths. The first four characteristics listed are identical to those for virtual channels. That is, quality of service, switched and semipermanent virtual paths, cell sequence integrity, and traffic parameter negotiation and usage monitoring are all also characteristics of a virtual path. There are a number of reasons for this duplication. First, this provides some flexibility in how the network manages the requirements placed upon it. Second, the network must be concerned with the overall requirements for a virtual path, and within a virtual path, may negotiate the establishment of virtual circuits with given characteristics. Finally, once a virtual path is set up, it is possible for the end users to negotiate the creation of new virtual channels. The virtual-path characteristics impose a discipline on the choices that the end users may make.

In addition, a fifth characteristic is listed for virtual paths:

- *Virtual-channel identifier restriction within a virtual path.* One or more virtual-channel identifiers, or numbers, may not be available to the user of the virtual path, but may be reserved for network use. Examples would be virtual channels used for network management.

Control Signaling   In narrowband ISDN, the D channel is provided for control signaling of calls on B and H channels. In B-ISDN, with its ATM interface, there is no simple fixed-rate structure of H, B, and D channels. Thus, a more flexible arrangement for control signaling is needed. The requirement is further complicated by the need for the establishment and release of two types of entities: virtual channels and virtual paths.

For virtual channels, I.150 specifies four methods for providing an establishment/release facility. One or a combination of these methods will be used in any particular network:

1. *Semipermanent virtual channels* may be used for user-to-user exchange. In this case, no control signaling is required.

2. If there is no preestablished call control signaling channel, one must be set up. For that purpose, a control signaling exchange must take place between the user and the network on some channel. Hence we need a permanent channel, probably of low data rate, that can be used to set up virtual channel that can be used for call control. Such a channel is called a *meta-signaling channel,* because the channel is used to set up signaling channels.

3. The meta-signaling channel can be used to set up a virtual channel between the user and the network for call control signaling. This *user-to-network signaling virtual channel* can than be used to set up virtual channels to carry user data.

4. The meta-signaling channel can also be used to set up a *user-to-user signaling virtual channel.* Such a channel must be set up within a preestablished virtual path. It can then be used to allow the two end users, without network intervention, to establish and release user-to-user virtual channels to carry user data.

For virtual paths, three methods are defined in I.150:

1. A virtual path can be established on a *semipermanent* basis by prior agreement. In this case, no control signaling is required.

2. Virtual path establishment/release may be *customer controlled.* In this case the customer uses a signaling virtual channel to request the virtual path from the network.

3. Virtual path establishment/release may be *network controlled.* In this case the network establishes a virtual path for its own convenience. The path may be network-to-network, user-to-network, or user-to-user.

ATM Cells

The asynchronous transfer mode makes use of fixed-size cells, consisting of a 5-octet header and a 48-octet information field. There are several advantages to the use of small, fixed-size cells. First, the use of small cells may reduce queuing delay for a high-priority cell, because it waits less if it arrives slightly behind a lower-priority cell that has gained access to a resource (e.g., the transmitter). Second, it appears that fixed-size cells can be switched more efficiently, which is important for the very high data rates of ATM.

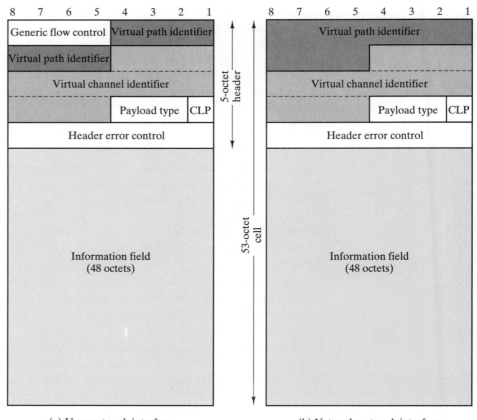

(a) User-network interface   (b) Network-network interface

FIGURE 8.9 ATM Cell Format.

Figure 8.9a shows the header format at the user–network interface, and Figure 8.9b shows the cell header format internal to the network. Internal to the network, the generic flow control field, which performs end-to-end functions, is not retained. Instead, the virtual-path identifier field is expanded from 8 to 12 bits. This allows support for an expanded number of VPCs internal to the network, to include those supporting subscribers and those required for network management.

Multiple terminals may share a single access link to the network. The *generic flow control field* is to be used for end-to-end flow control. The details of its application are for further study. The field could be used to assist the customer in controlling the flow of traffic for different qualities of service. One candidate for the use of this field is a multiple-priority-level indicator to control the flow of information in a service-dependent manner.

The virtual-path identifier and virtual-channel identifier fields constitute a routing field for the network. The *virtual-path identifier* indicates a user-to-user

TABLE 8-2 Payload Type Field Coding

PT Coding	Interpretation[a]
0 0 0	User data cell, AAU = 0, congestion not experienced
0 0 1	User data cell, AAU = 1, congestion not experienced
0 1 0	User data cell, AAU = 0, congestion experienced
0 1 1	User data cell, AAU = 1, congestion experienced
1 0 0	OAM segment associated cell
1 0 1	OAM end-to-end associated cell
1 1 0	Resource management cell
1 1 1	Reserved for future function

[a] *AAU, ATM user-to-ATM user indication; OAM, Operations, administration, and maintenance.*

or user-to-network virtual path. The *virtual-channel identifier* indicates a user-to-user or user-to-network virtual channel.

The *payload type* field indicates the type of information in the information field. Table 8-2 shows the interpretation of the PT bits. A value of 0 in the first bit indicates user information, that is, information from the next-higher layer. In this case, the second bit indicates whether congestion has been experienced; the third bit, known as the ATM-user-to-ATM-user (AAU) indication bit, is a one-bit field that can be used to convey information between end users. A value of 1 in the first bit indicates that this cell carries network management or maintenance information. This indication allows insertion of network-management cells into a user's virtual channel without affecting user's data. Thus, it can provide in-band control information.

The *cell loss priority* is used to provide guidance to the network in the event of congestion. A value of 0 indicates a cell of relatively higher priority, which should not be discarded unless no other alternative is available. A value of 1 indicates that this cell is subject to discard within the network. The user might employ this field so that extra information may be inserted into the network, with a CLP of 1, and delivered to the destination if the network is not congested. The network sets this field to 1 for any data cell that is in violation of a traffic agreement between the user and the network. In this case, the switch that does the setting realizes that the cell exceeds the agreed traffic parameters but that the switch is capable of handling the cell. At a later point in the network, if congestion is encountered, this cell has been marked for discard in preference to cells that fall within agreed traffic limits.

The *header error control (HEC)* field is an 8-bit error code that can be used to correct single-bit errors in the header and to detect double-bit errors. In the case of most existing protocols, such as LAPD and LAPB, the data field that serve as input to the error code calculation is in general much longer than the size of the resulting error code. This allows for error detection. In the case of ATM, the input to the calculation is only 32 bits, compared to 8 bits for the code. The fact that the input is relatively short allows the code to be used not only for error detection but, in some cases, for actual error correction. This is because there is sufficient redundancy in the code to recover from certain error patterns.

The error protection function provides both recovery from single-bit header errors, and a low probability of the delivery of cells with errored headers under bursty error conditions. The error characteristics of fiber-based transmission systems appear to be a mix of single-bit errors and relatively large burst errors. For some transmission systems, the error correction capability, which is more time consuming, might not be invoked.

ATM Traffic and Congestion Control

Congestion control techniques are vital to the successful operation of ATM-based networks. Without such techniques, traffic from user nodes can exceed the capacity of the network, causing memory buffers of ATM switches to overflow, leading to data losses.

ATM networks present difficulties in effectively controlling congestion that are not found in other types of networks, including frame relay networks. The high data rates and switching speeds mean that significant chunks of information can easily be lost. Furthermore, for data traffic, the loss of even one cell can require the retransmission of thousands of cells. The complexity of the problem is compounded by the limited number of overhead bits available for exerting control over the flow of user cells. This area is currently the subject of intense research, and no consensus has emerged for a full-blown traffic and congestion control strategy. Accordingly, ITU-T has defined a restricted initial set of traffic and congestion control capabilities aiming at simple mechanisms and realistic network efficiency; these are specified in I.371. The ATM Forum has published a somewhat more advanced version of this set in the ATM user–network interface (UNI), Traffic Specification 4.0.

A variety of congestion control techniques are used for ATM, based on the type of traffic being carried over particular virtual channels and virtual paths. Congestion control is tailored to provide desired characteristics to the throughput of the traffic. The user and the network negotiate the traffic characteristics of each connection and then the network does its best to support the agreed-on characteristics.

Four classes of service for ATM traffic have been defined (Figure 8.10):

FIGURE 8.10 ATM Bit Rate Services.

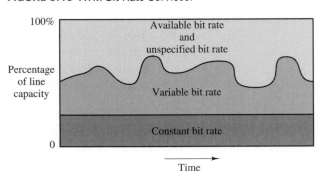

- *Constant bit rate (CBR):* requires that a fixed data rate be made available by the ATM provider. The network must ensure that this capacity is available and also polices the incoming traffic on a CBR connection to ensure that the subscribe does not exceed its allocation.

- *Variable bit rate (VBR):* offers somewhat more flexibility. Rather than a single rate, a VBR connection is defined in terms of a sustained rate for normal use and a faster burst rate for occasional use at peak periods. The faster rate is guaranteed, but it is understood that the user will not continuously require this faster rate.

- *Available bit rate (ABR):* provides the user with a guaranteed minimum capacity. When additional capacity is available, the user may burst above the minimum rate without risk of cell loss.

- *Unspecified bit rate (UBR):* a best-effort service. No amount of capacity is guaranteed, and any cells may be discarded.

CBR provides a service similar to a leased line of a dial-up switched circuit. A constant bit rate is maintained. VBR is useful for applications that run at an uneven rate but that require a given capacity on demand. An example is a voice connection or video teleconference in which there may be idle periods but in which a given data rate is needed to keep up with the flow of information at other times.

ABR and UBR support LAN internetworking and other types of data traffic. Typically, data traffic is much burstier than voice or video traffic. A constant or nearly constant delivery rate is not required. For the user, the concern is one of throughput, while for the network the concern is that bursts of traffic from many users at the same time could overwhelm switches, causing cells to be dropped. ABR is intended for applications in which delay is a concern, such as on-line sessions between a user and a server. UBR is directed at delay-tolerant applications, such as file transfer and electronic mail.

The main practical difference between ABR and UBR is that in the case of ABR, the network will provide congestion information to the user, enabling the user to reduce or increase sending rate to achieve high efficiency. No such feedback is provided for UBR, which increases the risk of discarded cells and therefore the amount of traffic that must be retransmitted.

The high speed, efficiency, and flexible traffic control of ATM make it attractive as a universal networking technology that can support all types of traffic. Figure 8.11 illustrates this universal nature, indicating the types of customer requirements that can be met with an ATM network. Typically, a public ATM network provider will maintain a core network of high-performance ATM switches interconnected with high-capacity trunks such as SONET. The network provider, or perhaps a third party, will also provide smaller ATM switches at the edge of the network, some of which provide conversion from other protocols and traffic types. The customer can connect voice and data equipment, including PBXs and LANs, as well as older systems designed to work with other technologies, such as frame relay and SMDS.

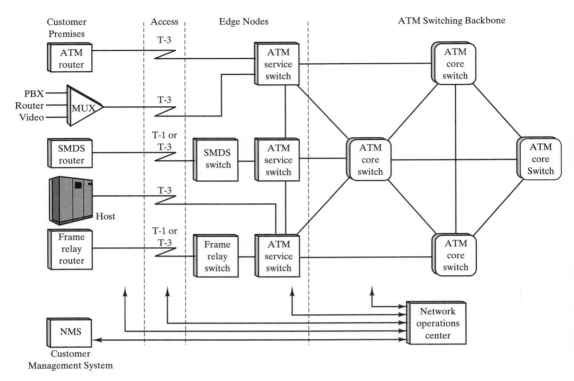

FIGURE 8.11 Public ATM Network [FELT94].

8.4 SWITCHED MULTIMEGABIT DATA SERVICE

Switched Multimegabit Data Service (SMDS)
A high-speed data transmission service offered by telecommunications carriers.

Switched multimegabit data service (SMDS) is a high-speed switched data service developed by Bellcore on behalf of the seven regional Bell operating companies (RBOCs). It was first introduced in late 1991 and is now widely available in the United States. It is also offered now by a number of public carriers in other countries.

As with frame relay and ATM, SMDS defines a service at the user–network interface. Unlike frame relay and ATM, which are connection-oriented services, SMDS is a connectionless, or datagram, type of service. It shares with frame relay and ATM an emphasis on streamlined processing to achieve high data rates.

The current specification for SMDS provides for user access at DS1 (1.544 Mbps) and DS3 (45 Mbps). As with other public switched services, access to the network is by means of a dedicated line. Internally, SMDS packets are switched from source to destination through one or more SMDS switches. These switches are connected by high-speed trunks, such as DSI or SONET transmission systems.

Customer equipment, such as a file server, a mainframe, or a gateway on a LAN, connects to a digital terminal (DT) device using a standardized subscriber–network interface (SNI). The DT links the customer site to the carrier's

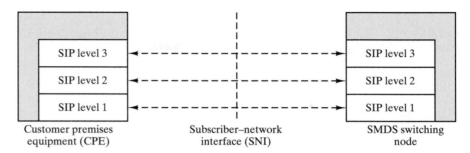

FIGURE 8.12 SMDS Interface Protocol (SIP) Architecture.

central office that serves this customer. The SMDS switch does not have to be located in the central office that is closest to the customer site. Instead, the nearest central office can act as a "serving" office, connecting the customer site to an SMDS switch at another central office. This helps to minimize the cost of the service, because SMDS switches can be placed at the points of greatest traffic and still be available to users in other areas.

The SMDS architecture consists of multiple protocol layers (Figure 8.12) and is based on the protocol architecture of the IEEE 802.6 metropolitan-area network (MAN) standard. However, SMDS is not just a MAN service. It is a full-fledged WAN service capable of covering arbitrarily large areas. Whereas the IEEE 802.6 defines a specific physical layer, consisting of a shared-access optical fiber bus, SMDS simply uses the IEEE 802.6 protocols to define the interface to the user and supports this interface internally with a switched network.

The highest layer (SIP-3) defines a data unit (datagram) of variable length up to 9188 octets. Thus, SMDS can encapsulate entire packets from most LANs. Each data unit contains a source and a destination address. The next-lower layer of the interface (SIP-2) breaks each data unit up into fixed 53-octet cells, the same size used in ATM. Because ATM is intended to be the transport mechanism for broadband ISDN, Bellcore sees SMDS as providing a service that eases transition to B-ISDN when it arrives. Because both B-ISDN and SMDS are based on the use of a 53-octet cell, this transition strategy is promising.

The SMDS specification includes several features that network managers should find appealing. An address screening capability can be used to restrict communication to a group of addresses. This allows the user to construct a logical private network over a public SMDS network. SMDS also provides network management information directly to the end user, including usage statistics.

8.5 BROADBAND ISDN

The planning for ISDN began as far back as 1976 and only in recent years has moved from the planning stage to prototypes and actual implementations. It will be a number of years before the full spectrum of ISDN services is widely available, and there will continue to be refinements and improvements to ISDN services and network facilities. However, most of the planning and design effort is

Broadband ISDN (B-ISDN)
A second-generation set of standards for ISDN. BISDN is characterized by the use of asynchronous transfer mode.

now directed toward a network concept that is far more revolutionary than ISDN itself. This new concept has been referred to as **broadband ISDN (B-ISDN)**.

In one of its first working documents on B-ISDN, ITU-T modestly defines B-ISDN as "a service requiring transmission channels capable of supporting rates greater than the primary rate." Behind this innocuous statement lie plans for a network and set of services that will have far more impact on business and residential customers than ISDN. With B-ISDN, services, especially video services, requiring data rates orders of magnitudes beyond those that can be delivered by ISDN will become available. To contrast this new network and these new services to the original concept of ISDN, that original concept is now being referred to as **narrowband ISDN**.

B-ISDN is designed to exploit the advances in technology discussed in Section 8.1. B-ISDN will achieve the integration of a wide range of communications facilities and the support of, in effect, universal communications with the following key characteristics:

- Worldwide exchange between any two subscribers in any medium or combination of media.
- Retrieval and sharing of massive amounts of information from multiple sources, in multiple media, among people in a shared electronic environment.
- Distribution, including switched distribution, of a wide variety of cultural, entertainment, and educational materials to home or office, virtually on demand.

Broadband ISDN Architecture

B-ISDN differs from narrowband ISDN in a number of ways. To meet the requirement for high-resolution video, an upper channel rate on the order of 150 Mbps is needed. To support one or more interactive services and distributive services (such as video-on-demand) simultaneously, a total subscriber line rate of about 600 Mbps is needed. In terms of today's installed telephone plant, this is a stupendous data rate to sustain. The only appropriate technology for widespread support of such data rates is optical fiber. Hence, the introduction of B-ISDN depends on the pace of introduction of fiber subscriber loops.

Functional Architecture   Figure 8.13 depicts the functional architecture of B-ISDN. As with narrowband ISDN, control of B-ISDN is based on common-channel signaling. B-ISDN must, of course, support all the 64-kbps transmission services, both circuit switching and packet switching, that are supported by narrowband ISDN. This protects the user's investment and facilitates migration from narrowband to broadband ISDN. In addition, broadband capabilities are provided for higher-data-rate transmission services. At the user–network interface, these capabilities will be provided with the connection-oriented asynchronous transfer mode (ATM) facility.

Transmission Structure   In terms of data rates available to B-ISDN subscribers, three new transmission services are defined. The first of these consists of a full-

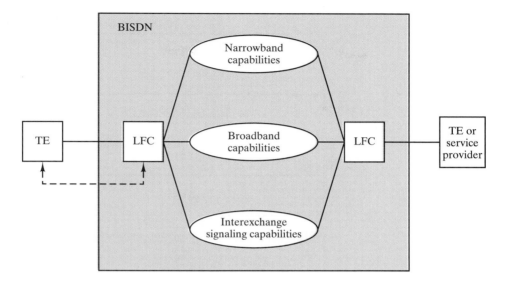

LEGEND

LFC = local function capabilities   TE = terminal equipment

FIGURE 8.13 B-ISDN Architecture.

duplex 155.52-Mbps service. The second service is asymmetrical, providing transmission from the subscriber to the network at 155.52 Mbps, and in the other direction at 622.08 Mbps. The highest-capacity service yet defined is a full-duplex 622.08-Mbps service.

A data rate of 155.52 Mbps can certainly support all the narrowband ISDN services. That is, it readily supports one or more basic or primary rate interfaces. In addition, it can support most of the B-ISDN services. At that rate, one or several video channels can be supported, depending on the video resolution and the coding technique used. Thus, the full-duplex 155.52-Mbps service will probably be the most common B-ISDN service.

The higher data rate of 622.08 Mbps is needed to handle multiple video distribution, such as might be required when a business conducts multiple simultaneous videoconferences. This data rate makes sense in the network-to-subscriber direction. The typical subscriber will not initiate distribution services and thus would still be able to use the lower, 155.52-Mbps, service. The full-duplex 622.08-Mbps service would be appropriate for a video distribution provider.

Broadband ISDN Protocols

The protocol architecture for B-ISDN introduces some new elements not found in the ISDN architecture, as depicted in Figure 8.14. For B-ISDN it is assumed that the transfer of information across the user–network interface will use asynchronous transfer mode (ATM).

The decision to use ATM for B-ISDN is a remarkable one. This implies that B-ISDN will be a packet-based network, certainly at the interface and almost

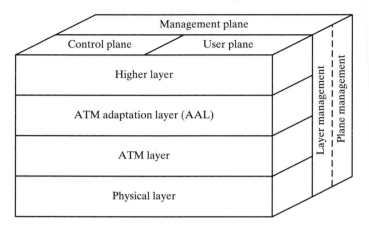

FIGURE 8.14 B-ISDN Protocol Reference Model.

certainly in terms of its internal switching. Although the recommendation also states that B-ISDN will support circuit-mode applications, this will be done over a packet-based transport mechanism. Thus, ISDN, which began as an evolution from the circuit-switching telephone network, will transform itself into a packet-switching network as it takes on broadband services.

Two layers of the B-ISDN protocol architecture relate to ATM functions. There is an ATM layer common to all services that provides packet transfer capabilities, and an ATM adaptation layer (AAL) that is service dependent. The AAL maps higher-layer information into ATM cells to be transported over B-ISDN, then collects information from ATM cells for delivery to higher layers. The use of ATM creates the need for an adaptation layer to support information transfer protocols not based on ATM. Two examples listed in I.121 are PCM voice and LAPD. PCM voice is an application that produces a stream of bits. To employ this application over ATM, it is necessary to assemble PCM bits into packets (called *cells* in the recommendation) for transmission and to read them out on reception in such a way as to produce a smooth, constant flow of bits to the receiver. For LAPD, it is necessary to map LAPD frames into ATM cells; this will probably mean segmenting one LAPD frame into a number of cells on transmission, and reassembling the frame from cells on reception. By allowing the use of LAPD over ATM, all of the existing ISDN applications and control signaling protocols can be used on B-ISDN.

The protocol reference model makes reference to three separate planes:

- *User plane:* provides for user information transfer, along with associated controls (e.g., flow control, error control).

- *Control plane:* performs call control and connection control functions.

- *Management plane:* includes plane management, which performs management functions related to a system as a whole and provides coordination between all the planes, and layer management, which performs management functions relating to resources and parameters residing in its protocol entities.

SUMMARY

A major change is occurring in the provision of wide-area telecommunications services. The increasing capacity requirements of distributed computing systems, coupled with the introduction of transmission facilities of high speed and high reliability, have led to the introduction of a variety of packet-switching services that far outstrip the capabilities of X.25 networks.

The most widely available such service is frame relay. Frame relay was developed initially as part of ISDN but is offered by a wide variety of providers for both public and private network configurations. Frame relay makes use of variable-sized packets, called frames, and a processing scheme that is considerably simpler than X.25. Data rates of up to 2 Mbps are readily achievable.

The switched multimegabit data service (SMDS) offers data rates of up to 45 Mbps and makes use of fixed-size packets called cells. The cell size for SMDS is the same as that used for ATM and B-ISDN. It is intended that SMDS will provide a transition path to ATM and B-ISDN.

Asynchronous transfer mode (ATM) is even more streamlined than frame relay and SMDS and is intended to provide capacity in the hundreds of Mbps and eventually in the Gbps range. ATM technology is finding use in a wide variety of offerings for both wide-area and local-area networking. In addition, ATM is the transmission technology used in broadband ISDN, which may be viewed as a package ATM offering that provides a variety of standardized services.

RECOMMENDED READING

A more technical and in-depth treatment of the topics in this chapter can be found in [STAL95a]. Other useful surveys of the technologies and applications covered in this chapter are [DUTT95] and [KUMA95].

DUTT95 DUTTON, H., and LENHARD, P. *High-Speed Networking Technology: An Introductory Survey.* Upper Saddle River, NJ: Prentice Hall, 1995.

KUMA95 KUMAR, B. *Broadband Communications: A Professional's Guide to ATM, Frame Relay, SMDS, SONET, and B-ISDN.* New York: McGraw-Hill, 1995.

STAL95a STALLINGS, W. *ISDN and Broadband ISDN, with Frame Relay and ATM,* 3rd ed. Upper Saddle River, NJ: Prentice Hall, 1995.

 ### *Recommended Web Sites*

- http://www.frforum.com: web site of the Frame Relay Forum, which is leading the effort to expand the functionality of frame relay networks.

- http://www.mot.com/MIMS/ISG/tech/frame-relay/resources.html: exhaustive source of information on frame relay.

- http://www.atmforum.com: web site of the ATM Forum, which is leading the effort to expand the functionality of ATM networks.

- http://www.sbexpos.com/sbexpos/associations/smds/home.html: web site of the SMDS Interest Group. Provides information on SMDS providers and interesting case studies.

- http://www.smds-ig.org/home.html
- http://www.cerf.net/smds: exhaustive source of information on SMDS, including technical reports, background information, and case studies.

KEY TERMS

Asynchronous Transfer Mode (ATM)	Committed Information Rate (CIR)	Switched Multimegabit Data Service (SMDS)
Broadband ISDN (B-ISDN)	Frame Relay	Virtual Channel
Cell Relay	Narrowband ISDN	Virtual Path

QUESTIONS

1. What are the key high-speed networking services available for wide-area networking?
2. How does frame relay differ from X.25?
3. What are the relative advantages and disadvantages of frame relay compared to X.25?
4. How is congestion control handled in a frame relay network?
5. How does ATM differ from frame relay?
6. What is the difference between a virtual channel and a virtual path?
7. What are the relative advantages and disadvantages of SMDS compared to frame relay and ATM?
8. What is broadband ISDN?

PROBLEMS

1. One key design decision for ATM was whether to use fixed- or variable-length cells. Let us consider this decision from the point of view of efficiency. We can define transmission efficiency as

$$N = \frac{\text{number of information octets}}{\text{number of information octets} + \text{number of overhead octets}}$$

   a. Consider the use of fixed-length packets. In this case the overhead consists of the header octets. Define:

   L = data field size of the cell in octets
   H = header size of the cell in octets
   X = number of information octets to be transmitted as a single message.

   Derive an expression for N. *Hint:* The expression will need to use the operator $|\cdot|$, where $|Y|$ is the the smallest integer greater than or equal to Y.

   b. If cells have variable length, overhead is determined by the header, plus the flags to delimit the cells or an additional length field in the header. Let Hv = additional overhead octets required to enable the use of variable-length cells. Derive an expression for N in terms of X, H, and Hv.

   c. Let $L = 48$, $H = 5$, and $Hv = 2$. Plot N versus message size for fixed- and variable-length cells. Comment on the results.

2. Another key design decision for ATM is the size of the data field for fixed-size cells. Let us consider this decision from the point of view of efficiency and delay.

   a. Assume that an extended transmission takes place, so that all cells are completely filled. Derive an expression for the efficiency *N* as a function of *H* and *L*.

   b. Packetization delay is the delay introduced into a transmission stream by the need to buffer bits until an entire packet is filled before transmission. Derive an expression for this delay as a function of *L* and the data rate *R* of the source.

   c. Common data rates for voice coding are 32 kbps and 64 kbps. Plot packetization delay as a function of *L* for these two data rates; use a left-hand *y* axis with a maximum value of 2 ms. On the same graph, plot transmission efficiency as a function of *L*; use a right-hand *y* axis with a maximum value of 100%. Comment on the results.

3. Consider the following applications. In each case indicate whether you would use X.25, frame relay, ATM, or SMDS facilities. Assume that the facilities are available and "competitively" priced; i.e., determine, in each case, whether the functional characteristics of the service offering matches well the requirements of the application. Explain in each case the reasons for your choice.

   a. You have a large number of locations in a metropolitan area. At each location there is a large number of real time data transactions processed. Information about the transactions must be sent independently and more or less randomly amongst the locations. That is, the transactions are not batched or do not occur in bunches. Performance requirements are such that the delay must be short. Volumes at each location are modest but in total range up to few megabits per second in total.

   b. You now have a national WAN with about a half dozen locations in relatively remote areas. The transmission facilities are varied and include radio links, satellite links, and phone links using modems. The data rates, are relatively modest.

   c. In this case, you have multimedia applications. They image communication and significant real time video and audio services. These are interspersed with a multitude of other data services. The number of locations is small, but with the image and video applications, the volume is quite large nearing gigabit per second ranges. There is also a large number of users and applications involved so that a large number of virtual circuits are needed even though the number of locations is small.

4. Consider compressed video transmission in an ATM network. Suppose standard ATM cells must be transmitted through 5 switches. The data rate is 43 Mbps.

   a. What is the transmission time for one cell through one switch?

   b. Each switch may be transmitting a cell from other traffic all of which we assume to have lower (non-preemptive for the cell) priority. If the switch is busy transmitting a cell our cell has to wait until the other cell completes transmission. If the switch is free our cell is transmitted immediately. What is the maximum time from when a typical video cell arrives at the first switch (and possibly waits) until it is finished being transmitted by the 5th and last one? Assume that you can ignore propagation time, switching time, and everything else but the transmission time and the time spent waiting for another cell to clear a switch.

   c. Now suppose we know that each switch is utilized 60% of the time with the other low priority traffic. By this we mean that with probability .6 when we look at a switch it is busy. Suppose that if there is a cell being transmitted by a switch, the average delay spent waiting for a cell to finish transmission is ??? a cell transmission time. What is the average time from the input of the first switch to clearing the fifth.

   d. However, the measure of most interest is not delay but jitter which is the variability in the delay. Use parts b) and c) calculate the maximum and average variability, respectively, in the delay.

In all cases assume that the various random events are independent of one another; for example, we ignore the burstiness typical of such traffic.

FLORIDA POWER AND LIGHT

Since 1990, Florida Power and Light (FPL) has relied on 767-mile SONET network to handle the bulk of its voice communications traffic. The network snakes north from Miami along both Florida coasts. Although this network has reduced communications cost over the company's previous leased-line arrangements, it has not helped to deal with burgeoning data communications costs. To further gain a grip on costs, FPL plans to build an ATM switching network on top of the SONET infrastructure, to handle voice and data traffic [BRUN96].

Figure 8.15 shows the layout of the SONET network and the planned ATM overlay. As a first step, an additional SONET link is to be installed between Daytona and Sarasota, creating a closed ring. This will provide improved connectivity and greater efficiency in the ATM traffic. ATM will also extend essential network services to sites that the SONET ring does not reach. For example, the ATM network will be used to carry supervisory control and data acquisition traffic and power station telemetry data—the type of information that lets engineers monitor power demand and deliver extra capacity to hot spots. Such data are critical to FPS's power delivery business unit, which operates out of a site in the Miami area not served by the SONET ring. To bring such spur sites into the SONET ring would involve millions of dollars in investment in new SONET optical lines. ATM can provide the connectivity by leasing T-1 and T-3 lines at far less cost.

FIGURE 8.15 Florida Power and Light's Network Plan.

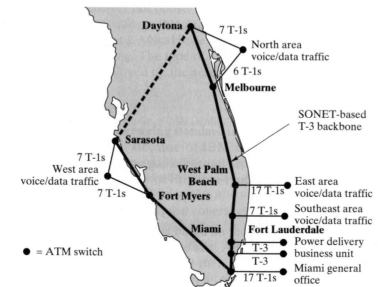

FPL plans for a relatively rapid rollover to the new ATM network. During the summer of 1996, FPL telecommunications personnel conducted site analysis to develop final estimates for traffic capacity. The plan calls for switch installation in the fall, then a one-month period to monitor a limited-traffic experiment, followed by complete cutover to the ATM network. This quick pace should minimize operational disruption. But behind this ambitious schedule is an intensive planning and analysis phase that took several years.

After an exhaustive analysis of its project requirements, FPL issued an RFP (request for proposals) that included more than 450 questions, filling 23 pages. A section in the RFP on "absolute requirements" lists 16 mandatory conditions, including the following statement: "The prospective vendor must take full and unconditional responsibility for satisfactory operation and performance of all system components upon turning the system over to the customer." Section 2 of the RFP maps out FPL's ATM objectives. It includes four diagrams that depict the initial ATM network topology and show how the switches will be used for future applications. A section on the product's switching hardware asks detailed questions about architecture, capacity, scalability, fault recovery, and automatic reroute functions, as well as inquiring about available voice, data, and video modules. The software section examines network management issues, routing and connection management, switched virtual circuits, and congestion control.

Once the responses were in, FPL spent many hours comparing functions and features in spreadsheet format and calling vendors to fill in missing pieces. FPL found that this process resulted in a far more detailed picture of each vendor's offering than what was presented in the initial responses. When the list had been narrowed down to a few finalists, FPL's evaluation team visited each vendor's facility for demonstrations. As of this writing, FPL is in the process of making its final decision and proceeding with contract award.

Discussion Questions

1. FPL spent a lot of time trying to nail down exact specifications for their system before issuing RFPs. An alternative would have been to (1) prepare a shorter, more general statement of requirements, (2) require each vendor to produce a detailed solution, and (3) have a small number of finalists actually field a prototype system. Discuss the relative merits of the two approaches.

2. What should FPL be looking for in the one-month trial period at the beginning of installation?

3. The use of a SONET/ATM infrastructure should result in substantial cost savings and improved network management compared to the mixture of leased line, dial-up facilities, and data networks used previously. Another potential benefit is that the network may provide the flexibility to respond to new products, new services, and new needs. Discuss the network's potential for providing this type of benefit.

9

Local-Area Networks

CHAPTER OBJECTIVES

After reading this chapter, you should be able to:

- Define the various types of local-area networks (LANs) and list the requirements that each is intended to satisfy.

- Give some representative examples of LAN applications.

- Explain why wire replacement is a prime motivation for the installation of a LAN.

- Discuss the topologies and transmission media commonly used for LANs and describe the combinations that are usually found.

- Explain how data processing devices are typically interfaced to a LAN.

- List the various options provided in current LAN standards, explain why the customer should limit purchase consideration to those standards, and describe the various application areas for which each option is most appropriate.

- Explain the functions of, and need for, bridges.

Local-Area Network (LAN)
A local network that makes use of a shared transmission medium and packet broadcasting. Companies.

W e turn now to a discussion of the **local-area networks (LANs)**. Whereas wide-area networks may be public or private, LANs usually are owned by the organization that is using the network to interconnect equipment. LANs have much greater capacity than wide-area networks, to carry what is generally a greater internal communications load.

A simple example of a LAN that highlights some of its characteristics is shown in Figure 9.1 All of the devices are attached to a shared transmission medium. A transmission from any one device can be received by all other devices attached to the same network. Traditional LANs have provided data rates in a range from about 1 to 20 Mbps. These data rates, though substantial, have become increasingly inadequate with the proliferation of devices, the growth in multimedia applications, and the increased use of the client–server architecture. As a result, much of the effort in LAN development has been in the development

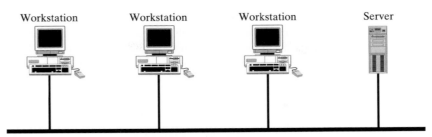

Shared transmission medium

FIGURE 9.1 A Simple Local Area Network.

of high-speed LANs, with data rates of 100 Mbps or more. In Chapter 10, we will see a number of examples of high-speed LANs.

In this chapter we look at the underlying technology of LANs and describe the most important lower-speed LANs. Chapter 10 is devoted to a discussion of high-speed and wireless LANs.

9.1 BACKGROUND

The variety of applications for LANs is wide. To provide some insight into the types of requirements that LANs are intended to meet, we discuss some of the most important general application areas for these networks and then look at the implications for LAN configuration.

LAN Applications

Personal Computer Local Networks   We start at one extreme, a system designed to support personal computers. With the relatively low cost of such systems, individual managers within organizations are independently procuring personal computers for departmental applications, such as spreadsheet and project management tools and Internet access.

But a collection of departmental-level processors will not meet all of an organization's needs; central processing facilities are still required. Some programs, such as econometric forecasting models, are too big to run on a small computer. Corporate-wide data files, such as accounting and payroll, require a centralized facility but should be accessible to a number of users. In addition, there are other kinds of files that, although specialized, must be shared by a number of users. Further, there are sound reasons for connecting individual intelligent workstations not only to a central facility but to each other as well. Members of a project or organization team need to share work and information. By far the most efficient way to do so is electronically.

Certain expensive resources, such as a disk or a laser printer, can be shared by all users of the departmental local network. In addition, the network can tie into larger corporate network facilities. For example, the corporation may have a building-wide local network and a wide-area private network. A communications server can provide controlled access to these resources.

Local networks for the support of personal computers and workstations have become nearly universal in organizations of all sizes. Even those sites that still depend heavily on the mainframe have transferred much of the processing load to networks of personal computers. Perhaps the prime example of the way in which personal computers are being used is to implement client-server applications.

For personal computer networks, a key requirement is low cost. In particular, the cost of attachment to the network must be significantly less than the cost of the attached device. Thus, for the ordinary personal computer, an attachment cost in the hundreds of dollars is desirable. For more expensive, high-performance workstations, higher attachment costs can be tolerated. In any case, this suggests that the data rate of the network may be limited; in general, the higher the data rate, the higher the cost.

Backend Networks   Backend networks are used to interconnect large systems such as mainframes, supercomputers, and mass storage devices. The key requirement here is for bulk data transfer among a limited number of devices in a small area. High reliability is generally also a requirement. Typical characteristics include:

- *High data rate.* To satisfy the high-volume demand, data rates of 100 Mbps or more are required.
- *High-speed interface.* Data transfer operations between a large host system and a mass storage device are typically performed through high-speed parallel I/O interfaces rather than slower communications interfaces. Thus, the physical link between station and network must be high speed.
- *Distributed access.* Some sort of distributed medium access control (MAC) technique is needed to enable a number of devices to share the medium with efficient and reliable access.
- *Limited distance.* Typically, a backend network will be employed in a computer room or a small number of contiguous rooms.
- *Limited number of devices.* The number of expensive mainframes and mass storage devices found in the computer room generally numbers in the tens of devices.

Typically, backend networks are found at sites of large companies or research installations with large data processing budgets. Because of the scale involved, a small difference in productivity can mean millions of dollars.

Consider a site that uses a dedicated mainframe computer. This implies a fairly large application or set of applications. As the load at the site grows, the existing mainframe may be replaced by a more powerful one, perhaps a multiprocessor system. At some sites, a single-system replacement will not be able to keep up; equipment performance growth rates will be exceeded by demand growth rates. The facility will eventually require multiple independent computers. Again, there are compelling reasons for interconnecting these systems. The cost of system interrupt is high, so it should be possible, easily and quickly, to shift applications to backup systems. It must be possible to test new procedures and applications without degrading the production system. Large bulk storage files must be accessible from more than one computer. Load leveling should be possible to maximize utilization and performance.

It can be seen that some key requirements for computer room networks are the opposite of those for personal computer local networks. High data rates are required to keep up with the work, which typically involves the transfer of large blocks of data. The electronics for achieving high speeds are expensive, on the order of tens of thousands of dollars per attachment. Fortunately, given the much higher cost of the attached devices, such costs are reasonable.

High-Speed Office Networks   Traditionally, the office environment has included a variety of devices with low- to medium-speed data transfer requirements. However, new applications in the office environment are being developed for which the limited speeds (up to 10 Mbps) of the typical LAN are inadequate. Desktop image processors could soon increase network data flow by an unprecedented amount. Examples of these applications include fax machines, document image processors, and graphics programs on personal computers and workstations. Consider that a typical page with 200 picture elements, or pels[1] (black or white points), per inch resolution (which is adequate but not high resolution) generates 3,740,000 bits (8.5 in. × 11 in. × 40,000 pels per square inch). Even with compression techniques, this will generate a tremendous load. In addition, disk technology and price/performance have evolved so that desktop storage capacities exceeding 1 Gbyte are not uncommon. These new demands require LANs with high speed that can support the larger numbers and greater geographic extent of offices systems over computer room systems.

Backbone Local Networks   The increasing use of distributed processing applications and personal computers has led to a need for a flexible strategy for local networking. Support of premises-wide data communications requires a networking service that is capable of spanning the distances involved and that interconnects equipment in a single (perhaps large) building or a cluster of buildings. Although it is possible to develop a single LAN to interconnect all the data processing equipment of a premises, this is probably not a practical alternative in most cases. There are several drawbacks to a single-LAN strategy:

- *Reliability.* With a single LAN, a service interruption, even of short duration, could result in a major disruption for users.
- *Capacity.* A single LAN could be saturated as the number of devices attached to the network grows over time.
- *Cost.* A single-LAN technology is not optimized for the diverse requirements of interconnection and communication. The presence of large numbers of low-cost microcomputers dictates that network support for

[1] A *picture element*, or *pel*, is the smallest discrete scanning-line sample of a facsimile system, which contains only black–white information (no gray scales). A *pixel* is a picture element that contains gray-scale information.

these devices be provided at low cost. LANs that support attachment at very low cost will not be suitable for meeting the overall requirement.

A more attractive alternative is to employ lower-cost, lower-capacity LANs within buildings or departments and to interconnect these networks with a higher-capacity network. This latter network is referred to as a *backbone network*. If confined to a single building or cluster of buildings, a high-capacity LAN can perform the backbone function.

LAN Configuration

Tiered Local-Area Networks   Consider the kinds of data processing equipment to be supported in a typical organization. In rough terms, we can group this equipment into three categories:

- *Personal computers and workstations.* The workhorse in most office environments is the microcomputer, including personal computers and workstations. Most of this equipment is found at the departmental level, used by individual professionals and secretarial personnel. When used for network applications, the load generated tends to be rather modest.
- *Servers.* Servers, used within a department or shared by users in a number of departments, can perform a variety of functions. Generic examples include support of expensive peripherals such as mass storage devices, providing applications that require large amounts of processor resources, and maintaining databases accessible by many users. Because of this shared use, these machines may generate substantial traffic.
- *Mainframes.* For large database and scientific applications, the mainframe is still the machine of choice. When the machines are networked, bulk data transfers dictate that a high-capacity network be used.

The requirements indicated by this spectrum suggest that a single local network will not, in many cases, be the most cost-effective solution. A single network would have to be rather high speed to support the aggregate demand. However, the cost of attachment to a local network tends to increase as a function of the network data rate. Accordingly, a high-speed local network would be very expensive for attachment of low-cost personal computers.

An alternative approach, which is becoming increasingly common, is to employ two or three tiers of local networks (Figure 9.2). Within a department, a low-cost, moderate-speed LAN supports a cluster of personal computers and workstations. Such departmental LANs are lashed together with a backbone local network of higher capacity. In addition, shared systems are also supported off this backbone. If mainframes are also part of the office equipment suite, a separate high-speed LAN supports these devices and may be linked, as a whole, to the backbone local network to support traffic between the mainframes and other office equipment. We will see that LAN standards and products address the need for all three types of local networks.

Evolution Scenario   One final aspect of the tiered architecture should be mentioned: the way in which such a networking implementation comes about in an

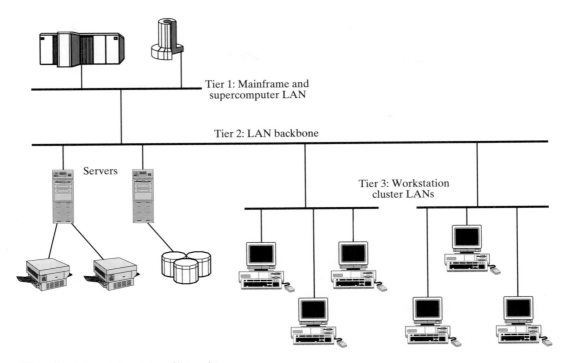

Tier 1: Mainframe and
supercomputer LAN

Tier 2: LAN backbone

Servers

Tier 3: Workstation
cluster LANs

FIGURE 9.2 Tiered Local Area Networks.

organization. This will vary widely from one organization to the next, but two general scenarios can be defined. It is useful to be aware of these scenarios because of their implications for the selection and management of local-area networks.

In the first scenario, the LAN decisions are made from the bottom up, with each department making decisions more or less in isolation. In this scenario, the particular application requirements of a department are typically well known. For example, an engineering department has very high data rate requirements to support its CAD environment; whereas the sale department has low data rate requirements for their order entry and order inquiry needs. Because the applications are well known, a decision can be made quickly as to which network to purchase. Departmental budgets usually can cover the costs of these networks, so approval of a higher authority is not required. The result is that each department will develop its own cluster network (tier 3). In the meantime, if this is a large organization, the central data processing organization may acquire a high-speed (tier 1) LAN to interconnect mainframes.

Over time, as many departments develop their own clusters, they realize that they have a need to interconnect with each other. For example, the marketing department may have to access cost information from the finance department as well as last month's order rate from sales. When cluster-to-cluster communication requirements become important, the company will make a conscious decision to provide interconnect capability. This interconnect capability is realized through the LAN backbone (tier 2).

The advantage of this scenario is that since the department manager is closest to the department's needs, local interconnect strategies can be responsive to the specific applications of the department, and acquisition can be timely. There are several disadvantages to this approach. First, there is the problem of suboptimization. If procurement is made on a company-wide basis, perhaps less total equipment will be acquired to satisfy the total need. In addition, larger-volume purchases may result in more favorable terms. Second, the company is eventually faced with the need to interconnect all of these departmental LANs. If there are a wide variety of such LANs from many different vendors, the interconnection problem becomes more difficult.

For these reasons, an alternative scenario is becoming increasingly common: a top-down design of a LAN strategy. In this case the company decides to map out a total local networking strategy. The decision is centralized because of its impact on the entire operation or company. The advantage of this approach is built-in compatibility to interconnect the users. The difficulty with this approach is, of course, the need to be responsive and timely in meeting needs at the departmental level.

9.2 LAN TECHNOLOGY

The key elements of a LAN are:

- *Topology:* bus, ring, or star
- *Transmission medium:* twisted pair, coaxial cable, or optical fiber
- *Layout:* linear or star
- *Medium access control:* CSMA/CD or token passing

Together, these elements determine not only the cost and capacity of the LAN but also the type of data that may be transmitted, the speed and efficiency of communications, and even the kinds of applications that can be supported. Table 9-1 provides an overview of these elements. In this section we survey the major technologies in the first three of these categories. It will be seen that there is an interdependence among the choices in different categories. Accordingly, a discussion of pros and cons relative to specific applications is best done by looking at preferred combinations. This, in turn, is best done in the context of standards, which is a subject of a later section.

Topologies

In the context of a communication network, the term *topology* refers to the way in which the end points, or stations, attached to the network are interconnected. The common topologies for LANs are bus, tree, ring, and star (Figure 9.3). The bus is a special case of the tree, with only one trunk and no branches; we shall use the term *bus/tree* when the distinction is unimportant.

Bus and Tree Topologies   Both bus and tree topologies are characterized by the use of a multipoint medium. For the **bus**, all stations attach, through appropriate

Bus
A LAN topology in which stations are attached to a shared transmission medium.

TABLE 9-1 LAN Technology Elements

Element	Options	Restrictions	Comments
Topology	Bus/tree Ring Star	Optical fiber not cost-effective Not CSMA/CD or broadband —	No active elements Supports fiber Conforms to standard building wiring practices
Transmission medium	Unshielded twisted pair Shielded twisted pair Baseband coaxial cable Broadband coaxial cable Optical fiber	Speed–distance limitation Speed–distance limitation — Not with ring Not cost-effective with bus	Inexpensive; prewired; noise vulnerability Relatively inexpensive Declining popularity High capacity; multiple channels; rugged; expensive Very high capacity; security
Layout	Linear Star	— —	Minimal cable Ease of wiring; availability
Medium access control	CSMA/CD Token passing	Not with ring —	Simple; widely implemented High throughput; priority

FIGURE 9.3 Local Area Network Topologies.

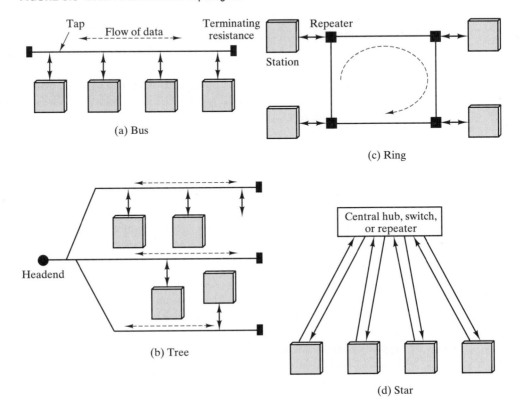

(a) Bus

(c) Ring

(b) Tree

(d) Star

hardware interfacing known as a *tap,* directly to a linear transmission medium, or bus. Full-duplex operation between the station and the tap allows data to be transmitted onto the bus and received from the bus. A transmission from any station propagates the length of the medium in both directions and can be received by all other stations. At each end of the bus is a terminator, which absorbs any signal, removing it from the bus.

The **tree** topology is a generalization of the bus topology. The transmission medium is a branching cable with no closed loops. The tree layout begins at a point known as the **headend**. One or more cables start at the headend, and each of these may have branches. The branches in turn may have additional branches to allow quite complex layouts. Again, a transmission from any station propagates throughout the medium and can be received by all other stations.

Two problems present themselves in this arrangement. First, because a transmission from any one station can be received by all other stations, there needs to be some way of indicating for whom the transmission is intended. Second, a mechanism is needed to regulate transmission. To see the reason for this, consider that if two stations on the bus attempt to transmit at the same time, their signals will overlap and become garbled. Or, consider that one station decides to transmit continuously for a long period of time.

To solve these problems, stations transmit data in small blocks, known as *frames.* Each frame consists of a portion of the data that a station wishes to transmit, plus a frame header that contains control information. Each station on the bus is assigned a unique address, or identifier, and the destination address for a frame is included in its header.

Figure 9.4 illustrates the scheme. In this example, station C wishes to transmit a frame of data to A. The frame header includes A's address. As the frame propagates along the bus, it passes B. Station B observes the address and ignores the frame. A, on the other hand, sees that the frame is addressed to itself and therefore copies the data from the frame as it goes by.

So the frame structure solves the first problem mentioned above: It provides a mechanism for indicating the intended recipient of data. It also provides the basic tool for solving the second problem, the regulation of access. In particular, the stations take turns sending frames in a cooperative fashion. This involves putting additional control information into the frame header.

With the bus or tree, no special action needs to be taken to remove frames from the medium. When a signal reaches the end of the medium, it is absorbed by the terminator.

Ring Topology   In the **ring** topology, the network consists of a set of *repeaters* joined by point-to-point links in a closed loop. The repeater is a comparatively simple device, capable of receiving data on one link and transmitting them, bit by bit, on the other link as fast as they are received, with no buffering at the repeater. The links are unidirectional; that is, data are transmitted in one direction only and all oriented in the same way. Thus, data circulate around the ring in one direction (clockwise or counterclockwise).

Tree
A LAN topology in which stations are attached to a shared, branching transmission medium.

Headend
The endpoint of a broadband bus or tree. Transmission from each station is toward the headend. Reception by each station is from the headend.

Ring
A LAN topology in which stations are attached to repeaters connected in a closed loop.

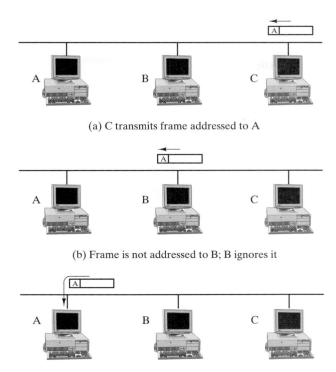

(a) C transmits frame addressed to A

(b) Frame is not addressed to B; B ignores it

(c) A copies frame as it goes by

FIGURE 9.4 Frame Transmission on a Bus LAN.

Each station attaches to the network at a repeater and can transmit data onto the network through the repeater. As with the bus and tree, data are transmitted in frames. As a frame circulates past all the other stations, the destination station recognizes its address and copies the frame into a local buffer as it goes by. The frame continues to circulate until it returns to the source station, where it is removed (Figure 9.5). Because multiple stations share the ring, medium access control is needed to determine at what time each station may insert frames.

Star Topology   In the **star** LAN topology, each station is connected directly to a common central node. Typically, each station attaches to a central node, referred to as the *star coupler,* via two point-to-point links, one for transmission in each direction.

In general, there are two alternatives for the operation of the central node. One approach is for the central node to operate in a broadcast fashion. A transmission of a frame from one station to the node is retransmitted on all the outgoing links. In this case, although the arrangement is physically a star, it is logically a bus: A transmission from any station is received by all other stations, and only one station at a time may transmit successfully. Another approach is for the central node to act as a frame switching device. An incoming frame is buffered in the node and then retransmitted on an outgoing link to the destination station.

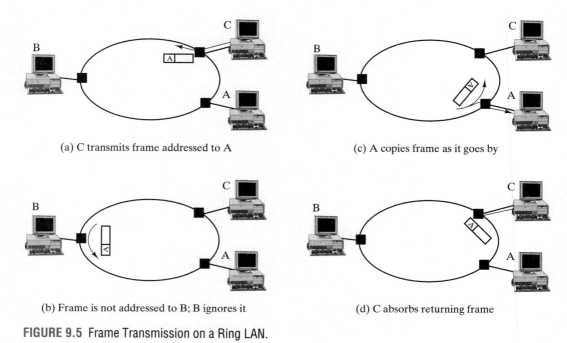

(a) C transmits frame addressed to A

(c) A copies frame as it goes by

(b) Frame is not addressed to B; B ignores it

(d) C absorbs returning frame

FIGURE 9.5 Frame Transmission on a Ring LAN.

Choice of Topology   The choice of topology depends on a variety of factors, including reliability, expandability, and performance. This choice is part of the overall task of designing a LAN. Accordingly, this choice cannot be made in isolation, independent of the choice of transmission medium, wiring layout, and access control technique. However, a few general remarks can be made at this point.

For moderate data-rate requirements, the bus/tree topology appears to be most flexible. It is able to handle a wide range of devices, in terms of number of devices, data rates, and data types. The tree topology is relatively easy to lay out, regardless of the physical configuration of the building and the location of wiring ducts or other cable pathways. Any time that an intersection is reached, the cable can simply be branched in all desired directions.

Very high speed links over considerable distances can be used for the ring topology. Hence, the ring has the potential of providing the best throughput of any topology. One disadvantage of the ring is that a single link or repeater failure could disable the entire network.

The star topology takes advantage of the natural layout of wiring in a building. It is generally best for short distances and can support a small number of devices at very high data rates.

Transmission Media

Three forms of transmission media have commonly been used for LANs: twisted pair, coaxial cable, and optical fiber. For both unshielded and shielded twisted pair, digital signaling is used, whereas for optical fiber, analog signaling is used. For coaxial cable, either digital or analog signaling can be used; in this case, the two forms of signaling are referred to as *baseband* and *broadband,* respectively. The use of these two forms of signaling in a bus or tree topology warrants further elaboration. In recent years, there has been increased interest in wireless LANs as well. We defer a discussion of these until Chapter 10.

Baseband
Transmission of signals without modulation.

Baseband Bus   A **baseband** bus uses digital signaling; that is, the binary data to be transmitted are inserted onto the cable as a sequence of voltage pulses, usually using Manchester or differential Manchester encoding (see Figure 5.5). The nature of digital signals is such that the entire frequency spectrum of the cable is consumed. Hence, it is not possible to have multiple channels (frequency-division multiplexing) on the cable. Transmission is bidirectional. That is, a signal inserted at any point on the medium propagates in both directions to the ends, where it is absorbed (Figure 9.6a). The digital signaling requires a bus topology. Unlike analog signals, digital signals cannot easily be propagated through the branching points required for a tree topology. Baseband bus LAN systems can extend only a limited distance, about 1 km at most. This is because the attenuation of the signal, which is most pronounced at higher frequencies, causes a blurring of the pulses and a weakening of the signal to the extent that communication over larger distances is impractical.

To extend the length of the network, repeaters may be used. This device works in a somewhat different fashion than the repeater on the ring. The bus repeater is not used as a device attachment point and is capable of transmitting in both directions. A repeater joins two segments of cable and passes digital signals in both directions between the segments. A repeater is transparent to the rest of the system; as it does no buffering, it does not logically isolate one segment from another. So, for example, if two stations on different segments attempt to transmit at the same time, their packets will interfere with each other (collide). To avoid multipath interference, only one path of segments and repeaters is allowed between any two stations. Figure 9.7 illustrates a multiple-segment baseband bus LAN.

Broadband
In local area networks, data transfer by means of analog (radio-frequency) signals.

Broadband Bus   In the context of LANs, the term **broadband** implies the use of analog signaling. Thus, frequency-division multiplexing is possible. The frequency spectrum of the cable can be divided into channels or sections of bandwidth. Separate channels can support separate and independent data traffic, television, and radio signals. Broadband components allow splitting and joining operations; hence both bus and tree topologies are possible. Much greater distances—some tens of kilometers—are possible with broadband compared to baseband. This is because the analog signals that carry the digital data can propagate greater distances before noise and attenuation damage the data.

Unlike baseband, broadband is inherently a unidirectional signaling technique; signals inserted onto the medium can propagate in only one direction. The primary reason for this is that it is not feasible to build amplifiers that will pass signals of one frequency in both directions. This unidirectional property means

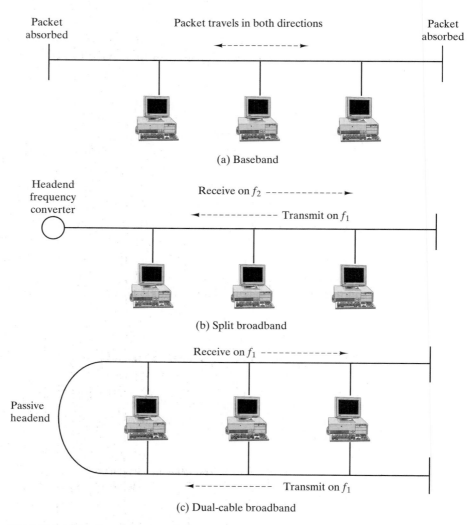

FIGURE 9.6 Baseband and Broadband Transmission Techniques.

that only those stations "downstream" from a transmitting station can receive its signals. How, then, can full connectivity be achieved?

Clearly, two data paths are needed. These paths are joined at the headend. For the bus topology, the headend is simply one end of the bus. For the tree topology, the headend is the root of a branching tree. All stations transmit on one path toward the headend (inbound). Signals arriving at the headend are then propagated along a second data path away from the headend (outbound). All stations receive on the outbound path.

Physically, two alternative configurations are used to implement the inbound and outbound paths (Figure 9.6b and c). On a *dual-cable* configuration, the inbound and outbound paths are separate cables, with the headend simply a

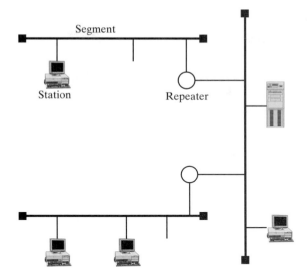

FIGURE 9.7 Baseband Configuration.

passive connector between the two. Stations send and receive on the same frequency. On a *split* configuration, the inbound and outbound paths are different frequencies on the same cable. Bidirectional amplifiers pass lower frequencies inbound and higher frequencies outbound. The headend contains a device, known as a *frequency converter,* for translating inbound frequencies to outbound frequencies.

Choice of Transmission Medium   The choice of transmission medium is determined by a number of factors. It is, we shall see, constrained by the topology of the LAN. Other factors come into play, including:

- *Capacity:* to support the expected network traffic
- *Reliability:* to meet requirements for availability
- *Types of data supported:* tailored to the application
- *Environmental scope:* to provide service over the range of environments required

We can make a few general observations. Unshielded twisted pair is an inexpensive, well-understood medium. Typically, office buildings are wired to meet the anticipated telephone system demand plus a healthy margin; thus there are no cable installation costs in the use of unshielded twisted pair. However, the data rate that can be supported is generally quite limited, with the exception of very small LAN. Unshielded twisted pair is likely to be the most cost-effective for single-building, low-traffic LAN installation.

Shielded twisted pair and baseband coaxial cable are more expensive than unshielded twisted pair but provide greater capacity. Broadband cable is even more expensive but provides even greater capacity. For the broad range of LAN requirements, these media are quite attractive. For most requirements, a system based on one of these media can be designed to meet current demand with plenty of room for expansion, at reasonable cost. Broadband coaxial cable systems excel when there are a lot of devices and a considerable amount of traffic. Examples include large data processing installations and sophisticated office automation systems, which may support facsimile machines, image processing systems, and graphics-intensive computing. In practice, both forms of coaxial cable have suffered declining popularity. Over short distances, twisted pair is more cost-effective, and for longer distances or high data rates, optical fiber has become competitive.

Optical fiber has a number of attractive features, such as electromagnetic isolation, high capacity, and small size, which have attracted a great deal of interest. As yet the market penetration of fiber LANs is low; this is due primarily to the high cost of fiber components and the lack of skilled personnel to install and maintain fiber systems. This situation is beginning to change rapidly as more products using fiber are introduced.

Relationship between Medium and Topology

The choices of transmission medium and topology are not independent. The ring topology requires point-to-point links between repeaters. Twisted-pair wire, baseband coaxial cable, and optical fiber can all be used to provide the links. However, broadband coaxial cable would not work well in this topology. Each repeater would have to be capable of receiving and transmitting data simultaneously on multiple channels. It is doubtful that the expense of such devices could be justified. Table 9-2a summarizes representative parameters for transmission media for commercially available ring LANs.

For the bus topology, twisted pair and both baseband and broadband coaxial cable are appropriate, and numerous products exist for each of these media. Until recently, optical fiber cable has not been considered feasible; the multipoint configuration was considered not cost-effective, due to the difficulty in constructing low-loss optical taps. However, recent advances have made the optical-fiber bus practical, even at quite high data rates.

The tree topology can be employed with broadband coaxial cable. The unidirectional nature of broadband signaling allows the construction of a tree architecture. On the other hand, the bidirectional nature of baseband signaling, on either twisted pair or coaxial cable, is not suited to the tree topology. Table 9-2b summarizes representative parameters for transmission media for commercially available bus and tree LANs.

The reader will note that the performance for a given medium is considerably better for the ring topology then for the bus/tree topology. In the bus/tree topology, each station is attached to the medium by a tap, and each tap introduces some attenuation and distortion to the signal as it passes by. In the ring, each station is attached to the medium by a repeater, and each repeater generates a new signal to compensate for effects of attenuation and distortion.

The star topology requires a point-to-point link between each device and the central node. Most recent activity for this topology has focused on the use of

TABLE 9-2 Characteristics of Transmission Media and Topologies for LANs

(a) RING TOPOLOGY			
Transmission Medium	*Data Rate (Mbps)*	*Repeater Spacing (km)*	*Number of Stations*
Unshielded twisted pair	4	0.1	70
Shielded twisted pair	16	0.3	250
Baseband coaxial cable	16	1.0	250
Optical fiber	100	2.0	250
Wireless	100	0.1	10's

(b) BUS/TREE TOPOLOGY			
Transmission Medium	*Data Rate (Mbps)*	*Range (km)*	*Number of Stations*
Unshielded twisted pair	1	<2	10's
Baseband coaxial cable	10; 50 with limitations	<3/<1	100's/10's
Broadband coaxial cable	50; 20 per channel	<30	100s–1000's
Optical fiber	45	<150	500
Wireless	10	<1	10's

(c) STAR TOPOLOGY			
Transmission Medium	*Data Rate (Mbps)*	*Radius (km)*	*Number of Stations*
Unshielded twisted pair	10–100	0.1	70
Shielded twisted pair	10–100	0.3	250
Baseband coaxial cable	16	1.0	250
Optical fiber	100–1000	1.0	250
Wireless	100	0.1	10's

twisted pair and optical fiber at high data rates over short distances. Table 9-2c summarizes representative parameters for transmission media for commercially available star LANs.

Structured Cabling

As a practical matter, the network manager needs a cabling plan that deals with the selection of cable and the layout of the cable in a building. The cabling plan should be easy to implement and accommodate future growth.

Cabling Standards To aid in the development of cabling plans, standards have been issued that specify the cabling types and layout for commercial buildings. These standards are referred to as **structured cabling** systems. A structured cabling system is a generic wiring scheme with the following characteristics:

1. The scheme refers to the wiring within a commercial building.
2. The scope of the system includes cabling to support all types of information transfer, including voice, LANs, video and image transmission, and other forms of data transmission.
3. The cabling layout and cable selection is independent of vendor and end-user equipment.
4. The cable layout is designed to encompass distribution to all work areas within the building, so that relocation of equipment does not require

rewiring but simply requires plugging the equipment into a preexisting outlet in the new location.

One advantage of such standards is that it provides guidance for preinstallation of cable in new buildings so that future voice and data networking needs can be met without the need to rewire the building. The standards also simplify cable layout design for network managers. Two standards for structured cabling systems have been issued: EIA/TIA-568, issued jointly by the Electronic Industries Association and the Telecommunications Industry Association, and ISO 11801, issued by the International Organization for Standardization. The two standards are quite similar; the details in this section are from the EIA/TIA-568 document.

A structured cabling strategy is based on the use of a hierarchical, star-wired cable layout. Figure 9.8 illustrates the key elements for a typical commercial building. External cables, from the local telephone company and from wide-area networks, terminate in an equipment room that is generally on the ground floor or a basement level. Patch panel and cross-connect equipment in the equipment room connects the external cables to internal distribution cable. Typically, the first level of distribution consists of backbone cables. In the simplest implementation, a single backbone cable or set of cables runs from the equipment room to telecommunications closets (called *wiring closets*) on each floor. A telecommunications closet differs from the equipment room only in that it is less complex; the telecommunications closet generally contains cross-connect equip-

FIGURE 9.8 Elements of a Structured Cabling Layout.

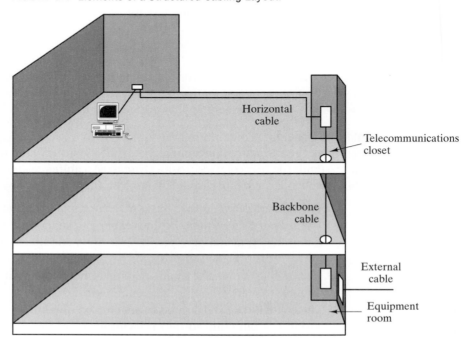

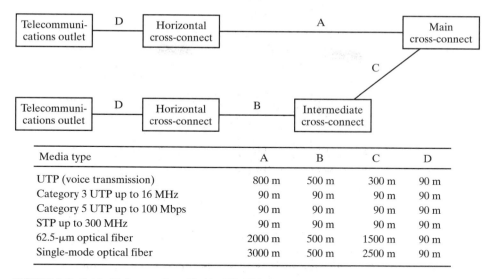

Media type	A	B	C	D
UTP (voice transmission)	800 m	500 m	300 m	90 m
Category 3 UTP up to 16 MHz	90 m	90 m	90 m	90 m
Category 5 UTP up to 100 Mbps	90 m	90 m	90 m	90 m
STP up to 300 MHz	90 m	90 m	90 m	90 m
62.5-μm optical fiber	2000 m	500 m	1500 m	90 m
Single-mode optical fiber	3000 m	500 m	2500 m	90 m

FIGURE 9.9 Cable Distances Specified in EIA-568-A.

ment for interconnecting cable to the backbone on a single floor. The cable distributed on a single floor is referred to as *horizontal cabling.* This cabling connects the backbone to wall outlets that service individual telephone and data equipment.

The use of a structured cabling plan enables an enterprise to use the transmission media appropriate for its requirements in a systematic and standardized fashion. Figure 9.9 indicates the media recommended for each portion of the structured cabling hierarchy. For horizontal cabling, a maximum distance of 90 m is recommended independent of media type. This distance is adequate to provide coverage for an entire floor for many commercial buildings. For buildings with very large floor space, backbone cable may be required to interconnect multiple telecommunications closets on a single floor. For backbone cabling, distances range from 90 to 3000 m, depending on cable type and position in the hierarchy.

Figure 9.10 indicates the current utilization of various transmission media for horizontal cabling. A few years ago it was anticipated that organizations would migrate from ordinary telephone wire (category 3 UTP) to optical fiber as high-speed LANs became increasingly popular. However, the standardization of category 5 UTP and the development of several LAN standards that use this inexpensive medium have resulted in the dominance of this medium over all others in corporate installations.

Wiring Closets versus Hubs There are two general strategies for laying out the LAN transmission medium: linear and star. The *linear* strategy attempts to provide the desired topology with the minimum cable, subject to the physical constraints of the building. The medium is installed to the subscriber locations, which may be some or all of the offices in the building. Any of the media that have been described can be used, and bus, tree, and ring topologies can be provided.

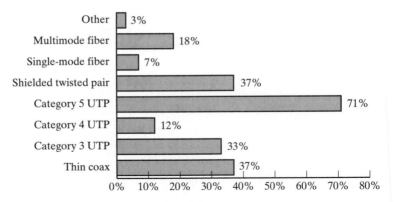

FIGURE 9.10 Corporate Horizontal Wiring Usage [*Source: Telcommunications Magazine, January 1996*].

The *star* layout strategy uses an individual cable from a concentration point to each subscriber location. The star layout is the obvious choice for a star topology LAN, but it can also be used for the bus and ring LAN topologies, as depicted in Figure 9.11. In the case of the bus topology, the bus is very short and resides at the concentration point; the drop cables to the attached devices are relatively long. In the case of the ring topology, the ring is distorted so that each link of the ring loops through the concentration point. Typically, the layout is used separately on each floor of a building. The concentration point is the **wiring closet**; some or all of the offices on the floor are connected to the closet on that floor. Connections between floors are provided by linking the closets. This type of layout is invariably used to support telephones in an office building and is becoming increasingly popular for LANs.

The preceding discussion provides the opportunity of clarifying a distinction seen in much of the literature between a wiring closet and a hub. When the central point of a star layout is an active node that accepts frames and regenerates the signal for transmission, the central node is referred to as a **hub**. We will see that hubs have become increasingly flexible and intelligent and can be used to interconnect different types of LANs.

9.3 LAN STANDARDS

IEEE 802
A committee of the Institute of Electrical and Electronics Engineers organized to produce local area network standards.

The key to the development of the LAN market is the availability of a low-cost interface. The cost to connect equipment to a LAN must be much less than the cost of the equipment alone. This requirement, plus the complexity of the LAN logic, dictates a solution based on the use of chips and very large scale integration (VLSI). However, chip manufacturers will be reluctant to commit the necessary resources unless there is a high-volume market. A widely accepted LAN standard assures that volume and also enables equipment from a variety of manufacturers to intercommunicate. This is the rationale of the **IEEE 802** committee.

The committee issued a set of standards, which were adopted in 1985 by the American National Standards Institute (ANSI) as American national standards.

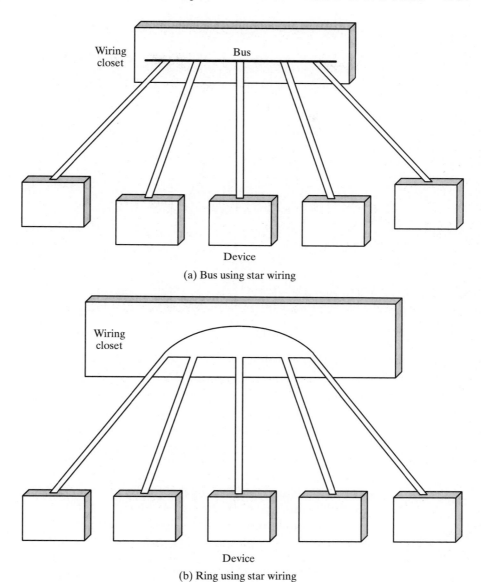

(a) Bus using star wiring

(b) Ring using star wiring

FIGURE 9.11 Bus and Ring Topologies Using Star Wiring.

The standards were subsequently revised and reissued as international standards by the International Organization for Standardization (ISO) in 1987, with the designation ISO 8802. Since then, the IEEE 802 committee has continued to revise and extend the standards, which are ultimately adopted by ISO.

Structure of the LAN Standards

Two conclusions were quickly reached by the committee: (1) the task of communication across the local network is sufficiently complex that it needs to be broken

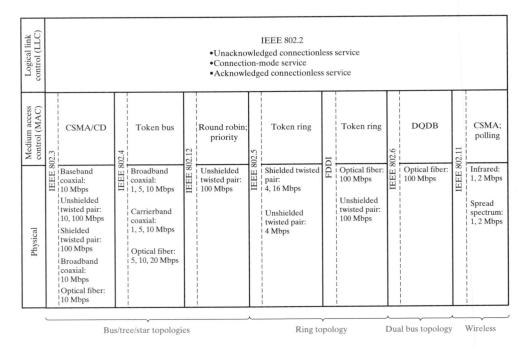

FIGURE 9.12 LAN/MAN Standards.

up into more manageable subtasks, and (2) no single technical approach will satisfy all requirements. The second conclusion was reached reluctantly when it became apparent that no single standard would satisfy all committee participants. There was support for various topologies, access methods, and transmission media. The response of the committee was to standardize all serious proposals rather than to attempt to settle on just one. Figure 9.12 summarizes the current state of standardization. The figure also includes the fiber distributed data interface (FDDI) standard, which was developed by ANSI. Although FDDI is not an IEEE 802 standard, it was developed to conform to the IEEE 802 reference model.

The standards are organized as a three-layer protocol hierarchy. Logical link control (LLC) is responsible for addressing and data link control. It is independent of the topology, transmission medium, and medium access control technique chosen, and was issued as a separate standard. Below logical link control are the medium access control (MAC) and physical layers. Because of the interdependence between medium access control, medium, and topology, these layers were organized into standards based on the medium access control algorithm, with the physical layer specified as part of the medium access control standard.

Logical Link Control (IEEE 802.2)

In the remainder of this section we provide an overview of **logical link control** (LLC), which is a common link protocol for all the LANs. The key medium access control protocols and their associated medium alternatives are explored in the remainder of this chapter and in Chapter 10.

LLC specifies the mechanisms for addressing stations across the medium and for controlling the exchange of data between two users. The operation and format of this standard is based on HDLC. Three services are provided as alternatives for attached devices using LLC:

- *Unacknowledged connectionless service.* This service is a datagram-style service. It is a very simple service that does not involve any of the flow- and error-control mechanisms. Thus, the delivery of data is not guaranteed. However, in most devices, there will be some higher layer of software that deals with reliability issues.
- *Connection-mode service.* This service is similar to that offered by HDLC. A logical connection is set up between two users exchanging data, and flow control and error control are provided.
- *Acknowledged connectionless service.* This is a cross between the two services outlined above. It provides that datagrams are to be acknowledged, but no prior logical connection is set up.

Typically, a vendor will provide these services as options that the customer can select when purchasing the equipment. Alternatively, the customer can purchase equipment that provides two or all three services and select a specific service based on application.

Unacknowledged connectionless service requires minimum logic and is useful in two contexts. First, it will often be the case that higher layers of software will provide the necessary reliability and flow-control mechanism, and it is efficient to avoid duplicating them. For example, either TCP or the ISO transport protocol standard would provide the mechanisms needed to ensure that data are delivered reliably. Second, there are instances in which the overhead cost to establish and maintain connection is unjustified or even counterproductive: for example, data collection activities that involve the periodic sampling of data sources, such as sensors and automatic self-test reports from security equipment or network components. In a monitoring application, loss of an occasional data unit would not cause distress, as the next report should arrive shortly. Thus, in most cases, unacknowledged connectionless service is the preferred option.

Connection-mode service could be used in very simple devices, such as terminal controllers, that have little software operating above this level. In these cases it would provide the flow control and reliability mechanisms normally implemented at higher layers of the communications software.

Acknowledged connectionless service is useful in several contexts. With connection-mode service, the logical link control software must maintain some sort of table for each active connection, to keep track of the status of that connection. If the user needs guaranteed delivery but there are a large number of destinations for data, connection-mode service may be impractical because of the large number of tables required. An example is a process control or automated factory environment where a central site may need to communicate with a large number of processors and programmable controllers. Another use of this is the handling of important and time-critical alarm or emergency control signals in a factory. Because of their importance, an acknowledgment is needed so that the sender can be assured that the signal got through. Because of the urgency of the signal, the user might not want to take the time to establish a logical connection before sending the data.

Medium Access Control

Medium Access Control (MAC)
Method of determining which station on a local area network has access to the transmission medium at any time.

All LANs and MANs consist of collections of devices that must share a network's transmission capacity. Some means of controlling access to the transmission medium is needed to provide an orderly and efficient use of that capacity. This is the function of a **medium access control (MAC)** protocol. Two techniques enjoy widespread acceptance and are described in this chapter: CSMA/CD and token passing.

The relationship between LLC and the MAC protocol can be seen by considering the transmission formats involved. User data are passed down to the LLC layer, which prepares a link-level frame known as an LLC protocol data unit (PDU). This PDU is then passed down to the MAC layer, where it is enclosed in a MAC frame.

The exact format of the MAC frame differs somewhat for the various MAC protocols in use. In general, all of the MAC frames have a format similar to that of Figure 9.13. The fields of this frame are:

- *MAC control:* field containing any protocol control information needed for functioning of the MAC protocol. For example, a priority level could be indicated here.
- *Destination MAC address:* the destination physical attachment point on the LAN for this frame.
- *Source MAC address:* the source physical attachment point on the LAN for this frame.

FIGURE 9.13 LLC PDU in a Generic MAC Frame Format.

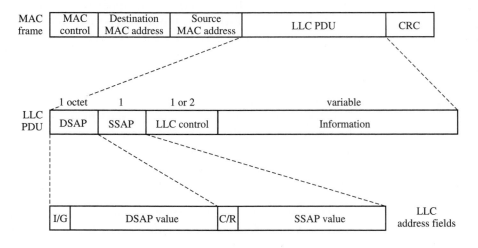

- *LLC PDU:* the LLC data from the next-higher layer. This includes the user data plus the source and destination service access point (SAPs), which indicate the user of LLC.
- *CRC:* the cyclic redundancy check field [also known as the frame check sequence (FCS) field]. This is an error-detecting code, as we have seen in HDLC and other data link control protocols (Chapter 5).

In most data link control protocols, the data link protocol entity is responsible not only for detecting errors using the CRC, but for recovering from those errors by retransmitting damaged frames. In the LAN protocol architecture, these two functions are split between the MAC and LLC layers. The MAC layer is responsible for detecting errors and discarding any frames that are in error. The LLC layer optionally keeps track of which frames have been received successfully and retransmits unsuccessful frames.

9.4 ETHERNET AND CSMA/CD

Within the IEEE 802 LAN standards committee, the 802.3 group has issued a set of standards with a common medium access control technique known as CSMA/CD. This set of standards grew out of the commercial product Ethernet, and the term *Ethernet* is still often used to refer to all the specifications. Collectively, the Ethernet-like LANs are the dominant force in the LAN market and are likely to remain so for a considerable time. As with the other IEEE 802 standards (except for LLC), IEEE 802.3 defines a medium access control layer and a number of transmission medium options.

Medium Access Control

CSMA/CD
A medium access control technique in which a station first senses the medium and transmits only if the medium is idle. The station ceases transmission if it detects a collision.

Ethernet
A 10-Mbps baseband local area network specification developed jointly by Xerox, Intel, and Digital Equipment.

The simplest form of medium access control for a bus or tree is **carrier-sense multiple access with collision detection (CSMA/CD)**. The original baseband version of this technique was developed by Xerox as part of the **Ethernet** LAN. The original broadband version was developed by MITRE as part of its MITREnet LAN. With CSMA/CD, a station wishing to transmit first listens to the medium to determine if another transmission is in progress (carrier sense). If the medium is idle, the station may transmit. It may happen that two or more stations attempt to transmit at about the same time. If this happens, there will be a collision; the data from both transmissions will be garbled and not received successfully. Thus, a procedure is needed that specifies what a station should do if the medium is found busy and what it should do if a collision occurs:

1. If the medium is idle, transmit.
2. If the medium is busy, continue to listen until the channel is idle, then transmit immediately.
3. If a collision is detected during transmission, cease transmitting immediately.
4. After a collision, wait a random amount of time, then attempt to transmit again (repeat from step 1).

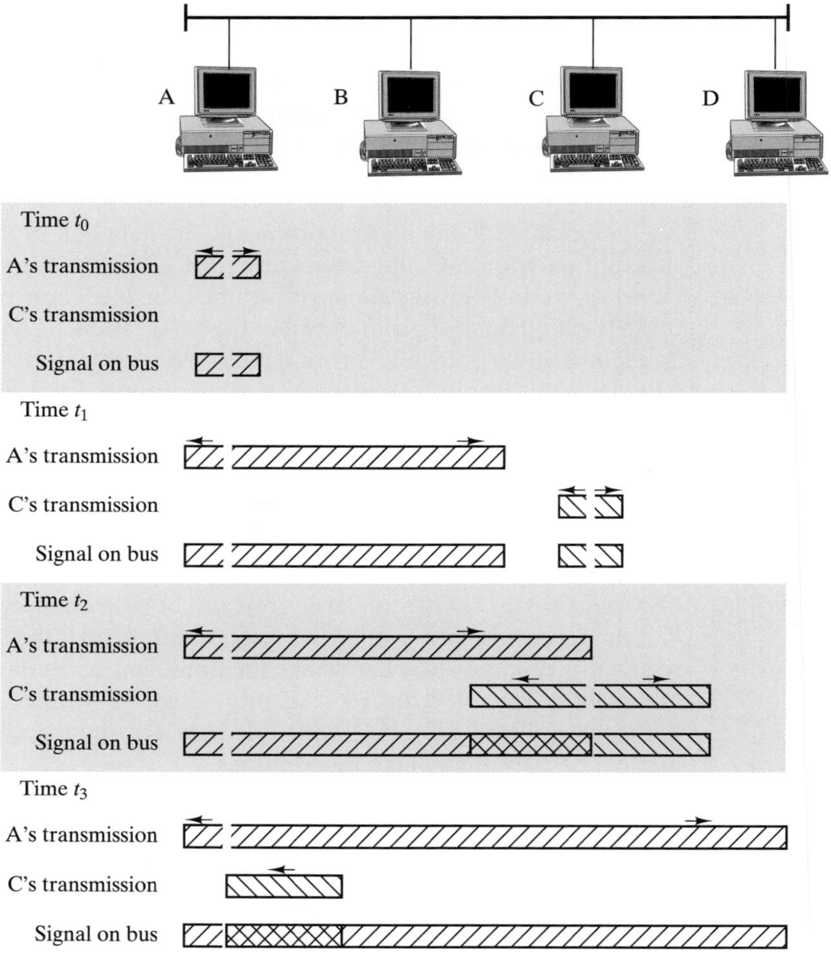

FIGURE 9.14 CSMA/CD Operation.

Figure 9.14 illustrates the technique. The upper part of the figure shows a baseband LAN layout. The remainder of the figure depicts activity on the bus at four successive instants in time. At time t_0, station A begins transmitting a packet addressed to D. At t_1, both B and C are ready to transmit. Station B senses a transmission and so defers. Station C, however, is still unaware of A's transmission and begins its own transmission. When A's transmission reaches C, at t_2, C detects the collision and ceases transmission. The effect of the collision propagates back to A, where it is detected some time later, t_3, at which time A ceases transmission.

The advantage of CSMA/CD is its simplicity. It is easy to implement the logic required for this protocol. Furthermore, there is little to go wrong in the execution of the protocol. For example, if for some reason a station fails to detect a collision, the worst that can happen is that it continues to transmit its frame, wasting some time on the medium. Once the transmission is over, the algorithm continues to function as before.

IEEE 802.3 Medium Options at 10 Mbps

The IEEE 802.3 committee has been the most active in defining alternative physical configurations. This is both good and bad. On the good side, the standard has been responsive to evolving technology. On the bad side, the customer, not to mention the potential vendor, is faced with a bewildering array of options. However, the committee has been at pains to ensure that the various options can easily be integrated into a configuration that satisfies a variety of needs. Thus, the user that has a complex set of requirements may find the flexibility and variety of the 802.3 standard to be an asset.

To distinguish the various implementations that are available, the committee has developed a concise notation:

<data rate in Mbps> <signaling method><maximum segment length in hundreds of meters>

In this chapter we consider the options that operate at 10 Mbps, the rate of the original commercial Ethernet; higher-speed options are discussed in Chapter 10. The alternatives are:

- 10BASE5
- 10BASE2
- 10BASE-T
- 10BROAD36
- 10BASE-F

Note that 10BASE-T and 10-BASE-F do not quite follow the notation: "T" stands for twisted pair and "F" stands for optical fiber. Table 9-3 summarizes these options.

TABLE 9-3 IEEE 802.3 10-Mbps Physical Layer Medium Alternatives

	10BASE5	*10BASE2*	*10BASE-T*	*10BROAD36*	*10BASE-FP*
Transmission medium	Coaxial cable (50 Ω)	Coaxial cable (50 Ω)	Unshielded twisted pair	Coaxial cable (75 Ω)	850-nm optical fiber pair
Signaling technique	Baseband (Manchester)	Baseband (Manchester)	Baseband (Manchester)	Broadband (DPSK)	Manchester/ on–off
Topology	Bus	Bus	Star	Bus/tree	Star
Maximum segment length (m)	500	185	100	1800	500
Nodes per segment	100	30	—	—	33
Cable diameter (mm)	10	5	0.4–0.6	0.4–1.0	62.5/125 μm

10BASE5 Medium Specification   10BASE5 is the original 802.3 medium specification and is based directly on Ethernet. 10BASE5 specifies the use of 50-Ω coaxial cable and uses Manchester digital signaling.[2] The maximum length of a cable segment is set at 500 m. The length of the network can be extended by the use of repeaters. A repeater is transparent to the MAC level; as it does no buffering, it does not isolate one segment from another. So, for example, if two stations on different segments attempt to transmit at the same time, their transmissions will collide. To avoid looping, only one path of segments and repeaters is allowed between any two stations. The standard allows a maximum of four repeaters in the path between any two stations, extending the effective length of the medium to 2.5 km.

10BASE2 Medium Specification   To provide a lower-cost system than 10BASE5 for personal computer LANs, 10BASE2 was added. As with 10BASE5, this specification uses 50-Ω coaxial cable and Manchester signaling. The principal difference is that 10BASE2 uses a thinner cable, which supports fewer taps over a shorter distance than does the 10BASE5 cable. Because they have the same data rate, it is possible to combine 10BASE5 and 10BASE2 segments in the same network by using a repeater that conforms to 10BASE5 on one side and 10BASE2 on the other side. The only restriction is that a 10BASE2 segment should not be used to bridge two 10BASE5 segments because a "backbone" segment should be as resistant to noise as the segments it connects.

10BASE-T Medium Specification   By sacrificing some distance, it is possible to develop a 10-Mbps LAN using the unshielded twisted pair medium. Such wire is often found prewired in office buildings as excess telephone cable and can be used for LANs. Such an approach is specified in the 10BASE-T specification. The 10BASE-T specification defines a star-shaped topology. A simple system consists of a number of stations connected to a central point, referred to as a multiport repeater, via two twisted pairs. The central point accepts input on any one line and repeats it on all of the other lines.

Stations attach to the multiport repeater via a point-to-point link. Ordinarily, the link consists of two unshielded twisted pairs. Because of the high data rate and the poor transmission qualities of unshielded twisted pair, the length of a link is limited to 100 m. As an alternative, an optical fiber link may be used. In this case the maximum length is 500 m.

In the simplest 10BASE-T arrangement, the central element of the star is an active element, referred to as the *hub*. Each station is connected to the hub by two twisted pairs (transmit and receive). The hub acts as a repeater: When a single station transmits, the hub repeats the signal, on the outgoing line to each station. Note that although this scheme is physically a star, it is logically a bus: A transmission from any one station is received by all other stations, and if two stations transmit at the same time, there will be a collision.

Multiple levels of hubs can be cascaded in a hierarchical configuration. Figure 9.15 illustrates a two-level configuration. There is one *header hub* (HHUB)

------

[2] See Section 5.2.

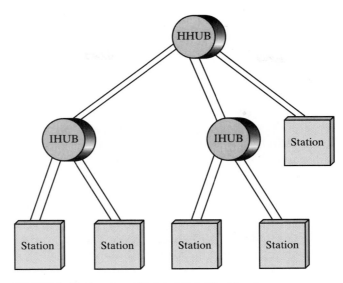

FIGURE 9.15 Two-Level Twisted-Pair Star Topology.

and one or more *intermediate hubs* (IHUBs). Each hub may have a mixture of stations and other hubs attached to it from below. This layout fits well with building wiring practices. Typically, there is a wiring closet on each floor of an office building, and a hub can be placed in each one. Each hub could service the stations on its floor.

10BROAD36 Medium Specification The 10BROAD36 specification is the only 802.3 specification for broadband. The medium employed is the standard 75-Ω CATV coaxial cable. Either a dual-cable or split-cable configuration is allowed. The maximum length of an individual segment, emanating from the headend, is 1800 m; this results in a maximum end-to-end span of 3600 m.

The signaling on the cable is differential phase-shift keying (DPSK). In ordinary PSK, a binary 0 is represented by a carrier with a particular phase, and a binary 1 is represented by a carrier with the opposite phase (180° difference). DPSK makes use of differential encoding, in which a change of phase occurs when a 0 occurs, and there is no change of phase when a 1 occurs. The advantage of differential encoding is that it is easier for the receiver to detect a change in phase than to determine the phase itself.

The characteristics of the modulation process are specified so that the resulting 10-Mbps signal fits into a 14-MHz bandwidth.

10BASE-F Medium Specification The 10BASE-F specification enables users to take advantage of the distance and transmission characteristics available with the use of optical fiber. The standard actually contains three specifications:

- *10-BASE-FP (passive):* a passive-star topology for interconnecting stations and repeaters with up to 1 km per segment.

- *10-BASE-FL (link):* defines a point-to-point link that can be used to connect stations or repeaters at up to 2 km.
- *10-BASE-FB (backbone):* defines a point-to-point link that can be used to connect repeaters at up to 2 km.

All three of these specifications make use of a pair of optical fibers for each transmission link, one for transmission in each direction. In all cases the signaling scheme involves the use of Manchester encoding. Each Manchester signal element is then converted to an optical signal element, with the presence of light corresponding to high and the absence of light corresponding to low. Thus, a 10-Mbps Manchester bit stream actually requires 20 Mbps on the fiber.

The 10-BASE-FP defines a passive star system that can support up to 33 stations attached to a central passive star. 10-BASE-FL and 10-BASE-FB define point-to-point connections that can be used to extend the length of a network. The key difference between the two is that 10-BASE-FB makes use of synchronous retransmission. With synchronous signaling, an optical signal coming into a repeater is retimed with a local clock and retransmitted. With conventional asynchronous signaling, used with 10-BASE-FL, no such retiming takes place, so that any timing distortions are propagated through a series of repeaters. As a result, 10BASE-FB can be used to cascade up to 15 repeaters in sequence to achieve greater length.

Hubs and Switches

Earlier, we referred to the term *hub* in reference to a star-topology LAN. This term is used to refer to a number of different types of devices. The most important distinction is between the shared-medium hub and the switched LAN hub. To clarify the distinction among types of hubs, let us consider Ethernet-style LANs. Figure 9.16a shows a typical layout of a traditional 10-Mbps Ethernet. A bus is installed that is laid out so as that all the devices to be attached are in reasonable proximity to a point on the bus. A transmission from any one station is propagated along the length of the bus and may be received by all other stations. In the figure, station B is transmitting. This transmission goes from B, across the lead from B to the bus, along the bus in both directions, and along the access lines of each of the other attached stations. In this configuration, all the stations must share the total capacity of the bus, which is 10 Mbps.

A shared-medium hub, such as specified by 10BASE-T, has a central hub, often in a building wiring closet. A star wiring arrangement is used to attach the stations to the hub. In this arrangement, a transmission from any one station is received by the hub and retransmitted on all of the outgoing lines. To avoid collision, only one station can transmit at a time. Again, the total capacity of the LAN is the same as that of the access lines from each station, 10 Mbps. The shared-medium hub has several advantages over the simple bus arrangement. It exploits standard building wiring practices in the layout of cable. In addition, the hub can be configured to recognize a malfunctioning station that is jamming the network and to cut that station out of the network. Figure 9.16b illustrates the operation of a shared-medium hub.

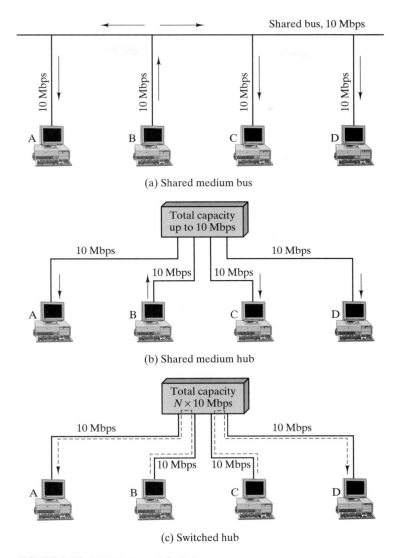

(a) Shared medium bus

(b) Shared medium hub

(c) Switched hub

FIGURE 9.16 LAN Hubs and Switches.

To achieve greater performance, a new form of hub, known as a *switching hub,* was introduced. In this case, the central hub acts as a switch, much as a packet switch or circuit switch. An incoming frame from a particular station is switched to the appropriate output line to be delivered to the intended destination. At the same time, other unused lines can be used for switching other traffic. Figure 9.16c shows an example in which station B is transmitting a frame to A and at the same time, C is transmitting a frame to D. So in this example, the current throughput on the LAN is 20 Mbps, although each individual device is limited to 10 Mbps. The switching hub has several attractive features:

1. No change is required to the software or hardware of the attached devices to covert a bus LAN or a shared-medium hub LAN to a switching-hub LAN. In the case of a CSMA/CD LAN, each attached device continues to use the CSMA/CD protocol to access the LAN. From the point of view of the attached devices, nothing has changed in the access logic.

2. Each attached device has a dedicated capacity equal to that of the entire original LAN, assuming that the hub has sufficient capacity to keep up with all attached devices. For example, in Figure 9.16c, if the hub can sustain a throughput of 20 Mbps, each attached device appears to have a dedicated capacity for either input or output of 10 Mbps.

3. The switching hub scales easily. Additional devices can be attached to the hub by increasing the capacity of the hub correspondingly.

Two types of switched hubs are available as commercial products:

- *Store-and-forward switch.* The hub accepts a frame on an input line, buffers it briefly, and then routes it to the appropriate output line.
- *Cut-through switch.* The hub takes advantage of the fact that the destination address appears at the beginning of the MAC frame (Figure 9.13). The hub begins repeating the incoming frame onto the appropriate output line as soon as the hub recognizes the destination address.

The cut-through switch yields the highest possible throughput but at some risk of propagating bad frames, because the switch is not able to check the CRC prior to retransmission. The store-and-forward switch involves a delay between sender and receiver but boosts the overall integrity of the network.

The discussion in this section has been in terms of Ethernet hubs and switched Ethernet LANs. However, the principle applies to any type of LAN, including token ring. The type of LAN is determined by the medium access control protocol employed on the access lines between hub and station.

9.5 TOKEN RING

Token Ring
A medium access control technique for ring LANs. A token circulates around the ring to regulate access.

The IEEE 802.5 **token ring** standard is an outgrowth of IBM's commercial token ring LAN product. Because of IBM's presence in the corporate marketplace, token ring LANs have gained broad acceptance. However, token ring has never achieved the popularity of Ethernet-type systems.

Medium Access Control

The token ring technique is based on the use of a small frame, called a *token*, that circulates when all stations are idle. A station wishing to transmit must wait until it detects a token passing by. It then seizes the token by changing one bit in the token, which transforms it from a token to a start-of-frame sequence for a data frame. The station then appends and transmits the remainder of the fields needed to construct a data frame.

When a station seizes a token and begins to transmit a data frame, there is no token on the ring, so other stations wishing to transmit must wait. The frame on the ring will make a round trip and be absorbed by the transmitting station. In the default operation, the transmitting station will insert a new token on the ring when both of the following conditions have been met:

- The station has completed transmission of its frame.
- The leading edge of the transmitted frame has returned (after a complete circulation of the ring) to the station.

If the bit length of the ring is less than the frame length, the first condition implies the second. If not, a station could release a free token after it has finished transmitting but before it begins to receive its own transmission; the second condition is not strictly necessary and is relaxed for the configuration option known as *early token release*. The advantage of imposing the second condition is that it ensures that only one data frame at a time may be on the ring and only one station at a time may be transmitting, simplifying error recovery procedures.

Once the new token has been inserted on the ring, the next station downstream with data to send will be able to seize the token and transmit. Figure 9.17 illustrates the technique. In the example, station A sends a frame to C, which receives it and then, once it has also received a token, sends its own frames to A and D.

Note that under lightly loaded conditions, there is some inefficiency with token ring because a station must wait for the token to come around before transmitting. However, under heavy loads, which is when it matters, the ring functions in a round-robin fashion, which is both efficient and fair. To see this, consider the configuration in Figure 9.17. After station A transmits, it releases a token. The first station with an opportunity to transmit is D. If D transmits, it then releases a token and C has the next opportunity, and so on.

The principal advantage of token ring is the flexible control over access that it provides. In the simple scheme just described, the access if fair. In addition, schemes can be used to regulate access to provide for priority and guaranteed bandwidth services. The principal disadvantage of token ring is the requirement for token maintenance. Loss of the token prevents further utilization of the ring. Duplication of the token can also disrupt ring operation. One station must be selected as a monitor to ensure that exactly one token is on the ring and to reinsert a free token if necessary.

Bridge
An internetworking device that connects two similar local area networks that use the same LAN protocols.

IEEE 802.5 Transmission Medium Options

The 802.5 standard specifies the use of shielded twisted pair with data rates of 4 and 16 Mbps using differential Manchester encoding. An earlier specification of a 1-Mbps system has been dropped from the most recent edition of the standard. A recent addition to the standard is the use of unshielded twisted pair at 4 Mbps.

9.6 BRIDGES

In virtually all cases there is a need to expand beyond the confines of a single LAN, to provide interconnection to other LANs and to wide-area networks. Two general approaches are used for this purpose: bridges and routers. The **bridge** is

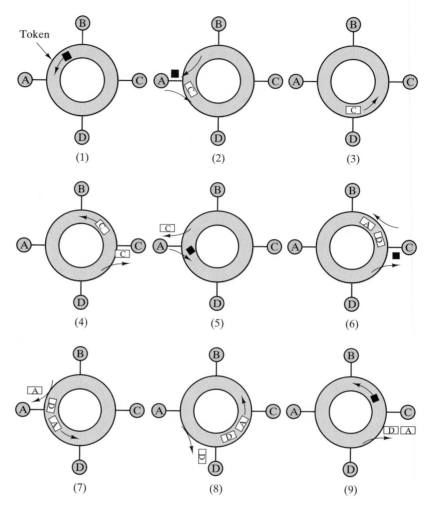

FIGURE 9.17 Token Ring Operation.

the simpler device and provides a means of interconnecting similar LANs. The router is a more general-purpose device, capable of interconnecting a variety of LANs and WANs. We explore bridges in this section and look at routers in Chapter 12.

The bridge is designed for use between LANs that use identical protocols for the physical and link layers (e.g., all conforming to IEEE 802.3 or all conforming to FDDI). Because the devices all use the same protocols, the amount of processing required at the bridge is minimal. More sophisticated bridges are capable of mapping from one MAC format to another (e.g., to interconnect an Ethernet and a token-ring LAN).

Because the bridge is used in a situation in which all the LANs have the same characteristics, the reader may ask: Why not simply have one large LAN? Depending on circumstance, there are several reasons for the use of multiple LANs connected by bridges:

- *Reliability.* The danger in connecting all data processing devices in an organization to one network is that a fault on the network may disable communication for all devices. By using bridges, the network can be partitioned into self-contained units.

- *Performance.* In general, performance on a LAN declines with an increase in the number of devices or the length of the wire. A number of smaller LANs will often give improved performance if devices can be clustered so that intranetwork traffic significantly exceeds internetwork traffic.

- *Security.* The establishment of multiple LANs may improve security of communications. It is desirable to keep different types of traffic (e.g., accounting, personnel, strategic planning) that have different security needs on physically separate media. At the same time, the different types of users with different levels of security need to communicate through controlled and monitored mechanisms.

- *Geography.* Clearly, two separate LANs are needed to support devices clustered in two geographically distant locations. Even in the case of two buildings separated by a highway, it may be far easier to use a microwave bridge link than to attempt to string coaxial cable between the two buildings.

Figure 9.18 illustrates the action of a bridge connecting two LANs, A and B, using the same MAC protocol. In this example, a single bridge attaches to both LANs; frequently, the bridge function is performed by two "half-bridges," one on each LAN. The functions of the bridge are few and simple:

- Read all frames transmitted on A and accept those addressed to any station on B.

- Using the medium access control protocol for B, retransmit each frame on B.

- Do the same for B-to-A traffic.

Several design aspects of a bridge are worth highlighting:

1. The bridge does not modify the content or format of the frames it receives, nor does it encapsulate them with an additional header. Each frame to be transferred is simply copied from one LAN and repeated with exactly the same bit pattern on the other LAN. Because the two LANs use the same LAN protocols, it is permissible to do this.

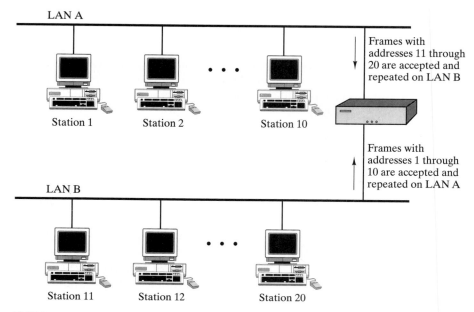

FIGURE 9.18 Bridge Operation.

2. The bridge must contain addressing and routing intelligence. At a minimum, the bridge must know which addresses are on each network to know which frames to pass. Further, there may be more than two LANs interconnected by a number of bridges. In that case a frame may have to be routed through several bridges in its journey from source to destination.

3. A bridge may connect more than two networks.

In summary, the bridge provides an extension to the LAN that requires no modification of the communications software in the stations attached to the LANs. It appears to all stations on the two (or more) LANs that there is a single LAN on which each station has a unique address. The station uses that unique address and need not explicitly discriminate between stations on the same LAN and stations on other LANs; the bridge takes care of that.

SUMMARY

The requirement for networking capability within the individual building is just as strong as the requirement for wide-area networking. Every business environment is populated with a large and growing collection of data processing equipment. Local-area networks are needed to tie this equipment together, both for intraoffice communications and to provide a cost-effective link to wide-area networks.

A LAN consists of a shared transmission medium and a set of hardware and software for interfacing devices to the medium and regulating the orderly access to the medium. The topologies that have been used for LANs are ring, bus, tree, and star. A ring

LAN consists of a closed loop of repeaters that allow data to circulate around the ring. A repeater may also function as a device attachment point. Transmission is generally in the form of frames. The bus and tree topologies are passive sections of cable to which stations are attached. A transmission of a frame by any one station can be heard by any other station. A star LAN includes a central node to which stations are attached.

The transmission media that are used for LANs are twisted pair, coaxial cable, and optical fiber. In the case of coaxial cable, two versions are in common use. The baseband LAN uses digital signaling. The broadband LAN uses analog signaling and allows multiple channels of data simultaneously. Video and other analog signals can also be simultaneously supported on the broadband cable. Both shielded and unshielded twisted pair are in use.

A set of standards has been defined for LANs that specifies a range of data rates and encompasses all of the topologies and transmission media just mentioned. These standards, the IEEE 802 and fiber distributed data interface (FDDI) standards, are widely accepted, and most of the products on the market conform to one of these standards.

In most cases an organization will have multiple LANs that need to be interconnected. The simplest approach to meeting this requirement is the bridge.

RECOMMENDED READING

The literature on LANs and MANs is vast. The material in this chapter is covered in much more depth in [STAL97b]. [MART94] and [MADR94] are also good book-length treatments of LANs.

MADR94   MADRON, T. *Local Area Networks: New Technologies, Emerging Standards.* New York: Wiley, 1994.

MART94   MARTIN, J., CHAPMAN, K., and LEBEN, J. *Local Area Networks: Architectures and Implementations.* Upper Saddle River, NJ: Prentice Hall, 1994.

STAL97b   STALLINGS, W. *Local and Metropolitan Area Networks,* 5th ed. Upper Saddle River, NJ: Prentice Hall, 1997.

Recommended Web Sites

- http://web.syr.edu/~jmwobus/lans: has links to most important sources of LAN information on the Internet, including all of the related FAQs (frequently-asked questions).

- http://wwwhost.ots.utexas.edu/ethernet: provides general Ethernet information, technical specifications, an Ethernet reading list, and an image of inventor Robert Metcalf's original 1976 Ethernet drawing.

- http://www.astral.org: site of the Alliance for Strategic Token Ring Advancement and Leadership, a vendor organization.

KEY TERMS

Baseband	Hub	Star
Bridge	IEEE 802	Structured Cabling
Broadband	Local-Area Network (LAN)	Token Ring
Bus	Logical Link Control (LLC)	Tree
CSMA/CD	Medium Access Control	Wiring Closet
Ethernet	(MAC)	
Headend	Ring	

QUESTIONS

1. How do the key requirements for computer room networks differ from those for personal computer local networks?
2. Compare and contrast the major functions of a personal computer, minicomputer, and mainframe in a company.
3. What is network topology?
4. What is the primary reason that baseband bus LAN systems can extend only about 1 km without repeaters?
5. Explain the difference between a dual-cable configuration and a split configuration for a broadband bus LAN.
6. Explain the difference between a linear strategy and a star strategy for LAN transmission media.
7. What is CSMA/CD?
8. Under heavy loads, how do CSMA/CD and token bus differ?

PROBLEMS

1. Instead of LLC, could HDLC be used as a data link control protocol for a LAN? If not, what is lacking?
2. Consider the transfer of a file containing 1 million characters from one station to another. Calculate the total elapsed time and effective throughput for the following cases:
   a. A circuit-switched, star-topology local network. Call setup time is negligible and the data rate on the medium is 64 kbps.
   b. A bus topology local network with two stations a distance D apart, a data rate of B bps, and a frame size of P with 80 bits of overhead per frame. Each frame is acknowledged with an 89-bit frame before the next is sent. The propagation speed on the bus is 200 m/μsec. Solve for:
      (1) $D = 1$ km, $B = 1$ Mbps, $P = 256$ bits
      (2) $D = 1$ km, $B = 10$ Mbps, $P = 256$ bits
      (3) $D = 10$ km, $B = 1$ Mbps, $P = 256$ bits
      (4) $D = 1$ km, $B = 50$ Mbps, $P = 10,000$ bits
   c. A ring topology local network with a total circular length of $2D$, with the two stations a distance D apart. Acknowledgment is achieved by allowing a frame to circulate past the destination station, back to the source station, with an acknowledgment bit set by the destination. There are N repeaters on the ring, each of which introduces a delay of one bit time. Repeat the calculation for each of b1 through b4 for $N = 10; 100; 1000$.
3. In the description of CSMA/CD, it was stated that after a collision, a station waits a random amount of time and then attempts to transmit again. This waiting period is defined as follows: The delay is an integral multiple of slot time. The number of slot times to delay before the nth retransmission attempt is chosen as a uniformly distributed random integer r in the range $0 < r < 2^K$, where $K = \min(n, 10)$. Slot time is, roughly, twice the round-trip propagation delay on the bus. Assume that two stations always have a frame to send. After a collision, what is the mean number of retransmission attempts before one station transmits successfully. What is the answer if three stations always have frames to send?

CHAPTER 9

Case Study

LEVI STRAUSS

*L*evi Strauss is a major apparel manufacturer headquartered in San Francisco, with annual revenue of nearly $5 billion. The headquarters complex consists of a five-building campus. As with many businesses, Levi has come to rely heavily on LANs. Unfortunately, and again as with many other companies, the LANs at Levi's corporate headquarters sprouted in an uncontrolled fashion as individual departments hired consultants, developed new applications or moved some existing applications off the mainframe, and set up their own networks. Each department had its own LAN administrator, applications, and environment [DOUG93]. This pattern was repeated beyond headquarters at other sites.

The driving force behind the proliferation of LANs was the proliferation of PCs. The company realized that someone with a PC and the skills to go along with the PC gets a better result than someone with a terminal and access to a mainframe. The result: with 32,000 employees, Levi Strauss is the proud possessor of over 10,000 PCs, and the ratio of employees to PCs is dropping.

Those PCs, of course, dictate the need for networks. In just a three-year period, beginning in 1988, the headquarters location went from an exclusively mainframe-based operation to a PC-based operation and a hodgepodge of 22 different LANs, with different technologies (Ethernet, token ring, etc.), different communications software platforms, and different file and database standards. Although the departments did have their own network administrators, they lacked the networking expertise to solve all support problems, particularly those that involved users accessing data or applications beyond the departmental LAN. As the number of LANs grew, with hundreds of users, the need for an enterprise strategy became evident.

In May 1991, Levi Strauss formed a task force of networking and MIS staff members to devise a strategy for the headquarters complex (short term) and the entire corporation (long term). The group inventoried the network equipment and connections already in place and interviewed users and administrators to determine needs and problems. Before attempting a design solution, the group developed "ten commandments" for information resources management that would guide their work:

1. Thou shalt employ a network architecture based on OSI protocols.
2. Thou shalt implement TCP/IP on each LAN and sub-LAN.
3. Thou shalt complete a corporate campus backbone network based on TCP/IP and FDDI.
4. Thou shalt implement star-wired LANs with Ethernet technology.
5. End-use access shall be graphical user interface (GUI) and display a "common look and feel" on a windowing workstation.
6. Thou shalt provide single sign-on access to all authorized systems unless security requires additional authentication.
7. Data shall be migrated to servers in the network.
8. All stations in the network shall have a common routing table and support the same routing table abstractions.
9. Thou shalt replace existing Intel-based file servers with general-purpose RISC-based Unix servers.

10. Thou shalt implement these commandments in a time-to-market fashion.

These commandments were used as the basis of a strategy to move the entire company's networking suite to a standard strategic platform that would support future technical and business needs. A LAN consulting group was set up to oversee and administer the evolution to the new regime.

However, much of the work of this new group would involve selling and not dictating. At the core of Levi Strauss's corporate culture is empowerment—employees assume responsibility for all aspects of their jobs, including computer needs [BROU92]. Accordingly, departments did not have to follow the 10 guidelines (not commandments!). As the head of the LAN consulting group put it: "If someone needs to do something to make their job easier, it's within the bounds of their responsibility to take care of it. It's a very distributed model. A typical user might feel: 'This is my information. I'm the one who needs it, and I shouldn't have to deal with a guy in a white castle in San Francisco.' "

The selling job involved, initially, a briefing of the 25 departmental LAN administrators and to interested groups to explain the 10-point plan. Then regular informal forums were set up for the LAN administrators to create a free flow of information and for the central LAN group to remain current on users' concerns. The central group set up a centralized purchasing service for network equipment. This relieved local administrators of a nuisance and built a relationship in which departments could begin to see the central group as a resource rather than an outsider.

In the long run, a client–server architecture seems ideally suited to the needs of Levi Strauss (see Chapter 14 for a discussion of client–server computing). It was felt that a client–server architecture based on open systems had the highest probability of making information more accessible to people who need it to make decisions and act on them. The first step in getting there, or indeed to any uniform architecture, is to rationalize the networking installation. To do this, the central group began rewiring all the headquarters buildings to support star-wired Ethernet-based LANs. As the wiring became available, the central group encouraged migration to the new LANs by offering network management support and hardware/software procurement support. By 1993, the wiring installation was complete. LANs in the five buildings at the headquarters complex are connected by a backbone FDDI network.

Users and department managers have responded positively to the plan. The opportunity to maintain local control of data and applications while offloading much of the network management and purchasing hassle to a centralized utility-type service is attractive. Accordingly, many of the departments have already moved over to new LANs that fit within the central plan.

With the networking scheme well in hand, Levi is looking toward opportunities to improve distributed application support. The key to this is to provide a client–server architecture based on a company-standard server platform. This approach would enable individual departments to purchase and/or implement their own applications but to rely on the use of servers that are maintained by the central office. One overall goal is that all major corporate systems, from personnel to purchasing to manufacturing, be able to communicate with each other [STEV92]. This goal is to be achieved with centralized standards but decentralized computing capability.

The choice of a single-server vendor has turned out to be more difficult than anticipated. Two companies were in the running: Sun Microsystems and Hewlett-Packard. In essence, the company felt that Sun had the better technology while HP offered superior sales support. However, in a process familiar to many network managers, the Levi Strauss people found themselves jumping back and forth between the two vendors in trying to make a decision.

To begin, after a needs assessment and a test of both products, Levi Strauss chose Sun because it appeared to provide faster response time and greater reliability. Then, because Sun could not provide adequate sales support in such areas as user training and maintenance, Levi Strauss decided to go with HP, which set up a 35-node network as a prototype. Unfortunately, the networking software had bugs and the price was turning out to be more than Levi Strauss wanted to spend. It took over a year to work out all these problems.

With the network and server architecture in hand, the company turned to the whole point of this exercise: migrating users to a common desktop application base. Individual groups were given the lead in acquiring equipment within a common boundary: Intel-based 486 or better PCs as standard for the desktop, with Microsoft Windows and Office for business applications. The goal is for everyone to have the same platform, the same look and feel, and consistent naming and addressing. By 1995, some 10,000 office workers in Levi Strauss's domestic and international offices and subsidiaries had a single computing platform for creating and sharing information [PARK95].

Although the application support area is slow in maturing, Levi Strauss is satisfied with the progress made so far. The centralization of key areas of LAN purchasing and management has accelerated the move from mainframe-based to LAN-based applications, which in turn fits better with Levi Strauss's distributed-authority corporate culture. While there are still many incompatibilities among the applications and equipment in use throughout the company, Levi Strauss is poised to evolve as platforms and software become available to support their overall strategy.

Discussion Questions

1. What would likely be the most compelling arguments that the central staff could make to encourage local LAN administrators to adopt the 10-point plan and yield some authority to the central group?

2. What are the probable difficulties and risk associated with the transition from mainframe-oriented to personal-computer oriented computing?

3. Do you anticipate any security concerns? If so, what precautions should the company take?

CHAPTER 10

High-Speed
and Wireless LANs

After reading this chapter, you should be able to:

- Understand the reasons for the interest in LANs that operate at data rates of 100 Mbps or more.

- Describe the most important types of high-speed LANs.

- Explain the continued interest in Ethernet-type systems at higher and higher data rates.

- Describe the FDDI LAN.

- Describe the Fibre Channel LAN.

- Discuss the role of ATM in local networking and its relationship to ATM WANs.

- Discuss the importance of wireless LANs.

- Describe the various approaches to wireless local networking.

*A*fter a decade or more of gradual refinement and evolution in LAN products, recent years have seen rapid change in the technology, design, and commercial applications for LANs. These changes fall into two categories: (1) a variety of new schemes for high-speed local networking, and (2) the development of practical, effective wireless LANs. In this chapter we examine these two types of LAN.

10.1 THE EMERGENCE OF HIGH-SPEED LANs

Personal computers and microcomputer workstations began to achieve widespread acceptance in business computing in the early 1980s and have now achieved virtually the status of the telephone: an essential tool for office workers. Until relatively recently, office LANs provided basic connectivity services: connecting personal computers and terminals to mainframes and midrange systems that ran corporate applications, and providing workgroup connectivity at the departmental or divisional level. In both cases, traffic patterns were relatively light, with an emphasis on file transfer and electronic mail. The LANs that were available for this type of workload, primarily Ethernet and token ring, are well suited to this environment.

In the 1990s, two significant trends have altered the role of the personal computer and therefore the requirements on the LAN:

1. The speed and computing power of personal computers has continued to enjoy explosive growth. In 1988, a 16-MHz 80286 platform with 2 MB of RAM was considered a high-end systems. In the latter part of the 1990s, a more typical system is a Pentium or PowerPC processor in the low hundreds of megahertz with built-in RAM of 64 MB or more. These more powerful platforms support graphics-intensive applications and ever-more elaborate graphical use interfaces to the operating system.

2. MIS organizations have recognized the LAN as a viable and indeed essential computing platform, resulting in the focus on network computing. This trend began with the client–server computing, which has become a dominant architecture in the business environment and the more recent intranetwork trend. Both of these approaches, which are discussed in Part 4, involve the frequent transfer of potentially large volumes of data in a transaction-oriented environment.

The effect of these trends has been to increase the volume of data to be handled over LANs and, because applications are more interactive, to reduce the acceptable delay on data transfers. The earlier generation of 10-Mbps Ethernets and 16-Mbps token rings are simply not up to the job of supporting these requirements.

The following are examples of requirements that call for higher-speed LANs:

- *Centralized server farms.* In many applications, there is a need for user, or client, systems to be able to draw huge amounts of data from multiple centralized servers, called *server farms.* An example is a color publishing operation, in which servers typically contain tens of gigabytes of image data that must be downloaded to imaging workstations. As the performance of the servers themselves has increased, the bottleneck has shifted to the network. Switched Ethernet alone would not solve this problem because of the limit of 10 Mbps on a single link to the client.

- *Power work groups.* These groups typically consist of a small number of cooperating users who need to draw massive data files across the network. Examples are a software development group that runs tests on a new software version, or a computer-aided design (CAD) company that regularly runs simulations of new designs. In such cases, large amounts of data are distributed to several workstations, processed, and updated at very high speed for multiple iterations.

- *High-speed local backbone.* As processing demand grows, LANs proliferate at a site, and high-speed interconnection is necessary.

TABLE 10-1 Characteristics of Some High-Speed LANs

	Fast Ethernet	*Gigabit Ethernet*	*FDDI*	*Fibre Channel*	*ATM LAN*
Data rate	100 Mbps	1 Gbps	100 Mbps	100–800 Mbps	25 Mbps–1.2 Gpbs
Transmission media	UTP, STP, optical fiber	Optical fiber	UTP, STP, optical fiber	Optical fiber	UTP, STP, optical fiber
Access method	CSMA/CD	CSMA/CD	Token ring	Switched	Switched
Supporting standard	IEEE 802.3	IEEE 802.3	ANSI X3T9.5	Fibre Channel Association	ATM Forum

To keep pace with the changing local networking needs of business, a number of approaches to high-speed LAN design have become commercial products. The most important of these are:

- *Fast Ethernet and Gigabit Ethernet.* The extension of 10-Mbps CSMA/CD to higher speeds is a logical strategy, as it tends to preserve the investment in existing systems.
- *ATM LAN.* The extension of ATM from wide-area networking into the LAN arena is attractive because of the ease of interconnection of ATM LANs and WANs.
- *Fibre Channel.* This approach is intended to provide a low-cost, easily scalable approach to achieving very high data rates in local areas.
- *Fiber distributed data interface (FDDI).* This token-ring scheme has actually been around for a long time. The maturity of its technology has made it a competitor in the high-speed LAN market.

Table 10-1 lists some of the characteristics of these various approaches.

10.2 FAST ETHERNET AND GIGABIT ETHERNET

If one were to design a high-speed (100 Mbps or more) LAN from scratch, one would not choose CSMA/CD as the basis for the design. CSMA/CD is simple to implement and robust in the face of faults, but it does not scale well. As the load on a bus increases, the number of collisions increases, degrading performance. Furthermore, as the data rate for a given system increases, performance also decreases. The reason for this is that at a higher data rate, a station can transmit more bits before it recognizes a collision, and therefore more wasted bits are transmitted.

These problems can be overcome. To accommodate higher loads, a system can be designed to have a number of different segments, interconnected with hubs. The hubs can act as barriers, separating the LAN into *collision domains*, so that a collision in one domain does not spread to other domains. The use of switched Ethernet hubs in effect eliminates collisions, further increasing efficiency. However, there are more efficient ways of achieving the same objectives, such as the use of token ring systems or a switched LAN strategy. We discuss two examples of the latter, Fibre Channel and ATM LANs, later in this chapter.

Despite some drawbacks to its use, Ethernet-style LANs have been developed that operate at 100 Mbps. The reasons for this are instructive. From the vendor's point of view, the CSMA/CD protocol is well understood and vendors have experience building the hardware, firmware, and software for such systems. Scaling the system up to 100 Mbps or even 1 Gbps may be easier than implementing an alternative protocol and topology. From the customer's point of view, it is relatively easy to integrate older systems running at 10 Mbps with newer systems running at higher speeds if all the systems use the same frame format and the same access protocol. In other words, the continued use of Ethernet-style systems is attractive because Ethernet is already there. This same situation is encountered in other areas of data communications. Vendors and customers do not always, or even in the majority of cases, choose the technically superior solution. Cost, ease of management, and other factors relating to the already existing base of equipment are more important factors in the selection. This is the reason that Ethernet-style systems continue to dominate the LAN market long after most observers predicted the demise of Ethernet.

In recent years, standards have been developed for 802.3 systems operating at 100 Mbps, generally referred to as **Fast Ethernet**. The Fast Ethernet systems have been accepted in the marketplace enthusiastically. Even more recently, systems operating at 1 Gbps, known simply as **Gigabit Ethernet**, have appeared. We look at both schemes in this section.

Fast Ethernet

Fast Ethernet refers to a set of specifications developed by the IEEE 802.3 committee to provide a low-cost, Ethernet-compatible LAN operating at 100 Mbps. The blanket designation for these standards is 100BASE-T. The committee defined a number of alternatives to be used with different transmission media.

Figure 10.1 shows the terminology used in labeling the specifications and indicates the media used. All of the 100BASE-T options use the IEEE 802.3 MAC protocol and frame format. 100BASE-X refers to a set of options that use

FIGURE 10.1 IEEE 802.3 100BASE-T Options.

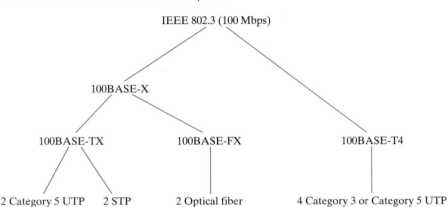

the physical medium specifications originally defined for fiber distributed data interface (FDDI; covered in the next section). All of the 100BASE-X schemes use two physical links between nodes; one for transmission and one for reception. 100BASE-TX makes use of shielded twisted pair (STP) or high-quality (category 5) unshielded twisted pair (UTP). 100BASE-FX uses optical fiber. For all of these schemes the distances involved between hubs and stations is on the order of a maximum of 100 to 200 m.

In many buildings, any of the 100BASE-X options requires the installation of new cable. To minimize costs for buildings that do not have the required cable in place, 100BASE-T4 defines a lower-cost alternative that can use category 3, voice-grade UTP in addition to the higher-quality category 5 UTP.[1] To achieve the 100-Mbps data rate over lower-quality cable, 100BASE-T4 dictates the use of four twisted-pair lines between nodes, with the data transmission making use of three pairs in one direction at a time. For all the 100BASE-T options, the topology is similar to that of 10BASE-T, namely a star-wire topology.

100BASE-X   For all of the transmission media specified under 100BASE-X, a unidirectional data rate of 100 Mbps is achieved transmitting over a single link (single twisted pair, single optical fiber). For all these media, an efficient and effective signal encoding scheme is required. The one chosen was originally defined for FDDI and is referred to as 4B/5B-NRZI. This encoding technique is more efficient than the Manchester technique used for 10-Mbps Ethernet and is therefore desirable at the higher data rate.

The 100BASE-X designation includes two physical medium specifications, one for twisted pair, known as 100BASE-TX, and one for optical fiber, known as 100-BASE-FX. 100BASE-TX makes use of two pairs of twisted-pair cable, one pair used for transmission and one for reception. Both STP and category 5 UTP are allowed. 100BASE-FX makes use of two optical fiber cables, one for transmission and one for reception.

100BASE-T4   100BASE-T4 is designed to produce a 100-Mbps data rate over lower-quality category 3 cable, thus taking advantage of the large installed base of category 3 cable in office buildings. The specification also indicates that the use of category 5 cable is optional. For 100BASE-T4 using category 3 voice-grade cable, it is not reasonable to expect to achieve 100 Mbps on a single twisted pair. Instead, 100BASE-T4 specifies that the data stream to be transmitted be split up into three separate data streams, each with an effective data rate of $33\frac{1}{3}$Mbps. Four twisted pair are used. Data are transmitted using three pairs and received using three pairs. Thus, two of the pairs must be configured for bidirectional transmission.

Configuration and Operation   In its simplest form, a 100BASE-T network is configured in a star-wire topology, with all stations connected directly to a central point referred to as a *multiport repeater*. In this configuration, the repeater rather

---

[1] See Section 4.3 for a discussion of category 3 and category 5 cable.

than the attached stations has the responsibility for detecting collisions. The repeater functions as follows:

- A valid signal appearing on any single input is repeated on all-output link.
- If two inputs occur at the same time, a jam signal is transmitted on all links.

The term *collision domain* is used to define a single CSMA/CD network. This means that if two stations transmit at the same time, a collision will occur. Stations separated by a simple multiport repeater are within the same collision domain, whereas stations separated by a bridge are in different collision domains. Figure 10.2 illustrates this difference. The bridge operates in a store-and-forward fashion and therefore participates in two CSMA/CD algorithms, one for each of the two collision domains that it connects.

The 100BASE-T standard defines two types of repeaters. A class I repeater can support unlike physical media segments, such as 100BASE-T4 and 100BASE-TX. In this case there is likely to be increased internal delay in the repeater to handle the conversion from one signaling scheme to another. Therefore, only a single class I repeater is used in a collision domain. A class II repeater is limited to a single physical media type, and two class II repeaters may be used in a single collision domain.

Full-Duplex Operation   A traditional Ethernet is half-duplex: A station can either transmit or receive a frame, but it cannot do both simultaneously. With full-duplex operation, a station can transmit and receive simultaneously. If a

FIGURE 10.2 100BASE-T Collision Domains.

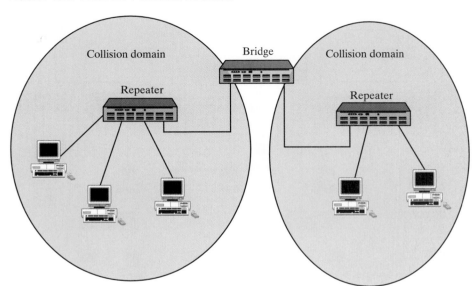

100-Mbps Ethernet ran in full-duplex mode, the theoretical transfer rate becomes 200 Mbps.

Several changes are needed to operate in full-duplex mode. The attached stations must have full-duplex rather than half-duplex adapter cards. The central point in the star wire cannot be a simple multiport repeater but rather, must be a switched hub. In this case each station constitutes a separate collision domain. In fact, there are no collisions and the CSMA/CD algorithm is no longer needed. However, the same 802.3 MAC frame format is used and the attached stations can continue to execute the CSMA/CD algorithm, even though no collisions can ever be detected.

Mixed Configuration   One of the strengths of the Fast Ethernet approach is that it readily supports a mixture of existing 10-Mbps LANs and newer 100-Mbps LANs. An example of what can be accomplished is shown in Figure 10.3, in which the 100-Mbps technology is used as a backbone LAN. Many of the stations attach to 10-Mbps hubs using the 10BASE-T standard. These hubs are in turn connected to switching hubs that conform to 100BASE-T and that can support both 10-Mbps and 100-Mbps links. Additional high-capacity workstations and servers attach directly to these 10/100 switches. These mixed-capacity switches are in turn connected to 100-Mbps hubs using 100-Mbps links. The 100-Mbps hubs provide a

FIGURE 10.3 Example 100-Mbps Ethernet Backbone Strategy [FELT96].

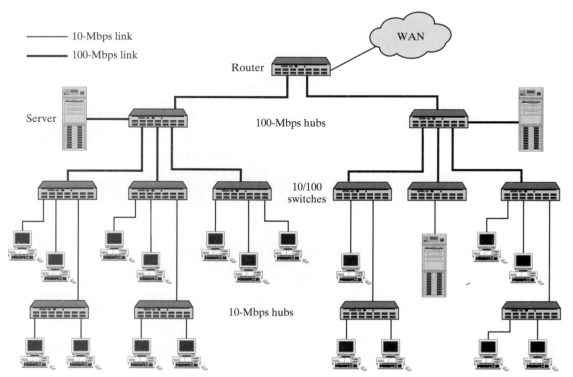

building backbone and are also connected to a router that provides connection to an outside WAN.

Gigabit Ethernet

In late 1995, the IEEE 802.3 committee formed a high-speed study group to investigate means for conveying packets in Ethernet format at speeds in the gigabits per second range. Since that time, there has been considerable work on the development of the Gigabit Ethernet concept.

The strategy for Gigabit Ethernet is the same as that for Fast Ethernet. While defining a new medium and transmission specification, Gigabit Ethernet retains the CSMA/CD protocol and Ethernet format of its 10-Mbps and 100-Mbps predecessors. It is compatible with 100BASE-T and 10BASE-T, preserving a smooth migration path. As more organizations move to 100BASE-T, putting huge traffic loads on backbone networks, demand for Gigabit Ethernet has intensified.

The medium and transmission specification for Gigabit Ethernet call for the use of optical fiber over relatively short distances. Rather than attempt to develop a tailored medium specification, Gigabit Ethernet borrows the physical layer specification from Fibre Channel, described later in this chapter.

Figure 10.4 shows a typical application of Gigabit Ethernet. A 1-Gbps switching hub provides backbone connectivity for central servers and high-speed workgroup hubs. Each workgroup hub supports both 1-Gbps links, to connect to the backbone hub and to support high-performance workgroup servers, and 100-Mbps links, to support high-performance workstations, servers, and 100-Mbps hubs.

The success of both Fast Ethernet and Gigabit Ethernet highlight the importance of network management concerns in choosing a network technology. Both ATM and Fibre Channel may be technically superior choices for a high-speed backbone because of their flexibility and scalability. However, the Ethernet alternatives offer compatibility with existing installed LANs, network management software, and applications. This compatibility has accounted for the survival of a 20-year-old technology (CSMA/CD) in today's fast-evolving network environment.

10.3 ATM LANs

A document on customer premises networks jointly prepared by Apple, Bellcore, Sun, and Xerox [ABSX92] identifies three generations of LANs:

- *First generation:* typified by the CSMA/CD and token-ring LANs. The first generation provided terminal-to-host connectivity and supported client–server architectures at moderate data rates.

- *Second generation:* typified by FDDI. The second generation responds to the need for backbone LANs and for support of high-performance workstations.

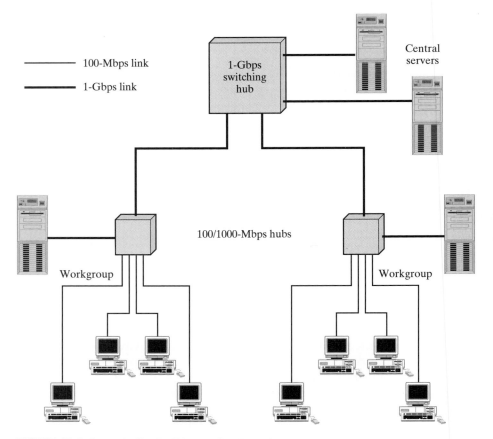

FIGURE 10.4 Example Gigabit Ethernet Configuration.

- *Third generation:* typified by ATM LANs. The third generation is designed to provide the aggregate throughputs and real-time transport guarantees that are needed for multimedia applications.

Typical requirements for a third-generation LAN include:

1. Support multiple, guaranteed classes of service. A live video application, for example, may require a guaranteed 2-Mbps connection for acceptable performance, whereas a file transfer program can utilize a "background" class of service.
2. Provide scalable throughput that is capable of growing both per host capacity (to enable applications that require large volumes of data in and out of a single host) and aggregate capacity (to enable installations to grow from a few to several hundred high-performance hosts).
3. Facilitate the interworking between LAN and WAN technology.

ATM is ideally suited to these requirements. Using virtual paths and virtual channels, multiple classes of service are easily accommodated, either in a preconfigured fashion (permanent connections) or on demand (switched connections). ATM is easily scalable by adding more ATM switching nodes and using higher (or lower) data rates for attached devices. Finally, with the increasing acceptance of cell-based transport for wide-area networking, the use of ATM for a premises network enables seamless integration of LANs and WANs.

The term **ATM LAN** has been used by vendors and researchers to apply to a variety of configurations. At the very least, an ATM LAN implies the use of ATM as a data transport protocol somewhere within the local premises. Among the possible types of ATM LANs:

- *Gateway to ATM WAN.* An ATM switch acts as a router and traffic concentrator for linking a premises network complex to an ATM WAN.
- *Backbone ATM switch.* Either a single ATM switch or a local network of ATM switches interconnect other LANs.
- *Workgroup ATM.* High-performance multimedia workstations and other end systems connect directly to an ATM switch.

These are all "pure" configurations. In practice, a mixture of two or all three of these types of networks is used to create an ATM LAN.

Figure 10.5 shows an example of a backbone ATM LAN that includes links to the outside world. In this example, the local ATM network consists of four

FIGURE 10.5 Example ATM LAN Configuration.

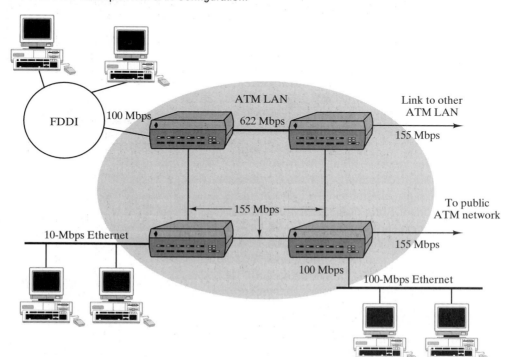

switches interconnected with high-speed point-to-point links running at the standardized ATM rates of 155 and 622. On the premises, there are three other LANs, each of which has a direct connection to one of the ATM switches. The data rate from an ATM switch to an attached LAN conforms to the native data rate of that LAN. For example, the connection to the FDDI network is at 100. Thus, the switch must include some buffering and speed conversion capability to map the data rate from the attached LAN to an ATM data rate. The ATM switch must also perform some sort of protocol conversion from the MAC protocol used on the attached LAN to the ATM cell stream used on the ATM network. A simple approach is for each ATM switch that attaches to a LAN to function as a bridge or router.

An ATM LAN configuration such as that shown in Figure 10.5 provides a relatively painless method for inserting a high-speed backbone into a local environment. As the on-site demand rises, it is a simple matter to increase the capacity of the backbone by adding more switches, increasing the throughput of each switch, and increasing the data rate of the trunks between switches. With this strategy, the load on individual LANs within the premises can be increased and the number of LANs can grow.

However, this simple backbone ATM LAN does not address all the needs for local communications. In particular, in the simple backbone configuration, the end systems (workstations, servers, etc.) remain attached to shared-media LANs, with the limitations on data rate imposed by the shared medium.

A more advanced and more powerful approach is to use ATM technology in a hub. Figure 10.6 suggests the capabilities that can be provided with this

FIGURE 10.6 ATM LAN Hub Configuration.

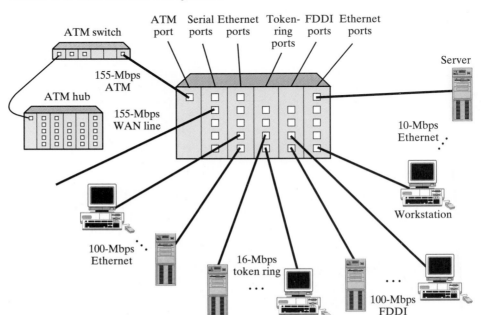

approach. Each ATM hub includes a number of ports that operate at different data rates and use different protocols. Typically, such a hub consists of a number of rack-mounted modules, with each module containing ports of a given data rate and protocol.

The key difference between the ATM hub shown in Figure 10.6 and the ATM nodes depicted in Figure 10.5 is the way in which individual end systems are handled. Notice that in the ATM hub, each end system has a dedicated point-to-point link to the hub. Each end system includes the communications hardware and software to interface to a particular type of LAN, but in each case, the LAN contains only two devices: the end system and the hub! For example, each device attached to a 10-Mbps Ethernet port operates using the CSMA/CD protocol at 10 Mbps. However, because each end system has its own dedicated line, the effect is that each system has its own dedicated 10-Mbps Ethernet. Therefore, each end system can operate at close to the maximum 10-Mbps data rate.

The use of a configuration such as that of either Figure 10.5 or Figure 10.6 has the advantage that existing LAN installations and LAN hardware, called *legacy LANs,* can continue to be used while ATM technology is introduced. The disadvantage is that the use of such a mixed-protocol environment requires the implementation of some sort of protocol conversion capability. A simpler approach, but one that requires that end systems be equipped with ATM capability, is to implement a "pure" ATM LAN.

One issue that was not addressed in our discussion so far has to do with the interoperability of end systems on a variety of interconnected LANs. End systems attached directly to one of the legacy LANs implement the MAC layer appropriate to that type of LAN. End systems attached directly to an ATM network implement the ATM and AAL protocols. As a result, there are three areas of compatibility to consider:

1. Interaction between an end system on an ATM network and an end system on a legacy LAN.
2. Interaction between an end system on a legacy LAN and an end system on another legacy LAN of the same type (e.g., two IEEE 802.3 networks).
3. Interaction between an end system on a legacy LAN and an end system on another legacy LAN of a different type (e.g., an IEEE 802.3 network and an IEEE 802.5 network).

A variety of approaches are possible to meet these requirements. In essence, what is involved is the use of a bridge plus protocol mapping between various MAC layers and mapping between MAC formats and ATM cells. For details, see [STAL97b].

10.4 FIBRE CHANNEL

As the speed and memory capacity of personal computers, workstations, and servers have grown, and as applications have become ever more complex with greater reliance on graphics and video, the requirement for greater speed in delivering data to the processor has grown. This requirement affects two methods of data communications with the processor: I/O channel and network communications.

An I/O channel is a direct point-to-point or multipoint communications link, predominantly hardware-based and designed for high speed over very short distances.. The I/O channel transfers data between a buffer at the source device and a buffer at the destination device, moving only the user contents from one device to another, without regard to the format or meaning of the data. The logic associated with the channel typically provides the minimum control necessary to manage the transfer plus hardware error detection. I/O channels typically manage transfers between processors and peripheral devices, such as disks, graphics equipment, CD-ROMs, and video I/O devices.

A network is a collection of interconnected access points with a software protocol structure that enables communication. The network typically allows may different types of data transfer, using software to implement the networking protocols and to provide flow control, error detection, and error recovery. As we have discussed, networks typically manage transfers between end systems over local, metropolitan, or wide-area distances.

Fibre Channel is designed to combine the best features of both technologies: the simplicity and speed of channel communications with the flexibility and interconnectivity that characterize protocol-based network communications. This fusion of approaches allows system designers to combine traditional peripheral connection, host-to-host internetworking, loosely coupled processor clustering, and multimedia applications in a single multiprotocol interface. The types of channel-oriented facilities incorporated into the Fibre Channel protocol architecture include:

- Data-type qualifiers for routing frame payload into particular interface buffers
- Link-level constructs associated with individual I/O operations
- Protocol interface specifications to allow support of existing I/O channel architectures, such as the Small Computer System Interface (SCSI)

The types of network-oriented facilities incorporated into the Fibre Channel protocol architecture include:

- Full multiplexing of traffic between multiple destinations
- Peer-to-peer connectivity between any pair of ports on a Fibre Channel network
- Capabilities for internetworking to other connection technologies.

Depending on the needs of the application, either channel or networking approaches can be used for any data transfer. The Fibre Channel Association, which is the industry consortium promoting Fibre Channel, lists the following ambitious requirements that Fibre Channel is intended to satisfy [FCA94]:

- Full-duplex links, with two fibers per link

- Performance from 100 to 800 Mbps on a single link (200 to 1600 Mbps per link)
- Support for distances up to 10 km
- Small connectors
- High-capacity utilization with distance insensitivity
- Greater connectivity than existing multidrop channels
- Broad availability (i.e., standard components)
- Support for multiple cost/performance levels, from small systems to supercomputers
- Ability to carry multiple existing interface command sets for existing channel and network protocols

The solution was to develop a simple generic transport mechanism based on point-to-point links and a switching network. This underlying infrastructure supports a simple encoding and framing scheme that in turn supports a variety of channel and network protocols.

Fibre Channel Elements

The key elements of a Fibre Channel network are the end systems, called *nodes*, and the network itself, which consists of one or more switching elements. The collection of switching elements is referred to as a *fabric*. These elements are interconnected by point-to-point links between ports on the individual nodes and switches. Communication consists of the transmission of frames across the point-to-point links.

The Fibre Channel network is quite different from the other LANs that we have examined so far. Fibre Channel is more like a traditional circuit-switched or packet-switched network than is the typical shared-medium LAN. Thus, Fibre Channel need not be concerned with medium access control (MAC) issues. Because it is based on a switching network, the Fibre Channel scales easily in terms of ports, data rate, and distance covered. This approach provides great flexibility. Fibre Channel can readily accommodate new transmission media and data rates by adding new switches and ports to an existing fabric. Thus, an existing investment is not lost with an upgrade to new technologies and equipment. Further, as we shall see, the layered protocol architecture accommodates existing I/O interface and networking protocols, preserving the preexisting investment.

Fibre Channel Protocol Architecture

The Fibre Channel standard is organized into five levels, illustrated in Figure 10.7. Each level defines a function or set of related functions. Levels FC-0 through FC-2 of the Fibre Channel hierarchy are currently defined in a standard referred to as Fibre Channel Physical and Signaling Interface (FC-PH). Currently, there is no final standard for FC-3. At level FC-4, individual standards have been produced for mapping a variety of channel and network protocols onto lower levels.

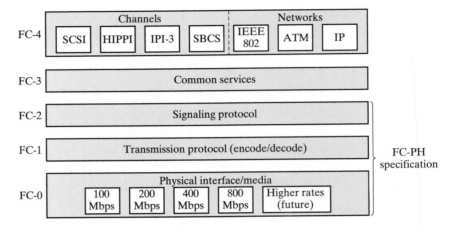

FIGURE 10.7 Fibre Channel Levels.

The five levels can be defined briefly as follows:

- *FC-0.* The physical interface and media level allows a variety of physical media and data rates.

- *FC-1.* The transmission protocol level defines the signal encoding technique used for transmission and for synchronization across the point-to-point link.

- *FC-2.* The framing protocol level deals with the transmission of data between ports in the form of frames, similar to other data link control protocols.

- *FC-3.* The common services level provides a set of services that are common across multiple ports of a node. One example is striping, which makes use of multiple ports in parallel to transmit a single information unit across multiple links simultaneously; this achieves higher aggregate throughput. A possible use is for transferring large data sets in real time, as in video-imaging applications.

- *FC-4.* The mapping level defines the mapping of various channel and network protocols to FC-PH. These include both channel specifications, such as the small computer system interface (SCSI) and network specifications, such as IEEE 802. Thus, existing equipment with other interfaces are readily accommodated with Fibre Channel.

Fibre Channel Physical Media and Topologies

One of the major strengths of the Fibre Channel standard is that it provides a range of options for the physical medium, the data rate on that medium, and the topology of the network.

TABLE 10-2 Maximum Distance for Fibre Channel Media Types

	800 Mbps	*400 Mbps*	*200 Mbps*	*100 Mbps*
Single-mode fiber	10 km	10 km	10 km	—
50-μm multimode fiber	0.5 km	1 km	2 km	10 km
62.5-μm multimode fiber	175 m	350 m	1500 m	1500 m
Video coaxial cable	25 m	50 m	75 m	100 m
Miniature coaxial cable	10 m	15 m	25 m	35 m
Shielded twisted pair	—	—	50 m	100 m

Transmission Media Table 10-2 summarizes the physical transmission-medium and data-rate options that are available under Fibre Channel. Each entry specifies the maximum point-to-point link distance (between ports) that is defined for a given transmission medium at a given data rate. These media may be mixed in an overall configuration. For example, a single-mode optical link could be used to connect switches in different buildings, with multimode optical links used for vertical distribution inside, and shielded twisted-pair or coaxial-cable links to individual workstations.

Topologies The most general topology supported by Fibre Channel is referred to as a *fabric* or *switched topology*. This is an arbitrary topology that includes at least one switch to interconnect a number of end systems. The fabric topology may also consist of a number of switches forming a switched network, with some or all of these switches also supporting end nodes.

Routing in the fabric topology is transparent to the nodes. Each port in the configuration has a unique address. When data from a node are transmitted into the fabric, the edge switch to which the node is attached uses the destination port address in the incoming data frame to determine the destination port location. The switch then either delivers the frame to another node attached to the same switch or transfers the frame to an adjacent switch to begin routing of the frame to a remote destination.

The fabric topology provides scalability of capacity: As additional ports are added, the aggregate capacity of the network increases, thus minimizing congestion and contention and increasing throughput. The fabric is protocol independent and largely distance insensitive. The technology of the switch itself and of the transmission links connecting the switch to nodes may be changed without affecting the overall configuration. Another advantage of the fabric topology is that the burden on nodes is minimized. An individual Fibre Channel node (end system) is only responsible for managing a simple point-to-point connection between itself and the fabric; the fabric is responsible for routing between ports and error detection.

In addition to the fabric topology, the Fibre Channel standard defines two other topologies. With the point-to-point topology there are only two ports, and

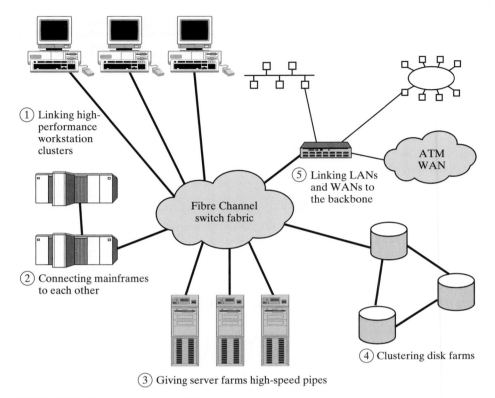

① Linking high-
performance
workstation
clusters

⑤ Linking LANs
and WANs to
the backbone

ATM
WAN

Fibre Channel
switch fabric

② Connecting mainframes
to each other

④ Clustering disk farms

③ Giving server farms high-speed pipes

FIGURE 10.8 Five Applications of Fibre Channel.

these are connected directly, with no intervening fabric switches. In this case there is no routing. The arbitrated loop topology is a simple, low-cost topology for connecting up to 126 nodes in a loop. The arbitrated loop operates in a manner roughly equivalent to the token ring protocols that we have seen.

Topologies, transmission media, and data rates may be combined to provide an optimized configuration for a given site. Figure 10.8 is an example that illustrates the principal applications of Fibre Channel.

Prospects for Fibre Channel

Fibre Channel is backed by an industry interest group known as the Fibre Channel Association, and a variety of interface cards for different applications are available. Fibre Channel has been most widely accepted as in improved peripheral device interconnect, providing services that can eventually replace such schemes as SCSI. It is a technically attractive solution to general high-speed LAN requirements but must compete with Fast Ethernet and ATM LANs. Cost and performance issues should dominate the manager's consideration of these competing technologies.

10.5 FIBER DISTRIBUTED DATA INTERFACE

Fiber Distributed Data Interface (FDDI)
A standard for 100-Mbps optical fiber ring local area network.

The oldest high-speed LAN standard is the **fiber distributed data interface (FDDI)**. The topology of FDDI is ring. The medium access control technique employed is token ring, with only minor differences from the IEEE token-ring specification. The medium specification specifically incorporates measures designed to ensure high availability.

Medium Access Control

Whereas early token release is an option in IEEE 802.5 token ring, it is mandatory in FDDI. Figure 10.9 gives an example of FDDI operation. After station A has seized the token, it transmits frame F1 and immediately transmits a new token. F1 is addressed to station C, which copies it as it circulates past. The frame eventually returns to A, which absorbs it. Meanwhile, B seizes the token issued by A and transmits F2 followed by a token. This action could be repeated any number of times, so that at any one time, there may be multiple frames circulating the ring. Each station is responsible for absorbing its own frames based on the source address field.

The reason that early token release is so important with FDDI is that at the higher data rate, a frame occupies only a relatively small part of a ring and so, if only one frame is allowed on the ring at a time, most of the ring would be idle at all times. Put another way, if the transmitting station must wait until its frame returns before releasing a token, many more bits could be transmitted during that delay at a higher data rate than at a lower data rate, and therefore the waste of capacity is greater at the higher data rate.

FDDI Physical Layer Specification

The FDDI standard specifies a ring topology operating at 100 Mbps. Two media are included: optical fiber and twisted-pair. Two twisted-pair media are specified: category 5 unshielded twisted pair and shielded twisted pair.

Prospects for FDDI

Although FDDI is a technically sound solution and has achieved respectable market share, it has never dominated the high-speed LAN market and is not likely to do so. Fast Ethernet equipment is less expensive and is compatible with the large installed base of Ethernet LANs. ATM LANs integrate well with the ATM WANs and are more suitable for multimedia traffic, especially video and voice than FDDI LANs.

10.6 WIRELESS LANs

In just the past few years, **wireless LANs** have come to occupy a significant niche in the local-area network market. Increasingly, organizations are finding that wireless LANs are an indispensable adjunct to traditional wired LANs, to satisfy

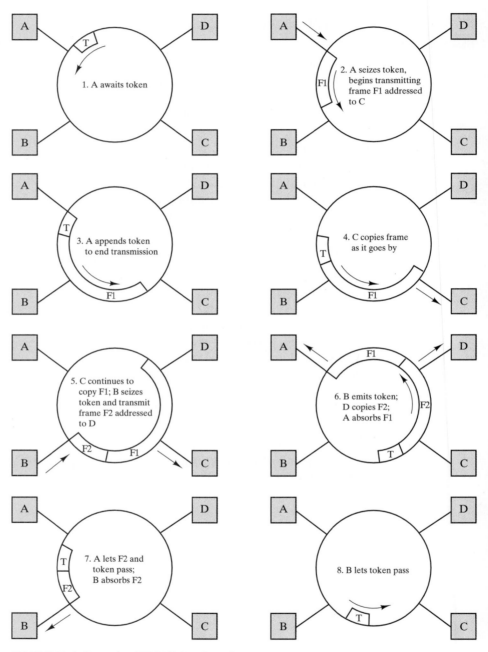

FIGURE 10.9 Example of FDDI Token Ring Operation.

requirements for mobility, relocation, ad hoc networking, and coverage of locations difficult to wire. As the name suggests, a wireless LAN is one that makes use of a wireless transmission medium. Until relatively recently, wireless LANs were little used because of high prices, low data rates, occupational safety concerns, and licensing requirements. As these problems have been addressed, the popularity of wireless LANs has grown rapidly.

Wireless LAN Applications

[PAHL95] lists four application areas for wireless LANs: LAN extension, cross-building interconnect, nomadic access, and ad hoc networks. Let us consider each of these in turn.

LAN Extension Early wireless LAN products, introduced in the late 1980s, were marketed as substitutes for traditional wired LANs. A wireless LAN saves the cost of the installation of LAN cabling and eases the task of relocation and other modifications to network structure. However, this motivation for wireless LANs was overtaken by events. First, as awareness of the need for LANs became greater, architects designed new buildings to include extensive prewiring for data applications. Second, with advances in data transmission technology, there is an increasing reliance on twisted-pair cabling for LANs and, in particular, category 3 unshielded twisted pair. Most older buildings are already wired with an abundance of category 3 cable. Thus, the use of a wireless LAN to replace wired LANs has not happened to any great extent.

However, in a number of environments, there is a role for the wireless LAN as an alternative to a wired LAN. Examples include buildings with large open areas, such as manufacturing plants, stock exchange trading floors, and warehouses; historical buildings with insufficient twisted pairs and where drilling holes for new wiring is prohibited; and small offices where installation and maintenance of wired LANs is not economical. In all these cases, a wireless LAN provides an effective and more attractive alternative. In most these cases, an organization will also have a wired LAN to support servers and some stationary workstations. For example, a manufacturing facility typically has an office area that is separate from the factory floor but which must be linked to it for networking purposes. Therefore, typically, a wireless LAN will be linked into a wired LAN on the same premises. Thus, this application area is referred to as *LAN extension.*

Figure 10.10 indicates a simple wireless LAN configuration that is typical of many environments. There is a backbone wired LAN, such as Ethernet, that supports servers, workstations, and one or more bridges or routers to link with other networks. In addition, there is a control module (CM) that acts as an interface to a wireless LAN. The control module includes either bridge or router functionality to link the wireless LAN to the backbone. In addition, it includes some sort of access control logic, such as a polling or token-passing scheme, to regulate access from the end systems. Note that some of the end systems are stand-alone devices, such as a workstation or a server. In addition, hubs or other user modules (UMs) that control a number of stations off a wired LAN may also be part of the wireless LAN configuration.

The configuration of Figure 10.10 can be referred to as a single-cell wireless LAN; all of the wireless end systems are within range of a single control module. Another common configuration, suggested by Figure 10.11, is a multiple-cell wireless LAN. In this case, there are multiple control modules interconnected by

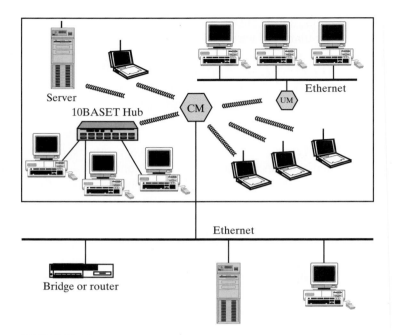

FIGURE 10.10 Example Single-Cell Wireless LAN Configuration.

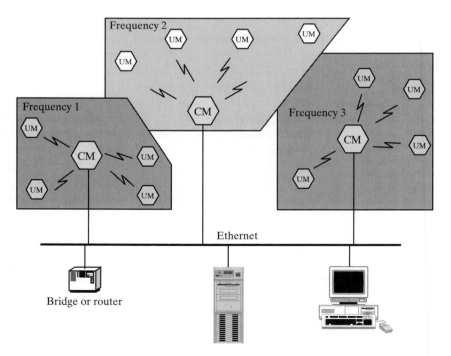

FIGURE 10.11 Example Multiple-Cell Wireless LAN Configuration.

a wired LAN. Each control module supports a number of wireless end systems within its transmission range. For example, with an infrared LAN, transmission is limited to a single room; therefore, one cell is needed for each room in an office building that requires wireless support.

Cross-Building Interconnect   Another use of wireless LAN technology is to connect LANs in nearby buildings, be they wired or wireless LANs. In this case, a point-to-point wireless link is used between two buildings. The devices so connected are typically bridges or routers. This single point-to-point link is not a LAN per se, but it is usual to include this application under the heading of wireless LAN.

Nomadic Access   Nomadic access provides a wireless link between a LAN hub and a mobile data terminal equipped with an antenna, such as a laptop computer or notepad computer. One example of the utility of such a connection is to enable an employee returning from a trip to transfer data from a personal portable computer to a server in the office. Nomadic access is also useful in an extended environment such as a campus or a business operating out of a cluster of buildings. In both of these cases, users may move around with their portable computers and may wish access to the servers on a wired LAN from various locations.

Ad Hoc Networking   An ad hoc network is a peer-to-peer network (no centralized server) set up temporarily to meet an immediate need. For example, a group of employees, each with a laptop or palmtop computer, may convene in a conference room for a business or classroom meeting. The employees link their computers in a temporary network just for the duration of the meeting.

Figure 10.12 suggests the differences between an ad hoc wireless LAN and a wireless LAN that supports LAN extension and nomadic access requirements. In the former case, the wireless LAN forms a stationary infrastructure consisting of one or more cells with a control module for each cell. Within a cell, there may be a number of stationary end systems. Nomadic stations can move from one cell to another. In contrast, there is no infrastructure for an ad hoc network. Rather, a peer collection of stations within range of each other may dynamically configure themselves into a temporary network.

Wireless LAN Requirements

A wireless LAN must meet the same sort of requirements typical of any LAN, including high capacity, ability to cover short distances, full connectivity among attached stations, and broadcast capability. In addition, there are a number of requirements specific to the wireless LAN environment. The following are among the most important requirements for wireless LANs:

- *Throughput.* The medium access control protocol should make as efficient use as possible of the wireless medium to maximize capacity.
- *Number of nodes.* Wireless LANs may need to support hundreds of nodes across multiple cells.
- *Connection to backbone LAN.* In most cases, interconnection with stations on a wired backbone LAN is required. For infrastructure wireless

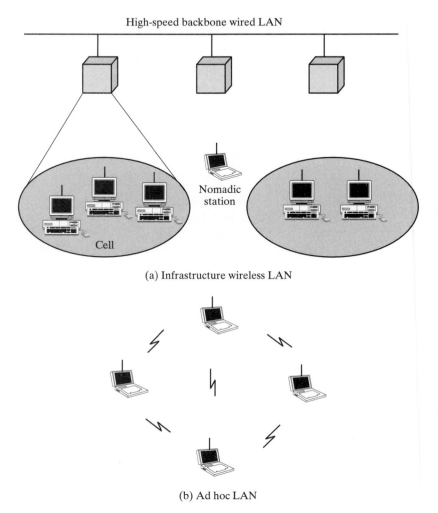

High-speed backbone wired LAN

Nomadic
station

Cell

(a) Infrastructure wireless LAN

(b) Ad hoc LAN

FIGURE 10.12 Wireless LAN Configurations.

LANs, this is easily accomplished through the use of control modules that connect to both types of LANs. There may also need to be accommodation for mobile users and ad hoc wireless networks.

- *Service area.* A typical coverage area for a wireless LAN may be up to a 300- to 1000-ft diameter.

- *Battery power consumption.* Mobile workers use battery-powered workstations that need to have a long battery life when used with wireless adapters. This suggests that a MAC protocol that requires mobile nodes to monitor access points constantly or to engage in frequent handshakes with a base station is inappropriate.

- *Transmission robustness and security.* Unless designed properly, a wireless LAN may be interference-prone and easily eavesdropped. The design of a wireless LAN must permit reliable transmission even in a noisy environment and should provide some level of security from eavesdropping.

- *Collocated network operation.* As wireless LANs become more popular, it is quite likely that two or more wireless LANs can operate in the same area or in an area where interference is possible between the LANs. Such interference may thwart normal operation of a MAC algorithm and may allow unauthorized access to a particular LAN.
- *License-free operation.* Users would prefer to buy and operate wireless LAN products without having to secure a license for the frequency band used by the LAN.
- *Handoff/roaming.* The MAC protocol used in the wireless LAN should enable mobile stations to move from one cell to another.
- *Dynamic configuration.* The MAC addressing and network management aspects of the LAN should permit dynamic and automated addition, deletion, and relocation of end systems without disruption to other users.

SUMMARY

High-speed LANs have emerged as a critical element of corporate information systems. Such LANs are needed not only to provide an on-premises backbone for linking departmental LANs, but to support the high-performance requirements of graphics-based client–server and intranet applications.

For most applications, Fast Ethernet and the emerging Gigabit Ethernet technologies dominate corporate high-speed LAN choices. These systems involve the least risk and cost for managers for a number of reasons, including compatibility with the existing large Ethernet installed base, maturity of the basic technology, and compatibility with existing network management and configuration software.

A more powerful and flexible approach is afforded by the ATM LAN. This type of LAN extends ATM technology and protocols from the wide-area environment to the corporate site. Such LANs are attractive because of ATM's ability to carry an integrated flow of voice, image, video, and data traffic, and because of the seamless connection to the increasingly available ATM WANs. Cost and the fact that this is a newer technology than Ethernet have slowed introduction of the ATM LAN.

Two other high-speed LAN approaches also have attracted considerable support. FDDI has been around for many years. This 100-Mbps token-ring system provides good support for data-only backbone applications. With the higher speeds available via Ethernet, ATM, and Fibre Channel, FDDI may experience declining acceptance. Fibre Channel is a technically attractive solution that provides solid performance; its ability to compete with Fast Ethernet and ATM remains to be seen as of this writing.

RECOMMENDED READING

[STAL97b] covers in greater detail all the LAN systems discussed in this chapter. A superb management-oriented treatment of high-speed LANs is [SAUN96], which provides practical guidance on selection, configuration, and performance issues. [JOHN96a] is an exhaustive treatment of Fast Ethernet, emphasizing the technical details. [BREY95] covers both switched 10-Mbps Ethernet and Fast Ethernet, with more emphasis on practical installation issues and providing a comparison with competing technologies.

Two detailed accounts of FDDI are [MILL95] and [SHAH94]; The former provides more detail on physical-layer issues, while the latter has more coverage of the MAC protocol. [KAVA95] and [NEWM94] are good survey articles on LAN ATM architecture and configurations. The most comprehensive description of Fibre Channel is [STEP95]. This book provides a detailed technical treatment of each layer of the Fibre Channel architecture. Also good is [BENN96].

BENN96   BENNER, A. *Fibre Channel: Gigabit Communications and I/O for Computer Networks.* New York: McGraw-Hill, 1996.

BREY95   BREYER, R., and RILEY, S. *Switched and Fast Ethernet: How It Works and How to Use It.* Emeryville, CA: Ziff-Davis Press, 1995.

JOHN96a   JOHNSON, H. *Fast Ethernet: Dawn of New Network.* Upper Saddle River, NJ: Prentice Hall, 1996.

KAVA95   KAVAK, N. "Data Communication in ATM Networks." *IEEE Network,* May/June 1995.

MILL95   MILLS, A. *Understanding FDDI.* Upper Saddle River, NJ: Prentice Hall, 1995.

NEWM94   NEWMAN, P. "ATM Local Area Networks." *IEEE Communications Magazine,* March 1994.

SAUN96   SAUNDERS, S. *The McGraw-Hill High-Speed LANs Handbook.* New York: McGraw-Hill, 1996.

SHAH94   SHAH, A., and RAMAKRISHNAN, G. *FDDI: A High-Speed Network.* Upper Saddle River, NJ: Prentice Hall, 1994.

STAL97b   STALLINGS, W. *Local and Metropolitan Area Networks,* 5th ed. Upper Saddle River, NJ: Prentice Hall, 1997.

STEP95   STEPHENS, G., and DEDEK, J. *Fibre Channel.* Menlo Park, CA: Ancot Corporation, 1995.

Recommended Web Sites

- http://www.iol.unh.edu: University of New Hampshire site for equipment testing for ATM, FDDI, Fast Ethernet, and other LANs.
- http://www.amdahl.com/ext/CARP/FCA/FCA.html: Web site of the Fibre Channel Association.
- http://www.wlana.com//index.html: Web site of the Wireless LAN Alliance. Gives an introduction to the technology, including a discussion of implementation considerations, and case studies from users. Links to related sites.

KEY TERMS

ATM LAN	Fiber Distributed Data	Fibre Channel
Fast Ethernet	Interface (FDDI)	Gigabit Ethernet
		Wireless LAN

QUESTIONS

1. Explain why a data rate of 10 Mbps on all LAN segments is increasingly inadequate for many businesses.
2. What are the transmission medium options for Fast Ethernet?
3. Other than the data rate, how does Fast Ethernet differ from 10BASE-T?
4. List the levels of Fibre Channel and the functions of each level.
5. How does FDDI differ from IEEE 802.5 token ring?

CHAPTER 10

Case Study

ROCK AND ROLL HALL OF FAME AND MUSEUM

The Rock and Roll Hall of Fame and Museum, established to preserve the history of rock music, opened in late 1995 in Cleveland. In addition to housing rock and roll memorabilia, such as John Lennon's spectacles and Hendrix's guitar, the hall of Fame devotes about 2000 square feet to interactive multimedia kiosks that feature real-time audio and video exhibits. Designing and implementing a system that would deliver audio and full-motion video to 25 multimedia kiosks turned out to be no small undertaking [KARV96]. The broad goal of the project was to be able to deliver streamed video over a fault-tolerant system to Macintosh workstations within 2 seconds of a request. The project was contracted out to CIBER (Consultants in Business, Engineering, and Research), a San Francisco-based systems integrator.

Phase One: Ethernet

CIBER initially felt that a 10BASE-T Ethernet system would be adequate for the job. The plan was to have two servers, each with an identical set of digitized audio and video clips on disk. This would allow one server to pick up the job if the other went down. With everything connected to the same Ethernet, there was full connectivity with a minimum of hardware. CIBER set up a demonstration for the customer. Unfortunately, as the load on the system was increased but still well within projected demand, the system began to drop packets due to congestion.

Phase Two: Token Ring

CIBER then moved to a 16-Mbps token ring. With its higher data rate and more efficient access control technique, token ring seemed poised to handle the load. With the museum's opening date approaching, CIBER went ahead with an installation that involved the token-ring LAN, dual servers, and Macintosh Quadra 840 workstations. After about a month of installation and shakedown, CIBER was ready for a "dress rehearsal" demonstration. Much to everyone's dismay, the new configuration also dropped packets. Full-motion video consists of 30 frames per second, and the system dropped about one-half of these frames. With the audio, the delivery was so choppy that the workstations would fill up a local cache until it was full, play part of the tune, and then have to wait for more data to arrive.

With less than three months to opening, CIBER needed to go into high gear. An analysis of the working configuration indicated both raw performance problems and problems in the way that the communications software and protocols were handling requests. For example, at the server end, the software was chopping the audio and video streams into very small packets and the Macintosh workstations were unable to reassemble them fast enough to provide real-time audio and video.

Phase Three: Switched Ethernet

At least, based on the live experiments, CIBER now had a better idea of capacity requirements. The order called for 10 kiosks to deliver audio and video and 15 to handle audio only. CIBER estimated they would need 2.6 Mbps of capacity to deliver video to each of 10 workstations and 0.9 Mbps to deliver audio to the other 15. This amounted to 40 Mbps required to meet their needs. They weren't going to get that from a shared Ethernet or even token ring, but switched Ethernet with a 100BASE-T backbone might do the trick, provided that the software was beefed up.

313

CIBER found a software solution that seemed to work. Starlight's StarWorks is a software package that runs on Sun workstations and provides efficient video delivery. For example, with Star-Works, video data are organized in *stripes*, on separate disks in a disk array. Pulling video from more than one drive speeds up access time and enables StarWorks to stream packets in long groups, cutting back on handshaking with the workstations.

With the software plan in hand, the task was to deploy a 100BASE-T backbone to link up the servers and 10BASE-T switched Ethernet to the Macintosh workstations. This would give each workstation a dedicated 10-Mbps link with a 100-Mbps capacity back to the servers. But this phase, too, ran into unexpected problems. The configuration used LANnet hubs that provided both 100BASE-T and 10BASE-T ports, but when these were linked up to the SunSPARC servers, many problems cropped up. Working with both the hub and server vendors, it is likely that the problems could eventually have been solved, but the team was working on a tight deadline. On another project, CIBER has integrated Sun servers with Cisco switches. Cisco switches were

FIGURE 10.13 Network Configuration for Rock and Roll Hall of Fame and Museum.

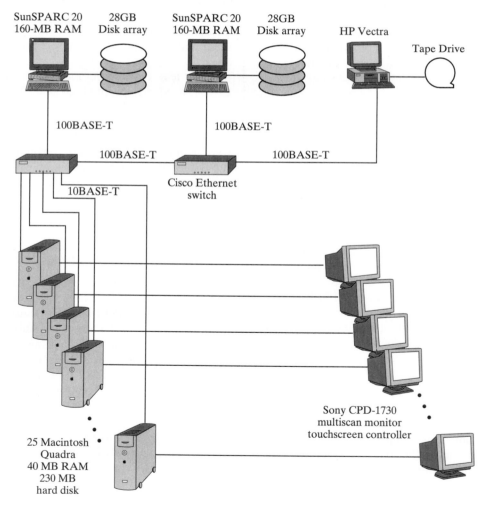

brought in that supported 25 switched 10BASE-T ports and nine 100BASE-T links.

Figure 10.13 shows the final configuration. The 25 kiosks are located in two exhibition areas. Each kiosk gets about 100 hours of use per week. Each kiosk includes a speaker and a touch-control monitor hooked up to a Macintosh workstation, at distances up to 500 ft. All the workstations and other network equipment are located in a control room. Once an option is chosen, the signal travels over video cable to the workstation. If video clips are requested, the request goes to one of the servers, which pumps the data down to the workstation. Data move from the server to the switch at 100 Mbps and then to a workstation at 10 Mbps. Each server stores all the audio and video clips, providing full redundancy. Finally, an HP Vectra with a large-capacity tape drive stores all the files in backup.

Recently, the museum has extended this networked approach to its Web site (http://www.rockhall.com/), spreading the rock'n' roll gospel to the networked masses on many platforms [HAWN96]. Web users can download the same audio and video clips available to museum visitors and play the clips using Apple's Quicktime. The site provides the Quicktime software for Apple and Windows platforms.

Discussion Questions

1. What lessons do you draw from the repeated false starts of the CIBER team?

2. How could the process have been managed better?

3. Comment on the final configuration. Can you suggest radically different configurations? If so, compare with the actual.

CHAPTER 11

Wireless Networks

CHAPTER OBJECTIVES

After reading this chapter, you should be able to:

- Identify the advantages and disadvantages of unguided (wireless communication) relative to guided communication.

- Distinguish among the three generations of mobile telephony.

- Understand the characteristics of time-division multiple access (TDMA) and code-division multiple access (CDMA) as used for mobile telephony.

- Describe the possibilities of Personal Communications Systems (PCS).

- Understand the properties of LEOS, HEOS, and GEOS satellites.

*A*s the applications of electronic information systems reach into every aspect of our lives, it becomes increasingly bothersome to be tethered to them by wires. Wireless communications offers us mobility and much else. Wireless communications should be considered when:

- Mobile communication is needed.
- Communication must take place in a hostile or difficult environment.
- A communication system must be deployed quickly.
- Communication facilities must be installed at low cost (but perhaps with lower performance).
- The same information must be broadcast to many locations.

On the other hand, wireless communication has disadvantages compared to guided media such as twisted pair, coaxial cable, or optical fiber. Wireless communication:

- Operates in a less controlled environment and is therefore more susceptible to interference, noise, and eavesdropping.
- Generally, the data rates are less in wireless facilities than in guided facilities.

- There can be more reuse of frequencies in guided media than in wireless media.

In this chapter we consider wireless systems, including mobile telephony, satellite applications, and third-generation wireless systems.

11.1 MOBILE TELEPHONY

One can categorize mobile telephone systems into generations. The first-generation systems are based on analog communication using frequency modulation. Due to the overwhelming popularity of the first-generation systems, systems that use the spectrum more efficiently became necessary. This requirement was addressed by the second generation, which uses digital techniques and time-division multiple access (TDMA) or code-division multiple access (CDMA). Advanced call processing features are present as well. The third generation will evolve from a number of second-generation wireless systems. The idea will be to integrate these services into one set of standards. It is expected that a single handset will support a wide variety of services, including voice, data, and video. We will describe one first-generation system, the Advanced Mobile Phone System (AMPS), which is common in North and South America, Australia, and China. We then look at a second-generation system, Global System for Mobile (GSM), which is very popular throughout Europe and is probably the fastest-growing mobile telephony technology. We then briefly discuss the relative merits of the FDMA, TDMA, and CDMA access methods, which have been fiercely debated in the United States. We conclude with an overview of the proposals for the third-generation systems.

11.2 ADVANCED MOBILE PHONE SERVICE

Since the early 1980s the most common mobile telephony system in North America is the **Advanced Mobil Phone Service (AMPS)** developed by AT&T. This approach is also common in South America, Australia, and China. Figure 11.1 gives a schematic view of the AMPS. The system has three basic types of devices: the *mobile*, the *base transceiver*, and the *mobile telephone switching office (MTSO)*. The mobile communicates with the base transceiver; the transceivers communicate with the mobiles and with the MTSO. The MTSO coordinates the activities of the base transceivers and also connects calls to the public wire telephone network. We describe these elements in more detail shortly, but first we look at the issue of efficient use of the spectrum.

As we have already observed, a problem with wireless communication is that you are limited in how often you can use the same frequency for different communications because the signals, not being constrained, can interfere with one another even if geographically separated. Systems supporting a large number of communications simultaneously need mechanisms to conserve spectrum.

Spectral Allocation

In North America, two 25-MHz bands are allocated to AMPS, one for transmission from the base station to the mobile unit (869–894 MHz), the other for

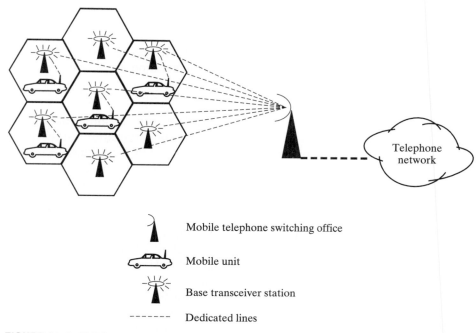

Mobile telephone switching office

Mobile unit

Base transceiver station

------- Dedicated lines

FIGURE 11.1 AMPS Layout.

transmission from the mobile to the base station (824–849 MHz). Each of these bands is split in two to encourage competition (i.e., so that in each market two operators could be accommodated). An operator is allocated only 12.5 MHz in each direction for its system. The channels are spaced 30 kHz apart, which allows a total of 416 channels for an operator. Twenty-one are usually allocated for control, leaving 395 to carry calls. The control channels are data channels operating at 10 kbps. The conversation channels carry the conversations in analog using frequency multiplexing. Control information is also sent on the conversation channels in bursts as data. This number of channels is inadequate for most major markets, so some way must be found either to use less bandwidth per conversation or to reuse frequencies. Both have been done. For AMPS, frequency reuse is exploited.

Spatial Allocation

As is common, we discuss the reuse of frequency in the idealized case of a hexagonal tessellation of the plane by cells (see Figure 11.1). Each cell has a base transceiver that is "responsible" for it. The power of communication is carefully controlled (to the extent that it is possible in the highly variable mobile communication environment) to allow communication within the cell using a given frequency while limiting the power at that frequency that escapes the cell into adjacent ones. The objective is to use the same frequency in another nearby cell, thus allowing the frequency to be used for multiple simultaneous conversations.

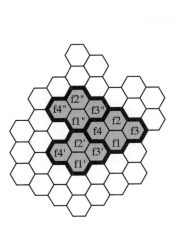

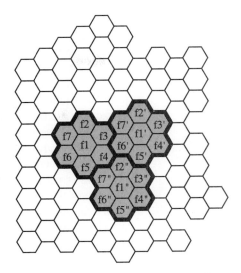

(a) Frequency reuse pattern for *n* = 4

(b) Frequency reuse pattern for *n* = 7

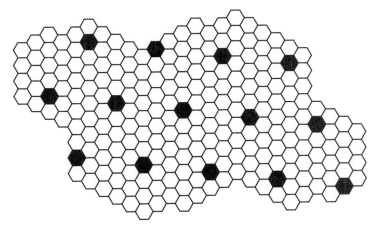

(c) Black cells indicate a frequency reuse for *n* = 19

FIGURE 11.2 Frequency Reuse Patterns.

Generally, 10 to 50 frequencies are assigned to each cell, depending on the traffic expected.

The essential issue, of course, is to determine how many cells must intervene between two cells using the same frequency so that the two cells do not interfere with each other. Various patterns of frequency reuse are possible. Some examples are shown in Figure 11.2. If the pattern consists of *n* cells and each cell is assigned the same number of frequencies, each cell can have N/n frequencies, where *N* is the total number of frequencies allotted to the system. For AMPS, $N = 395$, and $n = 7$ is the smallest size that can provide sufficient isolation between two uses of the same frequency. This implies that there can be at most 57 frequencies per cell on average.

In time, as more customers use the system, traffic may build up so that there are not enough frequencies assigned to a cell to handle its calls. Then new, smaller cells can be introduced within the old ones, each with its own set of frequencies to increase capacity. Generally, the original cells are about 4 to 8 miles in size. To introduce smaller cells within the larger ones, 60° or 120° directional antennas can be used. The smaller cells can themselves be split; however, 1-mile cells are close to the practical limit. To use a smaller cell, the power level used must be reduced to keep the signal within the cell. Also, as the mobiles move, they pass from cell to cell, which requires transferring of the call from one base transceiver to another. As the cells get smaller, these "handovers" become much more frequent. Figure 11.3 shows how cells can be divided to provide more capacity. More sophisticated management of the frequency is possible. In practice, the distribution of traffic and topographic features is not uniform. Thus the fixed uniform allocation of frequencies described above needs to be generalized. For example, a fixed allocation that is nonuniform is possible. The division of cells into smaller cells is one example of this. More dynamic assignments are also possible. In the simplest case, frequencies are "borrowed" from adjacent cells by congested cells. The frequencies can also be assigned to cells in a general, dynamic way. If this is all well managed, tens of thousands of simultaneous calls can be supported in one system.

FIGURE 11.3 Cell Splitting.

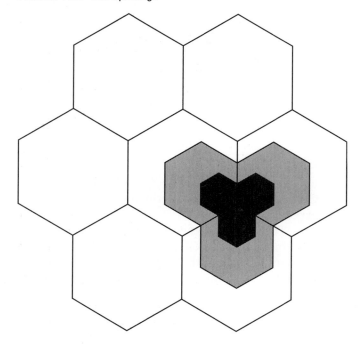

Mobile Units

Mobile units can be mobile (in vehicles) or portable (hand held). Each contains a modem that can switch between many frequencies (is frequency-agile). The hand-held terminals typically transmit an order of magnitude less maximum power than do the mobile units. The transmitting power of the mobile can be controlled by the system to match the size of the cell in which the mobile is operating.

Each mobile unit has three identification numbers. The *electronic serial number* is a 32-bit identifier assigned to the mobile when manufactured. Supposedly, the serial number is not easily modifiable and that attempts to change it would make the unit inoperable. The *system identification number* is a 15-bit code that identifies the system operator with which the mobile is associated. This allows the system to determine if the mobile is a "roamer," that is, a mobile operating outside the service area of the system operator with which the mobile subscriber has an account. Special authorization procedures must be carried out for roamers. Finally, the mobile unit has a *mobile identification number*, a 34-bit identifier representing the 10-digit telephone number of the mobile.

Base Transceiver

The base transceiver supports full-duplex communication with the mobile. The base transceivers are connected to a controlling MTSO, usually by microwave or by wire.

Mobile Telephone Switching Office

The mobile telephone switching office (MTSO) is the control and management element of an AMPS network. It is given the following responsibilities:

- Performing the switching functions for the mobile network (e.g., handovers as the mobile travels from cell to cell)
- Coordinating backup
- Providing the data collection to support billing
- Acting as test and monitoring facilities
- Connecting the mobile network to the wired public switched network

Operation

Logon　The portfolio of frequencies of each base transceiver is divided into control channels and conversation channels. When a mobile becomes operational it starts sensing the received control channels to determine the channel (and the base transceiver) the mobile receives best (with highest power). There is then an exchange of information with the MTSO. The mobile announces its system identification number, which defines the system to which it "belongs." If the home system is different from the one in which it is operating, it is a "roamer" and the MTSO must communicate with the mobile's home system for authorization of the mobile and to inform the mobile's home system where it is so that it can be reached by incoming calls from the wired public network.

Monitoring   The mobile then monitors that channel for calls destined to it. It also responds periodically to queries to confirm its presence to the system, and checks the power level of its control channel continuously to make sure that it is not leaving the cell (i.e., the signal become less than a threshold). It switches from control channel to control channel to maintain adequate signal strength.

Handling Calls   When the MTSO receives an incoming call from the public wired telephone network or, possibly, from a mobile in its region that is destined for another mobile in its area, it has all the base transceivers page their cells to locate the destination mobile. When the mobile detects an incoming call, it again samples the signals of the control channels from the various nearby base transceivers to find the most powerful on which to respond. The MTSO, through the corresponding base transceiver, assigns an inbound/outbound frequency pair for the conversation. Similarly, for a call originated by a mobile, the mobile finds the best control channel and communicates with the MTSO through the associated base transceiver. The MTSO responds with a frequency-pair assignment for the conversation (assuming that the call can be completed).

Handovers   When a mobile leaves a cell as it travels from cell to cell through the network area, the power received from the control channel it is monitoring may start to fade. When it sinks below a threshold, the mobile sends a message asking for a new assignment. The MTSO then has nearby base transceivers monitor the transmission of the mobile and report the power that they see. The MTSO then assigns the base transceiver, presumably with the strongest received signal, as the new transceiver for the mobile. In accessing each transceiver, handed-off calls have priority over originating calls, since it is assumed that users will find it more frustrating to have a call in process interrupted than to be told (by a "busy") that a new call cannot be accepted at the moment.

11.3 GLOBAL SYSTEM FOR MOBILE COMMUNICATIONS

Before the Global System for Mobile Communications (GSM) was developed, the countries of Europe used a number of incompatible cellular phone technologies. GSM was developed to provide a common second-generation technology for Europe so that the same subscriber units could be used throughout the continent. The technology has been extremely successful and is probably the most popular standard, worldwide, for new implementations. GSM first appeared in 1991 in Europe. Similar systems have now been implemented in South America, Asia, North Africa, the Middle East, and Australia. Over 126 operators in 75 countries use the system or its variants, DCS-1800 and DCS-1900. Second-generation systems such as GSM are based on the first-generation systems and share many characteristics. For that reason, we limit our discussion of the GSM system to features that are essentially different from those of AMPS.

Features

One attractive and novel feature of GSM is the *Subscriber Identity Module (SIM),* a portable device in the form of a smart card or plug-in module that stores the subscriber's identification number, the networks the subscriber is authorized to use, encryption keys, and other information specific to the subscriber. The GSM subscriber units are totally generic until a SIM is inserted. Therefore, a subscriber need only carry his or her SIM and then can use a wide variety of subscriber devices in many countries simply by inserting the SIM in the device to be used. In fact, except for certain emergency communications, the subscriber units will not work without a SIM inserted. Thus, the SIMs roam, not the subscriber devices.

GSM transmission is encrypted, so it is private; in contrast, AMPS transmission can easily be monitored. A stream cipher, A5, is used to encrypt the transmission from subscriber to base transceiver. However, the conversation is in the clear in the land-line network. Another cipher, A3, is used for authentication. Both are secret key systems (see Chapter 17). In addition to classical telephony services, GSM has been designed from the ground up to support data, and image services. These services are based on the ISDN model. User data rates at up to 9.6 kbps are supported.

System Overview

In general terms GSM is structured much as AMPS. Figure 11.4 indicates the major elements of GSM and a typical topology. The basic elements are the *subscriber* (we use the term *subscriber* rather than *mobile* for GSM because the SIM makes the subscriber the more relevant entity), a *base transceiver* for each cell, and the *base station controllers,* which may be collocated with the base transceivers or with the *mobile services switching center (MSSC),* which is the last

FIGURE 11.4 GSM Layout.

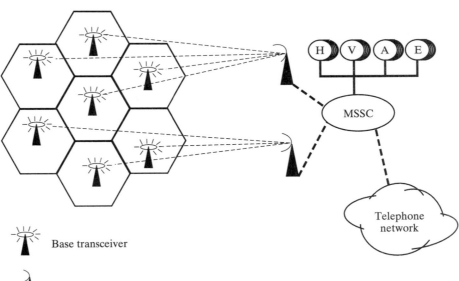

Base transceiver

Base station controller

element. In the case where base transceiver and base station controller are collocated, the pair is often called a *base station subsystem*. While the base station controller has much functionality, controlling handovers, power levels, and frequency assignments for the subscribers, the mobile services switching center is the heart of the system. It provides the interface to the public wired network and carries out the data collection for billing. It is supported by four databases that it controls.

The *home location register* database (H) stores information, both permanent and temporary, about each of the subscribers that "belong" to it (i.e., for which the subscriber has the telephone number associated with the switching center). One important temporary piece of information is the "location" of the subscriber. The location is determined by which *visitor location register* database (V) the subscriber is entered into. The visitor location register maintains information about subscribers that are physically in the region covered by the switching center. It records whether or not, the subscriber is active and other parameters associated with the subscriber.

For a call coming to the subscriber, the telephone number associated with the subscriber points to its switching center, which then can find in its home locator register the appropriate switching center where the subscriber is currently physically located. For a call coming from the subscriber, the visitor location register is used to initiate the call. Even if the subscriber is in the area covered by its home switching center, it is also represented in the switching center's visitors location register, for consistency.

The *authentication center* database (A) is used for authentication activities of the system; for example, it holds the authentication and encryption keys for all the subscribers in both the home and visitor location registers. The center controls access to user data as well as being used for authentication when a subscriber joins a network. Finally, the *equipment identity register* database (E) keeps track of the type of equipment that exists at the mobile station. It also plays a role in security (e.g., blocking calls from stolen mobile stations and preventing use of the network by stations that have not been approved).

Spectral Allocation

The GSM spectral allocation is 25 MHz for base transmission (935–960 MHz) and 25 MHz for mobile transmission (890–915 MHz). The bandwidth is accessed by users using a combination of frequency-division multiple access (FDMA) and time-division multiple access (TDMA) (both are discussed in the next section). There are radio-frequency carriers every 200 kHz, which provides for 124 full-duplex channels. The channels are modulated at a data rate of 270.833 kbps. As before, there are two types of channels, traffic and control.

Traffic channels can carry digitized speech or user data. Each carrier can carry up to eight conversations using time-division multiple access . Each analog voice signal is converted using linear predictive coding into a 13-kbps digital signal. (There are options at lower data rates as well.)

There are three general types of control channels: *broadcast*, *common control*, and *dedicated control*. Broadcast channels operate only from the base transceiver to the subscriber unit. These channels act as a reference signal for mobiles, identify the cell and network identity to mobiles, provide information on the status of the cell (e.g., channel availability and congestion information), and provide synchronization. The common control channels are used to page subscribers, receive asynchronous communications using slotted Aloha from subscribers, and assign channels to subscribers. The dedicated control channels provide signaling services to subscribers.

Two virtually identical systems, DCS-1800 and DCS-1900, are based on GSM and differ mainly in using spectral allocations at 1800 and 1900 MHz, respectively. DCS-1900 is used primarily in the United States.

11.4 MULTIPLE ACCESS

The primary motivation for the transition from the first-generation cellular telephones to the second was the need to conserve spectrum. The first-generation systems were extremely successful and the number of subscribers has been growing exponentially for years. However, use (and profit) is constrained by spectrum capacity. Hence there is a premium on the efficient use of spectrum. In the United States this interest has not been decreased by the recent policy of the FCC to auction spectrum (for very large sums of money) rather than give it away. For these reasons, it is of interest to examine in some detail how the spectrum is divided among users in current and planned systems. There are basically four ways to divide the spectrum among active users: frequency-division multiplexing (FDM), time-division multiplexing (TDM), code-division multiplexing (CDM), and space-division multiplexing (SDM). The first two types we discussed in Chapter 6; the remaining two we treat here.

Space-division multiplexing is simply the idea of using the same spectral band in two physically disjoint places. A simple example is the idea of frequency reuse in cells, as discussed in this chapter. By assigning the same frequency in two different cells, the frequency can be reused as long as the cells are sufficiently far apart. Another form of space division that has been proposed for cellular telephony is to use highly directional antennas so that the same frequency may be used for two communications. This idea can be carried further by using steered beam antennas, which can actually aim the antenna at a specific user. The ideas behind code-division multiplexing are a little more complex, but because of their importance, we discuss these next.

Code-Division Multiplexing

CDM is based on a (direct sequence) spread spectrum, which in turn is, based on the following rather counterintuitive notion. We take a signal that we wish to communicate that has a data rate of, say, D bits per second and we convert it for transmission into a longer message and transmit it at a higher rate say, kD, where k is called the *spreading factor*. It might be about 100. Several things can be gained from this apparent waste of spectrum. We can gain various kinds of noise and multipath immunity. The earliest applications of spread spectrum were military, where it was used for its immunity to jamming. It can also be used for hiding and encrypting signals. However, of interest to us is that several users can independently use the same (higher) bandwidth with very little interference. Let us see how that works. We start with a data signal with rate D, which we call the bit data rate. We break each bit into k *chips* according to a fixed pattern that is specific to each user, called the *user's code*, so that the new channel has a *chip data rate* of kD chips per second. As an illustration we consider a simple example with $k = 6$. It is simplest to characterize a code as a sequence of 1's and -1's. Figure 11.5 shows the codes for three users, A, B, and C, each of which is communicating with the same base station receiver, R. Thus, the code for user A is $c_A = <1, -1, -1, 1, -1, 1>$. Similarly, user B has code $c_B = <1, 1, -1, -1, 1, 1>$, and user C has $c_C = <1, 1, -1, 1, 1, -1>$.

We now consider the case of user A communicating with the base station. The base station is assumed to know A's code. For simplicity, we assume that communication is synchronous so that the base station knows when to look for codes. If A wants to send a 1 *bit,* A transmits its code as a chip pattern 1, -1, -1, 1, -1, 1. If a 0 bit is to be sent, A transmits the complement (1's and -1's reversed) of its code, -1, 1, 1, -1, 1, -1. At the base station the receiver decodes the chip patterns. In our simple version, if the receiver R receives a chip pattern $d = d1, d2, d3, d4, d5, d6$, and the receiver is seeking to communicate with a user

FIGURE 11.5 CDMA Example.

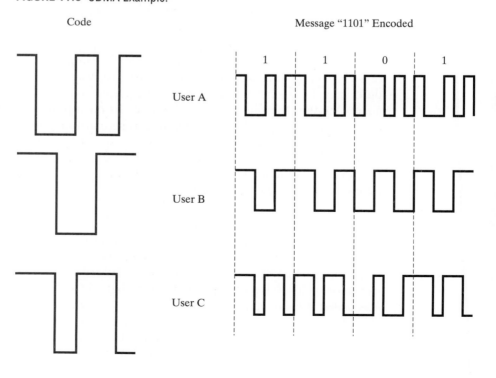

Code

Message "1101" Encoded

User A

User B

User C

u so that it has at hand *u*'s code, $c = c1, c2, c3, c4, c5, c6$, the receiver performs electronically the following decoding function:

$$S_u(d) = d1 \times c1 + d2 \times c2 + d3 \times c3 + d4 \times c4 + d5 \times c5 + d6 \times c6$$

The subscript *u* on *S* simply indicates that *u* is the user that we are interested in. Let's suppose the user *u* is actually A and see what happens. If A sends a 1 bit, then *d* is $1, -1, -1, 1, -1, 1$ and the computation above using S_A becomes

$$S_A(1, -1, -1, 1, -1, 1) = 1 \times 1 + (-1) \times (-1) + (-1) \times (-1)$$
$$+ 1 \times 1 + (-1) \times (-1) + 1 \times 1 = 6$$

If a sends a 0 bit that corresponds to $d = -1, 1, 1, -1, 1, -1$, we get

$$S_A(-1, 1, 1, -1, 1, -1) = -1 \times 1 + 1 \times (-1) + 1 \times (-1) + (-1) \times 1$$
$$+ 1 \times (-1) + (-1) \times 1 = -6$$

Please note that it is always the case that $-6 \le S_A(d) \le 6$ no matter what sequence of -1's and 1's that *d* is, and that the only *d*'s for which the extreme values of 6 and -6 result are for A's code and its complement, respectively. So if S_A produces a $+6$, we say that we have received a 1 bit from A, if S_A produces a -6, we say that we have received a 0 bit from user A; otherwise, we assume there is an error or that someone else is sending information. So why go through all this, one may ask. The reason becomes clear if we see what happens if user B is sending and we try to receive it with S_A, that is, decoding with the wrong code, A's. If B sends a 1 bit, then $d = 1, 1, -1, -1, 1, 1$. Then

$$S_A(1, 1, -1, -1, 1, 1) = (-1) \times 1 + (-1) \times (-1) + 1 \times (-1)$$
$$+ 1 \times 1 + (-1) \times (-1) + (-1) \times 1 = 0!$$

Thus, the unwanted signal (from B) does not show up at all. You can easily verify that if B had sent a 0 bit, that the decoder would produce 0 again. This means that if the decoder is linear and if A and B transmit signals s_A and s_B, respectively, at the same time, then $S_A(s_A + s_B) = S_A(s_A) + S_A(s_B) = S_A(s_A)$ since the decoder ignores B when it is using A's code. The codes of A and B that have the property that $S_A(c_B) = S_B(c_A) = 0$ are called *orthogonal*. Such codes are very nice to have but there are not all that many of them. More common is the case when $S_X(c_Y)$ is small in absolute value when $X \ne Y$. Then it is easy to distinguish between the two cases when $X = Y$ and when $X \ne Y$. In our example $S_A(c_C) = S_C(c_A) = 0$, but $S_B(c_C) = S_B(c_C) = 2$. In the latter case the C signal would make a small contribution to the decoded signal instead of 0. Using such a decoder, S_A, the receiver can sort out transmission from A even when there may be other users broadcasting in the same cell.

In practice, in CDM, the receiver can filter out the contribution from unwanted users or they appear as low-level noise. However, if there are many users competing for the channel with the one the receiver is trying to listen to, or if the signal power of one or more competing signals is too high, perhaps because it is very near the receiver (the "near/far" problem), the system breaks down. The coding gain we get, which is 6 in our simple example, is greater than 100 in practical systems, so that the ability of our decoder to filter out unwanted codes can be quite effective.

Which Access Method to Use

Besides the pure forms of splitting the channel (FDM, TDM, CDM, SDM), hybrids are also possible. For example, GSM uses FDM to divide the allotted spectrum into 124 carriers. Each carrier is then split in up to eight parts using TDM. The number of potential users in any one cell is potentially enormous. Any subscriber in the area could enter the cell; in addition, a whole world of roamers could show up. Fortunately, the number of customers who are in a given cell at one time and have their units registered with the system is usually quite modest. The problem is how to determine which users are active in a cell and how to assign them to vacant subchannels. Mobiles/subscribers entering a cell by a handover can be allocated a channel directly through the MTSO. The question remains what to do about mobiles/subscribers that are just becoming active. A common answer is to use an Aloha random access channel such as is described in the Alohanet Case Study, at the end of this chapter. Since the message from a mobile/subscriber announcing its presence is quite short and infrequent, poor utilization of Aloha channels is not a problem. Similarly, control information originating from a mobile/subscriber can be carried in the same random access mode. One control message is to assign the mobile/subscriber a dedicated channel when a conversation or data transfer is necessary.

With the addition of a random access scheme such as Aloha to dynamically assign subchannels to users, the multiplexing methods FDM, TDM, CDM, SDM become random access methods: frequency-division multiple access (FDMA), time-division multiple access (TDMA), code-division multiple access (CDMA), and space-division multiple access (SDMA), respectively. So the assignment of channels and other control functions that are relatively short and rare are initiated using a random access method, while the higher-traffic activities are carried out in dedicated subchannels derived by a multiplexing scheme.

The primary multiple access schemes used in cellular telephony (and satellite communications as well) are FDMA (e.g., AMPS), TDMA (e.g., GSM with some FDMA as well), and CDMA. They are listed in increasing complexity of implementation and also increasing spectral efficiency. The CDMA standard in North American IS-95 (adopted in December 1993). It was proposed by Qualcom. The TDMA candidate for digital mobile telephony is IS-54, "Digital AMPS." In this proposal the 30-kHz channels of AMPS are divided into three subchannels of 10 kHz each, giving 3:1 improvement in spectrum utilization. Qualcom claims a tenfold improvement for the IS-95 system over AMPS. CDMA uses *soft handoff*, wherein the power from the codes in the old and new cells is summed by the mobile. In the other direction, the two signals received by the two base transceivers can be compared to make better communication.

In the United States there is quite a controversy over the access method to use. FDMA, which was used in first-generation systems such as AMPS, is clearly too wasteful of spectrum. Moreover, with the development of inexpensive, high-performance digital signal processing chips, FDMA is no longer necessarily easier to implement than TDMA. But the choice for the second generation between TDMA and CDMA is fiercely debated. Adherents of IS-54, which is the U.S. standard for TDMA, argue that the theoretical advantages of the CDMA scheme, IS-95, are hard to realize in practice and that there is a lot more successful experience with TDMA. CDMA proponents argue that the theoretical advantages can be realized and that CDMA offers additional features as well. The TDMA systems have achieved an early lead in actual implementations worldwide. But large wireless providers are beginning to sign up with CDMA vendors.

11.5 THIRD-GENERATION WIRELESS COMMUNICATION

One of the driving forces of modern communication technology is the trend toward universal personal telecommunications and universal communications access. The first concept refers to the ability of a person to identify him- or herself easily and use conveniently any communication system in a large area (e.g., globally) over a continent or in an entire country in terms of a single account. The second refers to the capability of using one's terminal in a wide variety of environments to connect to information services (e.g., to have a portable terminal that will work in the office, on the street, and on airplanes equally well). This revolution in personal computing will obviously involve wireless communication in a fundamental way. The GSM cellular telephony with its subscriber identity module, for example, is a large step toward these goals.

Personal communications services (PCS) and **personal communication networks (PCN)** are names attached to this concept of global wireless communications. It has been estimated that "PCS is likely to be a \$50 billion industry by the close of the decade. The system will serve as many as 150 million people world wide and 60 million in the United States, including millions who will benefit from in-building PCS and PCS data transmission...." [WIMM92]

Generally, the technology planned is digital using time-division multiple access or code-division multiple access to provide efficient use of the spectrum and high capacity.

PCS handsets are designed to be low power and relatively small and light. Efforts are being made internationally to allow the same terminals to be used worldwide. Worldwide frequency allocations have been made for second-generation cordless telephones (CT-2) in the 800-MHz region and for more advanced personal communications in the 1.7- to 2.2-GHz region of the spectrum.

The 1992 World Administrative Radio Conference (WARC 92) resulted in worldwide allocations for future public land mobile telecommunications systems (FPLMTS). This concept includes both terrestrial and satellite-based services. In addition, allocations were made for low-earth-orbiting (LEO) satellite services which can be used to support personal communications.

Some proposed technologies that come under the umbrella of PCS are American Digital Cellular System, Japanese Digital Cellular System, second-generation cordless telephones (CT-2), the European Community's General Speciale

Mobile (GSM) for digital cellular service, and Digital European Cordless Telephone (DECT) for services such as advanced in-building wireless telephony, all supported by low-earth-orbit (LEO) satellites and geosynchronous satellites, as well as terrestrial antennas. The technology is developing rapidly; for example, it is now possible to make a TDMA/CDMA 1-watt spread spectrum transceiver using parts costing less than $25.

11.6 SATELLITE COMMUNICATION

Satellite transmission has the unique capability of providing global communication, including transmission to and from moving terminals (e.g., trucks, ships, and airplanes) without the need of an extensive terrestrial infrastructure.

Geosynchronous Satellites

Satellites can be characterized by the orbits they keep. The most common type today is the **geosynchronous** (or **geostationary**) **satellite (GEOS)** (see Figure 11.6). If the satellite is in a circular orbit 22,300 miles above the earth's surface and rotates in the equatorial plane of the earth, it will rotate at exactly the same angular speed as the earth, and will remain above the same spot on the equator. This configuration has many advantages to recommend it. Because the satellite is stationary relative to the earth, there is no problem with frequency changes due

FIGURE 11.6 Satellite Orbits.

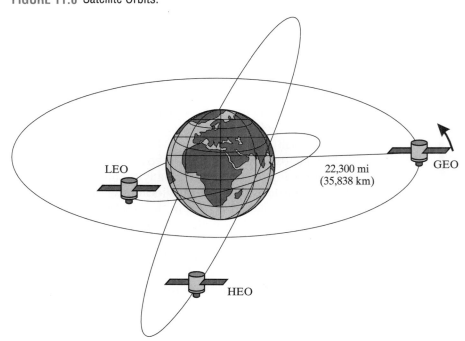

to relative motion of the satellite and antennas on earth. Moreover, the tracking of the satellite by its earth stations is simplified. Also, at that height it can communicate with roughly a fourth of the earth. On the other hand, there are some problems. The most obvious one is that the signal can get quite weak after traveling over 20,000 miles. Also, the polar regions and the far northern and southern hemispheres are poorly served by geosynchronous satellites. Moreover, even for signals traveling at the speed of light, 186,000 miles/sec, the delay in sending a signal from a point on the equator beneath the satellite 22,300 miles to the satellite and 22,300 miles back is substantial. The delay, in fact, is $(2 \times 22,300)/186,000 = 0.24$ sec. For other locations on earth of the sending and receiving earth stations, the delay is even longer. If the satellite link is used in a telephone, the delay between when one person speaks and the other responds is increased twofold, or almost 0.5 sec. This is definitely noticeable. Another feature of geosynchronous satellites is that they use their assigned frequencies over a very large area. For applications such as broadcasting TV programs, this can be desirable, but for point-to-point communications it is very wasteful of spectrum. Special spot and steered beam antennas which restrict the area covered by the satellite's signal can be used to control the "footprint" or signaling area. To solve some of these problems, other orbits have been designed for satellites. GEOS were discussed in Chapter 4. **Highly elliptic orbiting satellite (HEOS)** and, especially, **low earth orbiting satellites (LEOS)** (including space stations) are important for third-generation personal communications.

Highly Elliptic Orbiting Satellites

In northern Europe and in polar regions, the angle of geosynchronous satellites above the horizon can be uncomfortably low. At low angles satellite signals are easily obstructed by natural obstacles, hills and mountains, and by human-made ones such as buildings. In Russia this is a particularly pronounced problem. To deal with it, Russia uses highly elliptic orbits for some of its satellites. The prototype of this type of orbit was Russia's *Molniya* series of satellites. The *Molniya* orbit was designed to offer a better angle of inclination of the satellite to the horizon in the far northern hemisphere and the polar region. The orbit is elliptical and is inclined 65° with respect to the equator. It is at its farthest from the earth at its apogee of 24,856 miles (slightly more than the 22,300-mile height of a geosynchronous satellite) over the northern hemisphere, and is closest, 500 km, at its perigee in the southern hemisphere. Thus it has very good coverage over the northern hemisphere. Moreover, the satellite spends most of its 12-hr orbit over the northern hemisphere. Three satellites suffice for 24-hr coverage. A similar system has been proposed by the European Space Agency for digital audio broadcasting.

This type of satellite has little to recommend it beyond its coverage of polar regions. Because the orbit is not geosynchronous, multiple satellites are needed for 24-hr coverage. Moreover, to the extent that the apogee is greater than geosynchronous orbit altitude, the signal attenuation (loss) is even more.

Low Earth Orbiting Satellites

The original AT&T satellite proposal was for low earth orbiting satellites. However, most of the early satellites were geosynchronous. Nevertheless, low earth orbits have advantages, and many recent satellite proposals (e.g., Iridium; see Section 11.7) are based on them. The idea is to use constellations of inexpensive low earth orbiting satellites, sometimes called *lightsats.* They orbit at altitudes of about 200 to 700 miles above the earth's surface. Therefore, their signal is much stronger than that of geosynchronous satellites for given transmission power. Their coverage can be better localized so that spectrum can be conserved. For this reason, this technology is currently being proposed for communicating with mobile terminals and with personal terminals which need stronger signals to function. On the other hand, to provide broad coverage over 24 hrs., many satellites are needed. Sixty-six are being proposed by Motorola for their Iridium system.

A number of commercial proposals have been made to use clusters LEOSs to provide communications services. These proposals can be divided into two categories:

- *Little LEOSs:* intended to work at communication frequencies below 1 GHz using no more than 5 MHz of bandwidth and supporting data rates up to 10 kbps. These systems are aimed at paging, tracking, and low-rate messaging. Proposals of this type are summarized in Table 11-1.
- *Big LEOSs:* working at frequencies above 1 GHz and supporting data rates up to a few megabits per second. These systems tend to offer the same services as those of small LEOSs, with the addition of voice and positioning services. Table 11-2 summarizes many of the big LEOS proposals. We discuss in some detail the most advanced of these proposals, Motorola's Iridium.

11.7 IRIDIUM: A THIRD-GENERATION SATELLITE SYSTEM

Iridium is an ambitious proposal conceived of by Motorola in 1987 for a global network of up to 66 small LEOSs to provide voice, data, facsimile and paging service to users via hand-held wireless telephones and pagers any place in the world at any time. It is probably the most thoroughly developed of the big LEOSs and is the most ambitious. It is named for the element iridium, which contains 77 electrons, which corresponded to the 77 satellites originally planned for the system, although now, 66 satellites are planned. One of its novel features is its use of communication between its satellites to transport data through its network (see Figure 11.7). It is estimated that it will cost well over $3 billion to implement. It will be owned by an international consortium called Iridium, Inc. and built and operated by Motorola's Satellite Communications Division. Motorola itself has spent or committed well over a half billion dollars to the project.

Lockheed will build 125 spacecraft. There are expected to be 15 to 20 ground stations. Subscriber fees are estimated at $3 per minute, with a cost for the hand-held terminals of over $1500. Iridium expects at least 1.5 million

TABLE 11-1 Proposed LEO Systems below 1 GHz

	ORBCOMM (*Orbital Comm. Corp.*)	*STARNET* (*Starsys*)	*LEOSAT* (*Marcor*)	*VITASAT* (*Vita*)
Number of satellites	20	24	2	2
Class	LEOS	LEOS	LEOS	LEOS
Lifetime (years)	7	5	7	5
Orbit altitude (km)	970	1300	1000	815
Orientation	Circular-orthogonal	Circular	Circular	Circular
Initial geographic coverage	CONUS Offshore points U.S. Pacific islands Polar regions	CONUS Offshore points	North America Some areas of Central/South America	Global
Service markets	Emergency paging Tracking Messaging	Emergency paging Tracking Messaging	Vehicular monitoring Tracking Emergency paging Emissions Positioning Messaging	Heavy data transfer (100+ pages)
User terminal types	Hand-held Transportable Vehicular Fixed	Hand-held Vehicular Transportable Fixed	Vehicular	Fixed Transportable
Terminal estimated cost	$200	$75	$100	$5000
Wattage	2	1	10	
Uplink bands (MHz)	VHF 148–149.9	148–149.9	148–149.9	148–149.9
Downlink bands (MHz)	VHF 137–138	137–138	137–138	137–138
Method of access	FDMA	CDMA	CDMA	FDMA
Launch vehicle class	Pegasus	TBD	Ariane	Ariane
Projected operational date	Late 1994	Late 1995	Mid 1993	Early 1994

TABLE 11-2 Proposed LEO Systems above 1 GHz

	IRIDIUM™ (Motorola)	ODYSSEY (TRW)	ELLIPSAT (Ellipsat Corp.)	GLOBALSTAR (Loral and Qualcomm)	ARIES (CCI, Constellation Comm. Inc.)
Number of satellites	66	12	6	24	48
Class	LEOS	HEOS	LEOS	LEOS	LEOS
Lifetime (years)	5	10	3	7.5	5
Orbit altitude (km)	755	10,600	2903/426	1390	1000
Orientation	Circular	Circular	Elliptical	Elliptical	Circular
Initial geographic coverage	Global	CONUS Offshore U.S. Europe Asia/Pacific	CONUS Offshore U.S.	CONUS	CONUS Offshore U.S.
Service markets	Cellular-like voice Positioning-RDSS Paging Messaging Data transfer	Cellular-like voice Positioning-RDSS Paging Messaging Data transfer	Cellular-like voice Positioning-RDSS Paging Messaging	Cellular-like voice Positioning-RDSS Paging Messaging	Cellular-like voice Positioning-RDSS Paging Messaging
Voice cost/min	$3.00	$0.60	$0.40–$0.50	$0.30	N/A
User terminal types	Hand-held Vehicular Transportable	Hand-held Vehicular Transportable	Vehicular Transportable	Hand-held Vehicular Transportable	Vehicular Transportable
Terminal estimated cost	$3500	$250–350	$1000 or 300	$500–700	$1500
Wattage	0.4	0.5	6	1	2
Uplink bands	L-band (1616.5–1626.5 MHz)	L-band	L-band	L-band	L-band
Downlink bands	L-band	S-band (2483.5–2500 MHz)	S-band	L-band with C-band (5199.5–5216/6525–6541 MHz) feeder links or L-band S-band or L-band L-band with C-band and some S-band feeder links	S-band
Method of access	FDMA	CDMA	CDMA	CDMA	CDMA
Launch vehicle class	TBD	Atlas 2	Delta or Pegasus	Delta or Ariane	Delta or Atlas
Projected operational dates	1998	Mid-1996	Late 1993, first phase	Mid-1997	Early 1996

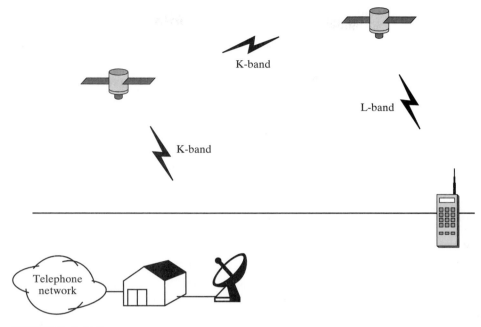

FIGURE 11.7 Iridium.

customers to make the enterprise profitable. Table 11-3 indicates the market that Motorola sees in various segments.

Services

Iridium is targeted primarily for personal communication services, including voice, paging, and messaging services. Radio determination satellite service (RDSS) is contemplated as well. The system is not envisaged as a replacement or

TABLE 11-3 Iridium Demand Projections (Number of Subscribers)

	YEAR 2001		YEAR 2006	
Market segment	*United States*	*Total*	*United States*	*Total*
Maritime	7,000	35,000	8,000	45,000
High-income business	180,000	448,000	270,000	800,000
Travel	210,000	820,000	335,000	1,515,000
Aeronautical	13,000	22,000	16,000	34,000
Industrial	50,000	140,000	70,000	230,000
Government	36,000	292,000	50,000	450,000
Rural	0	67,000	0	150,000
Total	496,000	1,824,000	749,000	3,224,000

substitution for cellular telephone service but rather, as a worldwide radio telephone service. The system is intrinsically more expensive than cellular and is designed for relatively low traffic densities. It is planned to provide mobile service where it is not now available. In areas where mobile service is provided by geosynchronous satellite, Iridium offers less delay, a stronger signal, and better reception. Iridium can also provide telephone service in areas where it is not presently available.

Iridium plans to sell bulk transmission capacity to licensed and authorized operators for resale in their authorized areas. Voice communication will be digital at 4.8 kbps, using vocoding technology which, it is claimed, provides quality comparable to today's land mobile radio equipment. Other planned services include:

- *Radiodetermination service and two-way messaging.* Except for some pagers, all units will have this capability as well as the ability to report position. Some units will support the global positioning service (GPS) as well.

- *Paging.* Alphanumeric direct to satellite paging throughout the world in a package only slightly bigger than that of today's pagers is planned.

- *Facsimile.* Mobile facsimile units that are integrated with the Iridium telephone and stand-alone units are planned.

- *Data.* An Iridium 2400-bps modem is being developed.

Satellites and Orbits

The 66 satellites will operate in nearly polar orbits. The number is sufficient so that at least one is in line of sight at virtually every location in the world at all times. They will orbit at an altitude of 420 nautical miles (778 km). The satellites are organized into six planes of 11 satellites each. The handovers between adjacent cells will take place a little more than once a minute, which is consistent with current cellular telephone technology.

A single satellite will sweep out 48 beams or cells over the earth's surface. The total peak capacity for each satellite is 960 channels; 780 are full duplex. The satellites are connected by direct microwave cross-links in space.

Communications

Communication between users and satellites will take place in the L-band of the spectrum, 1600 to 1700 MHz. The links between satellites and between satellites and gateways will use the area from 18 to 30 GHz of the K-band. The satellites will use phased-array antennas for L-band communication. Each antenna complex will support 48 interlaced spot beams (cells). The power of each beam can be controlled independently to maintain link quality in the face of variations of range, foliage, and similar factors. However, the spot **pattern** is fixed relative to the satellite.

The radio link between user and satellite uses space, time, and frequency multiplexing. Time-division multiplexing and the space multiplexing allowed by the cellular structure support extensive frequency reuse. For example, the same frequency could be used five times in the United States alone. A voice conversation can be supported by about 2 kHz of bandwidth. A single cell, on average, can service 236 simultaneous users, while a limited number of geometrically isolated cells can handle peak loads of two to three times that many. The worldwide system capacity is approximately 283,000 channels.

User Terminal Devices

Initially, development will focus on pagers, personal hand-held cellular-like units, and mobile units for automobile, boat, or aircraft. In particular, a design goal of the Iridium hand-held device is that it be consistent in size, weight, and battery life to terrestrial cellular units. The hand-held unit will operate for 24 hrs. on one charge, 1 hr of active calling and 23 hrs. of being able to receive calls. The transmitters will operate at less than 600 mW, also comparable to current cellular telephones. Several kinds of data transmission will be supported as well, ranging upward from 2400 bps asynchronous.

RECOMMENDED READING

The description of ALOHANET was taken from [ABRA85]. Much of the material on wireless was based on [BLAC96b], [FREE96], and [RAPP96].

ABRA85   ABRAMSON, N. "Development of the ALOHANET." *IEEE Transactions on Information Theory*, March 1985.
BLAC96b   BLACK, U. *Mobile and Wireless Networks*, Upper Saddle River, NJ: Prentice Hall, 1996.
FREE96   FREEMAN, R. *Telecommunication System Engineering*. New York: Wiley, 1996.
RAPP96   RAPPAPORT, T. *Wireless Communications*. Upper Saddle River, NJ: Prentice Hall, 1996.

KEY TERMS

Advanced Mobile Phone Service (AMPS)	Highly Elliptic Orbiting Satellite (HEOS)	Personal Communications Network (PCN)
Geosynchronous Satellites (GEOS)	Low Earth Orbiting Satellite (LEOS)	Personal Communications Services (PCS)

QUESTIONS

1. Compare and contrast the concepts of universal personal telecommunications and universal communications access.
2. Characterize the three generations of mobile telephony.
3. How does AMPS differ from GSM?

4. Under what circumstances would you use GEOS, HEOS, and LEOS, respectively?

5. What are some ways of achieving frequency reuse in wireless communications?

6. Explain what LEO, GEO, and HEO satellites are (including what the acronyms stand for). Compare the three types with respect to factors such as size and shape of orbits, signal power, frequency reuse, propagation delay, coverage of polar regions, number of satellites for global coverage, and handoff frequency.

ALOHANET

*I*n the late 1960s, information theorist Norm Abramson and his colleagues at the University of Hawaii were faced with the problem of providing data communication among the seven campuses of the University of Hawaii, spread over the four islands of Oahu, Kauai, Maui, and Hawaii (see Figure 11.8). The objective was to provide terminals at all the campuses with interactive access to the computer resources of the main campus. Therefore, most communications between the campuses had one end at the central computer. Using land lines to communicate among the islands was clearly not feasible, dedicated point-to-point leased radio facilities were too expensive, and given the bursty nature of the computer communications, sharing channels using frequency- or time-division multiplexing was inefficient, especially considering that the eventual plan was to support hundreds of terminals. Abramson and his colleagues then had the idea of using Oahu as a base station for radio broadcast communication to the other six campuses using two radio channels, that is, with a separate channel into Oahu and another channel out. The channels supported a data rate of 9600 bps in a bandwidth of 100 kHz. The problem of access to the channel had to be dealt with. How could one of the campuses, other than the one

FIGURE 11.8 The Aloha System.

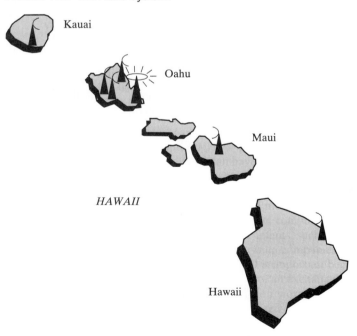

with the main computer, seize the inbound channel to the main computers? For a small number of locations, the transmitter at Oahu could sequentially and continually ask (poll) each station if it had something to send. However, Abramson had a better idea. Each of the remote stations would contend for the channel simply by transmitting its packets of information asynchronously and independent of the other stations. If the transmission was successful, the Oahu station would acknowledge successful receipt of the packet and all would be well. If two or more remote stations began transmission in overlapping intervals, the Oahu station, called Menehune (Hawaiian for "elf "), would not answer because it would not receive a valid packet. After an appropriate timeout interval, having not received positive acknowledgments, the stations would try again. It was important that with high probability the colliding stations waited different, usually random times, so that two colliding stations would not wait the same amount of time and collide again upon retransmitting. One could not assume that the remote stations could hear each other's communication, so the success of communication could only be determined by Menehune. The first channel was turned on in June 1971.

Discussion Questions

1. Why would frequency- or time-division multiplexing have been inefficient for the Hawaiian application?

2. Suppose that instead of a few remote stations, there were thousands. Would polling be a feasible option?

3. Suppose that instead of there being obstacles between the remote stations, so that the remote stations could not communicate with one another, all the stations could hear each other's communications. How would you improve the Aloha protocol? (*Hint:* Review the discussion of CSMA/CD in Chapter 9.)

4. Shortly after Abramson invented the Aloha protocol, Larry Roberts of ARPA pointed out that the chance of collision could be reduced if the system were synchronized in time slots that were a little longer than the maximum packet transmission time. That is, no transmission could start except at the beginning of a slot. Give a qualitative explanation of why this might be so. This variation is called *slotted Aloha* and the original scheme is called *pure Aloha.*

5. The Aloha scheme is simple and elegant; unfortunately, it does not make good use of the channel. In the idealized case of random packet transmissions from an infinite number of stations, the maximum utilization is about one-sixth of the total capacity of the channel. (Larry Robert's scheme doubled the utilization, but it was still small.) Can you think of a way to gain the flexibility of Aloha random access while still using the channel efficiently? (If you can't, review the section on channel access in this chapter.)

CHAPTER 11

Case Study

INDONESIA'S PALAPA SATELLITE

*I*ndonesia is an island nation—nearly 14,000 islands, in fact. Almost half of them are inhabited. Providing a communications infrastructure for the country is rather daunting. Copper will not do the job. In 1976 a 12-transponder satellite called Palapa went into geosynchronous orbit over Indonesia. By becoming the first developing country with its own satellite, at a stroke the Indonesian government established electronic connectivity throughout the country for television, telephone, facsimile, and data transmission. Indonesia is now using its third generation of Palapa satellites.

Discussion Question

1. Suppose that Indonesia wanted to use the Palapa, or some other satellite, to provide data communication among its thousands of islands. Would the Aloha access method be useful? If so, for what types of data traffic? How would application of the Aloha approach to satellite communication differ from its terrestrial applications?

PART 4

APPLICATIONS

CHAPTER 12

TCP/IP and Other Protocol Architectures

CHAPTER OBJECTIVES

After reading this chapter, you should be able to:

- Define the term *protocol architecture* and explain the need for and benefits of a communications architecture.

- Describe the TCP/IP protocol architecture and explain the functioning of each layer.

- Give a brief description of the open systems interconnection (OSI) architecture and each of its constituent layers.

- Explain the motivation for the development of a standardized protocol architecture and the reasons why a customer should use products based on a protocol architecture standard in preference to products based on a proprietary architecture.

- Describe IBM's system network architecture (SNA) and contrast it with TCP/IP and OSI.

- Explain the need for internetworking.

- Describe the operation of a router within the context of TCP/IP to provide internetworking.

*I*n Part 4 we focus on some of the most important distributed applications and examine the functions and services of those applications. The discussion describes the way in which application software modules in two separate computers could interact to perform the application. Implicit in the discussion is that there is some means to transfer messages and data reliably from one system to another. So before looking at specific applications in Chapters 12 and 13, in this chapter we examine the underlying communications software required to support those applications. We will see that the required software is substantial. To make the task of implementing this communications software manageable, a modular structure known as a protocol architecture is used.

We begin this chapter by introducing a simple protocol architecture consisting of just three modules, or layers. This will allow us to present the key characteristics and design features of a protocol architecture without getting bogged down in details. With this background, we are then ready to examine the most important architectures: TCP/IP, the open systems interconnection (OSI) architecture, and the systems network architecture (SNA). TCP/IP is an Internet-based standard and is the framework for developing a complete range of computer communications standards. Virtually all computer vendors now provide support for this architecture. OSI is another standardized architecture that is often used to describe communications functions, but that is now rarely implemented. SNA is the proprietary architecture used by IBM and is the most widely used proprietary architecture. Although IBM provides support for TCP/IP, it continues to use SNA, and the latter architecture will remain important for many years to come.

Following a discussion of protocol architectures, the important concept of internetworking is examined. Inevitably, a business will require the use of more than one communications network. Some means of interconnecting these networks is required, and this raises issues that relate to the protocol architecture.

12.1 SIMPLE PROTOCOL ARCHITECTURE

Need for a Protocol Architecture

When computers, terminals, and/or other data processing devices exchange data, the procedures involved can be quite complex.. Consider, for example, the transfer of a file between two computers. There must be a data path between the two computers, either directly or via a communication network. But more is needed. Typical tasks to be performed:

1. The source system must either activate the direct data communication path or inform the communication network of the identity of the destination system desired.
2. The source system must ascertain that the destination system is prepared to receive data.
3. The file transfer application on the source system must ascertain that the file management program on the destination system is prepared to accept and store the file for this particular user.
4. If the file formats used on the two systems are incompatible, one or the other system must perform a format translation function.

It is clear that there must be a high degree of cooperation between the two computer systems. Instead of implementing the logic for this as a single module, the task is broken up into subtasks, each of which is implemented separately. As an example, Figure 12.1 suggests the way in which a file transfer facility could be implemented. Three modules are used. Tasks 3 and 4 in the preceding list could be performed by a file transfer module. The two modules on the two systems exchange files and commands. However, rather than requiring the file transfer module to deal with the details of actually transferring data and commands, the file transfer modules each rely on a communications service module. This module is responsible for making sure that the file transfer commands and data are reliably exchanged between systems. Among other things, this module would per-

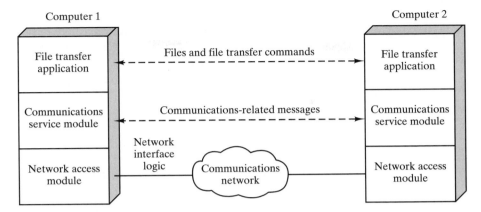

FIGURE 12.1 A Simplified Architecture for File Transfer.

form task 2. Now the nature of the exchange between systems is independent of the nature of the network that interconnects them. Therefore, rather than building details of the network interface into the communications service module, it makes sense to have a third module, a network access module, that performs task 1 by interacting with the network.

Let us try to summarize the motivation for the three modules in Figure 12.1. The file transfer module contains all the logic that is unique to the file transfer application, such as transmitting passwords, file commands, and file records. These files and commands must be transmitted reliably. However, the same sorts of reliability requirements are relevant to a variety of applications (e.g., electronic mail, document transfer). Therefore, these requirements are met by a separate communications service module that can be used by a variety of applications. The communications service module is concerned with assuring that the two computer systems are active and ready for data transfer and for keeping track of the data that are being exchanged to assure delivery. However, these tasks are independent of the type of network that is being used. Therefore, the logic for actually dealing with the network is separated out into a separate network access module. That way, if the network to be used is changed, only the network access module is affected.

Thus, instead of a single module for performing communications, there is a structured set of modules that implements the communications function. That structure is referred to as a **protocol architecture**. In the remainder of this section, we generalize the preceding example to present a simplified protocol architecture. Following that, we look at more complex, real-world examples.

Three-Layer Model

In very general terms, distributed data communications can be said to involve three agents: applications, computers, and networks. In Chapter 13 we look at several applications; examples include file transfer and electronic mail. These applications execute on computers that can often support multiple simultaneous applications. Computers are connected to networks, and the data to be exchanged are transferred by the network from one computer to another. Thus, the transfer of data from one application to another involves first getting the data to the computer in which the application resides and then getting it to the intended application within the computer.

With these concepts in mind, it appears natural to organize the communication task into three relatively independent layers:

- Network access layer
- Transport layer
- Application layer

The **network access layer** is concerned with the exchange of data between a computer and the network to which it is attached. The sending computer must provide the network with the address of the destination computer, so that the network may route the data to the appropriate destination. The sending computer may wish to invoke certain services, such as priority, that might be provided by the network. The specific software used at this layer depends on the type of network to be used; different standards have been developed for circuit switching, packet switching, local-area networks, and others. For example, X.25 is a standard that specifies the access to a packet-switching network; this standard is described in Chapter 7. It makes sense to separate those functions having to do with network access into a separate layer. By doing this, the remainder of the communications software, above the network access layer, need not be concerned about the specifics of the network to be used. The same higher-layer software should function properly regardless of the particular network to which the computer is attached.

Regardless of the nature of the applications that are exchanging data, there is usually a requirement that data be exchanged reliably. That is, we would like to be assured that all the data arrive at the destination application and that the data arrive in the same order in which they were sent. As we shall see, the mechanisms for providing reliability are essentially independent of the nature of the applications. Thus, it makes sense to collect those mechanisms in a common layer shared by all applications; this is referred to as the **transport layer**.

Finally, the **application layer** contains the logic needed to support the various user applications. For each different type of application, such as file transfer, a separate module is needed that is peculiar to that application.

Figures 12.2 and 12.3 illustrate this simple architecture. Figure 12.2 shows three computers connected to a network. Each computer contains software at the network access and transport layers and software at the application layer for one or more applications. For successful communication, every entity in the overall system must have a unique address. Actually, two levels of addressing are needed. Each computer on the network must have a unique network address; this allows the network to deliver data to the proper computer. Each application on a computer must have an address that is unique within that computer; this allows the transport layer to support multiple applications at each computer. The latter addresses are known as **service access points (SAPs)**, connoting the fact that each application is individually accessing the services of the transport layer.

Service Access Point (SAP)
A means of identifying a user of the services of a protocol entity.

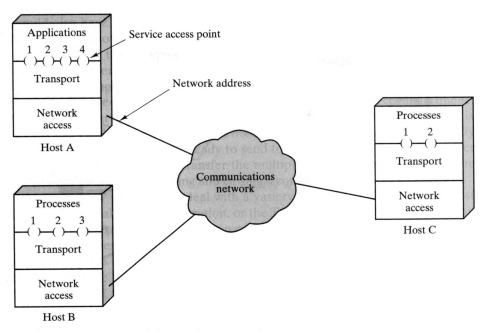

FIGURE 12.2 Communications Architectures and Networks.

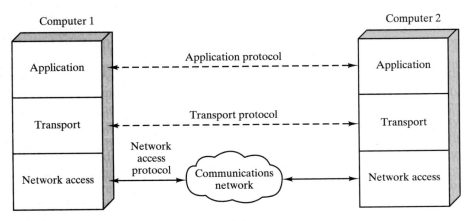

FIGURE 12.3 Protocols in a Simplified Architecture.

Figure 12.3 indicates the way in which modules at the same level on different computers communicate with each other: by means of a protocol. A protocol is the set of rules or conventions governing the ways in which two entities cooperate to exchange data. A protocol specification details the control functions that may be performed, the formats and control codes used to communicate those functions, and the procedures that the two entities must follow. We have already seen a number of examples of protocols: HDLC (Chapter 5), the packet level of X.25 (Chapter 7), frame relay (Chapter 8), and so on.

Let us trace a simple operation. Suppose that an application, associated with SAP 1 at computer A, wishes to send a message to another application, associated with SAP 2 at computer B. The application at A hands the message over to its transport layer with instructions to send it to SAP 2 on computer B. The transport layer hands the message over to the network access layer, which instructs the network to send the message to computer B. Note that the network need not be told the identity of the destination service access point. All that it needs to know is that the data are intended for computer B.

To control this operation, control information, as well as user data, must be transmitted, as suggested in Figure 12.4. Let us say that the sending application generates a block of data and passes this to the transport layer. The transport layer may break this block into two smaller pieces to make it more manageable. To each of these pieces the transport layer appends a transport header, containing protocol control information. The combination of data from the next-higher layer and control information is known as a *protocol data unit* (PDU); in this case, it is referred to as a *transport protocol data unit*. The header in each transport PDU contains control information to be used by the peer transport protocol at computer B. Examples of items that may be stored in this header include:

- *Destination SAP.* When the destination transport layer receives the transport protocol data unit, it must know to whom the data are to be delivered.

- *Sequence number.* Since the transport protocol is sending a sequence of protocol data units, it numbers them sequentially so that if they arrive out of order, the destination transport entity may reorder them.

- *Error detection code.* The sending transport entity may include a code that is a function of the contents of the remainder of the PDU. The receiving transport protocol performs the same calculation and compares

FIGURE 12.4 Protocol Data Units.

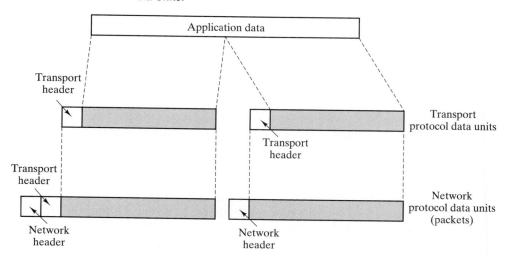

the result with the incoming code. A discrepancy results if there has been some error in transmission. In that case the receiver can discard the PDU and take corrective action.

The next step is for the transport layer to hand each protocol data unit over to the network layer, with instructions to transmit it to the destination computer. To satisfy this request, the network access protocol must present the data to the network with a request for transmission. As before, this operation requires the use of control information. In this case the network access protocol appends a network access header to the data it receives from the transport layer, creating a network access PDU. Examples of the items that may be stored in the header include:

- *Destination computer address.* The network must know to whom (which computer on the network) the data are to be delivered.
- *Facilities requests.* The network access protocol might want the network to make use of certain facilities, such as priority.

Figure 12.5 puts all of these concepts together, showing the interaction between modules to transfer one block of data. Let us say that the file transfer module in computer X is transferring a file one record at a time to computer Y. Each record is handed over to the transport layer module. We can picture this action as being in the form of a command or procedure call. The arguments of this procedure call include the destination computer address, the destination service access point, and the record. The transport layer appends the destination service access point and other control information to the record to create a transport PDU. This is then handed down to the network access layer by another procedure call. In this case the arguments for the command are the destination computer address and the transport protocol data unit. The network access layer uses this information to construct a network PDU. Suppose that the network is an

FIGURE 12.5 Operation of a Protocol Architecture.

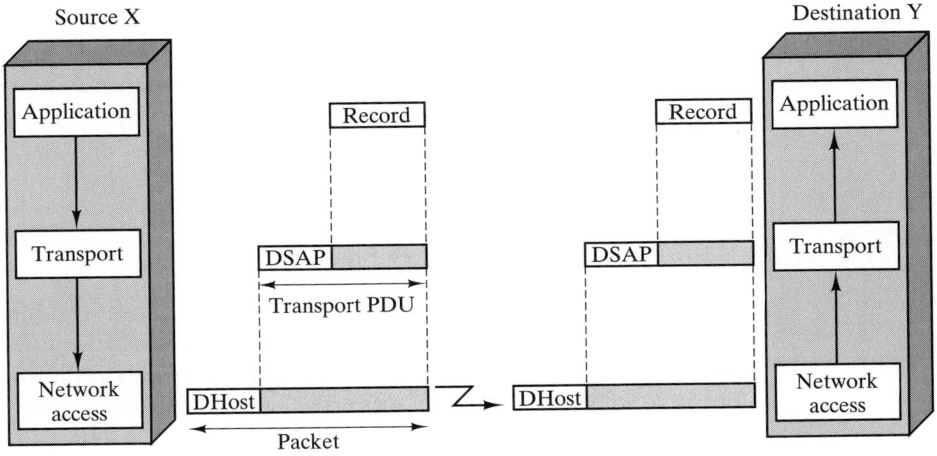

X.25 packet-switching network. In this case the network protocol data unit is an X.25 data packet (see Figure 7.15). The transport protocol data unit is the data field of the packet, and the packet header includes the virtual circuit number for a virtual circuit connecting *X* and *Y*.

The network accepts the network PDU from X and delivers it to Y. The network access module in Y receives the PDU, strips off the header, and transfers the enclosed transport PDU to X's transport layer module. The transport layer examines the transport protocol data unit header and on the basis of the SAP field in the header delivers the enclosed record to the appropriate application, in this case the file transfer module in Y.

This example will repay close study. In the remainder of the chapter we will be looking at more complex protocol architectures. However, these architectures are based on the same principles and mechanisms as those in this simple example.

Standardized Protocol Architectures

When communication is desired among computers from different vendors, the software development effort can be a nightmare. Different vendors use different data formats and data exchange protocols. Even within one vendor's product line, different model computers may communicate in unique ways.

As the use of computer communications and computer networking proliferates, a one-at-a-time special-purpose approach to communications software development is too costly to be acceptable. The only alternative is for computer vendors to adopt and implement a common set of conventions. For this to happen, standards are needed. Such standards would have two benefits:

- Vendors feel encouraged to implement the standards because of an expectation that because of wide usage of the standards, their products would be less marketable without them.
- Customers are in a position to require that the standards be implemented by any vendor wishing to propose equipment to them.

Two protocol architectures have served as the basis for the development of interoperable protocol standards: the TCP/IP protocol suite and the OSI reference model. TCP/IP is by far the most widely used interoperable architecture. OSI, though well known, has never lived up to its early promise. In the remainder of this chapter we introduce these two architectures and examine an important proprietary scheme: IBM's SNA.

12.2 TCP/IP PROTOCOL ARCHITECTURE

TCP/IP is a result of protocol research and development conducted on the experimental packet-switched network, ARPANET, funded by the Defense Advanced Research Projects Agency (DARPA), and is generally referred to as the TCP/IP protocol suite. This protocol suite consists of a large collection of protocols that have been issued as Internet standards by the Internet Architecture Board (IAB).

TCP/IP Layers

There is no official TCP/IP protocol model as there is in the case of OSI. However, based on the protocol standards that have been developed, we can organize the communication task for TCP/IP into five relatively independent layers:

- Application layer
- Host-to-host, or transport, layer
- Internet layer
- Network access layer
- Physical layer

The **physical layer** covers the physical interface between a data transmission device (e.g., workstation, computer) and a transmission medium or network. This layer is concerned with specifying the characteristics of the transmission medium, the nature of the signals, the data rate, and related matters.

The **network access layer** is concerned with the exchange of data between an end system and the network to which it is attached. The sending computer must provide the network with the address of the destination computer, so that the network may route the data to the appropriate destination. The sending computer may wish to invoke certain services, such as priority, that might be provided by the network. The specific software used at this layer depends on the type of network to be used; different standards have been developed for circuit switching, packet switching (e.g., X.25), local area networks (e.g., Ethernet), and others. Thus it makes sense to segregate functions having to do with network access into a separate layer. By doing this the remainder of the communications software, above the network access layer, need not be concerned about the specifics of the network to be used. The same higher-layer software should function properly regardless of the particular network to which the computer is attached.

The network access layer is concerned with access to and routing data across a network for two end systems attached to the same network. In those cases where two devices are attached to different networks, procedures are needed to allow data to traverse multiple interconnected networks. This is the function of the **internet layer**. The **internet protocol (IP)** is used at this layer to provide the routing function across multiple networks. This protocol is implement not only in the end systems but also in routers. A **router** is a processor that connects two networks and whose primary function is to relay data from one network to the other on its route from the source to the destination end system.

Regardless of the nature of the applications that are exchanging data, there is usually a requirement that data be exchanged reliably. That is, we would like to be assured that all the data arrive at the destination application and that the data arrive in the same order in which they were sent. As we shall see, the mechanisms for providing reliability are essentially independent of the nature of the applications. Thus, it makes sense to collect those mechanisms in a common layer shared by all applications; this is referred to as the *host-to-host layer,* or **transport layer**. The **transmission control protocol (TCP)** is the most commonly used protocol to provide this functionality.

Internet Protocol
An internetworking protocol that executes in hosts and routers to interconnect a number of packet networks.

Router
An internetworking device that connects two computer networks. It makes use of an internet protocol.

Finally, the **application layer** contains the logic needed to support the various user applications. For each different type of application, such as file transfer, a separate module is needed that is peculiar to that application.

TCP and UDP

For most applications running as part of the TCP/IP protocol architecture, the transport layer protocol is TCP. TCP provides a reliable connection for the transfer of data between applications. Figure 12.6a shows the header format for TCP, which is a minimum of 20 octets, or 160 bits. The source port and destination port fields identify the applications at the source and destination systems that are using this connection.[1] The sequence number, acknowledgment number, and window fields provide flow control and error control in a way similar to the mechanisms in HDLC, discussed in Chapter 5. The checksum is a 16-bit frame check sequence used to detect errors in the TCP segment.

In addition to TCP, there is one other transport-level protocol that is in common use as part of the TCP/IP protocol suite: the **user datagram protocol (UDP)**. The UDP provides a connectionless service for application-level procedures. UDP does not guarantee delivery, preservation of sequence, or protection against duplication. UDP enables a procedures to send messages to other procedures with a minimum of protocol mechanism. Some transaction-oriented appli-

FIGURE 12.6 TCP and UDP Headers.

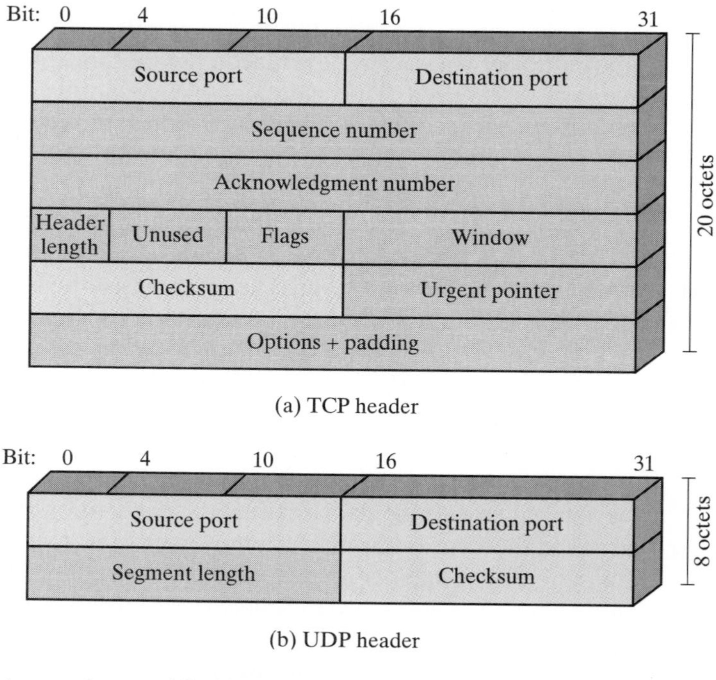

(a) TCP header

(b) UDP header

[1] The term *port* has essentially the same meaning as *service access point* (SAP), introduced in Section 12.1. The former is typically used in TCP/IP literature and the latter in OSI literature.

cations make use of UDP; one example is SNMP (simple network management protocol), the standard network management protocol for TCP/IP networks. Because it is connectionless, UDP has very little to do. Essentially, it adds a port addressing capability to IP. This is best seen by examining the UDP header, shown in Figure 12.6b.

IP and IPv6

For decades, the keystone of the TCP/IP protocol architecture has been the internet protocol (IP). Figure 12.7a shows the IP header format, , which is a minimum of 20 octets, or 160 bits. The header includes 32-bit source and destination addresses. The header checksum field is used to detect errors in the header to avoid misdelivery. The protocol field indicates whether TCP, UDP, or some

FIGURE 12.7 IP Headers.

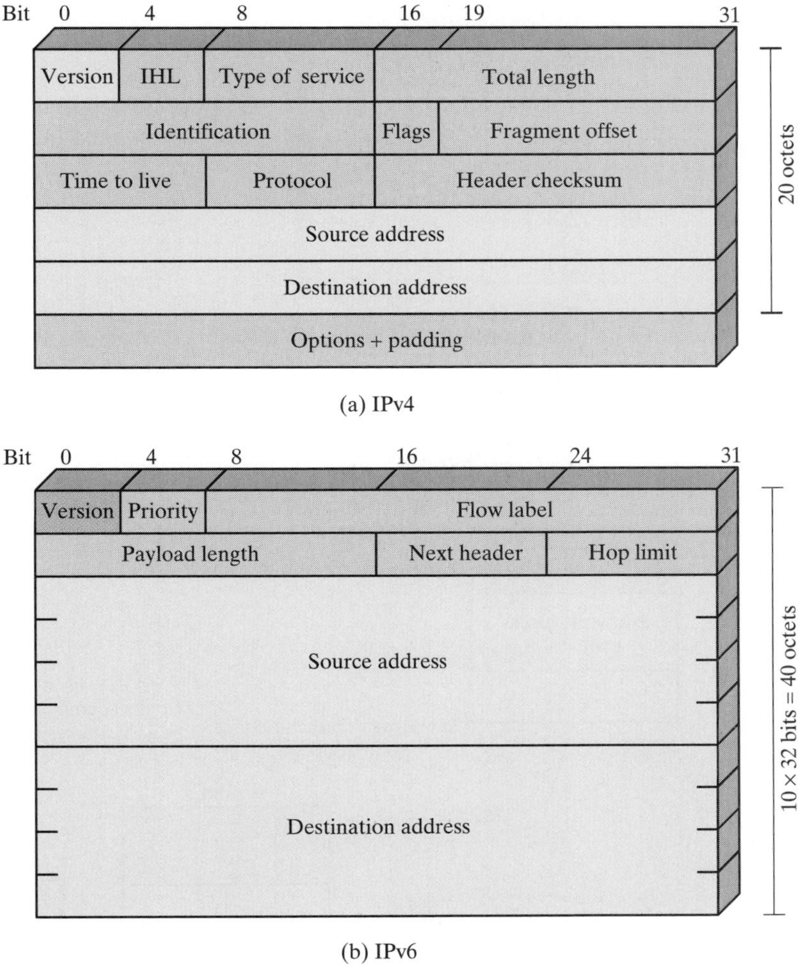

(a) IPv4

(b) IPv6

other higher-layer protocol is using IP. The flags and fragment offset fields are used in the fragmentation and reassembly process.

In 1995, the Internet Engineering Task Force (IETF), which develops protocol standards for the Internet, issued a specification for a next-generation IP, known then as IPng. This specification was turned into a standard in 1996 known as IPv6. IPv6 provides a number of functional enhancements over the existing IP, designed to accommodate the higher speeds of today's networks and the mix of data streams, including graphic and video, that are becoming more prevalent. But the driving force behind the development of the new protocol was the need for more addresses. The current IP uses a 32-bit address to specify a source or destination. With the explosive growth of the Internet and of private networks attached to the Internet, this address length became insufficient to accommodate all the systems needing addresses. As Figure 12.7b shows, IPv6 includes 128-bit source and destination address fields. Ultimately, all the installations using TCP/IP are expected to migrate from the current IP to IPv6, but this process will take many years if not decades.

Operation of TCP/IP

Figure 12.8 indicates how these protocols are configured for communications. To make clear that the total communications facility may consist of multiple net-

FIGURE 12.8 TCP/IP Concepts.

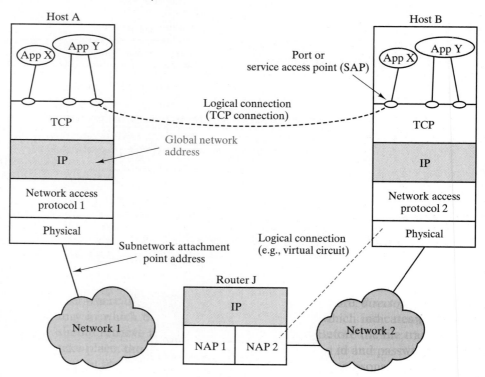

works, the constituent networks are usually referred to as *subnetworks*. Some sort of network access protocol, such as the Ethernet logic, is used to connect a computer to a subnetwork. This protocol enables the host to send data across the subnetwork to another host or, in the case of a host on another subnetwork, to a router. IP is implemented in all the end systems and the routers. It acts as a relay to move a block of data from one host, through one or more routers, to another host. TCP is implemented only in the end systems; it keeps track of the blocks of data to assure that all are delivered reliably to the appropriate application.

For successful communication, every entity in the overall system must have a unique address. Actually, two levels of addressing are needed. Each host on a subnetwork must have a unique global internet address; this allows the data to be delivered to the proper host. This address is used by IP for routing and delivery. Each application within a host must have an address that is unique within the host; this allows the host-to-host protocol (TCP) to deliver data to the proper process. The latter addresses are known as **ports**.

Let us trace a simple operation. Suppose that a process, associated with port 1 at host A, wishes to send a message to another process, associated with port 2 at host B. The process at A hands the message down to TCP with instructions to send it to host B, port 12. TCP hands the message down to IP with instructions to send it to host B. Note that IP need not be told the identity of the destination port. All it needs to know is that the data are intended for host B. Next, IP hands the message down to the network access layer (e.g., Ethernet logic) with instructions to send it to router X (the first hop on the way to B).

To control this operation, control information as well as user data must be transmitted, as suggested in Figure 12.9. Let us say that the sending process generates a block of data and passes this to TCP. TCP may break this block into

FIGURE 12.9 Protocol Data Units in the TCP/IP Architecture.

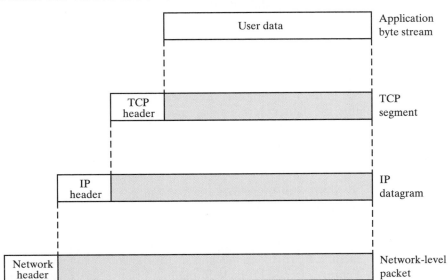

smaller pieces to make more manageable. To each of these pieces, TCP appends control information known as the TCP header (Figure 12.6a), forming a *TCP segment*. The control information is to be used by the peer TCP protocol entity at host B. Examples of items that are included in this header include:

- *Destination port.* When the TCP entity at B receives the segment, it must know to whom the data are to be delivered.
- *Sequence number.* TCP numbers the segments that it sends to a particular destination port sequentially, so that if they arrive out of order, the TCP entity at B can reorder them.
- *Checksum.* The sending TCP includes a code that is a function of the contents of the remainder of the segment. The receiving TCP performs the same calculation and compares the result with the incoming code. A discrepancy results if there has been some error in transmission.

Next, TCP hands each segment over to IP, with instructions to transmit it to host B. These segments must be transmitted across one or more subnetworks and relayed through one or more intermediate routers. This operation, too, requires the use of control information. Thus IP appends a header of control information (Figure 12.7) to each segment to form an *IP datagram*. An example of an item stored in the IP header is the destination host address (in this example, B).

Finally, each IP datagram is presented to the network access layer for transmission across the first subnetwork in its journey to the destination. The network access layer appends its own header, creating a packet, or frame. The packet is transmitted across the subnetwork to router X. The packet header contains the information that the subnetwork needs to transfer the data across the subnetwork. Examples of items that may be contained in this header include:

- *Destination subnetwork address.* The subnetwork must know to which attached device the packet is to be delivered.
- *Facilities requests.* The network access protocol might request the use of certain subnetwork facilities, such as priority.

At router X, the packet header is stripped off and the IP header examined. On the basis of the destination address information in the IP header, the IP module in the router directs the datagram out across subnetwork 2 to host B. To do this, the datagram is again augmented with a network access header.

When the data are received at B, the reverse process occurs. At each layer, the corresponding header is removed, and the remainder is passed on to the next higher layer, until the original user data are delivered to the destination process.

TCP/IP Applications

A number of applications have been standardized to operate on top of TCP. We mention three of the most common here.

The *simple mail transfer protocol (SMTP)* provides a basic electronic mail facility. It provides a mechanism for transferring messages among separate hosts. Features of SMTP include mailing lists, return receipts, and forwarding. The

SMTP protocol does not specify the way in which messages are to be created; some local editing or native electronic mail facility is required. Once a message is created, SMTP accepts the message and makes use of TCP to send it to an SMTP module on another host. The target SMTP module will make use of a local electronic mail package to store the incoming message in a user's mailbox.

The *file transfer protocol (FTP)* is used to send files from one system to another under user command. Both text and binary files are accommodated, and the protocol provides features for controlling user access. When a user wishes to engage in file transfer, FTP sets up a TCP connection to the target system for the exchange of control messages. These allow user ID and password to be transmitted and allow the user to specify the file and file actions desired. Once a file transfer is approved, a second TCP connection is set up for the data transfer. The file is transferred over the data connection, without the overhead of headers or control information at the application level. When the transfer is complete, the control connection is used to signal the completion and to accept new file transfer commands.

TELNET provides a remote logon capability, which enables a user at a terminal or personal computer to logon to a remote computer and function as if directly connected to that computer. The protocol was designed to work with simple scroll-mode terminals. TELNET is actually implemented in two modules: User TELNET interacts with the terminal I/O module to communicate with a local terminal. It converts the characteristics of real terminals to the network standard, and vice versa. Server TELNET interacts with an application, acting as a surrogate terminal handler so that remote terminals appear as local to the application. Terminal traffic between user and server TELNET is carried on a TCP connection.

12.3 OSI PROTOCOL ARCHITECTURE

Open Systems Interconnection (OSI) Reference Model
A seven-layer model of communications between cooperating devices.

The **open systems interconnection (OSI) reference model** was developed by the International Organization for Standardization (ISO) as a model for a computer protocol architecture, and as a framework for developing protocol standards. It consists of seven layers:

- Application
- Presentation
- Session
- Transport
- Network
- Data link
- Physical

Table 12-1 illustrates the OSI model and provides a brief definition of the functions performed at each layer. The intent of the OSI model is that protocols be developed to perform the functions of each layer.

The designers of OSI assumed that this model and the protocols developed within this model would come to dominate computer communications,

TABLE 12-1 OSI Layers

Application layer
   Provides access to the OSI environment for users and also provides distributed information services.

Presentation layer
   Provides independence to the application processes from differences in data representation (syntax)

Session layer
   Provides the control structure for communication between applications; establishes, manages, and terminates connections (sessions) between cooperating applications

Transport layer
   Provides reliable, transparent transfer of data between end points; provides end-to-end error recovery and flow control

Network layer
   Provides upper layers with independence from the data transmission and switching technologies used to connect systems; responsible for establishing, maintaining, and terminating connections

Data Link layer
   Provides for the reliable transfer of information across the physical link; sends blocks of data (frames) with the necessary synchronization, error control, and flow control

Physical layer
   Concerned with transmission of unstructured bit stream over physical medium; deals with the mechanical, electrical, functional, and procedural characteristics to access the physical medium

---

eventually replacing proprietary protocol implementations and rival multivendor models such as TCP/IP. This has not happened. Although many useful protocols have been developed in the context of OSI, the overall seven-layer model has not flourished. Instead, the TCP/IP architecture has come to dominate. There are a number of reasons for this outcome. Perhaps the most important is that the key TCP/IP protocols were mature and well tested at a time when similar OSI protocols were in the development stage. When businesses began to recognize the need for interoperability across networks, only TCP/IP was available and ready to go. Another reason is that the OSI model is unnecessarily complex, with seven layers to accomplish what TCP/IP does with fewer layers.

Figure 12.10 illustrates the layers of the TCP/IP and OSI architectures, showing roughly the correspondence in functionality between the two. The figure also suggests common means of implementing the various layers.

12.4 IBM's System Network Architecture

The era of the true protocol architecture began with the announcement in 1974 by IBM of its **systems network architecture (SNA)**. SNA was developed by IBM to protect its customer base and allow its customers to take advantage of new IBM offerings. The problem was that there was a proliferation of communications protocols and user access methods on IBM machines. Customers developed complex applications and were unable easily to incorporate new computers into their operation. Many of the communications techniques were inefficient, and a flourishing business in communications processors designed to support IBM users

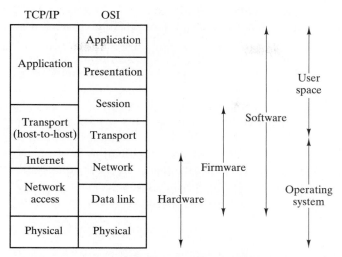

FIGURE 12.10 A Comparison of the TCP/IP and OSI Protocol Architectures.

developed among minicomputer and communication vendors These factors led to the development of an architecture that would provide efficient user access to a network of computers and terminals. This architecture has two facets:

- *Network architecture:* the network elements and configurations possible within SNA.
- *Protocol architecture:* the protocols and their interrelationships needed to support communications across an SNA network.

SNA is important because even with the success of TCP/IP, it is a widely used networking and protocol architecture, used on virtually all IBM installations and on most plug-compatible machines.[2]

Network Architecture

SNA is sufficiently general-purpose to encompass the requirements of virtually any user. From the user's point of view, the key elements of the network are terminals and application programs. The user interacts with the network from a terminal, and the principal concern of the user is the execution of applications on host computers. In some cases a terminal may be a stand-alone device with some communications processing capability, but in many cases, one or more terminals connect to the network by means of a terminal controller device. This device contains the communications logic to interact with the rest of the network. Similarly, a host system may contain communications logic for participating in the network. However, particularly on larger machines, it makes sense to remove the communications processing burden from the host and house it in a front-end processor.

---

[2] These are computers that have the same hardware characteristics as an IBM machine. Amdahl is an example of a mainframe vendor offering plug-compatible systems. In the microcomputer realm, such machines are referred to as *clones.* In either case, they allow the user to take advantage of IBM software on a hardware base from a different vendor.

These elements (hosts, terminals, communications processors) are the nodes of an SNA network. Nodes may be interconnected by direct transmission links or by networks, such as an X.25 packet-switching network. In the latter case, the network is a part of the SNA network only as a means of data transport. The internal elements and functions of the communications network are of no concern to SNA.

As an architecture, SNA provides a formal specification, or set of rules, to manage communications. This specification is implemented as a collection of software modules in the various nodes of the network. In SNA terminology, the implementation of the specification is in terms of *network addressable units (NAUs)*. These are the logical network components that provide communications interfaces through which end users can gain access to each other and through which the network is managed. There are three types of NAU:

- *System services control point (SSCP):* provides network management functions.
- *Physical unit (PU):* manages the physical resources of a node.
- *Logical unit (LU):* provides an interface to end users.

All NAUs reside within SNA nodes. NAUs are logical locations within an SNA network that have associated with them unique network names and addresses. A network consists of one or more domains. Each domain contains a host with an SSCP to manage and control communications in that domain. Each node in the network usually contains a single physical unit. Finally, each node that supports end users contains one or more logical units. A node that is a pure communications processor, such as a front-end processor, contains no logical units. Figure 12.11 illustrates the configuration of the various NAUs.

SNA defines the interaction of NAUs and the operation of the transmission subsystem (transmission links and communications networks). NAUs communicate with each other by means of sessions. A session is simply a temporary liaison between two NAUs for the purpose of exchanging data in a controlled manner (flow control and error control). Sessions that connect end-user application programs or devices directly are called LU–LU sessions. All other sessions are control sessions between the SSCP and other SSCPs, PUs, or LUs.

Until the early 1980s, the SNA dictated a hierarchical architecture. Each domain contained a mainframe host and a variety of communications and terminal controllers. All session setup required the mediation of the SSCP in the host. Sessions between end users in different domains required the cooperation of the respective SSCPs. With the explosive growth in the use of IBM personal computers, an exclusively hierarchical approach became untenable. In some networks there would be many personal computers with a requirement to exchange data with each other. To mediate all exchanges through a central host would create an inefficient bottleneck. Furthermore, some local-area network installations might consist solely of personal computers with no mainframe. To meet this new requirement, IBM developed a new capability referred to as LU 6.2, or advanced program-to-program communication (APPC). Because of the importance of

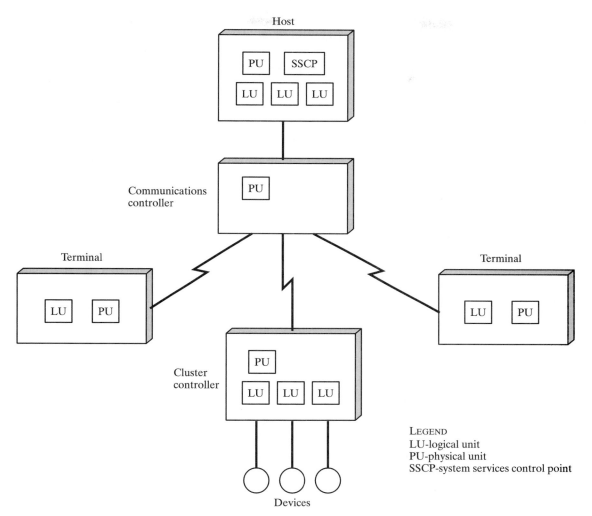

FIGURE 12.11 Locations of Various Types of NAU.

this specific member of the NAU family, it is worth expanding briefly on these concepts.

Advanced Program-to-Program Communication

Advanced program-to-program communication (APPC) is IBM's umbrella term for the set of SNA facilities designed to provide enhanced support for distributed transaction processing. The APPC standard is contained in the SNA definitions for physical unit type 2.1 (PU2.1) and logical unit type 6.2 (LU6.2). PU2.1 was designed for implementation in personal computers and minicomputers. It supports superior capabilities over previous PU specifications, which give it extended connectivity ability. There are two aspects to this extended capability:

- It can connect a node to other network nodes in two ways. It can link to a mainframe in a hierarchical manner. It can also connect to another PU2.1 node in a peer-to-peer relationship. The significance of this is that distributed intelligent nodes can use PU2.1 to connect directly, without mainframe connection.

- It allows multiple links, as well as parallel session support, an improvement in resource sharing and efficiency.

LU2.1 is designed to provide communications services to applications residing on PU2.1 nodes. It supports features useful for transaction processing applications. Also, it contains an interface specification that makes it easy for users to write their own applications.

Protocol architecture

As with OSI, SNA's protocol architecture is defined in terms of a set of layers, each of which performs part of the communications function. The layers are:

- Physical
- Data link control
- Path control
- Transmission control
- Data flow control
- Presentation services
- Transaction services

These layers correspond roughly to the seven OSI layers, with some differences. A brief description of each SNA layer follows.

The **physical control layer** specifies the physical interface between nodes, which may be serial or parallel. A serial interface is a communications link of the type discussed throughout this book. The term *serial* refers to the fact that bits are transmitted one at a time. A parallel interface, on the other hand, provides multiple transmission paths, and a number of bits (usually 8, 16, or 32) are transmitted in parallel. The parallel interface is typical of I/O channel connections between mainframes and front-end processors.

The **data link control layer** provides for the reliable transfer of data across a physical link. The protocol specified for serial communication links is synchronous data link control (SDLC). SDLC was the model for HDLC, which was covered in Chapter 5; in functional terms, SDLC is a subset of HDLC.

The **path control layer** creates logical connections between network addressable units (NAUs). The path control layer is divided into three sublayers that perform different functions related to setting up and using a logical connection:

- *Transmission group control.* Between any pair of connected nodes in a network, there may be one or more physical links. If there are multiple links, they are treated as a transmission group and an outgoing block of data can be transmitted on any link of the group. This provides increased reliability and load balancing to improve throughput.

- *Explicit route control.* This is the routing function. A route from the source node to the destination node through zero or more intermediate nodes is established.

- *Virtual route control.* When data are exchanged between end nodes across an explicit route, a logical connection, called a virtual route, is established. This is similar to a virtual circuit and includes a flow control capability.

The **transmission control layer** is responsible for establishing, maintaining, and terminating SNA sessions. A session is a logical relationship between end-points (NAUs). This layer guarantees the reliable delivery of data and corresponds to the OSI transport layer.

The **data flow control layer** provides session-related services that are visible and of interest to end-user processes and terminals. The principal functions are in the following categories:

- *Send/receive mode.* Full duplex or half duplex may be specified.

- *Chaining.* This is, in effect, a checkpointing mechanism that supports recovery.

- *Bracketing.* Whereas chaining is used to delimit a sequence of data units transmitted in one direction, bracketing deals with a sequence of exchanges and supports recovery in transaction-oriented applications.

- *Response options.* Three acknowledgments may be specified. For each block of data: (1) do not send an acknowledgment, (2) send an acknowledgment only in case of an exception, and (3) always send an acknowledgment.

- *Quiesce/shutdown.* A temporary or permanent halt in the flow of data may be requested.

The **presentation services layer** includes the following functions:

- *Format translation.* This service allows each endpoint to have a different view of the data exchanged and provides the necessary translation or reformatting functions.

- *Compression.* Data can be compressed at the bit or byte level using specified procedures to reduce transmission volume.

- *Transaction program support.* This service controls conversation-level communication between transaction programs by (1) loading and invoking transaction programs, (2) maintaining send and receive mode protocols, and (3) enforcing correct parameter usage and sequencing restrictions.

The **transaction services layer** is intended primarily to provide network management services. The following are included:

- *Configuration services:* allow an operator to start up or reconfigure a network by activating and deactivating links.

- *Network operator services:* include such nonconfiguration operator functions as the collection and display of network statistics and the communication of data from users and processes to the network operator.

- *Session services:* support the activation of a session on the behalf of end users and applications. In effect, this is the user interface to the transmission control layer.

- *Maintenance and management services:* provide for the testing of network facilities and assist in fault isolation and identification.

12.5 INTERNETWORKING

In most cases, a LAN or MAN is not an isolated entity. An organization may have more than one type of LAN at a given site to satisfy a spectrum of needs. An organization may have multiple LANs of the same type at a given site to accommodate performance or security requirements. And an organization may have LANs and possibly MANs at various sites and need them to be interconnected for central control of distributed information exchange.

An interconnected set of networks, from a user's point of view, may appear simply as a larger network. However, if each of the constituent networks retains its identity, and special mechanisms are needed for communicating across multiple networks, the entire configuration is often referred to as an *internet,* and each of the constituent networks as a *subnetwork.* These terms are defined briefly in Table 12-2. The most important example of an internet is referred to simply as the Internet. As the Internet has evolved from its modest beginnings as a research-oriented packet-switching network, it has served as the basis for the

TABLE 12-2 Internetworking Terms

Communication network
A facility that provides a data transfer service among stations attached to the network.

Internet
A collection of communication networks interconnected by bridges and/or routers.

Subnetwork
Refers to a constituent network of an internet. This avoids ambiguity since the entire internet, from a user's point of view, is a single network.

Bridge
A device used to connect two LANs that use similar LAN protocols. The bridge acts as an address filter, picking up packets from one LAN that are intended for a destination on another LAN and passing those packets on. The bridge does not modify the contents of the packets and does not add anything to the packet. The bridge operates at layer 2 of the OSI model.

Router
A device used to connect two subnetworks that may or may not be similar. The router employs an internet protocol present in each router and each end system of the network. The router operates at layer 3 of the OSI model.

development of internetworking technology and as the model for private internetworks within organizations.

Table 12-2 also defines two sorts of devices used to interconnect subnetworks in an internet. These devices provide a communications path and the necessary logic so that data can be exchanged between subnetworks. The differences between them have to do with the types of protocols used for the **internetworking** logic. We looked at the role and functions of bridges in Chapter 9. The role and functions of routers were introduced in the context of the internet protocol (**IP**) earlier in this chapter. However, because of the importance of routers in the overall networking scheme, it is worth providing additional comment in this section.

Routers

The bridge is only applicable to a configuration involving a single type of LAN. Of course, in many cases, an organization will need access to devices on a variety of networks. For example, as Figure 9.2 illustrates, an organization may have a tiered LAN architecture, with different types of LANs used for different purposes within an organization. There may also need to be access to devices on a wide-area network. Examples of the latter are systems on other LANs owned by the organzition at another geographic location, a public information source or database for query and transaction applications, a customer or supplier computer for transferring ordering information, and the Internet.

Internetworking is achieved by using intermediate systems, or routers, to interconnect a number of independent networks. Essential functions that the router must perform include:

1. Provide a link between networks.
2. Provide for the routing and delivery of data between processes on end systems attached to different networks.
3. Provide these functions in such a way as not to require modifications of the networking architecture of any of the attached subnetworks.

Point 3 means that the router must accommodate a number of differences among networks, such as:

- *Addressing schemes.* The networks may use different schemes for assigning addresses to devices. For example, an IEEE 802 LAN uses either 16-bit or 48-bit binary addresses for each attached device; an X.25 public packet-switching network uses 12-digit decimal addresses (encoded as 4 bits per digit for a 48-bit address). Some form of global network addressing must be provided, as well as a directory service.

- *Maximum packet sizes.* Packets from one network may have to be broken into smaller pieces to be transmitted on another network, a process known as *segmentation.* For example, Ethernet imposes a maximum packet size of 1500 bytes; a maximum packet size of 1000 bytes is common on X.25 networks. A packet that is transmitted on an Ethernet system and picked up by a router for retransmission on an X.25 network may have to segment the incoming packet into two smaller ones.

- *Interfaces.* The hardware and software interfaces to various networks differ. The concept of a router must be independent of these differences.
- *Reliability.* Various network services may provide anything from a reliable end-to-end virtual circuit to an unreliable service. The operation of the routers should not depend on an assumption of network reliability.

The requirements above are best satisfied by an internetworking protocol such as IP, which is implemented in all end systems and routers.

Internetworking Example

Figure 12.12 depicts a configuration that we will use to illustrate the interactions among protocols for internetworking. In this case we focus on a server attached to a frame relay WAN and a workstation attached to an IEEE 802 LAN, with a router connecting the two networks. The router will provide a link between the server and the workstation that enables these end systems to ignore the details of the intervening networks.

Figures 12.13 through 12.15 outline typical steps in the transfer of a block of data, such as a file or a web page, from the server, through a network, and ultimately to an application in the workstation. In this example, the message passes through just one router. Before data can be transmitted, the application and transport layers in the server establish, with the corresponding layer in the workstation, the applicable ground rules for a communication session. These include character code to be used, error-checking method, and the like. The protocol at each layer is used for this purpose and then is used in the transmission of the message.

FIGURE 12.12 Configuration for TCP/IP Example.

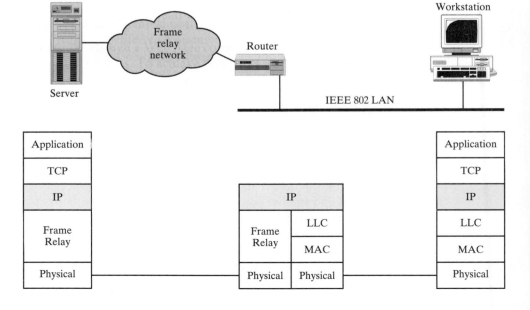

1. Preparing the data. The application protocol prepares a block of data for transmission: for example, an E-mail message (SMTP), a file (FTP), or a block of user input (TELNET).

2. Using a common syntax. If necessary, the data are converted to a form expected by the destination. This may include a different character code, the use of encryption, and/or compression.

3. Segmenting the data. TCP may break the data block into a number of segments, keeping track of their sequence. Each TCP segment includes a header containing a sequence number and a frame check sequence to detect errors.

4. Duplicating segments. A copy is made of each TCP segment, in case the loss or damage of a segment necessitates retransmission. When an acknowledgment is received from the other TCP entity, a segment is erased.

5. Fragmenting the segments. IP may break a TCP segment into a number of datagrams to meet size requirements of the intervening networks. Each datagram includes a header containing a destination address, a frame check sequence, and other control information.

6. Framing. A frame relay header and trailer is added to each IP datagram. The header contains a connection identifier and the trailer contains a frame check sequence.

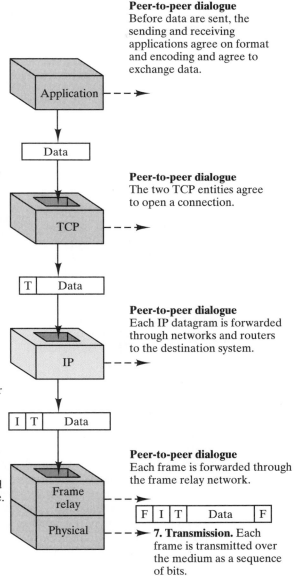

Peer-to-peer dialogue
Before data are sent, the sending and receiving applications agree on format and encoding and agree to exchange data.

Peer-to-peer dialogue
The two TCP entities agree to open a connection.

Peer-to-peer dialogue
Each IP datagram is forwarded through networks and routers to the destination system.

Peer-to-peer dialogue
Each frame is forwarded through the frame relay network.

7. Transmission. Each frame is transmitted over the medium as a sequence of bits.

FIGURE 12.13 Operation of TCP/IP: Action at Sender.

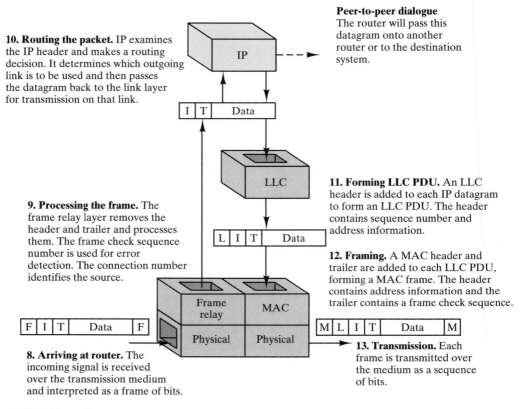

10. Routing the packet. IP examines the IP header and makes a routing decision. It determines which outgoing link is to be used and then passes the datagram back to the link layer for transmission on that link.

Peer-to-peer dialogue
The router will pass this datagram onto another router or to the destination system.

9. Processing the frame. The frame relay layer removes the header and trailer and processes them. The frame check sequence number is used for error detection. The connection number identifies the source.

11. Forming LLC PDU. An LLC header is added to each IP datagram to form an LLC PDU. The header contains sequence number and address information.

12. Framing. A MAC header and trailer are added to each LLC PDU, forming a MAC frame. The header contains address information and the trailer contains a frame check sequence.

8. Arriving at router. The incoming signal is received over the transmission medium and interpreted as a frame of bits.

13. Transmission. Each frame is transmitted over the medium as a sequence of bits.

FIGURE 12.14 Operation of TCP/IP: Action at Router.

SUMMARY

The communication functionality required for distributed applications is quite complex. This functionality is generally implemented as a structured set of modules. The modules are arranged in a vertical, layered fashion, with each layer providing a particular portion of the needed functionality and relying on the next-lower layer for more primitive functions. Such a structure is referred to as a protocol architecture.

One motivation for the use of this type of structure is that it eases the task of design and implementation. It is standard practice for any large software package to break the functions up into modules that can be designed and implemented separately. After each module is designed and implemented, it can be tested. Then the modules can be combined and tested together. This motivation has led computer vendors to develop proprietary layered protocol architectures. An example of this is the systems network architecture (SNA) of IBM.

A layered architecture can also be used to construct a standardized set of communication protocols. In this case the advantages of modular design remain, but in addition, a layered architecture is particularly well suited to the development of standards. Standards can be developed simultaneously for protocols at each layer of the architecture. This

20. Delivering the data. The application performs any needed transformations, including decompression and decryption, and directs the data to the appropriate file or other destination.

19. Reassembling user data. If TCP has broken the user data into multiple segments, these are reassembled and the block is passed up to the application.

18. Processing the TCP segment. TCP removes the header. It checks the frame check sequence and acknowledges if there is a match and discards for mismatch. Flow control is also performed.

17. Processing the IP datagram. IP removes the header. The frame check sequence and other control information are processed.

16. Processing the LLC PDU. The LLC layer removes the header and processes it. The sequence number is used for flow and error control.

15. Processing the frame. The MAC layer removes the header and trailer and processes them. The frame check sequence number is used for error detection.

14. Arriving at destination. The incoming signal is received over the transmission medium and interpreted as a frame of bits.

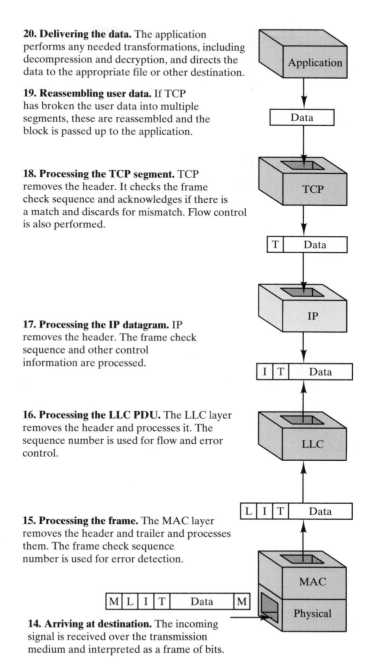

FIGURE 12.15 Operation of TCP/IP: Action at Receiver.

breaks down the work to make it more manageable and speeds up the standards-development process. The TCP/IP protocol architecture is the standard architecture used for this purpose. This architecture contains five layers. Each layer provides a portion of the total communications function required for distributed applications. Standards have been developed for each layer. Development work continues, particularly at the top (application) layer, where new distributed applications are still being defined.

Another standardized architecture is the open systems interconnection (OSI) model. This seven-layer model was intended to be the international standard that would govern all protocol design. However, OSI never achieved market acceptance and has yielded to TCP/IP.

RECOMMENDED READING

[STAL97a] is a detailed description of the TCP/IP model and of the standards at each layer of the model. The material is also covered in [TANE96], which averages about one chapter per layer. Both books also cover OSI. An excellent treatments of SNA is [MART87]; it is detailed, complete, and clearly written.

MART87 MARTIN, J., and CHAPMAN, K. *SNA: IBM's Networking Solution.* Upper Saddle River, NJ: Prentice Hall, 1987.

STAL97a STALLINGS, W. *Data and Computer Communications,* 5th ed. Upper Saddle River, NJ: Prentice Hall, 1997.

TANE96 TANENBAUM, A. *Computer Networks.* Upper Saddle River, NJ: Prentice Hall, 1996.

 ### *Recommended Web Site*

- http://playground.sun.com/pub/ipng/html/ipng-main.html: contains information about IPv6 and related topics.

KEY TERMS

Application Layer	Path Layer	Systems Network
Data Flow Layer	Physical Layer	Architecture (SNA)
Data Link Layer	Port	Transmission Control
Internet Layer	Presentation Layer	Protocol (TCP)
Internet Protocol (IP)	Protocol Architecture	Transmission Layer
Internetworking	Router	Transport Layer
Network Access Layer	Service Access Point	User Data Protocol
Open Systems Interconnection	(SAP)	(UDP)
(OSI) Reference Model	Session Layer	

QUESTIONS

1. What is the major function of the network access layer?
2. What tasks are performed by the transport layer?
3. What is a protocol?
4. What is a protocol data unit (PDU)?
5. What are the major services provided by the data link layer of the OSI model?

6. What is TCP/IP?

7. Under IBM's system network architecture (SNA), what are network addressible units (NAUs)?

8. Because SNA was developed primarily around a master–slave relationship, how can computers achieve a peer-to-peer relationship?

9. What is a router?

PROBLEMS

1. OSI has seven layers. Design an architecture with eight layers and make a case for it. Design one with six layers and make a case for that.

2. A TCP segment consisting of 1500 bits of data and 160 bits of header is sent to the IP layer, which appends another 160 bits of header. This is then transmitted through two networks, each of which uses a 24-bit packet header. The destination network has a maximum packet size of 800 bits. How many bits, including headers, are delivered to the network layer protocol at the destination?

CHAPTER 13

Distributed Applications

CHAPTER OBJECTIVES

After reading this chapter, you should be able to:

- Discuss the applications for electronic mail.

- Explain that basic functionality of SMTP.

- Explain the need for MIME as an enhancement to ordinary E-mail.

- Describe the key elements of MIME.

- Define electronic data interchange (EDI) and explain its importance to business.

- Specify the components of an EDI system.

- Discuss the relationship between electronic mail and EDI.

- Describe the basic functionality of the World Wide Web.

- Explain the role of HTTP and HTML in the operation of a Web application.

As we discussed in Chapters 2 and 3, distributed information processing is essential in virtually all businesses. Much of the distributed processing is tailored to specific types of data and is supported by proprietary vendor software. However, there is a growing use of distributed applications for both intracompany and intercompany exchange that are general purpose in nature and that are defined by international standards or by industry de facto standards. These applications can have a direct impact on the efficiency and competitiveness of a business. In this chapter we look at three of the most important and widespread of these distributed applications:

- Electronic mail
- Electronic data interchange
- Web-based applications

In each case, international standards have been developed. As these standards become more widely implemented by computer vendors and software houses, these applications become increasingly important and useful in the business environment.

■ Illustration: Problem Statement

The port authority at a major U.S. seaport is seeking ways of increasing the flow of cargo through the port. One problem area is the time to process documents. The movement of goods involves steamship companies, customhouse brokers, terminal operators, and trucking companies. Currently, documents such as arrival notices and inspection receipts must be mailed from one company to the next. Often, shipping firms must wait days and wade through huge stacks of mail to find and complete necessary forms that track the movement of cargo.

One approach the port authority considered was the acquisition of a mainframe and the use of a database management system on the mainframe. All companies that use the port would be required to enter information into the central database. A set of software packages would be provided on the mainframe to meet typical needs, and all communications between companies would be via the central port authority database.

This plan was rejected by the port users. Each company already had its own computerized system for tracking goods and had invested in the hardware and software to implement and maintain the system. Furthermore, the company system typically contained a lot of proprietary information that could not be disclosed. Thus, each company would have to continue to maintain its own information base on its own computer and reenter the necessary information into the port authority computer. This was an unnecessary waste of resources and introduced the potential for errors. Furthermore, because the various companies used a variety of computer systems, from personal computers to mainframes, there was no obvious way to standardize the database used by each.

What other approach to increase automation is promising? (The problem solution appears at the end of the chapter.) ■

13.1 ELECTRONIC MAIL

Electronic Mail
Correspondence in the form of messages transmitted between work stations over a network.

Electronic mail is a facility that allows users at workstations and terminals to compose and exchange messages. The messages need never exist on paper unless the user (sender or recipient) desires a paper copy of the message. Some electronic mail systems serve users on a single computer; others provide service across a network of computers. Table 13-1 lists some of the common features provided by an electronic mail facility. In Chapter 2 we briefly outlined the need for and benefits of electronic mail. In this section we look at the basic functioning of electronic mail, its use in a distributed environment, and the international standards for electronic mail.

Public versus Private Electronic Mail

A public electronic mail service is one provided by a third-party electronic mail vendor. The service is usually available over one or more public networks, especially the dial-up public telephone network. Users gain access to the facility from a terminal or personal computer by connecting to the facility across the public

TABLE 13-1 Typical Electronic Mail Facilities

Message Preparation

Word processing

Facilities for the creation and editing of messages. Usually, these need not be as powerful as a full word processor, since electronic mail documents tend to be simple. However, most electronic mail packages allow "off-line" access to word processors: the user creates a message using the computer's word processor, stores the message as a file, and then uses the file as input to the message preparation function of the word processor.

Annotation

Messages often require some sort of short reply. A simple technique is to allow the recipient to attach annotation to an incoming message and send it back to the originator or on to a third party.

Message Sending

User directory

Used by the system. May also be accessible to users to be able to look up addresses.

Timed delivery

Allows the sender to specify that a message be delivered before, at, or after a specified date/time. A message is considered delivered when it is placed in the recipient's mailbox.

Multiple addressing

Copies of a message are sent to multiple addressees. The recipients are designated by listing each in the header of the message or by the use of a distribution list. The latter is a file containing a list of users. Distribution lists can be created by the user and by central administrative functions.

Message priority

A message may be labeled at a given priority level. Higher-priority messages will be delivered more rapidly, if that is possible. Also, the recipient will be notified or receive some indication of the arrival of high-priority messages.

Status information

A user may request notification of delivery or of actual retrieval by the recipient. A user may also be able to query the current status of a message (e.g., queued for transmission, transmitted but receipt confirmation not yet received).

Interface to other facilities

These would include other electronic systems, such as telex, and physical distribution facilities, such as couriers and the public mail service (e.g., U.S. Postal Service).

Message Receiving

Mailbox scanning

Allows the user to scan the current contents of mailbox. Each message may be indicated by subject, author, date, priority, and so on.

Message selection

The user may select individual messages from the mailbox for display, printing, storing in a separate file, or deletion.

Message notification

Many systems notify an on-line user of the arrival of a new message and indicate to a user during logon that there are messages in his or her mailbox.

Message reply

A user may reply immediately to a selected message, avoiding the necessity of keying in the recipient's name and address.

Message rerouting

A user who has moved, either temporarily or permanently, may reroute incoming messages. An enhancement is to allow the user to specify different forwarding addresses for different categories of messages.

network. Messages can be sent to any other registered subscriber. Thus, a corporation could use a public mail system for internal electronic mail communication and could also exchange messages with customers and suppliers who are also registered with this facility. Examples of public mail systems are MCI Mail, available over the MCI public telecommunications network, and the mail systems provided by on-line services such as Compuserve.

A private electronic mail facility is one that is integrated with the user's computer equipment. This may be in the form of software from an independent software house that runs on the equipment of one or more computer vendors. More commonly, the electronic mail facility is provided by the computer vendor, often as part of an integrated office system such as those from DEC (All-in-One) or IBM (PROFS). As the name implies, private electronic mail facilities are owned and operated by a company for its own internal messaging requirements; for external messaging, a connection to other systems is required.

In general, the services offered on private and public electronic mail systems are quite similar. One factor in deciding between the two is cost. For private systems, there is the initial cost of the software and hardware. If the facility is implemented on computers already used for other purposes, the only hardware costs will be additional terminals and their connections for users who need the terminal only for electronic mail. For public systems, the cost is number and length of messages transmitted and stored in mailboxes on the system. Other factors to consider: Private mail systems are able to offer better integration with customer-owned computer systems, whereas public mail systems are able to offer a wider range of delivery options (e.g., links to telex and courier services) and a broader community of users.

Internet electronic mail does not fit into either of the categories just discussed. Strictly speaking, Internet mail is not a complete electronic mail facility but merely the transfer mechanism for exchanging mail among subscribing systems. This distinction is explained in the next subsection.

Single-Computer versus Multiple-Computer Electronic Mail

The simplest form of electronic mail is the single-system facility (Figure 13.1a). This facility allows all the users of a shared computer system to exchange messages. Each user is registered on the system and has a unique identifier, usually the person's last name. Associated with each user is a mailbox. The electronic mail facility is an application program available to any user logged onto the system. A user may invoke the electronic mail facility, prepare a message, and "send" it to any other user on the system. The act of sending simply involves putting the message in the recipient's mailbox. The mailbox is actually an entity maintained by the file-management system and is in the nature of a file directory. One mailbox is associated with each user. Any "incoming" mail is simply stored as a file under that user's mailbox directory. The user may later go and fetch that file to read the message. The user reads messages by invoking the mail facility and "reading" rather than "sending." In most systems, when the user logs on, he or she is informed if there is any new mail in that user's mailbox.

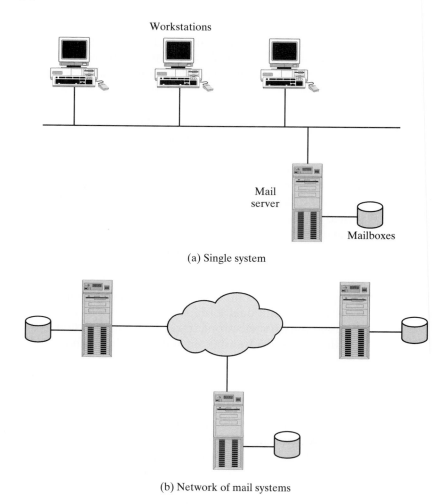

FIGURE 13.1 Electronic Mail Configurations.

Many public mail systems are single-computer systems, with a single host system maintaining all the mailboxes of all users. In the private context, a single central host may support single-computer mail. More typically, in a LAN configuration, the central mail system is a dedicated mail server or a mail facility on a multipurpose server. In the latter case, the software for preparing and processing mail may be on each person's workstation, while the mailboxes themselves are on the server.

With a single-system electronic mail facility, messages can only be exchanged among users of that particular system. Clearly, this is too limited. In a distributed environment, we would like to be able to exchange messages with users attached to other systems. Thus, we would like to treat electronic mail as a distributed application.

For a distributed mail system, a number of mail handlers (e.g., mail servers) connect over a network facility (e.g., public or private WAN or the Internet) and exchange mail (Figure 13.1b). With this configuration, it is useful to group electronic mail functions into two distinct categories: user agent and message transfer agent.

The user agent functions are visible to the electronic mail user. These include facilities for preparing and submitting messages for routing to the destination(s), as well as utility functions to assist the user in filing, retrieving, replying, and forwarding. The message transfer agent accepts messages from the user agent for transmission across a network or internetwork. The message transfer agent is concerned with the protocol operation needed to transmit and deliver messages.

The user does not interact directly with the message transfer agent. If the user designates a local recipient for a message, the user agent stores the message in the local recipient's mailbox. If a remote recipient is designated, the user agent passes the message to the message transfer agent for transmission to a remote message transfer agent and ultimately to a remote mailbox.

Many vendors offer a network version of their basic electronic mail facility. However, this will only allow the user to send mail to users on systems of the same vendor. Several forms of interconnection are needed. It is most desirable to provide an interconnection between a private electronic mail network and a public electronic mail service. Also desirable is the ability to interconnect private systems based on computers from different vendors. To provide these interconnections, a set of standards is needed, a topic to which we now turn.

Simple Mail Transfer Protocol

The **simple mail transfer protocol (SMTP)** is the standard protocol for transferring mail between hosts in the TCP/IP protocol suite; it is defined in RFC 821. Although messages transferred by SMTP usually follow the format defined in RFC 822, described later, SMTP is not concerned with the format or content of messages themselves, with two exceptions. This concept is often expressed by saying that SMTP uses information written on the *envelope* of the mail (message header), but does not look at the contents (message body) of the envelope. The two exceptions:

1. SMTP standardizes the message character set as 7-bit ASCII.
2. SMTP adds log information to the start of the delivered message that indicates the path the message took.

Basic Electronic Mail Operation   Figure 13.2 illustrates the overall flow of mail in a typical system. Although much of this activity is outside the scope of SMTP, the figure illustrates the context within which SMTP typically operates. To begin, mail is created by a user agent program in response to user input. Each created message consists of a header that includes the recipient's E-mail address and other information, and a body containing the message to be sent. These messages are then queued in some fashion and provided as input to an SMTP Sender program, which is typically an always-present server program on the host.

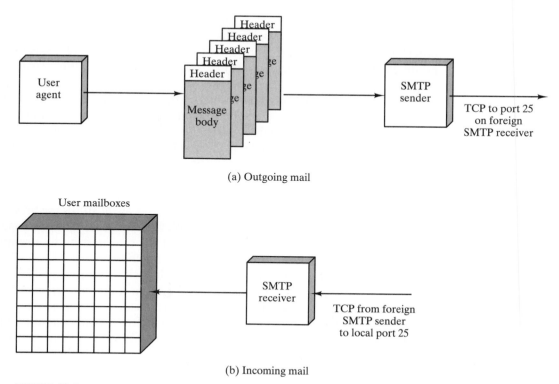

(a) Outgoing mail

(b) Incoming mail

FIGURE 13.2 SMTP Mail Flow.

Although the structure of the outgoing mail queue will differ depending on the host's operating system, each queued message conceptually has two parts:

1. The message text, consisting of:
   - The RFC 822 header: This constitutes the message envelope and includes an indication of the intended recipient or recipients.
   - The body of the message, composed by the user.
2. A list of mail destinations.

The list of mail destinations for the message is derived by the user agent from the 822 message header. In some cases, the destination or destinations are literally specified in the message header. In other cases, the user agent may need to expand mailing list names, remove duplicates, and replace mnemonic names with actual mailbox names. If any blind carbon copies (BCCs) are indicated, the user agent needs to prepare messages that conform to this requirement. The basic idea is that the multiple formats and styles preferred by humans in the user interface are replaced by a standardized list suitable for the SMTP send program.

The *SMTP sender* takes messages from the outgoing mail queue and transmits them to the proper destination host via SMTP transactions over one or more TCP connections to port 25 on the target hosts. A host may have multiple SMTP senders active simultaneously if it has a large volume of outgoing mail, and should also have the capability of creating SMTP receivers on demand so that mail from one host cannot delay mail from another.

Whenever the SMTP sender completes delivery of a particular message to one or more users on a specific host, it deletes the corresponding destinations from that message's destination list. When all destinations for a particular message are processed, the message is deleted from the queue. In processing a queue, the SMTP sender can perform a variety of optimizations. If a particular message is to be sent to multiple users on a single host, the message text need to be sent only once. If multiple messages are ready to send to the same host, the SMTP sender can open a TCP connection, transfer the multiple messages, and then close the connection, rather than opening and closing a connection for each message.

The SMTP sender must deal with a variety of errors. The destination host may be unreachable, out of operation, or the TCP connection may fail while mail is being transferred. The sender can requeue the mail for later delivery but give up after some period rather than keep the message in the queue indefinitely. A common error is a faulty destination address, which can occur due to user input error or because the intended destination user has a new address on a different host. The SMTP sender must either redirect the message if possible or return an error notification to the message's originator.

The *SMTP protocol* is used to transfer a message from the SMTP sender to the SMTP receiver over a TCP connection. SMTP attempts to provide reliable operation but does not guarantee to recover from lost messages. No end-to-end acknowledgment is returned to a message's originator that a message is delivered successfully to the message's recipient, and error indications are not guaranteed to be returned either. However, the SMTP-based mail system is generally considered reliable.

The *SMTP receiver* accepts each arriving message and either places it in the appropriate user mailbox or copies it to the local outgoing mail queue if forwarding is required. The SMTP receiver must be able to verify local mail destinations and deal with errors, including transmission errors and lack of disk file capacity.

The SMTP sender is responsible for a message up to the point where the SMTP receiver indicates that the transfer is complete; however, this simply means that the message has arrived at the SMTP receiver, not that the message has been delivered to and retrieved by the intended recipient. The SMTP receiver's error-handling responsibilities are generally limited to giving up on TCP connections that fail or are inactive for very long periods. Thus, the sender has most of the error recovery responsibility. Errors during completion indication may cause duplicate, but not lost, messages.

In most cases, messages go directly from the mail originator's machine to the destination machine over a single TCP connection. However, mail will occasionally go through intermediate machines via an SMTP forwarding capability, in which case the message must traverse multiple TCP connections between source and destination. One way for this to happen is for the sender to specify a route to the destination in the form of a sequence of servers. A more common event is forwarding required because a user has moved.

It is important to note that the SMTP protocol is limited to the conversation that takes place between the SMTP sender and the SMTP receiver. SMTP's main function is the transfer of messages, although there are some ancillary functions dealing with mail destination verification and handling. The rest of the mail-handling apparatus depicted in Figure 13.2 is beyond the scope of SMTP and may differ from one system to another.

We now turn to a discussion of the main elements of SMTP.

SMTP Overview   Operation of SMTP consists of a series of commands and responses exchanged between the SMTP sender and receiver. The initiative is with the SMTP sender, which establishes the TCP connection. Once the connection is established, the SMTP sender sends commands over the connection to the receiver. Each command generates exactly one reply from the SMTP receiver.

Basic SMTP operation occurs in three phases: connection setup, exchange of one or more command-response pairs, and connection termination. We examine each phase in turn.

Connection Setup   An SMTP sender will attempt to set up a TCP connection with a target host when it has one or more mail messages to deliver to that host. The sequence is quite simple:

1. The sender opens a TCP connection with the receiver.
2. Once the connection is established, the receiver identifies itself with "220 Service Ready."
3. The sender identifies itself with the HELO command.
4. The receiver accepts the sender's identification with "250 OK."

If the mail service on the destination is unavailable, the destination host returns a "421 Service Not Available" reply in step 2 and the process is terminated.

Mail Transfer   Once a connection has been established, the SMTP sender may send one or more messages to the SMTP receiver. There are three logical phases to the transfer of a message:

1. A MAIL command identifies the originator of the message.
2. One or more RCPT commands identify the recipients for this message.
3. A DATA command transfers the message text.

The *MAIL command* gives the reverse path which can be used to report errors. If the receiver is prepared to accept messages from this originator, it returns a "250 OK" reply. Otherwise, the receiver returns a reply indicating failure to execute the command or an error in the command.

The *RCPT command* identifies an individual recipient of the mail data; multiple recipients are specified by multiple use of this command. A separate reply is returned for each RCPT command, with one of the following possibilities:

1. The receiver accepts the destination with a 250 reply; this indicates that the designated mailbox is on the receiver's system.

2. The destination will require forwarding and the receiver will forward.
3. The destination requires forwarding but the receiver will not forward; the sender must resend to the forwarding address.
4. A mailbox does not exist for this recipient at this host.
5. The destination is rejected due to some other failure to execute or an error in the command.

The advantage of using a separate RCPT phase is that the sender will not send the message until it is assured that the receiver is prepared to receive the message for at least one recipient, thereby avoiding the overhead of sending an entire message only to learn that the destination is unknown. Once the SMTP receiver has agreed to receive the mail message for at least one recipient, the SMTP sender uses the *DATA command* to initiate the transfer of the message. If the SMTP receiver is still prepared to receive the message, it returns a start message; otherwise, the receiver returns a reply indicating failure to execute the command or an error in the command. If the Start reply is returned, the SMTP sender proceeds to send the message over the TCP connection as a sequence of ASCII lines. The end of the message is indicated by a line containing only a period. The SMTP receiver responds with an OK reply if the message is accepted, or with the appropriate error code.

An example, taken from RFC 821, illustrates the process:

```
S: MAIL FROM:<Smith@Alpha.ARPA>
R: 250 OK

S: RCPT TO:<Jones@Beta.ARPA>
R: 250 OK

S: RCPT TO:<Green@Beta.ARPA>
R: 550 No such user here

S: RCPT TO:<Brown@Beta.ARPA>
R: 250 OK

S: DATA
R: 354 Start mail input; end with <CRLF>.<CRLF>
S: Blah blah blah...
S: ...etc. etc. etc.
S: <CRLF>.<CRLF>
R: 250 OK
```

The SMTP sender is transmitting mail that originates with the user Smith@Alpha.ARPA. The message is addressed to three users on machine Beta.ARPA, namely, Jones, Green, and Brown. The SMTP receiver indicates that it has mailboxes for Jones and Brown but does not have information on Green. Because at least one of the intended recipients has been verified, the sender proceeds to send the text message.

Connection Closing The SMTP sender closes the connection in two steps. First, the sender sends a QUIT command and waits for a reply. The second step is to initiate a TCP close operation for the TCP connection. The receiver initiates its TCP close after sending its reply to the QUIT command.

RFC 822 RFC 822 defines a format for text messages that are sent using electronic mail. The SMTP standard adopts RFC 822 as the format for use in constructing messages for transmission via SMTP. In the RFC 822 context, messages are viewed as having an envelope and contents. The envelope contains whatever information is needed to accomplish transmission and delivery. The contents compose the object to be delivered to the recipient. The RFC 822 standard applies only to the contents. However, the content standard includes a set of header fields that may be used by the mail system to create the envelope, and the standard is intended to facilitate the acquisition of such information by programs.

An RFC 822 message consists of a sequence of lines of text and uses a general "memo" framework. That is, a message consists of some number of header lines, which follow a rigid format, followed by a body portion consisting of arbitrary text.

A header line usually consists of a keyword, followed by a colon, followed by the keyword's arguments; the format allows a long line to be broken up into several lines. The most frequently used keywords are From, To, Subject, and Date. Here is an example message:

```
Date: Thur, 16 Jan 1997 10:37:17 (EST)
From: "William Stallings" <ws@host.com>
Subject: The Syntax in RFC 822
To: Smith@Other-host.com
Cc: Jones@Yet-Another-Host.com

Hello. This section begins the actual message body, which
is delimited from the message heading by a blank line.
```

Another field that is commonly found in RFC 822 headers is message-ID. This field contains a unique identifier associated with this message.

Multipurpose Internet Mail Extension

The **multipurpose internet mail extension (MIME)** is an extension to the RFC 822 framework that is intended to address some of the problems and limitations of the use of SMTP and RFC 822 for electronic mail. The following are the limitations of the SMTP/822 scheme:

1. SMTP cannot transmit executable files or other binary objects. A number of schemes are in use for converting binary files into a text form that can be used by SMTP mail systems, including the popular Unix uuencode/uudecode scheme. However, none of these is a standard or even a de facto standard.

2. SMTP cannot transmit text data that includes national language characters because these are represented by 8-bit codes with values of 128 decimal or higher, and SMTP is limited to 7-bit ASCII.

3. SMTP servers may reject mail messages over a certain size.

4. SMTP gateways that translate between ASCII and the character code EBCDIC do not use a consistent set of mappings, resulting in translation problems.
5. SMTP gateways to X.400 electronic mail networks cannot handle nontextual data included in X.400 messages.
6. Some SMTP implementations do not adhere completely to the SMTP standards defined in RFC 821. Common problems include:
   - Deletion, addition, or reordering of carriage return and linefeed.
   - Truncating or wrapping lines longer than 76 characters.
   - Removal of trailing white space (tab and space characters).
   - Padding of lines in a message to the same length.
   - Conversion of tab characters into multiple space characters.

These limitations make it difficult to use encryption with electron mail and to use SMTP to carry multimedia objects and electronic data interchange (EDI) messages. MIME is intended to resolve these problems in a manner that is compatible with existing RFC 822 implementations. The specification is provided in RFC 1521 and 1522.

Overview The MIME specification includes the following elements:

1. Five new message header fields are defined, which may be included in an RFC 822 header. These fields provide information about the body of the message.
2. A number of content formats are defined, thus standardizing representations that support multimedia electronic mail.
3. Transfer encodings are defined that enable the conversion of any content format into a form that is protected from alteration by the mail system.

In this subsection we introduce the five message header fields. The next two subsections deal with content formats and transfer encodings. The five header fields defined in MIME are:

- *MIME-Version:* Must have the parameter value 1.0. This field indicates that the message conforms to RFC 1521 and 1522.
- *Content-Type:* describes the data contained in the body with sufficient detail that the receiving user agent can pick an appropriate agent or mechanism to represent the data to the user or otherwise deal with the data in an appropriate manner.
- *Content-Transfer-Encoding:* indicates the type of transformation that has been used to represent the body of the message in a way that is acceptable for mail transport.
- *Content-ID:* Used to uniquely identify MIME entities in multiple contexts.
- *Content-Description:* A plain text description of the object with the body; this is useful when the object is not readable (e.g., audio data).

Any or all of these fields may appear in a normal RFC 822 header. A compliant implementation must support the MIME-version, content-type, and content-transfer-encoding fields; the content-ID and content-description fields are optional and may be ignored by the recipient implementation.

MIME Content Types   The bulk of the MIME specification is concerned with the definition of a variety of content types. This reflects the need to provide standardized ways of dealing with a wide variety of information representations in a multimedia environment. Table 13-2 lists the content types specified in RFC 1521. There are seven different major types of content and a total of 14 subtypes. In general, a content type declares the general type of data, and the subtype specifies a particular format for that type of data.

For the *text type* of the body, no special software is required to get the full meaning of the text, aside from support of the character set indicated. RFC 1521 defines only one subtype: plain text, which is simply a string of ASCII characters or ISO 8859 characters. An earlier version of the MIME specification included a *richtext* subtype, which provides greater formatting flexibility. It is expected that this subtype will reappear in a later RFC.

The *multipart type* indicates that the body contains multiple, independent parts. The content-type header field includes a parameter, called *boundary,* that defines the delimiter between body parts. This boundary should not appear in any parts of the message. Each boundary starts on a new line and consists of two hyphens followed by the boundary value. The final boundary, which indicates the

TABLE 13-2 MIME Content Types

Type	*Subtype*	*Description*
Text	Plain	Unformatted text; may be ASCII or ISO 8859.
Multipart	Mixed	The different parts are independent but are to be transmitted together. They should be presented to the receiver in the order in which they appear in the mail message.
	Parallel	Differs from mixed only in that no order is defined for delivering the parts to the receiver.
	Alternative	The different parts are alternative versions of the same information. They are ordered in increasing faithfulness to the original and the recipient's mail system should display the "best" version to the user.
	Digest	Similar to mixed, but the default type/subtype of each part is message/rfc822
Message	rfc822	The body is itself an encapsulated message that conforms to RFC 822.
	Partial	Used to allow fragmentation of large mail items, in a way that is transparent to the recipient.
	External-body	Contains a pointer to an object that exists elsewhere.
Image	jpeg	The image is in JPEG format, JFIF encoding.
	gif	The image is in GIF format.
Video	mpeg	MPEG format.
Audio	Basic	Single-channel 8-bit ISDN mu-law encoding at a sample rate of 8 kHz.
Application	PostScript	Adobe Postscript.
	octet-stream	General binary data consisting of 8-bit bytes.

end of the last part, also has a suffix of two hyphens. Within each part there may be an optional ordinary MIME header.

Here is a simple example of a multipart message, containing two parts both consisting of simple text (taken from RFC 1521):

```
From: Nathaniel Borenstein <nsb@bellcore.com>
To: Ned Freed <ned@innosoft.com>
Subject: Sample message
MIME-Version: 1.0
Content-type: multipart/mixed; boundary="simple boundary"

This is the preamble. It is to be ignored, although it
is a handy place for mail composers to include an
explanatory note to non-MIME conformant readers.
--simple boundary

This is implicitly typed plain ASCII text. It does NOT
end with a linebreak.
--simple boundary
Content-type: text/plain; charset=us-ascii

This is explicitly typed plain ASCII text. It DOES end
with a linebreak.

--simple boundary--
This is the epilogue. It is also to be ignored.
```

There are four subtypes of the multipart type, all of which have the same overall syntax. The *multipart/mixed subtype* is used when there are multiple independent body parts that need to be bundled in a particular order. For the *multipart/parallel subtype,* the order of the parts is not significant. If the recipient's system is appropriate, the multiple parts can be presented in parallel. For example, a picture or text part could be accompanied by a voice commentary that is played while the picture or text is displayed.

For the *multipart/alternative subtype,* the various parts are different representations of the same information. The following is an example:

```
From: Nathaniel Borenstein <nsb@bellcore.com>
To: Ned Freed <ned@innosoft.com>
Subject: Formatted text mail
MIME-Version: 1.0
Content-Type: multipart/alternative; boundary=boundary42

--boundary42

Content-Type: text/plain; charset=us-ascii

  ...plain text version of message goes here....
--boundary42
Content-Type: text/richtext
```

```
 .... RFC 1341 richtext version of same message goes
here ...
--boundary42--
```

In this subtype, the body parts are ordered in terms of increasing prefer-ence. For this example, if the recipient system is capable of displaying the mes-sage in the richtext format, this is done; otherwise, the plain text format is used.

The *multipart/digest subtype* is used when each of the body parts is inter-preted as an RFC 822 message with headers. This subtype enables the construc-tion of a message whose parts are individual messages. For example, the moderator of a group might collect E-mail messages from participants, bundle these messages, and send them out in one encapsulating MIME message.

The *message type* provides a number of important capabilities in MIME. The *message/rfc822 subtype* indicates that the body is an entire message, includ-ing header and body. Despite the name of this subtype, the encapsulated message may be not only a simple RFC 822 message, but any MIME message.

The *message/partial subtype* enables fragmentation of a large message into a number of parts, which must be reassembled at the destination. For this subtype, three parameters are specified in the content-type: message/partial field:

- *id:* a value that is common to each fragment of the same message, so that the fragments can be identified at the recipient for reassembly, but unique across different messages.

- *number:* a sequence number that indicates the position of this fragment in the original message. The first fragment is numbered 1, the second 2, and so on.

- *total:* the total number of parts. The last fragment is identified by having the same value for the *number* and *total* parameters.

The *message/external-body subtype* indicates that the actual data to be con-veyed in this message are not contained in the body. Instead, the body contains the information needed to access the data. As with the other message types, the message/external-body subtype has an outer header and an encapsulated mes-sage with its own header. The only necessary field in the outer header is the con-tent-type field, which identifies this as a message/external-body subtype. The inner header is the message header for the encapsulated message.

The content-type field in the outer header must include an access-type para-meter, which has one of the following values:

- *ftp:* the message body is accessible as a file using the file transfer protocol (FTP). For this access type, the following additional parameters are mandatory: *name*, the name of the file; and *site*, the domain name of the host where the file resides. Optional parameters are: *directory*, the direc-tory in which the file is located; and *mode*, which indicates how FTP should retrieve the file (e.g., ASCII, image). Before the file transfer can take place, the user will need to provide a used id and password. These are not transmitted with the message for security reasons.

- *tfpt:* the message body is accessible as a file using the trivial file transfer protocol (TFTP). The same parameters as for ftp are used, and the user id and password must also be supplied.
- *anon-ftp:* identical to ftp, except that the user is not asked to supply a user id and password. The parameter *name* supplies the name of the file.
- *local-file:* the message body is accessible as a file on the recipient's machine.
- *afs:* the message body is accessible as a file via the global AFS (Andrew file system). The parameter *name* supplies the name of the file.
- *mail-server:* the message body is accessible by sending an E-mail message to a mail server. A *server* parameter must be included that gives the E-mail address of the server. The body of the original message, known as the *phantom body,* should contain the exact command to be sent to the mail server.

The *image type* indicates that the body contains a displayable image. The subtype, jpeg or gif, specifies the image format. In future, more subtypes will be added to this list.

The *video type* indicates that the body contains a time-varying picture image, possibly with color and coordinated sound. The only subtype so far specified is mpeg.

The *audio type* indicates that the body contains audio data. The only subtype, basic, conforms to an ISDN service known as "64-kbps, 8-kHz structured, usable for speech information," with a digitized speech algorithm referred to as μ-law PCM (pulse-code modulation). This general type is the typical way of transmitting speech signals over a digital network. The term μ-*law* refers to the specific encoding technique; it is the standard technique used in North America and Japan. A competing system, known as *A-law,* is standard in Europe.

The *application type* refers to other kinds of data, typically either uninterpreted binary data or information to be processed by a mail-based application. The *application/octet-stream subtype* indicates general binary data in a sequence of octets. RFC 1521 recommends that the receiving implementation should offer to put the data in a file or use it as input to a program.

The *application/postscript subtype* indicates the use of Adobe PostScript.

13.2 ELECTRONIC DATA INTERCHANGE

Electronic data interchange (EDI) is the direct computer-to-computer exchange of information normally provided on standard business documents, such as invoices, bills of lading, and purchase orders. It has become one of the most visible and widely implemented of the distributed applications.

Figure 13.3 contrasts the use of electronic data interchange to a nonelectronic environment. Without EDI, any business transaction, such as the order of goods, depends on the exchange of paper documents. As part (a) of the figure illustrates, such a transaction may involve a number of people in two different companies. Furthermore, if each company has computer-based procedures, the following sequence is involved.

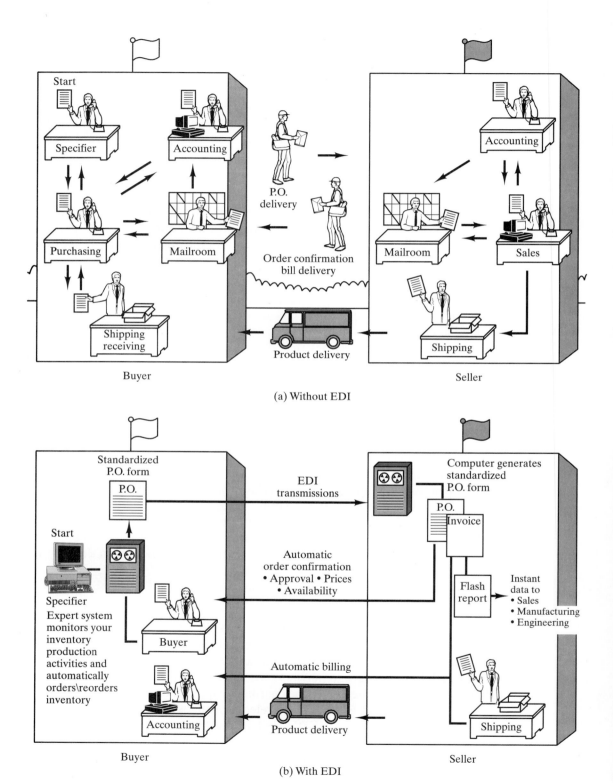

FIGURE 13.3 EDI Versus Paper.

1. Company A prints out a filled-out form (e.g., purchase order) and mails it to company B.
2. Company B enters data from the form into a computer system.

This cumbersome procedure can be avoided if the two companies agree on an electronic format for the form. That is the key to electronic data interchange.

Although electronic data interchange can be used for intracompany data exchange, its strength—and appeal—is that it may be used between companies that can agree on EDI formats. Some of the major benefits of electronic data interchange:

- *Cost savings.* EDI can save countless employee hours in entering data on forms, entering data into a computer from a form, and handling the forms. Mail and courier costs are also reduced as physical document transfer is replaced with cheaper electronic document transfer.

- *Speed.* Electronic document exchange can occur instantaneously if two computer systems enjoy an active link or channel across a communications facility. Even if the parties involved are not always hooked into the network, the transmission will occur on a schedule dictated only by the frequency of network connection.

- *Reduction of errors.* Because communication is computer-to-computer, rekeying of data is eliminated. In addition, there are no problems of lost or misrouted mail, because communication is direct and immediately verifiable.

- *Security.* When documents are transferred physically, there are a number of opportunities for obtaining or altering the contents of the document, for intercepting and preventing delivery of the document, and for introducing false documents. With a fully electronic document transfer, some of the security techniques outlined in Chapter 17 can provide superior security to that of manual techniques.

- *Integration with other office automation applications.* Arriving electronic documents can trigger application programs that make use of the incoming data. The ability to receive and act rapidly on documents such as purchase orders and invoices can give a company a competitive edge over companies not using electronic data interchange.

- *Just-in-time deliveries.* A number of companies, primarily in the automotive and electronics industries, have made just-in-time production a major thrust. Just-in-time is a manufacturing method in which goods are produced and made available by prior operations just in time to be further fabricated, assembled, or sold. Each operation produces only what is necessary to satisfy the demands of the succeeding operation. Although substantial cost savings may be made from internal implementation alone, complete use of just-in-time requires that every manufacturer in the value-added chain produce just-in-time. By speeding up communications, EDI provides the necessary foundation for intercompany just-in-time operations.

In simple terms, this is how electronic data interchange is used for the exchange of electronic documents between two companies:

1. Prior to any computer work, representatives of the two companies meet to specify the applications that they will implement. The companies must agree on the common formats to be exchanged and the actions to be taken on document receipt. The means of communications must also be decided. This can be as simple as a dial-up connection between systems. Other alternatives are the use of a third-party network specializing in the transmittal of EDI data or the use of electronic mail (described subsequently).

2. Each company adds EDI software to its computer to translate company data into standard formats for transmission and for the reverse translation of the data it receives.

3. As often as operationally required, the two companies exchange data electronically in the standard formats.

Electronic data interchange began to be implemented in the early 1980s and is now enjoying explosive growth. Indeed, it has reached the point where EDI is no longer an option for large and medium-sized companies. Many large companies, such as General Motors and IBM, are urging and in some cases demanding that their suppliers use EDI. Even when major customers are not insistent on this point, those suppliers that can use the EDI system of a customer will have a competitive advantage.

EDI Standards

In a number of cases, ad hoc EDI formats have been developed, but these are being quickly abandoned in favor of standards. In the United States, EDI was initially developed in the transportation industry as early as 1975. The grocery industry, in response to a study that showed that savings in the hundreds of millions of dollars could be achieved, became heavily involved in 1981, and since that time a number of industries have participated in the development of standards.

Much of the standardization effort is now being performed by the American National Standards Institute (ANSI), which has issued a series of standards with the general designation of X.12. These standards define forms and related procedures for applications relevant to a variety of industries. For each application, major units of information are defined as *transaction sets,* which are the structure for communicating information between systems. Each transaction set in EDI equates to a form in a paperwork system. An application may have a number of different transaction sets defined. For example, Table 13-3 lists the transaction sets, or forms, for two applications that have been developed as X.12 standards.

The standard for a transaction set encompasses two specifications:

- *Content of the transaction set.* These are the actual items of information that the transaction set contains. These correspond to fields on forms. Any given transaction set will contain all the items normally found useful

TABLE 13-3 Example EDI Applications (ANSI X.12)

Transportation Applications	*General Business Applications*
Space reservation	Invoice
Space cancelation or revision	Payment order/remittance advice
Space confirmation, container release and	Planning schedule with release capability
movement	Price sales catalog
Shipping instructions	Request for quotation
Detailed freight invoices	Response to RFQ
Summary freight invoices	Inventory advice
Inbound consolidator reports	Purchase order
Outbound consolidator reports	Purchase order acknowledgment
Shipment tracing inquiry	Ship notice/manifest
Shipment tracing report	Purchase order change request
Outbound shipment movement reports	Purchase order change request acknowledgment
Inbound shipment movement reports	Receiving advice
Order payment	Product transfer and resale
Debit payment request	
Freight payment	
Waybill data exchange	
Export control reports	
Import manifest reports	
Repetitive shipment pattern maintenance	
Container transfer	

in a particular business form. Many of the items will be optional and may be ignored in a particular application.

- *Format of the transaction set.* A computer-readable format is defined to allow exchange of information between computers.

Each transaction set (form) consists of a number of *segments* (line or box of information on the form), and each segment is defined in terms of *data elements* (individual field within a line or box). An example, one of the simplest, of a transaction set is shown in Table 13-4. Most of the segments correspond to lines or areas on a form. In addition, there are a header and a trailer to delimit the entire transaction set. Also, some of the segments may be repeated; this is referred to as a *loop.* If one loop is nested inside another, a loop header and trailer are needed to delimit the outer loop. Each segment is in turn broken down into a number of data elements (not shown). These are meant to encompass all the possible items of information that might be useful on such a form.

All segments and data elements are classified as mandatory, conditional, or optional. A *mandatory item* must be present in the transaction set. A *conditional item* is mandatory under certain conditions, either by nature of the other information in a filled-in form or by agreement between two EDI participants. An *optional item* may be used at the discretion of the sender; it is never required by the receiver.

Each item in a transaction set is variable length, but the information is structured so that it may be constructed by one computer system and interpreted and

TABLE 13-4 EDI Form 820: Payment Order/Remittance Advice

Segment	Requirement[a]	Max Use[b]	Loop Index[c]	Purpose
Transaction set header	M	1	—	Indicate start of form and assign control number.
Beginning segment	M	1	—	Indicate total amount and enable automated funds transfer.
Note/special instruction	O	100	—	Comment or special instructions in free format.
Currency	O	1	—	Specify details of currency used in transaction.
Reference numbers	M	5	—	Transmit reference numbers associated with named party.
Date/time reference	M	10	—	Specify pertinent dates and times.
Name	O	1	200	Identify party by organization type, name, and code.
Additional name information	O	2	—	Additional names or names longer than 35 characters.
Address information	O	2	—	Location of named party.
Geographic location	O	1	—	Geographic place of named party.
Reference numbers	O	12	—	Transmit reference numbers associated with named party.
Administrative contact	O	3	—	To whom administrative communications should be directed.
Loop header	M	1	—	Indicates that next segment begins a loop.
Name	M	1	10,000	Identify party by organization type, name, and code.
Remittance advice	M	1	10,000	Detail on items being paid.
Currency	O	1	—	Specify details of currency used in transaction.
Reference numbers	O	5	—	Transmit reference numbers associated with named party.
Data/time reference	O	10	—	Specify pertinent dates and times.
Loop trailer	M	1	—	Indicates completion of a loop.
Transaction set trailer	M	1	—	Indicates end of form and segment count.

[a] *M, mandatory; O, optional.*

[b] *Maximum number of times a segment may be used in succession, exclusive of any loop specification.*

[c] *Maximum number of times a loop may be used in succession.*

processed by another. Thus, each item has a unique code and is specified by a data length and a data value. In most cases, certain syntactic rules are imposed (e.g., a data element may need to be numeric).

Components of an EDI System

To send/receive EDI documents effectively, the trading partner's internal information systems must contain three fundamental elements: the application, the translation software, and the communications network.

The *application* is the function in which business information is either generated or needed. Order-entry and accounts-payable systems are examples of applications. Depending on the level of computer sophistication of the company, the application may be paper-based, computerized, or a combination of the two.

The second element of an EDI system is *translation software.* Most companies with computerized applications have their own in-house format for data storage, which is usually incompatible with the corresponding EDI specification. A company need not convert all internal processing and storage to the standard format but will require software to convert the internal format to the message standard, and vice versa. The message standard, just described, defines the elements and formats of individual transaction sets and defines a number of transaction sets for a given application. A number of message standards have been developed for various industries, such as:

- Ocean transportation
- Trucking
- Rail transportation
- Motor transportation
- Electrical
- Warehouse
- Grocery
- Banking
- General business

Each industry standard is developed by representatives of that industry, within the overall framework of the EDI standard. As each standard is developed and stabilized, it is issued by ANSI as an X.12 standard.

Translation software may also provide other secondary functions, such as the ability to enter a transaction directly rather than retrieve data from a central database. This provides support for paper-based applications. For many of the common database management, spreadsheet, and business packages, translation software is available from a variety of software vendors. In other cases, the user may need to develop in-house translation software. This is generally the biggest expense associated with the implementation of an electronic data interchange scheme.

EDI messages are transmitted over an existing public or private *communications network.* Any communications facility can be used that interconnects the companies that wish to exchange data. What is required, however, is the logic for routing and delivery of messages. In general, this is an electronic mail function. An EDI delivery system can be implemented as an added feature of a general-purpose electronic mail system. Alternatively, a special-purpose electronic mail facility intended only for EDI messages can be used.

Maximum EDI benefits are attainable only when all three of the elements just described are completely computerized and information flows from sender's application to recipient's application without human intervention. This is referred to as *application-to-application EDI.* The common types of configurations that provide application-to-application EDI include:

- Application, translator, and communications software residing on a mainframe computer or a server system

■ Application on mainframe or minicomputer and translator and communications software on a personal computer

The appeal of the latter configuration is that it allows a new EDI user to start small, by purchasing inexpensive microcomputer EDI software. The microcomputer, in this case, functions as a "front end" to the larger computer.

Personal computers, as stand-alone systems, have not been commonly used to support application-to-application EDI completely. More recent, more powerful personal computers can provide such support, and this configuration is likely to become popular.

Third-Party Network Services

A third-party network service can serve as an intermediary between EDI partners as part of the electronic data interchange. The alternative is direct links between two EDI partners. Such direct links cause difficulties for both partners, including:

■ Precise document exchange times must be prearranged between partners, a requirement that becomes increasingly difficult as the number of trading partners increases.

■ Documents must be transmitted one by one to each partner, a costly process.

■ Data communication hardware and software must be compatible between partners, a requirement that becomes increasingly difficult as the number of trading partners increases.

For most EDI users, the most cost-effective mode of EDI communication is through a third-party network service. Each user attaches to the network and may exchange documents with any other user. The network will provide a mailbox storage facility, so that it is not necessary for two partners to be on line at the same time. When a document is transmitted, it will be delivered to the destination user immediately if that user's computer is available. Otherwise, the document is stored in the destination user's mailbox until it is retrieved by that user. The network may also provide translation services to map from one EDI format to another.

The benefits of a third-party service, compared to direct links, include:

■ Flexibility in communications by providing electronic document storage and by supporting multiple line speeds and computer protocols.

■ Savings in time and effort to initiate EDI with new trading partners.

■ Reduced need to buy/develop translation software.

Costs of using an EDI third-party service vary widely among service providers and defy comparison. This is partly because of price competition and partly due to the fact that a number of the providers offer other services, such as electronic mail and time-sharing services, and have evolved a pricing structure that encompasses a variety of activities.

13.3 WORLD WIDE WEB

World Wide Web
A networked,
graphically
oriented
hypermedia
system.

The **World Wide Web** is an Internet-based hypertext system initially developed in 1989 by Tim Berners Lee at the European Laboratory for Particle Physics, CERN, in Switzerland. The release in 1993 of Mosaic, the first graphical user interface to the Web, marked the beginning of a sustained exponential growth in the number of Web sites and the amount of Web traffic. This explosive growth is the prime cause for the widespread use of the Internet and the intense business interest in exploiting the Internet. In this section we provide an overview of basic Web technology. The use of the Web for Internet and intranet applications is explored in Chapters 14 and 15.

Operation of the World Wide Web

The Web is, in essence, an architecture for sharing information. The information is in the form of linked *pages* that reside at various sites around the Internet. An individual page can contain text, graphic images, and even links to voice and video. A page may be passive, simply providing a static collection information on demand. A page may also be dynamic, in several ways:

- A page can contain a form for the user to fill out.
- A page can, on user request, trigger a search of a database or file.
- A page can contain information that is dynamically updated.
- A page can contain *applets*, which are small platform-independent applications that can be transferred to a user's machine for execution.

Figure 13.4a illustrates the key ingredients of the Web that are visible to the user. A user accesses the Web by means of a **Web browser** program, such as Netscape or Mosaic, running on the user's system. The browser can connect to a **Web server** across the Internet (or a corporate intranet). The server maintains a database of information in the form of linked pages. The pages at a server generally are organized into a hierarchical tree of pages. Further, any page may have a pointer to pages on other servers anywhere on the Internet. Each server, and indeed each page, has a unique address that is used by the browser to navigate through this global, cross-linked collection of pages.

Figure 13.4b shows the key underlying components that support the Web. On the server side, there is a collection of pages with links between them plus links to pages on other servers. Each page contains information that is defined using the hypertext markup language (HTML). Each page is identified by an address known as a **uniform resource locator (URL)**, which is unique across all the pages on all the servers connected to the Internet. Some of the information on a server's pages may reflect information maintained at the site in a database or file system. In that case the server requires a mapping function that automatically and dynamically keeps the information on the pages current as it changes in the database, and vice versa.

Communication between a browser and a server is in the form of one or more transactions. A transaction occurs over a TCP connection and consists of a

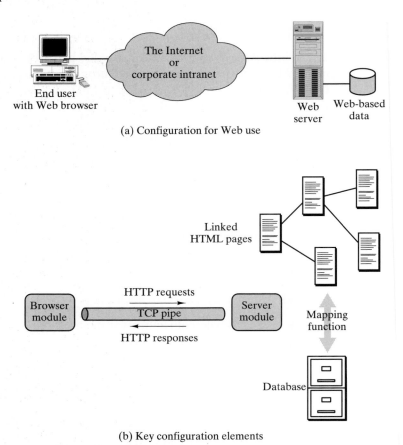

FIGURE 13.4 Configuration for Web-Based Applications.

request from the browser and a response from the server. The request/response exchange uses the hypertext transfer protocol (HTTP).

In the remainder of this section, we elaborate on three key elements of Web operation: URLs, HTML, and HTTP.

Uniform Resource Locator

A key concept in the operation of the Web is that of uniform resource locator (URL). In the defining documents (RFC 1738, 1808), the URL is characterized as follows:

> A uniform resource locator (URL) is a compact representation of the location and access method for a resource available via the Internet. URLs are used to locate resources, by providing an abstract identification of the resource location. Having located a resource, a system may perform a variety of operations on the resource, as might be characterized by such words

as access, update, replace, find attributes. In general, only the access method needs to be specified for any URL scheme.

A resource is any object that can be accessed by the Internet, and includes file directories, files, documents, images, audio or video clips, and any other data that may be stored on an Internet-connected computer. The term *resource* in this context also includes electronic mail addresses, the results of a finger or archie command, USENET newsgroups, and individual messages in a USENET newsgroup.

With a few exceptions (such as the E-mail address represented as a URL value), we can think of a URL as a networked extension of a filename. The URL provides a pointer to any object that is accessible on any machine connected to the Internet. Furthermore, because different objects are accessible in different ways (e.g., via Web, ftp, gopher, etc.), the URL also indicates the access method that must be used to retrieve the object.

The general form of a URL is as follows:

```
<scheme>:<scheme-specific-part>
```

The URL consists of the name of the access scheme being used followed by a colon and then by an identifier of a resource whose format is specific to the scheme being used.

Although the scheme-specific formats differ, they have a number of points in common. In particular, many of the access schemes support the use of hierarchical structures, similar to hierarchical directory and file structures common to files systems such as Unix. For the URL, the components of the hierarchy are separated by "/", similar to the Unix approach.

The most heavily used type of URL, in the Web context, is the HTTP URL. This URL scheme designates Internet resources accessible using the HTTP protocol, and in particular designates Web sites. In its simplest form, an HTTP URL has the following format:

```
http://<host>:<port>/<path>
```

The default port number for HTTP is 80. If the <path> portion is omitted, the URL points to the top-level resource, such as a home page. For example,

```
http://www.shore.net
```

points to the home page of the Internet site "www.shore.net." A more complex path points to hierarchically subordinate pages. For example,

```
http://www.shore.net/~ws/BDC3e.html
```

points to the home page for this book on the www.shore.net computer. An HTTP URL can also point to a document available via the Web, such as

```
http://www.w3.org/pub/WWW/Addressing/rfc1738.txt
```

TABLE 13-5 Uniform Resource Locator Schemes

Scheme	Default Port	Syntax
http	80	http://\<host\>:\<port\>/\<path\>?\<searchpart\>
ftp	21	ftp://\<user\>:\<password\>@\<host\>:\<port\>/\<cwd1\>/\<cwd2\>/.../\<cwdN\>/ \<name\>;type=\<typecode\>
gopher	70	gopher://\<host\>:\<port\>/\<selector\> or gopher://\<host\>:\<port\>/\<selector\>%09\<search\> or gopher://\<host\>:\<port\>/\<selector\>%09\<search\>%09\<gopher+_string\> or
mailto	—	mailto:\<rfc822-addr-spec\>
news	—	news:\<newsgroup-name\> or news:\<message-id\>
telnet	23	telnet://\<user\>:\<password\>@\<host\>:\<port\>

This is the URL for RFC 1738, available through the Web site of the WWW consortium.

Table 13-5 lists the general format of the most important URL schemes. In addition to Web URLs, URLs can point to ftp and gopher sites, to E-mail addresses, to USENET news groups, and to sites accessible by remote logon using TELNET.

Hypertext Markup Language

The **hypertext markup language (HTML)** is the language used to define the content of Web pages. In its basic structure, HTML is quite simple, consisting of tags that precede or bracket various types of information. We can think of the contents of a Web page as consisting of text that obeys the syntax of HTML. A Web browser is able to read the HTML language on a page and translate it a displayable image.

Although a Web page consists of text, the displayed version of the page may include images. To achieve this effect, the Web page may contain the address of images that are stored in a binary format. When the page is displayed, the browser reads in the image file and incorporates it into the displayed page.

As an example, Figure 13.5 shows a browser display of the original version of the Web page for this book. The HTML content of the page is shown in Figure 13.6. As with all HTML documents, this one begins with the tag \<HTML\> and ends with the tag \</HTML\>. Everything between these tags is either a tag or other text.

All tags in HTML are delimited by angle brackets. There are two types of tags: single and paired. A single tag provides an instruction to the browser. For example, the tag \<HR\> tells the browser to insert a horizontal rule or line in the display. Two paired tags bracket a portion of the pages content and provide some instruction on how to interpret the bracketed text. The ending tag of the pair

---

Welcome to the
Course Web Site for Business Data
Communications, Third Edition

This site will provide support for instructors and students using the book.

UNDER CONSTRUCTION

Grand opening planned for early 1997. The following are planned

- Links to relevant web sites, organized by chapter.
- Link to the errata sheet for the book.
- Link via ftp to an on-line set of viewgraphs.
- Information for subscribing to the on-line mailing list for the book.

If you have any other suggestions for site content, please contact either of the authors. Thanks!

For more information about the book, visit its Prentice Hall page.

Bill Stallings

Richard Van Slyke

FIGURE 13.5 Display of a Web Page.

always includes a forward slash after its beginning bracket. For example, the HTML fragment

<TITLE>Business Data Communications, Third Edition</TITLE>

defines the phrase "Business Data Communications, Third Edition" as the title of this page; it will appear at the top of the graphical browser display when the page is displayed.

Figure 13.6 illustrates the use of a number of tags, which we describe briefly. A Web page is divided into two parts: the head and the body. The head, delimited by HEAD tags, contains descriptive information about the page, such as TITLE. The body, delimited by BODY tags, is the displayable content of the page.

```
<HTML><HEAD><TITLE>Business Data Communications, Third Edition</TITLE></HEAD
><BODY><IMG SRC="orangebar.gif" WIDTH= "640" HEIGHT="11" ALIGN=bottom
NATURALSIZEFLAG="3">
<H1><CENTER>Welcome to the<BR>
Course Web Site for Business Data Communications, Third Edition</CENTER></H1>
<IMG SRC="orangebar.gif" WIDTH="640" HEIGHT="11" ALIGN=bottom NATURALSIZEFLAG=
"3">
<H3>This site will provide support for instructors and students using the
book.</H3>
<H3><CENTER><IMG SRC="const.gif" WIDTH="168" HEIGHT="64" ALIGN=bottom
NATURALSIZEFLAG="3"><BR>UNDER CONSTRUCTION</CENTER></H3>
<H3><BR>
Grand opening planned for early 1997. The following are planned</H3>
<UL>
<LI>Links to relevant web sites, organized by chapter.
<LI>Link to the errata sheet for the book.
<LI>Link via ftp to an on-line set of viewgraphs.
<LI>Information for subscribing to the on-line mailing list for the book.
</UL>
<H3><BR>
If you have any other suggestions for site content, please contact either
of the authors. Thanks!<BR><BR>
For more information about the book, visit its
<A HREF="http://www.prenhall.com/002/u66219/u6621-9.html" >Prentice
Hall page</A>.<BR><BR>
<A HREF="mailto:ws@shore.net">Bill Stallings</A><BR><BR>
<A HREF="mailto:rvslyke@poly.edu">Richard Van Slyke</A></H3>
</BODY></HTML>
```

FIGURE 13.6 HTML for Web Page Displayed in Figure 13.5.

The IMG tag contains a pointer to a binary image file that is to be read and displayed at this point in the page. There are three such tags in this example. The first two both point to the image with the file name orangebar.gif. The suffix indicates that this file is in the GIF format, which is one of the standardized image formats used on the Web.

In general, the HTML author cannot control the text font or size that is displayed by a browser. However, the header tags provides a way to add impact to a display by indicating relative font size. Six levels of header are provided from the largest (level 1 indicated by the tag H1) to the smallest (level 6 indicated by the tag H6). HTML also provides a number of tags for formatting text layout. For example, although Web browsers do handle word wrap, so that text automatically wraps down to the next line, most do not recognize carriage returns to start a new line or paragraph. The new line tag, BR, starts a new line on the display. The CENTER tag pair indicates that the enclosed text is to be centered.

HTML provides a facility for creating lists, one of the most common elements on a Web page. For an unnumbered, or unordered, list the Web browser puts a bullet in front of each list entry. The entire list is defined by a UL tag pair, and each list entry is preceded by an LI tag. A numbered, or ordered, list is defined with an OL tag pair; in this case, the browser puts sequential numbers in front of the list entries.

An essential part of virtually all Web pages is the ability to link to other Web pages and to other Internet resources, such as ftp sites and E-mail addresses. Our example contains two types of links:

<A HREF="mailto:ws@shore.net">ws@shore.net</A>
<A HREF="http://www.prenhall.com/002/u66219/u6621-9.html">
Prentice Hall page</A>

In both cases, the leading tag includes a hypertext reference. In the first case, the mailto: label indicates that this is an electronic mail address, and in the second case, the http: label indicates that this is an HTTP address. The bracketed text is highlighted in some way by the browser (typically underlined), so that the user can click on that text to invoke the link. Table 13-6 summarizes the tags we have discussed.

TABLE 13-6 Common HTML Tags

Tag	Description
<HTML>...</HTML>	Brackets an HTML page
<HEAD>...</HEAD>	Head of page
<TITLE>...</TITLE>	Title of page
<BODY>...</BODY>	Body of page
<H*n*>...</H*n*>	Level *n* header
 	New line
<CENTER>...</CENTER>	Center the enclosed content
<HR attributes>	Horizontal rule
<IMG SRC = "...">	Insert image here
<A HREF="...">...</A>	Hypertext link defined by a URL
<OL>...</OL>	Ordered (numbered) list
<UL>...</UL>	Unordered (bulleted) list
<LI>	List item follows

Hypertext Transfer Protocol

The **hypertext transfer protocol (HTTP)** is the foundation protocol of the Web and can be used in any client–server application involving hypertext. The name is somewhat misleading in that HTTP is not a protocol for transferring hypertext; rather, it is a protocol for transmitting information with the efficiency necessary for making hypertext jumps. The data transferred by the protocol can be plain text, hypertext, audio, images, or any Internet-accessible information.

HTTP is a transaction-oriented client–server protocol. The most typical use of HTTP is between a web browser and a web server. To provide reliability, HTTP makes use of TCP. Nevertheless, HTTP is a "stateless" protocol: Each transaction is treated independently. Accordingly, a typical implementation will create a new TCP connection between client and server for each transaction and then terminate the connection as soon as the transaction completes, although the specification does not dictate this one-to-one relationship between transaction and connection lifetimes.

The stateless nature of HTTP is well suited to its typical application. A normal session of a user with a Web browser involves retrieving a sequence of Web pages and documents. The sequence is, ideally, performed rapidly, and the locations of the various pages and documents may be a number of widely distributed servers.

Another important feature of HTTP is that it is flexible in the formats that it can handle. When a browser issues a request to a server, it may include a prioritized list of formats that it can handle, and the server replies with the appropriate format. For example, a lynx browser cannot handle images, so a Web server need not transmit any images on Web pages. This arrangement prevents the transmission of unnecessary information and provides the basis for extending the set of formats with new standardized and proprietary specifications.

In the typical case, the browser opens a TCP connection that is end to end between the browser and the server. The browser then issues an HTTP request. The request consists of a specific command, referred to as a method, a URL, and a MIME-like message containing request parameters, information about the browser, and perhaps some additional content information.

When the server receives the request, it attempts to perform the action requested and then returns an HTTP response. The response includes status information, a success/error code, and a MIME-like message containing information about the server, information about the response itself, and possible body content. The TCP connection is then closed. Table 13-7 lists the commonly used HTTP requests, or methods, with a brief definition of each.

■ Illustration: Problem Solution

The Port Authority decided to implement an electronic data interchange network. A third-party network service will be used, and companies will be required to use message formats that are compliant with the X12 standards. The Port Authority will maintain mailbox space for all Port users. Each company simply has to develop or acquire translation software for converting from their own formats to the EDI format and communications software for linking to the third-party network. ■

SUMMARY

Standardized distributed applications are becoming increasingly important to businesses, for three main reasons:

- Standardized applications are more readily acquired and used than special-purpose software that may have inadequate support and is accompanied by inadequate training.

TABLE 13-7 HTTP Request Methods

Method	Description
GET	A request to retrieve the information identified in the URL and to return it in a entity body. A GET is conditional if the if-modified-since header field is included, and is partial if a range header field is included.
HEAD	Identical to a GET, except that the server's response must not include an entity body; all the header fields in the response are the same as if the entity body were present. This enables a client to get information about a resource without transferring the entity body.
POST	A request to accept the attached entity as a new subordinate to the identified URL. The posted entity is subordinate to that URL in the same way that a file is subordinate to a directory containing it, a news article is subordinate to a newsgroup to which it is posted, or a record is subordinate to a database.
PUT	A request to accept the attached entity and store it under the supplied URL. This may be a new resource with a new URL, or a replacement of the contents of an existing resource with an existing URL.
DELETE	Requests that the origin server delete the resource identified by the URL in the request-line.
LINK	Establishes one or more link relationships from the resource identified in the request-line. The links are defined in the link field in the entity-header.
UNLINK	Removes one or more link relationships from the resource identified in the request-line. The links are defined in the link field in the entity-header.

- Standardized software allows the user to procure computers from a variety of vendors and yet have those computers work together.
- Standards promote the ability for different companies to exchange data.

This chapter examines three important applications. For all of these distributed applications, standards have been developed and the use of the application is growing rapidly.

A general-purpose electronic mail facility provides a means of exchanging unstructured messages, usually text messages. Electronic mail is a rapid and convenient method for communication, supplementing and, in many instances, replacing telephone and paper communications. Because electronic mail is so general purpose in nature, it is perhaps the most popular distributed application and can have the most widespread benefits.

The most widely used protocol for the transmission of electronic mail is SMTP. SMTP assumes that the content of the message is a simple text block. The recent MIME standard expands SMTP to support transmission of multimedia information

Electronic data interchange (EDI) is the direct computer-to-computer exchange of data normally provided on standard business documents, such as invoices, bills of lading, and purchase orders. EDI is designed for use between companies but can also find application for internal company communications. EDI is important because virtually all business between companies is transacted on the basis of an exchange of forms. Because most businesses now automate most of their information storage and processing, electronic form exchange can take place if there is a standardized computer-readable format for the forms. The standard must encompass all items of data that are required for business communications. Accordingly, there are a wide variety of EDI standards for different industries, encompassing most of the forms that are useful within each industry.

An electronic mail facility can be used as the delivery system for EDI documents. These are two separate capabilities and two separate standards. EDI deals primarily with the format and content of forms. Some means of exchanging those forms is required, and electronic mail is the most attractive alternative.

The rapid growth in the use of the Web is due to the standardization of all the elements that support Web applications. The URL is a standardized, universal addressing scheme for global, unique identification of Web pages and other Internet resources. HTML provides a language for creating Web pages. Finally, HTTP is the protocol for the exchange of Web-based information between Web browsers and Web servers.

RECOMMENDED READING

More detail on SMTP, MIME, URLs, and HTTP can be found in [STAL97a]. These topics are also covered in [TANE96].

STAL97a STALLINGS, W. *Data and Computer Communications,* 5th ed. Upper Saddle River, NJ: Prentice Hall, 1997.

TANE96 TANENBAUM, A. *Computer Networks.* Upper Saddle River, NJ: Prentice Hall, 1996.

Recommended Web Site

- http://www.w3.org/pub/WWW: Web site of the World Wide Web Consortium, containing up-to-date information on HTTP, HTML, and URLs.

KEY TERMS

Electronic Data Interchange (EDI)	Hypertext Transfer Protocol (HTTP)	Uniform Resource Locator (URL)
Electronic Mail	Multipurpose Internet Mail Extensions (MIME)	Web Browser
Hypertext Markup Language (HTML)	Simple Mail Transfer Protocol (SMTP)	Web Server
		World Wide Web

QUESTIONS

1. With a single-system mail facility or native mail facility, what major elements are needed?
2. What are the SMTP and MIME standards?
3. What is electronic data interchange (EDI)?
4. What are some major benefits of electronic data interchange?
5. Describe three key components of an EDI system.
6. What are the major ingredients of a Web system?
7. How are URLs used to identify Internet resources?
8. How is the content of a Web page specified?
9. How does HTTP operate to support Web exchanges between browsers and servers?
10. What is the role of TCP in the World Wide Web? What is the role of IP?

PROBLEM

1. Electronic mail systems differ in the manner in which multiple recipients are handled. In some systems the originating user agent or mail sender makes all the necessary copies and these are sent out independently. An alternative approach is to determine the route for each destination first. Then a single message is sent out on a common portion of the route and copies are made only when the routes diverge; this process is referred to as *mail-bagging*. Discuss the relative advantages and disadvantages of the two methods.

R.J. REYNOLDS TOBACCO CO.

R.J. Reynolds Tobacco Co. is a $9 billion company that places more than 80,000 orders with 2300 suppliers world wide, for a total expenditure of more than $1 billion annually. Remarkably, all of that purchasing is done by means of EDI [HAIG93]. Reynolds has pursued a goal of 100% EDI purchases since 1986 and finally reached that goal in 1993. The motivation is simple: With EDI, the company is saving more than $5 million a year in inventory costs, as well as making the whole purchasing process faster and more effective.

For example, consider the purchasing cycle time. Instead of negotiating particular purchases, buyers now negotiate long-term contracts. Most Reynolds' suppliers provide electronic sales catalogs, which the company puts into its on-line purchasing system. When someone in the company who is authorized to order goes on-line, all that has to be filled out on the company's electronic form is the part number, the quantity, and what account should be charged. These orders are transmitted immediately to the supplier, with most of the orders received within hours. The supplier then sends back an acknowledgment, with the quantity, price, and delivery date. Because the accounting system is integrated with the purchasing system, numbers are entered only once, reducing error.

The result of this system has been a substantial speed-up. For example, in one category of materials, referred to as maintenance, repair, and operating items, it used to take 30 to 45 days from the time a spare part was ordered until it arrived. The turnaround time is now 2 days. As a result, Reynolds has been able to drastically slash its inventory of spare parts. Cost is another big area of savings. The company estimates that the overhead cost of a typical EDI order is just 93 cents, compared to $75 for a comparable paper order.

When Reynolds began this process, it encouraged its suppliers to get on the system. Reynolds maintained a package that can translate between alternative formats, solving one of the big technical problems with EDI. As the use of EDI spread to more of its suppliers, Reynolds became more insistent with the others. In some cases, EDI was a difficult sale. As Reynolds' purchasing manager puts it: "EDI is not part of traditional executive management thinking. Because it's electronic, they perceive it only as an MIS tool. They don't realize it changes the whole way you do business. People in the operations area have to understand how it changes business dramatically, and they have to sell it up the line well. People are reticent to change what works today. Internally, we had battles with our buyers. They wanted the forms printed out the way they had always been. So you have resistance at all levels, from suppliers and internally, and you require some resources to overcome that."

Slowly, Reynolds overcame resistance first with persuasion and then with insistence. By 1992, 86% of all orders were placed over EDI. Most of these, however, were to 560 major suppliers. About 1500 of the company's 2300 suppliers, mostly small companies, were still outside the system. To move these suppliers over, Reynolds decided to employ a service bureau. The procedure works in the following way. When Reynolds places an order to a supplier that is not hooked up, it sends the order via EDI to the service bureau. The bureau prints out the order and faxes it to the supplier. The supplier faxes back an acknowledgment, which the bureau types into an EDI acknowledgment form, which is then transmitted back to Reynolds. Although this approach does not capitalize on all the benefits of

EDI, because the supplier does not change its way of doing business, Reynolds benefits by doing its transactions one way.

Beyond the direct benefits of EDI, Reynolds is beginning to exploit the use of EDI to achieve additional benefits by literally changing some of its business practices. For example, Reynolds is in the process of implementing a scheme that will make it unnecessary for suppliers to send invoices in many cases. On items where the price is known, Reynolds can post the order and receive an acknowledgment but not an invoice. When the goods are received, the appropriate information is put into the system and payment is made automatically. This cuts the disbursement process out of the loop, eliminating processes and reducing costs.

The almost total reliance on electronic forms for its external information transfer has also had an impact on paperwork practices within the company [BRON95]. In the early 1990s, Reynolds was spending several million dollars annually producing, sorting, storing, distributing, and managing 4500 different kinds of forms, everything from expense reports and vacation requests to contracts and specialized order forms. Paper is a slow way to move information, one that creates storage and duplication problems. Management found that departments would wait to reorder critical forms until the last one was gone, often forcing staff to place expensive rush orders. Inspired by the success with EDI, Reynolds began looking for ways to automate forms processing. The company acquired software that runs on DOS, Windows, and Macintosh that comes in two parts: a system for creating electronic forms and linking them to databases over a LAN; and a user front end for filling out and routing these electronic forms.

Currently, most personnel use the electronic forms system for many of the old paper forms. So far, Reynolds has reduced its budget for printing paper forms by approximately 25%, and expects savings to increase annually as the system expands. They have also reduced the cost of storage and distribution by the same percentage and hope to reduce paper costs by 50% within five years.

Discussion Questions

1. Why doesn't Reynolds simply absorb the functions of the service bureau, eliminating the middleman and hence saving costs?

2. What security concerns are raised by Reynolds' EDI strategy?

3. The company plans to tie electronic funds transfer (ETF) to its EDI relationships as well. This will enable Reynolds to transfer funds automatically when goods are received. By getting their money on time or even early, suppliers will lower their accounts receivable and gain faster use of their money. In return, Reynolds expects the suppliers to be willing to offer better terms. What pitfalls do you see for this strategy?

14

Client–Server
and Intranet Computing

CHAPTER OBJECTIVES

After reading this chapter, you should be able to:

- Discuss the reasons for the growing interest in and availability of client–server computing systems.

- Describe the features and characteristics of client–server computing.

- Describe the architecture of client–server applications.

- Explain the role of middleware in client–server systems.

- Assess the networking requirements and implications of client–server computing.

- Define intranet and contrast it with Internet.

- Compare client–server and intranet approaches to distributed computing.

A number of distributed applications, such as those discussed in Chapter 13, involve what might be referred to as a *peer interaction between systems*. There is also a fundamentally different style of distributed computing, one that is having a profound impact on the way in which businesses use computers: client–server computing.

We begin this chapter with a general description of the client–server philosophy and the implications for businesses. Next, we examine the nature of the application support provided by the client–server architecture. Then we look at the rather fuzzy but very important concept of middleware. Following this survey of client–server computing, we examine a more recent approach referred to as an intranet. An intranet uses Internet technology and applications (especially Web-based applications) to provide in-house support for distributed applications.

14.1 GROWTH OF CLIENT–SERVER COMPUTING

One of the hottest computer buzzwords of the 1990s is **client–server**. Virtually every hardware and software vendor has something to say on the subject. Examples:

- Workstation vendors such as Sun and Hewlett-Packard emphasize the performance and reliability of their products used as server platforms.

- Operating-system vendors emphasize the client–server support features in their systems. Example: Microsoft's Windows NT is targeted specifically at the server market.

- Application-level and database management system vendors such as Bachman and Sybase push client–server solutions to business problems.

As with other new waves in the computer field, client–server computing comes with its own set of jargon words. Table 14-1 lists some of the terms that are commonly found in descriptions of client–server products and applications.

TABLE 14-1 Client–Server Terminology

Applications programming interface (API)
   A set of function and call programs that allow clients and servers to intercommunicate.

Client
   A networked information requester, usually a PC or workstation, that can query database and/or other information from a server.

Middleware
   A set of drivers, APIs, or other software that improves connectivity between a client application and a server.

Relational database
   A database in which information access is limited to the selection of rows that satisfy all search criteria.

Server
   A computer, usually a high-powered workstation, a minicomputer, or a mainframe, that houses information for manipulation by networked clients.

Structured Query Language (SQL)
   A language developed by IBM and standardized by ANSI for addressing, creating, updating, or querying relational databases.

What Is Client–Server?

Client–server computing has clearly arrived. Although the "spin" from various vendors varies, there is nevertheless fairly good agreement about what client–server computing is. Table 14-2 quotes some of the definitions that have been proposed for the client–server concept. It is worthwhile to take the time to read these definitions carefully. From all of these definitions some general themes emerge.

Figure 14.1 attempts to capture the essence of these themes. As the term suggests, a client–server environment is populated by clients and servers. The client machines are generally single-user PCs or workstations that provide a highly user-friendly interface to the end user. The client-based station generally presents the type of graphical interface that is most comfortable to users, including the use of windows and a mouse. Common examples of such interfaces are provided by Microsoft Windows and Macintosh. Client-based applications are tailored for ease of use and include such familiar tools as the spreadsheet.

TABLE 14-2 Definitions of Client–Server

Client–server computing

Involves splitting an application into tasks and putting each task on the platform where it can be handled most efficiently. This usually means putting the processing for the presentation on the user's machine (the client) and the data management and storage on a server. Depending on the application and the software used, all data processing may occur on the client or be split between the client and the server. The server is connected to its clients via a network. Server software accepts requests for data from client software and returns the results to the client. The client manipulates the data and presents the results to the user. [DEWI93]

Client–server

A network environment where the control of data is established at a server node and is available for access, but not update, at other nodes. [INMO91]

Client–server computing model

Implies a cooperative processing of requests submitted by a client, or requester, to the server, which processes the requests and returns the results to the client. In this model, application processing is divided (not necessarily evenly) between client and server. The processing is actually initiated and partially controlled by the client, but not in a master–slave fashion. Instead, both client and server cooperate to execute an application successfully. [BERS96]

Client–server

A model for the interaction between concurrently executing software processes. Client processes send requests to a server process, which responds with results to those requests. As the name implies, server processes provide services to their clients, usually by way of specific processing that only they can do. The client process, freed from the complexity and overhead of processing the transaction, is able to perform other useful work. The interaction between the client and server processes is a cooperative, transactional exchange in which the client is proactive and the server is reactive. [RENA96]

Client–server computing

Any application in which the requestor of action is on one system and the supplier of action is potentially on another. In addition, most client–server solutions have a many-to-one design—that is, more than one client typically makes requests of the server. [MOSK93]

Each server in the client–server environment provides a set of shared user services to the clients. The most common type of server currently is the database server, usually controlling a relational database. The server enables many clients to share access to the same database and enables the use of a high-performance computer system to manage the database. In addition to clients and servers, the third essential ingredient of the client–server environment is the network. Client–server computing is distributed computing. Users, applications, and resources are distributed in response to business requirements and linked by a single LAN or WAN or by an internet of networks.

How does a client–server configuration differ from any other distributed processing solution? There are a number of characteristics that stand out, and that together, make client–server distinct from ordinary distributed processing:

- There is a heavy reliance on bringing user-friendly applications to the user on his or her own system. This gives the user a great deal of control over the timing and style of computer usage and gives department-level managers the ability to be responsive to their local needs.

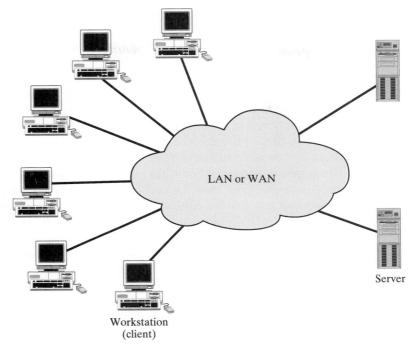

LAN or WAN

Server

Workstation
(client)

FIGURE 14.1 Generic Client–Server Environment.

- Although the applications are dispersed, there is an emphasis on centralizing corporate databases and many network management and utility functions. This enables corporate management to maintain overall control of the total capital investment in computing and information systems, enabling corporate management to provide interoperability so that systems are tied together. At the same time it relieves individual departments and divisions of much of the overhead of maintaining sophisticated computer-based facilities but enables them to choose just about any type of machine and interface they need to access data and information. The case study of Levi Strauss in Chapter 9 is one example of this blend of central and distributed control.

- There is a commitment, by both user organizations and vendors, to open and modular systems. This means that the user has greater choice in selecting products and in mixing equipment from a number of vendors.

- Networking is fundamental to the operation. Thus, network management and network security have a high priority in organizing and operating information systems.

Client–server computing is on the one hand a natural solution from the product point of view, because it exploits the growing availability and affordability of microcomputers and networks. On the other hand, client–server computing may be the ideal choice to support the direction that business is taking in the organization of work.

The latter point deserves elaboration. The success of client–server computing in the marketplace is not just a matter of new jargon on top of old solutions. Client–server computing is indeed a new technical approach to distributed computing. But beyond that, client–server computing is responsive to, and indeed creates the conditions for, new ways of organizing business. Let us consider two significant trends in industry that illustrate the point.

The first of these is the permanent shedding of jobs by companies in an effort to downsize and streamline for success in a fiercely competitive market. The graphs in Figure 14.2 confirm this trend. A hallmark of the end of each U.S. recession in the past 30 years has been a strong growth in productivity. It is this growth that has enabled companies to climb out of the recession and contribute to the growth in the gross domestic product. Traditionally, each recovery has been accompanied by waves of hiring, as business expands to meet increased demand. However, following the most recent recession, although productivity growth has occurred, job growth has not. In this recovery, businesses have squeezed payrolls to remain competitive.

Why have companies needed to shed jobs to remain competitive, and how have they managed to increase productivity so fast as to have sales growth without payroll growth? Figure 14.2c suggests the answer. The cost per employee is rising rapidly, with wage increases coupled to mandated benefits increases. At the same time, business equipment, especially computer and network equipment and services, have suffered only modest cost increases. This has led, as one might expect, to substantial increases in investment in computers and other information technology in an effort to compensate for a smaller employee base. As *Business Week* [FARR93] put it: "It is the lethal combination of global competition, expensive workers, and cheap computers that has severed the link between economic growth and jobs growth." This trend occurs in small as well as large businesses, and is affecting middle managers as well as clerical staff. What client–server computing provides is a way of automating tasks and of eliminating barriers to information that allows companies to eliminate layers of management and to add work without adding workers.

Another trend that illustrates the effectiveness of client–server computing is the *internal market movement*. This is a movement that affects primarily large businesses, which seek to combine entrepreneurial zeal with corporate might to have the best of both worlds: the economies of scale of a large business with the agility of a small business. In an era of rapid technological and market changes, many large companies are tearing down traditional functional hierarchies and replacing them with collections of relatively independent business units. These units must then compete with external companies for business from other units. In an internal market, every business unit operates as an independent company. Each decides to buy its inputs from internal sources (other units of the corporation) or from outside suppliers. Even traditional "overhead" departments, such as information systems, accounting, and legal must sell their services to other units and compete with outside providers.

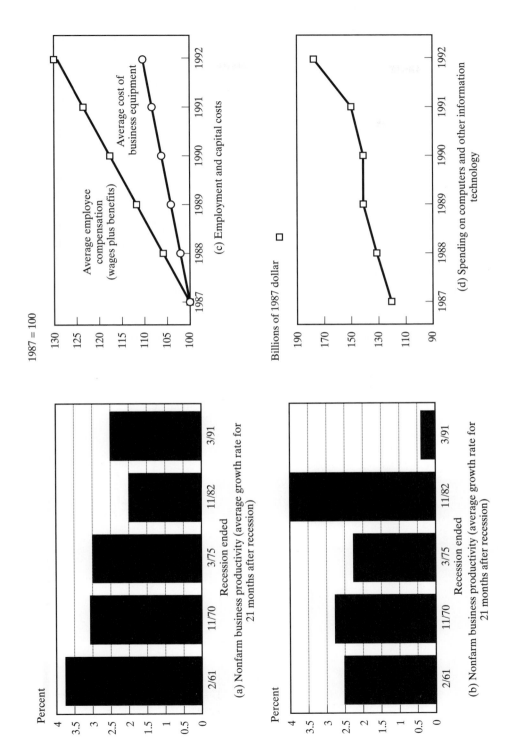

FIGURE 14.2 U.S. Employment and Computer Purchasing Trends (Business Week, February 22, 1993).

This dose of internal competition is designed to correct the flaws of the traditional way of doing business. As Jay Forrester of MIT observes [ROTH93]: "American corporations are some of the largest socialist bureaucracies in the world. They have central planning, central ownership of capital, central allocation of resources, subjective evaluation of people, lack of internal competition, and decisions made at the top in response to political pressures."

Internal markets have already transformed some companies and promise to have a major impact on others. But until recently there has been a formidable obstacle to implementing such a scheme. In a large company, the use of an internal market can result in thousands of teams making agreements among themselves and with outsiders. Somehow, the ledgers for all the resulting transactions have to be reconciled. Analyses of this situation have suggested that the cost and complexity of bookkeeping would overwhelm the benefits of an internal market. The evolution of computing technology has overcome this obstacle. Today, a number of multinationals are using the latest database software running on client–server networks to set up internal markets [ROTH93].

These and other business trends have spurred investment in client–server technology. A survey of 930 information systems managers shows that database applications are the most common to be supported on client–server environments, but many other applications have also been moved to the client–server regime (Figure 14.3).

FIGURE 14.3 Applications Supported Using Client–Server Computing.

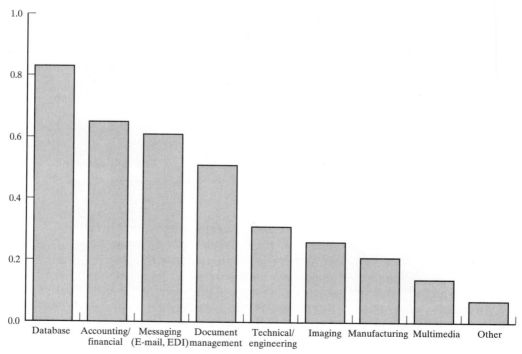

TABLE 14-3 Client–Server Pros and Cons

(a) ADVANTAGES

Feature	*Benefit*
Networked web of small, powerful machines	If one machine goes down, your business stays up.
Computer arrays with thousands of MIPS	The system provides the power to get things done without monopolizing resources. End users are empowered to work locally.
Some workstations are as powerful as mainframes but cost an order of magnitude less	By giving you power for less money, the system offers you the flexibility to make other purchases or to increase your profits.
Open systems	You can pick and choose hardware, software, and services from various vendors.
Systems grow easily	It is easy to modernize your system as your needs change.
Individual client operating environments	You can mix and match computer platforms to suit the needs of individual departments and users.

(b) DISADVANTAGES

Downside	*What it means for you*
Maintenance nightmares	Parts don't always work together. There are several possible culprits when something goes wrong.
Support tools lacking	With the client–server architecture, you must often locate or build support tools yourself.
Retraining required	The software development philosophy for the Mac or Windows is different from that of COBOL or C.

Of course, as with any major change in computing configuration, the move to client–server is neither risk free or pain free. Table 14-3 shows that users report, in addition to many perceived benefits, a number of pitfalls in moving to client–server. Nevertheless, with the falling cost and proliferation of microcomputers and the competitive forces acting on industry, client–server seems destined to be the dominant style of corporate computing for the foreseeable future.

Evolution of Client–Server Computing

The way in which client–server computing has evolved is worth noting. This style of organizing computer resources began at the work group and departmental level. Departmental managers found that relying on central, mainframe-based applications hindered their ability to respond rapidly to business demands. Application development time within the central IS shop was too slow, and the results were not tailored to the specific needs of the department. The deployment of PCs enabled workers to have computing power and data at their command and enabled department-level managers to select needed applications quickly.

However, if a pure PC environment, cooperation among users was difficult. Even within the department, there needed to be a departmental-level database and departmental formatting and data usage standards. The solution to these requirements is a departmental-level client–server architecture. Typically, such an architecture involves a single LAN, a number of PCs, and one or two servers.

The success of departmental-level client–server systems paved the way for the introduction of enterprise-wide client–server computing. Ideally, such an architecture will enable the integration of departmental and IS organization resources, allowing for applications that give individual users ready but controlled access to corporate databases. The dominant theme of such architectures is the reestablishment of control over data by the central IS organization but in the context of a distributed computing system.

14.2 CLIENT–SERVER APPLICATIONS

The central feature of a client–server architecture is the allocation of application-level tasks between clients and servers. Figure 14.4 illustrates the general case. In both client and server, of course, the basic software is an operating system running on the hardware platform. The platforms and the operating systems of client and server may differ. Indeed, there may be a number of different types of client platforms and operating systems and a number of different types of server platforms and operating systems in a single environment. As long as a particular client and server share the same communications protocols and support the same applications, these lower-level differences are irrelevant.

It is the communications software that enables client and server to interoperate. Examples of such software include TCP/IP, OSI, and various proprietary

FIGURE 14.4 Generic Client–Server Architecture.

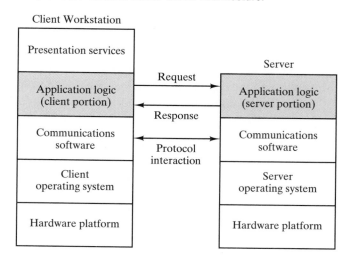

architectures such as SNA. Of course, the point of all this support software (communications and operating system) is to provide a base for distributed applications. Ideally, the actual functions performed by the application can be split up between client and server in a way that optimizes platform and network resources and that optimizes the ability of users to perform various tasks and to cooperate with one another in using shared resources. In some cases these requirements dictate that the bulk of the applications software executes at the server, while in other cases, most of the application logic is located at the client.

Finally, an essential factor in the success of a client–server environment is the way in which the user interacts with the system as a whole. Thus, the design of the user interface to the client machine is critical. In most client–server systems, there is heavy emphasis on providing a **graphical user interface (GUI)** that is easy to use, easy to learn, yet powerful and flexible. Thus, we can think of a presentation services module[1] in the client workstation responsible for providing a user-friendly interface to the distributed applications available in the environment.

Database Applications

As an example that illustrates the concept of splitting application logic between client and server, let us consider the most common family of client–server applications: those that make use of relational databases. In this environment, the server is essentially a database server. Interaction between client and server is in the form of transactions in which the client makes a database request and receives a database response.

Figure 14.5 illustrates, in general terms, the architecture of such a system. The server is responsible for maintaining the database, for which purpose a complex database management system software module is required. A variety of applications that make use of the database can be housed on client machines. The "glue" that ties client and server together is software that enables the client to make requests for access to the server's database. A popular example of such logic is the structured query language (SQL).

Figure 14.5 suggests that all of the application logic—the software for "number crunching" or other types of data analysis—is on the client side, while the server is only concerned with managing the database. Whether such a configuration is appropriate depends on the style and intent of the application. For example, suppose that the primary purpose is to provide on-line access for record lookup. Figure 14.6a suggests how this might work. Suppose that the server is maintaining a database of 1 million records (called *rows* in relational database jargon), and the user wants to perform a lookup that should result in zero, one, or at most a few records. The user could search for these records using a number of search criteria (e.g., records older than 1992, records referring to residents of Ohio, records referring to a specific event or characteristic, etc.). An initial client query may yield a server response that there are 100,000 records that satisfy the

---

[1] Not to be confused with the presentation layer of the OSI model. The presentation layer is concerned with the formatting of data so that it can be interpreted properly by the two communicating machines. A presentation services module is concerned with the way in which the user interacts with an application and with the layout and functionality of what is presented to the user on his/her screen.

Client Workstation

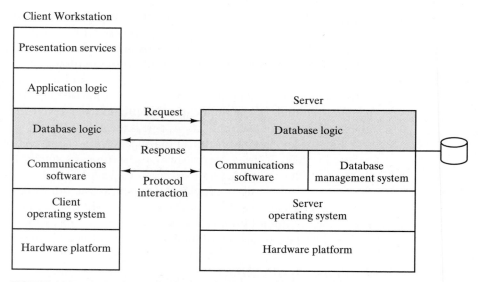

FIGURE 14.5 Client–Server Architecture for Database Applications.

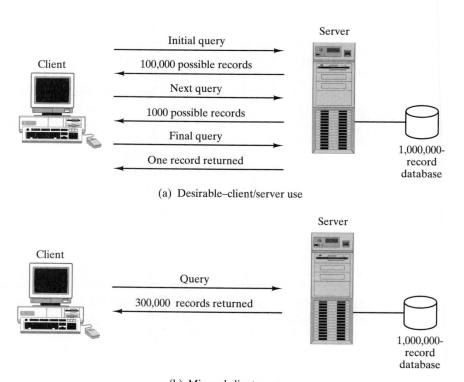

(a) Desirable–client/server use

(b) Misused client–server

FIGURE 14.6 Client–Server Database Usage.

search criteria. The user then adds additional qualifiers and issues a new query. This time, a response indicating that there are 1000 possible records is returned. Finally, the client issues a third request with additional qualifiers. The resulting search criteria yield a single match, and the record is returned to the client.

The application above is well suited to a client–server architecture for two reasons:

1. There is a massive job of sorting and searching the database. This requires a large disk or bank of disks, a high-speed CPU, and a high-speed I/O architecture. Such capacity and power is not needed and is too expensive for a single-user workstation or PC.

2. It would place too great a traffic burden on the network to move the entire 1 million record file to the client for searching. Therefore, it is not enough for the server just to be able to retrieve records on behalf of a client; the server needs to have database logic that enables it to perform searches on behalf of a client.

Now consider the scenario of Figure 14.6b, which has the same 1 million record database. In this case, a single query results in the transmission of 300,000 records over the network. This might happen if, for example, the user wishes to find the grand total or mean value of some field across many records or even the entire database.

Clearly, the latter scenario is unacceptable. One solution to this problem, that maintains the client–server architecture with all its benefits, is to move part of the application logic over to the server. That is, the server can be equipped with application logic for performing data analysis as well as data retrieval and data searching.

Classes of Client–Server Applications

Within the general framework of client–server, there is a spectrum of implementations that divide the work between client and server differently. The exact distribution of data and application processing depends on the nature of the database information, the types of applications supported, the availability of interoperable vendor equipment, and the usage patterns within an organization. Figure 14.7 illustrates in general terms some of the major options for database applications. Other splits are possible and the options may have a different characterization for other types of applications. In any case it is useful to examine this figure to get a feeling for the kind of trade-offs possible.

The figure depicts four classes:

- *Host-based processing.* Host-based processing is not true client–server computing as the term is generally used. Rather, *host-based processing* refers to the traditional mainframe environment in which all or virtually all of the processing is done on a central host. Often the user interface is via a dumb terminal. Even if the user is employing a microcomputer, the user's station is generally limited to the role of a terminal emulator.

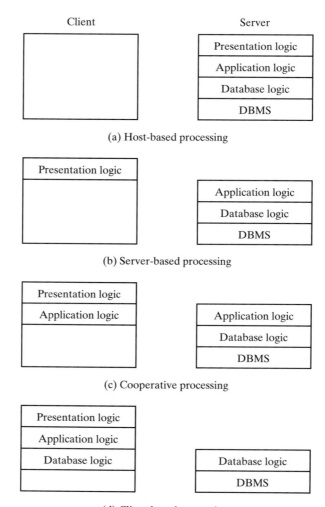

FIGURE 14.7 Classes of Client–Server Applications.

- *Server-based processing.* The most basic class of client–server configuration is one in which the client is principally responsible for providing a graphical user interface, while virtually all of the processing is done on the server.

- *Client-based processing.* At the other extreme, virtually all application processing may be done at the client, with the exception of data validation routines and other database logic functions that are best performed at the server. Generally, some of the more sophisticated database logic functions are housed on the client side. This architecture is perhaps the most common client–server approach in current use. It enables the user to employ applications tailored to local needs.

■ *Cooperative processing.* In a cooperative processing configuration, the application processing is performed in an optimized fashion, taking advantage of the strengths of both client and server machines and of the distribution of data. Such a configuration is more complex to set up and maintain, but in the long run, this type of configuration may offer greater user productivity gains and greater network efficiency than those of other client–server approaches.

Figure 14.7c and d correspond to configurations in which a considerable fraction of the load is on the client. This so-called *fat client* model has been popularized by application development tools such as Powersoft Corp.'s PowerBuilder and Gupta Corp.'s SQL Windows. Applications developed with these tools are typically departmental in scope, supporting between 25 and 150 users [ECKE95]. The main benefit of the fat client model is that it takes advantage of desktop power, offloading application processing from servers and making them more efficient and less likely to be bottlenecks.

There are, however, several disadvantages to the fat client strategy. The addition of more functions rapidly overloads the capacity of desktop machines, forcing companies to upgrade. If the model extends beyond the department to incorporate many users, the company must install high-capacity LANs to support the large volumes of transmission between the thin servers and the fat clients. Finally, it is difficult to maintain, upgrade, or replace applications distributed across tens or hundreds of desktops.

Figure 14.7b is representative of a *fat server* approach. This approach more nearly mimics the traditional host-centered approach and is often the migration path for evolving corporate-wide applications from the mainframe to a distributed environment.

14.3 MIDDLEWARE

The development and deployment of client–server products has far outstripped efforts to standardize all aspects of distributed computing, from the physical layer up to the application layer. This lack of standards makes it difficult to implement an integrated, multivendor, enterprise-wide client–server configuration. Because much of the benefit of the client–server approach is tied up with its modularity and the ability to mix and match platforms and applications to provide a business solution, this interoperability problem must be solved.

To achieve the true benefits of the client–server approach, developers must have a set of tools that provide a uniform means and style of access to system resources across all platforms. This will enable programmers to build applications that not only look and feel the same on various PCs and workstations but that use the same method to access data regardless of the location of that data.

The most common way to meet this requirement is by the use of standard programming interfaces and protocols that sit between the application above and communications software and operating system below. Such standardized interfaces and protocols have come to be referred to as **middleware**. With standard programming interfaces, it is easy to implement the same application on a variety of server types and workstation types. This obviously has benefit to the customer, but vendors are also motivated to provide such interfaces. The reason is that customers buy applications, not servers; customers will only choose among those server products that run the applications they want. The standardized protocols are needed to link these various server interfaces back to the clients that need access to them.

There are a variety of middleware packages ranging from the very simple to the very complex. What they all have in common is the capability to hide the complexities and disparities of different network protocols and operating systems. Client and server vendors generally provide a number of the more popular middleware packages as options. Thus, a user can settle on a particular middleware strategy and then assemble equipment from various vendors that support that strategy.

Middleware Architecture

Figure 14.8 suggests the role of middleware in a client–server architecture. The exact role of the middleware component will depend on the style of client–server computing being used. Referring back to Figure 14.7, recall that there are a number of different client–server approaches, depending on the way in which application functions are split up. In any case, Figure 14.8 gives a good general idea of the architecture involved.

Note that there is both a client and server component of middleware. The basic purpose of middleware is to enable an application or user at a client to access a variety of services on servers without being concerned about differences among servers. To look at one specific application area, the structured query language (SQL) is supposed to provide a standardized means for access to a rela-

FIGURE 14.8 The Role of Middleware in a Client–Server Architecture.

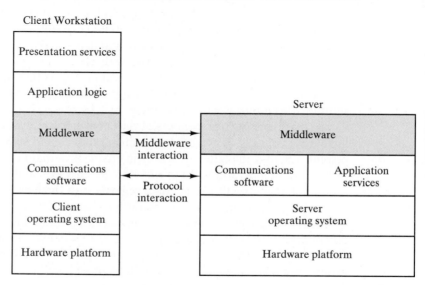

tional database by either a local or remote user or application. However, many relational database vendors, although they support SQL, have added their own proprietary extensions to SQL. This enables vendors to differentiate their products but also creates potential incompatibilities.

As an example, consider a distributed system used to support, among other things, the personnel department. The basic employee data, such as employee name, address, and so on, might be stored on a Gupta database, whereas salary information might be contained on an Oracle database. When a user in the personnel department requires access to particular records, that user doesn't want to be concerned with which vendor's database contains the records needed. Middleware provides a layer of software that enables uniform access to these differing systems.

It is instructive to look at the role of middleware from a logical rather than an implementation point of view. This viewpoint is illustrated in Figure 14.9. Middleware enables the realization of the promise of distributed client–server computing. The entire distributed system can be viewed as a set of applications and resources available to users. Users need not be concerned with the location of data or indeed the location of applications. All applications operate over a uniform **applications programming interface (API)**. The middleware, which cuts across all client and server platforms, is responsible for routing client requests to the appropriate server.

FIGURE 14.9 Logical View of Middleware [BERN96b].

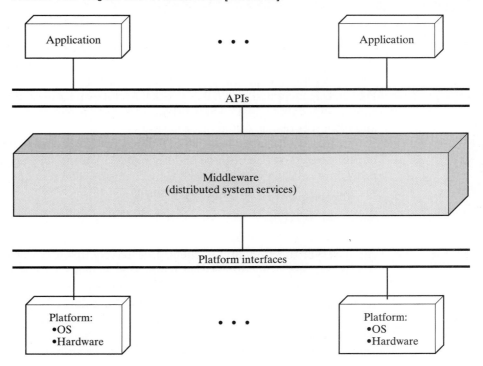

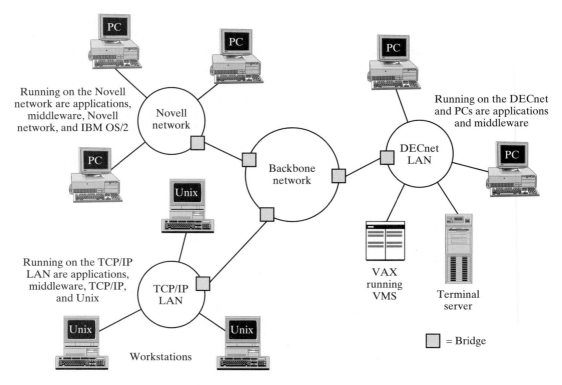

Running on the Novell network are applications, middleware, Novell network, and IBM OS/2

Running on the DECnet and PCs are applications and middleware

Running on the TCP/IP LAN are applications, middleware, TCP/IP, and Unix

Workstations

□ = Bridge

FIGURE 14.10 Example of Middleware Functionality.

An example of how middleware is used to integrate disparate products is the installation depicted in Figure 14.10. In this case, middleware is used to overcome network and operating-system incompatibilities. A backbone network links DECnet, Novell, and TCP/IP networks. Middleware, running on each network component, ensures that all network users have transparent access to applications and resources on any of the three networks.

Although there is a wide variety of middleware products, these products are typically based on one of three underlying mechanisms: message passing, remote procedure calls, and object-oriented mechanisms. The remainder of this section provides an overview of these mechanisms.

Message Passing

Figure 14.11a shows the use of distributed message passing to implement client–server functionality. A client process requires some service (e.g., read a file, print) and sends a message containing a request for service to a server process. The server process honors the request and sends a message containing a reply. In its simplest form, only two functions are needed: send and receive. The send function specifies a destination and includes the message content. The receive function tells from whom a message is desired (including "all") and provides a buffer where the incoming message is to be stored.

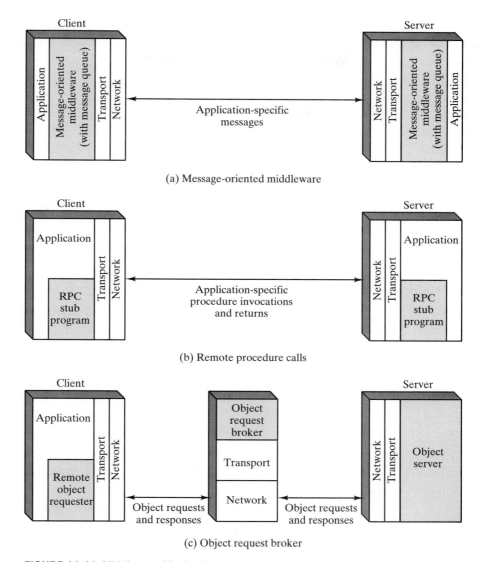

FIGURE 14.11 Middleware Mechanisms.

Figure 14.12 suggests an implementation approach for message passing. Processes make use of the services of a message-passing module. Service requests can be expressed in terms of primitives and parameters. A primitive specifies the function to be performed, and the parameters are used to pass data and control information. The actual form of a primitive depends on the message-passing software. It may be a procedure call or it may itself be a message to a process that is part of the operating system.

The send primitive is used by the process that desires to send the message. Its parameters are the identifier of the destination process and the contents of the

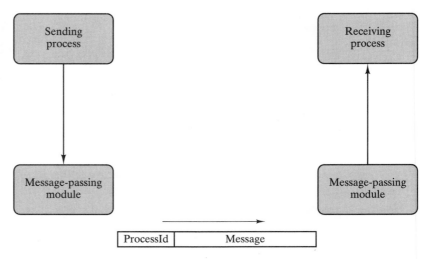

FIGURE 14.12 Basic Message-Passing Primitives.

message. The message-passing module constructs a data unit that includes these two elements. This data unit is sent to the machine that hosts the destination process, using some sort of communications facility, such as TCP/IP. When the data unit is received in the target system, it is routed by the communications facility to the message-passing module. This module examines the processId field and stores the message in the buffer for that process.

In this scenario the receiving process must announce its willingness to receive messages by designating a buffer area and informing the message-passing module by a receive primitive. An alternative approach does not require such an announcement. Instead, when the message-passing module receives a message, it signals the destination process with some sort of receive signal and then makes the received message available in a shared buffer.

Several design issues are associated with distributed message passing, and these are addressed in the remainder of this subsection.

Reliability versus Unreliability   A reliable message-passing facility is one that guarantees delivery if possible. Such a facility would make use of a reliable transport protocol or similar logic and would perform error-checking, acknowledgment, retransmission, and reordering of misordered messages. Because delivery is guaranteed, it is not necessary to let the sending process know that the message was delivered. However, it might be useful to provide an acknowledgment back to the sending process so that it knows when delivery has taken place. In either case, if the facility fails to achieve delivery (e.g., persistent network failure, crash of destination system), the sending process is notified of the failure.

At the other extreme, the message-passing facility may simply send the message out into the communications network but will report neither success nor failure. This alternative greatly reduces the complexity and processing and communications overhead of the message-passing facility. For those applications that require confirmation that a message has been delivered, the applications themselves may use request and reply messages to satisfy the requirement.

Blocking versus Nonblocking With nonblocking, or asynchronous, primitives, a process is not suspended as a result of issuing a send or receive. Thus, when a process issues a send primitive, the operating system returns control to the process as soon as the message has been queued for transmission, or a copy has been made. If no copy is made, any changes made to the message by the sending process before or even while it is being transmitted are made at the risk of the process. When the message has been transmitted, or copied to a safe place for subsequent transmission, the sending process is interrupted to be informed that the message buffer may be reused. Similarly, a nonblocking receive is issued by a process which then proceeds to run. When a message arrives, the process is informed by interrupt, or it can poll for status periodically.

Nonblocking primitives provide for efficient, flexible use of the message-passing facility by processes. The disadvantage of this approach is that it is difficult to test and debug programs that use these primitives. Irreproducible, timing-dependent sequences can create subtle and difficult problems. The alternative is to use blocking, or synchronous, primitives. A blocking send does not return control to the sending process until the message has been transmitted (unreliable service) or until the message has been sent and an acknowledgment received (reliable service). A blocking receive does not return control until a message has been placed in the allocated buffer.

Remote Procedure Calls

A variation on the basic message-passing model is the remote procedure call. This is now a widely accepted and common method for encapsulating communication in a distributed system. The essence of the technique is to allow programs on different machines to interact using simple procedure call/return semantics, just as if the two programs were on the same machine. That is, the procedure call is used for access to remote services. The popularity of this approach is due to the following advantages:

1. The procedure call is a widely accepted, used, and understood abstraction.

2. The use of remote procedure calls enables remote interfaces to be specified as a set of named operations with designated types. Thus, the interface can be clearly documented and distributed programs can be statically checked for type errors.

3. Because a standardized and precisely defined interface is specified, the communication code for an application can be generated automatically.

4. Because a standardized and precisely defined interface is specified, developers can write client and server modules that can be moved among computers and operating systems with little modification and recoding.

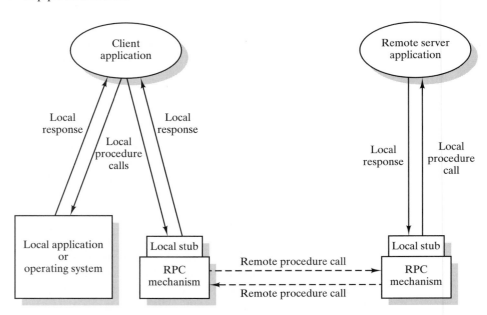

FIGURE 14.13 Remote Procedure Call Mechanism.

The remote procedure call mechanism can be viewed as a refinement of reliable, blocking message passing. Figure 14.11b illustrates the general architecture, and Figure 14.13 provides a more detailed look. The calling program makes a normal procedure call with parameters on its machine. For example,

$$\text{CALL P(X,Y)}$$

where

      P = procedure name
      X = passed arguments
      Y = returned values

It may or may not be transparent to the user that the intention is to invoke a remote procedure on some other machine. A dummy or stub procedure P must be included in the caller's address space or be dynamically linked to it at call time. This procedure creates a message that identifies the procedure being called and includes the parameters. It then sends this message to a remote system and waits for a reply. When a reply is received, the stub procedure returns to the calling program, providing the returned values.

At the remote machine, another stub program is associated with the called procedure. When a message comes in, it is examined and a local CALL P(X,Y) is generated. This remote procedure is thus called locally (on the target machine), so its normal assumptions about where to find parameters, the state of the stack, and so on, are identical to the case of a purely local procedure call.

Client–Server Binding Binding specifies how the relationship between a remote procedure and the calling program will be established. A binding is formed when two applications have made a logical connection and are prepared to exchange commands and data.

Nonpersistent binding means that a logical connection is established between the two processes at the time of the remote procedure call and that as soon as the values are returned, the connection is dismantled. Because a connection requires the maintenance of state information on both ends, it consumes resources. The nonpersistent style is used to conserve those resources. On the other hand, the overhead involved in establishing connections makes nonpersistent binding inappropriate for remote procedures that are called frequently by the same caller.

With *persistent binding,* a connection that is set up for a remote procedure call is sustained after the procedure return. The connection can then be used for future remote procedure calls. If a specified period of time passes with no activity on the connection, the connection is terminated. For applications that make many repeated calls to remote procedures, persistent binding maintains the logical connection and allows a sequence of calls and returns to use the same connection.

Object-Oriented Mechanisms

As object-oriented technology becomes more prevalent in operating-system design, client–server designers have begun to embrace this approach. In this approach, clients and servers ship messages back and forth between objects. Object communications may rely on an underlying message or RPC structure or be developed directly on top of object-oriented capabilities in the operating system.

A client that needs a service sends a request to an object request broker, which act as a directory of all the remote service available on the network (Figure 14.11c). The broker calls the appropriate object and passes along any relevant data. Then the remote object services the request and replies to the broker, which returns the response to the client.

The success of the object-oriented approach depends on standardization of the object mechanism. Unfortunately, there are several competing designs in this area. One is Microsoft's common object model (COM), the basis for object linking and embedding (OLE). This approach has the support of Digital Equipment Corporation, which has developed COM for Unix. A competing approach, developed by the Object Management Group, is the common object request broker architecture (CORBA), which has wide industry backing. IBM, Apple, Sun, and many other vendors support the CORBA approach.

14.4 INTRANETS

Intranet
A corporate internetwork that provides the key Internet applications, especially the World Wide Web.

Intranet is a term used to refer to the implementation of Internet technologies within a corporate organization rather than for external connection to the global Internet. This concept, unknown until a few years ago, has resulted in the most rapid change of direction in the history of business data communications. By any measure, including product announcements by vendors, statements of intent by customers, actual deployment of products, and even books on the shelves of bookstores, intranets have enjoyed a more rapid penetration of the corporate consciousness than personal computers, client–server computing, or even the Internet and the World Wide Web.

What accounts for this growth is a long list of attractive features and advantages of an intranet-based approach to corporate computing, including:

- Rapid prototyping and deployment of new services (can be measured in hours or days).
- Scales effectively (start small, build as requirements dictate).
- Virtually no training required on the part of users and little training required of developers, because the services and user interfaces are familiar from the Internet.
- Can be implemented on virtually all platforms with complete interoperability.
- Open architecture means large and growing number of add-on applications available across many platforms.
- Supports a range of distributed computing architectures (few central servers or many distributed servers).
- Structured to support integration of "legacy" information sources (databases, existing word processing documents, groupware databases).
- Supports a range of media types (audio, video, interactive applications).
- Inexpensive to start, requires little investment in either new software or infrastructure.

The enabling technologies for the intranet are the high processing speed and storage capacity of personal computers, together with the high data rates of LANs. Although the term *intranet* refers to the entire range of Internet-based applications, including network news, gopher, and ftp, it is Web technology that is responsible for the almost-instant acceptance of intranets. Thus, the bulk of this section is devoted to a discussion of Web systems. At the close of the section, we briefly mention other intranet applications.

Intranet Web

The web browser has become the universal information interface. An increasing number of employees have had experience using the Internet Web and are comfortable with the access model it provides. The intranet web takes advantage of this experience base.

Web Content An organization can use the intranet web to enhance management–employee communication and to provide job-related information easily and quickly. Figure 14.14 suggests, at a top level, the kinds of information that can be provided by a corporate web. Typically, there is an internal corporate home page that serves as an entry point for employees into the corporate intranet. From this home page, there are links to areas of interest company-wide or to large groups of employees, including human resources, finance, and infor-

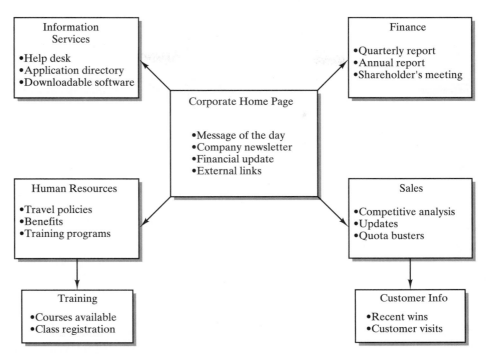

FIGURE 14.14 Example Corporate Web Page Structure.

mation system service. Other links are to areas of interest to groups of employees, such as sales and manufacturing.

Beyond these broad-based web services, an intranet web is ideal for providing departmental- and project-level information and services. A group can set up its own web pages to disseminate information and to maintain project data. With the widespread availability of easy-to-use WYSIWYG page authoring tools, such as Adobe Pagemill, it is relatively easy for employees outside the information services group to develop their own web pages for specific needs.

Web/Database Applications Although the web is a powerful and flexible tool for supporting corporate requirements, the HTML used to construct web pages provides a limited capability for maintaining a large, changing base of data. For an intranet to be truly effective, many organizations will want to connect the web service to a database with its own database management system.

Figure 14.15 illustrates a general strategy for web/database integration in simple terms. To begin, a client machine (running a web browser) issues a request for information in the form of a URL reference. This reference triggers a program at the web server that issues the correct database command to a database server. The output returned to the web server is converted into an HTML format and returned to the web browser.

[WHET96] lists the following advantages of a web/database system compared to a more traditional database approach:

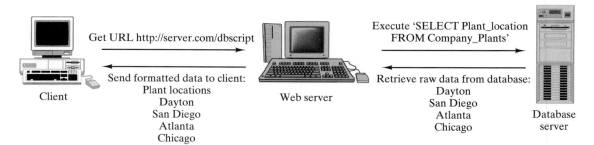

FIGURE 14.15 Web/Database Connectivity.

- *Ease of administration.* The only connection to the database server is the web server. The addition of a new type of database server does not require configuration of all the requisite drivers and interfaces at each type of client machine. Instead, it is only necessary for the web server to be able to convert between HTML and the database interface.

- *Deployment.* Browsers are already available across almost all platforms, which relieves the developer of the need to implement graphical user interfaces across multiple customer machines and operating systems. In addition, developers can assume that customers already have and will be able to use browsers as soon as the intranet web server is available, avoiding deployment issues such as installation and synchronized activation.

- *Development speed.* Large portions of the normal development cycle, such as deployment and client design, do not apply to web-based projects. In addition, the text-based tags of HTML allow for rapid modification, making it easy continually to improve the look and feel of the application based on user feedback. By contrast, changing form or content of a typical graphical-based application can be a substantial task.

- *Flexible information presentation.* The hypermedia base of the web enables the application developer to employ whatever information structure is best for a given application, including the use of hierarchical formats in which progressive levels of detail are available to the user.

These advantages are compelling in the decision to deploy a web-based database interface. However, managers need to be aware of potential disadvantages, also listed in [WHET96]:

- *Functionality.* Compared to the functionality available with a sophisticated graphical user interface (GUI), a typical web browser interface is limited. For example, it is difficult with HTML to generate graphical forms with buttons, text fields, and selection menus whose content depend on user input.

- *Stateless operation.* The nature of HTTP is such that each interaction between a browser and a server is a separate transaction, independent of prior or future exchanges. Typically, the web server keeps no information between transactions to track the state of the user. Such history information can be important. For example, consider an application that allows the user to query a database of parts for cars and trucks. Once the user has indicated that he or she is looking for a specific truck part, subsequent menus should show only parts that pertain to trucks. It is possible to work around this difficulty, but it is awkward.

Intranet Webs versus Traditional Client–Server   Although traditional client–server systems have become increasingly widespread and popular, displacing older corporate computing models, their use is not without problems, including:

- Long development cycles
- Difficulty of partitioning applications into client and server modules and the even greater difficulty in modifying the partition in response to user feedback
- Effort involved in distributing upgrades to clients
- Difficulty in scaling the servers to respond to increased load in a distributed environment
- Continuous requirement for increasingly powerful desktop machines

Much of this difficulty can be traced to the typical client–server design, which puts much of the load on the client; this fat client strategy corresponds to Figure 14.7c and d. As we mentioned earlier, this strategy may not scale well to corporate-wide applications. Thus, many companies opt for a fat server approach. An intranet web can be viewed as one realization of the fat server.

Viewed as an alternative to other fat server schemes, the intranet web has the advantages of ease of deployment, use of a small number of widely accepted standards, and integration with other TCP/IP-based applications. However, it is unlikely that the intranet web will kill or even slow down traditional client–server deployment, at least in the near term. Longer term, the intranet web may come to dominate corporate computing or it may simply be a widely used alternative to other client–server strategies that also flourish. No one can yet predict the outcome.

Other Intranet Technologies

The centerpiece of any intranet strategy is the intranet web. However, other Internet technologies can also play a key role in the success of an intranet. Perhaps the two most important, after the web, are electronic mail and network news.

Electronic Mail   Electronic mail is already the most heavily used network application in the corporate world. However, traditional E-mail is generally limited and inflexible. Intranet mail products provide simple, standard, methods for attaching documents, sound, images, and other multimedia to mail messages. In addition to supporting multimedia, intranet mail systems generally make it easy to create and manage an **electronic mailing list**. A mailing list is really nothing more than an alias that has multiple destinations. Mailing lists are usually created to discuss specific topics. Anyone interested in that topic may join that list. Once a user has been added to a list, he or she receives a copy of every message posted to the list. A user can ask a question or respond to someone else's question by sending a message to the list address. The mailing list is thus an effective way of supporting project-level communication.

Network News   Most readers of this book are familiar with **USENET**, otherwise known as **network news**. USENET is a collection of electronic bulletin boards that work in much the same way as the Internet mailing lists. If you subscribe to a particular news group, you receive all messages posted to that group, and you may post a message that is available to all subscribers. One difference between USENET and Internet mailing lists has to do with the mechanics of the systems. USENET is actually a distributed network of sites that collect and broadcast news group entries. To access a news group, for read or write, one must have access to a USENET node. Another, more significant difference is the way in which messages are organized. With an electronic mailing list, each subscriber receives messages one at a time, as they are sent. With USENET, the messages are archived at each news site and organized by subject matter. Thus, it is easier to follow the thread of a particular discussion with USENET. This ability to organize and store messages in threads makes USENET ideal for collaborative work.

As with other Internet technologies, USENET is readily adapted to form an intranet news service. The news messages can be stored on a single news servers, or multiple servers within the organization can act as news repositories. New groups are created as needed by departments and projects.

SUMMARY

Client–server computing is the key to realizing the potential of information systems and networks to significantly improve productivity in organizations. With client–server computing applications are distributed to users on single-user workstations and personal computers. At the same time, resources that can and should be shared are maintained on server systems that are available to all clients. Thus, the client–server architecture is a blend of decentralized and centralized computing.

Typically, the client system provides a graphical user interface (GUI) that enables a user to exploit a variety of applications with minimal training and relative ease. Servers support shared utilities, such as database management systems. The actual application is divided between client and server in a way intended to optimize ease of use and performance.

Because there are no generally accepted standards for client–server networking, a number of products have been developed to bridge the gap between client and server and to enable users to develop multivendor configurations. Such products generally are referred to as middleware. Middleware products are based on either a message-passing or a remote-procedure-call mechanism.

Recently, a new organizational model has arrived to compete with the client–server model: the intranet. An intranet leverages existing Internet applications, especially the

Web, to provide an internal suite of applications suited to the needs of an organization. Intranets are easy to set up, involve standardized software, can be deployed on multiple platforms, and require virtually no user training.

RECOMMENDED READING

[BERS96] both provides a good technical discussion of the design issues involved in allocating applications to client and server and in middleware approaches; the book also discusses products and standardization efforts. [RENA96] is oriented toward the management aspects of installing client–server systems and selecting applications for that environment. [SIMO95] describes the principles and mechanisms of client–server computing and middleware in the context of two detailed case studies, one for Windows and one for Unix.

[EVAN96] provides a practical, detailed how-to manual on setting up a corporate intranet; the book covers a wide spectrum of applications and gives concrete guidance for implementation. [ECKE96] is another good treatment, although somewhat less detailed. A more informal but very enlightening treatment is [BERN96a]; this book provides a management-level discussion of the advantages of web intranets and strategies for building and exploiting them.

BERN96a   BERNARD, R. *The Corporate Intranet.* New York: Wiley, 1996.
BERS96   BERSON, A. *Client/Server Architecture.* New York: McGraw-Hill, 1996.
ECKE96   ECKEL, G. *Intranet Working.* Indianapolis, IN: New Riders, 1996.
EVAN96   EVANS, T. *Building an Intranet.* Indianapolis, IN: Sams, 1996.
RENA96   RENAUD, P. *Introduction to Client/Server Systems.* New York: Wiley, 1996.
SIMO95   SIMON, A., and WHEELER, T. *Open Client/Server Computing and Middleware.* Chestnut Hill, MA: AP Professional Books, 1995.

Recommended Web Site

- http://www.intranetjournal.com: home of the on-line *Intranet Journal,* which includes news and features as well as links to intranet vendors and other intranet-related sites.

KEY TERMS

Applications Programming Interface (API)	Graphical User Interface (GUI)	Network News USENET
Client–Server	Intranet	
Electronic Mailing List	Middleware	

QUESTIONS

1. What is client–server computing?
2. What distinguishes client–server computing from any other form of distributed data processing?

3. Discuss the rationale for locating applications on the client, the server, or split between client and server.

4. What are fat clients and fat servers, and what are the differences in philosophy of the two approaches?

5. Suggest pros and cons for fat client and fat server strategies.

6. What is middleware?

7. Since we have standards such as TCP/IP and OSI, why is middleware needed?

8. What is an intranet?

9. What is the distinction between client–server and intranet?

BURLINGTON COAT FACTORY

Burlington Coat Factory is a fast-growing retailer offering low-priced apparel in a no-frills environment. The company's sales have doubled in the past five years, and topped $1 billion in 1992, operating out of 190 stores in 38 states. For the immediate future, Burlington has adopted a position that appears consistent with the fiscal philosophy of the 1990s [JEFF92]. The company plans to slow unit growth slightly while trying to bolster profits and analyze productivity on a unit-by-unit basis. Efficient and effective computer support is the key to this strategy. For example, a typical store offers 10,000 to 20,000 outerwear garments from as many as 300 makers. This variety dictates heavy reliance on automation of inventory control, purchasing, sales analysis, and a host of other inter-locking functions required to keep Burlington competitive.

Throughout the 1980s, Burlington relied on a traditional computer support model, based on a centralized operation with all applications running on a headquarters mainframe [ULLM93]. All store transactions were typed into a small, multiuser Altos micro (Figure 14.16). Transactions were sent via modem to an X.25 wide-area network and then to the headquarters mainframe. In addition, a number of dumb terminals were connected to network PADs (packet assembler/disassemblers); these devices were used for data queries (but not updates) of central databases.

To cut costs and to provide greater flexibility, Burlington began a migration to a client–server

FIGURE 14.16 Burlington Coat Factory: Early 1980s Configuration.

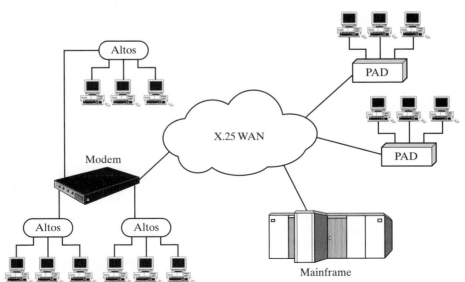

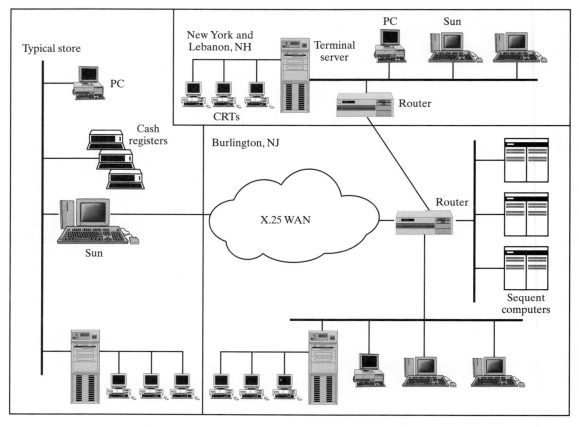

FIGURE 14.17 Burlington Coat Factory: Mid-1990s Configuration.

environment, a process that culminated in the departure of its venerable mainframe in early 1992. In this new environment (Figure 14.17), central databases and applications are maintained by a battery of six Sequent computers. The Altos systems have been replaced with IBM-compatible PCs and with powerful Sun workstations. Dumb terminals remain to provide access to central resources that does not require client–server functionality.

The company has ended up with a configuration that provides far more aggregate computing power at a reasonable cost compared to the mainframe approach. But beyond cost savings, the client–server architecture provides the company with improved range and availability of data and applications. This has changed the way peo-

ple can work with data. For example, users no longer have to ask for MIS reports, because client–server computing enables them to access the databases themselves. Users can feed information from the databases into spreadsheets or word processors on their desktop systems, integrating the remote data with local tools.

Burlington's computer applications are based virtually 100% on client–server: everything from conveyor-belt scanners that generate database transaction to graphical workstations on which decision-makes enter queries. In a typical store, the basic transactions are entered into cash registers that are MS-DOS machines. These transactions are routed to a Sun workstation that acts as a file server and a communications gateway to the central computers.

Each store is connected to the headquarters complex via a VSAT (very small aperture satellite terminal) link that employs TCP/IP over X.25. Thus, Burlington maintains its own private WAN. Through the WAN, access is provided to the host systems, which maintain central databases and other services, such as gateway to VISA/MasterCard for credit card verification.

One major benefit of this new architecture is its modularity, which makes it easy to expand the system to meet growing needs. As demand rises, Burlington can add capacity to existing servers, add more servers, and add more clients. Because all interaction is based on coordinated transactions, this growth does not require retooling existing machines and applications.

The company saw benefits from the new client–server strategy by the end of the first full year of operation [COX94], especially in meeting the demands of the 1993 holiday season. The client–server system enabled Burlington to ship products sooner, buy smarter, sell more, and open more stores. The company also found that workers are depending on the new distributed system almost completely to perform their jobs. Decision support systems that enable purchase or selling decisions based on the latest data are having a large effect on corporate revenues and are among the biggest reasons for justifying the move to a client–server architecture.

Discussion Questions

1. List some advantages of the new computing environment over the old for handling Burlington's day-to-day business.

2. With broader access provided to central databases, what security and data integrity measures should be taken to protect the database?

3. If satellite service is interrupted, the communications link between individual stores and headquarters is unavailable. What requirements does this impose on a store's computing complex?

WISCONSIN DEPARTMENT OF NATURAL RESOURCES

The Wisconsin Department of Natural Resources (DNR) has a wide scope of responsibility, ranging from resource management to gaming licenses and air- and water-quality testing. The agency maintains a networking infrastructure that connects different DNR offices and various related state agencies, federal agencies, and universities. The basic model for all the DNR applications is client–server computing [POWE96].

The DNR places great importance on the staff's comprehension of various PC hardware and software technologies. Many years ago the DNR outsourced training for its 4000 employees at a cost of about $125 per half day of class time per person, regardless of topic. The high cost and complaints on the general nature of the training led the state agency to explore in-house training. The in-house training program the DNR developed has surpassed all hopes for its success. Now in place since 1992, the curriculum has proven to be less expensive and of superior quality to that of any third-party training available. DNR updates the network configuration and the courseware continually to keep its staff up to date.

At one point DNR explored a training program based on videotape and character-based computer-based training (CBT) for much of its instruction, but this was unsatisfactory. Many attendees found the videotapes boring, and the CBT format lacked elements, such as sound full-motion video, and animation, that make self-paced courses stimulating.

DNR now bases its instructions on multimedia courseware. There are a number of off-the-shelf courses, with publishers offering extensive libraries of information technology classes. Such courseware needs a reliable and fast server, and

DNR chose an Alpha from Digital Equipment running Windows NT for this role (Figure 14.18). Courses are loded from CDs to the server. Sixty minutes of courseware consumes 500 MB of disk space. Course topics include Microsoft Office, Windows 3.1, Windows 95, Windows for Workgroups, TCP/IP, and Oracle.

The server supports a multimedia FDDI LAN with workstations that support video input. In addition, the server is hooked into the department's wide-area network to provide access to users at other state sites. The client workstations are Pentium PCs running Windows for Workgroups. Each workstation has 24 MB of RAM, a 21-inch Viewsonic monitor, its own CD-ROM and disk drives, and a Realmagic MPEG decoder for compressed video input.

The NT server has lived up to its hype, proving to be a very efficient and effective operating system with good tools for managing system resources and access. As a result, installation and maintenance has been handled in-house. This lessens users' reliance on technical support staff for installations, upgrades, and routine problem resolution.

Most courses require between two and four CDs, and each takes 30 minutes to load. It takes only a few minutes to create the files for the front end, however. With all 12 clients viewing active MPEG video streams, utilization has proven to be surprisingly low—just 25% of the processor, LAN capacity, and server memory.

Disk utilization approaches 65 to 70% if all 12 clients are served off a single disk. This is close to the levels typically viewed as the point at which saturation occurs and disk performance can be expected to decline. DNR avoids this problem by using additional channels and by configuring the data on an array of disks to distribute the load.

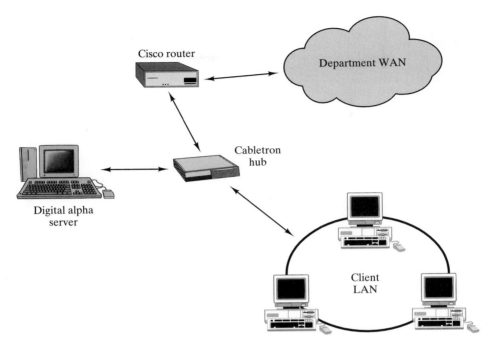

FIGURE 14.18 Network at Wisconsin Department of Natural Resources.

With this design the current configuration can support more than 30 clients.

The application software includes a data capture function to track user activity. The DNR uses the data for billing, updating personnel training records, and tracking use of the courseware. Based on an analysis of historical data and the anticipated volume of training, manually performing course registration, courseware checkout, and courseware return would require the equivalent of one full-time employee.

Discussion Questions

1. List the various ways of providing in-house training on the topics covered by DNR. Is the multimedia approach selected by DNR a good choice?

2. Discuss performance issues related to design of the courseware network.

PART 5

MANAGEMENT ISSUES

CHAPTER 15

Doing Business on the Internet

CHAPTER OBJECTIVES

After reading this chapter, you should be able to:

- Explain why the Internet is, potentially, an attractive market.

- Identify and discuss the different modes of commerce on the Internet.

- Describe the applications of the Internet that can be used for commerce.

- Explain the importance of the World Wide Web to Internet commerce.

- Identify what is needed to make the World Wide Web useful for commerce.

- Understand the role of security and privacy in Internet commerce.

- List the payment functions needed to support commercial use of the Internet.

- Understand the role of payment systems in Internet commerce.

On very rare occasions, technology dramatically transforms the way we live our lives; examples include the printing press, the automobile, integrated circuitry, and fiber optic communications. The Internet, and more specifically its World Wide Web (WWW or the Web) service, may be such a transforming technology. The Web has made an already exponentially growing phenomenon, the Internet, into an even-faster-growing one, causing a transformation from a techy sandbox into a popular fad. But it will last.

In 1969, the Internet began as ARPANET with four nodes. Today the number of hosts is in the millions, the number of users in the tens of millions, and the number of countries participating is nearing 200. The number of connections to the Internet has roughly doubled each year for the last 15 years (Figure 15.1). The Web started in 1989, with the first popular browser appearing in 1992, and it is growing at exponential rates as well. Obviously, the Web offers great commercial opportunities. Today you cannot avoid advertisements and product packaging with Web addresses on them. But doing business on the Internet is different from standard commercial practice. Obviously, commercial opportunities

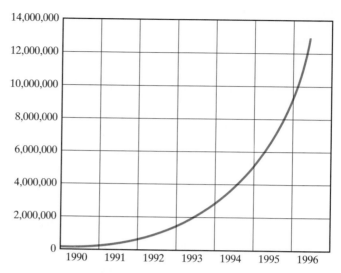

FIGURE 15.1 Number of Internet Hosts.

abound, but dangers to established companies are no fewer. Companies as large and powerful as AT&T, IBM, and Microsoft have seen careful and extensive marketing plans made worthless in a period of months by the Web phenomenon. However, novel technological advances in communications, encryption, privacy, and payment systems are essential to realization of Internet commerce. We will look at all these issues and more, but first we look at how the Internet came to be.

15.1 THE INTERNET

The Internet evolved from the ARPANET, which was developed in 1969 by the Advanced Research Projects Agency (ARPA) of the U.S. Department of Defense. It was the first operational packet-switched network. ARPANET began operations in four locations: UCLA, University of Santa Barbara, the University of Utah, and SRI (Stanford Research Institute). Previously, the two primary paradigms for electronic communications were *circuit switching* (essentially, voice communication; see Section 7.3), and *message switching* (telegraph and telex). In circuit switching (Figure 15.2), if source S was to communicate with destination D, through a network a dedicated path of transmission facilities would be established (S, a, c, e, D) connecting S to D. All of these facilities would be held for the duration of the "call." In particular, if there are lulls in the conversation, the path of facilities would remain unused during these periods. On the other hand, after the connection is established there is minimal delay through the network. Moreover, once the call was set up, the network could basically be passive. Since switching was often electromechanical, this was a big plus.

In message switching, a message is sent from S to D in stages (see Figure 15.2). First the transmission facility from S to a might be seized and the message transmitted from S to a, where it is stored temporarily. At this point the S to a channel is released. Then a channel from a to c is accessed and the message is

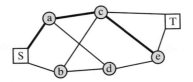

(a) Circuit switching holds all channels

Message switching

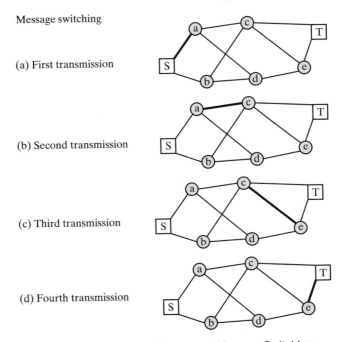

(a) First transmission

(b) Second transmission

(c) Third transmission

(d) Fourth transmission

FIGURE 15.2 Circuit Switching versus Message Switching.

sent to *c*, and so on. In this case the transmission channels are used only when they are needed, not wasted when they are not needed. In exchange for this more efficient use of transmission, the delay can be substantial and quite variable. The messages were frequently stored at each intermediate location on slow peripheral processors such as disks, magnetic drums, or in the early days, on punched paper tapes. These peripherals are slow. Moreover, each time the message is transmitted, a transmission time equal to the length of the message divided by the channel's data rate was incurred, so very long messages would incur very long delays on each hop. There would be one such delay for each hop on the path connecting the source to the destination, so the delay due to transmissions would vary widely depending on the length of the message and the number of hops on the path connecting source to destination.

Packet switching is a special case of message switching with special properties. First the transmitted data unit, the packet, was limited in length, say, to about 1000 bits. If a message was bigger than the maximum packet size, it would be broken up into a number of packets. Second, when the packets were passed from switch to switch they were stored in high-speed random access memory (RAM) rather than in the slower peripherals ordinarily used in message-switching systems. This idea had several obvious advantages. The delay was much shorter. The delay of the first packet to arrive would be only the transmission time of the first packet times the number of hops on the path used. The subsequent packets would follow in sequence immediately behind. If high-speed channels were used, the delay, even across the United States, would be a few hundred milliseconds. The ARPANET used 50-kbps links. Thus for a path with five or fewer hops and a packet length of less than 1000 bits, the transmission time would be less than $1000 \times 8/50,000 = 0.16$ sec. At the same time, the channels were used as efficiently as for message switching. Despite its obvious advantages (the idea was being explored at the National Physics Laboratory in England at about the same time), it probably could not have been implemented effectively except for the recent development of large-scale-integrated circuitry, especially the microprocessor, which made the rapid and computationally intensive switching possible.

The ARPANET technology offered other new advantages. When circuit switching is used for data transmission it is essential that the data rates of the transmitting device and the receiving device be the same. With packet switching this was not necessary. A packet could be sent at the data rate of the transmitting device into the network, travel through the network at a variety of different data rates, usually higher than the transmitter's rate, and then be metered out at the data rate that the receiver was expecting. The packet-switched network and its interfaces can buffer backed-up data to make speed conversion from a higher rate to a lower one possible. It was not just differing data rates that made interconnections difficult at the time of ARPANET's invention; the complete lack of open communication standards made it virtually impossible for a computer made by one manufacturer to communicate electronically with a computer made by another. Of particular interest to its military sponsors, ARPANET also offered adaptive routing. Each packet, individually, was routed to its destination by whatever route seemed fastest at the time of its transmission. Thus, if parts of the network got congested or failed, packets would automatically be routed around the obstacles.

Some of the early applications developed for the ARPANET also offered new functionality. The first two important applications were TELNET and FTP. The first, TELNET, provided a *lingua franca* for remote computer terminals. When the ARPANET was introduced, each different computer system needed a different terminal. The TELNET application provided a common-denominator terminal. If software was written for each type of computer to support the "TELNET terminal," one terminal could interact with all computer types. The file transport protocol (FTP) offered a similar open functionality. FTP allowed the transparent transfer of files from one computer to the other over the network. This is not as trivial as it may sound since various computers had different word sizes, stored their bits in different orders, and used different word formats. However, the first "killer ap" for the ARPANET was electronic mail. Before

ARPANET there were electronic mail systems, but they were all single-computer systems. In 1972, Ray Tomlinson of Bolt Beranek and Newman (BBN) wrote the first system to provide distributed mail service across a computer network using multiple computers. As early as 1973, an ARPA study had found that three-fourths of all ARPANET traffic was E-mail [HAFN96].

The technology was so successful that ARPA applied the same packet-switching technology to tactical radio communication (Packet Radio) and to satellite communication (SATNET). Because the three networks operated in very different communication environments, the appropriate values for certain parameters such as maximum packet size were different in each case. Faced with the dilemma of integrating these networks, Vint Cerf and Bob Kahn of ARPA started to develop methods and protocols for *internetting*, that is, communicating across arbitrary, multiple, packet-switched networks. They published a very influential paper in May 1974 [CERF74] outlining their approach to a transmission control protocol. The proposal was refined and details filled in by the ARPANET community, with major contributions from participants from European networks such as Cyclades (France) and EIN, eventually leading to the TCP and IP protocols, which, in turn, formed the basis for what eventually became the TCP/IP protocol suite. This provided the foundation for the Internet. In 1982–1983, ARPANET converted from the original NCP protocol to TCP/IP. Many networks then were connected using this technology throughout the world. Nevertheless, use of the ARPANET was generally restricted to ARPA contractors.

National Science Foundation Takes on a Role

Then NSF extended support to other computer science research groups with CSNET in 1980–1981; in 1986, NSF extended Internet support to all the disciplines of the general research community with the NSFNET backbone. Originally, NSFNET was designed to interconnect six NSF-funded supercomputer centers across the country and the centers to supercomputer users nationwide. Eventually, NSF offered interconnection through its backbone to regional packet-switched networks across the country. In 1990 the ARPANET was shut down.

Acceptable Use Policies

The astonishing growth of the Internet did not go unnoticed by the commercial world. However, in many countries (including the United States up until 1995) the national governments subsidized the Internet backbone for their countries. Many of these governments have *acceptable use* policies that limit commercial activities; often, Internet communications over these facilities are limited to research and educational use. Since NSF was subsidizing the Internet backbone in the United States, there was strong feeling by some that the use of the backbone should be restricted to research, education, and government use. This was codified in a voluntary acceptable use policy for the Internet (Table 15-1). The "culture" of the Internet also imposed additional informal limitations on commercial uses.

TABLE 15-1 NSFNET Backbone Services Acceptable Use Policy (June 1992)

General Principle

1. NSFNET backbone services are provided to support open research and education in and among U.S. research and instructional institutions, plus research arms of for-profit firms when engaged in open scholarly communication and research. Use for other purposes is not acceptable.

Specifically Acceptable Uses

2. Communication with foreign researchers and educators in connection with research or instruction, as long as any network that the foreign user employs for such communication provides reciprocal access to U.S. researchers and educators.
3. Communication and exchange for professional development, to maintain currency, or to debate issues in a field or subfield of knowledge.
4. Use for disciplinary-society, university-association, government-advisory, or standards activities related to the user's research and instructional activities.
5. Use in applying for or administering grants or contracts for research or instruction but not for other fund-raising or public relations activities.
6. Any other administrative communications or activities in direct support of research and instruction.
7. Announcements of new products or services for use in research or instruction but not advertising of any kind.
8. Any traffic originating from a network of another member agency of the Federal Networking Council if the traffic meets the acceptable use policy of that agency.
9. Communication incidental to otherwise acceptable use, except for illegal or specifically unacceptable use.

Unacceptable Uses

10. Use for for-profit activities, unless covered by the General Principle or as a specifically acceptable use.
11. Extensive use for private or personal business.

This statement applies to use of the NSFNET Backbone only. NSF expects that connecting networks will formulate their own use policies. The NSF Division of Networking and Communications Research and Infrastructure will resolve any questions about this policy or its interpretation.

NSFNET backbone services are provided to support open research and education in and among U.S. research and instructional institutions, plus research arms of for-profit firms when engaged in open scholarly communication and research. User for other purposes is prohibited.

Internet Interconnection Points

In 1991, General Atomics, which operated CERFnet (a California regional network), Performance Systems International, operating PSINet (a commercial spin-off from New York's regional network, NYSERnet), and UUNET technologies, a commercial internet service provider that owned Alternet, provided nearly all the commercial TCP/IP services in the United States. On their own networks, since they did not use the NSF backbone, they were not subject to NSF's acceptable use policy. However, to communicate between their networks they had been using the NSF backbone, which brought them under the policy. To get around this problem they formed the Commercial Information Interchange (CIX). Originally, it was a mechanism for the networks of the three founders to interchange traffic carried on their networks at a U.S. west coast router so that each network's customers would have access to customers on other's networks at no extra

FIGURE 15.3 U.S. Internet Access Points.

charge. As other providers entered the market, they too found the concept useful and joined the exchange. By 1996, CIX had 147 member networks. One feature of the CIX is that there are no *settlements*, that is, no **traffic-based** fees for use of the interchange. A similar interconnection point was formed in 1994 in England, the London Internet Exchange (LINX); in 1996, it had 24 member networks. Also in 1991, the U.S. government announced that it would no longer subsidize the Internet after 1995. As part of the privatization plan, the government mandated interconnection points called *network access points*. There are now three, near New York, Chicago, and San Francisco, respectively. There are also metropolitan area exchanges, MAE East and MAE West (Figure 15.3). When the U.S. government privatized the national backbone in 1995, at least the U.S. part of the Internet was opened to virtually unlimited commercial activity. For the last several years the commercial domain, ".com," has been the fastest-growing, outstripping the educational domain, ".edu," which previously dominated Internet host registrations.

The World Wide Web

In the spring of 1989, at CERN (the European Laboratory for Particle Physics), Tim Berners-Lee proposed the idea of a distributed hypermedia technology to facilitate the international exchange of research findings using the Internet. Almost exactly two years later a prototype World Wide Web (WWW or the Web, for short) was developed at CERN using the NeXT computer as a platform. By the end of 1991, they released a line-oriented *browser* or reader to a limited population. But the really explosive growth of the technology came with the development at the first *graphically* oriented browser, *Mosaic*, developed at the NCSA Center at the University of Illinois by Mark Andreasson and others in 1993. Two million copies of Mosaic were delivered over the Internet. Today, less than a decade later, the characteristic Web addresses, the URLs, are ubiquitous. One

TABLE 15-2 Number of Web Sites

Date	Number of Web Sites	Percent .com Sites
6/93	130	1.5
12/93	623	4.6
6/94	2,738	13.5
12/94	10,022	18.3
6/95	23,500	31.3
1/96	100,000	50
6/96 (est.)	230,000	NA[a]

Source: Matthew Gray of MIT, URL = http://www.mit.edu:8001/people/mkgray/net/.
[a] *NA, not available.*

cannot read a newspaper or watch TV without seeing the addresses everywhere. Table 15-2 shows the exponential growth of the WWW. It also shows the increased commercial use of the Web.

The Web is a system consisting of an internationally distributed collection of *multimedia files* supported by clients (users) and servers (information providers). Each file is addressed in a consistent manner using its *universal resource locator (URL)*. The files from the providers are viewed by the clients using *browsers* such as Mosaic, Netscape Navigator, or Microsoft's Internet Explorer. Most common browsers have graphical display and support multimedia: text, audio, image, video. The user can move from file to file by clicking with a mouse or other pointing device on specially highlighted text or image elements on the browser display; the transfer from one file to the next is called a *hyperlink*. The layout of the browser display is controlled by the *Hyptertext Markup Language* (HTML) standard, which defines embedded commands in text files which specify features of the browser display, such as the fonts, colors, images, and their placement on the display, and the location of the locations where the user can invoke the hyperlinks and their targets. The last important feature of the Web is the hypertext transfer protocol (HTTP), which is a communications protocol for use in TCP/IP networks for fetching the files from the appropriate servers as specified by the hyperlinks. For more, see Section 13.3.

What the Internet Looks Like Today

Users now ordinarily connect to the Internet through an Internet service provider (ISP). For home users the provider is often one of the major on-line services such as American Online and Compuserve. Today, most residential users connect to the ISPs over voice-grade lines using modems at data rates of, at most, 28.8 kbps using PPP or SLIP. This is perfectly adequate for E-mail and related services but marginal for graphics-intensive Web surfing. The most available migration path to increased bandwidth is through ISDN, which, in the simplest case, can support connections at up to 128 kbps (Section 7.6). However, availability is spotty. Further in the future, cable TV companies are developing cable modems that will be able to operate at a peak rate in the low megabits per second range, although the channels will be shared among users.

Users who connect to the Internet through their work often use workstations or PCs connected to their employer-owned LANs, which in turn connect through shared organizational trunks to an ISP. In these cases, the shared circuit is often a T-1 connection, while for very large organizations T-3 connections are sometimes found. Smaller organizations may use 56-kbps or ISDN connections.

The ISPs are connected by "wholesalers," which we can call network service providers. They, in turn, interconnect using Internet connection points such as CIX, MAE East and West, and the network access points (Figure 15.3). The network service providers use transmission at T-3 rates, with some moving up to ATM connections at rates 155 Mbps up to, in the future, 622 Mbps.

The commercial uses of the Internet came in stages. In the early days, limited by the access rules of the ARPANET and later, by the acceptable usage policy, commercial use was limited to R&D or other technical units using the Net for research and educational uses, although some informational activities that could be considered marketing where carried on under the name of research and education. When the Internet was privatized in 1995, the first new applications were mainly informational ones for sales and marketing information and public relations. EDI transactions for intercompany invoices, billing, and the like, which were originally designed for use on dedicated wide-area networks and commercial public networks, began to be carried on the Internet. Commercial networks, especially Compuserve, have long played a customer service role by providing bulletin board services dealing with technical and usage problems in using products. These activities were gradually extended to the Internet as well. The most tempting activity is direct sales to the tens of millions of Internet users throughout the world. However, the initial infrastructure of the Internet did not support online transactions well. There were three limitations: lack of an easy-to-use graphical user interface, lack of security, and lack of effective payment systems. The most popular and easy-to-use interface, the World Wide Web and its browsers, did not become commonly available until 1994. In its early incarnations there was very little support to allow the client browser to submit information (forms) to the server. Moreover, there were not many options for payment for on-line ordering, and all the options were insecure. One obvious payment method is to use credit card accounts. However, most people are uncomfortable about sending credit card numbers over the Internet, with good reason, because of the lack of security. For example, if the credit card information is not encrypted it is very easy to "listen in" on Internet communications. Moreover, several files of customers' credit card numbers on merchants' computers have been compromised. The ease of collecting and integrating information on customer transactions when they are in electronic form also raises privacy concerns for customers. One of the hottest application areas in financial information systems is "data mining," which often involves collecting large amounts of customer transaction information to improve the targeting of marketing efforts. These limitations are beginning to be ameliorated. The latest browsers support communication with the server by the user filling in forms.

Secure on-line credit card transactions do not address one of the most tempting markets on the Internet. Huge volumes of free information are available on the Internet. Especially in the early years, the information was made available through the intellectual openness and enthusiasm of its initial participants, fed by the psychic benefits of having an audience for one's words. But another reason so much information is free is that there is no effective way to charge the relatively small amounts that would be involved in buying such information. Many Net surfers would gladly pay a few cents for useful information to compensate the contributor for his or her effort. Given the many people using the Net, the accumulated gross sales could be quite large for popular information even if each individual charge was modest. However, the cost of a credit card transaction for each sale would dwarf a reasonable price for the information. What is needed is a *micropayment* system.

15.2 SECURITY FOR COMMERCE ON THE INTERNET

Perhaps the greatest barrier to mass retail electronic commerce on the Internet is its lack of security. Many initiatives have been proposed to deal with the problem. We consider two general-purpose approaches that are broadly representative and probably the most important as well: the Secure Socket Layer (SSL) from Netscape and Secure HTTP (S-HTTP) from Enterprise Integration Technology. In the next section we consider two *payment systems* that provide strong security for Internet purchases of goods and services. The first is Secure Electronic Transactions (SET), proposed for bankcard transactions by MasterCard and Visa. The second is a more sophisticated payment system that attempts to emulate many of the properties of cash transactions, particularly in anonymity. The system is E-cash, invented by David Chaum and marketed and developed by DigiCash in Amsterdam.

Secure Socket Layer

Of the four systems, Secure Socket Layer (SSL) provides security at the lowest level of the protocol hierarchy. The security furnished is transparent to the user; it is provided at a level just above the basic TCP/IP service. Software using TCP often specifies a "socket" at each end of a communication which maps the software processes at each end to the communication. At this level SSL can encrypt all communication between the sockets on the fly and transparently. Therefore, it can support security for virtually any Internet application. In particular, electronic mail, TELNET, and FTP transactions as well as Web interchanges can be protected using SSL. SSL provides security on a link or channel basis for client–server interactions of general type rather than on a document or transaction basis. Netscape developed this protocol and implemented it in their browsers. It has been submitted as an Internet draft.

Most of the SSL process is involved with the initial exchange of information (handshake) to set up the secure channel. The protocol begins with the client requesting authentication from the server. The request from the client specifies the encryption algorithms it understands and also has some challenge text. (Challenge text is essentially random material that is returned in encrypted material to prevent retransmission of earlier ciphertext, which would have different challenge text.) The authentication that is returned by the server is in the form of a certificate with a public-key signature of the server. The authentication also includes the server's preferences for encryption algorithms. The client then generates a master key and encrypts with the server's public key and sends the result to the server. The server then returns a message encrypted with the master key. This key is used to generate the keys used to send messages. There is an optional second part to this handshake process in which the customer is authenticated to the server. To do this, the server sends a "challenge" message to the client. The client authenticates itself by returning a message with the client's digital signature on the challenge as well as its public-key certificate. The digital signatures used in the initialization are based on RSA public-key encryption. However, after the handshaking is completed, several (single-key) encryption systems can be used including DES, Triple DES, and IDEA (see Chapter 17). To obtain a document from a server using an SSL secured channel, another access method, https, is used; that is, one simply uses "https" in the URL instead of "http."

Secure HTTP

Secure HTTP (S-HTTP) was developed by Enterprise Integration Technology (EIT) as part of the CommerceNet Project in Silicon Valley but has been released as a public specification. EIT first proposed the system publicly in an Internet Draft in June 1994. Terisa Systems is now developing this technology. The system provides security enhancements to the Web transport standard, hypertext transfer protocol (HTTP). It allows client and server to negotiate independently encryption, authentication, and digital signature methods, in any combination, in both directions. It supports a variety of encryption algorithms, including RSA, MOSS, PGP, DES cipher block chaining, triple DES, and others (see Chapter 17). The use of S-HTTP begins with an exchange of messages that specify security management information such as the encryption, hash, and signature algorithms to be used in each direction. These can be specified separately for header and content information. S-HTTP can provide confidentiality, authentication, integrity guarantees, and nonrepudiability on an individual file basis. Table 15-3 shows a representative header block for a server given as an illustration in the May 1996 Internet draft. The first instruction states that the server will accept at the sender's option MOSS or PKCS-7, which are two methods of encapsulating message parts that are treated cryptographically. The second instruction

TABLE 15-3 Secure HTTP Sample Header

```
SHTTP-Privacy-Domains: recv-optional=MOSS, PKCS-7;
     orig-required=PKCS-7
SHTTP-Certificate-Types: recv-optional=X.509;
     orig-required=X.509
STTP-Key-Exchange-Algorithms: recv-required=RSA;
     orig-optional=Inband,RSA
SHTTP-Signature-Algorithms: orig-required=RSA;
     recv-required=RSA
SHTTP-Privacy-Enhancements: orig-required=sign;
     orig-optional=encrypt
```

states that the certificates may be in the ITU X.509 format in the direction from the client to the server, and is mandatory from server to client. The third instruction characterizes the key exchange method. For client to server the RSA method is mandatory, while from server to client RSA can be used or keys can be sent in-band. The in-band option allows the proving of privacy enhancements when only one of the parties has a public-key pair. This is important for spontaneous transactions. The fourth instruction indicates that RSA is required in both directions for digital signatures. The last instruction indicates the services to be used are authentication, signature, and/or encryption. In this case the server announces that it will send a signature and may encrypt. Several other specifications are made implicitly through defaults. At least in principle, S-HTTP can ride on top of SSL (see Figure 15.4).

15.3 ELECTRONIC PAYMENT SYSTEMS

The basic purpose of money is to make it possible for the provider and consumer of a good or service to perform their half of a transaction (delivery of the good or service, and the acceptance of it, respectively) at different places and different times. This avoids the necessity of face-to-face real-time bartering to accomplish trade. Moreover, the use of money distributes trade. Thus, if a maker of chairs needs some eggs to cook for breakfast, the chairmaker does not have to look for someone who both has hens and wants a chair in order to have breakfast. Using money, the chairmaker can sell her chairs to a chair buyer, long before breakfast time, and use the money to buy eggs when she needs them.

The relation of a monetary system to barter is analogous to the relation of electronic mail to face-to-face conversation. If Alice, who lives in Tokyo, wishes to communicate with Bob, who lives in New York, electronic mail allows them to communicate at a great distance and at different times.

FIGURE 15.4 Layered Security Mechanisms.

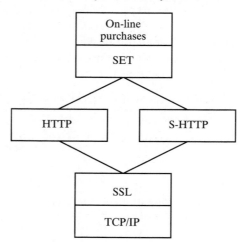

Often, it is inconvenient or unsafe to transfer large sums of money or to be physically in the same place to transfer money. A payment system provides mechanisms for transferring *money* or *money equivalents* from place to place and time to time. Common types of nonelectronic payment systems are cash, checks, credit cards, debit cards, and electronic funds transfers.

The Internet provides a massive potential market. It is used effectively for advertising, customer service, and many other commercial activities today. But to make money directly (i.e., to make large-scale retail sales), an effective electronic payment system is necessary. The lack of such a system is the largest impediment to making money directly through retail activities on the Internet. Related to the lack of effective electronic payment systems is the other major barrier to commercial use of the Internet: security. The very benefits of the Internet—its broad distribution, its accessibility, its electronic speeds—make it a dangerous place to do business. Thus, it is not surprising that the security mechanisms discussed in Section 15.2 and in Chapter 17 play major roles in electronic payment systems.

We will discuss mainly financial transactions that are between a vendor and a consumer. Other kinds of transactions, such as those between large customers and their suppliers, will have established procedures for payment that may well already be electronic through electronic fund transfer (EFT), EDI (Section 13.2), or other means. For established financial relations, standard methods are in place for checking creditworthiness and other parameters of the transaction which do not differ markedly from nonelectronic transactions. But a casual transaction between a consumer who may not have dealt with the vendor previously poses new problems.

Many electronic payment systems have been proposed for on-line commerce. Undoubtedly, there will be a substantial shake-out, with many of the proposals falling by the wayside. Nevertheless, several systems will remain, because there are applications with different requirements. In this section we introduce SET (Secure Electronic Transactions), which is being developed by MasterCard and Visa to map bankcard transactions onto the Internet. This will make possible the on-line use of already existing banking relationships embodied in credit and debit cards. This is perhaps the most straightforward transition from current practice to on-line sales of products and services. However, there are payment applications that can be met better in other ways. For example, cash has many virtues that would also be attractive on the Internet. David Chaum and his Digi-Cash proposal address many of these. One important and controversial aspect of cash is its anonymity—cash does not ordinarily leave an audit trail. Another natural marketing opportunity on the Internet is the offering of information, much of which is now offered free, for lack of a payment mechanism, to Internet "surfers." It is essential that the overhead of the payment system be very modest so as to not dwarf the fees that can be charged. Such payment systems are called *micropayment systems.* After some general remarks on on-line payment systems we will look at DigiCash's E-cash system as an example of a sophisticated electronic cash system.

Characteristics of On-Line Payment Systems

We first look at what aspects characterize an on-line payment system. We can characterize a system by five aspects: (1) by the type of transactions supported, (2) by the means of settlement, (3) by the operational characteristics, (4) by privacy and security characteristics, and (5) by who takes on what risks.

Transaction Types   Relevant transaction characteristics are whether the system supports micropayments, large payments, and transactions that are consummated immediately, such as deliver of on-line information for payment, as opposed to transactions in which delivery is at a later date.

Means of Settlement   At least in the near term, tokens that are delivered for payment must be backed by traditional forms of money and money substitutes, such as cash, credit (presumably from banks or other traditional lending agencies, perhaps through bankcards—credit and debit cards), and electronic funds transfer.

Operational Characteristics   Payment systems can be on-line systems or off-line systems. That is, when a customer attempts to consummate a transaction, does there have to be an active on-line connection to a financial institution or other third party to validate the payment? This can often be inconvenient. However, on the other hand, systems involving secured and tamperproof devices that can store money without requiring on-line verification raise significant security issues. Another operational issue is whether the customer and the merchant need to have a preexisting business relationship or will the payment system support "impulse" buying. For example, does the customer have to have a key certificate before using the system? When does the user of a token pay for it? Prepayment is used in smart cards and electronic purses that store money. The money can be paid on a debit basis; that is, the user's "account" is debited at the time of the transaction. Finally, the user can pay on a credit or postpaid basis, where the payment is made at some time after the transaction. Credit cards and electronic checks are mechanisms of that type.

Privacy and Security   How much privacy should the system provide? Should an audit trail be provided for all transactions? What happens when a token is "lost"? Is secrecy of the contents at issue, authentication, nonrepudiation?

Who Takes Risks?   What happens if no one will accept the tokens? If the token is submitted for payment, suppose the delivery is not made or is unsatisfactory?

Complications   The power of modern cryptography promises to make electronic payment systems more reliable in many ways than the traditional systems they replace. However, intrinsic to on-line systems are challenges that must be dealt with. For, example, on-line "money" is basically information, and information can be replicated endlessly. Often, there may be no tangible, physical record of the transaction, only transitory electronic phenomena. Also, the Internet now connects nearly 200 countries, and there is little to limit on-line commerce between any of the countries. This gives rise to sovereignty issues, foreign exchange risk, and problems of resolving disputes.

Secure Electronic Transactions

Secure electronic transactions (SET) is a payment protocol sponsored by MasterCard International and Visa International with a number of technology partners, including GTE, IBM, Microsoft, Netscape, SAIC, Terisa Systems, and VeriSign, to support the payment for goods and services over the Internet using bankcards (credit and debit cards). It is being developed as an open industry standard and current specifications can be obtained from the Web pages of MasterCard and Visa (http://www.mastercard.com/ and http://www.visa.com/). It was announced in February 1996, and the third revision of the standard was announced in June 1996. It uses RSA public-key encryption technology and DES single-key technology (see Chapter 17). The idea is that software developers will develop software implementing SET which will be tested by MasterCard and Visa for conformance.

Figure 15.5 shows the participants of SET and their relations. The *cardholder*, the *merchant*, and the merchant's *financial institution* are involved directly in the payment process. In addition, *certificate authorities* are needed to handle the public-key authentication and related issues. It should be noted that the SET protocol provides for secrecy and other security features only for the *financial* information. *Order* information will be protected by other means.

Cardholder   The SET "cardholder" is actually the workstation of the person holding the card. This workstation can support all the activities outlined in Table 15-4, but SET is concerned only with the financial aspects in steps 5, 6, and 8. The

FIGURE 15.5 Participants and Interactions.

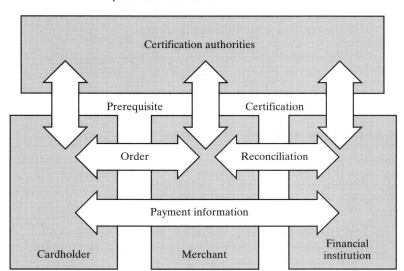

TABLE 15-4 Model for Electronic Shopping

1. **Shopping and browsing**
   The cardholder will use electronic shopping and browsing tools to locate merchants offering the desired item(s) much as advertisements and telephone directories are used today.

2. **Item and merchant selection**
   Using the information gained in step 1, the cardholder selects the item(s) and the merchant.

3. **Ordering and negotiation**
   The cardholder fills in and reviews the electronic order form to verify the items ordered and their prices. Discounts and other special options for payment and price may be negotiated at this point based on quantity ordered and other circumstances.

4. **Payment selection**
   The cardholder and the merchant agree on means of payment.

5. **Payment authorization and transport**[a]
   The cardholder initiates payment. This is where SET begins.

6. **Confirmation and delivery**[a]
   When the merchant receives the purchase request from the cardholder, the merchant requests authorization from SET. The merchant also sends a confirmation and status report to the cardholder.

7. **Delivery of goods**
   When the authorization is received, the merchant ships the item(s) to the cardholder.

8. **Merchant reimbursement**[a]
   After the items are shipped, the merchant may use SET to initiate a request for reimbursement.

[a] *Steps handled by SET.*

cardholder workstation deals with SET through its connection to the merchant (Figure 15.5). The cardholder also communicates indirectly through the merchant with the merchant's financial institution. In fact, data fields sent to the financial institution via the merchant are encrypted with the financial institution's public key so that the merchant cannot view them. One virtue of this is that the financial institution can then provide assurance that the cardholder is dealing with a card-approved merchant. The cardholder also may deal directly with a certification authority for public-key certificates.

Merchant   The merchant connects with the cardholder. It also connects with its financial institution for authorization and reimbursement. The merchant also requests its public key certificates and its renewals to support security functions from the Merchant Certificate Authority (MCA).

Certificate Authority Hierarchy   SET calls for a trusted hierarchy of certificate authorities that begins with a root certificate authority (RCA), which certifies brand-specific certificate authorities (BCAs), which may in turn certify geopolitical certificate authorities (GCAs).

Security Services   SET uses both single and public key cryptography to protect the confidentiality of its financial information. Optionally, confidential communication between the merchant's financial institution back to the cardholder can be provided for indicating reasons for transactions being declined, or to request the cardholder to call the issuer of its card. Authentication using digital signatures, and integrity guarantees using hashing algorithms, are provided. However, nonrepudiation is not supplied.

Certificates In general, certificates authenticate the public key as belonging to a particular entity: cardholder, merchant, or financial institution. The public/private key pairs are generally used for digital signatures (see Chapter 17). SET uses the ITU standard for certificates, X.509. In the case of the cardholder, the signature certificate, if the cardholder has one, effectively binds the public key to the cardholder's primary account number. However, cryptographic methods are used to obscure the account number from all but the cardholder's certificate authority, and the issuing financial institution. Moreover, even the cardholder's name is kept private from all but the foregoing entities. The merchant needs two certificates, one to sign its messages, another to exchange keys with. The merchant's financial institution needs two also. To get a certificate the cardholder requests one from the cardholder certificate authority (CCA). The CCA responds with an encryption certificate for the cardholder to use when transmitting its account number to the CCA. The CCA responds with a certificate registration form appropriate for the payment card being used. The cardholder completes the registration and returns it to the CCA, along with the cardholder's public key. The CCA verifies the information with the issuing financial institution. It then generates the certificate and sends it to the cardholder. Similar, but somewhat simpler procedures are used by the merchant to get its certificates from the merchant certifying authority. Certificates for both the cardholder and the merchant are renewed periodically. Certificate revocation lists are used to inform parties of certificates that have been revoked because they have been compromised, information contained in the certificate has been changed, the authorization is terminated, or for other reasons. Table 15-4 summarizes the important steps in electronic shopping. SET deals with payment authorization and transport, confirmation and inquiry, and merchant reimbursement.

To use SET, one needs SET-enabled software, presumably a browser, and an account with a financial institution that supports SET. From the user's point of view, a user can choose products and/or services to buy at a Web site and order them simply using the browser's graphical user interface. Table 15-5 gives the steps involved behind the scenes.

Electronic Cash

Electronic or digital cash ideally should have the following characteristics [SCHN96]:

1. *Independence.* The security of E-cash should not be dependent on its physical location, and it should be possible to communicate it over electronic networks.
2. *Security.* It should not be possible to copy or reuse the money.
3. *Privacy.* The privacy of the user should be protected so that the relationship between the user and the user's purchases should not be traceable.

TABLE 15-5 SET Procedure

I. Prior Arrangements
    1. The customer opens an account with a financial institution that supports electronic payments using SET.
    2. The customer receives a certificate which acts like a bankcard for on-line transactions. It includes the user's public key. The certificate is digitally signed by the customer's financial institution to validate the certificate.
    3. Merchants also have certificates for digital signatures and key exchanges, respectively, signed by its financial institution to authenticate it.

II. Transaction Steps
    1. The customer places an order, by E-mail, Web browser, or other electronic means. At some point the customer has been presented by the merchant with a form summarizing the contents of the order and whatever arrangement has been made for payment, such as installment plans.
    2. The first step in the SET part of the ordering process is for the customer to send a message to the merchant indicating which brand of bankcard the customer wishes to use and requesting a copy of the merchant's certificate signed by the financial institution of the merchant with the merchant's public key and the public key of the merchant's financial institution.
    3. The merchant returns a message with a transaction number and the certificates requested.
    4. After verifying the certificates, the user's software then sends the merchant a signed message that contains (a) summary order information (this may be encrypted but is not required by SET), which includes a message digest signed with the customer's private key; (b) the payment information, which is encrypted with the public key of the merchant's financial institution—this has the advantage of not allowing the merchant to see the payment information, and (c) a message digest, which links together the order and payment information so that the payment cannot be used for another order, called a *dual signature*. Note that the order information in this step does not include the details of the transaction, such as amounts and types of products or services purchased; this information was exchanged (step II.1) before the SET operations were started.
    5. When the merchant receives the information it verifies the customer's digital signature and checks the signed digest to verify that the order summary was not modified. Then the merchant generates and signs a acknowledgment message responding to the customer. This message includes the merchant's public-key certificate.
    6. The merchant then contacts its financial institution to authenticate the customer.
    7. The merchant sends a message to its financial institution signed by the merchant and encrypted with the institution's public key. The message includes the payment information, including the customer's cardholder account number, still encrypted so that the merchant can't "see" it.
    8. When it receives the merchant's message, the merchant's financial institution verifies the merchant and checks the signature to make sure that the message is authentic and unmodified.
    9. The institution then turns to the payment information and opens it up using its private key. Then the institution verifies that the payment has money behind it.
    10. The bank authorizes the payment to the merchant and the merchant ships the goods.
    11. The merchant collects its reimbursement.

---

    4. *Off-line payment.* It should be possible for the user to make a purchase without the user and/or the merchant having to be connected to a third party on-line for authorization or validation.
    5. *Transferability.* It should be possible to transfer the E-cash to other users so that they can make purchases with it.
    6. *Divisibility.* It should be possible to "make change," that is, to subdivide the E-cash value into smaller amounts.

However, most systems that are proposed for actual use usually provide only a subset of the properties. The properties of electronic cash were first studied systematically by David Chaum. We look in some detail at his E-cash proposal.

E-Cash David Chaum is one of the major innovators in electronic payment systems. He has started a company, DigiCash, in Amsterdam in 1990 to commercialize some of his ideas. His *E-cash* product is an electronic payment system that seeks to emulate many of the properties of cash. Most important, his system provides, at least, the anonymity that is characteristic of cash transactions. While the cryptographic protocols that are used are sophisticated, E-cash is straightforward to use. It is easier to use than most ATM systems. The Mark Twain Bank in the United States, and financial institutions in Finland, Sweden, France, and Germany have signed on to try the system.

Each user of E-cash maintains a central E-cash account with the financial institution supporting E-cash. Each customer also has a DigiCash "Wallet" on the hard disk of his or her workstation which contains "digital coin" tokens subtracted from the account. These coins are simply packets of bits created by a digital cash algorithm.

The system is set up in such a way that if the token is spent only once, anonymity is provided in the sense that there is no way to link the user with his or her purchases. On the other hand, if the user tries to spend the money twice, with very high probability the user can be identified.

There has been a certain amount of controversy surrounding the anonymity property of digital cash and related systems. Specters of tax evasion, money laundering, untraceable kidnapping ransoms, and funding for terrorist activities have been raised as reasons for having traceability.

How to Use It We illustrate its use by following a possible scenario of its use on Windows-based PCs (http://www.digicash.com/ecash/). Before using the system the user must have an *E-cash account* with a financial institution supporting E-cash. Once the user starts her E-cash program, it runs in the background on her PC. A small window is displayed that shows the amount in E-cash "coins" stored on her hard disk; the window also has buttons arranged on a toolbar for the fundamental functions of the system.

To use E-cash to make purchases, the user needs E-cash coins on her hard drive. Withdrawing cash from your account to your hard drive is much like using an ATM machine. Upon pushing the correct button on the toolbar, a dialogue box appears. The same dialogue box is used for withdrawals and deposits, so the user indicates that she wants to withdraw money from her account to her hard disk. She then indicates the amount. In the most usual case, this is all that need be done.

Money can be spent in two ways. A payment can be requested by someone else or the user can initiate the payment herself. In the case that someone else presents a request for payment, the user simply indicates "yes," she will pay, or "no," she will not. She also has the opportunity to instruct the system to respond automatically to future similar requests. This automatic response can be qualified by the user in several different ways; she can restrict automatic payment to requests with the same account ID, the same payment amount, and/or the same payment description. Upper bounds can also be placed on the total amount paid under the instruction, the payment per request, and the number of requests to honor.

To initiate a payment, the user hits the payment icon on the E-cash toolbar and fills in the blanks, much like writing a check in the resulting dialogue box. This box also does double duty as a request for payment box. There are fields for the account ID, the amount, a description, and a pair of communication options.

The receiver of a payment has the option of depositing the "money" in the E-cash account or have the E-cash coins put on his hard drive for future use. The receiver indicates that he wishes to receive the payment (or indicates not, if he doesn't) and whether he wishes the money credited to his account or stored as E-cash coins on his hard drive. As in the other cases, there is an automatic processing option that accepts the payments and disposes of them in the same way as for the current transaction.

At any time, E-cash coins can be deposited into the user's E-cash account. The same dialogue box is used as for withdrawals. Another button on the toolbar calls up a dialogue box which displays various statements of the user's account, including payments made and payments received. It is also possible to use the system to cancel payments if the merchant has not deposited the payment. Finally, if the user's computer crashes and stored E-cash coins are lost along with records of recent transactions, another special procedure can be used to recreate the account to its proper state using records of the user's account.

How It Is Implemented   A digital coin is a string of bits stored on the user's hard drive. Each such string has an amount associated with it. A "purse" of these strings are managed by the user's E-cash software. This software determines how the collection of denominations are managed; for example, which ones are spent in a particular transaction. When the user makes a purchase by sending the appropriate E-cash coin strings to a merchant. The merchant's software automatically sends the coins to the merchant's bank for deposit. The merchant does not ship the merchandise or send a receipt until the coins are accepted by the bank.

To prevent coins from being spent more than once, the financial institution backing the coins keeps the serial numbers of each coin spent in a database. However, the original user of the coin is not associated with the serial number in the database. If the serial number of the coin that the merchant submits is already in the database, the merchant is told that he has a useless copy. On the other hand, if the number is not in the database, the financial institution informs the merchant that the coin is valid and the coins are deposited to the merchant's account.

If a user makes an E-cash payment to another user, the other user may want to have the E-cash received on her hard disk rather than deposited. The exchange in this case is the same as the process with the merchant up until the payment is accepted by the second user's financial institution; at this point, the financial institution sends back new E-cash in the same amount to the second user's hard disk. From the second user's perspective, the E-cash has simply been transferred from the first user to the second.

To make this all work by providing security for the parties concerned and privacy for the users, sophisticated cryptography techniques are needed, several of them invented and patented by David Chaum founder of DigiCash. We sketch briefly three of the most important techniques.

It is necessary to prevent the financial institution that digitally signs E-cash coins attesting to their validity from knowing the user who spent them when they are presented for payment. To do this, a "blind signature" technique is used. When the user requests a transfer from her E-cash account to E-cash coins on her hard disk, it is actually the user who generates a random number identifying the coin. Then the user's software encrypts the coin with a digital envelope which makes the coin unreadable by the financial institution. The financial institution then signs the coin digitally. The envelope is constructed so that the user can remove it without disturbing the financial institution's signature. Therefore, the financial institution will be able to recognize the coin as one that it signed when it is presented for payment but will not know which user it came from. This gives rise to at least two concerns.

First, how does the financial institution know that it is authorizing a coin of the correct amount? To accomplish this, the user actually presents a number of potential coins to her E-cash financial institution, each hidden in a separate digital envelope. The financial institution then randomly selects one of the potential coins to become the real one. The user must then provide the means to unwrap the remainder of the potential coins, the idea being that the financial institution can check to see if all but the one randomly chosen candidate coin has the right amount. Presumably, it would be prohibitively risky for the user to misstate the amount and face the high probability of being caught.

A second concern is how the financial institution prevents the user (or the merchant) from copying the bit string representing the E-cash coin and using it again. As we have already seen, the financial institution keeps a list of the serial numbers of the coins presented for redemption. However, there are two concerns. If a coin is presented twice, how does one identify the "correct" copy? For example, suppose that a merchant accepts an E-cash coin for merchandise and then gives a copy of the coin to a confederate merchant who presents it for redemption before the correct copy? Or suppose that the user presents copies of the same coin at two or more places? To deal with this, there is a cryptographic technique called *secret splitting* which allows the bank, with high probability, to identify the user if she presents copies of her coin at two or more places: If she presents it only once, her anonymity is preserved, but if she presents it more than once, it is stripped away. In the simplest form of secret sharing, a message is kept secret by being locked cryptographically with two keys so that both are needed to reveal the message. In E-cash the identification of the user of the E-cash coin is kept in n key pairs so that if both parts of any of the key pairs are available, the user is revealed. When the user submits the coin for payment, the merchant's software generates a random binary string with n bits. If the ith bit is a 0, the left half of the key pair is associated with the coin; if it is a 1, the right. If the user submits the coin again, another random string will be chosen by the second merchant. The probability that both randomly chosen strings turn out to be the same is quite small for reasonably large n. So if the financial institution receives two coins with same serial number, if they were copies submitted by the user, with high probability, the two strings of half-keys will have at least one where both halves are available, thereby identifying the user. On the other hand, if the key halves are identical, again with high probability, the merchant did the copying.

Now let us review which of the six desiderata for electronic cash E-cash satisfies. It definitely travels digitally, it resists forgery, and it offers strong privacy. However, it does not work off-line. The last two properties—transferrable to other people and capable of being divided into change—is debatable. From the outside it appears that both functionalities are offered, although in implementation both features are simulated by reissuing E-cash coins.

RECOMMENDED READING

The cryptographic protocols for electronic commerce can be somewhat intimidating; fortunately, however, computers are very good at carrying out such things. Many of the cryptographic techniques introduced here are discussed in more detail in Chapter 17. Even more comprehensive discussions can be found in [SCHN96] and [WAYN96]. [KALA96] is a comprehensive, general survey of electronic commerce. The DigiCash scenario was based on [http://www.digicash.com/publish/E-cash_intro.html]. The SET specifications are available at http://www.mastercard.com/ and http://www.visa.com/. Our description of SET was based on the third version of the specifications.

KALA96   KALAKOTA, R., and WHINSTON, A. B. *Frontiers of Electronic Commerce.* Reading, MA: Addison-Wesley, 1996.

SCHN96   SCHNEIER, B. *Applied Cryptography.* New York: Wiley, 1996.

WAYN96   WAYNER, P. *Digital Cash: Commerce on the Net.* New York: Academic Press, 1996.

KEY TERMS

Electronic Cash	Internet Service Provider	Network Access Point
Electronic Payment	(ISP)	Secure Electronic
Systems	Metropolitan Area	Transaction (SET)
Internet	Exchange	World Wide Web

QUESTIONS

1. What is the relation of the ARPANET to the Internet?
2. What are "acceptable use" policies for network use?
3. What has been the fastest growing domain of the Internet in recent years?
4. What are the most important barriers to the use of the Internet for on-line retail transactions?
5. In what layers in the protocol hierarchy do Secure Socket Layer (SSL) and Secure HTTP (S-HTTP) reside?
6. What five features characterize an on-line payment system?
7. What are the classes of participants in SET transactions?
8. What is the most controversial aspect of E-cash? Why?

CHAPTER 15

Case Study

FLORIDA DEPARTMENT OF MANAGEMENT SERVICES

*B*y the early 1990s the Florida Department of Management Service (DMS) had built up a large information systems network that served state government agencies in 10 regional sites and connected these to the data center in Tallahassee. The network was based on the use of the proprietary systems network architecture (SNA) from IBM and a mainframe at the data center that housed most of the applications.

Although relatively happy with the SNA operation, DMS saw a need to expand applications and services by providing TCP/IP capability and Internet access. The goal was met in a remarkably short time. Over the course of 30 months, DMS built a statewide TCP/IP network, began offering Internet services to local and state agencies, and created a suite of Internet applications that will ultimately move personnel, accounting, and billing systems on-line [JOHN96b]. To complete the success story, DMS managed to accomplish all that while saving the state of Florida more than $4 million. The breakdown is shown below.

The aim of this upgrade was to exploit the Internet. Internet connectivity, together with key Internet applications such as the Web, could make it easier for agencies across the state to communicate with each other, with suppliers,

and with users, thereby improving employee productivity.

IP Infrastructure

The first step was to build an IP infrastructure. The then-current configuration, based on SNA, made heavy use of telephone-company (telco)-supplied equipment and services. DMS considered the possibility of outsourcing the IP capability but rejected this for the following reasons:

1. None of the telcos had a router-based service at that time, which meant that DMS would have to wait for the carrier to build its own network.

2. DMS wanted to select the routers. The telcos wouldn't purchase the products picked by DMS because they did not fit in with their plans. Finally, a regulatory prohibition against colocation meant that user-owned equipment couldn't be installed at telco central offices.

3. The existing SNA network could easily be adapted to TCP/IP.

The existing configuration had been put in place to allow some 6000 users throughout the state to access mainframe application in Tallahassee. SNA network control processors (NCP)

What Was Spent		What Was Not Spent	
Personnel	$ 450,000	Terminal upgrades	$ 150,000
Application development	300,000	Mainframe application	1,000,000
Software (including Web software, databases, and development tools)	850,000	development	
		Mainframe hardware upgrades	6,000,000
		Mainframe software upgrades	600,000
Hardware (servers, routers, telco services)	1,525,000	**Total**	$7,750,000
Maintenance	450,000		
Total	$3,575,000		

in 10 cities were linked via T-1 (1.544 Mbps) and T-3 (45 Mbps) lines to a communications controller on a token ring LAN in the DMS data center. The communications controller handled SNA traffic into and out of the mainframe. The token ring also supported SNA terminals, personal computers, and other equipment.

To transform the SNA backbone into a router network, all DMS had to do, in essence, was deploy routers at each site, connect the boxes, and link them to a central-site router at the data center (Figure 15.6). Put that way, it sounds easy, and in fact the installation and startup went remarkably smoothly.

DMS chose the Cisco 7000 as its backbone router, with one deployed at each of the 10 regional sites. The Cisco gear came with strong

network management and could be booted and configured centrally. At each site the Cisco router and the NCP are hooked to a digital access cross-connect switch (DACS). This switch segregates SNA from TCP/IP traffic and directs it accordingly. The DACS now provide the T-1/T-3 link to the SNA communications controller at the data center. In addition, each DACS is connected to the DACS at each of the nine other regional centers to create a mesh for IP traffic. Finally, there is a link from each DACS to a router at the data center.

At the regional center, SNA traffic is handled as before from IBM 3270 terminals. This traffic only goes from the regional center to the mainframe at the data center. For connection to the IP backbone and the Internet applications, each

FIGURE 15.6 Network Configuration for Florida Department of Management Services.

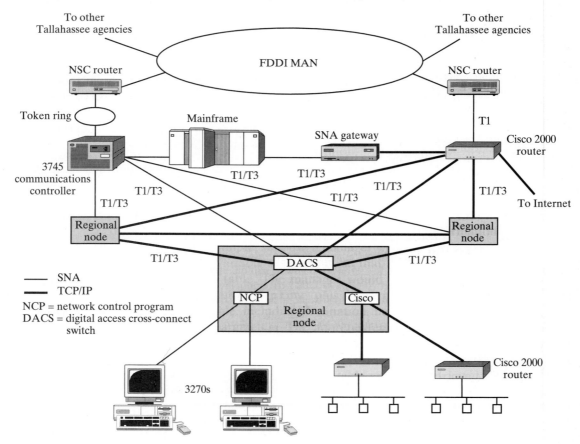

regional center is equipped with Cisco 2000 routers to connect up workstations, personal computers, and servers via LANs.

At the data center, there is a high-capacity Cisco 2000 router that has a direct leased link to each of the 10 regional centers. This router is also connected to the Internet and provides the entry point for the entire far-flung DMS network into the Internet. Finally, there are several Network Systems Corp. routers that connect the data center to the Tallahassee MAN, which is an FDDI ring owned and operated by Sprint Corp. The MAN gives agencies located throughout Tallahassee access to the data center and to each other.

Applications

Once the IP infrastructure was in place, DMS began to add applications. The first, and still the most popular, application was a client–server employment system. The original system stored information about some 125,000 state employees on the mainframe. About 1200 users throughout the state accessed it over the SNA network. Although the system was secure and reliable, services were slow and the interface clumsy. The applications around the database had been developed and installed in the early 1980s and were batch-mode with fixed-transaction access. Users couldn't configure their own request and searches on the fly. If they wanted anything out of the ordinary, they had to contact mainframe programmers, who might take days or weeks to develop what was needed. The new application makes use of a Unix server at the data center that is hooked to the mainframe and downloads the employee database at least weekly to store in its own server database. Users at workstations at the various agencies and centers access the server over the IP network running an application Copesview.

Another client–server application that generates a lot of traffic over the IP network is Spursview, a purchasing application. Like Copesview, it was adapted from a mainframe application—SPURS (statewide purchasing system). SPURS, which was used by roughly 4000 employees, stored information on the mainframe about products purchased by the site, including vendor, model number, and price. Here again,

users were limited as to the type of searches they could perform. With Spursview, users gained a variety of new capabilities, such as wild-card searches on any parameters (data of purchase, vendor, type of product, etc.). They can also create graphs and bar charts and import data directly into PC-based spreadsheets.

Intranet and Internet Applications

The data center maintains a link to the Internet through which all traffic between their IP network and the Internet pass. This link is equipped with a firewall that prevents unauthorized access.

With the Internet link and the IP network up, DMS was in a position to offer Internet access to state employees as well as to set up web services for both intranet and Internet access. Like the servers in the client–server configuration, the web server has a link to the mainframe and is able to construct databases accessible from web browsers.

One of the most popular web-based applications is a job-posting service that lets users search for vacancies within the state system by location, salary ranges, and type of work. The state has about 8000 job vacancies on any given day. Applicants can fill out an on-line job application and store it for multiple submissions. This application averages about 100,000 hits per week.

Another well-used site eliminates the need for state employees to process information regarding government contracts and suppliers. Previously, when a vendor won a bid, it submitted pricing and product data on floppy disks. The DMS employed several people full time just to review that information, format it, and enter it onto the mainframe. That information is now available on the web. Users can access this information on the DMS web server and on web servers at vendor sites. For example, users can search for contracted suppliers that offer computers priced below $2000. The search generates a list of names, each of which is a web link. Because the data resides on the vendors' web servers, it is up to the suppliers, not the DMS, to make sure that all data are accurate and up to date.

DMS is also working on an on-line purchasing system running over the web. Users not only would be able to view vendor information but also could order products on-line. This application will take a lot of coordination, because it involves the purchasing department, comptroller's office, and accounting. It also involves authenticating users to ensure that they are authorized to make purchases.

DMS has not neglected those who pay their salaries: the citizens of Florida. The web service available to the public is called the Florida Community Network, and it has been a success story and a model for other states [REGE96]. The FCN is currently averaging 1 million hits per month. On-line access to information can in many cases eliminate two or three layers of bureaucracy and provide a self-service connection to the government. For example, one of the projects under development is automatic fishing and gaming licensing. Mrs. X in Palm Beach wants to go fishing but knows she needs a license. She logs on to the FCN site, chooses the search option, and types "fishing." Within seconds, a form appears that lets Mrs. X apply and pay for a license from the comfort of her home. She fills out the form, submits it, and moments later a license is e-mailed to her. No clerks, no lines, no trips to the office of the tax collector or a sporting goods store. Yet another popular web service is the statewide telephone directory, which includes listings for state and local government, universities, community colleges, and school boards.

The DMS web site is undergoing constant evolution and refinement. It is located at http://fcn.state.fl.us/dms.

Discussion Questions

1. What security mechanisms are needed to protect the DMS systems from both state employees and users accessing over the Internet?

2. Visit the DMS web site and list the major services found there. Discuss the relative merits of each.

3. Suggest improvements to existing services and suggest new services that should be added.

16

Network Management

CHAPTER OBJECTIVES

After reading this chapter, you should be able to:

■ List and define the key requirements that a network management system should satisfy.

■ Explain the central role of indicators in a network management system and list and discuss the most important service- and efficiency-oriented indicators.

■ Describe the concept of performance monitoring, explain its importance, and discuss approaches to providing technical control.

■ Give an overview of the architecture of a network management system and explain each of its key elements.

■ Describe the IBM approach to network management, embodied in NetView.

■ Describe the standardized approach to network management in a TCP/IP environment.

■ Describe SNMP and list the differences between versions 1 and 2.

*N*etworks and distributed processing systems are of critical and growing importance in enterprises of all sorts. The trend is toward larger, more complex networks supporting more applications and more users. As these networks grow in scale, two facts become painfully evident:

■ The network and its associated resources and distributed applications become indispensable to the organization.

■ More things can go wrong, disabling the network or a portion of the network or degrading performance to an unacceptable level.

A large network cannot be put together and managed by human effort alone. The complexity of such a system dictates the use of automated network management tools. The urgency of the need for such tools is increased, and the difficulty of supplying such tools is also increased if the network includes equipment from multiple vendors. Moreover, the increasing decentralization of network services as exemplified by the growing importance of workstations and client–server computing makes coherent and coordinated network management increasingly difficult. In such complex information systems, many significant network assets are dispersed far from network management personnel.

This chapter provides an overview of network management. We begin by looking at the requirements for network management. This should give some idea of the scope of the task to be accomplished. To manage a network, it is fundamental that one must know something about the current status and behavior of that network.

For either LAN management alone or for a combined LAN/WAN environment, what is needed is a network management system that includes a comprehensive set of data gathering and control tools and that is integrated with the network hardware and software. We look at the general architecture of a network management system and then examine the most widely used standardized software package for supporting network management: SNMP.

16.1 NETWORK MANAGEMENT REQUIREMENTS

Table 16-1 lists key areas of network management as suggested by the International Organization for Standardization (ISO). These categories provide a useful way of organizing our discussion of requirements.

Fault Management

Overview To maintain proper operation of a complex network, care must be taken that systems as a whole, and each essential component individually, are in proper working order. When a fault occurs, it is important, as rapidly as possible, to:

- Determine exactly where the fault is.
- Isolate the rest of the network from the failure so that it can continue to function without interference.

TABLE 16-1 OSI Management Functional Areas

Fault management
The facilities that enable the detection, isolation, and correction of abnormal operation of the OSI environment.

Accounting management
The facilities that enable charges to be established for the use of managed objects and costs to be identified for the use of those managed objects.

Configuration and name management
The facilities that exercise control over, identify, collect data from, and provide data to managed objects for the purpose of assisting in providing for continuous operation of interconnection services.

Performance management
The facilities needed to evaluate the behavior of managed objects and the effectiveness of communication activities.

Security management
Addresses those aspects of OSI security essential to operate OSI network management correctly and to protect managed objects.

- Reconfigure or modify the network in such a way as to minimize the impact of operation without the failed component or components.
- Repair or replace the failed components to restore the network to its initial state.

Central to the definition of fault management is the fundamental concept of a fault. Faults are to be distinguished from errors. A **fault** is an abnormal condition that requires management attention (or action) to repair. A fault is usually indicated by failure to operate correctly or by excessive errors. For example, if a communications line is physically cut, no signals can get through. Or a crimp in the cable may cause wild distortions so that there is a persistently high bit error rate. Certain errors (e.g., a single bit error on a communication line) may occur occasionally and are not normally considered to be faults. It is usually possible to compensate for errors using the error control mechanisms of the various protocols.

User Requirements Users expect fast and reliable problem resolution. Most end users will tolerate occasional outages. When these infrequent outages do occur, however, the user generally expects to receive immediate notification and expects that the problem will be corrected almost immediately. To provide this level of fault resolution requires very rapid and reliable fault detection and diagnostic management functions. It is imperative for a credible operation that fault detection be proactive. Incipient faults must be recognized before service is degraded if possible; in any case, faults must be determined by the system rather than by user complaints. The impact and duration of faults can also be minimized by the use of redundant components and alternate communication routes, to give the network a degree of "fault tolerance." The fault management capability itself should be redundant to increase network reliability.

Users expect to be kept informed of the network status, including both scheduled and unscheduled disruptive maintenance. Users expect reassurance of correct network operation through mechanisms that use confidence tests or analyze dumps, logs, alerts, or statistics. After correcting a fault and restoring a system to its full operational state, the fault management service must ensure that the problem is truly resolved and that no new problems are introduced. This requirement is called problem tracking and control. As with other areas of network management, fault management should have minimal effect on network performance.

Accounting Management

Overview In many enterprise networks, individual divisions or cost centers, or even individual project accounts, are charged for the use of network services. These are internal accounting procedures rather than actual cash transfers, but nevertheless, they are important to the participating users. Furthermore, even if no such internal charging is employed, the network manager needs to be able to track the use of network resources by user or user class for a number of reasons, including:

- A user or group of users may be abusing their access privileges and burdening the network at the expense of other users.
- Users may be making inefficient use of the network, and the network manager can assist in changing procedures to improve performance.
- The network manager is in a better position to plan for network growth if user activity is known in sufficient detail.

User Requirements   The network manager needs to be able to specify the kinds of accounting information to be recorded at various nodes, the desired interval between sending the recorded information to higher-level management nodes, and the algorithms to be used in calculating the charging. Accounting reports should be generated under network manager control. To limit access to accounting information, the accounting facility must provide the capability to verify users' authorization to access and manipulate that information.

Configuration and Name Management

Overview   Modern data communication networks are composed of individual components and logical subsystems (e.g., the device driver in an operating system) that can be configured to perform many different applications. The same device, for example, can be configured to act either as a router or as an end system node or both. Once it is decided how a device is to be used, the configuration manager can choose the appropriate software and set of attributes and values (e.g., a transport layer retransmission timer) for that device.

Configuration management is concerned with initializing a network and gracefully shutting down part or all of the network. It is also concerned with maintaining, adding, and updating the relationships among components and the status of components themselves during network operation.

User Requirements   Startup and shutdown operations on a network are the specific responsibilities of configuration management. It is often desirable for these operations on certain components to be performed unattended (e.g., starting or shutting down a network interface unit). The network manager needs the capability to identify the components that comprise the network and to define the desired connectivity of these components. Those who regularly configure a network with the same or a similar set of resource attributes need ways to define and modify default attributes and to load these predefined sets of attributes into the specified network components. The network manager needs the capability to change the connectivity of network components when users' needs change. Reconfiguration of a network is often desired in response to performance evaluation or in support of network upgrade, fault recovery, or security checks.

Users often need to, or want to, be informed of the status of network resources and components. Therefore, when changes in configuration occur, users should be notified of these changes. Configuration reports can be generated either on some routine periodic basis or in response to a request for such a report. Before reconfiguration, users often want to inquire about the upcoming status of resources and their attributes. Network managers usually want only authorized users (operators) to manage and control network operation (e.g., software distribution and updating).

Performance Management

Overview   Modern data communications networks are composed of many and varied components, which must intercommunicate and share data and resources. In some cases it is critical to the effectiveness of an application that the communication over the network be within certain performance limits. Performance management of a computer network comprises two broad functional categories: monitoring and controlling. Monitoring is the function that tracks activities on the network. The controlling function enables performance management to make adjustments to improve network performance. Some of the performance issues of concern to the network manager:

- What is the level of capacity utilization?
- Is there excessive traffic?
- Has throughput been reduced to unacceptable levels?
- Are there bottlenecks?
- Is response time increasing?

    To deal with these concerns, the network manager must focus on some initial set of resources to be monitored to assess performance levels. This includes associating appropriate metrics and values with relevant network resources as indicators of different levels of performance. For example, what count of retransmissions on a transport connection is considered to be a performance problem requiring attention? Performance management must, therefore, monitor many resources to provide information in determining network operating level. By collecting this information, analyzing it, and then using the resultant analysis as feedback to the prescribed set of values, the network manager can become more and more adept at recognizing situations indicative of present or impending performance degradation.

User Requirements   Before using a network for a particular application, a user may want to know such things as the average and worst-case response times and the reliability of network services. Thus performance must be known in sufficient detail to assess specific user queries. End users expect network services to be managed in such a way as consistently to afford their applications good response time.

    Network managers need performance statistics to help them plan, manage, and maintain large networks. Performance statistics can be used to recognize potential bottlenecks before they cause problems to the end users. Appropriate corrective action can then be taken. This action can take the form of changing routing tables to balance or redistribute traffic load during times of peak use or when a bottleneck is identified by a rapidly growing load in one area. Over the long term, capacity planning based on such performance information can indicate the proper decisions to make, for example, with regard to expansion of lines in that area.

Security Management

Overview   Security management is concerned with generating, distributing, and storing encryption keys. Passwords and other authorization or access control information must be maintained and distributed. Security management is also concerned with monitoring and controlling access to computer networks and access to all or part of the network management information obtained from the network nodes. Logs are an important security tool, and therefore, security management is very much involved with the collection, storage, and examination of audit records and security logs, as well as with the enabling and disabling of these logging facilities.

User Requirements   Security management provides facilities for protection of network resources and user information. Network security facilities should be available for authorized users only. Users want to know that the proper security policies are in force and effective and that the management of security facilities is itself secure.

16.2 NETWORK MANAGEMENT SYSTEMS

Architecture of a Network Management System

A **network management system** is a collection of tools for network monitoring and control that is integrated in the following senses:

- A single operator interface with a powerful but user-friendly set of commands for performing most or all network management tasks.
- A minimal amount of separate equipment. That is, most of the hardware and software required for network management is incorporated into the existing user equipment.

A network management system consists of incremental hardware and software additions implemented among existing network components. The software used in accomplishing the network management tasks resides in the host computers (e.g., workstations, servers, mainframes) and communications processors (e.g., front-end processors, terminal cluster controllers, bridges, routers). A network management system is designed to view the entire network as a unified architecture, with addresses and labels assigned to each point and the specific attributes of each element and link known to the system. The active elements of the network provide regular feedback of status information to the network control center.

Figure 16.1 suggests the architecture of a network management system. Each network node contains a collection of software devoted to the network management task, referred to in the diagram as a network management entity (NME). Each NME performs the following tasks:

- Collect statistics on communications and network-related activities.
- Store statistics locally.

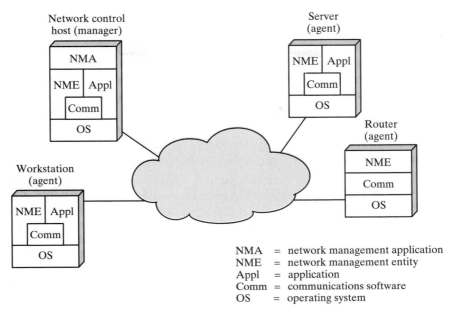

FIGURE 16.1 Elements of a Network Management System.

- Respond to commands from the network control center, including commands to:
  1. Transmit collected statistics to network control center.
  2. Change a parameter (e.g., a timer used in a transport protocol).
  3. Provide status information (e.g., parameter values, active links).
  4. Generate artificial traffic to perform a test.
- Send messages to the network control center when local conditions undergo a signficant change.

At least one host in the network is designated as the network control center, or **manager**. In addition to the NME software, the network control host includes a collection of software called the network management application (NMA), which controls network management activity throughout the network. The NMA includes an operator interface to allow an authorized user to manage the network. The NMA responds to user commands by displaying information and/or by issuing commands to NMEs throughout the network. This communication is carried out using an application-level network management protocol that employs the communications architecture in the same fashion as any other distributed application.

Each other node in the network that is part of the network management system includes a NME and, for purposes of network management, is referred to as an **agent**. Agents include end systems that support user applications as well as nodes that provide a communications service, such as front-end processors, cluster controllers, bridges, and routers.

Several observations are in order:

1. Since the network management software relies on the host operating system and on the communications architecture, most offerings to date are designed for use on a single vendor's equipment. As mentioned, standards in this area are still evolving. However, recent years have seen the emergence of standardized network management systems designed to manage a multiple-vendor network.

2. As depicted in Figure 16.1, the network control host communicates with and controls the NMEs in other systems.

3. For maintaining high availability of the network management function, two or more network control hosts are used. In normal operation, one of the centers is idle or simply collecting statistics, while the other is used for control. If the primary network control host fails, the backup system can be used.

In the remainder of this section, we introduce a widely used proprietary network management system.

IBM Network Management Architecture and NetView

IBM's systems network architecture (SNA) includes a network management architecture. As the types of networks built on SNA have grown in size and complexity and have come to include non-IBM equipment, the software tools for network management have undergone a similar evolution, culminating in the 1986 announcement of NetView, NetView/PC, and open network management as the basis for satisfying the need for network management. The IBM approach is bold. Simply put, IBM wants to provide the single, unifying framework into which all other network management products feed and from which all the equipment in a user's network can be controlled.

It is useful to examine the IBM approach for two reasons. First, the range of capabilities provided in the IBM scheme provides a good idea of the types of tools desirable in a network management system. Second, the IBM scheme is the most widely used network management system. Because it is linked to SNA, IBM's network management scheme is quickly spreading into customer SNA environments; furthermore, IBM has published specifications that allow other vendors to interface their network management gear to an IBM host-based network management controller. Thus, implementations of the IBM approach have proliferated.

We look first at the various aspects of network management under IBM's scheme and then at the products from which a network management system can be constructed.

Network Management Categories   As we have seen, network management covers many functions that are necessary to manage a communications network. The SNA network management is comprised of the following major categories:

- Problem management
- Change management
- Configuration management
- Performance and accounting management

Figure 16.2 shows the key subtasks in each category.

Problem management is the process of managing network problems from initial detection through final resolution. The initial step is *problem determination*: the automated or manual process that detects a hardware, software, or firmware component problem. *Diagnosis* determines the problem's cause, and *bypass and recovery* provide either a partial or a complete bypass until final resolution can be enacted. *Resolution* is the corrective measure taken to eliminate the detected problem or an impending one. *Tracking and control* is the process of recording the history of the problem.

Each node (host, front-end processor, cluster controller) in the network is responsible for its own error analysis to determine whether a problem exists and whether local recovery action can be performed. This responsibility extends to controlling line monitors attached to lines emanating from the node. If a problem exists that cannot be resolved locally, the node sends an alert signal to the network control center software to indicate that a component in the network is unavailable and that intervention is required. For example, the network control center may reroute all virtual circuits that pass through the affected area.

Change management applies to additions, deletions, and modifications to networked hardware, software, and microcode resources. *Software change control* directs and documents activities such as installation, removal, modification, and temporary program fixes. *Microcode change control* keeps tabs on microcode installation, removal of temporary fixes, engineering changes, or feature changes. *Hardware change control* notes the hardware installation, removal, engineering changes, or other updates.

Configuration management is the process concerned with the generation and maintenance of a configuration database that contains knowledge of all physical and logical network resources and their relationships. *Physical and logical resource identification* records physical network resources. Resources can include such devices as host computers, front-end processors, cluster controllers, modems, multiplexers, and protocol converters. Each resource is coded by such categories as line types, serial numbers, inventory numbers, telephone numbers, real and virtual memory allocations, and program numbers. The term *logical resource* refers to SNA-defined entities such as system service control points, physical units, and logical units (see Figure 12.11). *Resource relationship identification* is the process of identifying and recording the physical and logical configuration of network resources.

Performance and accounting management quantifies, reports, and controls the use and charges associated with network components. *Response-time monitoring* measures end-user session response times and generates problem notifications if predetermined thresholds are exceeded. *Availability monitoring* reports component availability. *Utilization monitoring* keeps tabs on network

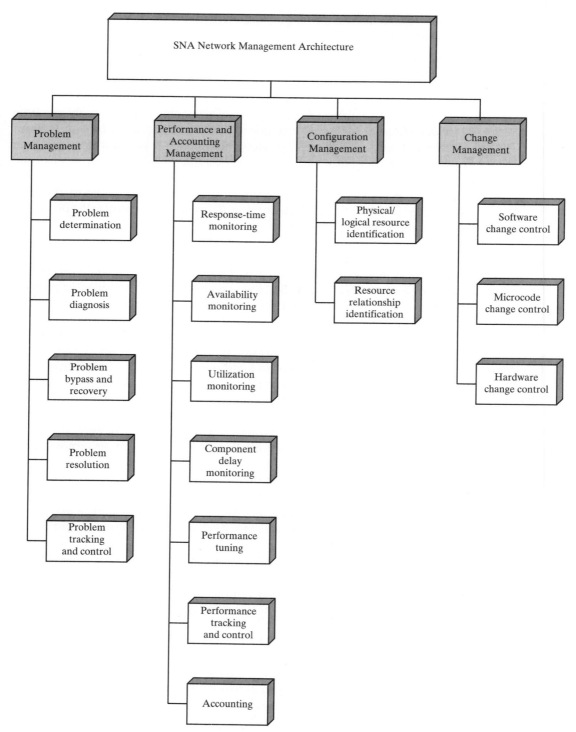

FIGURE 16.2 IBM's Philosophy of Network Management.

resource–server use; it generates unsolicited problem notification if preset threshold values are exceeded. *Component delay monitoring* tracks critical component delays; it initiates unsolicited problem notification if predetermined service levels are exceeded. *Performance tuning* is the process of modifying critical network performance parameters to improve throughput. *Performance tracking and control* is the process of recording and tracking performance events or alerts. *Accounting* records, allocates, and tracks network resources in an effort to allocate costs properly.

NetView   To support all the tasks discussed in the preceding subsection, IBM has developed a number of software and hardware tools designed to work with and in an SNA network. All these were consolidated into a single product line with the introduction of **NetView**. The underlying theme of NetView is that a very sophisticated degree of network monitoring and control can be focused at a single location (operating on a mainframe local to that location), yet can call on resources distributed throughout the network as "eyes" and "hands" to perform its functions. The NetView architecture is in general terms that of Figure 16.1. There is a network control center on a mainframe that communicates and controls network management software and hardware elements throughout the network.

NetView is intended to operate across multiple networks, where the networks may not all be SNA-based but may include token-ring LANs, X.25 packet-switching networks, and even non-IBM wide-area networks. To that end, some of the interfaces and operating details of NetView have been published to permit other suppliers to build NetView "handles" and "extensions" into their products, so that those non-IBM products can nevertheless be part of NetView's network management continuum. Moreover, recently IBM has released products to support network elements managed by SNMP and TCP/IP. This concept is referred to as *open network management.*

One of these "open systems" provisions is **NetView/PC**, a software product that is in an IBM personal computer or IBM PC-compatible product. NetView/PC makes it possible for the personal computer in question, despite running autonomous applications (from the mainframe perspective), to interface with the mainframe's network management capabilities and participate with the mainframe in the overall management of the network.

Figure 16.3 depicts the major software elements of NetView and NetView/PC. The NetView software on the mainframe that acts as the network control center consists of the following key elements:

- *Control facility:* provides the capability to operate the network. It uses NetView commands to control such network resources as modems and protocol converters.
- *Hardware monitor:* actually, a software package that collects notifications of failures or significant events affecting physical network or computer resources. These notifications, as well as recommended actions, may be displayed.

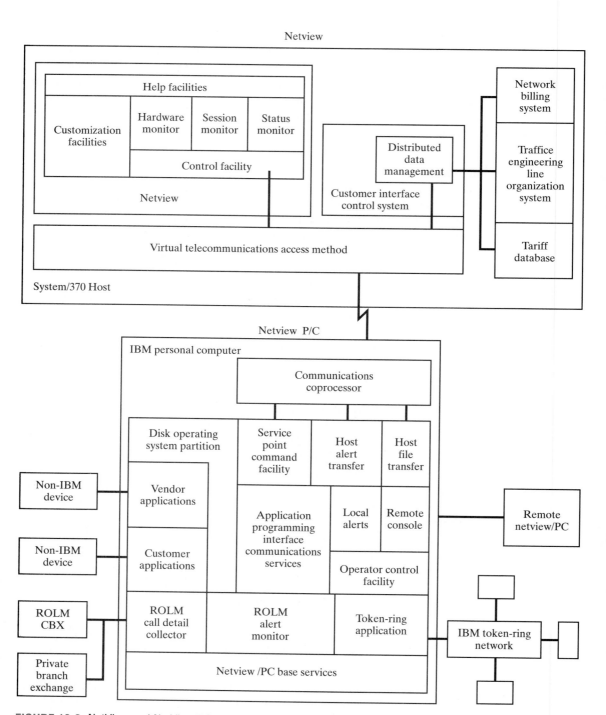

FIGURE 16.3 NetView and NetView/PC.

- *Session monitor:* collects session-related information on the resources of the logical components of the network, such as physical units (PUs), logical units (LUs), and system services control points (SSCPs). It includes measurements of data on response time and session failure.

- *Status monitor:* displays status information on network resources; also automatically reactivates network resources following failures.

- *Help facilities:* provided at several levels for commands, messages, and codes. Descriptions of fields on displays are included, and a systematic problem-solving facility guides the use through the various steps of particular network management tasks.

- *Customization facilities:* permits a user to tailor NetView. Information not needed can be suppressed. Information can be changed to accommodate a user's procedures. Additional functions can be added to increase a user's network management capabilities.

The software just listed applies primarily to computer and data network management. In addition, an IBM host can contain software that specifically relates to the management of digital PBX and voice network resources. The host software consists of the following:

- *Network billing system:* provides the user with a clear accounting of PBX costs and use categorized by department, by long-distance carrier, and by equipment.

- *Traffic engineering line organization system:* allows the user to analyze call-detail records received from the PBX. It helps to determine cost-effective ways to configure a site's telecommunications network, both voice and data, and also helps to identify such network problems as over-capacity, undercapacity, and isolated links.

- *Tariff database:* provides tariff information for U.S. long-distance carriers.

The remaining NetView-related software is in a personal computer and is referred to as NetView/PC. This software can be used for stand-alone network management. For example, NetView/PC can perform specific device tests locally and record the results in a local disk file. In addition, NetView/PC can send information to NetView on a host, which can then take additional measures.

A key application that is part of NetView/PC deals with token-ring local-area networks (LANs). The token-ring application records network errors in an event log. Other network events, such as stations joining and withdrawing from the LAN, can be recorded in the log to assist the user in problem determination. Logged events may be displayed and printed for a specified station or period. Alert conditions are immediately signaled to the operator via audible alarms and highlighted indicators on the display. At the same time, an alert message can be transmitted to NetView in the host. The token-ring application can operate as a stand-alone application. In addition, NetView/PC's remote-console support allows an operator at a remote PC to use the local token-ring network manager.

NetView/PC also provides documented software interfaces so that non-IBM vendors and customers can write additional network management applications and link these to the NetView scheme.

16.3 TECHNICAL CONTROL

The most important characteristic of a network and its services is availability. As the use of distributed systems has increased within organizations, there has come to be increasing reliance on networks, and the cost of network "downtime" has increased dramatically. Thus, the most important aspect of network management is that part that contributes to availability. In particular, the following are needed:

- Automatic and remote testing and monitoring of the system, to reduce downtime due to the need to locate service personnel
- Restoring and/or reconfiguring the system upon failure in real time
- Providing network performance and functioning statistics to facilitate planning and management for high availability

This aspect of network management is often referred to as **network technical control**.

The first task of network technical control is to locate faults. As the number of network nodes and connections grows, this becomes an increasingly difficult task. A commonsense approach is first to check out the devices at either end of the troublesome communication facility because access is usually easiest at the endpoints. That failing, the next logical step is to examine the closest transmission facility and then proceed, segment by segment, until the problem is located. Although this tactic may look good on paper, it may not be that easy in practice. Network managers can only hope that when the fault is finally located, it is in a network segment to which they have ready access.

As the number of transmission options has mushroomed since then (e.g., LANs, alternative public carriers, digital leased lines, private microwave, etc.), diagnosing problems has become something of a shell game. Diagnostic and test equipment has had to keep pace with the transition and grow in functionality and scope, yet remain affordable. Further complicating the network manager's task is the mixture of multiple vendors' equipment found in most networks.

A wide variety of network technical control products, systems, and components are commercially available. These range in functionality and price from a $100 breakout box, designed to diagnose a single physical interface, to an elaborate centralized network technical control center that may cost several hundred thousand dollars. Technical control approaches, and the equipment that support them, can be grouped into two categories: component-level technical control and network technical control systems.

Component-Level Technical Control

Component-level technical control equipment is typically concerned with monitoring network activity at the point of attachment of host systems to the network. Most of the devices marketed for this area perform a line-monitoring function; more recently, there has been increasing use of protocol analyzers.

Line Monitors   A line monitor captures the signal between a host system and the network; generally, these devices are employed only on the network end, not on the host end. The large variety of equipment in this area can be categorized as being digital, analog, or a combination.

A *digital line monitor* traps and displays data and control characters to provide a precise picture of line activity. In addition, the monitor permits interface control signals (e.g., those of the EIA-232 interface; see Chapter 5) to be checked when there are problems in establishing and maintaining message exchanges. Some units also provide test messages for polling and responding, which are used in end-to-end network tests. Parity indications and counts, also common features, are used both in checking out specific problems and in determining line quality.

An *analog line monitor* can be used in a situation where data are transmitted and received through a modem attached to an analog transmission facility. While a digital bit-error rate test conducted over an analog line will help generally determine whether a channel is functioning properly, analog test gear is required to diagnose the cause of the problem. The monitor measures various parameters of the analog signal, such as attenuation, distortion, and other impairments of the signal. The use of this type of device requires some understanding of signal properties, and it is consequently not as accessible for customer testing and monitoring. Analog monitors have traditionally been oriented toward telephone line testing, but similar equipment is available to diagnose broadband/CATV channels, microwave and satellite circuits, and even optical fiber links. For a given medium, and function for function, analog line monitors are typically more expensive than the digital counterparts. The user's needs will determine whether it is satisfactory simply to identify a circuit as having problems, or whether it is necessary to learn precisely why the analog channel is exhibiting data transmission problems.

Protocol Analyzers   As networks grow in complexity and sophistication, line monitors have evolved to include a range of active capabilities. The user cannot only passively monitor data traffic, but can also simulate various network components, such as modem, terminal, and processor, to perform interactive tests in a variety of simulated operating environments. Communication protocols and codes can also be tested. With these additional capabilities, the device is often referred to as a protocol analyzer. Typically, up to layer 3 of the OSI architecture (e.g., all three levels of X.25) is handled.

Network Technical Control Systems

The individual line monitor or protocol analyzer is useful for testing a particular line and the equipment attached to that line. In a large, distributed network, a number of such devices are needed, and these will be scattered throughout the network. It is clearly impractical to attempt to manage a network by means of these devices alone. What is needed is some way to integrate the devices and centralize the control of the network. Network technical control systems are intended for this purpose.

Network technical control systems are supplied by traditional suppliers of patching, switching, and modem equipment. These systems offer access to remote sites via leased or dial-up lines or through the use of a secondary channel on modems. A network technical control center offers centralized testing and control by integrating the supplier's data line monitors with the accompanying line of patching and switching equipment at the central site. Control of monitoring and testing at remote sites can be performed from the central site without the need for any manual intervention at the remote site.

Switching equipment forms the basis of a network technical control system by providing the following functions:

- Fall back to standby or spare facilities in the event of a failure.
- Test and monitor the network by switching diagnostic equipment into the required circuits.
- Reconfigure the network to isolate a fault or when the network changes in design or expands.

Figure 16.4 shows a typical network technical control system configuration. A network control center, usually attached to a central host, provides centralized control of all technical control equipment and activities. It communicates with special electronic modules added to each modem, line monitor, and other technical control device in the network. The control center gathers status and operational data from its associated equipment and responds to commands from the operator at the console. The control center provides the operator with the means

FIGURE 16.4 Example Network Technical Control System.

T   = terminal
LMU = line monitor unit

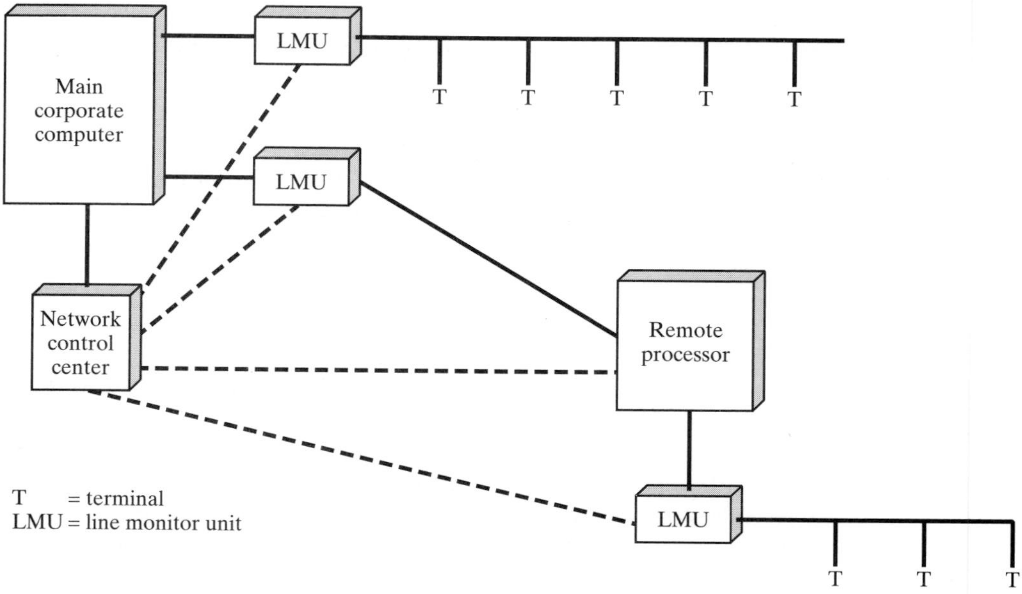

of diagnosing a problem, isolating the faulty unit, and restoring network operation while the failed element is being repaired or replaced.

The figure uses dashed lines to indicate communication between the network control center and associated equipment. These could be separate leased or dial-up communication links. An alternative for leased analog lines is the use of a secondary channel. The standard voice channel extends from 300 to 3000 Hz. Within that channel, the actual frequency band used by a modem for transmitting data is typically a much narrower band centered at 1800 Hz. Hence it is possible to provide a separate channel for control signals and status information within the larger bandwidth.

The test and control functions performed by a network technical control system can be divided into the following categories:

- Nonintrusive tests
- Intrusive tests
- Remedial functions
- Analog measurements

Nonintrusive tests make use of the secondary channel and do not interfere with the main-channel data traffic. Therefore, these tests do not disrupt network operation and are invisible to users and applications. To gain more precise information, intrusive tests, which do employ the main channel, must be performed periodically. Remedial functions restore and reconfigure the network to bypass any fault that has been identified and localized. Analog measurements can provide supplementary information about line quality that can aid in fault diagnosis.

16.4 PERFORMANCE MONITORING

After availability, the second most important characteristic of a network is performance. For interactive applications, we have seen that a response time suited to the application is critical for satisfactory productivity. Many applications that are not necessarily sensitive to response time, such as file transfer, disk backup, and bulk printer output, are sensitive to throughput; that is, the amount of data to be transferred is so great that a steady high throughput is necessary. Thus, a major task of network management is the collection of data on response time, throughput, and utilization. When problems develop, from the user's point of view, such performance data must be available in sufficient detail to be able to assess the bottleneck that is causing the problem and to plan appropriate remedial action. This aspect of network management is often referred to as **performance monitoring**.

The task of performance monitoring is a complex one. For the information to be useful in diagnosis and planning, the performance monitoring function must be able to isolate the bottlenecks that can occur in a network environment. As with the area of technical control, performance monitoring approaches, and the equipment that support them, can be grouped into two categories: component-level performance monitoring and network monitoring systems.

Component-Level Performance Monitoring

Component-level performance monitoring equipment is typically concerned with measuring performance-related indicators for single components or segments of the network. The following types of devices are common:

- Response-time monitors
- Hardware monitors
- Software monitors

Response-Time Monitors   There are a number of products on the market that provide, at reasonable cost, a direct measurement of the user's response time. These devices are typically portable and easy to use.

The response-time monitor measures the interval from the time that the user hits a SEND or equivalent key that causes the transmission of a transaction request to the host until the response is received from the host. For terminals that are specially equipped with a transaction-indicator light, the monitor can be optically coupled to the indicator light. For other terminals, the monitor must be coupled electronically to the terminal or to the communication interface (e.g., EIA-232) of the terminal and analyze the electrical signals to determine the start and finish of a transaction.

A response-time monitor measures and displays the response time of each transaction and the average response time. It also retains and displays the number of transactions and the response time of the minimum, maximum, and last transactions. Although these devices are useful in measuring the most important indicator, overall response time, the components of the response time are not broken out.

Hardware Monitors   The inputs to a hardware monitor are sensors that measure signal voltage transitions in the circuitry of various pieces of hardware in the network. These measurements can be used to derive performance-related information. Using these devices, any hardware of any manufacturer can be measured, including central-system hardware, lines, terminal controllers, storage devices, front-end processors, and minicomputers and microcomputers. Two basic types of measurements are gathered:

- *Events:* accumulation of the number of occurrences of specific events
- *Timing:* timing the duration of a specific signal

Table 16-2 gives examples of typical hardware monitor measurements. By carefully collating and analyzing results, a great deal can be learned about the performance of components and lines in a network. Furthermore, a hardware monitor introduces no overhead into the network or any of the processors; it is a passive monitoring technique that does not consume processor resources or transmission capacity.

The interest in hardware monitors is declining, although the devices are still much in use. Their main disadvantages are:

TABLE 16-2 Typical Hardware Monitor Measurements

System profile

Used for evaluating a computer system, including host, front-end processor, and terminal controller. In most cases, processor- and I/O-related parameters are included. Overlap between I/O or communications operations and computer processing can be determined.

Memory mapping

Indicates the activity of selected memory regions. This is a guide to which software modules are being executed, including I/O and communications modules.

Data layout

The access history of data regions on disk can be monitored. The access pattern may cause extreme disk arm movements, which slow response time. Reorganization of disk memory or placement of critical data in main computer memory may improve performance.

Teleprocessing

Special-purpose measurements on communications controllers, lines, and terminals can be accomplished. These measurements are of signals inside hardware equipment and are more cumbersome than measurements taken by line monitors.

- High prices
- Difficulties in accessing critical signals
- High level of skill and training required for setting up measurement, operating the device, and evaluating the results

Software Monitors   A software monitor is a software package resident in main memory on a host (e.g., workstation, server) or a communications processor (e.g., front-end processor, packet switch, terminal cluster controller) that can gather and report statistics on hardware and systems and applications software activity. Because the monitor functions by being executed by the processor on which it is resident, it consumes processor time and hence slows down the operation of that which is being measured. Accordingly, the monitor can be active or inactive, usually under user control. When the network manager needs to gather statistics, various software monitors are activated; at other times they are inactive and do not interfere with normal operation.

When a software monitor is active, its execution is triggered by a timer or an event, either of which causes an interrupt. For example, the monitor could be triggered every time a virtual circuit is set up or torn down, or every time there is disk access from a particular application. Or the monitor could be triggered at regular intervals to take a snapshot of conditions, such as the number of virtual circuits active or the size of the queue of frames waiting to be transmitted over a data link.

The software monitor focuses on the behavior of an individual node in the network and generates statistics that can be used to fine-tune the operating system and applications so as to improve the performance of that node. This is of critical importance, because in a typical network situation, delays internal to a node account for 70 to 80% of the user's response time, with the rest made up by communications delays.

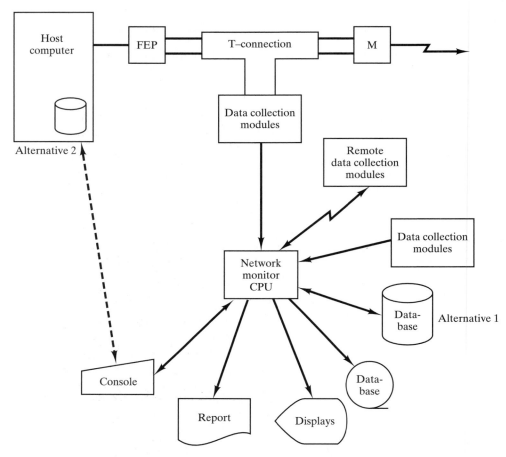

FIGURE 16.5 Network-Monitoring Architecture [TERP92].

Network Monitoring Systems

The purpose of a network monitor is to continuously measure and analyze the most important communications-related parameters in a network. Figure 16.5 shows a general architecture of a network monitor. There is a central network monitor computer that controls a variety of data collection modules. The data collection module is a microcomputer that monitors multiple communications lines. Typically, a data collection module can gather statistics on raw traffic as well as data link and packet-level statistics. At the packet level, events of significance, in addition to total packet traffic, include call clearing, reset, and restart packets (see Chapter 7), can be recorded. These modules are passive and hence do not interfere with or degrade normal communications. A separate communications facility is needed to hook the modules into the central network monitor computer.

The network monitoring system can be completely independent of the computers, terminals, and other equipment in the network and thus is vendor-inde-

TABLE 16-3 Typical Performance Indicators Reported by a Network Monitor

Service Parameters	*Efficiency Parameters*
Availability Overall network availability Line availability User-level availability	**Throughput** Transmit Number of transactions Number of messages Number of characters Longest message Average message length Number of packets (X.25) Receive Number of transactions Number of messages Number of characters Longest message Average message length Number of packets (X.25)
Response time Network delay Host delay Average response time Maximum response time Minimum response time Alternatives at the user's level Up to the first character Up to complete information arrival Up to terminal unlocking Modem turnaround Poll-list cycle time	
	Polling Number of positive polls Number of negative polls Polling delay
Accuracy and integrity Number of troubles by network elements Hit list for most frequent troubles Number of messages lost Number of messages duplicated Number of messages arrived but not delivered Number of NAKs Number of retransmissions Number of timeouts Number of incomplete transmissions	**Utilization** Communication controller Cluster controller Terminal device Link idle Link utilization Software utilization Contention

Source: [TERP92].

pendent. The data collection modules attach to standardized digital interfaces, such as EIA-232. To interpret traffic, however, the data collection modules must be programmed to recognize the data link and network protocols. The only system dependencies occur if the network monitor makes use of a central user host to store database and data processing facilities.

The network monitor will analyze the incoming performance data to prepare ongoing snapshot displays and summary reports. Table 16-3 shows typical performance indicators that may be reported.

16.5 SIMPLE NETWORK MANAGEMENT PROTOCOL

The **simple network management protocol (SNMP)** was developed for use as a network management tool for networks and internetworks operating TCP/IP. It has since been expanded for use in all types of networking environments. The term *simple network management protocol* is actually used to refer to a collection of specifications for network management that include the protocol itself, the definition of a database, and associated concepts.

Basic Concepts

Network Management Architecture   The model of network management that is used for SNMP includes the following key elements:

- Management station
- Management agent
- Management information base (MIB)
- Network management protocol

The **management station** is typically a stand-alone device, but may be a capability implemented on a shared system. In either case the management station serves as the interface for the human network manager into the network management system. The management station will have, at minimum:

- A set of management applications for data analysis, fault recovery, and so on
- An interface by which the network manager may monitor and control the network
- The capability of translating the network manager's requirements into the actual monitoring and control of remote elements in the network
- A database of information extracted from the MIBs of all the managed entities in the network

Only the last two elements are the subject of SNMP standardization.

The other active element in the network management system is the **management agent**. Key platforms, such as hosts, bridges, routers, and hubs, may be equipped with SNMP so that they may be managed from a management station. The management agent responds to requests for information from a management station, responds to requests for actions from the management station, and may asynchronously provide the management station with important but unsolicited information.

The means by which resources in the network may be managed is to represent these resources as objects. Each object is, essentially, a data variable that represents one aspect of the managed agent. The collection of objects is referred to as a **management information base (MIB)**. The MIB functions as a collection of access points at the agent for the management station. These objects are standardized across systems of a particular class (e.g., bridges all support the same management objects). A management station performs the monitoring function by retrieving the value of MIB objects. A management station can cause an action to take place at an agent or can change the configuration settings of an agent by modifying the value of specific variables.

The management station and agents are linked by a **network management protocol**. The protocol used for the management of TCP/IP networks is the simple network management protocol (SNMP). This protocol includes the following key capabilities:

- *Get:* enables the management station to retrieve the value of objects at the agent.

- *Set:* enables the management station to set the value of objects at the agent.
- *Trap:* enables an agent to notify the management station of significant events.

There are no specific guidelines in the standards as to the number of management stations or the ratio of management stations to agents. In general, it is prudent to have at least two systems capable of performing the management station function, to provide redundancy in case of failure. The other issue is the practical one of how many agents a single management station can handle. As long as SNMP remains relatively "simple," that number can be quite high, certainly in the hundreds.

Network Management Protocol Architecture   SNMP is an application-level protocol that is part of the TCP/IP protocol suite. As Figure 16.6 illustrates, SNMP operates over the user datagram protocol (UDP). For a stand-alone management station, a manager process controls access to the central MIB at the management station and provides an interface to the network manager. The manager process achieves network management by using SNMP, which is implemented on top of UDP, IP, and the relevant network-dependent protocols (e.g., Ethernet, ATM, X.25).

FIGURE 16.6 The Role of SNMP.

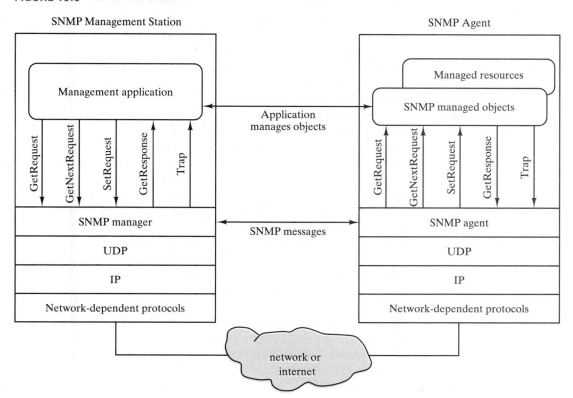

Each agent must also implement SNMP, UDP, and IP. In addition, there is an agent process that interprets the SNMP messages and controls the agent's MIB. For an agent device that supports other applications, such as FTP, TCP as well as UDP is required.

From a management station, three types of SNMP messages are issued on behalf of a management applications: GetRequest, GetNextRequest, and SetRequest. The first two are two variations of the get function. All three messages are acknowledged by the agent in the form of a GetResponse message, which is passed up to the management application. In addition, an agent may issue a trap message in response to an event that affects the MIB and the underlying managed resources.

Because SNMP relies on UDP, which is a connectionless protocol, SNMP is itself connectionless. No ongoing connections are maintained between a management station and its agents. Instead, each exchange is a separate transaction between a management station and an agent.

Trap-Directed Polling   If a management station is responsible for a large number of agents and if each agent maintains a large number of objects, it becomes impractical for the management station to regularly poll all agents for all their readable object data. Instead, SNMP and the associated MIB are designed to encourage the manager to use a technique referred to as *trap-directed polling*.

The recommended strategy is this. At initialization time, and perhaps at infrequent intervals, such as once a day, a management station can poll all the agents it knows of for some key information, such as interface characteristics and perhaps some baseline performance statistics, such as average number of packets sent and received over each interface over a given period of time. Once this baseline is established, the management station refrains from polling. Instead, each agent is responsible for notifying the management station of any unusual event, such as the agent crashing and being rebooted, the failure of a link, or an overload condition as defined by the packet load crossing a threshold. These events are communicated in SNMP messages known as **traps**.

Once a management station is alerted to an exception condition, it may choose to take some action. At this point, the management station may direct polls to the agent reporting the event and perhaps to some nearby agents in order to diagnose any problem and to gain more specific information about the exception condition.

Trap-directed polling can result in substantial savings of network capacity and agent processing time. In essence, the network is not made to carry management information that the management station does not need, and agents are not made to respond to frequent requests for uninteresting information.

Proxies   The use of SNMP requires that all agents, as well as management stations, must support UDP and IP. This limits direct management to such devices and excludes other devices, such as some bridges and modems, that do not support any part of the TCP/IP protocol suite. Further, there may be numerous small systems (personal computers, workstations, programmable controllers) that do implement TCP/IP to support their applications but for which it is not desirable to add the additional burden of SNMP, agent logic, and MIB maintenance.

To accommodate devices that do not implement SNMP, the concept of **proxy** was developed. In this scheme an SNMP agent acts as a proxy for one or more other devices; that is, the SNMP agent acts on behalf of the proxied devices. The management station sends queries concerning a device to its proxy agent. The proxy agent converts each query into the management protocol that is used by the device. When a reply to a query is received by the agent, it passes that reply back to the management station. Similarly, if an event notification of some sort from the device is transmitted to the proxy, the proxy sends that on to the management station in the form of a trap message.

Protocol Specification

With SNMP, information is exchanged between a management station and an agent in the form of an SNMP message. Each message includes a version number, indicating the version of SNMP, a community name to be used for this exchange, and one of five types of protocol data units. This structure is depicted in Figure 16.7, and the constituent fields are defined in Table 16-4. Note that the GetRequest, GetNextRequest, and SetRequest PDUs have the same format as the GetResponse PDU, with the error-status and error-index fields always set to 0. This convention reduces the number of different PDU formats that the SNMP entity must deal with.

The GetRequest and GetNextRequest PDUs are both commands from a manager to retrieve data from an agent. The difference is that the GetRequest lists a specific variable or variables to be retrieved, while the GetNextRequest is

FIGURE 16.7 SNMP Formats.

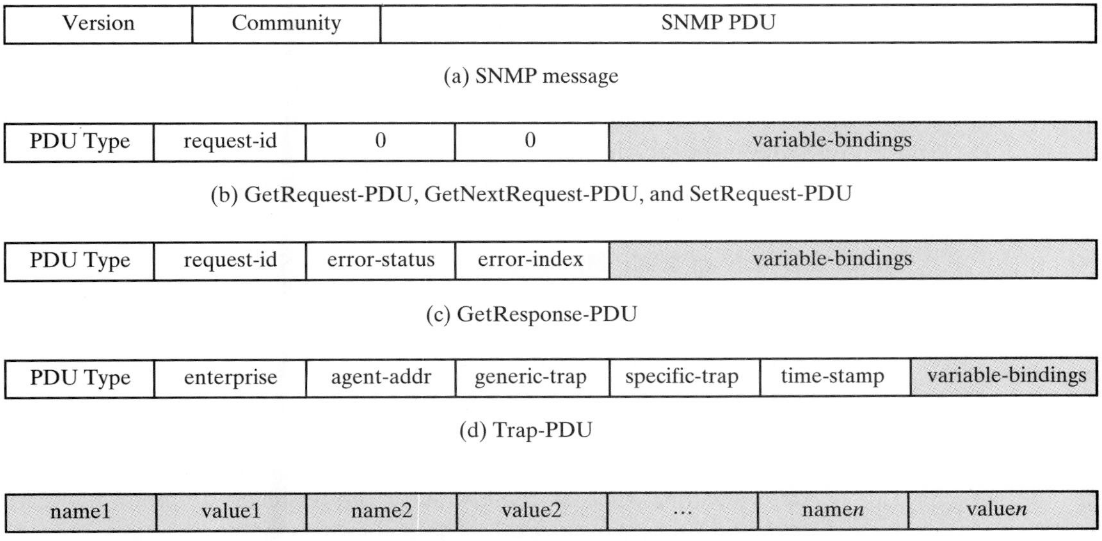

Version	Community	SNMP PDU

(a) SNMP message

PDU Type	request-id	0	0	variable-bindings

(b) GetRequest-PDU, GetNextRequest-PDU, and SetRequest-PDU

PDU Type	request-id	error-status	error-index	variable-bindings

(c) GetResponse-PDU

PDU Type	enterprise	agent-addr	generic-trap	specific-trap	time-stamp	variable-bindings

(d) Trap-PDU

name1	value1	name2	value2	...	name*n*	value*n*

(e) variable-bindings

TABLE 16-4 SNMP Message Fields

Field	Description
version	SNMP version; RFC 1157 is version 1.
community	A pairing of an SNMP agent with some arbitrary set of SNMP application entities. The name of the community functions as a password to authenticate the SNMP message.
request-id	Used to distinguish among outstanding requests by providing each request with a unique ID.
error-status	Used to indicate that an exception occurred while processing a request. Values are: noError (0), tooBig (1), noSuchName (2), badValue (3), readOnly (4), genErr (5).
error-index	When error-status is nonzero, error-index may provide additional information by indicating which variable in a list caused the exception. A variable is an instance of a managed object.
variable-bindings	A list of variable names and corresponding values. In some cases (e.g., GetRequest-PDU) the values are null.
enterprise	Type of object generating trap; based on sysObjectID.
agent-addr	Address of object generating trap.
generic-trap	Generic trap type. Values are: coldStart (0), warmStart (1), linkDown (2), linkUp (3), authenticationFailure (4), egpNeighborLoss (5), and enterpriseSpecific (6).
specific-trap	Specific trap code.
time-stamp	Time elapsed between the last (re)initialization of the network entity and the generation of the trap; contains the value of sysUpTime.

used as a way of exploring a management information base (MIB). In essence, a MIB exhibits a tree structure, and the GetNextRequest gets the next element to be encountered in traversing the tree. For both GetRequest and GetNextRequest, the values, if available, are returned in a GetResponse PDU. The Set command is a command from a manager to update variables in an agent; in this case the GetResponse PDU provides an acknowledgment. Finally, the Trap PDU is a notification from an agent to a manager.

Transmission of an SNMP Message In principle, an SNMP entity performs the following actions to transmit one of the five PDU types to another SNMP entity.

1. The PDU is constructed.
2. This PDU is then passed to an authentication service, together with the source and destination transport addresses and a community name. The authentication service then performs any required transformations for this exchange, such as encryption or the inclusion of an authentication code, and returns the result. The community name is a value that indicates the context for this authentication procedure.

3. The protocol entity then constructs a message, consisting of a version field, the community name, and the result from step 2.
4. This message is passed to the transport service.

In practice, authentication is not typically invoked.

Receipt of an SNMP Message   In principle, an SNMP entity performs the following actions upon reception of an SNMP message.

1. It does a basic syntax check of the message and discards the message if it fails to parse.
2. It verifies the version number and discards the message if there is a mismatch.
3. The protocol entity then passes the user name, the PDU portion of the message, and the source and destination transport addresses (supplied by the transport service that delivered the message) to an authentication service.
   a. If authentication fails, the authentication service signals the SNMP protocol entity, which generates a trap and discards the message.
   b. If authentication succeeds, the authentication service returns the PDU.
4. The protocol entity does a basic syntax check of the PDU and discards the PDU if it fails to parse. Otherwise, using the named community, the appropriate SNMP access policy is selected and the PDU is processed accordingly.

In practice, the authentication service merely serves to verify that the community name authorizes receipt of messages from the source SNMP entity.

Variable Bindings   All SNMP operations involve access to scalar objects. However, it is possible in SNMP to group a number of operations of the same type (get, set, trap) into a single message. Thus, if a management station wants to get the values of all the scalar objects in a particular group at a particular agent, it can send a single message requesting all values, and get a single response, listing all values. This technique can greatly reduce the communications burden of network management.

To implement multiple-object exchanges, all SNMP PDUs include a variable bindings field. This field consists of a sequence of references to object instances, together with the value of those objects. Some PDUs are concerned only with the name of the object instance (e.g., get operations). In this case the value entries in the variable bindings field are ignored by the receiving protocol entity.

SNMPv2

SNMP has proliferated rapidly because it is what it claims to be: a simple tool for network management. SNMP provides a bare-bones set of functions that is easy to implement, relatively easy to use, and if used sensibly, imposes minimal overhead on network operations. Essentially, the SNMP specification defines a syntax for representing management information and a protocol for retrieving and updating that information. The popularity of SNMP eventually caught up with it. Now that (human) managers are used to the level of control available with SNMP, they see its flaws and want more functionality. Among the most noteworthy areas needing improvement were support for decentralized network management strategies, efficient transfer of large blocks of data, and security. All of these areas are addressed in the next generation, version 2, known as **SNMPv2**. A draft set of standards for SNMPv2 were issued in 1993. These were subsequently withdrawn for an overhaul. In 1996, a new edition, still called SNMPv2, was published. This new edition covers all aspects of SNMP except security, which was deferred for later study. This subsection provides a general overview of SNMPv2 functionality.

Decentralized Network Management   In a traditional centralized network management scheme, one host in the configuration has the role of a network management station; there may possibly be one or two other management stations in a backup role. The remainder of the devices on the network contain agent software and a MIB, to allow monitoring and control from the management station. As networks grow in size and traffic load, such a centralized system is unworkable. Too much burden is placed on the management station, and there is too much traffic, with reports from each agent having to wend their way across the entire network to headquarters. In such circumstances, a decentralized, distributed approach works best (e.g., Figure 16.8). In a decentralized network management scheme, there may be multiple top-level management stations, which might be referred to as *management servers.* Each such server might directly manage a portion of the total pool of agents. However, for many of the agents, the management server delegates responsibility to an intermediate manager. The intermediate manager plays the role of manager to monitor and control the agents under its responsibility. It also plays an agent role to provide information and accept control from a higher-level management server. This type of architecture spreads the processing burden and reduces total network traffic.

An essential element of a decentralized network management scheme is a powerful and flexible capability for cooperation among managers. To support manager-to-manager cooperation, SNMPv2 introduces two new features: an Inform command and a manager-to-manager MIB.

A manager uses the Inform command to send unsolicited information to another manager. For example, using the Inform command, a manager can notify another manager when some unusual event occurs, such as the loss of a physical link, or an excessive rate of traffic at some point in the network. Such unsolicited notifications provide an ideal tool for configuring a decentralized network management scheme. Higher-level managers need not concern themselves with the details of remote parts of the network; for example, when a local event that requires central attention occurs, the local manager can use the Inform command to alert the central manager. This ability for one manager to alert another is lacking in SNMP.

SNMPv2 also includes a manager-to-manager MIB, which defines tables that can be used to set up an event-reporting scheme. A manager can be config-

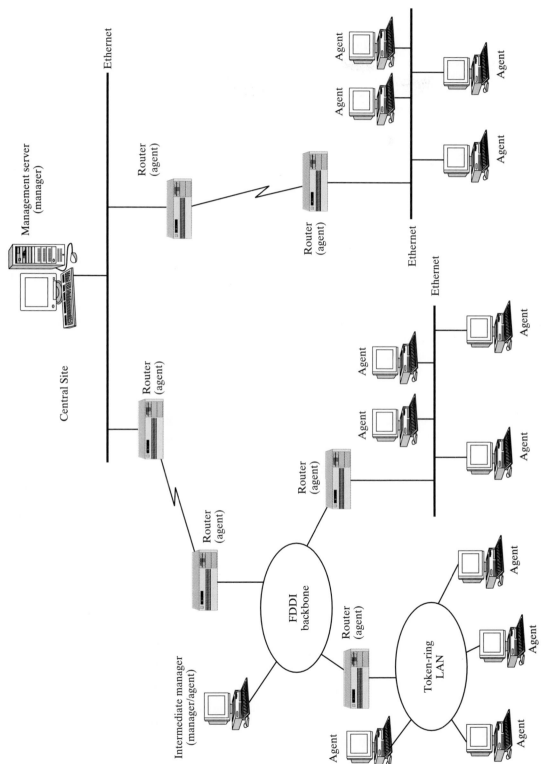

FIGURE 16.8 Example Distributed Network Management Configuration.

ured to issue notifications when something unusual happens, such as a surge in local traffic, and line failure, and so on. The MIB specifies which events will trigger a notification, what information is to be provided in the notification, and which manager or managers are to receive the notification. The notification information is transmitted in an Inform command. The advantage of this scheme, which again is lacking in the original SNMP, is that it is an easy matter to configure a distributed network management strategy in which low-level management stations will deal with ordinary network management tasks and alert a higher-level management station when a predefined event occurs.

Data Transfer One of the concerns that users have had with the original SNMP is the amount of traffic that can be generated as managers communicate with agents. With SNMP, only a limited amount of data can be exchanged in a single transaction, thus frequently forcing management workstations and agents to generate multiple transactions. The result can be a heavy load on the network that can affect response time for end-user applications.

To streamline these exchanges, SNMPv2 adds a new command, the GetBulk command, and introduces an improved version of SNMP's Get command. The GetBulk command targets the one area of information exchange capable of generating the most traffic: retrieval of tables. A table represents a related set of information about a resource (e.g., a router) or activity (e.g, the traffic over a TCP connection). It is organized as a collection of rows of variables, with each row having the same sequence of variables.

For example, each router in a configuration maintains a routing table with one row for each destination. The row is indexed by the destination address and includes a field for the next hop to take to get to the destination and the amount of time since this routing information was last changed. All the rows have the same format, with one row per destination.

With the original SNMP, it is only possible to retrieve information from such a table one row at a time. If a manager needs to see an entire routing table, for example, a tedious series of get/response transactions is needed, one for each row. With the GetBulk command, the manager can retrieve the entire table with one transaction and even retrieve additional nontable information in that same transaction. For example, suppose a manager wished to retrieve the entire routing table plus the variable sysUpTime, so that it could associate a system time with the retrieved table. The manager would issue a getBulk command that would list the variable sysUpTime, plus the variables that correspond to each of the fields in the table, including destination, next hop, and age. The command also includes two parameters. The nonrepeaters parameter indicates how many of the listed variables are to return just one value; in this case there is only one such variable, sysUpTime, so nonrepeaters is set to 1. The max-repetitions parameter indicates how many rows of the table are to be retrieved. If the manager knows the number of rows, max-repetitions is set to that value. Otherwise, the manager makes an educated guess and, if necessary, issues additional GetBulk commands to get additional rows.

Another feature of SNMPv2 that offers to improve the efficiency of data transfer is the nonatomic Get command. Management stations in both SNMP and SNMPv2 use the Get command to obtain the value of one or more variables. In SNMP, if a Get command lists multiple variables and if the agent is unable to return a value for even one of those variables, the entire command is rejected. If this happens, the manager must reissue the Get command with fewer variables. SNMPv2's nonatomic Get command allows partial results to be returned (hence the term *nonatomic*); that is, the agent will return those values that it can and ignore the rest of the variables in the command. Again, this improves efficiency by reducing the number of exchanges across the network.

Security Features The most substantial planned improvement of SNMPv2 over the original SNMP is the addition of security features. This deals with one of the major concerns that users of SNMP have expressed: its lack of effective security. Specifically, users want to know that only authorized personnel are able to perform network management functions (e.g., disable/enable a line) and that only authorized personnel are able to read network management information (e.g., contents of a configuration file). When SNMPv2 was first issued in 1993, a complete security facility was included in the specification. However, this facility was discovered to contain a number of drawbacks and was not included in the 1996 documents. Two competing approaches to providing security for SNMPv2 are under study at the time of this writing. Both approaches provide substantially the same functionality, and this is described in what follows.

The three new security features to be provided by SNMPv2 are authentication, secrecy, and access control. Authentication enables an agent to verify that an incoming command is from an authorized manager and that the contents of the command have not been altered. To achieve this, each manager and agent that wish to communicate must share a secret key. The manager uses this key to calculate a message authentication code that is a function of the message to be transmitted and appends that code to the message. When the agent receives the message, it uses the same key and calculates the message authentication code once again. If the agent's version of the code matches the value appended to the incoming message, the agent knows that the message can only have originated from the authorized manager and that the message was not altered in transit.

The secrecy facility enables managers and agents to encrypt messages to prevent eavesdropping by third parties. Again, manager and agent share a secret key. In this case, if the two are configured to use the secrecy facility, all traffic between them is encrypted using the data encryption standard (DES).

Finally, the access control facility makes it possible to configure agents to provide different levels of access to different managers. Access can be limited in terms of the commands that the agent will accept from a given manager and also in terms of the portion of the agent's MIB that a given manager may access. The access control policy to be used by an agent for each manager must be preconfigured and essentially consists of a table that details the access privileges of the various authorized managers. Figure 16.9 highlights the SNMPv2 security features.

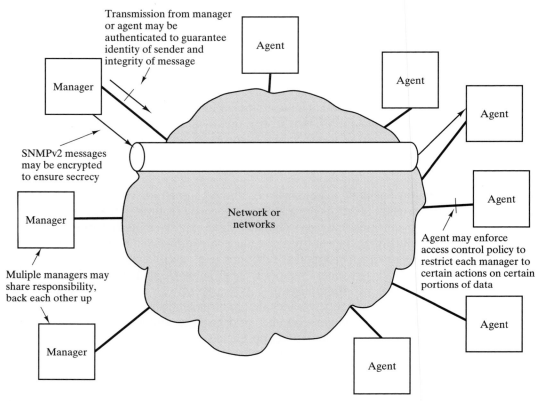

FIGURE 16.9 Features of SNMPv2 Security.

SUMMARY

As with security, the need for network management grows with the growing complexity and scale of a network. Network management covers a number of areas, the most important being:

- *Fault management.* The most important function of network management is to maintain high availability of network services and resources. For this purpose it is necessary to monitor the network for faults, to isolate the faults, and to recover from the faults.

- *Accounting management.* Divisions, cost centers, or projects may be charged for the use of network resources. Effective planning for network expansion requires an understanding of usage patterns. For both these areas, an accounting of network usage is needed.

- *Configuration and name management.* The resources of the network must be initialized and the intended relationships established for proper network operation.

- *Performance monitoring.* To provide efficient service with acceptable response times and throughput, it is necessary to monitor the performance of the network.

- *Security management.* The various schemes employed for security must be managed in a reliable and secure fashion.

To perform these functions in a modern, complex information network in an efficient and practical fashion, a full-fledged network management system is needed. For a network management system, software that provides network management functions is embedded into the software suite of every node in the network. Hardware monitoring or controlling devices are controlled by software in one or more network nodes. A central network control center is able to communicate with the network management software in all other nodes and with any specialized hardware. A good example of a mature network management system is the NetView product of IBM.

The operation of any network management system is based on information about the status and behavior of the network. Various network management tools are available for collecting these data.

Technical control is that part of network management that specifically relates to the requirement for providing high availability. Component-level technical control devices, such as line monitors and protocol analyzers, can be very useful in monitoring critical network areas. However, for broad and continuous coverage, a comprehensive network technical control system is needed. Such a system includes a collection of software and hardware added onto and integrated with network resources.

Performance monitoring is another critical area of network management and is involved in assessing the performance characteristics of the network, locating or anticipating bottlenecks and modifying the network to maintain an acceptable level of service. Again, component-level products, such as response-time monitors, hardware monitors, and software monitors, can provide useful information at critical network points. However, system-wide, detailed information requires a network monitoring system that is incorporated into the network at every node.

The most important standardized scheme for supporting network management applications is the simple network management protocol (SNMP). The original version of SNMP is available on a wide array of products and is widely used. SNMPv2 contains a number of enhancements to SNMP and is expected to supplant it.

RECOMMENDED READING

[STAL96] provides a comprehensive and detailed examination of network management protocol standards, including SNMP and SNMPv2; the book also provides an overview of network management technology. One of the few textbooks on the subject of network management is [TERP92]; this book contains a wealth of practical information about products and management strategies.

STAL96   STALLINGS, W. *SNMP, SNMPv2, and RMON: Practical Network Management.* Reading, MA: Addison-Wesley, 1996.
TERP92   TERPLAN, K. *Communication Networks Management.* Upper Saddle River, NJ: Prentice Hall, 1992.

Recommended Web Sites

- http://smurfland.cit.buffalo.edu/NetMan/index.html: good overall site for information on network management topics. This site has links to many of the vendors who offer SNMP, RMON, and other network management products.

- http://snmp.cs.utwente.nl: known as the Simple Web site. It is a good source of information on SNMP, including pointers to many public-domain implementations.

- http://www.nmf.org: home page for the Network Management Forum (NMF), a nonprofit organization whose members are vendors, customers, and others concerned with standardizing network management protocol and services. Although the original focus of NMF was OSI network management, it has since expanded its charter to include the promotion of SNMP-based products and solutions.

KEY TERMS

Agent	NetView/PC	Performance Monitoring
Capacity Planning	Network Management	Proxy
Fault	System	Simple Network Management
Manager	Network Management	Protocol (SNMP)
Management Information	Protocol	SNMPv2
Base (MIB)	Network Technical Control	Trap
NetView		

QUESTIONS

1. How does a fault differ from an error?

2. How is fault tolerance achieved?

3. What are the major categories of SNA network management?

4. Explain IBM's concept of open network management.

5. How can a non-IBM vendor link its product to NetView for network management?

6. What is network technical control?

7. What functions are performed by a network control system?

8. What is a software monitor?

9. What functions are provided by SNMP?

10. What is the difference between SNMPv1 and SNMPv2?

PROBLEM

1. The original (version 1) specification of SNMP has the following definition of a data type known as Gauge:

> This application-wide type represents a non-negative integer, which may increase or decrease, but which latches at a maximum value. This standard specifies a maximum value of 2^{32-1} (4294967295 decimal) for gauges.

Unfortunately, the word *latch* is not defined, and this resulted in two different interpretations. The SNMPv2 standard cleared up the ambiguity with the following definition:

The value of a Gauge has its maximum value whenever the information being modeled is greater than or equal to that maximum value; if the information being modeled subsequently decreases below the maximum value, the Gauge also decreases.

a. What is the alternative interpretation?
b. Discuss the pros and cons of the two interpretations.

17

Network Security

CHAPTER OBJECTIVES

After reading this chapter, you should be able to:

- List the most important security threats faced by a distributed data processing installation and indicate where those threats can occur.

- Define conventional and public-key encryption and compare the uses of the two methods.

- Explain the relevance of the DES and RSA encryption algorithms.

- Discuss the problems of key distribution and management.

- Indicate approaches to incorporating encryption in a network, including the use of link encryption and end-to-end encryption.

- Discuss applications of encryption to network security.

- Describe Web security threats.

*I*n a recent attack on the Texas A&M University computer complex, which consists of over 12,000 interconnected PCs, workstations, minicomputers, mainframes, and servers, a well-organized team of hackers were able to take virtual control of the complex. The computer center was notified that one of their machines was being used to attack computers at another location via the Internet. By monitoring activity, the computer center personnel learned that there were several outside intruders involved, who were running password-cracking routines on various computers (the site consists of a total of 12,000 interconnected machines). The center disconnected affected machines, plugged known security holes, and resumed normal operation. A few days later, one of the local system managers detected that the intruder attack had resumed. It turned out that the attack was far more sophisticated than had originally been believed. Having broken in by running password-cracking programs, the intruders then modified login software to enable them to capture additional passwords of users logging on to systems. The team compiled files containing hundreds of captured passwords, including some on major and supposedly secure servers. One local machine was set up as a hacker bulletin board, which the hackers used to contact each other, to discuss techniques and progress, and to disseminate the captured passwords. The team gained access to E-mail servers, enabling them to capture and read mail traveling to and from dial-in personal computers used by staff, faculty, and students.

An analysis of this attack revealed that there were actually two levels of hackers. The high level were sophisticated users with a thorough knowledge of the technology; the low level were the "foot soldiers," who merely used the supplied cracking programs, with little understanding of how they worked. This teamwork combined the two most serious weapons in the intruder armory: sophisticated knowledge of how to intrude and a willingness to spend countless hours "turning doorknobs" to probe for weaknesses.

What lessons can a network manager or information systems executive in the business world draw from this account? You could say that this incident occurred at a university computer complex and that university computing centers are notoriously open and provide ready access through dial-in lines and across the network and therefore are uniquely vulnerable. This conclusion would be wrong. True, university computer sites are generally open to Internet and dial-in access, but most businesses provide at least some level of remote access to their systems.

You could say that there is a sort of culture of free access to all information that is characteristic of the educational complex that is not repeated in the business world, and that therefore the university center is a more inviting and easier target. Again, this would be wrong. Universities have become quite sophisticated in their ability to use security tools to protect information and resources and university computer personnel are among the most sophisticated in using these tools and keeping up with the nature of the threat as it evolves. You could also ask many of the major telephone service providers or defense computer complexes whether they feel more secure than their university counterparts. Based on the number of successful attacks against those institutions, a feeling of greater security is hardly warranted.

Finally, you might say that these attacks are generally carried out by young people for kicks, with no intent to damage or steal, and that (1) they are more aware of the university facilities and will attack them and that (2) even if my facility is successfully breached, no harm is likely to be done. This attitude is wrong in all its facets. First, many of these young people are not so young anymore and may have graduated to more sophisticated targets; second, if your company's systems are on the Internet, attackers can easily find them; and finally, the benign culture of the "hacker" has changed and is no longer particularly benign.

You need to know that there is a risk, that this risk is multidimensional and serious, and that it is growing as companies become more dependent on networking and distributed systems. We begin this chapter with an introduction to the threats posed to business information systems and communication in a networked environment. Then we introduce encryption, which is a fundamental tool at the heart of virtually all security mechanisms, and look at some of the nuts and bolts of encryption techniques. The remainder of the chapter is devoted to various security services and applications based on encryption.

17.1 SECURITY THREATS

In broad terms, **security threats** can be classified as passive and active. **Passive attacks** have to do with eavesdropping on, or monitoring, transmissions. Electronic mail, file transfers, and client–server exchanges are examples of transmissions that can be monitored. **Active attacks** include the modification of transmitted data and attempts to gain unauthorized access to computer systems. We examine these two areas in turn.

Passive Attacks

Consider a user workstation in a typical business organization. Figure 17.1 suggests the types of communications facilities that might be employed by such a workstation and therefore gives an indication of the points of vulnerability to eavesdropping.

In most organizations, workstations are attached to local-area networks (LANs). Typically, the user can reach other workstations, hosts, and servers directly on the LAN or on other LANs in the same building that are interconnected with bridges and routers. Here, then, is the first point of vulnerability. In this case, the main concern is eavesdropping by another employee. Typically, a

FIGURE 17.1 Points of Vulnerability.

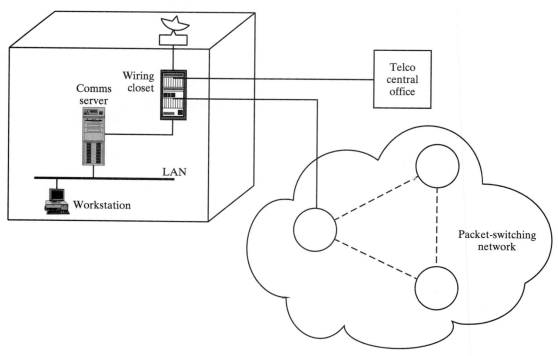

LAN is a broadcast network: transmission from any station to any other station is visible on the LAN medium to all stations. Data are transmitted in the form of frames, with each frame containing the source and destination address. An eavesdropper can monitor the traffic on the LAN and capture any traffic desired on the basis of source and destination addresses. Furthermore, the eavesdropper need not necessarily be an employee in the building. If the LAN, through a communications server or one of the hosts on the LAN, offers a dial-in capability, it is possible for an intruder to gain access to the LAN and monitor traffic.

Access to the outside world from the LAN is almost always available in the form of a router, a bank of dial-out modems, or some other type of communications server. From the communications server, there is a line leading to a wiring closet. The wiring closet serves as a patch panel for interconnecting internal data and phone lines and for providing a staging point for external communications.

The wiring closet itself is vulnerable. If an intruder can penetrate to the closet, he or she can tap into each wire to determine which are used for data transmission. After isolating one or more lines, the intruder can attach a low-power radio transmitter. The resulting signals can be picked up from a nearby location (e.g., a parked van or a nearby building).

Several routes out of the wiring closet are possible. A standard configuration provides access to the nearest central office of the local telephone company. Wires in the closet are gathered into a cable, which is usually consolidated with other cables in the basement of the building. From there, a larger cable runs underground to the central office.

In addition, the wiring closet may provide a link to a microwave antenna, either an earth station for a satellite link or a point-to-point terrestrial microwave link. The antenna link can be part of a private network, or it can be a local bypass to hook in to a long-distance carrier such as AT&T or MCI.

The wiring closet may also provide a link to a node of a packet-switching network. This link can be a leased line, a direct private line, or a switched connection through a public telecommunications network such as ISDN. Inside the network, data pass through a number of nodes and links between nodes until it arrives at the node to which the destination end system is connected.

An attack can take place at any of the communications links. The communications links involved can be cable (telephone twisted pair, coaxial cable, or optical fiber), microwave links, or satellite channels. Twisted pair and coaxial cable can be attacked using either invasive taps or inductive devices that monitor electromagnetic emanation. Invasive taps allow both active and passive attacks, whereas inductive taps are useful for passive attacks. Neither type of tap is particularly useful with optical fiber, which is one of the advantages of this medium. The fiber does not generate electromagnetic emanations and hence is not vulnerable to inductive taps. Physically breaking the cable seriously degrades signal quality and is therefore detectable. Microwave and satellite transmissions can be intercepted with little risk to the attacker. This is especially true of satellite transmissions, which cover a broad geographic area. Active attacks on microwave and satellite are also possible, although they are more difficult technically and can be quite expensive.

Thus, there are a large number of locations at which an attack can occur. Furthermore, for wide-area communications, many of these locations are not under the physical control of the end user. Even in the case of local-area networks, in which physical security measures are possible, there is always the threat of the disgruntled employee.

Active Attacks

Many organizations are just beginning to realize the scale and seriousness of the threats inherent in reliance on networks and distributed processing, and many still discount that threat. Intruder attacks range from the benign to the serious. At the benign end of the scale, there are many people who simply wish to explore the Internet and see what is out there. At the serious end are individuals who are attempting to read privileged data, perform unauthorized modifications to data, or disrupt the system.

Benign intruders might be tolerable, although they do consume resources and may slow performance for legitimate users. However, there is no way in advance to know whether an intruder will be benign or malign. Consequently, even for systems with no particularly sensitive resources, there is a motivation to control this problem. Furthermore, serious attacks from intruders are a real and growing problem. Some of the reasons for this trend:

- *Globalization.* The pressures of international competition have spawned a number of recent cases of industrial espionage. There is also evidence that a number of the "hacker clubs" are beginning to sell their services for this purpose.

- *Move to client–server architecture.* Companies have traditionally kept most of their data either on mainframes, which can be guarded with sophisticated security software, or on stand-alone PCs, which usually have not been accessible remotely. But as client/server architectures become increasingly popular, both barriers are removed. Most servers run Unix, which is notorious for its lack of mainframe-style security features and is a particular favorite of hackers.

- *Hackers' steep learning curve.* Hackers love to share information. Underground bulletin boards are used to exchange dial-in port phone numbers, compromised passwords, security holes in systems, and intrusion techniques. Because of a natural reluctance of security and systems personnel to share security-related information, especially concerning vulnerabilities, intruders are better able than their adversaries to stay abreast of the latest tricks of the trade and corporate vulnerabilities. Furthermore, when security personnel do exchange information about vulnerabilities, attackers can often eavesdrop and exploit these vulnerabilities before the holes are plugged on all affected systems.

An example of this last point is the Texas A&M incident discussed at the opening of this chapter. One of the results of the growing awareness of the intruder problem has been the establishment of a number of computer emergency response teams (CERTs). These cooperative ventures collect information about system vulnerabilities and disseminate it to systems managers. Unfortunately, intruders can also gain access to CERT reports. In the Texas A&M incident, later analysis showed that the intruders had developed programs to test the attacked machines for virtually every vulnerability that had been announced by CERT. If even one machine had failed to respond promptly to a CERT advisory, it was wide open to such attacks.

Most of those who acquire hacking or intruding skills come by them as teenagers or even younger. But remember that this has been going on for a number of years. There are plenty of grown-ups out there who acquired these skills when younger and are now in a position to use them. An employee can use intrusion techniques against his or her own company or might use these skills against a competitor to advance within his or her company. In some cases, a company may deliberately adopt a policy of attacking the computer systems of a competitor, either to gain information or to disrupt operations.

There is no simple way to quantify the threat posed by those skilled in breaching computer and network security, but two points should be kept in mind. First, the high level of dependence of organizations on computerized information and distributed processing means that the cost of a security failure can be very high; and second, the growing population of users of the Internet and other networking and dial-in facilities provides a growing opportunity for unauthorized access to computerized resources.

While the scale of the threat is difficult to quantify, the degree of vulnerability of information systems is all too apparent. A recent study by the US. General Accounting Office (GAO) found that Department of Defense computers are extremely vulnerable. Figure 17.2 shows the results of a series of attacks orchestrated by the Defense Information Systems Agency (DISA). DISA gained access 65% of the time. Of these successful attacks, only about 4% were detected by the target organization. Of those detected, only about 27% were reported to the appropriate security officials. Given the relative sophistication of Defense

FIGURE 17.2 Results of GAO Vulnerability Assessment [GAO96].

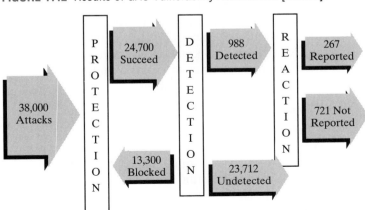

Department systems and computer personnel, the extract from the GAO report that follows should make sober reading for any business manager.

■ Illustration: Attacks on Information Systems

Attacks on Department of Defense computer systems are a serious and growing threat. The exact number of attacks cannot be readily determined because only a small portion are actually detected and reported. However, Defense Information Systems Agency (DISA) data implies that Defense may have experienced as many as 250,000 attacks last year. DISA information also shows that attacks are successful 65 percent of the time, and that the number of attacks is doubling each year, as Internet use increases along with the sophistication of hackers and their tools.

According to Defense officials, attackers have obtained and corrupted sensitive information—they have stolen, modified, and destroyed both data and software. They have installed unwanted files and "back doors" which circumvent normal system protection and allow attackers unauthorized access in the future. They have shut down and crashed entire systems and networks, denying service to users who depend on automated systems to help meet critical missions. Numerous Defense functions have been adversely affected, including weapons and supercomputer research, logistics, finance, procurement, personnel management, military health, and payroll.

In addition to the security breaches and service disruptions they cause, these attacks are expensive. The 1994 Rome Laboratory incident alone cost Defense over $500,000 to assess the damage to its systems, ensure the reliability of the information in the systems, patch the vulnerabilities in its networks and systems, and attempt to identify the attackers and their locations. Although Defense has not estimated the total cost of repairing damage caused by the thousands of attacks experienced each year, it believes they are costing tens or possibly even hundreds of millions of dollars. ■

Source: GAO Report 96-84, *Information Security: Computer Attacks at Department of Defense Pose Increasing Risks,* May 1996.

17.2 ENCRYPTION METHODS

The essential technology underlying virtually all automated network and computer security applications is cryptography. Two fundamental approaches are in use: conventional encryption, also known as symmetric encryption, and public-key encryption, also known as asymmetric encryption. The section provides an overview of both types of encryption, together with a brief discussion of some important encryption algorithms.

Conventional Encryption
A form of cryptosystem in which encryption and decryption are performed using the same key.

Conventional Encryption

Conventional encryption, also referred to as *symmetric encryption* or *single-key encryption,* was the only type of encryption in use prior to the introduction of public-key encryption in the late 1970s. Conventional encryption has been used for secret communication by countless individuals and groups, from Julius Caesar to the German U-boat force to present-day diplomatic, military, and commercial users. It remains by far the more widely used of the two types of encryption.

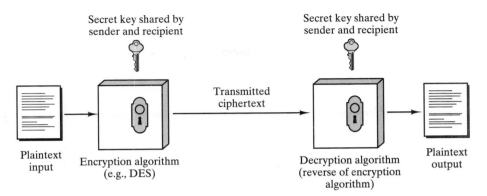

FIGURE 17.3 Conventional Encryption.

A conventional encryption scheme has five ingredients (Figure 17.3):

- *Plaintext.* This is the readable message or data that is fed into the algorithm as input.

Encryption
To convert plain text or data into unintelligible form by means of a reversible mathematical computation.

- *Encryption algorithm.* The **encryption** algorithm performs various substitutions and transformations on the plaintext.

- *Secret key.* The secret key is also input to the algorithm. The exact substitutions and transformations performed by the algorithm depend on the key.

- *Ciphertext.* This is the scrambled message produced as output. It depends on the plaintext and the secret key. For a given message, two different keys will produce two different ciphertexts.

- *Decryption algorithm.* This is essentially the encryption algorithm run in reverse. It takes the ciphertext and the same secret key and produces the original plaintext.

There are two requirements for secure use of conventional encryption:

1. We need a strong encryption algorithm. At a minimum, we would like the algorithm to be such that an opponent who knows the algorithm and has access to one or more ciphertexts would be unable to decipher the ciphertext or figure out the key. This requirement is usually stated in a stronger form: The opponent should be unable to decrypt ciphertext or discover the key even if he or she is in possession of a number of ciphertexts together with the plaintext that produced each ciphertext.

2. Sender and receiver must have obtained copies of the secret key in a secure fashion and must keep the key secure. If someone can discover the key and knows the algorithm, all communication using this key is readable.

There are two general approaches to attacking a conventional encryption scheme. The first attack is known as *cryptanalysis.* Cryptanalytic attacks rely on the nature of the algorithm plus perhaps some knowledge of the general characteristics of the plaintext or even some sample plaintext–ciphertext pairs. This type

TABLE 17-1 Average Time Required for Exhaustive Key Search

Key Size (bits)	Number of Alternative Keys	Time Required at 1 Encryption/μsec	Time Required at 10^6 Encryptions/μsec
32	$2^{32} = 4.3 \times 10^9$	2^{31} μsec = 35.8 minutes	2.15 milliseconds
56	$2^{56} = 7.2 \times 10^{16}$	2^{55} μsec = 1142 years	10.01 hours
128	$2^{128} = 3.4 \times 10^{38}$	2^{127} μsec = 5.4×10^{24} years	5.4×10^{18} years

of attack exploits the characteristics of the algorithm to attempt to deduce a specific plaintext or to deduce the key being used. Of course, if the attack succeeds in deducing the key, the effect is catastrophic: All future and past messages encrypted with that key are compromised.

The second method, known as the *brute-force* attack, is to try every possible key on a piece of ciphertext until an intelligible translation into plaintext is obtained. On average, half of all possible keys must be tried to achieve success. Table 17-1 shows how much time is involved for various key sizes. The table shows results for each key size, assuming that it takes 1 microsecond to perform a single decryption, a reasonable order of magnitude for today's computers. With the use of massively parallel organizations of microprocessors, it may be possible to achieve processing rates many orders of magnitude greater. The final column of the table considers the results for a system that can process 1 million keys per microsecond. As one can see, at this performance level, a 56-bit key can no longer be considered computationally secure.

Data Encryption Standard   The most widely used encryption scheme is defined in the **data encryption standard (DES)**, adopted in 1977 by the National Bureau of Standards, now the National Institute of Standards and Technology (NIST), as Federal Information Processing Standard 46 (FIPS PUB 46). In 1994, NIST "reaffirmed" DES for federal use for another five years; NIST recommends the use of DES for applications other than the protection of classified information (e.g., financial and other business applications).

As with any encryption scheme, there are two inputs to the DES encryption function: the plaintext to be encrypted and the key. With DES, the plaintext must be 64 bits and the key 56 bits. Longer blocks of plaintext are encrypted in blocks of 64 bits.

In essence, DES processes plaintext by passing each 64-bit input through 16 iterations, producing an intermediate 64-bit value at the end of each iteration. Each iteration is essentially the same complex function that involves a permutation of the bits and substituting one bit pattern for another. The input at each stage consists of the output of the previous stage plus a permutation on the key bits, where the permutation is known as a *subkey*.

The process of decryption with DES is essentially the same as encryption: Use the ciphertext as input to the DES algorithm, but use the subkeys generated for each iteration in reverse order (i.e., use the sixteenth subkey for the first iteration, the fifteenth subkey for the second iteration, etc.).

Strength of DES   Since DES was adopted as a federal standard, there have been lingering concerns about the level of security it provides. These concerns, by and large, fall into two areas: the nature of the algorithm and the key size.

For many years, the more important concern was the possibility of exploiting the characteristics of the DES algorithm to perform cryptanalysis. Because the design criteria for the algorithm have never been made public, there is a suspicion that the algorithm was constructed in such a way that cryptanalysis is possible for an opponent who knows its weaknesses. This assertion is tantalizing and over the years a number of regularities and unexpected behaviors in the algorithm have been discovered. However, no one so far has succeeded in discovering the supposed fatal weaknesses in DES. Indeed, as advances in cryptanalytic techniques have taken place, the underlying strength of the DES algorithm has become all the more apparent. As of this writing, no practical cryptanalytic attack method for DES has been published. Given that the algorithm has survived years of intensive scrutiny unscathed, it is probably safe to say that DES is one of the strongest encryption algorithms ever devised.

The more serious concern today is the key size. With a key length of 56 bits, there are 2^{56} possible keys, which is approximately 7.6×10^{16} keys. On the face of it, therefore, a brute-force attack appears impractical. Assuming that on average half the key space has to be searched, a single machine performing one DES encryption per microsecond would take more than 1000 years to break the cipher.

But the assumption of one encryption per microsecond is overly conservative. As far back as 1977, Whitfield Diffie and Martin Hellman, who were the first to describe public-key encryption in the open literature, postulated that the technology existed to build a parallel machine with 1 million encryption devices, each of which could perform one encryption per microsecond. The authors estimated that the cost would be about $20 million in 1977 dollars.

The most rigorous recent analysis of the problem was performed by Michael Wiener of Bell-Northern Research and is based on a known plaintext attack; that is, it is assumed that the attacker has at least one plaintext–ciphertext pair. Wiener takes care to provide the details of his design in his paper [WIEN93]: "There have been numerous unverifiable claims about how fast the DES key space can be searched. To avoid adding to this list of questionable claims, a great deal of detail in the design of a key search machine is included in the appendices. This detailed work was done to obtain an accurate assessment of the cost of the machine and the time required to find a DES key. There are no plans to actually build such a machine."

Wiener reports on the design of a chip that uses pipelined techniques to achieve a key search rate of 50 million keys per second. Using 1993 costs, he designed a module that costs $100,000 and contains 5760 key search chips. With this design, the following results are obtained:

Key Search Machine Unit Cost	*Expected Search Time*
$ 100,000	35 hours
$ 1,000,000	3.5 hours
$10,000,000	21 minutes

In addition, Wiener estimates a one-time development cost of about $500,000.

The Wiener design represents the culmination of years of concern about the security of DES and may in retrospect have been a turning point. The time has come to investigate alternatives for conventional encryption. The most widely accepted candidate for replacing DES is triple DES.

Triple DES   Given the potential vulnerability of DES to a brute-force attack, there has been considerable interest in finding an alternative. One approach, which preserves the existing investment in software and equipment, is to use multiple encryption with DES and multiple keys. The most popular form of multiple DES is referred to as **triple DES**. Triple DES uses two keys and three executions of the DES algorithm. The function follows an encrypt–decrypt–encrypt (EDE) sequence (Figure 17.4).[1] Although only two keys are used, three instances of the DES algorithm are required. It turns out that there is a simple technique, known as a meet-in-the-middle attack, that would reduce a double DES system with two keys to the relative strength of ordinary single DES. With three iterations of the DES function, the effective key length is 112 bits.

Public-Key Encryption

Public-Key Encryption
A method in which encryption and decryption are performed using two different keys, one of which is referred to as the public key and one of which is referred to as the private key.

Public-key encryption, first publicly proposed by Diffie and Hellman in 1976, is the first truly revolutionary advance in encryption in literally thousands of years. For one thing, public-key algorithms are based on mathematical functions rather than on simple operations on bit patterns. More important, public-key cryptography is asymmetric, involving the use of two separate keys, in contrast to the symmetric conventional encryption, which uses only one key. The use of two keys has profound consequences in the areas of confidentiality, key distribution, and authentication.

Before proceeding, we should first mention several common misconceptions concerning public-key encryption. One is that public-key encryption is more secure from cryptanalysis than conventional encryption. In fact, the security of any encryption scheme depends on the length of the key and the computational work involved in breaking a cipher. There is nothing in principle about either

FIGURE 17.4 Triple DES.

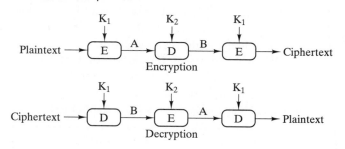

---

[1] There is no cryptographic significance to the use of decryption for the second stage. Its only advantage is that it allows users of triple DES to decrypt data encrypted by users of the older single DES simply by repeating the same key in each of the three stages.

conventional or public-key encryption that makes one superior to another from the point of view of resisting cryptanalysis. A second misconception is that public-key encryption is a general-purpose technique that has made conventional encryption obsolete. On the contrary, because of the computational overhead of current public-key encryption schemes, there seems no foreseeable likelihood that conventional encryption will be abandoned. Finally, there is a feeling that key distribution is trivial when using public-key encryption, compared to the rather cumbersome handshaking involved with key distribution centers for conventional encryption. In fact, some form of protocol is needed, often involving a central agent, and the procedures involved are no simpler nor any more efficient than those required for conventional encryption.

A public-key encryption scheme has six ingredients (Figure 17.5):

- *Plaintext.* This is the readable message or data fed into the algorithm as input.

- *Encryption algorithm.* The encryption algorithm performs various transformations on the plaintext.

- *Public and private key.* This is a pair of keys that have been selected so that if one is used for encryption, the other is used for decryption. The exact transformations performed by the encryption algorithm depend on the public or private key that is provided as input.

- *Ciphertext.* This is the scrambled message produced as output. It depends on the plaintext and the key. For a given message, two different keys will produce two different ciphertexts.

- *Decryption algorithm.* This algorithm generates the ciphertext and the matching key and produces the original plaintext.

The process works (produces the correct plaintext on output) regardless of the order in which the pair of keys is used. As the names suggest, the public key of the pair is made public for others to use, while the private key is known only to its owner.

Now, say that Bob wants to send a private message to Alice and suppose that he has Alice's public key and Alice has the matching private key (Figure 17.5a). Using Alice's public key, Bob encrypts the message to produce ciphertext. The ciphertext is then transmitted to Alice. When Alice gets the ciphertext, she decrypts it using her private key. Because only Alice has a copy of her private key, no one else can read the message.

Public key encryption can be used in another way, as illustrated in Figure 17.5b. Suppose that Bob wants to send a message to Alice and although it isn't important that the message be kept secret, he wants Alice to be certain that the message is indeed from him. In this case Bob uses his own private key to encrypt the message. When Alice receives the ciphertext, she finds that she can decrypt it with Bob's public key, thus proving that the message must have been encrypted by Bob: No one else has Bob's private key and therefore no one else could have created a ciphertext that could be decrypted with Bob's public key.

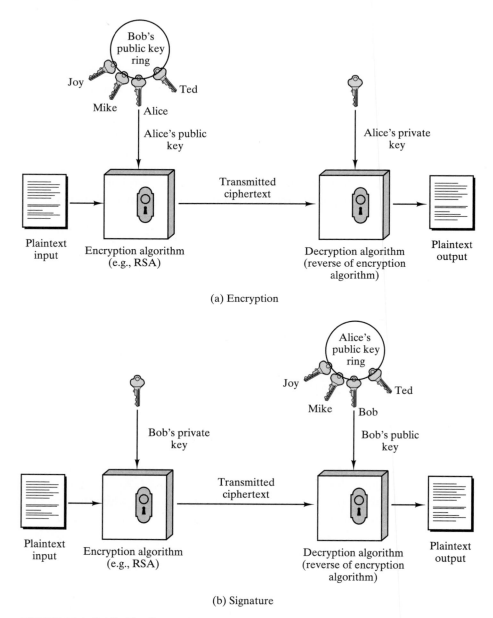

(a) Encryption

(b) Signature

FIGURE 17.5 Public-Key Encryption.

A general-purpose public-key cryptographic algorithm relies on one key for encryption and a different but related key for decryption. Furthermore, these algorithms have the following important characteristics:

- It is computationally infeasible to determine the decryption key given only knowledge of the cryptographic algorithm and the encryption key.

- Either of the two related keys can be used for encryption, with the other used for decryption.

The essential steps are the following:

1. Each user generates a pair of keys to be used for the encryption and decryption of messages.
2. Each user places one of the two keys in a public register or other accessible file. This is the public key. The companion key is kept private. As Figure 17.5 suggests, each user maintains a collection of public keys obtained from others.
3. If Bob wishes to send a private message to Alice, Bob encrypts the message using Alice's public key.
4. If Bob wishes to send an authenticated message to Alice, Bob encrypts the message using Bob's private key.

With this approach, all participants have access to public keys, and private keys are generated locally by each participant and therefore need never be distributed. As long as a user protects his or her private key, incoming communication is secure. At any time, a user can change the private key and publish the companion public key to replace the old public key.

What's the Advantage of Public-Key Encryption?

Compared to the typical conventional encryption algorithm, public-key encryption is painfully slow. So what is the point of this new method? The answer is that public-key encryption provides us with tremendous flexibility to perform a number of security-related functions. Two areas in particular stand out: key management and digital signatures. These are discussed later in the chapter.

Rivest–Shamir–Adleman (RSA) Algorithm   One of the first public-key schemes was developed in 1977 by Ron Rivest, Adi Shamir, and Len Adleman at MIT. The **RSA Algorithm** has since that time reigned supreme as the only widely accepted and implemented approach to public-key encryption. RSA is a cipher in which the plaintext and ciphertext are integers between 0 and $n - 1$ for some n. Encryption involves modular arithmetic. The strength of the algorithm is based on the difficulty of factoring numbers into their prime factors.

17.3 ENCRYPTION MANAGEMENT

In this section we examine two issues related to the management of the encryption function. First we look at the issue of where in the communication process encryption should be carried out. Then we look at the issue of key distribution.

Location of Encryption Devices

Recall from Figure 17.1 that in an information network there are many locations at which security threats may occur. If encryption is to be used to counter these threats, we need to decide what to encrypt and where the encryption gear should

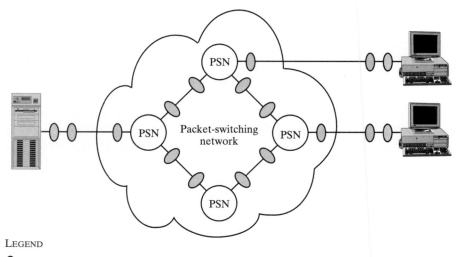

LEGEND

    = end-to-end encryption device

    = link encryption device

PSN = packet-switching node

FIGURE 17.6 Encryption Across a Packet-Switching Network.

be located. As Figure 17.6 indicates, there are two fundamental alternatives: link encryption and end-to-end encryption.

With *link encryption,* each vulnerable communications link is equipped on both ends with an encryption device. Thus, all traffic over all communications links is secured. Although this requires a lot of encryption devices in a large network, the number is still much smaller than the number of sender–receiver pairs that use such a network. One disadvantage of this approach is that at least part of the message must be decrypted each time it enters a packet switch; this is necessary because the switch must read the virtual circuit number in the packet header in order to route the packet. Thus, the message is vulnerable at each switch. If this is a public packet-switching network, the user has no control over the security of the nodes. Moreover, link encryption at broadband channel rates is currently beyond the state of the art, further limiting its applicability.

With *end-to-end encryption,* the encryption process is carried out at the two end systems. The source host or terminal encrypts the data. The data, in encrypted form, are then transmitted unaltered across the network to the destination terminal or host. The destination shares a key with the source and so is able to decrypt the data. This approach would seem to secure the transmission against attacks on the network links or switches. There is, however, still a weak spot.

Consider the following situation. A host connects to an X.25 packet-switching network, sets up a virtual circuit to another host, and is prepared to transfer data to that other host by using end-to-end encryption. As you know, data are transmitted over such a network in the form of packets, consisting of a header and some user data. What part of each packet will the host encrypt? Suppose that the host encrypts the entire packet, including the header. This will not work because, remember, only the other host can perform the decryption. The packet-switching node will receive an encrypted packet and be unable to read the header. Therefore, it will not be able to route the packet! It follows that the host may encrypt only the user data portion of the packet and must leave the header in the clear, so that it can be read by the network.

Thus, with end-to-end encryption, the user data are secure. However, the traffic pattern is not, because packet headers are transmitted in the clear. To achieve greater security, both link and end-to-end encryption can be used, as shown in Figure 17.6.

Key Distribution

Different problems arise for key distribution in the case of conventional encryption and public-key encryption. This subsection provides an overview of the issues for both cases.

Conventional Encryption   For conventional encryption to work, the two parties to an exchange must have the same key, and that key must be protected from access by others. Furthermore, frequent key changes are usually desirable to limit the amount of data compromised if an attacker learns the key. Therefore, the strength of any cryptographic system rests with the key distribution technique, a term that refers to the means of delivering a key to two parties that wish to exchange data, without allowing others to see the key. Key distribution can be achieved in a number of ways. For two parties, A and B:

1. A key could be selected by party A and physically delivered to party B.
2. A third party could select the key and physically deliver it to parties A and B.
3. If parties A and B have previously and recently used a key, one party could transmit the new key to the other, encrypted using the old key.
4. If parties A and B each have an encrypted connection to a third party C, C could deliver a key on the encrypted links to parties A and B.

Options 1 and 2 call for manual delivery of a key. For link encryption, this is a reasonable requirement, because each link encryption device is only going to be exchanging data with its partner on the other end of the link. However, for end-to-end encryption, manual delivery is awkward. In a distributed system, any given host or terminal may need to engage in exchanges with many other hosts and terminals over time. Thus, each device needs a number of keys, supplied dynamically. The problem is especially difficult in a wide-area distributed system.

Option 3 is a possibility for either link encryption or end-to-end encryption, but if an attacker ever succeeds in gaining access to one key, all subsequent keys are revealed. Even if frequent changes are made to the link encryption keys, these should be done manually. To provide keys for end-to-end encryption, option 4 is preferable.

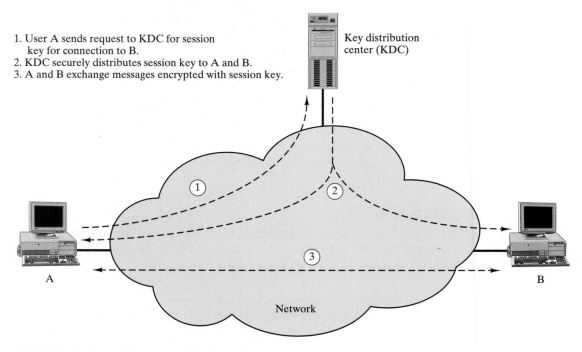

1. User A sends request to KDC for session key for connection to B.
2. KDC securely distributes session key to A and B.
3. A and B exchange messages encrypted with session key.

Key distribution center (KDC)

A

B

Network

FIGURE 17.7 Secure Conventional Key Distribution.

Figure 17.7 illustrates an implementation that satisfies option 4 for end-to-end encryption. In the figure, link encryption is ignored. This can be added, or not, as required. For this scheme, two kinds of keys are identified:

- *Session key.* When two end systems (hosts, terminals, etc.) wish to communicate, they establish a logical connection (e.g., virtual circuit). For the duration of that logical connection, all user data are encrypted with a one-time session key. At the conclusion of the session, or connection, the session key is destroyed.

- *Permanent key.* A permanent key is a key used between entities for the purpose of distributing session keys.

This approach relies on a **key distribution center (KDC)**, which determines which systems are allowed to communicate with each other. When permission is granted for two systems to establish a connection, the key distribution center provides a one-time session key for that connection.

The steps involved in establishing a connection are shown in the figure. When one host (e.g., a workstation or server) wishes to set up a connection to another host, it transmits a request to the KDC for permission to establish the connection (step 1). The communication between the host and the KDC is encrypted using a master key shared only by that host and the KDC. If the KDC approves the connection request, it generates the session key and delivers it to the two appropriate users, using a unique permanent key for each (step 2). All subsequent user data exchanged between the two end systems are encrypted using the one-time session key.

The automated key distribution approach provides the flexibility and dynamic characteristics needed to allow a number of terminal users to access a number of hosts and for the hosts to exchange data with each other. This approach is used in a number of networking applications. Perhaps the best known is Kerberos, which provides authentication and secure communication in a client–server environment.

Public-Key Encryption The need for secure distribution of keys is not absent from public-key encryption schemes. Suppose that Bob and Alice wish to exchange messages using public-key encryption. One approach would simply be for Bob to encrypt every message to Alice using Alice's public key. This approach is not used because of the high computational cost of encrypting entire messages with public-key algorithms. Instead, an ingenious combination of conventional and public-key encryption is used.

If Bob wants to correspond with Alice and other people, he generates a single pair of keys, one private and one public. He keeps the private key secure and broadcasts the public key to all and sundry. If Alice does the same, Bob has Alice's public key, Alice has Bob's public key, and they can now communicate securely. When Bob wishes to communicate with Alice, Bob can do the following (Figure 17.8):

1. Prepare a message.
2. Encrypt that message using conventional encryption with a one-time conventional session key.
3. Encrypt the session key using public-key encryption with Alice's public key.
4. Attach the encrypted session key to the message and send it to Alice.

Only Alice is capable of decrypting the session key and therefore of recovering the original message. This general approach to encryption and key distribution is in common use, especially for E-mail applications. Perhaps the best-known electronic mail application that uses this approach is Pretty Good Privacy (PGP).

It is important to note that we have replaced one problem with another. Bob's private key is secure because he need never reveal it; however, Alice must be sure that the public key with Bob's name written all over it is in fact Bob's public key. Someone else could have broadcast a public key and said it was Bob's. The solution to this problem is something known as a public-key certificate, which we discuss later in the chapter.

17.4 DIGITAL SIGNATURES

Suppose that Bob and Alice share a secret key for conventional encryption and that Alice receives an encrypted message that is allegedly from Bob. Alice decrypts the message and recovers intelligible plaintext. Conclusion: This is a genuine message from Bob, since Bob is the only person other than Alice who knows the shared secret key.

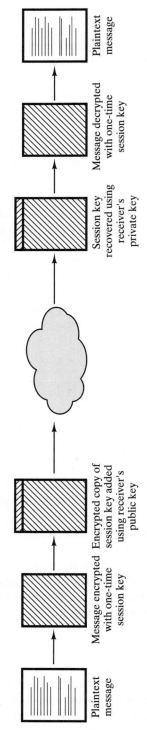

FIGURE 17.8 One-Time Session Key Encrypted with Public Key.

One weak spot in this arrangement is that Bob can send Alice a message and later deny it. What would be the point? Well, suppose that Bob is an investor and Alice a broker. On Monday Bob sends Alice a message with instructions to buy 1000 shares of Speculative Unlimited. On Tuesday the stock drops 10 points on bad news. On Wednesday Bob gets a written confirmation of the Monday trade and promptly denies that he ever gave such instructions. Can Alice prove otherwise? No, because Alice could have easily generated the buy order, encrypted it with the key she shares with Bob, and then decrypted her own message!

Public-key encryption solves this problem. This time, let us say that Bob sends a message to Alice encrypted with his private key. Alice decrypts the message, using Bob's public key, but also retains the encrypted version. If Bob later denies he sent the message, all Alice has to do is present a judge or other arbitrator with the ciphertext, the plaintext, and Bob's public key. The arbitrator can confirm that the ciphertext translates into the plaintext in question with Bob's public key and that the ciphertext must therefore have been created by Bob with his private key. Case closed!

Digital Signature Use

The scheme for authentication just described is impractical for the simple reason that public-key encryption of large blocks of data is painfully slow. We want to avoid having to encrypt thousands or tens of thousands or even millions of bits using RSA or a similar algorithm; it is just plain unwieldy. To get around this problem we may use a technique known as the **digital signature**. This scheme depends on not only public-key encryption but also another kind of algorithm known as a *secure hash function.*

Figure 17.9 illustrates the digital signature scheme. Bob has a message that needs to be authenticated. To do this with as little overhead as possible, Bob calculates a function of the text, called a *message digest,* or *hash code.* The purpose of the hash code is to produce a fingerprint for a message that is for all practical purposes unique to that message; any change in the message results in a different hash code. Next Bob encrypts the hash code with his private key; the result is a *digital signature.* Finally, Bob attaches the digital signature to the message and sends the whole thing to Alice.

On Alice's end, she is presented with a message and a signature. This gives Alice the opportunity to verify that the message is from Bob. First Alice uses the same hash function that Bob used to calculate the hash code for this message. Alice sets this aside temporarily and turns to the signature. Using Bob's public key, Alice decrypts the signature to recover a hash code. Finally, Alice compares the decrypted hash code with the one that she calculated; if there is a match, Alice can conclude that the message is from Bob and could only have come from Bob. Why? Well, let's look at the possibilities:

1. Suppose that an opponent (we'll call him X) prepares a message and attempts to forge Bob's signature. X can generate the hash code for the fraudulent message, but since X doesn't know Bob's private key, X cannot properly encrypt the message. So X cannot forge Bob's signature.

Digital Signature
An authentication mechanism that enables the creator of a message to attach a code that guarantees the source and integrity of the message.

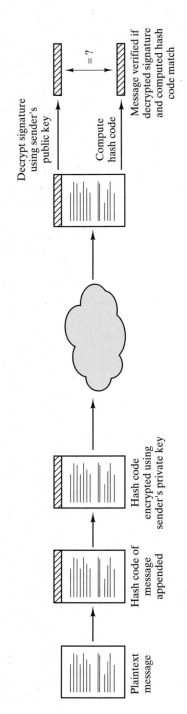

FIGURE 17.9 The Digital Signature Process.

2. Suppose instead that X intercepts a message from Bob. Now he has a message *and* a signature. Can X discard the message, create another message, and attach the stolen signature to this new message? No, because the new message will have a different hash code from the old message, and therefore the hash code in the signature won't match the hash code of the message.

3. Again, suppose that X intercepts the message, but this time he just makes a slight alteration to the message (e.g., inserting or deleting the word *not* in a critical place). Once again, this cannot succeed, because any change in the message will change the hash code and therefore result in a signature mismatch.

The digital signature is one of the great innovations in the history of cryptography. The recipient of a signed message knows that the message is in fact from the alleged source and that the message hasn't been altered in any way after it was signed. The digital signature makes possible a whole range of security services that are impractical using conventional encryption.

Public-Key Certificates

As was mentioned earlier, the use of public-key encryption does not eliminate the need to address the issue of key distribution. In the context of public-key encryption, the issue is one of authenticity: Someone can create a public–private key pair and publish the public key under someone else's name. Until such time as the victim discovers the forgery and alerts all potential correspondents, the attacker is able to read all encrypted messages intended for the victim and can use the forged keys for authentication.

The common way to overcome this problem is simply to use public-key encryption to authenticate the public key. This assumes the existence of some trusted signing authority or person, and works as follows:

1. A public key is generated by Bob and submitted to agency X for certification.
2. X determines by some procedure, such as a face-to-face meeting, that this is authentically Bob's public key.
3. X appends a timestamp to the public key, generates the hash code of the result, and encrypts that result with X's private key forming the signature.
4. The signature is attached to the public key.

Anyone equipped with a copy of X's public key can now verify that Bob's public key is authentic.

17.5 WEB SECURITY

Vulnerabilities of the Web

As the risk to data and systems increases, so does the number of companies opening themselves up to outsiders. Businesses are flocking to the Internet in droves to achieve a global presence and become more accessible to partners and customers. But while companies may create a World Wide Web site to draw attention to themselves, some of that attention may be the wrong kind.

The simplest use of the Web by businesses is as a means of disseminating information. A Web site, anchored by a home page, can contain a corporate profile, description of products and services, and information on how to them. In this simple application, the obvious concern is that the data at the Web site not be altered by unauthorized users. In this regard it is important to note that a Web site is not some kind of new or different computer system or operating system. A Web site consists of an application (the Web server) that runs on the local operating system and data (Web pages) that are stored in the local database or file management system. As such, the Web site is vulnerable to all the techniques that intruders have developed over the years for attacking operating systems and databases.

A more significant source of concern is that businesses are increasingly moving toward the use of the Web for electronic commerce. Users can access a Web site to place orders, using credit cards or digital cash. Now the stakes become higher, and both the company and customers need high levels of security for this system to operate. The solution here involves a number of basic security mechanisms together with application-specific adaptations of those mechanisms.

Let's look specifically at the types of threats inherent in running a Web site. There are four categories:

- Unauthorized alteration of data at the Web site
- Unauthorized access to the underlying operating system at the Web server
- Eavesdropping on messages passed between a Web server and a Web browser
- Impersonation

At the present time, it is this first two categories that present the greatest risk. At first glance, it may seem to the owner of the Web server that these threats are minimal. After all, if the server is set up to only accept WWW-style access, the potential intruder is limited to the use of the relatively simple Web commands, which only allow viewing Web page information and filling in Web page forms.

But already, several weak points in this system have been discovered. For example, many versions of the Mosaic server running on a Unix have several potential vulnerabilities. One flaw allows an intruder to put rogue code onto a Web server by overrunning a software buffer. Once that code is in place, the intruder may be able to get access to the operating system in the account under which the server is running. Another flaw enables an intruder to embed a Unix command into a Web request in such a way that the Web server is tricked into passing that command on to the operating system. Such a command could give the intruder access to the operating system for further commands or could be used to introduce a virus. Once these flaws were discovered, patches were introduced into the Web software to fix the problem. But older versions of the software still running out on the Internet are still vulnerable. Furthermore, the various Web server packages are bound to have other weak spots that have not yet been discovered by the server vendor.

Eavesdropping on messages between a Web server and client also presents a security risk. For example, some Web applications enable a user to set up an account with the company that manages the Web site to purchase products and to transfer credit card information for future purchases. If an eavesdropper intercepts the initial sign-on dialogue, he or she can later come back to the site, change the shipping address, and order products using the stolen account information. There are really two facets to this threat: (1) someone gains unauthorized access to transactions between a Web server and a Web browser, and (2) someone impersonates another user to perform unauthorized transactions.

How to Secure Your Web Site

In any plan for computer or network security, the manager needs to evaluate the costs versus the benefits. In a nutshell, you can achieve any desired level of security at the cost of increased expenditures on hardware, software, and personnel, and at the cost of increased inconvenience for users. As things now stand with respect to Web security, there are some reasonable steps that can be taken to provide a very high level of security. But keep in mind that this is an ongoing arms race between those building security tools to hold the fort and those honing their skill to breach that security. No security plan can be static; it must be subject to periodic review and assessment.

There are two basic lines of attack to improving Web security: securing the Web site itself, and securing the Web application. Both lines of attack are essential. Let's look first at the Web site. In many cases, Web servers are running on Unix machines. Unfortunately, Unix is full of security holes. In addition, people rarely have a machine that is only the Web server. Usually, the Web server computer has other uses, such as office E-mail. Thus, the first step to implementing a secure WWW server is to install all operating system security patches recommended by the OS vendor, crisis emergency response teams, and Department of Energy Computer Incident Advisory Capability (CIAC). Once this is done, the system operator at the site must keep up with the latest security advisories and promptly install all patches to plug newly discovered security holes.

In addition to keeping the underlying operating system as secure as possible, the system administrator should install the Web server software with minimal system privileges. A simple mistake is to install the software with full privileges. In such a case, if an intruder is able to get past the server and into the server's file directory, he or she has access to everything on the system, including files for other applications, password files, and other critical information.

A better solution is to use a more secure platform, such as Windows NT. Windows NT was designed to have a high level of security and is a much tougher nut to crack than Unix. However, although Windows NT will avoid many of the Unix-based weaknesses, it will probably have its own family of vulnerabilities. Its relative newness and small market share have kept it off the hackers' radar screen for now. So, although security will be better using Windows NT, this no cause for complacency on the part of the system manager.

Web Security Products

Once the site is secured to the desired level, attention needs to turn to the Web software itself. Fortunately, significant progress has been made in building secure Web servers and browsers. Drawing on the experience in recent years in developing other secure Internet protocols and applications, WWW designers have implemented several powerful security features in the latest generation of Web software.

The two **security mechanisms** that have achieved the most widespread acceptance are known as secure hypertext transport protocol (SHTTP) and secure sockets layer (SSL). The most important feature of these protocols is that they allow the client and server to negotiate acceptable levels of security for a particular transaction or a particular session. A variety of different network security techniques can be negotiated. For most purposes, some form of public-key encryption is used. Using public-key encryption, if the Web server and Web client each know the other's public key, secure exchange of messages and information is assured.

Initially, there was some confusion about which security approach to take, since there were two schemes competing for standardization. Fortunately, a consensus has developed that the two protocols should be used in combination. Key players in the development of the two protocols have formed a consortium known as Terisa systems to promote the use of SHTTP and SSL. Members include RSA, the patent holder on the RSA public-key encryption system; Netscape, maker of the most popular Web server and browser products, Compuserve/Spry, maker of the commercial Mosaic Web products; and Enterprise Integration Technologies. Terisa has developed a toolkit aimed at developers of secure server products. Spry, Netscape, Tandem, OpenMarket, and similar companies license the toolkit product for integration into their servers. The presence of Terisa has accelerated the introduction of standardized secure server features. A company looking to set up a Web site should acquire a Web server package that includes both SHTTP and SSL. Fortunately, the list of such packages is long and growing.

Web Security: A Corporate Responsibility

In setting up a Web server and connecting it to the Internet, a company runs the risk of eavesdropping, intrusion, theft of data, even alteration of data. Full responsibility for controlling these threats falls on the company. There is no Internet entity to appeal to if something goes wrong.

Compounding the problem is that the culture of the Internet—openness, ease of access, lack of controls—so easily penetrates the companies connected to the Internet. Corporate IS is often left out of Web planning and implementation. To cite several examples, Ragu's popular culinary Web site was launched and is maintained by the marketing arm of Ragu, not the corporate IS of the parent Van den Bergh Foods Co.; the Reebock Web site is run by their marketing group and was built by an outside contractor.

The potential for security problems is obvious in these cases. These Web sites may run on systems that are connected through internal LANs and WANs with other corporate computing assets. Yet it is the local unit running the Web site that is responsible for the security of that site, which is a potential point of entry into the entire corporate IS apparatus. The message is clear: Corporate IS must be Internet savvy, must understand the need for and means of implementing Web security, and must enforce Web security policies across the company.

SUMMARY

The increasing reliance by business on the use of data processing systems and the increasing use of networks and communications facilities to build distributed systems have resulted in a strong requirement for computer and network security. Computer security relates to mechanisms inside and related to a single computer system. The principal object is to protect the data resources of that system. Network security deals with the protection of data and messages that are communicated. This chapter deals with network security.

The requirements for security are best assessed by examining the various security threats faced by an organization. We can organize these threats into two main categories. Passive threats, sometimes referred to as wiretapping or eavesdropping, involve attempts by an attacker to obtain information relating to a communication. In most cases, the most serious such threat is the disclosure of files, messages, or documents in transit to an unauthorized party. The other category of threats includes a variety of active threats. These involve some modification of the transmitted data or the creation of false transmissions.

By far the most important automated tool for network and communications security is encryption, a process that conceals meaning by changing intelligible messages into unintelligible messages. Most commercially available encryption equipment makes use of conventional encryption, in which the two parties share a single encryption–decryption key. The principal challenge with conventional encryption is the distribution and protection of the keys. The alternative is a public-key encryption scheme, in which the process involves two keys, one for encryption and a paired key for decryption. One of the keys is kept private by the party that generated the key pair, and the other is made public.

Conventional encryption and public-key encryption are often combined in secure networking applications to provide a spectrum of security services. Conventional encryption is used to encrypt transmitted data, often using a one-time or short-term session key. The session key can be distributed by a trusted key distribution center or transmitted in encrypted form using public-key encryption. Public-key encryption also is used to create digital signatures, which authenticate the source of transmitted messages.

One critical application area that encompasses most of the security threats encountered by businesses is an Internet Web site. The Web manager must be alert to unauthorized alteration of content, to disclosure of confidential transactions, and to other forms of attach through the Web site.

RECOMMENDED READING

The topics in this chapter are covered in greater detail in [STAL95b]. For coverage of cryptographic algorithms, [SCHN96] is an essential reference work; it contains descriptions of virtually every cryptographic algorithm and protocol published in the last 15 years.

Two very good collections of papers are [SIMM92], which provides a rigorous, mathematical treatment of cryptographic protocols and algorithms, and [ABRA95], which deals with the issues at more of a system level.

ABRA95   ABRAMS, M., JAJODIA, S., and PODELL, H., eds. *Information Security.* Los Alamitos, CA: IEEE Computer Society Press, 1995.

SCHN96   SCHNEIER, B. *Applied Cryptography.* New York: Wiley, 1996.

SIMM92   SIMMONS, G., ed. *Contemporary Cryptology: The Science of Information Integrity.* Piscataway, NJ: IEEE Press, 1992.

STAL95b   STALLINGS, W. *Network and Internetwork Security: Principles and Practice.* Upper Saddle River, NJ: Prentice Hall, 1995.

Recommended Web Site

- http://world.std.com/~franl/crypto.html: Comprehensive set of links related to cryptography and network security.

KEY TERMS

Active Attacks	Key Distribution Center	Security Mechanism
Conventional Encryption	(KDC)	Security Threat
Data Encryption Standard	Passive Attacks	Triple DES
(DES)	Public-Key Encryption	
Digital Signature	RSA Algorithm	

QUESTIONS

1. Explain the difference between conventional encryption and public-key encryption.
2. What are DES and triple DES?
3. Why is there an issue about the distribution of public keys, which, after all, are supposed to be made public?
4. What is a digital signature?
5. Describe two uses of digital signatures.

PROBLEMS

1. One of the simplest forms of encryption is a substitution cipher. A substitution cipher is an encryption technique in which the letters of plaintext are replaced by other letters or by numbers or symbols. In a famous story by Edgar Allan Poe, the following cipher-text was generated using a simple substitution algorithm:

   ```
   53‡‡†305))6*;4826)4‡.)4‡);806*;48†8¶60))85;;]8*;:‡*8†83
   (88)5*†;46(;88*96*?;8)*‡(;485);5*†2:*‡(;4956*2(5*—4)8¶8*
   ;4069285));)6†8)4‡‡;1(‡9;48081;8:8‡1;48†85;4)485†528806*81
   (‡9;48;(88;4(‡?34;48)4‡;161;:188;‡?;
   ```

   Decrypt this message. *Hints:*

   a. The most frequently occurring letter in English is e. Therefore, the first or second (or perhaps third?) most common character in the message is likely to stand for e.

Also, e is often seen in pairs (e.g., meet, fleet, speed, seen, been, agree, etc.). Try to find a character in the ciphertext that decodes to e.

b. The most common word in English is "the." Use this fact to guess the characters that stand for t and h.

c. Decipher the rest of the message by deducing additional words.

Warning: The resulting message is in English but may not make much sense on a first reading.

2. One way to solve the key distribution problem is to use a line from a book that both the sender and the receiver possess to generate the key for a substitution cipher. Typically, at least in spy novels, the first sentence of a book serves as the key. The particular scheme discussed in this problem is from one of the best suspense novels involving secret codes, *Talking to Strange Men*, by Ruth Rendell. Work this problem without consulting that book! Consider the following message:

SIDKHKDM AF HCRKIABIE SHIMC KD LFEAILA

This ciphertext was produced using the first sentence of *The Other Side of Silence* (a book about the spy Kim Philby): "The snow lay thick on the steps and the snowflakes driven by the wind looked black in the headlights of the cars."

a. What is the encryption algorithm?

b. How secure is it?

c. To make the key distribution problem simple, both parties can agree to use the first or last sentence of a book as the key. To change the key, they simply need to agree on a new book. The use of the first sentence would be preferable to the use of the last. Why?

3. In one of his cases, Sherlock Holmes was confronted with the following message.

534 C2 13 127 36 31 4 17 21 41
DOUGLAS 109 293 5 37 BIRLSTONE
26 BIRLSTONE 9 127 171

Although Watson was puzzled, Holmes was immediately able to deduce the type of encryption algorithm. Can you?

APPENDIX A

Standards and Standards-Setting Organizations

*A*n important concept that recurs frequently in this book is standards. This appendix provides some background on the nature and relevance of standards and looks at the principal organizations involved in developing standards for networking and communications.

A.1 IMPORTANCE OF STANDARDS

It has long been accepted in the telecommunications industry that standards are required to govern the physical, electrical, and procedural characteristics of communication equipment. In the past, this view has not been embraced by the computer industry. Whereas communication equipment vendors recognize that their equipment will generally interface to and communicate with other vendors' equipment, computer vendors have traditionally attempted to monopolize their customers. The proliferation of computers and distributed processing has made that an untenable position. Computers from different vendors must communicate with each other, and with the ongoing evolution of protocol standards, customers will no longer accept special-purpose protocol conversion software development. The result is that standards now permeate all the areas of technology discussed in this book.

There are a number of advantages and disadvantages to the standards-making process. We list here the most striking ones. The principal advantages of standards are:

- A standard assures that there will be a large market for a particular piece of equipment or software. This encourages mass production and, in some cases, the use of large-scale-integration (LSI) or very-large-scale-integration (VLSI) techniques, resulting in lower costs.
- A standard allows products from multiple vendors to communicate, giving the purchaser more flexibility in equipment selection and use.

The principal disadvantages are:

- A standard tends to freeze the technology. By the time a standard is developed, subjected to review and compromise, and promulgated, more efficient techniques are possible.

- There are multiple standards for the same thing. This is not a disadvantage of standards per se but of the current way things are done. Fortunately, in recent years the various standards-making organizations have begun to cooperate more closely. Nevertheless, there are still areas where multiple conflicting standards exist.

A.2 STANDARDS AND REGULATION

It is helpful for the reader to distinguish three concepts:

- Voluntary standards
- Regulatory standards
- Regulatory use of voluntary standards

Voluntary standards are developed by standards-making organizations, such as those described in the next section. They are voluntary in that the existence of the standard does not compel its use. That is, manufacturers voluntarily implement a product that conforms to a standard if they perceive a benefit to themselves; there is no legal requirement to conform. These standards are also voluntary in the sense that they are developed by volunteers who are not paid for their efforts by the standards-making organization that administers the process. These volunteers are generally employees of interested organizations, such as manufacturers and government agencies.

Voluntary standards work because they are generally developed on the basis of broad consensus and because the customer demand for standard products encourages the implementation of these standards by the vendors.

In contrast, a regulatory standard is developed by a government regulatory agency to meet a public objective, such as economic, health, and safety objectives. These standards have the force of regulation behind them and must be met by providers in the context in which the regulations apply. Familiar examples of regulatory standards are in areas such as fire codes and health codes. But regulations can apply to a wide variety of products, including those related to computers and communications. For example, the Federal Communications Commission regulates electromagnetic emissions.

A relatively new, or at least newly prevalent, phenomenon is the regulatory use of voluntary standards. A typical example of this is a regulation that requires that the government purchase of a product be limited to those that conform to a referenced set of voluntary standards. This approach has a number of benefits:

- It reduces the rule-making burden on government agencies.
- It encourages cooperation between government and standards organizations to produce standards of broad applicability.
- It reduces the variety of standards that providers must meet.

A.3 STANDARDS-SETTING ORGANIZATIONS

Throughout this book we describe the most important standards in use or being developed for various aspects of data and computer communications. Various organizations have been involved in the development or promotion of these standards. This appendix provides a brief description of the most important (in the current context) of these organizations:

- Internet Engineering Task Force (IETF)
- International Organization for Standardization (ISO)
- International Telecommunications Union—Telecommunication Standardization Sector (ITU-T)

Internet Standards and the IETF

Many of the protocols that make up the TCP/IP protocol suite have been standardized or are in the process of standardization. By universal agreement, an organization known as the Internet Architecture Board (IAB) is responsible for the development and publication of these standards, which are published in a series of documents called requests for comments (RFCs). This subsection provides a brief description of the way in which standards for the TCP/IP protocol suite are developed.

The Internet and Internet Standards   The Internet is a large collection of interconnected networks all of which use the TCP/IP protocol suite. The Internet began with the development of ARPANET and subsequent support by the Defense Advanced Research Projects Agency (DARPA) for the development of additional networks to support military users and government contractors.

The IAB is the coordinating committee for Internet design, engineering, and management. Areas covered include operation of the Internet itself and the standardization of protocols used by end systems on the Internet for interoperability. The IAB has two principal subsidiary task forces: the Internet Engineering Task Force (IETF) and the Internet Research Task Force (IRTF). The actual work of these task forces is carried out by working groups. Membership in a working group is voluntary; any interested party may participate.

The IETF is responsible for publishing the RFCs, which are the working notes of the Internet research and development community. A document in this series may be on essentially any topic related to computer communications and may be anything from a meeting report to the specification of a standard.

The final decision of which RFCs become Internet standards is made by the IAB, on the recommendation of the IETF. To become a standard, a specification must meet the following criteria:

- Be stable and well understood
- Be technically competent
- Have numerous independent and interoperable implementations with operational experience
- Enjoy significant public support
- Be recognizably useful in some or all parts of the Internet

The key difference between these criteria and those used for international standards is the emphasis here on operational experience.

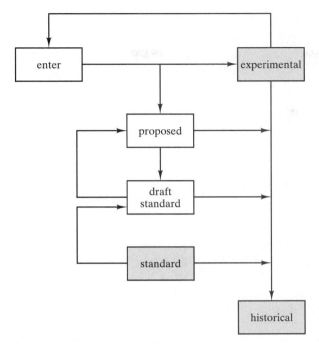

FIGURE A.1 IAB Standards Track Diagram.

Standardization Process Figure A.1 shows the series of steps, called the *standards track*, that a specification goes through to become a standard. The steps involve increasing amounts of scrutiny and testing. At each step the IETF must make a recommendation for advancement of the protocol, and the IAB must ratify it. The white boxes in the diagram represent temporary states, which should be occupied for the minimum practical time. However, a document must remain a proposed standard for at least six months and a draft standard for at least four months to allow time for review and comment. The shaded boxes represent long-term states that may be occupied for years.

A protocol or other specification that is not considered ready for standardization may be published as an experimental RFC. After further work, the specification may be resubmitted. If the specification is generally stable, has resolved known design choices, is believed to be well understood, has received significant community review, and appears to enjoy enough community interest to be considered valuable, the RFC will be designated a proposed standard.

For a specification to be advanced to draft standard status, there must be at least two independent and interoperable implementations from which adequate operational experience has been obtained. After significant implementation and operational experience has been obtained, a specification may be elevated to standard. At this point, the specification is assigned an STD number as well as an RFC number. Finally, when a protocol becomes obsolete, it is assigned to the historic state.

International Organization for Standardization

The International Organization for Standardization (ISO) is an international agency for the development of standards on a wide range of subjects. It is a voluntary, nontreaty organization whose members are designated standards bodies of participating nations, plus nonvoting observer organizations. Although ISO is not a governmental body, more than 70% of ISO member bodies are governmental standards institutions or organizations incorporated by public law. Most of the remainder have close links with the public administrations in their own countries. The U.S. member body is the American National Standards Institute.

ISO was founded in 1946 and has issued more than 5000 standards in a broad range of areas. Its purpose is to promote the development of standardization and related activities to facilitate international exchange of goods and services and to develop cooperation in the sphere of intellectual, scientific, technological, and economic activity. Standards have been issued to cover everything from screw threads to solar energy. One important area of standardization deals with the open systems interconnection (OSI) communications architecture and the standards at each layer of the OSI architecture.

In the areas of interest in this book, ISO standards are actually developed in a joint effort with another standards body, the International Electrotechnical Commission (IEC). IEC is concerned primarily with electrical and electronic engineering standards. In the area of information technology, the interests of the two groups overlap, with IEC emphasizing hardware and ISO focusing on software. In 1987, the two groups formed Joint Technical Committee 1 (JTC 1), which has the responsibility of developing the documents that ultimately become ISO (and IEC) standards in the area of information technology.

The development of an ISO standard from first proposal to actual publication of the standard follows a seven-step process. The objective is to ensure that the final result is acceptable to as many countries as possible. The steps are described here briefly (time limits are the minimum time in which voting could be accomplished, and amendments require extended time):

1. A new work item is assigned to the appropriate technical committee, and within that technical committee, to the appropriate working group. The working group prepares the technical specifications for the proposed standard and publishes these as a draft proposal (DP). The DP is circulated among interested members for balloting and technical comment. At least three months are allowed, and there may be iterations. When there is substantial agreement, the DP is sent to the administrative arm of ISO, known as the central secretariat.

2. The DP is registered at the central secretariat within two months of its final approval by the technical committee.

3. The central secretariat edits the document to ensure conformity with ISO practices; no technical changes are made. The edited document is then issued as a draft international standard (DIS).

4. The DIS is circulated for a six-month balloting period. For approval, the DIS must receive a majority approval by the technical committee mem-

bers and 75% approval of all voting members. Revisions may occur to resolve any negative vote. If more than two negative votes remain, it is unlikely that the DIS will be published as a final standard.

5. The approved, possibly revised DIS is returned within three months to the central secretariat for submission to the ISO council, which acts as the board of directors of ISO.

6. The DIS is accepted by the council as an international standard (IS).

7. The IS is published by ISO.

As can be seen, the process of issuing a standard is a slow one. Certainly, it would be desirable to issue standards as quickly as the technical details can be worked out, but ISO must ensure that the standard will receive widespread support.

ITU Telecommunication Standardization Sector

The ITU Telecommunications Standardization Sector (ITU-T) is a permanent organ of the International Telecommunication Union (ITU), which is itself a United Nations specialized agency. Hence the members of ITU-T are governments. The U.S. representation is housed in the Department of State. The charter of the ITU is that it "is responsible for studying technical, operating, and tariff questions and issuing Recommendations on them with a view to standardizing telecommunications on a worldwide basis." Its primary objective is to standardize, to the extent necessary, techniques and operations in telecommunications to achieve end-to-end compatibility of international telecommunication connections, regardless of the countries of origin and destination.

The ITU-T was created as of March 1, 1993 as one consequence of a reform process within the ITU. It replaces the International Telegraph and Telephone Consultative Committee (CCITT), which had essentially the same charter and objectives as the new ITU-T.

ITU-T is organized into 15 study groups that prepare recommendations:

1. Service description
2. Network operation
3. Tariff and accounting principles
4. Network maintenance
5. Protection against electromagnetic environment effects
6. Outside plant
7. Data network and open systems communications
8. Terminal equipment and protocols for telematic services
9. Television and sound transmission
10. Languages for telecommunication applications
11. Switching and signaling
12. End-to-end transmission performance
13. General network aspects

14. Modems and transmission techniques for data, telegraph, and telematic services

15. Transmission systems and equipment

Work within ITU-T is conducted in four-year cycles. Every four years, a World Telecommunications Standardization Conference is held. The work program for the next four years is established at the assembly in the form of questions submitted by the various study groups, based on requests made to the study groups by their members. The conference assess the questions, reviews the scope of the study groups, creates new or abolishes existing study groups, and allocates questions to them.

Based on these questions, each study group prepares draft recommendations. A draft recommendation may be submitted to the next conference, four years hence, for approval. Increasingly, however, recommendations are approved when they are ready, without having to wait for the end of the four-year study period. This accelerated procedure was adopted after the study period that ended in 1988. Thus, 1988 was the last time that a large batch of documents was published at one time as a set of recommendations.

GLOSSARY

Some of the definitions in this glossary are from the *American National Standard Dictionary of Information Technology*, ANSI Standard X3.172, 1995. These are marked with an asterisk.

Analog Data*   Data represented by a physical quantity that is considered to be continuously variable and whose magnitude is made directly proportional to the data or to a suitable function of the data.

Analog Signal   A continuously varying electromagnetic wave that may be propagated over a variety of media.

Analog Transmission   The transmission of analog signals without regard to content. The signal may be amplified, but there is no intermediate attempt to recover the data from the signal.

Application Layer   Layer 7 of the OSI model. This layer determines the interface of the system with the user and provides useful application-oriented services.

Asynchronous Transfer Mode (ATM)   A form of packet switching in which fixed-size cells of 53 octets are used. There is no network layer and many of the basic functions have been streamlined or eliminated to provide for greater throughput.

Asynchronous Transmission   Transmission in which each information character is individually synchronized, usually by the use of start elements and stop elements.

Authentication*   A process used to verify the integrity of transmitted data, especially a message.

Automatic Repeat Request (ARQ)   A feature that automatically initiates a request for retransmission when an error in transmission is detected.

Availability   The percentage of time that a particular function or application is available for users.

Bandwidth*   The difference between the limiting frequencies of a continuous frequency band.

Baseband   Transmission of signals without modulation. In a baseband local-area network, digital signals (1's and 0's) are inserted directly onto the cable as voltage pulses. The entire spectrum of the cable is consumed by the signal. This scheme does not allow frequency-division multiplexing.

Bell Operating Company (BOC)   Before the divestiture of AT&T, the 22 BOCs were AT&T

subsidiaries that built, operated, and maintained the local and intrastate networks and provided most of the day-to-day service for customers. After divestiture, the BOCs retain their identity within seven regional companies (RBOCs) and are responsible for local service as defined by local access and transport areas (LATAs).

Bit Stuffing   The insertion of extra bits into a data stream to avoid the appearance of unintended control sequences.

Bridge   An internetworking device that connects two similar local-area networks that use the same LAN protocols.

Broadband   In local-area networks, the use of coaxial cable for providing data transfer by means of analog (radio-frequency) signals. Digital signals are passed through a modem and transmitted over one of the frequency bands of the cable.

Broadband ISDN (BISDN)   A second-generation set of standards for ISDN. BISDN is characterized by the use of asynchronous transfer mode and by the provision of very high data rates to end users.

Bus   A LAN topology in which stations are attached to a shared transmission medium. The medium is a linear cable; transmissions propagate the length of the medium and are received by all stations.

Byte   A group of bits, usually 8, used to represent a character of other data.

Cell Relay   Another term for *asynchronous transfer mode.*

Centrex   A service offered by operating telephone companies that provides, from the telephone company office, functions and features comparable to those provided by a PBX.

Ciphertext   The output of an encryption algorithm; the encrypted form of a message or data.

Circuit Switching   A method of communicating in which a dedicated communications path is established between two devices through one or more intermediate switching nodes. Unlike

with packet switching, digital data are sent as a continuous stream of bits. Data rate is guaranteed, and delay is essentially limited to propagation time.

Coaxial Cable   A cable consisting of one conductor, usually a small copper tube or wire, within and insulated from another conductor of larger diameter, usually copper tubing or copper braid.

Codec   Coder–decoder. Transforms analog data into a digital bit stream (coder) and digital signals into analog data (decoder).

Common Carrier   In the United States, companies that furnish long-distance telecommunication services to the public. Common carriers are subject to regulation by federal and state regulatory commissions.

Common-Channel Signaling   Technique in which network control signals (e.g., call request) are separated from the associated voice or data path by placing the signaling from a group of voice or data paths on a separate channel dedicated to signaling only.

Communications Architecture   The hardware and software structure that implements the communications function.

Conventional Encryption   A form of cryptosystem in which encryption and decryption are performed using the same key.

CSMA/CD   Carrier-sense multiple access with collision detection. A medium access control technique for bus and tree LANs. A station wishing to transmit first senses the medium and transmits only if the medium is idle. The station ceases transmission if it detects a collision.

Cyclic Redundancy Check (CRC)   An error-detecting code in which the code is the remainder resulting from dividing the bits to be checked by a predetermined binary number.

Data Circuit-Terminating Equipment (DCE)   In a data station, the equipment that provides the signal conversion and coding between the data terminal equipment (DTE) and the line. The DCE may be separate equipment or an integral part of the DTE or of intermediate equipment. The DCE may perform other functions that are normally performed at the network end of the line.

Data Compression The process of eliminating gaps, empty fields, redundancies, and unnecessary data to shorten the length of records or blocks.

Datagram In packet switching, a self-contained packet, independent of other packets, that carries information sufficient for routing from the originating data terminal equipment (DTE) to the destination DTE without relying on earlier exchanges between the DTEs and the network.

Data Link Layer Layer 2 of the OSI model. Converts an unreliable transmission channel into a reliable one.

Data Terminal Equipment (DTE)* Equipment consisting of digital end instruments that convert the user information into data signals for transmission or reconvert the received data signals into user information.

Digital Data* Data represented by discrete values or conditions.

Digital Data Switch A local network consisting of a central switch that uses circuit switching.

Digital PBX A private branch exchange (PBX) that operates internally on digital signal. Thus, voice signals must be digitized for use in the PBX.

Digital Signal A discrete or discontinuous signal, such as a sequence of voltage pulses.

Digital Signature An authentication mechanism that enables the creator of a message to attach a code that acts as a signature. The signature guarantees the source and integrity of the message.

Digital Transmission The transmission of digital data or analog data that have been digitized, using either an analog or digital signal, in which the digital content is recovered and repeated at intermediate points to reduce the effects of impairments, such as noise, distortion, and attenuation.

Digitize* To convert an analog signal to a digital signal.

Direct Inward Dialing* A service feature that allows inward-directed calls to a PBX to reach a specific PBX station without attendant assistance.

Distributed Data Processing Data processing in which some or all of the processing, storage, and control functions, in addition to input–output functions, are dispersed among data processing stations.

Electronic Data Interchange The direct computer-to-computer exchange of information normally provided on standard business documents, such as invoices, bills of lading, and purchase orders.

Electronic Mail Correspondence in the form of messages transmitted between workstations over a network. The most common protocol used to support electronic mail is the simple mail transfer protocol (SMTP).

Encapsulation The addition of control information by a protocol entity to data obtained from a protocol user.

Encryption To convert plain text or data into unintelligible form by means of a reversible mathematical computation.

Error-Detecting Code* A code in which each data signal conforms to specific rules of construction, so that departures from this construction in the received signal can be detected automatically.

Error Rate* The ratio of the number of data units in error to the total number of data units.

Ethernet A 10-Mbps baseband local-area network specification developed jointly by Xerox, Intel, and Digital Equipment. It is the forerunner of the IEEE 802.3 CSMA/CD standard.

Exchange Area A geographical area within which there is a single uniform set of charges for telephone service. A call between any two points within an exchange area is a local call.

Fiber Distributed Data Interface (FDDI) A standard for a 100-Mbps optical fiber ring local-area network.

Flow Control   A function performed by a receiving entity to limit the amount or rate of data sent by a transmitting entity.

Frame Check Sequence   An error-detecting code inserted as a field in a block of data to be transmitted. The code serves to check for errors upon reception of the data.

Frame Relay   A form of packet switching based on the use of variable-length link layer frames. There is no network layer, and many of the basic functions have been streamlined or eliminated to provide for greater throughput.

Frequency-Division Multiplexing (FDM) Division of a transmission facility into two or more channels by splitting the frequency band transmitted by the facility into narrower bands, each of which is used to constitute a distinct channel.

Full-Duplex Transmission   Transmission of data in both directions at the same time.

Half-Duplex Transmission   Data transmission in either direction, one direction at a time.

Hash function   A function that maps a variable-length data block or message into a fixed-length value called a hash code. The function is designed in such a way that, when protected, it provides an authenticator to the data or message. Also referred to as a *message digest.*

Headend   The endpoint of a broadband bus or tree local-area network. Transmission from each station is toward the headend. Reception by each station is from the headend.

Header   System-defined control information that precedes user data.

IEEE 802   A committee of the Institute of Electrical and Electronics Engineers organized to produce local area network standards.

Inchannel Signaling   A technique in which the same channel is used to carry network control signals as is used to carry the call to which the control signals relate.

Integrated Digital Network (IDN)   The integration of transmission and switching functions using digital technology in a circuit-switched telecommunications network.

Integrated Services Digital Network (ISDN) Worldwide telecommunication service that uses digital transmission and switching technology to support voice and digital data communications.

Internet   A worldwide internetwork based on TCP/IP that interconnects thousands of public and private networks and millions of users.

Internet Protocol   An internetworking protocol that executes in hosts and routers to interconnect a number of packet networks.

Internetwork   A collection of data networks, possibly including both LANs and WANs, interconnected physically by routers and logically by an internetwork protocol.

Internetworking   Communication among devices across multiple networks.

Intranet   A corporate internetwork that provides the key Internet applications, especially the World Wide Web. An intranet operates within the organization for internal purposes and can exist as an isolated, self-contained internetwork, or may have links to the Internet.

Layer*   A group of services, functions, and protocols that is complete from a conceptual point of view, that is, one of a set of hierarchically arranged groups, and that extends across all systems that conform to the network architecture.

Local Access and Transport Areas (LATA) A geographic area generally equivalent to a Standard Metropolitan Statistical Area. The territory served by the Bell system was divided into approximately 160 LATAs at divestiture. Intra-LATA services are provided by the Bell operating companies.

Local-Area Network (LAN)   A local network that makes use of a shared transmission medium and packet broadcasting. A packet transmitted by one station is received by all other stations. Typically, a LAN has a bus, tree, or ring topology.

Local Loop   A transmission path, generally twisted pair, between the individual subscriber and the nearest switching center of a public telecommunications network. Also referred to as a *subscriber loop.*

Medium Access Control (MAC) For a local-area network, the method of determining which station has access to the transmission medium at any time. CSMA/CD, token bus, and token ring are common access methods.

Modem Modulator/demodulator. A device that converts digital data to an analog signal that can be transmitted on a telecommunication line and converts the analog signal received to data.

Multiplexing* In data transmission, a function that permits two or more data sources to share a common transmission medium such that each data source has its own channel.

Network Layer Layer 3 of the OSI model. Responsible for routing data through a communication network.

Network Terminating Equipment (NTE) A grouping of ISDN functions at the boundary between the ISDN and the subscriber.

Noise Unwanted signals that combine with and hence distort the signal intended for transmission and reception.

Octet* A group of 8 bits, usually operated upon as an entity.

Open Systems Interconnection (OSI) Reference Model A model of communications between cooperating devices. It defines a seven-layer architecture of communication functions.

Optical Fiber A thin filament of glass or other transparent material through which a signal-encoded light beam may be transmitted by means of total internal reflection.

Packet Switching A method of transmitting messages through a communications network, in which long messages are subdivided into short packets. Each packet is passed from source to destination through intermediate nodes. At each node, the entire message is received, stored briefly, and then passed on to the next node.

Parity Bit* A check bit appended to an array of binary digits to make the sum of all the binary digits, including the check bit, always odd or always even.

Physical Layer Layer 1 of the OSI model. Concerned with the electrical, mechanical, and timing aspects of signal transmission over a medium.

Piggybacking The inclusion of an acknowledgment of a previously received protocol data unit in an outgoing protocol data unit.

Pixel* The smallest element of a digital image that can be assigned a gray level. Equivalently, a pixel is an individual dot in a dot-matrix representation of a picture.

Point-to-Point A configuration in which two and only two stations share a transmission path.

Postal, Telegraph, and Telephone (PTT) A government organization that operates a nationalized public telecommunications network.

Presentation Layer Layer 6 of the OSI model. Concerned with data format and display.

Private Branch Exchange (PBX) A telephone exchange on the user's premises. Provides a circuit-switching facility for telephones on extension lines within the building and access to the public telephone network.

Private Network A facility in which the customer leases circuits and, sometimes, switching capacity for the customer's exclusive use. Access may be provided to a public switched telecommunications service.

Protocol A set of semantic and syntactic rules that determines the behavior of functional units in achieving communication.

Protocol Data Unit (PDU)* Information that is delivered as a unit between peer entities of a network and may contain control information, address information, or data.

Public Data Network (PDN) A packet-switched network that is publicly available to subscribers. Usually, the term connotes government control or national monopoly.

Public-Key Encryption   A form of cryptosystem in which encryption and decryption are performed using two different keys, one of which is referred to as the *public key* and one of which is referred to as the *private key*.

Pulse-Code Modulation (PCM)   A process in which a signal is sampled and the magnitude of each sample with respect to a fixed reference is quantized and converted by coding to a digital signal.

Reference Configuration   A combination of functional groups and reference points that shows possible network arrangements.

Reference Point   A conceptual point at the conjunction of two nonoverlapping functional groupings.

Repeater   A device that receives data on one communication link and transmits it, bit by bit, on another link as fast as the data are received, without buffering.

Response Time*   In a data system, the elapsed time between the end of transmission of an enquiry message and the beginning of the receipt of a response message, measured at the enquiry terminal.

Ring   A LAN topology in which stations are attached to repeaters connected in a closed loop. Data are transmitted in one direction around the ring and can be read by all attached stations.

Router   An internetworking device that connects two computer networks. It makes use of an internet protocol and assumes that all attached devices on the networks use the same communications architecture and protocols.

Service Access Point (SAP)   A means of identifying a user of the services of a protocol entity. A protocol entity provides one or more SAPs, for use by higher-level entities.

Session Layer   Layer 5 of the OSI model. Manages a logical connection (session) between two communicating processes or applications.

Signaling   The exchange of information specifically concerned with the establishment and control of connections, and with management, in a telecommunication network.

Sliding-Window Technique   A method of flow control in which a transmitting station may send numbered protocol data units (PDUs) within a window of numbers. The window changes dynamically to allow additional PDUs to be sent.

Software-Defined Network (SDN)   A facility based on a public circuit-switched network that gives the user the appearance of a private network. The network is "software defined" in the sense that the user provides the service supplier with entries to a database used by the supplier to configure, manage, monitor, and report on the operation of the network.

Space-Division Switching   A circuit-switching technique in which each connection through the switch takes a physically separate and dedicated path.

Specialized Common Carrier   In the United States, a telecommunications common carrier other than AT&T and the Bell Operating Companies, authorized to provide a variety of transmission services.

Spectrum   Refers to an absolute, contiguous range of frequencies.

Statistical Time-Division Multiplexing   A method of TDM in which time slots on a shared transmission line are assigned to devices on demand.

Subscriber Loop   See *Local Loop.*

Switched Multi-megabit Data Service (SMDS)   A high-speed data transmission service offered by telecommunications carriers. SMDS is characterized by the use of fixed-size cells of 53 octets.

Synchronous Time-Division Multiplexing   A method of TDM in which time slots on a shared transmission line are assigned to devices on a fixed, predetermined basis.

Synchronous Transmission   Data transmission in which the time of occurrence of each signal representing a bit is related to a fixed time frame.

TDM Bus Switching A form of time-division switching in which time slots are used to transfer data over a shared bus between transmitter and receiver.

Telecommunication Service That which is offered by an administration or RPOA to its customers to satisfy a specific telecommunications requirement. Bearer service, teleservice, and teleaction service are types of telecommunication service.

Teleconference* A conference between persons remote from one another but linked by a telecommunication system.

Teleservice A type of telecommunication service that provides the complete capability, including terminal equipment functions, for communication between users according to protocols established by agreement between administrations and/or RPOAs.

Time-Compression Multiplexing A means for providing full-duplex digital data transmission over a single twisted pair. Data are buffered at each end and are sent across the line at approximately double the subscriber data rate, with the two ends taking turns.

Time-Division Multiplexing (TDM) The division of a transmission facility into two or more channels by allotting the common channel to several different information channels, one at a time.

Time-Division Switching A circuit-switching technique in which time slots in a time-multiplexed stream of data are manipulated to pass data from an input to an output.

Time-Multiplexed Switching (TMS) A form of space-division switching in which each input line is a TDM stream. The switching configuration may change for each time slot.

Time-Slot Interchange (TSI) The interchange of time slots within a time-division multiplexed frame.

Token Bus A medium access control technique for bus and tree LANs. Stations form a logical ring, around which a token is passed. A station receiving the token may transmit data and then must pass the token on to the next station in the logical ring.

Token Ring A medium access control technique for ring LANs. A token circulates around the ring. A station may transmit data by seizing the token, inserting a packet onto the ring, and then retransmitting the token.

Transmission Medium The physical medium that conveys data between data stations.

Transport Layer Layer 4 of the OSI model. Provides reliable, sequenced transfer of data between endpoints.

Tree A LAN topology in which stations are attached to a shared transmission medium. The medium is a branching cable emanating from a headend, with no closed circuits. Transmissions propagate from any station to the headend and then throughout the medium and are received by all stations.

Twisted Pair A transmission medium that consists of two insulated conductors twisted together to reduce noise.

Value-Added Network (VAN) A privately owned packet-switched network whose services are sold to the public.

Videoconference A teleconference involving video. The video may be full-motion video or some lesser-quality scheme.

Virtual Circuit A packet-switching mechanism in which a logical connection (virtual circuit) is established between two stations at the start of transmission. All packets follow the same route, need not carry a complete address, and arrive in sequence.

White Noise Noise that has a flat, or uniform, frequency spectrum in the frequency range of interest.

World Wide Web A networked, graphically oriented hypermedia system. Information is stored on servers, exchanged between servers and browsers, and displayed on browsers in the form of pages of text and images.

REFERENCES

ABRA85 ABRAMSON, N. "Development of the ALO-HANET." *IEEE Transactions on Information Theory,* March 1985.

ABRA95 ABRAMS, M., JAJODIA, S., and PODELL, H., eds. *Information Security.* Los Alamitos, CA: IEEE Computer Society Press, 1995.

ABSX92 APPLE COMPUTER, BELLCORE, SUN MICROSYSTEMS, and XEROX. *Network Compatible ATM for Local Network Applications, Version 1.01.* October 19, 1992 (available at parcftp.xerox.com/pub/latm).

ASH90 ASH, G. "Design and Control of Networks with Dynamic Nonhierarchical Routing." *IEEE Communications Magazine,* October 1990.

BELL90 BELLCORE (Bell Communications Research). *Telecommunications Transmission Engineering.* Three volumes. 1990.

BELL91 BELLAMY, J. *Digital Telephony.* New York: Wiley, 1991.

BENN96 BENNER, A. *Fibre Channel: Gigabit Communications and I/O for Computer Networks.* New York: McGraw-Hill, 1996.

BERN96a BERNARD, R. *The Corporate Intranet.* New York: Wiley, 1996.

BERN96b BERNSTEIN, P. "Middleware: A Model for Distributed System Services." *Communications of the ACM,* February 1996.

BERS96 BERSON, A. *Client/Server Architecture.* New York: McGraw-Hill, 1996.

BERT92 BERTSEKAS, D., and GALLAGER, R. *Data Networks.* Upper Saddle River, NJ: Prentice Hall, 1992.

BHUS85 BHUSHAN, B., and OPDERBECK, H. "The Evolution of Data Switching for PBXs." *IEEE Journal on Selected Areas in Communications,* July 1985.

BLAC93 BLACK, U. *Data Link Protocols.* Upper Saddle River, NJ: Prentice Hall, 1993.

BLAC95 BLACK, U. *The V Series Recommendations: Standards for Data Communications over the Telephone Network.* New York: McGraw-Hill, 1995.

BLAC96a BLACK, U. *Physical Level Interfaces and Protocols.* Los Alamitos, CA: IEEE Computer Society Press, 1995.

BLAC96b BLACK, U. *Mobile and Wireless Networks,* Upper Saddle River, NJ: Prentice Hall, 1996.

BREY95 BREYER, R., and RILEY, S. *Switched and Fast Ethernet: How It Works and How to Use It.* Emeryville, CA: Ziff-Davis Press, 1995.

BRON95 BRONWYN, F. "Formulating a Forms Strategy." *PC World,* February 1995.

BROU92 BROUSSELL, D., APPLETON, E., and MOAD, J. "Levi Strauss's CIO on the Technology of Empowerment." *Datamation,* June 1, 1992.

BRUN96 BRUNO, C. "Hook a Ride on an ATM Project." *Network World,* June 10, 1996.

CARR90 CARR, E. "The Message Makers." *Economist,* March 10, 1990.

CASA94 CASAVANT, T., and SINGHAL, M., eds. *Distributed Computing Systems.* Los Alamitos, CA: IEEE Computer Society Press, 1994.

CERF74 CERF, V., and KAHN, R. "A Protocol for Packet Network Interconnection," *IEEE Transactions on Communications,* May 1974

COUC97 COUCH, L. *Digital and Analog Communication Systems.* Upper Saddle River, NJ: Prentice Hall, 1997.

COUL94 COULOURIS, G., DOLLIMORE, J., and KINDBERG, T. *Distributed Systems: Concepts and Design.* Reading, MA: Addison-Wesley, 1994.

COX94 COX, J., and RIGNEY, T. "Distributed Systems Put to the Test." *Communications Week,* January 10, 1994.

COX95 COX, N., MANLEY, C., and CHEA, F. *LAN Times Guide to Multimedia Networking.* New York: Osborne/McGraw-Hill, 1995.

DEWI93 DEWIRE, D. *Client/Server Computing.* New York: McGraw-Hill, 1993.

DOUG93 DOUGHERTY, E. "Not by the Seat of the Pants." *LAN Magazine,* January 1993.

DUTT95 DUTTON, H., and LENHARD, P. *High-Speed Networking Technology: An Introductory Survey.* Upper Saddle River, NJ: Prentice Hall, 1995.

DWYE92 DWYER, S., ET AL. "Teleradiology Using Switched Dialup Networks." *IEEE Journal on Selected Areas in Communications,* September 1992.

ECKE95 ECKERSON, W. "Client Server Architecture." *Network World Collaboration,* Winter 1995.

ECKE96 ECKEL, G. *Intranet Working.* Indianapolis, IN: New Riders, 1996.

EVAN96 EVANS, T. *Building an Intranet.* Indianapolis, IN: Sams, 1996.

FARR93 FARR, C. "The Scary Math of New Hires." *Business Week,* February 22, 1993.

FCA94 FIBRE CHANNEL ASSOCIATION. *Fibre Channel: Connection to the Future.* Austin, TX: Fibre Channel Association, 1994.

FELT94 FELTMAN, C. "ATM Takes Off." In McMullen, M., ed. *Networks 2000: Internet, Information Super-highway, Multimedia Networks, and Beyond.* San Francisco: Miller Freeman Books, 1994.

FELT96 FELTMAN, C. "Ethernet Earns Its Wings." *LAN Magazine,* January 1996.

FREE91 FREEMAN, R. *Telecommunication Transmission Handbook.* New York: Wiley, 1991.

FREE94 FREEMAN, R. *Reference Manual for Telecommunications Engineering.* New York: Wiley, 1994.

FREE96 FREEMAN, R. *Telecommunication System Engineering.* New York: Wiley, 1996.

GAO96 GENERAL ACCOUNTING OFFICE. *Information Security: Computer Attacks at Department of Defense Pose Increasing Risks.* Report GAO/AIMD-96-84, May 1996.

GARE95 GAREISS, R. "AAA Shifts Gears for Corporate Connectivity." *Data Communications,* November 1995.

GUYN88 GUYNES, J. 1988. "Impact of System Response Time on State Anxiety." *Communications of the ACM,* March 1988.

HAFN96 HAFNER, K., and LYON, M. *Where Wizards Stay up Late.* New York: Simon & Schuster, 1996.

HAIG92 HAIGHT, T. "The Dynamic Desktop." *Network Computing,* June 1992.

HAIG93 HAIGHT T. "100 Percent Electronic Purchasing!" *Network Computing,* May 1993.

HARB92 HARBISON, R. "Frame Relay: Technology for Our Time." *LAN Technology,* December 1992.

HAWN96 HAWN, M. "Finally, Rock Computes." *Macworld,* January 1996.

HELD96 HELD, G. *Data and Image Compression: Tools and Techniques.* New York: Wiley, 1996.

HELG91 HELGERT, H. *Integrated Services Digital Networks: Architectures, Protocols, and Standards.* Reading, MA: Addison-Wesley, 1991.

INMO91 INMON, W. *Developing Client/Server Applications in an Architected Environment.* Boston: QED, 1991.

JAYA92 JAYANT, N. "Signal Compression: Technology, Targets, and Research Directions." *IEEE Journal on Selected Topics in Communications,* June 1992.

JEFF92 JEFFREY, A. "Burlington Coat Factory: Original Off-Prices." *Discount Store News,* March 16, 1992.

JOHN96a JOHNSON, H. *Fast Ethernet: Dawn of New Network.* Upper Saddle River, NJ: Prentice Hall, 1996.

JOHN96b JOHNSON, J. "Tech Team." *Data Communications,* February 1996.

KALA96 KALAKOTA, R., and WHINSTON, A. B., *Frontiers of Electronic Commerce.* Reading, MA: Addison-Wesley, 1996.

KARV96 KARVE, A. "Multimedia Takes the Stage." *LAN Magazine,* May 1996.

KAVA95 KAVAK, N. "Data Communication in ATM Networks." *IEEE Network,* May/June 1995.

KESS93 KESSLER, G. *ISDN: Concepts, Facilities, and Services.* New York: McGraw-Hill, 1993.

KUMA95 KUMAR, B. *Broadband Communications: A Professional's Guide to ATM, Frame Relay, SMDS, SONET, and B-ISDN.* New York: McGraw-Hill, 1995.

LIEB95 LIEBMANN, L. "Keeping Inn Control." *LAN Magazine,* June 1995.

LYLE92 LYLES, J., and SWINEHART, D. "The Emerging Gigabit Environment and the Role of the Local ATM." *IEEE Communications Magazine,* April 1992.

MADR94 MADRON, T. *Local Area Networks: New Technologies, Emerging Standards.* New York: Wiley, 1994.

MART87 MARTIN, J., and CHAPMAN, K. *SNA: IBM's Networking Solution.* Upper Saddle River, NJ: Prentice Hall, 1987.

MART88 MARTIN, J., and LEBAN, J. *Principles of Data Communication.* Upper Saddle River, NJ: Prentice Hall, 1988.

MART90 MARTIN, J. *Telecommunications and the Computer.* Upper Saddle River, NJ: Prentice Hall, 1990.

MART94 MARTIN, J., CHAPMAN, K., and LEBEN, J. *Local Area Networks: Architectures and Implementations.* Upper Saddle River, NJ: Prentice Hall, 1994.

MCEL93 MCELROY, M. *The Corporate Cabling Guide.* Boston: Artech House, 1993.

MILL95 MILLS, A. *Understanding FDDI.* Upper Saddle River, NJ: Prentice Hall, 1995.

MOSK93 MOSKOWITZ, R. "What Are Clients and Servers Anyway?" *Network Computing,* Special Issue on Client/Server Computing, Spring 1993.

MULL93 MULLENDER, S., ed. *Distributed Systems.* New York: ACM Press, 1993.

NELS96 NELSON, M., and GAILLY, J. *The Data Compression Book.* New York: M&T Books, 1996.

NEWM94 NEWMAN, P. "ATM Local Area Networks." *IEEE Communications Magazine,* March 1994.

PAHL95 PAHLAVAN, K., PROBERT, T., and CHASE, M. "Trends in Local Wireless Networks." *IEEE Communications Magazine,* March 1995.

PARK95   PARKER, R. "For Levi Strauss, Standard Network Is a Perfect Fit." *InfoWorld*, February 13, 1995.

PAUL96   PAUL, L. "Levi Finds Gold Mine of Data." *PC Week*, May 13, 1996.

PETT95   PETTERSSON, G. "ISDN: From Custom to Commodity Service." *IEEE Spectrum*, June 1995.

POWE96   POWERS, P. "Training on a Fast LAN." *LAN Magazine*, March 1996.

RAPP96   RAPPAPORT, T. *Wireless Communications.* Upper Saddle River, NJ: Prentice Hall, 1996.

REEV95   REEVE, W. *Subscriber Loop Signaling and Transmission Handbook.* Piscataway, NJ: IEEE Press, 1995.

REGE96   REGE, J. "A New Face for Florida." *Oracle Magazine*, July/August 1996.

RENA96   RENAUD, P. *Introduction to Client/Server Systems.* New York: Wiley, 1996.

ROTH93   ROTHSCHILD, M. "Coming Soon: Internal Markets." *Forbes ASAP*, June 7, 1993.

SAUN96   SAUNDERS, S. *The McGraw-Hill High-Speed LANs Handbook.* New York: McGraw-Hill, 1996.

SCHN96   SCHNEIER, B. *Applied Cryptography.* New York: Wiley, 1996.

SEVC96   SEVCIK, P. "Designing a High-Performance Web Site." *Business Communications Review*, March 1996.

SEYE91   SEYER, M. *RS-232 Made Easy: Connecting Computers, Printers, Terminals, and Modems.* Upper Saddle River, NJ: Prentice Hall, 1991.

SHAH94   SHAH, A., and RAMAKRISHNAN, G. *FDDI: A High-Speed Network.* Upper Saddle River, NJ: Prentice Hall, 1994.

SHNE84   SHNEIDERMAN, B. "Response Time and Display Rate in Human Performance with Computers." *ACM Computing Surveys*, September 1984.

SIMM92   SIMMONS, G., ed. *Contemporary Cryptology: The Science of Information Integrity.* Piscataway, NJ: IEEE Press, 1992.

SIMO95   SIMON, A., and WHEELER, T. *Open Client/Server Computing and Middleware.* Chestnut Hill, MA: AP Professional Books, 1995.

SMIT88   SMITH, M. "A Model of Human Communication." *IEEE Communications Magazine*, February 1988.

SPIR88   SPIRAM, K., and WHITT, W. "Characterizing Superposition Arrival Processes in Packet Multiplexers for Voice and Data." *IEEE Journal on Selected Areas in Communications,* September 1988.

SPOH93   SPOHN, D. *Data Network Design.* New York: McGraw-Hill, 1994.

SPRA91   SPRAGINS, J., HAMMOND, J., and PAWLIKOWSKI, K. *Telecommunications Protocols and Design.* Reading, MA.: Addison-Wesley, 1991.

STAL95a   STALLINGS, W. *ISDN and Broadband ISDN, with Frame Relay and ATM,* 3rd ed. Upper Saddle River, NJ: Prentice Hall, 1995.

STAL95b   STALLINGS, W. *Network and Internetwork Security: Principles and Practice.* Upper Saddle River, NJ: Prentice Hall, 1995.

STAL96   STALLINGS, W. *SNMP, SNMPv2, and RMON: Practical Network Management.* Reading, MA: Addison-Wesley, 1996.

STAL97a   STALLINGS, W. *Data and Computer Communications,* 5th ed. Upper Saddle River, NJ: Prentice Hall, 1997.

STAL97b   STALLINGS, W. *Local and Metropolitan Area Networks,* 5th ed. Upper Saddle River, NJ: Prentice Hall, 1997.

STAL98   STALLINGS, W. *High-Speed Networks: TCP/IP and ATM Design Principles.* Upper Saddle River, NJ: Prentice Hall, 1998.

STEI95   STEINKE, S. "Middleware Meets the Network." *LAN Magazine*, December 1995.

STEP95   STEPHENS, G., and DEDEK, J. *Fibre Channel.* Menlo Park, CA: Ancot Corporation, 1995.

STEV92   STEVENS, L. "Systems Development vs. the Tower of Babel." *Bobbin*, June 1992.

TANE96   TANENBAUM, A. *Computer Networks.* Upper Saddle River, NJ: Prentice Hall, 1996.

TEGE95   TEGER, S. "Multimedia: From Vision to Reality." *AT&T Technical Journal*, September/October 1995.

TERP92   TERPLAN, K. *Communication Networks Management.* Upper Saddle River, NJ: Prentice Hall, 1992.

THAD81   THADHANI, A. "Interactive User Productivity." *IBM Systems Journal*, No. 1, 1981.

ULLM93   ULLMAN, E. "Client/Server Frees Data." *Byte,* June 1993.

WAYN96   WAYNER, P., *Digital Cash: Commerce on the Net.* New York: Academic Press, 1996.

WHET96   WHETZEL, J. "Integrating the World Wide Web and Database Technology." *AT&T Technical Journal*, March/April 1996.

WIEN93   WIENER, M. "Efficient DES Key Search." *Proceedings, Crypto '93*. Springer-Verlag, 1993.

WIMM92   WIMMER, K., and JONES, J. "Global Development of PCS," *IEEE Communications Magazine*, June 1992.

INDEX

INDEX

ACRONYMS

AAL	ATM Adaptation Layer
AM	Amplitude Modulation
AMI	Alternate Mark Inversion
ANS	American National Standard
ANSI	American National Standard Institute
ARQ	Automatic Repeat Request
ASCII	American Standard Code for Information Interchange
ASK	Amplitude-Shift Keying
ATM	Asynchronous Transfer Mode
B-ISDN	Broadband ISDN
BOC	Bell Operating Company
CBR	Constant Bit Rate
CCITT	International Consultative Committee on Telegraphy and Telephony
CIR	Committed Information Rate
CRC	Cyclic Redundancy Check
CSMA/CD	Carrier Sense Multiple Access with Collision Detection
DDP	Distributed Data Processing
DES	Data Encryption Standard
DCE	Data Circuit-Terminating Equipment
DES	Data Encryption Standard
DTE	Data Terminal Equipment
FCC	Federal Communications Commission
FCS	Frame Check Sequence
FDDI	Fiber Distributed Data Interface
FDM	Frequency-Division Multiplexing
FSK	Frequency-Shift Keying
FTP	File Transfer Protocol
FM	Frequency Modulation
HDLC	High-Level Data Link Control
HTTP	Hypertext Transfer Protocol
HTML	Hypertext Markup Language
ICMP	Internet Control Message Protocol
IDN	Integrated Digital Network
IEEE	Institute of Electrical and Electronics Engineers
IETF	Internet Engineering Task Force
IP	Internet Protocol
IPng	Internet Protocol - Next Generation
ISDN	Integrated Services Digital Network
ISO	International Organization for Standardization
ITU	International Telecommunication Union